The Oxford Critical Guide

OXFORD CRITICAL GUIDES

Oxford Critical Guides provide authoritative and reader-friendly introductions to ancient literature. Individual chapters are dedicated to each book or section of the ancient work, offering a step-by-step reading and a helpful guide. Each chapter provides a summary of the book, a survey of key themes, and an overview of important scholarship. The chapters are specially commissioned and written by leading academics in the field. The volumes are designed to be completely accessible to readers without Greek or Latin.

TITLES PUBLISHED IN THIS SERIES INCLUDE

The Oxford Critical Guide to Homer's *Iliad*
Edited by Jonathan L. Ready

The Oxford Critical Guide to Tacitus

Edited by

SALVADOR BARTERA

KELLY E. SHANNON-HENDERSON

OXFORD
UNIVERSITY PRESS

OXFORD
UNIVERSITY PRESS

Great Clarendon Street, Oxford, OX2 6DP,
United Kingdom

Oxford University Press is a department of the University of Oxford.
It furthers the University's objective of excellence in research, scholarship,
and education by publishing worldwide. Oxford is a registered trade mark of
Oxford University Press in the UK and in certain other countries

Published in the United States of America by Oxford University Press
198 Madison Avenue, New York, NY 10016, United States of America

British Library Cataloguing in Publication Data

Data available

Library of Congress Control Number: 2025930030

ISBN 9780192894038 (hbk)
ISBN 9780198967583 (pbk)

DOI: 10.1093/9780191915086.001.0001

Printed and bound by
CPI Group (UK) Ltd, Croydon, CR0 4YY

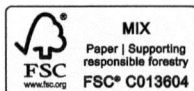

MIX
Paper | Supporting
responsible forestry
FSC www.fsc.org   FSC® C013604

The manufacturer's authorised representative in the EU for product safety is
Oxford University Press España S.A. of El Parque Empresarial San Fernando de Henares,
Avenida de Castilla, 2 – 28830 Madrid (www.oup.es/en or
product.safety@oup.com). OUP España S.A. also acts as importer into Spain
of products made by the manufacturer.

Acknowledgments

Tacitus is a difficult author to teach for many reasons: the subject matter of his works, his intricate and idiosyncratic prose style, and the fragmentary state of his major historical works. Both of us have taught Tacitus many times and have wished for introductions to individual works that were accessible, especially to today's undergraduates. And so, when Charlotte Loveridge of Oxford University Press approached us about putting together this volume for the new "Critical Guide" series, we wholeheartedly embraced the challenge because of the benefit we hoped the volume could bring to a new generation of students of Tacitus. Our thanks go first and foremost to Charlotte for her support of the project from its very beginnings.

Many people have contributed to making this volume possible. We are grateful to all our contributors for taking on the task of writing for this new type of handbook and for the engaging essays they have produced. We would also like to thank for their generous support the Department of Classics at the University of Tennessee-Knoxville and the Semple Fund of the Department of Classics at the University of Cincinnati. Elizabeth Vandiver performed a valuable service with her careful work on the bibliography, as did Scott Garner in preparing the index. We also thank the Oxford University Press editorial team for their excellent work handling production of the book.

We both learned to read Tacitus at the University of Virginia, where we had the incredible good fortune to have Tony Woodman as our mentor. Tony has continued his mentorship of us both for twenty years now; in addition to being the foremost scholar of Tacitus of his generation, he has been a marvelous friend, support, and guide to us both. We could never have asked for more, and it is safe to say this volume never could have existed without him. And so it is to him that we dedicate it, with utmost gratitude.

optimo magistro

Salvador Bartera & Kelly E. Shannon-Henderson
Knoxville & Cincinnati

Contents

Introduction   1
Salvador Bartera and Kelly E. Shannon-Henderson

1. *Agricola*   13
   Sergio Audano

2. *Germania*   24
   Katherine Clarke

3. *Dialogus de oratoribus*   36
   Christopher S. van den Berg

4. *Histories* 1   48
   Cynthia Damon

5. *Histories* 2   62
   Lydia Spielberg

6. *Histories* 3   76
   S. P. Oakley

7. *Histories* 4   89
   Timothy A. Joseph

8. *Histories* 5   101
   René Bloch

9. *Annals* 1   112
   Victoria Emma Pagán

10. *Annals* 2   124
    Aske Damtoft Poulsen

11. *Annals* 3   133
    Olivier Devillers

12. *Annals* 4   145
    Bram ten Berge

13. *Annals* 5 and 6   159
    Kelly E. Shannon-Henderson

14. *Annals* 11 and 12   175
    Caitlin Gillespie

15. *Annals* 13   188
    Alain M. Gowing

16. *Annals* 14   200
    Christopher Whitton

17. *Annals* 15   215
    Rhiannon Ash

18. *Annals* 16   229
    Salvador Bartera

Bibliography   245
Index   265
About the Contributors   269

Introduction

Salvador Bartera and Kelly E. Shannon-Henderson

Tacitus and his Works

Cornelius Tacitus, who has cast so long a shadow over the study of the history of the principate and of historiography in general, is himself a rather shadowy figure. Neither his first name (probably Publius), nor his birthplace (usually thought to be somewhere in Gallia Cisalpina or Narbonensis), nor his date of birth (probably no earlier than 58 CE) is known for certain.[1] We know that he was of senatorial rank and held all the political offices up to and including the highest, the consulship. His date of death is unknown; the latest confirmed date in his life is 112/13 CE, when he can be confirmed from the evidence of inscriptions to have been in Mylassa (modern Milâs in southwestern Turkey) during his term as proconsular governor of the province of Asia.

The question of Tacitus' political career and how it shaped his historical outlook has always been one of the animating forces of Tacitean scholarship. At the beginning of the *Histories*, Tacitus famously writes, "I would not deny that my political career was begun by Vespasian, increased by Titus, and further advanced by Domitian; but those who profess uncorrupted truthfulness must speak of everyone not with love and without hatred" (*H.* 1.1.3: *dignitatem nostram a Vespasiano inchoatam, a Tito auctam, a Domitiano longius provectam non abnuerim*: *sed incorruptam fidem professis neque amore quisquam et sine odio dicendus est*).[2] Other writers of the post-Flavian era, and Tacitus himself at times (e.g. *Agr.* 1–3; see further Audano, Chapter 1 in this volume), look back on the principate of Domitian in particular as a time of tyranny that had a chilling effect on historical literature, as writers feared to compose works that might draw the ire of the regime and invite a capital trial or summary execution.[3] Tacitus did wait until after the principate of Nerva had begun to publish his first work, the *Agricola* (see below),[4] suggesting that he felt similarly despite his surviving and even thriving under Domitian. By this time, he had already attained a significant reputation as an orator,[5] and the literary qualities of his works, which the chapters in this volume seek to highlight and explain, are informed by his legal-rhetorical career. They were also shaped by the political system of the Principate and the individual emperors under whom he lived, on which his outlook is generally taken to be strongly negative. His claims to avoid bias and favoritism, both in the *Histories* proem quoted above and at the beginning of the *Annals*, where he promises to narrate "without anger and enthusiasm, the causes of which I keep far away" (*Ann.* 1.1.3: *sine ira et studio,*

---

[1] The classic work on Tacitus' life is Birley (2000). See also "Cornelius Tacitus," *TE* 301–5 (A. J. Woodman).
[2] On the proem of the *Histories*, see Damon, Chapter 4 in this volume.   [3] See e.g. Wilson (2003).
[4] See further Audano, Chapter 1 in this volume.
[5] Pliny *Ep.* 2.1.6, dated to 97 CE, refers to Tacitus as "a most eloquent eulogist" (*laudator eloquentissimus*).

quorum causas procul habeo), should be read not as a claim to scholarly "objectivity" in a modern sense, but rather as a promise to avoid letting his account be colored by personal favoritism or animus—both of which he claims dogged previous writers of imperial history, so as to make their accounts useless repositories of extreme flattery or criticism.[6]

Agricola

The *Agricola* is Tacitus' first work, probably written when Trajan had been adopted by Nerva (late 97 CE, around the time of Tacitus' consulship and funeral speech for Verginius Rufus) but before he became emperor (late January 98 CE), and published shortly thereafter. He may, however, have planned this work when Domitian was still emperor. The *Agricola* is essentially a biography, but not a traditional one, for it blends several genres, including ethnography and the consolatory genre. It is also indebted to a type of literature that became famous in this period, the *exitus illustrium virorum et feminarum*, "the deaths of illustrious men and women," a genre that certainly also influenced the later books of the *Annals*.[7] As Sergio Audano points out in Chapter 1, Tacitus firmly places himself in the Greco-Roman historical tradition, for the *Agricola* opens with a clear allusion to the Elder Cato, the "father" of Roman prose, as well as to Sallust, Tacitus' main model, whose moralizing historiography influenced Tacitus' approach to history. But his influences also include Thucydides (via Sallust), as well as Seneca (especially his *Consolatio ad Marciam*),[8] Caesar (most evidently in the ethnographic excursus on Britain), Cicero (the timely death of Agricola recalls the *De oratore*), Livy, and probably many other authors who have not survived.

Why Tacitus chose to praise his father-in-law has no obvious answer. Apart from his duty as a son-in-law, he may have felt the need to offer an official tribute to a man whose funeral he could not attend (as he says at *Agr.* 45.4–5). But there is more. Tacitus' *Agricola* makes Agricola an *exemplum* of how to behave under a tyrant. A distinguished military man who conquered Britain and never withdrew his support for the emperor, even when Domitian's hostility toward him became obvious, provided an ideal model of civic behavior, proving that it was possible to be a good man even under a bad *princeps* (42.4). The publication of the *Agricola* coincided with a new period of hope after one of the darkest moments in Roman history, during which Tacitus had made his political impact, which perhaps required some justification in the eyes of his contemporaries. His father-in-law provided the best example of loyalty to the new form of government, the Principate, without necessarily approving the princeps who represented such a system. Tacitus had chosen a similar path. Unlike Agricola, he had not only survived but thrived under Domitian. His *Agricola*, therefore, is to a certain extent an autobiography too.

One of the most interesting aspects of this work is how Tacitus portrays the peoples and culture of Britain in their clashing with the Romans. Despite some common, mainly literary motifs, which can be paralleled in similar ethnographic descriptions, he is perhaps the first to offer an "objective" assessment of the nature of Roman imperialism, whose benefits he does not deny but whose hypocrisy is voiced in the famous speech of the British

---

[6] See esp. Griffin (2009), 176.   [7] See Bartera on *Annals* 16, Chapter 18 in this volume.
[8] On Seneca in Tacitus, see Pliotis (2023), 116–79.

chieftain Calgacus before the final battle against the Romans: "They make a desert and call it peace" (30.5: *ubi solitudinem faciunt pacem appellant*). Tacitus was not the first to point out the predatory nature of Roman conquests, but the depth of Calgacus' analysis is unparalleled, at least among surviving texts.[9] Yet it remains a matter of dispute to what extent Calgacus' criticism of Roman conquest represents Tacitus' own voice (cf. Maternus' speech in the *Dialogus*). The exceptional pride of Calgacus' words notwithstanding, Agricola's army easily prevails, imposing Roman order on British chaos.

With the *Agricola*, Tacitus made a significant impact on the Roman literary tradition and complemented his already distinguished political career, in the best tradition of senatorial historiography. With the biography of his father-in-law, Tacitus offered his contemporaries an example to imitate, and perhaps a warning that principate and *libertas* ("freedom/independence") could hardly coexist.

Germania

While it is relatively simple mentally to draw a straight line between the critique of Domitian in *Agricola* and the themes of the *Histories* and *Annals*, Tacitus' second work, usually referred to as *Germania*,[10] feels like a perplexing turn away from political narrative into ethno-geographical analysis in the tradition of Pliny the Elder or Pomponius Mela, in which Tacitus' attention is aimed at the furthest reaches of the known world. The history of Roman military activity in the region, famous as an arena of spectacular failures at conquest, intrudes into the text only in a limited way.[11] It is usually said that one of the text's most politically "relevant" aspects is the way Tacitus constructs the Germans as being, despite their undoubted barbarism, repositories of an old-fashioned morality no longer accessible at Rome.[12] This aspect of *Germania* would go on to have a long and often dark reception history, as German nationalism in the nineteenth century and Nazism in the twentieth reworked this image of superiority for increasingly evil ends.[13]

Germania also has a long history of being used as a source text by scholars of the Bronze Age and early Middle Ages in Northern Europe, who put Tacitus in dialogue with archaeological remains and historical and legal texts dealing with early medieval Northern Europe in an attempt to understand a society that left no written records of its own.[14] Yet given Tacitus' strongly literary agenda, it is very difficult to use *Germania* to explain specific historical phenomena. For another striking feature of the text is the extent to which its depictions of Germans dovetail with the descriptions by other Roman writers (such as Caesar) of other "northerners" (such as Gauls and Britons), creating a powerful web of associations and stereotypes that Christopher Krebs has termed "borealism."[15] Indeed, the tensions between the generalizations Tacitus makes about Germans as a whole in the first half of *Germania* and the more specific observations on the customs of individual peoples

---

[9] Cf. e.g. the speech of Critognatus at Caesar *BG* 7.77, with Krebs (2023), ad loc.

[10] Its original title may have been *De situ et originibus Germanorum* (*On the Location and Origins of the Germans*); see Rives (1999), 99.

[11] See especially Tan (2014); McNamara (2021).   [12] See especially O'Gorman (1993).

[13] See Krebs (2011b).

[14] The commentary of Rives (1999) engages such scholarship throughout and is a great introduction to these approaches and their limitations.

[15] Krebs (2011a).

described in the second half of the text raise questions for the reader about how they are to understand Germans: in the broad-brush big picture that depicts all of them as largely similar, or through a microscope that reveals the nuances of individual tribes and their particular customs? This is perhaps particularly relevant if we conceive of a reader who would go on to the *Histories* and *Annals*, where military campaigns against Germans and other "northerners" were often a major feature.[16]

For the reader of *Germania*, then, whether ancient or modern, the text is perhaps best approached not as documentation for "actual" cultural practices or geographical informa- tion, but rather as a representation of first-century Roman understandings of the edges of the known world, in all their barbarity and marvelousness.[17] As Katherine Clarke shows in Chapter 2, there are further literary layers to Tacitus' *Germania* along these lines that have not been fully appreciated. She illuminates how Tacitus' text interfaces with the works of previous Greek historians and geographical writers, especially Herodotus and Posidonius. Read in this way, the *Germania* becomes significant not only as a depiction of Rome's "Other," but also as evidence for Tacitus as a polymath who could incorporate Greek geographical learning to create a striking portrait of a region of the world that was politically of the utmost significance while also remaining at the fringes of Roman knowledge.

Dialogus de oratoribus

The *Dialogus de oratoribus* is Tacitus' most enigmatic work. It distinguishes itself in genre (a dialogue modeled after those of Cicero), subject matter (the history and state of con- temporary oratory), and language (a neo-Ciceronian manner that is quite "un-Tacitean," compared to the *Histories* and *Annals*). For these reasons, its authenticity has often been questioned, although nowadays the consensus is that this work is indeed by Tacitus, who, trained in rhetoric and himself a renowned orator, was capable of writing in a manner that suited the topic of oratory. What the *Dialogus* means in the context of Tacitus' oeuvre, however, is still a matter of debate. Why did Tacitus, after writing a biography and an ethnographic treatise, decide to turn to a completely different genre? Is this dialogue a political reflection on the importance of freedom of speech, a literary manifesto of a sort, or what, exactly? The dramatic date is the mid-70s CE, when Tacitus, who appears in the dialogue, was about to begin his political career. Was it written in those years and only later published, or was it composed in the first years of the second century after the publi- cation of *Agricola* and *Germania*, as most scholars believe? The work is dedicated to Fabius Justus, consul in 102 CE.

The dialogue's discussion takes place at the house of Maternus, where three pairs of speeches are delivered: Marcus Aper in defense of oratory and Curiatius Maternus of poetry; Aper in defense of modern orators and Vipstanus Messalla against modern orators; Messalla's critique of modern education and Maternus' of modern oratorical ven- ues. The last speech is perhaps the most significant because it is generally thought to

---

[16] See Ash (2014).

[17] For the idea of the "edges of the earth," see Romm (1992). There are several recent treatments of wonder in *Germania*: see Lightfoot (2020); McNamara (2022); Shannon-Henderson (2022).

represent Tacitus' opinion, for Messalla identifies the loss of Republican *libertas* as the main cause for the decline of modern oratory. The debate, however, is not finished. The *Dialogus* ends without resolution.

The *Dialogus* is complex because none of the speeches is clearly victorious, and every speech puts forward ideas that Tacitus could have shared or criticized. Each speech has faults and merits, and Tacitus purposely structured them in these terms to create the tension that a proper debate required. His main model was Cicero, as most scholars agree, but Quintilian, too, played a significant role.

In Chapter 3, Christopher van den Berg stresses the complexity of this sophisticated and intellectually demanding work, challenging the *communis opinio* that Maternus' speech offers Tacitus' point of view—that is, that the decline of modern oratory is to be blamed on the imperial political system, since good oratory could thrive only in the Republic. Van den Berg focuses on Cicero's *De Republica* as Tacitus' model for his conception of statehood. The two dialogues have much in common, both structurally and thematically, and they both show ambivalence. Neither offers a univocal solution, only tentative conclusions. How sincere is Maternus' last speech? Cicero praised the mixed constitution as the best form of government; Maternus, drawing on Cicero's language, identified the Principate as the best solution to achieve order, with the emperor capable of restoring the disorder that the late Republic had caused. He famously twists Cicero's words (*Brut.* 45, *Rep.* 1.68.2, 3.23.3, *de Orat.* 2.35) to state that "eloquence nurses license, which fools call freedom" (40.2: *eloquentia alumna licentiae, quam stulti libertatem vocant*). Neither Cicero nor Tacitus endorsed extreme *libertas*, which they saw as detrimental to the constitutional order. When Maternus praises the *princeps* as the one who can guarantee order, he is therefore indirectly endorsing Cicero's civic savior and idealized monarch.

In the end, the *Dialogus* remains enigmatic in terms of what message it advocates. Tacitus does not condemn contemporary oratory but questions how oratory can function in the new form of government, the Principate. This work is not his farewell to oratory, which he continued to practice, both literally and metaphorically in his subsequent historical works.

Histories

After adopting three different genres in relatively short treatises, Tacitus made the conscious choice to turn to historical writing.[18] His approach to history is not revolutionary: he is aware of writing within a well-established tradition which started with Cato the Elder and had among its most prominent examples Sallust and Livy, whose influence on Tacitus is undeniable (see also above). Unfortunately, besides Sallust, Livy, and Tacitus, the works of almost no first-century historians have survived except in a very fragmentary state; but Tacitus' debt to his predecessors is evident, whether he is borrowing a single word, a particular syntactical device, or a whole narrative section. The most famous cases are perhaps the opening words of the *Annals* and the character portrayal of Sejanus at the beginning of *Annals* 4, both influenced by Sallust's *Catiline*. From Livy, he borrows the

---

[18] For an introduction to the Latin historians, see e.g. Kraus and Woodman (1997); Feldherr (2009b).

annalistic structure of his histories (i.e. a yearly account of domestic and foreign affairs), but he manipulates this format, which was traditionally associated with Republican historiography, to reflect the exceptional historical period that he chose to narrate: the Principate.[19] More than his predecessors, he borrows from poetry, especially epic poetry, Vergil especially, whether the allusion is but a single word (a *mot juste* to describe a particular event or character) or a special episode, which he "colors" with Vergilian flavor for dramatic purposes.[20]

When Tacitus planned his *Histories*, Trajan was emperor. The outlook was good, certainly better than the last years of Domitian. And indeed, Tacitus says at the opening of Book 1 that his future plan is to write of the post-Flavian period (*H.* 1.1.4). But he never did. Whether this change of mind was dictated by a certain disillusionment with Trajan, or whether Tacitus had developed a keen interest in the period that preceded the civil war of 69 CE, cannot be known (see also below). In their original plan, the *Histories* were to cover the entire Flavian dynasty (69–96 CE). Book 1 begins on January 1, 69 CE, the famous Year of the Four Emperors, which followed the death of Nero in June 68 CE, one of the most confusing and critical periods of Roman imperial history. Since the *Annals*, too, are incomplete, we can only guess how the last book of the *Annals* would have linked to the *Histories*, but it is evident from what survives that Tacitus conceived of his two major works as interdependent narratives. This is especially clear in *Annals* 16, where some of the characters who would play a major role in the *Histories* are encountered.[21]

What survives of the *Histories* is an extremely detailed account of little more than one year of Roman history, since Book 5, in itself fragmentary, adds little to the historical progression of Book 4. It is instead mainly a digression on the Jews that provides background information on one of the greatest military successes of the Flavians, the capture of Jerusalem, whose spoils funded a large part of the Flavians' building program, including the restoration of the Capitol, significantly paid for by the destruction of the Jewish temple.

Tacitus' account of the year 69 is as fascinating as it is complex and confusing: the mess (and repetitiveness) of the civil war surfaces on every page, creating disorder and turmoil, where it is often unclear who is fighting whom, who is allied with whom, and what happens when. Tacitus' narrative, which does not always follow a clear chronological order, contributes to this sense of disorder, where the Flavians, constantly in the background and gradually emerging as the narrative unfolds, are indicated as the ones who will eventually bring peace to Rome. But this is of course a deceptive hope because the relatively good reign of Vespasian was to be followed, after the brief, almost idealized principate of Titus, by the darkest period of Tacitus' personal experience, the reign of Domitian. As many scholars have observed, it also deeply influenced his treatment of the Julio-Claudians, especially of Nero, with whom Domitian was often compared.

Tacitus' relationship with the Flavians is ambiguous. As he admits at the opening of the *Histories* (see also above), he benefited from them for his political career, which began under Vespasian and advanced without interruption until he served as suffect consul in 97, his nomination perhaps owed to Domitian. When Vespasian emerged victorious after the three short-lived emperors, his main goal was to guarantee stability and prepare for

---

[19] See n. 21 below.   [20] See esp. Joseph (2012c).
[21] On the structure and book number of *Histories* and *Annals*, see Bartera, Chapter 18 in this volume, "Post Scriptum."

the succession of his elder son Titus. Thus the Flavians adopted propaganda designed to portray them as "liberators" rather than "conquerors," and as legitimate heirs of Augustus, canceling the memory of Nero. Vespasian did not challenge Vitellius for personal gain, it suggested, but to save Rome from his debauchery. This official image was adopted by court writers and can best be observed in Josephus, whose treatment of the Judaic War is undoubtedly influenced by Flavian propaganda.[22] When Tacitus came to historical writing, he had to face this problem, hence his profession of "independence" at the opening of both *Histories* and *Annals* (see also above). But his narrative is so ambiguous that it is often difficult to understand what he truly thought about the Flavians, and, more generally, about the Principate. It is therefore unsurprising that, since his texts re-emerged in the Renaissance, Tacitus has been seen as a supporter of the imperial system as well as nostalgic for the Republic.

In the *Histories*, Tacitus' narrative is neither straightforwardly pro-Flavian nor openly critical. The three emperors that followed Nero's death—Galba, Otho, and Vitellius—represent a downward spiral. If Galba is doomed because he behaves as though unaware that times have changed, and Otho, despite his dubious lifestyle, somewhat redeems himself with his heroic suicide, Vitellius embodies the utter degeneration of the civil wars, when loyalty becomes dangerous and disloyalty is rewarded with honor and money. As the three emperors fight each other, the Flavians skillfully move in the background and gradually emerge from the mess that the others have created. Tacitus' narrative, however, is careful never to implicate them directly. In Book 3, for example, when the Vitellians assault the Capitol, defended by Vespasian's brother Sabinus, the Temple of Jupiter catches fire, symbolizing the fall of the old Republic. Tacitus' narrative alone casts some doubt as to who was responsible for the fire; Flavian propaganda, naturally enough, blamed the Vitellians. Book 4 marks the beginning of Flavian rule, and yet the narrative focuses on questionable characters who had become notorious under Nero, many of whom appear in the surviving narrative of *Annals* 16. Among them, Helvidius Priscus the Elder stands out: he was Thrasea Paetus' son-in-law and "political heir." Having returned from his exile after Nero's death, he embodied the old Republican ideal of senatorial "independence" (*libertas*), and was a thorn in Vespasian's side, who tolerated him at first but eventually put him to death (this section of the *Histories*, however, does not survive).

The five chapters in this volume on the *Histories* illustrate well some of the themes and characters that Tacitus develops in the work. In Chapter 4, Cynthia Damon focuses on Tacitus' historiographical program, the parallel tradition and some of his literary techniques. In Chapter 5, Lydia Spielberg explores the uncertainty that pervades Book 2, a book of transition, when the Flavians make their first significant move, and in Chapter 6, Stephen Oakley emphasizes the brilliance of the climactic Book 3, dominated by two men, the Flavian general Antonius Primus and the degenerate Vitellius. Timothy Joseph turns to Book 4 in Chapter 7, where the action alternates between Rome, where the Flavians assert their power through their generals, and military operations abroad, aimed at consolidating the Flavians' victory. The fragmentary Book 5 is dominated by the Jewish excursus, which René Bloch examines in all its aspects in Chapter 8, including some hypotheses as to the content of the lost portion of the book.

---

[22] See Bartera (forthcoming b).

One of the most common feelings when reading Tacitus' *Histories* is frustration: a large amount of the narrative is lost, and what survives is so good that one wonders how Tacitus would have dealt with the historical period in which he played a leading role. How would he have narrated the destruction of Pompeii, for example, the dedication of the Colosseum, the rebuilding of the Capitol, his own role in Domitian's Secular Games (hinted at in *Annals* 11.11), or the terrible year 93? Perhaps we would know more about his personal life too. We get glimpses of some of this from the *Agricola*, but the rest is destined to remain one of the most unfortunate losses of Latin literature.

Annals

The *Annals* are Tacitus' last work, which he seems to have begun writing in the 110s CE. After completing the *Histories*, instead of following up on his avowed intention to write a work dealing with the post-Flavian emperors (*H.* 1.1.4; see also above), he instead returned to the previous dynasty, the Julio-Claudians. The reason for this apparent reversal is unknown (if indeed we are to take Tacitus' comments in the *Histories* seriously).

As the name *Annals* suggests (although it was perhaps not the work's original title),[23] the text operates in the tradition of annalistic historiography, works that were structured year-by-year.[24] Readers could expect the account of each year to begin with the names of the consuls, and to include details about foreign affairs and military campaigns, descriptions of political developments at Rome, and religious material. But, as scholars have observed, Tacitus was by no means restricted by this framework; rather, he reshaped it creatively to suit his own literary needs, reporting events out of chronological sequence in order to create significant or suggestive juxtapositions.[25] The part of the text that survives does not include all of books 5 or 11, any of books 7–10, or anything after the fragment of Book 16.

Tacitus' decision to begin the *Annals* when he did—at the moment of Tiberius' succession upon Augustus' death in 14 CE, with "a few things about Augustus and his final period" (*Ann.* 1.1.3: *pauca de Augusto et extrema*) included—was a deliberate and surprising literary choice. Why not include Augustus' entire principate, or even its beginnings, and give readers a picture of how the monarchical system of rule by emperors came to be?[26] But, as Victoria Pagán shows in Chapter 9 on *Annals* 1, Tacitus' choice of starting-place in fact allows him to reflect in interesting ways both on Augustus' legacy and on what is distinctive about Tiberius. By showing not the first but the second *princeps* in a hereditary system of power, Tacitus underlines that in 14 CE monarchy was already a foregone conclusion; return to the *libertas* of the Republican period was no longer possible (and it is doubtful such a prospect would even have been considered seriously at the time). The work that follows will be about a period where that "freedom" was, if not yet totally extinct, an increasingly endangered species.

---

[23] The text's heading in the First Medicean manuscript is *Ab excessu divi Augusti*, "From the departure of the divine Augustus." See e.g. Bartera (2016), 113–20.

[24] On these, see recently "Annales," *TE*: 54–5 (A. J. Woodman).   [25] See Ginsburg (1981); Bartera (2011).

[26] At *Ann.* 3.24.3, Tacitus seems to promise treatment of the Augustan period in a future work. Ronald Syme famously criticized Tacitus for not beginning in 4 CE; see further O'Gorman (1995a) and Pagán, Chapter 9 in this volume.

As our contributors show, subsequent books in the *Annals'* Tiberian "hexad"[27] continue to exploit these themes of dynasty and freedom. Aske Damtoft Poulsen, in Chapter 10, shows how Book 2, characterized by motifs of deceit and deception and focused on the figure of Germanicus—Tiberius' nephew, foil, heir, and possible rival for imperial power—continually raises and then dashes the reader's hope for an alternative Rome that might have been less gloomy than the actual one ruled by Tiberius. In a similar vein, for Olivier Devillers in Chapter 11, Book 3 is "the book of *libertas*" because of its focus, particularly in the latter half, on senatorial business, transacted with an almost-Republican level of activity, and some intimations of restraint on Tiberius' part. Yet this *libertas* is at the same time circumscribed by *delatio* ("denunciation" of private citizens in court on charges related to allegedly seditious acts) and *adulatio* ("flattery"), the lingering fallout of Germanicus' death, and the repeated invocation of the precedent of Augustus, founder of the freedom-restricting system of the Principate.

Things turn markedly for the worse in *Annals* 4 with the rise to prominence of Tiberius' minion Sejanus, who would push for the extermination of Germanicus' remaining family members and who descends to ever-greater atrocities after Tiberius' fateful withdrawal to Capri: "Suddenly fortune began to throw things into confusion, Tiberius himself to be savage or to lend strength to the savage" (*Ann.* 4.1.1: *repente turbare fortuna coepit, saevire ipse aut saevientibus vires praebere*). Bram ten Berge, in Chapter 12, shows that, beginning from this ominous opening paragraph and continuing throughout the rest of the book, Tacitus remixes motifs and wording from his earlier works, especially the *Histories*, to create the suggestive implication that the savagery here unleashed for the first time would continue for several more decades, underlining the inherent brutality of the Principate no matter who was at its helm. This downward arc continues in the mutilated books 5 and 6, as Kelly E. Shannon-Henderson, in Chapter 13, shows: we see the executions of Sejanus' associates, both presumed and real, after his demise, that show the dangers of traditional friendship; Tiberius' descent into ever more tyrannical behavior; the terrifying question of who will succeed him; and his ignominious end. Then in the final chapter of the hexad, she argues, Tacitus pulls us up short with an "obituary" of the emperor that forces the reader to think again about everything that has come before; no doubt a fitting end, even if we are doomed to remain unsure of how it would have prepared the reader for Tacitus' now-lost account of Caligula and the early years of Claudius.

When our text of the *Annals* resumes, Tacitus is apparently an enthusiastic participant in the historiographical tradition that was overwhelmingly hostile to Claudius, as Caitlin Gillespie shows in Chapter 14 on *Annals* 11–12. While we are shown some things this emperor gets right, including a healthy respect for traditional ceremonies and a famous speech in the Senate, Tacitus' narrative is dominated by Claudius' failures, particularly in the domestic realm; thus the Claudian books, as Gillespie shows, become a place where imperial women like Messalina and Agrippina the Younger dominate, always with negative consequences. *Annals* 12 closes in exactly the same way as the *Annals* began: with a dynastic transition of power engineered by a woman, as Agrippina the Younger's son Nero succeeds his stepfather.

---

[27] On the term and its significance as an organizational principle, see Bartera, Chapter 18 in this volume, "Post Scriptum."

Imperial women remain a common theme throughout the first two books on Nero's reign. As Alain Gowing shows, in Chapter 15, while Tacitus does give Nero credit for positive aspects of his reign's *quinquennium* (first five years), the first of the Neronian books admirably sets the tone for what will follow. Tacitus shows us an emperor who, while he may have advisors (Burrus, Seneca) who temper his worst impulses for the moment, will experience a degradation of his behavior and character as the narrative continues to unfold. Even from the beginning, there are hints of his end. Another major theme of Book 13 is Nero's relationships with the women in his life: domineering Agrippina, doomed Octavia, and his eventual wife Poppaea. They will continue to dominate Book 14. In Chapter 16, Christopher Whitton illuminates the book's increasing gloom, with a special focus on women's deaths: Agrippina's death-sequence, recalling earlier dark episodes in Julio-Claudian history; the pathos of the execution of Nero's young wife Octavia; and the violent suppression of the revolt of Boudica in Britain, which provides a "sideshadow" of the powerful women back in Rome.

Annals 15 plays with geography, as Rhiannon Ash shows in Chapter 17: Tacitus' narrative first sends the reader to the edges of the empire with an account of the eastern campaigns of Corbulo (whose forced suicide must have been a major feature of the now-lost end of the *Annals*) before being inevitably sucked back in to the imperial center in Rome, arena of further disgraceful behavior from Nero, the catastrophic fire of Rome in 64, the failed Pisonian conspiracy, and its bloody aftermath. Finally, as Salvador Bartera's analysis of Book 16 in Chapter 18 demonstrates, the last part of the *Annals* that we have reinforces the idea, which has been building over the previous two books, that Nero's reign has been increasing in its destructiveness, since the book is dominated by several significant forced suicides. Meanwhile, the end of the Julio-Claudian family line is foreshadowed, notably with Nero's killing of his pregnant wife Poppaea.

How exactly Tacitus concluded the *Annals* has been lost to time. Accordingly, Bartera closes his chapter with a "Post Scriptum" on the structure of the *Annals*, reviewing the evidence for and trying out various hypotheses related to the work's original length. We do not know for certain how many books the *Annals* originally comprised, or when Tacitus completed the *Annals*—if in fact he did, since it may have been interrupted by his death.

How to Use This Book

Like those of the other volumes in the *Oxford Critical Guide* series, these chapters are designed so that each can stand alone. Readers who find themselves studying only one of the minor works of Tacitus or one book of the *Annals* or *Histories* should find that the relevant chapter of the *Oxford Critical Guide to Tacitus* is intelligible and helpful even if they are experiencing no other part of Tacitus' texts.

In each chapter, readers will find a detailed analysis of the text under consideration that proceeds (mostly) straight through from beginning to end, introducing them to relevant interpretive issues, both historical and literary. They will also find cross-references to other parts of Tacitus, and to other *Critical Guide* chapters, that are designed to help them situate their book/work within Tacitus' larger *oeuvre*, as well as suggestions for further reading in the scholarly literature. In particular, we encourage use of the *Critical Guide* alongside previous handbook and companion volumes whose chapters are organized thematically, such as Woodman (2009a) and Pagán (2012), and in conjunction with the recent (2023) *Tacitus Encyclopedia* (*TE*; ed. Pagán), an exhaustive compendium of all things Tacitean.[28]

We hope that our approach in this volume will not only provide new insights to readers who already know Tacitus well but will also be especially helpful for undergraduate and graduate student readers approaching Tacitus for the first time in the context of a course where only one book or minor work has been assigned.

This should be true whether you read Tacitus in English or in Latin. Tacitus and other ancient texts are quoted both in the original language and in translation,[29] so as to render the volume accessible but at the same time not to obscure the idiosyncratic and masterful nature of Tacitus' Latin prose. We hope that this may inspire the reader who has not (yet) studied Latin to pursue training in the language and read Tacitus in the original—and if so, we hope that you derive as much delight and intellectual stimulation from reading Tacitus' prose as we have done over the years.

Further Reading

Commentaries

Commentaries are the ideal complement to critical studies of individual books. In English, the standard commentaries on Tacitus' works are the following:[30]

Agricola: Ogilvie and Richmond (1967); Woodman (2014)
Germania: Anderson (1938); Rives (1999)
Dialogus: Mayer (2001)
Histories:

   Books 1–2, Chilver (1979)
   Book 1, Damon (2003)
   Book 2, Ash (2007b)
   Book 3, Wellesley (1972)
   Books 4–5, Chilver and Townend (1985)

Annals:

   Book 1, Miller (1959); Goodyear (1972 [1.1–54]) and (1982 [1.55–81])
   Book 2, Goodyear (1981)
   Book 3, Woodman and Martin (1996)
   Book 4, Martin and Woodman (1989); Shotter (1989); Woodman (2018)
   Books 5–6, Martin (2001); Woodman (2017)
   Book 11, Malloch (2013)

---

[28] For a collection of "classic" articles on Tacitus, see Ash (2012).
[29] The Latin texts of Tacitus are quoted according to Winterbottom and Ogilvie (1975) for the *opera minora*, Wellesley (1989) for the *Histories*, Heubner (1994) for the *Annals*, unless otherwise stated (but "u" is printed as "v" throughout). Translations are by the individual authors of each chapter.
[30] In German, Heubner produced a commentary on the *Agricola* (1984) and *Histories* 1–5 (1963–82); Gudeman (1914) and Güngerich (ed. Heubner, 1980) on the *Dialogus*; Koestermann on the whole of the *Annals* (1963–8). There are numerous commentaries in German on the *Germania*, of which the most recent is Lund (1988); Much (1967) is still influential.

Book 12, Malloch (forthcoming a)
Book 13 Millband (2022 [chs. 15–25])
Book 14, Woodcock (1939); Whitton (forthcoming e)
Book 15 Miller (1973); Ash (2018)
Book 16, Fratantuono (2018); Bartera (forthcoming a)

English Translations

The entire works of Tacitus are available in the Loeb Classical Library editions (1914–70): Hutton (rev. Ogilvie) for the *Agricola*; Hutton (rev. Warmington) for the *Germania*, Peterson (rev. Winterbottom) for the *Dialogus*; Moore for the *Histories*; Jackson for the *Annals*.

More recently: Birley (1999) for *Agricola* and *Germania*; Fyfe (rev. Levene) (1997) and Wellesley (rev. Ash) (2009) for the *Histories*; Woodman (2004), Yardley and Barrett (2008), and Damon (2012) for the *Annals*.

Salvador Bartera and Kelly E. Shannon-Henderson, *Introduction* In: *The Oxford Critical Guide to Tacitus*.
Edited by: Salvador Bartera and Kelly E. Shannon-Henderson, Oxford University Press. © Oxford University Press 2025.
DOI: 10.1093/9780191915086.003.0001

1

Agricola

Sergio Audano

The *Agricola* and the Literary Beginnings of Tacitus

Tacitus' literary beginnings remain unknown. There is no information regarding the reasons why he decided to complement his senatorial career with that of a writer and historian. Some information, albeit fragmentary, comes from his friend Pliny the Younger.[1] He describes Tacitus as *laudator eloquentissimus*, "a most eloquent orator" (*Ep.* 2.1.6),[2] explaining how Tacitus as *consul suffectus* ("suffect consul") in 97 CE delivered a much-praised eulogy for Verginius Rufus. Rufus was a well-respected general and three-time consul who had refused to become emperor after the death of Nero in 68 and, thanks to his influence on the troops, had facilitated Nerva's rise to power just a few months earlier in 96.[3]

Some scholars believe this to be the background of Tacitus' first work, the *Agricola*, known as *De vita Iulii Agricolae liber* (or *De vita et moribus Iulii Agricolae*), dedicated to his father-in-law Agricola, who conquered and governed Britain. Agricola died under mysterious circumstances in 93 after returning to Rome; he was most likely the victim of the emperor Domitian's despotism. It is probable that Tacitus conceived the project of a complete and detailed biography of his father-in-law between the brief reign of Nerva (96–8) and the rise of Trajan. His aim may have been to restore, in the new emperor's eyes, the credibility of part of the ruling class, to which he himself belonged, after it had been severely undermined during Domitian's reign.[4] The image of Agricola was well-suited for this undertaking: he was a skillful governor, an excellent military man—just like Trajan—and also impeccable in his private life. Moreover, despite having served under Domitian, he was nevertheless a victim of the emperor's tyrannical despotism. Many, including Tacitus himself, could relate to the image of Agricola; thanks to his ethics, he became a true role model that withstood the test of time.

Of course, Tacitus' work played a key part in making Agricola a role model. It is important to examine, therefore, the literary elements that make the *Agricola* an interesting and unusual work.[5] First, its structure: the work comprises forty-six chapters, usually divided into six sections. The first section (chapters 1–4) serves as a preface and introduces the reader to both the biography of Agricola and the historical-political context of Domitian's empire (81–96). The second section (chapters 5–9) describes the youth of the future general and the initial stages of his *cursus honorum* ("political career"). It then focuses on his

---

[1] On the relationship between Tacitus and Pliny, in addition to the fundamental "Tacitus and Pliny" of Syme (1958a), 59–131, see more recently Marchesi (2008); Woodman (2009b); Whitton (2012); and Geisthardt (2015).
[2] See Whitton (2013), 74–5.   [3] On Pliny's characterization of Verginius Rufus, see Klodt (2015).
[4] See now the judicious assessment of Szoke (2019). See also Sailor (2008).
[5] See especially Woodman (2014), 1–11.

moral upbringing and on how Agricola acquired the ethical values that would guide him for his entire life. The third section (chapters 10–17) suspends the biographical part of the work by inserting an excursus on Britain. Here Tacitus offers a dense ethno-anthropological analysis and recounts the stages of the long process of the Romanization of Britain. The fourth section (chapters 18–38) is the longest, as it recounts Agricola's years as governor of Britain, which came to an end with the Romans' decisive victory over the rebels led by Calgacus at the battle of Mons Graupius in 84.[6] On this occasion, Calgacus delivers his famous speech just before the battle, perhaps the most famous passage of the *Agricola*. The two final sections cover the final, dramatic years of the general's life. The fifth (chapters 39–43) recounts his return to Rome and cold welcome by Domitian, who was jealous of his success. This section clearly shows the political climate of suspicion and terror caused by *delationes* ("denunciations") and the persecution of senators. The work then continues with Agricola's death in 93, for which the emperor may have been responsible. Tacitus dedicates the sixth and final section (chapters 44–6) to consecrating the image of his father-in-law to posterity, thus turning him into a highly moral *exemplum*.

Tacitus and the Genre of Biography

In terms of literary genre, the *Agricola* meets all the requirements of a biography.[7] Indeed, Tacitus starts recounting the life of his father-in-law from his youth and describes his psychological traits, dwelling on his moral upbringing. He recounts his *facta* (i.e. his military undertakings) and his successes, and draws to a close with Agricola's sudden and mysterious death.

The biography as a literary genre originates in Greek literature with important examples of lives of illustrious men (e.g. Isocrates' *Evagoras*), especially philosophers, in the fourth century BCE, and was further developed over the following centuries. By the time Tacitus started writing, biographies had become very popular, as is shown by the series of contemporary collections by Plutarch and Suetonius.

As most critics have noted, however, the *Agricola* is perhaps something more than just a traditional biography. The typical features of the genre are harmoniously combined with ancient Roman tradition, which already in the Republican era began adapting biography to the political contexts and typical practices of the senatorial aristocracy. In archaic times it was already common among the most illustrious families and ancient nobility to celebrate the *paterfamilias* upon his death: it was a traditional rite which reinforced both the sense of belonging within the family and the relationships with other families of the same social and political standing. A funeral, therefore, normally featured the *elogium*, "eulogy," and in particular the *laudatio*, "funeral speech," which celebrated the moral merits of the deceased, his victorious deeds, and his political successes, thus carrying on the legacy of success left by his equally glorious and commendable ancestors.[8] It is no coincidence that

---

[6] The dense narrative of this battle is thoroughly analyzed by Ash (2007a). For the more strictly military aspects (and also for problems of chronology), see Campbell (2010) and Smith (2015).

[7] For a thorough examination of the problems relating to the literary nature of the *Agricola*, see Steinmetz (2000).

[8] For a rhetorical analysis of the *laudatio*, as well as for an extensive historical and literary discussion, see Pepe (2015).

the *laudatio* was also accompanied by the display of the *imagines* of the deceased and of his ancestors: death would thus become a "show," where techniques belonging to the theatrical world were used, and the dead intermingled with the living in order to reaffirm the never-ending continuity of family identity and of social and political relations.[9] Moreover, these rituals also helped build a collective memory (*memoria*): the deceased's accomplishments were not only tied to him as a person or to his family, but they also became a heritage shared by his social group, who could fully relate to the biography of the deceased. Given the small amount of surviving evidence, the exact boundaries separating the two genres of *elogium* and *laudatio* remain unclear. Both were of course tied to death: they were speeches made during funerals, therefore first intended for oral delivery, but then written down to be more widely circulated.

Tacitus' intention of evoking this great Republican tradition clearly emerges in his first words: *clarorum virorum facta moresque posteris tradere, antiquitus usitatum, ne nostris quidem temporibus quamquam incuriosa suorum aetas omisit* (1.1: "In past times it was customary to pass down the deeds and behaviors of famous men for posterity. Even our present age, though indifferent to its own affairs, has not abandoned it").[10] Here Tacitus makes an intertextual reference to the beginning of the Elder Cato's *Origines* (fr. 2 Cornell),[11] the first historical work written in Latin, with a marked moralistic tone (and there may also be a reference to another fragment of Cato, fr. 113 Cornell: *clarorum virorum laudes atque virtutes*: "actions worthy of praise and virtue of famous men").[12] But the nexus *facta moresque*, "deeds and behaviors," seems to be a reference to Sallust (*Cat.* 55.6: *moribusque factisque*), who was also an author especially dear to Tacitus and with whom he shared an archaizing style. The final chapters, 44–6, are heavily influenced by the *laudatio* tradition, which Tacitus blends with elements typical of related genres such as the *consolatio*. One example is the theme of the *mors opportuna*, "timely death," which spared Agricola from having to witness the criminal degeneration of Domitian's empire (44.5: *festinatae mortis grande solacium tulit evasisse postremum illud tempus, quo Domitianus non iam per intervalla ac spiramenta temporum, sed continuo et velut uno ictu rem publicam exhausit*, "Yet it brought effective relief for his premature death to have avoided that last period, when Domitian, no longer at intervals and with breathing-spaces, but in a continuous and as it were single onslaught drained the blood of the State").

As is often the case with Tacitus (as can be seen more clearly in the *Germania*, written around the same time), the use of the past serves to criticize the present more or less explicitly. In the preface, Tacitus accuses his contemporaries of disregarding virtue, which is crushed by the weight of ignorance of what is right and by malice (1.1: *quotiens magna aliqua ac nobilis virtus vicit ac supergressa est vitium parvis magnisque civitatibus commune, ignorantiam recti et invidiam*, "every time a great and noble virtue wins and overcomes a vice common to small and large states: ignorance of what is right and jealousy"). Afterwards he comes to the pessimistic conclusion that writing a biography of a deceased man now actually requires a justification: "But as I am now about to write the life of a dead man I must seek a forgiveness that an attack upon him would not require. These times are so cruel and hostile to virtues" (1.4: *at nunc narraturo mihi vitam defuncti*

---

[9] On the Roman noble funeral, see Flower (1996) and Bettini (2015).
[10] Here and elsewhere translations are my own.   [11] See Woodman (2014), ad loc.
[12] The importance of Cato as a model for Tacitus is highlighted by Heubner (1984), 5 and Oniga (2003), 804.

hominis venia opus fuit, quam non petissem incusaturus: tam saeva et infesta virtutibus tempora). Here Tacitus himself, by defining his work as a *vita*, seems to provide us with the information necessary to classify it easily as a biography. Tacitus writes during the first months of the reign of Trajan, which at last provides some respite after the dramatic years of Domitian's tyranny, as he writes at the beginning of chapter 3 (*nunc demum redit animus*, "now at last spirits are reviving"). The new emperor, like his predecessor Nerva, has the difficult task of bringing together two opposite elements, the principate and freedom. Tacitus is, however, aware that although a *beatissimum saeculum*, "a most fortunate age" has just begun, "remedies are slower than diseases" (*tardiora sunt remedia quam mala*, 3.1) owing to humanity's inherent wickedness. Besides, there was still great hatred and resentment toward the past regime: many, including Tacitus and Agricola himself, had been tied in different ways to Domitian. Tacitus was therefore forced to make radical innovations in his biography, not only describing the actions his father-in-law performed but also giving the work a moral dimension, where strong ethical values led to glorious, memorable deeds, based on the model of the great protagonists of the Republican era.

Agricola, however, is not a shadowy figure from the past. He is instead a contemporary man whom readers still remember. Moreover, he enjoys the unproven yet very plausible fame of being a martyr of the emperor. It is no coincidence that, starting from chapter 39,[13] Tacitus has the biography genre interact with the tradition of the *exitus illustrium virorum*, "the deaths of illustrious men," which would later also be featured in his *Annales*, where he described the many victims of the Julio-Claudian emperors.[14] This is yet another significant innovation that confirms that Tacitus wanted to experiment with a new form of biography precisely because he intended to offer a new model to the ruling class that was being formed afresh in the reign of Trajan. Agricola is a reassuring role model: linked to the best tradition, he was able to combine *mores* with *facta*; he was a loyal servant of the empire, but not of the emperor, by whom he was repaid for the brilliant conquest of Britain only with ingratitude and perhaps even death. For such a character, a traditional biography was certainly not enough, in Tacitus' view. With the *Agricola* he carried out an innovative experiment unique in all of Latin literature.

The Literary Models of the *Agricola*

As regards *Agricola*'s literary models, Tacitus can be compared to Thucydides owing to his interest in contemporary history and especially in a specific time period, in this case the biography of his father-in-law, the subject of his in-depth analysis. But there are also other similarities. In chapters 30–2, before the battle of Mons Graupius, Tacitus compares the speech of the British commander Calgacus to his troops with the speech delivered by Agricola himself. The use of speeches in historiography owes much to Thucydides, but some elements of Tacitus' speeches transcend their traditional model. Tacitus, just like his Greek predecessor, uses speeches to shed light on underlying realities, especially when he dwells on the justification of violence of the strongest and the overpowering of the weakest. Consider, for instance, the famous dialogue between the Athenians and the Melians

---

[13] This perhaps begins already from ch. 2, as argued by Pigón (1987).
[14] See "*exitus illustrium virorum*," *BNP* 5: 269 (U. Eigler); Ronconi (2013); and Bartera on *Annals* 16 in Chapter 18 in this volume.

(Thuc. 5.85–113),[15] where the imperial power of Athens asserts itself with dramatic violence on the small and neutral island, whose population is destroyed in the name of the principle of the "natural" superiority of the strongest over the weakest. As we will see, Tacitus uses speeches to similar effect in the *Agricola*.

Even more than the Athenian historian, however, Tacitus' source of inspiration is Sallust, who, like Tacitus, is the author of two monographs closely related to contemporary political history, the *Bellum Catilinae* and the *Bellum Jugurthinum*, as well as a work of contemporary history of broader scope, the *Historiae*.[16] Sallust offers Tacitus many insights. His historical narrative is delivered with a moralistic tone, with a stark sense of distrust toward political institutions and more generally toward his contemporaries, who are guilty of abominable vices such as *avaritia*, *luxuria*, or *lubido* ("avarice, luxury, lust") and almost invariably devoid of any moral scruples. The moral corruption of the present justifies, for both Sallust and Tacitus, the creation of a past which is more imaginary than real, when all the virtues that led to Rome's greatness still prevailed. Consider, for example, Tacitus' need to appeal to the Republican tradition by alluding at the very beginning of the *Agricola* to Cato the Censor, the quintessential hero of the traditional values associated with the *mos maiorum* ("the custom of the ancestors"). Yet Sallust is not merely a model of morality and nostalgia for the past: he is above all a brave and original experimenter responsible for radical innovations in Latin historiography. It was indeed his excursus on Africa in the *Bellum Jugurthinum* (17–19)[17] that inspired Tacitus' long geo-ethnographic section on Britain (chapters 10–17), which will be discussed below. Tacitus staunchly emulated Sallust and framed his long digression on Britain from an ethno-anthropological perspective, but he was also attentive to the political dimension. (Likewise influential was Caesar, especially Books IV and V of the *Bellum Gallicum*, which covered the two Roman invasions of Britain in 55 and 54 BCE.) Furthermore, Sallust was known for his asymmetrical, archaic, hectic style, a style that focused on the characters' psychology and that was very distant from *concinnitas*, the orderly and regularly structured sentences that Cicero was known for.[18]

But Tacitus follows different models of style, not just the Sallustian. In the final section (chapters 44–6) in particular, when the deceased Agricola becomes a role model, Cicero's influence becomes apparent, more specifically *De Oratore* 3.8, to which Tacitus alludes in the penultimate chapter of the *Agricola*. Agricola's *mors opportuna* ("timely death"), introduced by *non vidit*, "he did not see" (45.1), recalls the sudden, and therefore "timely," death of the orator L. Licinius Crassus, whose death prevented him from witnessing the massacres of the Social Wars. It is no coincidence that, owing to Cicero's influence, the style of the *Agricola* seems calmer and more solemn in the concluding chapters.

In the final chapter of the *Agricola*, where the influence of consolatory literature becomes greater, Tacitus wishes to stress how the memory of Agricola's moral virtues will ensure that posterity will remember him. To do so, he uses the phrase *contemplatio virtutum*, "contemplation of virtues," which he most likely took from Seneca's *Consolatio ad Marciam* (24.4). The phrase is consistent with the rhetoric of *consolationes* and evokes the motif of the survival of the soul after death, an argument that often marked the end of

---

[15] See Canfora (1999).   [16] See Sailor (2004).
[17] See Oniga (1995); Mambwini Kivuila and Nsuka Nkoko (2017).
[18] On the language and style of the *Agricola*, see Woodman (2014), 30–5; on the language of Sallust, see Woodman (forthcoming).

consolatory writings.[19] In the *Agricola*, however, Tacitus wants to stress how only constant meditation on the qualities of his father-in-law will enable his memory to withstand the test of time from a more personal perspective. Tacitus' choice of literary models, therefore, proves to be very flexible. Sallust's influence is indeed remarkable: he is the main model, for he places Tacitus in the same tradition as Thucydides' interest in contemporary political history, but Tacitus also uses other models when building his arguments, for instance by alluding to Seneca and above all Cicero.

Excursus on Britain: Between Ethnography and Geopolitics

Chapters 10–17 constitute a new section of the monograph centered on the geographical, ethnographic, and above all "geopolitical" description of Britain.[20] On a literary level, Tacitus ultimately follows the model of Sallust's *Bellum Jugurthinum*. At the beginning of chapter 10 (10.1: *Britanniae situm populosque multis scriptoribus memoratos* [...] *referam*, "I will set out the position and the peoples of Britain already mentioned by many writers"), Tacitus follows Sallust's ethnographic section (*Jug*. 17.1: *res postulare videtur Africae situm paucis exponere...adtingere*, "My subject seems to require of me a brief account...of the situation of Africa"). But Tacitus also includes the peoples of Britain in his description, connecting the island's physical dimension with an anthropological description, which was a well-established practice in geographical literature (see the many instances in Pomponius Mela, e.g. at 1.68).

Apart from this intertext, many other Greek and Roman authors before Tacitus showed different degrees of interest in this region, such as the controversial Pytheas of Massalia, the first author ever to explore Britain; Posidonius; Caesar's famous excursus in *BG* 4–5; Livy; and Fabius Rusticus, whom Tacitus mentions at *Agr.* 10.3. Tacitus is also informed by an equally significant tradition of geo-ethnographic literature, starting at least from Herodotus and stretching, via Aristotle, up to Strabo and Pliny the Elder.[21] It is difficult indeed to establish how much exactly Tacitus knew about these works and how much each of these sources influenced the *Agricola*. Certainly Tacitus' geographical description of the island largely follows the model of his predecessors, in particular Caesar (*BG* 5.13.3) and Pliny the Elder (*NH* 4.102), who believed that the Iberian Peninsula extended northward, forming with Gaul and Germany a sort of inlet that had Britain at its center. Tacitus most likely uses the authority of Livy, who allegedly described the island in his lost Book 105, dedicated to Caesar's expedition to Britain.

At any rate, it is clear that Tacitus places himself in this geographical tradition, from which he employs many literary elements. This becomes especially apparent in chapters 10–12, which follow a clear order that he will largely employ again in the *Germania*, a work with which the *Agricola* shares many narrative features:[22] physical description (*Ag.* 10), ethno-anthropological analysis of the populations of the island (*Ag.* 11), and

---

[19] See especially Audano (2015).

[20] For an anthropological approach to the Roman perception of Britons, see Borca (2004). For an excellent overview, see Woodman (2014), 11–15.

[21] See Chapter 2 in this volume for Clarke's contribution on the *Germania*. For a general overview of geography in classical antiquity, see Dueck (2012).

[22] This is perhaps a sign that the two works were written around the same time.

considerations on the climate, agricultural production, and wealth of land and sea (*Ag.* 12). The main theme of chapter 11, however, is the population's autochthony. This thesis, in the case of the Britons, is challenged because of their barbaric nature and the frequent migrations of this type of population, which was often accustomed to changing names as well as location, as Posidonius had already written (fr. 62a Theiler). Tacitus records the most plausible explanation, which most modern scholars share based on archaeological evidence and comparative analyses: that there is a great similarity with the Gauls, and that this was the result of Celtic peoples' migration to the island. This is demonstrated not only by linguistic similarities but especially by similar cultural practices and religious beliefs, including the rites of the Druids and human sacrifices.

In chapter 12, Tacitus follows the usual *topos* of the rainy and foggy weather of northern territories. This climate-related characterization creates an implicit otherness compared with the Mediterranean areas, which include, among other things, the production of vines and olive trees, the absence of which is explicitly mentioned for Britain.

The second part of the British excursus (chapters 13–17) is more geopolitical in nature and focuses on the complex process of Romanization of the island, first attempted by Caesar, then resumed with mixed results by Claudius in 43, and at last accomplished thanks to Agricola's vigorous military action.[23] Interestingly, as a further guarantee of credibility, Tacitus emphasizes his direct contact with his father-in-law, an on-the-ground expert in places, facts, and people, and consequently a more reliable witness than much of the literature on Britain, which was written almost exclusively "abstractly." Tacitus explicitly notes this at the beginning of chapter 10, with the phrase *rerum fide*, "the trustworthiness of facts." Tacitus believes that the process of Romanization must be analyzed by adopting two perspectives. The first is purely political, since the whole narrative, which is ideological in nature, exalts the imperial destiny of Rome, whose aim (as defined by Vergil in the famous passage at *Aen.* 6.851–3) is *parcere subiectis et debellare superbos*, "to spare the conquered and subdue the proud." The second perspective, on the other hand, has been defined as "strategic," since Tacitus aims to emphasize the details of the military operations carried out by his father-in-law not only to illustrate his merits, but also to highlight the undeniable difficulty of a long and complex process of conquest that was achieved not only through open war but also through a clash of cultures and civilizations. This will become clear later, in chapter 21, when Agricola skillfully uses the pleasures of *humanitas*, the refined way of life of the Romans, to achieve not only the military but also the psychological submission of his enemies: indeed, he enticingly and non-violently—and therefore more permanently—eradicates their customs, culture, and language.

Thoughts on Roman Imperialism and the Speeches by Calgacus and Agricola

After tracing the history of the conquest of the island, Tacitus develops a broader reflection on the nature of imperialism, which he observes not just in Britain specifically, but as an absolute category of history. Tacitus does not condemn Roman expansionism, nor does he

---

[23] For a concise but accurate history of the Roman conquest of Britain, see Rutledge (2013); Birley (2005) is also important. On the Romanization process, see Woolf (2011).

intend to dissociate himself from the military and political reasons behind it. He remains a staunch advocate of senatorial ideology, which justified the occupation of foreign territories through the propagandistic celebration of the superiority of Roman civilization, portrayed as the expression of a just and superior moral order favored by the gods.

Roman expansionism largely coincided with the ideal of *pax*, "peace," which propaganda exalted as the result of "just" and morally legitimate wars. But this was an ancient debate: back in 155 BCE the philosopher Carneades, after arriving in Rome on an embassy, stated that the Romans fought *aliena cupiendo atque rapiendo*, as Cicero writes (*Rep.* 3.12.20: "coveting and plundering other people's goods").[24] There are many other texts that Tacitus was certainly familiar with, including the speech of the noble Gaul Critognatus in Caesar's *BG* 7.77 aimed at demonstrating the greedy and cruel behavior of the Romans, similar to the behavior of all conquerors. Tacitus surely also knew the letter of Mithridates, king of Pontus, to Arsaces, ruler of the Parthians, which is part of the surviving fragments of Sallust's *Historiae* (Book 4, fr. 69 Maurenbrecher), where the Romans are defined as *latrones gentium*, "robbers of [all] races," an idea that Tacitus reworks as *raptores orbis*, "predators of the whole world," in Calgacus' speech (30.4) to the British troops before the decisive battle of Mons Graupius (chapters 30–2). Calgacus, the otherwise unknown chieftain of the Britons (whom some have even argued Tacitus invented),[25] is introduced at the end of a tragic scene which features the unanimous participation in war of both young and old. To emphasize his outstanding personality, which is quite different from that of treacherous foreign enemies such as Hannibal or Jugurtha, Tacitus highlights his courage and noble origins. Calgacus' speech, a true manifesto against Roman imperialism and its slogans (starting with *pax*), falls under the rhetorical tradition of orations to exhort the troops before a battle.[26] Its structure follows a precise order in accordance with the rules of epideictic oratory: preface, central argumentation, and final exhortation.

Calgacus' words, however, immediately acquire strong political undertones, as can be noted from the speech's opening, when the unity of the various tribes is hailed as *initium libertatis*, "the beginning of freedom" (30.1), for all of Britain; there have been many who have seen here a projection of the attitude of many Roman senators fighting for their freedom against Domitian.[27] To Tacitus, who lends his voice to an enemy, the Roman conquest is one of the many possible examples of the dramatic and frightening manifestations of imperialism. In Tacitus' pessimistic view, there is an insatiable, arrogant greed for power and wealth that drives the strongest to exploit the weakest, using force as an instrument of conquest and domination. But the force of arms alone is not enough: Calgacus' words denounce how the violent and unnatural brutality of the conquerors takes away the dignity of the defeated along with freedom, erases their identity, disrupts their natural and environmental habitat, and destroys family and emotional ties. The thirst for conquest is a monster that feeds on the annihilation of the other, with no chance to escape. While violence and force are expressions of the savage nature of mankind, Tacitus also denounces how imperialism is disguised by those who prevail with a propaganda that exalts and justifies every cruelty through slogans such as peace, justice, and civilization.

---

[24] The passage, quoted by Lactantius (*Inst.* 6.9), is usually accepted as Ciceronian in editions of *De Republica*.
[25] See Fick (1994); Rutherford (2010); and Adler (2011).
[26] On this ancient practice, see Abbamonte (2009).
[27] See Lavan (2011) and especially Damtoft Poulsen (2017).

Some questions, however, may be raised: Does Tacitus, through Calgacus' speech, truly condemn Roman imperialism and its ideological repertoire? Or is he simply offering an analysis, however lucid and ruthless, of his enemies' view of Roman expansionist policy, of which his father-in-law was among the greatest protagonists, and which was firmly supported by the senatorial class to which Tacitus belongs and of which he is certainly a spokesman? Although these issues have been amply debated, it is not possible to give certain answers. Perhaps Tacitus himself saw the violence of the strongest as a frightening, inhumane, yet necessary evil, just as the rule of one man, the emperor, was equally frightening and inhumane, yet necessary. In this respect, freedom is depicted as a luxury that victors and vanquished, as much as they wish to have it, fool themselves into believing they have achieved even when they have not. All that remains, in the words of Calgacus, is the bitter acknowledgment of the devastating consequences of the Roman invasion, with the famous *sententia, ubi solitudinem faciunt pacem appellant*, "They make a desert and call it peace" (30.5).[28]

In chapters 33–4, then, Agricola delivers his speech to the Roman soldiers. Several scholars, when comparing it with that of Calgacus, with which it shares the same structure (proem, central argumentation, and final exhortation), have deemed Agricola's speech excessively conventional and artificial,[29] for example in the use of the initial address *commilitones*, "fellow soldiers" (33.2), which Caesar, as Suetonius writes (*Iul.* 67), had used to emphasize the sharing of the dangers of war between general and soldiers. With his words, Agricola wants to legitimize the civilizing function of this conquest. In his eyes, this is achieved thanks to the traditional discipline of the Roman army, which is completely different from the barbaric chaos of the Britons.

Agricola as an *exemplum*

Agricola's speech displays many elements of the protagonist's personality which Tacitus outlines throughout the work. But his focus in the final section is on Agricola's transformation into an *exemplum* for his contemporaries and especially for posterity.[30] Agricola, as portrayed by his son-in-law, stands out for his pragmatism, which derives from the connection of his actions with Roman *mores* (i.e. the moral code that regulates the actions of the individual within society).

When he outlines Agricola's moral values in chapter 4, Tacitus presents his father-in-law's youthful passion for philosophy as a sort of family secret, later interrupted by his mother, who deemed the "professional" study of this discipline unsuitable for an individual like him. Tacitus identifies *modus*, "a sense of proportion," as the defining trait that derived from that long-ago experience of study, which was later enriched by maturity and knowledge (4.3: *mox mitigavit ratio et aetas, retinuitque, quod est difficillimum, ex sapientia modum*; "Soon age and reason calmed him and, what is most difficult, from philosophy he retained moderation"). *Modus*, which refers specifically to the tradition of Aristotle's golden mean, is transformed from an abstract philosophical principle into a

---

[28] See Giannotti (2018), with rich bibliography.
[29] For a detailed comparison of the two speeches, see Audano (2017), xxxviii–xl.
[30] See Sailor (2012), 38–9 and Audano (2017), xl–lxviii.

concrete attitude of measured balance that Agricola applies to various circumstances in both the public and private sphere. An example of the latter is Agricola's reaction to the early death of his son in the middle of the expedition in Britain (chapter 29). In this painful circumstance, Agricola's characteristic *modus* enables him to manage the pain he feels. This shows Agricola's respect for decorum and moderation in his personal demeanor and public behavior. Agricola's personality embodies an ethical model based on individual virtue, which Tacitus wishes to turn into an *exemplum*. *Modus*, practiced in a concrete way by Agricola in his daily life, now becomes the highest expression of a solid inner balance, characterized by authentic *humanitas*, in which there is no room for any form of irrationality.

Such a view can also be observed in the epilogue of the monograph (chapters 44–6), where critics have identified clear elements that derive from the consolatory genre. The transformation of Agricola into a role model for posterity occurs through the *contemplatio* of his *virtutes* (46.1: *ad contemplationem virtutum tuarum*, "to contemplate your virtues").[31] As was mentioned above, Tacitus takes this expression from Seneca's *Consolatio ad Marciam*. While formally respecting the traditions of the consolatory genre, Tacitus puts Agricola's *virtutes* at the center and turns them into an element that can ensure the consolation of his relatives and the memory of the deceased among contemporaries and posterity alike. It is possible that Tacitus made a personal choice to rework the *topos* of the survival of the soul, a commonplace in *consolationes*, into a more rational vision, whereby Agricola's virtues are strong enough to turn him into an *exemplum* via constant *contemplatio*, thus guaranteeing his survival in the collective memory.

Tacitus' rejection of philosophical or religious idealization makes the *Agricola* a truly innovative work of literature. Since Tacitus focuses on the concrete actions that his father-in-law carried out, which derive from his many excellent qualities, the image of Agricola portrayed by Tacitus at the end of his work (46. 3–4) is not like a physical *imago* (i.e. the death mask of a deceased ancestor that patrician families usually placed in the atria of their houses as a visible sign of their social and political identity) but rather a moral representation that the general was able to instill in the minds of those who knew him. Tacitus wishes to hand Agricola's exemplum down to posterity, in the belief that his memory will not disappear over time thanks to his own *Agricola*. This work thus becomes a new form of biography, which, although in line with even the most ancient literary tradition, is nevertheless original and relevant to the times of Trajan. Agricola, whose ethical model is pragmatic and virtuous in equal measure, is therefore the best role model for the ruling class that supports the emperor in the management of power. And in this respect, to quote Tacitus' final words (46.4), *Agricola posteritati narratus et traditus superstes erit* ("Agricola, because he has been narrated and handed down to posterity, will survive").

Further Reading

For thorough introductions to the *Agricola* and its relation to Tacitus' other writings, see the relevant essays in the *Companions* of Woodman and Pagán, especially Birley (2009), Krebs (2012), and

---

[31] Birley (2009), 49–50 points out the meaning of *virtus*, as the synthesis of Agricola's public and personal qualities.

Sailor (2012). For further readings, the numerous commentaries published over the last fifty years are useful: they are often different in their approach, but complement each other well. The "classic" commentaries of Ogilvie and Richmond (1967) and Heubner (1984), although outdated in some respects, are still valuable. Among the most recent commentaries, Woodman (2014) undoubtedly stands out for its clarity and completeness, paying particular attention to Tacitus' linguistic and stylistic aspects. Soverini (2004) is useful for his in-depth philological and textual discussions, while Oniga (2003) stands out for its anthropological approach; Audano (2017) focuses more on ideological aspects and intertextual dynamics.

Sergio Audano, Agricola In: *The Oxford Critical Guide to Tacitus*. Edited by: Salvador Bartera and Kelly E. Shannon-Henderson, Oxford University Press. © Oxford University Press 2025. DOI: 10.1093/9780191915086.003.0002

2

Germania

Katherine Clarke

Ipse eorum opinionibus accedo qui Germaniae populos nullis aliis aliarum nationum conubiis infectos propriam et sinceram et tantum sui similem gentem extitisse arbitrantur.

As for me, I concur with those who believe that the peoples of Germany, not tainted by marriage with any other tribes, have existed as one-of-a-kind and unalloyed, a people like none but themselves.

(Tacitus, *Germania* 4)

This striking assertion of the insularity and consequent purity and uniqueness of the German peoples, so visibly prone to misuse and misappropriation, is emblematic of a scholarly tendency to marginalize and isolate the *Germania* itself as anomalous, generically problematic, and difficult to contextualize.[1] As a stand-alone work of ethnography, it defies the traditional ancient practice of embedding ethnographic material within works of geography or history.[2] In spite of Pagán's provocative assertion that the *Germania* is "arguably the most important work for understanding Tacitus,"[3] it is frequently omitted from discussions of Tacitus' political discourse, which appear to find more significant overlap between the *Annals*, *Histories*, and *Agricola*. Themes of autocratic power, kingship, and liberty which characterize such political analyses do find a place in the *Germania*, but its minimal incorporation into broader treatments of Tacitus' political thought is indicative of its outlier status.[4] The discourse of political power in *Germania* in relation to Tacitus' other works undoubtedly deserves further attention, but in this chapter I shall focus primarily on the *Germania*'s literary context. I shall argue that Syme's judgment of *Germania* as "unique but not original,"[5] while critical in intent, captures a grain of truth that can be more positively interpreted as describing a work which is deeply embedded in the ethnographical tradition. Rives' description of *Germania* as "the most marginal of Tacitus' works" will be shown to apply to its geographical location, but not to its literary context.[6] Far from being isolated, or linked only to predictable Latin

---

[1] On nationalist misuse of the text, see Krebs (2009), especially 295; Audano (2020) discusses *Germania*'s reception, including cxxxvi–cxlviii on "Il mito nazista della 'purezza della razza'"; also Rives (1999), 67–74.

[2] See Murphy (2004), 79 for *Germania* as "the only surviving ancient book devoted entirely to ethnography"; Rives (1999), 48–56 on *Germania*'s stand-alone nature; van Broeck (2018), 201.

[3] Pagán (2017), 78.

[4] *Germania* is, however, frequently used as a foil for Rome: see Goodyear (1970), 10; Martin (1981), 57 and 58; O'Gorman (1993). By contrast, the German humanist tradition focused on *Germania* as an accurate reflection of its Anglo-Saxon forerunners: cf. Toswell (2010).

[5] Syme (1958a), 126–7.

[6] Rives (2012), 59. Rives (2002) argues for *Germania* being embedded in its contemporary diplomatic and political context, rather than its literary heritage.

forerunners such as Caesar and Pliny the Elder, Tacitus' *Germania* finds extremely close structural and substantive parallels with parts of Herodotus' *Histories*, as well as specific echoes of the works of the great Hellenistic polymath Posidonius.[7] These literary interfaces generate a depth of meaning that makes the *Germania* not only unique but also original, and may also have consequences for our reading of related material in Tacitus' other works.

A Trio of Literary Models

Germania omnis a Gallis Raetisque et Pannoniis Rheno et Danuvio fluminibus, a Sarmatis Dacisque mutuo metu aut montibus separatur; cetera Oceanus ambit, latos sinus et insularum inmensa spatia complectens, nuper cognitis quibusdam gentibus ac regibus, quos bellum aperuit.

The whole of Germany is kept apart from the Gauls and the Raetians and Pannonians by a pair of rivers, the Rhine and Danube, and from the Sarmatians and Dacians by mutual fear or mountains: as for the rest, it is circumscribed by the Ocean, which embraces broad peninsulas and a vast expanse of islands, where we have recently become aware of certain nations and kings, whom war has revealed.

(Tacitus, *Germania* 1.1)

The very first sentence of the *Germania* alludes to several of Tacitus' literary forerunners. After a nod to Caesar's opening of the *De Bello Gallico* (1.1.1: *Gallia est omnis divisa in tres partes*: "The whole of Gaul is divided into three parts") carefully modified to indicate Germany's confinement and isolation (not least from the Gauls) brought by the surrounding rivers rather than its partitioning,[8] Tacitus moves immediately to a more Herodotean register. The demarcation of the landscape by rivers, here the Rhine and Danube, evokes Herodotus' persistent use of rivers to mark out the space of his narrative, particularly that of Scythia,[9] whose significance for the *Germania* will later become clear. Furthermore, the observation that Germany is kept apart from the Sarmatians and Dacians by mountains and "by mutual fear" (*mutuo metu*) recalls Herodotus' description of the Greeks and Easterners being kept apart by the same emotion (Herodotus 8.132.3):[10] "And so it happened that the barbarians were too disheartened to dare to sail farther west than Samos, and at the same time the Greeks dared to go at the Chians' request no farther east than

---

[7] Thomas (2009), 59 stresses *Germania*'s ethnographical context, but focuses on Latin authors. See Toswell (2010), 32 for *Germania* as rooted in the *Greek* ethnographical tradition of Hecataeus, Herodotus, and Posidonius, although he does not offer specific textual parallels. The current chapter seeks to do precisely that.

[8] Tan (2014), 182 contrasts the justification of conquest in *De Bello Gallico* with Tacitus' assertion of Germany's intact and uncontrollable status. *Contra* rivers as delimiters, note McNamara (2022), 181 stressing the *ease* of river-crossings in *Germania* (e.g. *G.* 28.1–3; 41.1).

[9] See Clarke (2018), 93–109. Herodotus 4.82 claims rivers as the dominant marvel of Scythia (cf. 4.47–57). See Thomas (1982), 15–16 on rivers in the ethnographic tradition; Thomas (2009) on Tacitus' use of rivers to define Germany.

[10] Tan (2014), 184 overplays Tacitus' originality here. The Herodotean echo is intensified by mention of the Sarmatians. Although Rives (1999), ad loc. sees the choice of Sarmatians and Dacians as Germany's eastern neighbors as unremarkable, the mention of Sarmatians here seems significant in light of chapter 46 discussed below.

Delos. Thus, fear guarded the middle ground between them." Thirdly, Germania's Oceanic littoral (*Oceanus ambit*) acknowledges the work of the great late Hellenistic polymath Posidonius and his works *On Ocean* and *Histories*.[11] Caesar's division of Gaul into three parts is thus transformed into Tacitus' tripartite contextualization of Germany, alluding to his three most significant literary predecessors in writing about the peoples and places of northern climes—Herodotus, Posidonius, and Caesar himself—making the *Germania* a heavily embedded, rather than an isolated, work.

Dipping a Toe in the Ocean: The Posidonian Backdrop

Tacitus' maritime take on Germany continues strongly beyond the first chapter, linking the *Germania* thematically to Posidonius' *On Ocean*. Certain aspects of this depiction clearly chime with elements of Tacitus' own monograph *Agricola* with its focus on the eponymous character's exploits in Britain. The sinuous nature of Germania's littoral (*G.* 1.1) mirrors Tacitus' own description of Britain's sea-girt status (*Agr.* 10.6: *mare...influere penitus atque ambire*, "The sea streams in and circles around far inland"). Hints at the fictional nature of Odysseus' journey to the shores of Germany (*G.* 3.2: *longo illo et fabuloso errore*, "by that long and legendary wandering") echo the barely credible nature of stories concerning a near-miss encounter between Agricola and Domitian's envoy in the English Channel (*Agr.* 40.2: *fictum ac compositum*, "invented and made up") or the equally incredible tale of the Usipi around Britain's shores (*Agr.* 28.1: *ut miraculum*, "like an object of wonder").[12] Tacitus' own development of this maritime world within his works is particularly marked in interplay between the *Germania* and *Agricola*: his description of the sea beyond the Suiones as "hard-going and almost motionless" (*G.* 45.1: *pigrum ac prope immotum*) unmistakably resembles the sea around Britain which is "hard-going and heavy to row through" (*Agr.* 10.5: *pigrum et grave remigantibus*).[13] Tacitus' later work, the *Annals*, will contribute further to the composite picture of a watery Germany, in which the Rhine estuary acts as a key entry point to Germany for Germanicus' cavalry (*Ann.* 1.63.3), just as it acts as an exit point to the Atlantic Ocean in *Germania* 34.2: *ipsum quin etiam Oceanum illa temptavimus* ("We have even ventured out from there into the Ocean").

The literary context of Tacitus' German portrait extends, however, far beyond his own works. Underpinning his claim to Germany's isolation and purity is the argument that ships "from our world" (*G.* 2.1: *ab orbe nostro*) ventured out into that vast Ocean only rarely, rendering contact unlikely. Tacitus' subsequent reference to inconclusive claims that Odysseus "was carried into this Ocean and came to the lands of Germany" (*G.* 3.2: *in hunc Oceanum delatum adisse Germaniae terras*) further reinforces the sense that it is the maritime façade which defines the connectivity or isolation of Germany. This dominance of the Ocean in defining Germany for Tacitus clearly alludes to Posidonius' work *On*

---

[11] Rives (1999), ad loc. mentions the Oceanic theories of Herodotus and Pliny, but not of Posidonius. Note Romm (1992), 16–17 for the association of fear with Oceanic expanses, linking the latter two of my three points here.

[12] On the Usipi, see Ash (2010a) and Clarke (2001), 109–10. But McNamara (2022), 176–7 contrasts this sole and brief wonder in the *Agricola* with the more widespread but complex wonders of the *Germania*, ambiguously caught between reality and fiction.

[13] See Shannon-Henderson (2022), 24–5 for the mixing of land and sea here as a paradoxographical motif, an *adynaton* which enhances the sense of otherness.

Ocean, about which frustratingly little is known, except through the testimony of Strabo in his *Geography*. Whether Tacitus used Posidonius' work directly has been questioned by those who view Pliny the Elder as a key intermediary author.[14] However, while Pliny's knowledge of Posidonius is beyond doubt,[15] direct engagement with the great Hellenistic polymath on the part of Tacitus himself seems certain. Indeed, Tacitus must surely be referring in part to Posidonius in the *Agricola* where he notes that "to investigate the nature of the Ocean and its tides is not germane to this work, and many writers have discussed it" (*Agr.* 10.6: *naturam Oceani atque aestus neque quaerere huius operis est, ac multi rettulere*).

In many points of detail, as well as in overall concept, Posidonius permeates Tacitus' *Germany*.[16] The relationship between Posidonius' work *On Ocean* and his *Histories* remains tantalizingly unclear,[17] but the extant fragments of the *Histories* contain ethnographic details which recur in Tacitus' *Germania*, suggesting direct interplay with that work as well as with *On Ocean*. At *Germania* 22–3, for example, Tacitus discusses the eating habits of the Germans, not least their predilection for meat early in the day and for all-night banquets leading to drunken violence. The meat-eating habit of the Celts, "a great deal of meat boiled or roasted on charcoal or on spits," were noted by Posidonius in Book 23 of his *Histories* (F 67 Edelstein–Kidd). Such generalities might seem unremarkable, but it is striking how close the comparisons run. Tacitus' note of the Germans' unceremonious approach to food (*G.* 23) sits neatly alongside Posidonius' claim that they eat voraciously, taking whole joints of meat in both hands and gnawing pieces off (F 277b E–K). Tacitus' description of the Germans using banquets to conduct state business echoes the picture in Posidonius of large dinner parties described in terms that resemble a formal council of war or peace,[18] although Posidonius' orderly occasion is transformed by Tacitus into a drunken brawl (*G.* 22.1): *crebrae, ut inter vinolentos, rixae raro conviciis, saepius caede et vulneribus transiguntur* ("Their frequent quarrels, as commonly happens with intoxicated people, are seldom fought out with mere insults, but more often with wounds and bloodshed").

The likelihood that Tacitus has drawn directly on Posidonius in his German ethnography is supported by further correspondences. Both Posidonius and Tacitus detail the drinking habits of the Germans. Posidonius notes that the wealthy drink wine from Italy or Massilia in Southern France, while the poor drink beer made from wheat with honey added (F 67 E–K). Tacitus observes the same two drinks in use (*G.* 23: *umor ex hordeo aut frumento*, "a liquor made from barley or other grain"), fermented to make it resemble wine, or, for those who live on the banks of the Rhine, wine itself. Furthermore, both authors move on to "games" which are played to the death—in Posidonius' case, the duels that are fought during feasts (F 68 E–K), and in Tacitus' *Germania* games of dice (*alea*) on

---

[14] Benario (1999) focuses on Caesar and Pliny, but see Gudeman (1900), 100–5 *against* the assumption that Pliny's *Natural History* (as opposed to his lost *Bella Germaniae*) was a major source for *Germania*; Murphy (2004), 165–93 points to divergences between Pliny and Tacitus on the Chauci; Rives (2012), 49 is sceptical of a significant relationship with Pliny.

[15] Paparazzo (2011) notes explicit citations of Posidonius at Pliny *NH* 2.85–7 and *NH* 6.57–8; see also Paparazzo (2005).

[16] Gudeman (1900) insists that Posidonius was a (possibly *the*) major source for Tacitus' *Germania*, despite thinking that "direct indebtedness cannot, of course, be demonstrated" (107). This chapter aims to underpin Gudeman's arguments from probability and instinct with specific correspondences.

[17] On this, see Clarke (1999), 129–92. [18] *G.* 22.1. Cf. Posidonius F 67 E–K.

which the players stake their lives (*G.* 24.2). And Posidonius' comments on the spurning of gold in favor of silver among the Celtic Scordistae (F 240a E–K) are echoed by Tacitus with his note that "they likewise prefer silver to gold" (*G.* 5.3: *argentum quoque magis quam aurum sequuntur*).

These frequent points of contact with Posidonius' *Histories*, which encompassed the history and ethnography of the northwest corner of Rome's world,[19] are complemented by interaction with *On Ocean*. This double debt to Posidonius through both his "historical" and "geographical" works illustrates the permeability of such boundaries on Posidonius' part but also the embedded, rather than isolated, nature of Tacitus' *Germania* itself. Indeed, Tacitus' description of the renowned Cimbri at *G.* 37 offers a neat illustration of his interaction with both Posidonian works. We know from two mentions in Strabo's *Geography* that Posidonius devoted attention to this northern people. Strabo first cites Posidonius' conjecture in *On Ocean* that the Cimbrian migration did *not* arise from a single great sea-flood (Strabo 2.3.6 = F 49 E–K). He then returns several books later to Posidonius' treatment of the Cimbri as part of his wider discussion of northern migrations. Here Strabo attributes an alternative theory to Posidonius to explain the mobility of the Cimbrians, namely their innate nomadic tendencies (Strabo 7.2.2 = F 272). The successive and aggressive wanderings of the Cimbri, which Strabo directly attributes to Posidonius, involve them attacking the Boii in the Hercynian Forest, then going down to the Ister and the lands of various Galatian peoples, and on to the Helvetii, some of whom are so excited and inspired by Cimbrian plunder that they join them in their wanderings. This middle-European frenzy of mobility and pillaging is put down only by intervention by the Romans, who subdue "both the Cimbri themselves and those who had joined their expeditions" on both sides of the Alps, before their rampage reaches any further into Italy (Strabo 7.2.2 = F 272).

The closeness of this "Posidonian" fragment cited by Strabo with Tacitus' account of the Cimbri (*G.* 37) is striking. Tacitus stresses the renown of this fabled people, which contrasts with their current diminished scale and status (*G.* 37.1: *parva nunc civitas, sed gloria ingens*, "a small state now, but great in glory"). For Tacitus, the scale of their military operations could be gauged by the physical remains of their entrenchments, by contrast with Posidonius' focus on their mobility. However, just as for Posidonius, the Cimbri take on for Tacitus an exceptional status as troublemakers in the region, especially for Rome. Among the extant fragments of Posidonius, it is rare to find comment on any specific historical or military event,[20] as indeed it is in Tacitus' *Germania*. Indeed, Tacitus' account of the Roman campaigns to put down the Cimbri includes the only dates to appear in the *Germania*, noting that "in the six hundred and fortieth year of our city of Rome…during the consulship of Caecilius Metellus and Papirius Carbo" (*G.* 37.2 *sescentesimum et quadragesimum annum urbs nostra agebat…Caecilio Metello ac Papirio Carbone consulibus*) was when the Cimbri first came to Rome's attention. This double-dating strategy serves to reinforce the momentous nature of this clash between two powers, and the bookending of Rome's struggle against the Germans by reference to yet another date, the second

---

[19] This is not surprising if we accept Dobesch (1995) on Posidonius' major contribution to the integration of northern Europe into a systematic world view. Rives (1999), 21–4 sees Posidonius as a key figure in turning the "Germani" into a distinctive group worthy of attention.

[20] This lack of historical material may reflect the preoccupations of later excerptors more than the original balance of Posidonius' works.

consulship of the emperor Trajan (*G.* 37.2), sets the seal on a supremely important episode in the work, where the watery, Odyssean, semi-fictional Ocean world of Germany comes, through the Cimbri, into sharp and very real focus as a direct military threat to Rome. Tacitus' account of the 210-year German campaigns in *G.* 37.3–5 adopts a distinctively different tone from that of the rest of the work, far exceeding in historical content and detail any other chapter in the *Germania*. As Tacitus notes, the scale of the threat posed by the Germans exceeds that of all Rome's other notorious foes—the Samnites, Carthaginians, both Spains, all the nations of Gaul, and even Parthians included. And the losses incurred here have been the greatest as well, outstripping the famed Parthian defeat of Crassus (*G.* 37.4): *at Germani Carbone et Cassio et Scauro Aurelio et Servilio Caepione Maximoque Mallio fusis vel captis quinque simul consularis exercitus populo Romano, Varum trisque cum eo legiones etiam Caesari abstulerunt* ("But the Germans have deprived the Roman people of five armies, all commanded by consuls; the Germans have routed or taken the commanders of these armies, Carbo, and Cassius, and Scaurus Aurelius, and Servilius Caepio, and also Maximus Mallius; the Germans have snatched away from even the Emperor Augustus himself Varus and three legions"). Even Rome's successes here have come at great cost (*G.* 37.4): *nec impune C. Marius in Italia, divus Iulius in Gallia, Drusus ac Nero et Germanicus in suis eos sedibus perculerunt* ("Not without loss did Gaius Marius in Italy, or the deified Julius in Gaul, or Drusus or Tiberius or Germanicus defeat them in their native territories"). Recent gains can be regarded with only guarded satisfaction (*G.* 37.5): *triumphati magis quam victi sunt* ("We have gained a triumph over them rather than a victory").

Although the fragmentary nature of Posidonius' *Histories* makes it impossible to say how much of Tacitus' account of hostile German interactions with Rome was owed to this work,[21] the Cimbri and their regional neighbors clearly struck a note of dread into both authors. The heart of Tacitus' "history" of Germany lies here, anchored to the migrations and campaigns of the fabled Cimbri.[22] The fact that Strabo's extensive citation of Posidonius' account of the Cimbri moves on to other ethnographic details that are not attributed to a particular source (7.2.3) and are not included by Tacitus suggests that the latter was drawing directly on Posidonius, rather than on Strabo as intermediary. Strabo's ongoing account of the northern Germans that extend along the Ocean might seem to prefigure Tacitus' litany of northern peoples which occupies chapters 38–46 of the *Germania*. However, Strabo's uncertainty over who inhabits this Oceanic fringe sits in contrast to the detail offered by Tacitus' account, reinforcing the likelihood that Posidonius rather than Strabo was Tacitus' main source for this information. And the Oceanic nature of this part of Tacitus' account is never absent for long, whether it is the worship of Mother Earth on an island in the Ocean (*G.* 40.2) or the Rugians and Lemovians with their distinctive round shields, short swords, and "obedience towards kings" (*G.* 44.1: *erga reges obsequium*), whose location further inland is articulated in terms of their relationship to the sea (*G.* 44.1: *protinus deinde ab Oceano*, "immediately next to the Ocean"). The maritime nature of this part of Germany escalates toward the end of the work, as the Suiones

---

[21] Posidonius treated at least part of Marius' career; see F 255 E–K, on his seventh consulship and death.

[22] This may explain Tacitus' slip in ascribing the defeat of Lucius Cassius Longinus to the Germans in the context of Cimbrian agitation (in fact he was defeated by the Gallic Tigurini in 107 BCE). Perl (2005), 174 suggests that the prominent defeat of the Tigurini in declamatory exercises led to their being readily elided with other groups troublesome for Rome.

turn out to live actually "in the Ocean" (*G.* 44.2: *ipso in Oceano*), powerful through their specially adapted ships (*G.* 44.2).

In the penultimate chapter of the *Germania*, the Ocean theme acquires a new intensity as Tacitus announces the transition beyond the Suiones to another sea, "hard-going and almost motionless," as noted above, "by which the world is thought to be bounded and enclosed" (*G.* 45.1: *quo cingi claudique terrarum orbem*). Our arrival at the edge of the earth is reinforced by the claim that nature itself finds its limit here (*G.* 45.1: *illuc usque…tantum natura*: "only to this point…does nature reach").[23] A clearer reference to the all-encircling Ocean of Homeric fame could not be found.

Through the Looking Glass: The Herodotean Mirror

The sea's importance here revives thoughts of a second major literary alignment with the Greek historian Herodotus.[24] The practice of amber-extraction in the shallows or on the shore, which Tacitus here describes in detail, is used to illustrate both the alien nature of this region, in the Suebi's failure to recognize the potential value of the amber, and its connectivity to Rome, which offers a market.[25] But the intellectual backdrop is also of considerable interest, with Tacitus' discussion of amber-harvesting evoking that of Herodotus at *Histories* 3.115.[26] Herodotus cloaks his whole discussion of amber in uncertainty. It is only a *logos*, after all, that amber was collected from the outflow of the Eridanus River into the northern sea, a nebulous landscape which sits alongside that of the equally dubious Tin Islands. Herodotus has suspicions about the existence of any of these geographical features, displaying greater confidence in the wonders of the East, and it is striking that he casts doubt on the very Ocean which has proved so dominant in Tacitus' *Germania*: "Nor, in spite of all my efforts over this, have I been able to hear from someone who has seen that there is a sea beyond Europe (3.115.2)."

But the correspondences between Herodotus and Tacitus here exceed the single point of contact in the extraction of amber. Tacitus' ongoing discussion of amber as resembling a tree-sap leads him to set up a geographical symmetry between East and West (*G.* 45.5):

> *Fecundiora igitur nemora lucosque, sicut Orientis secretis, ubi tura balsamaque sudantur, ita Occidentis insulis terrisque inesse crediderim, quae vicini solis radiis expressa atque liquentia in proximum mare labuntur ac vi tempestatum in adversa litora exundant.*

---

[23] See Romm (1992), 141–9 for the Ocean throughout Tacitus' works as an inaccessible and semi-mythical venue, lying outside the human world, let alone that controlled by Rome. Woolf (2013), 137 contrasts the human world of Germany with the bestial world of *G.* 46.

[24] Hartog's *Le Miroir d'Hérodote* (Hartog (1988)), alluded to in the title of this section, offers the classic treatment of Herodotus' generation of a sense of the "other," a technique also ascribed to Tacitus by Woodman (1992a).

[25] For the ambiguous status of this wonder, as part of a current economic reality but located in a semi-mythical location, see McNamara (2022), 183. As Shannon-Henderson (2022), 27–8 comments, Tacitus' explanation of amber-production enhances rather than diminishes its paradoxographical status, and focuses attention on the process of historical enquiry.

[26] Rives' (1999), ad loc. claim that "Pliny provides the only literary evidence for this important trade" seems to be belied by Herodotus.

I would therefore imagine that, just as in the furthest reaches of the East, where frankincense and balsam exude, there are in the islands and lands of the West fruitful woods and groves, which, acted upon by the close rays of the sun, flow in a liquid state into the adjacent sea, and are washed up on the opposite shores by the force of storms.

The balance here between opposing parts of the world recalls the many instances where Herodotus invokes such symmetries between rivers or whole regions.[27] Furthermore, the particular examples given of eastern frankincense and balms directly echo the very passage in Herodotus Book 3 in which he contrasts the exploitation of amber, tin, and other products of Europe such as gold (3.115–16) with the methods used to extract the exotic resources of the East such as frankincense, myrrh, and cassia in Arabia (3.107, 3.110–11), and the mysterious *ledanon* gum, which is produced in the beards of he-goats (3.112). It seems hardly coincidental to find this combination of amber and frankincense in both Herodotus and Tacitus, set within an explicitly East–West frame. For Herodotus, tin and amber are the products of the "most distant part" of Europe (3.115.2: ἐξ ἐσχάτης), just as for Tacitus, frankincense and balm represent "the furthest reaches of the East" (*G.* 45.5: *Orientis secretis*). The two passages are, in effect, mirror images of each other.[28]

The idea that the worlds of Herodotus and Tacitus are in conversation, but as neighbors rather than co-habitants, is reinforced by the final chapter of the *Germania*. Here the question arises as to whether the Peucinians, the Venedians, and the Fennians belong to the Germans or the Sarmatians. The determining factor, Tacitus suggests, is their lack of nomadism (*G.* 46.2):

Hi tamen inter Germanos potius referuntur, quia et domos figunt et scuta gestant et pedum usu ac pernicitate gaudent: quae omnia diversa Sarmatis sunt in plaustro equoque viventibus.

These, however, are rather counted among the Germans, in so far as they have fixed houses, and carry shields, and prefer travelling on foot, and delight in swiftness. All of these practices are different from those of the Sarmatians, who live in a wagon with a horse.

The nomadic wagon-dwelling Sarmatians naturally evoke Herodotus' Sauromatae, a subset of the Scythians (*Histories* 4.46, 4.110–17). Tacitus' clear criterion for determining whether the most remote peoples mentioned in his *Germania* truly belong to that work or more properly belong to the world of the Sarmatians is suggestive of a distinct boundary, where the worlds of Tacitus and Herodotus meet.[29] The dividing line between the Germani and the Sarmatians lies near the limit of Tacitus' theme; for all the clear-cut nature of this distinction in terms of nomadism or settlement, Tacitus opens this final chapter on a note of uncertainty (*G.* 46.1: *dubito*: "I doubt") as he nears the outer reaches of his knowledge.[30] We have, in any case, already gone beyond the limits of nature itself, which were arrived at in the previous chapter. The mirror on either side of which Tacitus

[27] See Clarke (2018), 57–8, 72–3, 160–1.

[28] McNamara (2022), 184, however, notes the additional intertext of Vergil, *Georgics* 2.112–23.

[29] Pomponius Mela 1.19 and 3.25 has Germany and Sarmatia sharing a border. Rives (1999), 18–21 notes how, in Greek ethnography, Celts and Scythians occupied the northern part of the known world, forming a backdrop against which the Germani were superimposed.

[30] Krebs (2011b), 205 notes that the ability to name Germany's neighbors gives a false sense of clarity about an elusive boundary.

and Herodotus adopt their respective viewpoints may be placed about here. This is where Herodotus admits defeat in his own enquiries concerning the extraction of amber and tin; this is where Tacitus from the opposite side concludes his work with a parallel expression of historiographical ignorance: "This, as something unknown, I shall leave open" (*G.* 46.4: *quod ego ut incompertum in medium relinquam*), a striking ending indeed, and even more resonant if the spatial metaphor of the phrase *in medium* might hint at the continuation of what appeared to be the edge of the earth into the world behind the mirror, that of Herodotus' Sauromatae and beyond.[31]

In fact, the worlds on either side of the mirror turn out to be overlapping rather than strictly contiguous. Just as Tacitus' gaze extends to the "recesses of the East" where exotic frankincense and balms are to be found, thereby trespassing onto Herodotean territory, so too does Tacitus invite Herodotus across the border, as it were, and he does so repeatedly throughout the text. Herodotus and his influence run through *Germania* from its first sentence. Here Tacitus' reference to the Rhine and Danube as demarcators of Germany from the surrounding areas evokes Herodotus' frequent use of rivers as geographical boundaries; but more particularly, Tacitus' outlining of a river network whose component parts are vividly traced from their mountain sources to their outlets into the seas recalls Herodotus' similar creation of a complex and extensive landscape articulated by rivers from their sources to the sea (*G.* 1.2):[32]

> *Rhenus, Raeticarum Alpium inaccesso ac praecipiti vertice ortus, modico flexu in occidentem versus septentrionali Oceano miscetur. Danuvius, molli et clementer edito montis Abnobae iugo effusus, pluris populos adit donec in Ponticum mare sex meatibus erumpat; septimum os paludibus hauritur.*

> The Rhine rising in the Rhaetian Alps from a summit that is inaccessible and sheer, after winding slightly towards the west, blends into the northern Ocean. The Danube, pouring down from the gently and gradually rising ridge of Mount Abnoba, traverses many peoples, until it bursts in six streams into the Pontic Sea; its seventh outlet is absorbed by the marshes.

From the outset, strands of Herodotean thought weave their course through the *Germania* in spite of the focus of many modern scholars on Latin literary models.[33] The theme of authorial uncertainty, noted above in relation to the final chapter of the *Germania*, runs through the work. In chapter 3, where Tacitus airs various traditions concerning the visits to Germany of Hercules and Odysseus, he concludes by refusing to commit himself to either confirming or refuting the tales: "These statements I have no intention of sustaining by proofs, or of refuting; everyone may believe or disbelieve them using his own critical

---

[31] McNamara (2021), 214 interprets this *aposiopesis* as Tacitus throwing the text out at the readers "before their eyes." McNamara (2022), 180 offers a different interpretation, suggesting that Tacitus implies "such tales could easily have continued, despite the absence of evidence." Audano (2020), ad loc. sees the abrupt ending as a reminder of the sudden start (*in medias res*) and therefore as a deliberate piece of Caesarian emulation.

[32] Herodotus 1.189.1 for the full course of the Gyndes.

[33] Woodman (1992a) offers a notable exception, convincingly reading Tacitus' account of Nero's Rome as heavily embedded in Herodotean paradoxography. See also Shannon-Henderson (2022), 29 on interaction between Herodotus and Tacitus *Annals* 2.61.1 over the depth of springs feeding the Nile, "to which most commentators agree Tacitus is indebted."

faculties" (*G.* 3.3: *quae neque confirmare argumentis neque refellere in animo est: ex ingenio suo quisque demat vel addat fidem*). This is particularly striking given that it follows directly on from another Herodotean topos which pulls in the opposite direction, namely the mention of material evidence in support of the presence of Odysseus in the region: an altar to the hero, inscribed also with the name of Laertes, and "monuments and tombs inscribed with Greek letters" (*G.* 3.2: *monumentaque et tumulos quosdam Graecis litteris inscriptos*).[34] As the text progresses, the Herodotean tone deepens. The chapter with which we started, in which the "pure" traits of the Germans are attributed to a lack of interaction with other peoples, goes on to explain some of their hardy characteristics explicitly through their location, claiming that they have grown accustomed to hunger and cold through "their climate and soil" (*G.* 4: *caelo solove*) in an obvious echo of Herodotus' closing chapter (9.122) and the theory of geographical determinism voiced by Cyrus the Great, claiming that "soft lands breed soft men."

In addition to these broadly Herodotean methods and approaches, echoes of Herodotus' account of the northerly Scythians in Book 4 of his *Histories* run through the *Germania*.[35] This starts in the second chapter with Tacitus' account of the claims to autochthony made by the Germans. Tacitus describes an earth-born god, Tuisto, and his son, Mannus, who are celebrated as "the origin and founders of the people" (*originem gentis conditoresque*), and the three sons of Mannus after whom the different population groups are named. This offers an unmistakable echo of Herodotus' presentation of Scythian claims to be born from their land, with their descent from Targitaus, born of Zeus and the daughter of the river Borysthenes, through his three sons Lipoxais, Arpoxais, and Colaxais who gave rise to the various Scythian peoples (Herodotus 4.5.1). In both cases, these myths of autochthony and descent from the triple line of an earth-born originator are juxtaposed with visits to the region by Hercules (*G.* 3.1 and *Histories* 4.8.1). As in the case of the collection of amber, it is the same combinations of ideas in Tacitus as in Herodotus, rather than single points of reference, which are suggestive of direct engagement with this important model for writing about the northern part of the world.

All in all, the intensity of Herodotean motifs which characterizes the end of the *Germania* might be seen as a natural escalation or an accumulation of allusions, both general and specific, to his northern world. When we reach in the final chapter the official boundary between Tacitus' Germans and Herodotus' wagon-dwelling Sarmatians, it is hard to see that demarcator as anything more than a two-way looking glass, through which it is easy to pass.

Summus Auctorum? The Caesarian Blind-alley

Far from being an isolated work, Tacitus' *Germania* partakes of a multilayered and richly textured literary milieu. Indeed, the sheer literariness of this work might encourage us to

---

[34] See e.g. Herodotus 8.39.2 for physical evidence as verification of a story.

[35] Small points of detail reinforce this: the female dress-custom of the Germans which leaves the nearest part of the breast exposed (*G.* 17.2) recalls Herodotus' bare-breasted Amazons. The special relationship between the Germans and their horses (*G.* 10.2; *G.* 32) echoes that enjoyed by the Scythians and other inhabitants of the Asian landmass in Herodotus' *Histories* (cf. 3.84–6 for the Persian royal succession determined by the neighing of horses).

approach the appearance of its inhabitants in other, more explicitly historical, works of Tacitus with caution. Thomas reads the ethnographic vignettes in *Germania* as heavily influenced by the ethnographic passages in the works of Latin poets such as Vergil.[36] This need not contradict the idea of the *Germania* as a work deeply embedded in a much longer literary tradition that goes back at least to Herodotus, spans both Greek and Latin works, and orientates itself primarily toward the ill-understood and semi-mythical Oceanic rim. As Ash has argued, an episode in Tacitus' *Histories* involving the Rhoxolani,[37] a tribe from central Europe who had moved westwards from Sarmatia, just beyond the world of Tacitus' *Germania*, also shows strong intertextual links with Vergil's Scythian ethnography in the *Georgics*. Her observations remind us that the fluidity and mobility of the northern peoples could lead to elision and confusion over their identity and location.[38] Tacitus' neat demarcation of Germany at the start of the work, which contributes to the misappropriated sense of its isolation and "purity," is belied by the messiness of its ethnographic picture and the impossibility of placing any of the peoples mentioned accurately on a map. It is debatable whether this geographical vagueness in *Germania* and elsewhere is due to a deliberate wish on Tacitus' part to stress the unconquerable nature of this area of the Roman world in the face of the emperor Domitian's repeated claims to have tamed Germany,[39] or simply to the geographically imprecise nature of the ethnographic tradition in which the *Germania* is embedded. In a sense, the two options merge if we recall the untamable Scythians, the obvious Herodotean parallel for geographical fluidity as an anti-imperial device.[40] Here, as ever, the Scythians provide a model on the other side of the looking glass for understanding the northern world of the *Germania*.

But is *Germania*'s intellectual and literary milieu even the one which Tacitus' opening sentence appears to promise? The strongly Oceanic themes that run through the text and the persistent echoes of Herodotus' Scythian description point us to a natural home for the *Germania* within the context of works devoted to the northern, semi-maritime world of Herodotus, Posidonius, and Strabo. The tendency of modern scholars to look for the literary backdrop of the *Germania* primarily in the predictable Latin works of Pliny and Caesar risks overlooking a rich and relevant ethnographic backdrop provided by Greek writers on this part of the world. The nod to Caesar's opening of the *De Bello Gallico* should be seen as just that, and nothing more.[41] Caesar is present in the work only as an unfulfilled promise. The closeness of some passages of *Germania* to ethnographic fragments of Posidonius' *Histories* sends us momentarily scurrying inland, even as far as northern Italy. But this is a false alignment to the world of Caesar's Gallic and civil wars, and we are allowed only a glimpse into northern Italy and Rome's various military engagements (G. 37) before being quickly reoriented back to the northern perimeter of the world and the Oceanic rim, back to the intellectual context of Posidonius' *On Ocean*, which

[36] Thomas (2009), 66. For *Germania*'s rich poetic interfaces, see Audano (2020), lxxxvi–xcix.
[37] Ash (2010b). Also see McNamara (2022), 184 for parallels between *Germania* and *Georgics*.
[38] Interplay between Vergil's Scythian ethnography and the *Germania* itself may be present at chapter 23 on substitutes for wine (Vergil, *Georgics* 3.379–80); see Rives (1999), ad loc.
[39] See Tan (2014), *passim* and especially 200; van Broeck (2018) on Tacitus' creation of a deliberately uncontrollable Germany by stressing fluidity in its geography and history.
[40] See Purves (2006) on amorphous, nomadic, untamable Scythia pitted against Darius, the bureaucratic controller par excellence of the Persian Empire.
[41] Rives (1999), ad 28.1 argues for Tacitus' alignment with Caesar, but see Gudeman (1900), 96, criticising the assumption that Caesar, the only author mentioned by name in *Germania*, is used extensively. McNamara (2021), 202–6 argues for the *Germania* as a direct *inversion* of Caesar's ethnography.

takes us around to the world of Herodotus' Scythia, not into Rome's heartland of Italy. Caesar may be *summus auctorum* and even *divus* (*G.* 28.1), but for all his boasts that the Gauls of his campaigns were once more powerful than Germany, the world of Tacitus' *Germania* does not belong to him.[42]

Whatever Tacitus claims in *G.* 4 about the isolation and integrity of the German peoples, this image is belied by the text, which resonates with stories of migration and intermingling. But the famous Cimbrian migrations, which orient us on a north–south axis and seem so consistent with the well-established habit of reading the *Germania* as an unsatisfactory part of the Roman ethnographic tradition (and the more modern preoccupation of reading it as a mirror to Rome), are in fact confined to one chapter. Far more pervasive is the east–west axis represented by the Sarmatians of the Greek tradition, who appear in both the first and the last chapter of the work and sweep commandingly not only across the indefinable expanses of northern Europe, but also across the whole extent of Tacitus' text.*

Further Reading

Krebs (2011b); McNamara and Pagán (2022); O'Gorman (1993) = Ash (2012) Chapter 3; Rives (1999); Romm (1992).

Katherine Clarke, Germania In: *The Oxford Critical Guide to Tacitus*. Edited by: Salvador Bartera and Kelly E. Shannon-Henderson, Oxford University Press. © Oxford University Press 2025. DOI: 10.1093/9780191915086.003.0003

---

[42] See Krebs (2011b) for Tacitus' direct rejection of Caesar's contribution to the notion of "Borealism" by reuniting the northern sweep which Caesar had split up to create the image of a distinct German people that served his political and military ends. Cf. Rives (1999), 26–7.

* Dedicated to the Sarmatians of our time, the people of Ukraine, migrating westward with their lives reduced to what they can carry.

3

Dialogus de oratoribus

Christopher S. van den Berg

Narratives of decline typically follow an alluring but misleading formula: anxious beliefs about the failures of today become hopeful beliefs about the successes of yesterday. This complex process of valorizing the past inevitably distorts not only the historical complexity of a bygone era but also the similar complexity of the seemingly woeful present. Authors and politicians ancient and modern have all too often fallen under the spell of such mystifying accounts. Was Tacitus, when he wrote the *Dialogus*, also one of the enchanted?

We are unlikely ever to know the answer with certainty, in part because it is unclear whether Tacitus had an unequivocal answer and, if so, whether he wished to share it. The *Dialogus De oratoribus* is a sophisticated, textually rich, and intellectually demanding series of debates on the history and state of oratory from the perspective of the late first/early second century CE. It begins with what seems like a straightforward question in the mouth of Lucius Fabius Iustus, who, Tacitus claims, often asked why so many ancient orators found fame while the modern day scarcely knows either orators or eloquence (1.1). The response that emerges becomes increasingly unclear as the issues are discussed in increasing depth. The conversation attributed to Tacitus' role models wanders through a remarkable range of topics; Marcus Aper's defense of oratory is vigorous and well-argued, as is Curiatius Maternus' defense of poetry. All three of the dialogue's speakers offer dubious or contradictory claims and counterclaims. Aper cites questionable role models to prove oratory's power; Maternus conceives of poetry in naively idealistic terms, and his historical analysis of Republican and imperial oratory is factually suspect; and Vipstanus Messalla's complaints about modern pedagogy and oratorical training rely heavily on Cicero's ideas, but his criticisms confuse Ciceronian ideals with Republican practice. All the while, Tacitus never chimes in to endorse any of the positions; the dialogue ends not with resolution but with a call to renew debate.[1]

A happy consensus among interpreters of the *Dialogus* once existed (a scholarly Golden Age?). It went something like this: Tacitus believed in the decline of oratory, and Maternus in his last speech offers the (Tacitean) historical explanation of decline, laying blame at the door of the emperors and the political system they embodied. Only in the Republic could oratory thrive. Aper is largely a boorish, ambitious, or venal advocate; Messalla's citation of education and training, which draws from the theoretical works of Cicero and Quintilian, pales in comparison to Maternus' vivid and damning political insights.[2]

---

[1] Luce (1993) elucidates problems in the speeches, although his explanation—that they are set pieces with considerable rhetorical latitude—fails to explain crucial aspects of the dialogue, such as the close interconnections of the speeches with one another and with other literary texts.

[2] See Mayer (2001) for such an account; challenged by Goldberg (1999) and van den Berg (2014); Keeline (2018), 223–76 tries to revive it. Champion (1994) soberly assesses Aper's values.

This line of thought has been challenged in recent decades by scholars who offer new ways of thinking about how and what the *Dialogus* might mean and what Tacitus accomplished by writing it. Unless we have already decided up front that Tacitus espoused decline and sought to offer an apparently historical answer in the mouth of the last speaker, then it is reasonable to conclude as Tacitus concludes the dialogue: by acknowledging that the oft-discussed question has yet to receive a satisfactory answer. We need more.[3]

Rather than directly rehearse the modern opinions and disagreements about the work (whom might Tacitus endorse, was there decline and if so what caused it, is Aper serious, Maternus savagely ironic, Messalla foolishly earnest?) this chapter considers Tacitus' reworkings of Cicero's *De Republica* ("On the Republic"). There Cicero conceptualizes and defines central civic institutions of the late Republic, especially oratory and the Roman constitution, even as he ponders whether such institutions were threatened or even irretrievably lost. Tacitus draws on Cicero's language and ideas with varying degrees of recognizability. These similarities, as well as consideration of Tacitus' brief musings on constitutional forms in his historical works, can help us to better understand his conception of statehood and eloquence under the Principate.

Tacitus turned to Cicero's dialogue when conceptualizing the Roman state, even if the influence is less obvious at first than that of rhetorical texts such as *De Oratore* or *Brutus*. Tacitus evokes the dialogue formally with the late arrival of Messalla (14.1), a touch partly modeled on the late arrival of Laelius in *De Republica* (1.18.1).[4] Structurally, the *Dialogus* contains three pairs of two speeches and can thus be thought of as a miniature of the three pairs of dialogue discussions in *De Republica*. Conceptually, Maternus' final speech shows the greatest affinities with this Ciceronian text by explaining the Republic and Principate in terms familiar from *De Republica*. Much of the shared language has yet to be examined in full, although a few intertextual reworkings have long since been recognized. Exploring the commonalities and divergences will help us to understand Tacitus' conception of statehood in the *Dialogus*.

Cicero's *De Republica*

De Republica outlines the Roman *res publica* ("public thing," especially the state or its government) in theoretical and practical terms. At a theoretical level, it examines the different types of constitutions, including the ideal "mixed" constitution, in Book 1.[5] Book 2 turns to the practical embodiment of that ideal in Roman history, detailing the evolution of Rome's constitution from its origins. Much of the rest of the work is lost or heavily fragmentary. Books 3 and 4 contain a debate on the utility and necessity of justice for the state and the means by which to educate a Roman citizen. Book 5 examines the ideal citizen and Book 6 concludes the work with the riveting account of "Scipio's Dream," a quasi-mythical depiction of the ideal statesman, which emulates Plato's Myth of Er at the end of his *Republic*.

[3] Marincola (1999) is a salutary examination of the theme of decline in Tacitus' historical prefaces.
[4] See also Rutledge (2000) for Alcibiades in Plato's *Symposium* as background.
[5] On the mixed constitution, see Lintott (1997), and more generally Lintott (1999).

How the broad range of allusions to Cicero's text ultimately shapes the message of the *Dialogus* is not immediately clear.[6] Yet it is perhaps unreasonable to expect clarity from Tacitus' citation of Cicero's *De Republica*. Ambivalence was built into many of Cicero's works of the 50s (and 40s) BCE just as it was built into the *Dialogus*. Cicero's *De Republica* and *De Oratore* ("On the Orator," Cicero's grand treatise on the ideal orator–statesman) and Tacitus' *Dialogus* all offer discussions that ultimately prove unsatisfactory and require further examination of differing viewpoints. All three works end on contradictory, but not necessarily irreconcilable, notes of resignation and optimism, in some sense building their optimism on top of a pessimistic foundation. In Cicero, the political crises of the Gracchi and of the impending Social and Civil Wars might be resolved by the ideal statesman in his pursuit of renown (*De Republica*). And Cicero's elder colleague, Hortensius, offers hope for oratory's future in *De Oratore* (it is set in 91 BCE).[7] For Tacitus, the assessment of modern oratory leads to the claim that one should embrace the different possibilities of different eras and to appreciate what's best in each age (41.5). These commonalities reflect a prominent feature of Greco-Roman dialogues, which so often refuse to deliver a uni-vocal message and instead explore a complex issue in order to arrive at only tentative conclusions.

Despite such general similarities, the relationship of the *Dialogus* to Cicero's *De Republica* is hardly straightforward. Maternus draws on and seems to endorse Cicero's constitutional explanations, highlighting the peaceful conditions of the present in patently Ciceronian terms. At the same time, he contradicts Cicero's requirement that orators ensure the flourishing of the civic order.[8] What emerges is not a full-scale rejection of the imperial system or celebration of republican government, but rather an impressive medi-tation on the relationship between constitutional order and oratorical practice. For all the sheer power of Maternus' arguments, we are left with as many questions as answers. Is the new order worth the threat it poses to eloquence, to the artistic ideal that so animated Cicero's definitions of elite moral and civic activity? And how reliable is Maternus' assess-ment of either the political order or the practice of oratory?

In turning to the *Dialogus* I would like for our purposes to set aside for now the vexed question of Maternus' sincerity, that is, whether his final speech is ironic in its praise of imperial rule.[9] Instead, I consider how his speech draws in various ways on Cicero's con-ception of the Republic and kingship in *De Republica*. The greatest focus thus far has been on the mixture of allusions in 40.2 (discussed further below). Maternus also repeatedly employs key vocabulary from Cicero when he discusses the ideals and realities of the Roman Republic, engaging with Cicero's ideas and analyzing the changed conditions of Roman statehood.

The broader interest in constitutional forms emerges in Maternus' mention of "the best constitution" (*optimus civitatis status*, 37.5), the very language that introduced the main topic of Cicero's *De Republica* (*optimum statum civitatis*, 1.33; cf. *de optimo civitatis statu*,

---

[6]   Koestermann (1930) offers detailed treatment. See also Keeline (2018), 270–3.

[7]   The ending of *De Oratore* is based on the end of Plato's *Phaedrus* (279a), in which the interlocutors predict the rise of Isocrates to prominence in philosophical rhetoric.

[8]   It is unfortunate that we possess so little of Book 5 of *De Republica*, in which Cicero's discussion of the ora-torical statesman may have been a significant point of reference.

[9]   On this question, see Luce (1993); Bartsch (1994), 98–115; Gowing (2005), 109–17.

1.70, 2.40, 2.65).¹⁰ Maternus depicts the present dispensation in terms of orderly peace (*quies*, "calm"; *otium*, "leisure"; *tranquilitas*, "tranquility"; *disciplina*, "order"; and *pax*, "peace(fulness)"; 38.2).¹¹ The first two terms, *quies* and *otium*, are central to the definition of constitutional order, joined with the notion of felicity (*beatus*, "happy" or "blessed"). Maternus remarks on the "ordered, calm, and flourishing Republic" (*composita et quieta et beata re publica*, 36.2). Cicero stressed the importance of order in similar terms (*beatus, otium, Rep.* 1.52.5; *pax, otium, Rep.* 2.26.1, 2.43.4).

Opposed to this in both works is the people's recklessness, most commonly denoted through the loaded political and moral term *licentia* (*D.* 36.2, 40.2; *Rep.* 1.44.5, 1.67.3, 1.68.2, 3.23.3). Such "license" or "recklessness" is produced by, and in turn produces, civic chaos (*perturbatio, mixtis omnibus*, essentially "commotion" and "general confusion," 36.2; *turbidis et inquietis temporibus*, "unruly and turbulent conditions," 37.6; *turbatis atque permixtis*, "turbulent and intemperate," *Rep.* 1.44; *turba et confusio*, "mass disorder," 1.63; *perturbatio*, "disorder," 2.63.1; cf. *perturbatam rem publicam*, "a disordered Republic," 6.11.5). The metaphorical language of disorder, especially those terms denoting improper mixing, can be traced back through Cicero to Plato's analogy in the *Republic* to the unmixed wine that produces psychological disturbance (*Rep.* 1.66–7 creatively translates Plat. *Rep.* 8.562c–563e1).

Such turbulence can only be dampened or rectified by the imposition of orderly moderation. Here the metaphorical language of haphazardly mixed disorder gives way to the proper mixing which Cicero expressed with terms such as *moderatum et permixtum* ("temperately blended," *Rep.* 1.45.3). These metaphors describe the ideal of the "mixed" constitution (*in hac iuncta moderateque permixta constitutione rei publicae*, "in this united and temperately blended state of the Republic," *Rep.* 1.69). For Cicero this involved distributing power—unequally and according to inherited hierarchical structures—to the people, the aristocracy, and the king-like figures who occupy the highest magistracies. Maternus picks up on this Ciceronian language when he praises the *modus et temperamentum*, "measured restraint," which was instituted by the Principate and found wanting in the Republic (40.4, 41.5).¹²

Cicero also discusses the regular need for select individuals to act as guardians or restorers of the constitutional order. Such a figure is the "moderator of the Republic" (*moderator rei publicae, Rep.* 5.8; cf. the metaphorical use at 6.17.3, with *temperatio*, "due mingling," and 6.26.3). He also discusses "that director of public matters" (*ille rector rerum publicarum, Rep.* 5.6; cf. *De Orat.* 1.211). Tacitus' Maternus employs similar language when describing the turmoil of the late Republic that would (implicitly) be rectified by the emperor: "with everything in disarray and in need of a single guide" (*mixtis omnibus et moderatore uno carentibus*, 36.2).¹³

---

¹⁰ The phrase is rare, and prior to Tacitus is attested (outside of Cicero) only at Sen. *Ben.* 2.20.2, whose language Tacitus repeats exactly (cf. Gell. *NA* 5.13.7). Tantalizingly, Seneca remarked: "Since the best condition of the state arises under the rule of a just king" (*cum optimus civitatis status sub rege iusto sit*). Cf. 40.2 (below) for similar language of statehood, *in bene constitutis civitatibus*.
¹¹ *Pax* is understood in the verb <*de*>*pacaverat*.
¹² See Wallace-Hadrill (1981) and (1982) on the emperor's virtues and the notion of the *civilis princeps*.
¹³ Powell (1994) discusses the *rector*. See Zarecki (2014) more generally.

Maternus' Versions of the *Respublica*

Several negative definitions of the late Republic fill out the picture of statehood that Maternus paints. When describing the final years of the Republic (40.4), he uses terms such as *partes*, *dissensiones*, and *discordiae* ("factions," "disagreements," and "enmities"). The late Republic lacked peace (*pax*) in the Forum, agreement (*concordia*) in the senate, respect (*reverentia*) for superiors, and restraint (*modus*) among magistrates. Essential to good governance is the discipline (*disciplina*) instilled by laws (*leges*, 40.3) and the order that prevails "among moral character ready to comply with a ruler" (*inter bonos mores et in obsequium regentis paratos*, 41.3). Compliance may well seem to slip too far in the direction of autocracy, but Tacitus looked kindly on the moral restraint expressed by *obsequium*, for example in praising the conduct of his father-in-law Agricola under Domitian.[14] Under the Principate, senatorial leaders quickly come to agreement (*cum optimi cito consentiant*, 41.3) and the wisdom of single rule replaces uninformed mob rule (41.4).

Such unvarnished praise of imperial control may make us question Maternus' position. While there is considerable overlap in the constitutional vision laid out in *De Republica* and the ideals expressed by Maternus, crucial differences also cannot be ignored. Maternus makes no attempt to suggest that the Principate is the mixed tripartite constitution so praised by Scipio, which carefully balances elements of monarchy, aristocracy, and democracy. His praise of the emperor as *sapientissimus et unus* ("uniquely wise," 41.4; cf. *moderatore uno*, "the sole guide," 36.2) is taken from a similar idea in *De Republica*, but from a passage that defines and praises monarchy: "Its condition is such that the safety, equality, and tranquility of the citizens is guided by the uninterrupted power and justice of a single man, and by his wisdom alone" (*is est autem status, ut unius perpetua potestate et iustitia uniusque sapientia regatur salus et aequabilitas et otium civium*, *Rep.* 2.43.4).[15] When Maternus appeals to the virtues of moderation and restraint, he likens the emperor to the extraordinary figure of state salvation who, for Cicero, temporarily intervenes amid civic crisis. The new granting of emergency powers in perpetuity to the emperor is a far cry from the temporary or extraconstitutional measures that Cicero endorsed. Several other key ingredients from Cicero's state recipe are wanting: there is no mention of a general sense of shared justice (*ius* or *aequitas*), and while the best men (*optimi*) may have a say in deliberations, Cicero envisioned shared deliberation (*consilium*) as a cornerstone of a functional *res publica*, and this expectation is absent in Maternus' praise.[16]

The difficulty of defining the imperial constitution and its effects on oratory are best seen in one of the most famous and intertextually rich moments of Maternus' speech (40.2):

---

[14] Tac. *Agr.* 8.1, 8.3, 42.4 and cf. *Ann.* 6.8.4 (on which see chapters 1 and 13 in this volume).

[15] This unique *sapientia* is ironically contrasted with the widespread and destructive knowledge of republican demagogues: "Each orator knew as much as sufficed to persuade a reckless populace" (*tantum quisque orator saperet quantum erranti populo persuaderi poterat*, *D.* 36.2). On the *errans populus*, cf. *Rep.* 1.52.4, *error et temeritas populorum*.

[16] Schofield (2021), 61–104 provides a succinct overview of Cicero's main expectations. Messalla, rather than Maternus, succinctly touches on these aspects of Cicero's political theory in *de Republica* and *de Legibus*: laws, *senatus consulta*, law of citizenship (or civil law), wisdom, and the precepts of the wise (*leges, senatus consulta, ius civitatis, sapientia*, and *praecepta prudentium*, 32.3). Messalla consistently recycles Ciceronian theory only to regret its practical absence, making it hard to interpret his excessive pessimism, which is often contradicted by other parts of the dialogue, or by historical fact. It should also be noted that Aper's speech does emphasize the role of premier orators as *amici* (8.1–4), that is, as part of the *consilium principis* that advised the emperor.

*non de otiosa et quieta re loquimur et quae probitate et modestia gaudeat, sed est magna
illa et notabilis eloquentia alumna licentiae, quam stulti libertatem vocant, comes seditio-
num, effrenati populi incitamentum, sine obsequio sine severitate, contumax temeraria
arrogans, quae in bene constitutis civitatibus non oritur.*

I am not speaking of some inactive and calm matter that enjoys uprightness and restraint,
but that great and notorious eloquence is the nursling of license, which fools call freedom; it is the companion of seditious actions, the goad of an unbridled people, lacking
compliance, lacking sternness, defiant, reckless, arrogant, and it does not arise in well-
ordered states.

The passage is stuffed with Ciceronian reminiscences that playfully subvert the original
meanings. Maternus reverses Cicero's association of eloquence and peace: "Eloquence is
the companion of peace, the associate of leisure, and the nursling, as it were, of a well-
ordered state" (*pacis est comes otique socia et iam bene constitutae civitatis quasi alumna
quaedam eloquentia, Brut.* 45).[17] He then borrows and combines two passages from *de
Republica* on the false equation of license with liberty: *ex hac nimia licentia, quam illi
solam libertatem putant* ("from this excessive license which they consider merely freedom," 1.68.2) and *dicitur illa libertas, est vero licentia* ("it is called liberty but is in fact
license," 3.23.3).[18] And last comes the pointed rebuff to Antonius' remarks on the power of
oratory to control the people: *et languentis populi incitatio et effrenati moderatio* ("both a
spur for the listless and bridle for the intemperate," *De Orat.* 2.35).

Maternus' praise may hide some ambivalence. It has recently been suggested that
Maternus points the reader to a damning ironic criticism that was latent in one of the passages he cites from *De Republica*. *Rep.* 1.68.2, one of two passages alluded to, continues as
follows: "[from this excessive license Plato] describes how a tyrant springs up as from the
root and is born" (*ait ille ut ex stirpe quadam existere et quasi nasci tyrannum*). Neither
the intended allusion nor its meaning is straightforward. Cicero carefully pieced together
disparate statements from his textual forerunner (Plato) just as Tacitus does here by drawing on multiple versions of this statement in *De Republica*.[19] The original context is also
crucial, since at *Rep.* 1.68.2 Cicero details how a demagogue manipulates popular unrest
only to assume the position of tyrant, the devolution of ochlocracy into tyranny.[20] The
transition of the demagogue into a tyrant was a commonplace of anti-democratic rhetoric
going back as far as Herodotus' debate over the three forms of government (3.80–2; cf.
Arist. *Pol.* 1310b14).

While the most pointed allusion, *Rep.* 1.68.2, is suggestive when read as the only possible
forerunner, other allusions and the broader context within *De Republica* are equally
crucial, and they do little to illuminate the transition from Republic to Empire or the
devolution of the emperor into a tyrant. In describing the rising tyrant, Cicero seems

---

[17] On the topos of oratory's connection to tranquil statehood, see also *De Orat.* 1.14, 1.30, 2.33; *Orat.* 141; and
Arist. *Pol.* 8.6 1341a 28–32 (on the flourishing of arts more generally after the Persian Wars), with van den Berg
(2021), 250–2. On the language of the ordered state, see also *civitas bene constituta* (*Rep.* 5.7).

[18] At *Rep.* 1.66–8 Scipio loosely translates and paraphrases Plat. *Rep.* 8.562c–63e. I return to the passage below.

[19] Cicero draws his agricultural image from a sentence a bit later, Plat. *Rep.* 565d1–2. Cic. *Rep.* 1.68.2 is
certainly the most similar forerunner, but not the only one.

[20] Keeline (2018), 271 remarks that the passage "describes how a tyranny develops out of a democracy," which
is true enough, although the passage cannot be an analogy for Rome's transition from Republic to Principate.

particularly to have in mind a demagogical figure like Clodius who, according to Cicero, aspired to tyranny, rather than figures like Caesar, Pompey, or (later) Octavian.[21] These charismatic personalities built their power on *Realpolitik* and military success rather than by demagogically seizing control from an enraged populace, as Clodius had, in the manner of several tribunes of the people before him. Furthermore, Plato's original argument had been a defense of monarchy over democracy, much as Scipio finds monarchy to be the best of the three individual forms of rule. Earlier in his adaptation of Plato, Cicero even railed against the people's tendency to overindulge in false liberty and to label powerful rulers as tyrants (*praepotentes reges tyrannos vocat*, *Rep.* 1.66.1). Cicero elsewhere is adamant that kings can become tyrants, but at this point in *De Republica*, like Plato before him, he deplores the dangers of the populace and its captivation by the charms of demagogues, who often use their power against monarchs or the aristocracy. As textual forerunners, Plato and Cicero justify monarchy at least as much as they criticize monarchy turned tyranny.[22]

Although Tacitus draws on Cicero's *De Republica* to conceptualize statehood, he remains far removed from Cicero, both temporally and in understanding the governance of the Roman state. Cicero undoubtedly would have thought Augustus a tyrant and his system tyranny. But history and experience had given Tacitus a different perspective. Among all the representations, theorizations, and criticisms of the emperors, the durability of the system was hardly in doubt. As Carlos Noreña remarks, "We can discern an unspoken but nevertheless pervasive assumption that this state of affairs was permanent."[23] Augustus, as Peter Brunt once argued, ultimately resuscitated much of what Cicero desired for the Republic.[24]

Tacitus on the *Respublica*

When assessing the realities of the imperial system, Tacitus' acknowledgment of its necessity is evident: "After war was finished at Actium and it served the peace to have all power accrue to one man,..." (*postquam bellatum apud Actium atque omnem potentiam ad unum conferri pacis interfuit*, *H.* 1.1.1; cf. Quint. 3.8.47). This is hardly a ringing endorsement, but Tacitus would later expand on the nature of the monarchical constitution with references again to Cicero (*Ann.* 4.33.1–2):

> *Nam cunctas nationes et urbes populus aut primores aut singuli regunt. (delecta ex iis et conflata rei publicae forma laudari facilius quam evenire, vel si evenit, [haud] diuturna esse potest.) Igitur ut olim, plebe valida vel cum patres pollerent, noscenda vulgi natura et*

---

[21] In the nearly contemporary *pro Milone* Cicero calls (the recently murdered) Clodius a *tyrannus* (*Mil.* 35; cf. *Mil.* 80 on honoring tyrannicides in Greece). More generally, see Gildenhard (2011), 74–98.

[22] Had Tacitus wished to have Maternus ironically praise kingship while intertextually decrying tyranny, several far better passages in *De Republica* were available. For example: "But if the people itself kills or drives out a tyrant, it is more restrained, to the extent that it is sensibly wise, and it rejoices in its deed and wishes to protect the state that it has set up" (*sin per se populus interfecit aut eiecit tyrannum, est moderatior, quoad sentit et sapit, et sua re gesta laetatur, tuerique vult per se constitutam rem publicam*, 1.65.3). One could well imagine a speech containing strong allusions to the second half of this sentence that would encourage us to hear an unexpressed allusion to the first half and its endorsement of tyrannicide.

[23] Noreña (2009), 267.   [24] Brunt (1988), 56–68.

quibus modis temperanter haberetur, senatusque et optimatium ingenia qui maxime per-
didicerant callidi temporum et sapientes credebantur, sic, converso statu neque alia
<salute> rerum quam si unus imperitet, haec conquiri tradique in rem fuerit, quia pauci
prudentia honesta ab deterioribus, utilia ab noxiis discernunt, plures aliorum eventis
docentur.[25]

Either the people, the aristocracy, or individuals rule all nations and cities (a form of the
Republic that is selected and composed from among these can be praised more easily
than it can arise or endure when it does arise). And so, just as previously when the people
were strong or the aristocracy powerful, one had to discern the nature of the mob and the
means by which it could be restrained in moderation, and those who had best learned the
temperaments of the senate and of the best men were thought to be clever concerning
their times and wise, in the same way, since the constitution has changed and the state's
security rests on one-man rule, it will have been useful to investigate and hand down
these things, since few men prudently distinguish honorable things from baser ones, useful from harmful, and many are taught by others' outcomes.

Praising the form of the Republic nods to Cicero's *De Republica* and its praise of Rome's
mixed constitution.[26] The passage also reflects several other features of *De Republica*. The
mention of the need to control and moderate the people is a running theme there.[27]
Mention of wise men (*sapientes*) of old (*olim*) who understand state affairs describes perfectly the idealized interlocutors of *De Republica*, who themselves describe and recall
instances of *sapientia* at Rome and in Greece. Cicero insisted that the ideal statesman
must understand the twists and turns of government in order to anticipate crises and disasters. Tacitus also integrates foresight (*prudentia*) into the historian's task, making it part
of the traditional exemplary purpose of observing and writing imperial history and align-
ing the historian's and the statesman's duties. The utility of Tacitus' history lies in docu-
menting the events that will help others to understand the nature and predict or even
influence the vicissitudes of the new order. Such political *prudentia*—a key term in Cicero's
conception of the statesman—encapsulated both "wisdom" and "foresight" (*providentia*)
(*Rep.* 2.45.2):[28]

> *id enim est caput civilis prudentiae, in qua omnis haec nostra versatur oratio, videre itinera*
> *flexusque rerum publicarum, ut cum sciatis quo quaeque res inclinet, retinere aut ante pos-*
> *sitis occurrere.*[29]

This is the chief matter of civil prudence (the topic of our whole conversation): to see the
twisting paths of states, so that you can anticipate or hold each event once you know
where it is headed.

---

[25] I follow here the text of Woodman (2018) rather than Heubner (1994), but prefer *<salute>* to *<fiducia>*.
[26] See Woodman (2018), 178–180 on allusions to *De Republica*.
[27] Tacitus may also include a meaningful pun when he says *quibus modis temperanter haberetur*; *modus* is a
key term to indicate restraint, connected to *moderatio*.
[28] The latent sense of vision in Tacitus' use of *prudentia* emerges perhaps in *discernunt* at 4.33.2.
[29] Cf. *Rep.* 1.45.2: *prospicere impendentes* and *in gubernanda re publica moderantem cursum atque in sua*
potestate retinentem; 6.1(fr.).1: *totam igitur expectas prudentiam huius rectoris, quae ipsum nomen hoc nacta est ex*
providendo. On *prudentia* as a key idea in Cicero's conception of the statesman and its connection to privileged
vision, see Cole (2013); Santangelo (2013), 56–68; Traversa (2015); Santangelo (2020).

Cicero's ideal statesman understood the nature of constitutional change and civic develop-ments and knew when to intervene. This required oratory, which was inextricable from civic virtue: his ideal statesman was an orator just as his ideal orator was a statesman. But can we say the same for Tacitus, especially in light of Maternus' persuasive claims about the abeyance of oratory? Another way of putting this, to return to the question of this essay's opening paragraph, is: Did Tacitus's conception of the new order and his role in it, even as a historian, also mean condemning oratory and espousing the thesis of decline?

Tacitus' allusions to *De Republica* may put us in mind of a shared concern in both authors: monarchy, whatever its potential qualities, can quickly become tyranny. Maternus paints an idealized picture of Roman rule in its monarchical form, even noting the aris-tocracy's (albeit limited) role in political deliberation (*cum optimi cito consentiant*, 41.4).[30] Yet the text to which he sends us back repeatedly stresses the preeminence of monarchy relative to other simple forms of government, democracy and oligarchy.[31] Cicero also emphasized its instability, the ease with which it could devolve into the worst form of government: in imperial terms, however laudable a Vespasian at a given moment, the pos-sibility of a Tiberius, Nero, or Domitian is always lurking.[32] Indeed, the model of swift devolution from the just—or at least competent—ruler to the savage overlord memorably fits Tacitus' depiction of degeneracy in the Neronian books of the *Annals*. They exemplify the transition from promising monarch to rank tyrant, a moral arc that culminates in and joins the narrative arc spanning the Julio-Claudian dynasty.[33] Such a concern, though ever present, need not preclude sincere praise for a Vespasian or a Nerva of the sort that we find in the speeches of Aper and Maternus, in the *Agricola*, or at the beginning of the *Histories*.[34] Nor is such praise of good monarchy inconsistent with insistence on the loss of the appropriate forms of *libertas* (as opposed to the extreme liberty of ochlocracy, the cor-rupt form of democracy).[35]

Again, the complex portrayal of Maternus points the way. He partly clothes the imperial monarch in the attire of Cicero's civic savior in times of crisis and in that of the idealized monarch. There is little doubt that Cicero opposed monarchy and believed in the virtues and stability of the mixed constitutional order.[36] What he required, like Tacitus, was a functioning moral community as part of that civic order.[37] And on this point we may again find a commonality in the historical perspectives across Tacitus' works. *Ann.* 3.26–8 reflects on the relationship between lawmaking and the demise of the Republic, with par-ticular criticism of the proliferation of new laws in the last hundred or so years of the Republic: "At the height of corruption in the Republic we had a great many laws"

---

[30] As Cic. *Rep.* 2.15.1–2 notes, the monarch will call on the best citizens (*optimus quisque*) for advice, but this is still kingship (the example is Romulus, compared to the Spartan Lycurgus). Scipio at this point is outlining the early origins of the mixed constitution, which is still in development. It is worth noting that Maternus' panegyric partly forgoes a *topos* of imperial panegyric, the assertion of the senate's (mostly) restored role in decision making.

[31] On monarchy as the best form of the simple constitution, see *Rep.* 1.54.2–3, 1.61.6.

[32] To use Cicero's terms: a lovable Cyrus can morph into a savage Phalaris (*Rep.* 1.44.3). On the easy slide from monarchy into tyranny, see *Rep.* 1.44.3, 1.64.5, 1.65.2, 2.43.2, 2.47–50.

[33] Tacitus later claims that Vespasian was the only emperor whose character improved upon assumption of the purple (*H.* 1.50.4). See Levick (1999b) on Vespasian.

[34] On the *Realpolitik* limits of combining *libertas et principatus*, see, however, Spielberg (2019).

[35] See Wirszubski (1950); Vielberg (1987); Morford (1991); Strunk (2017) on *libertas*.

[36] He believed neither Caesar nor Pompey wanted to restore constitutional order. See the discussion of *Rep.* 5.8 in *Epist. Att.* 8.11.2.

[37] Zetzel (2017), xvi–xxii.

(*corruptissima re publica plurimae leges*, *Ann.* 3.27.5). His depiction of the late Republic in the *Dialogus* also notes the constant passage of laws (*leges assiduae*, 38.2). In both works the legal reforms of Pompey in his third consulship (52 BCE) are singled out for discussion.[38] In the *Annals* they seem to be a failed precursor for the successful reforms of Augustus, who "instituted laws by which we might have peace and a princeps" (*deditque iura quis pace et principe uteremur*, 3.28.2). In the *Dialogus* Pompey's laws constrained eloquence and forced all business to be conducted in the forum, before the praetors, and in accordance with the law (*ut omnia in foro, omnia legibus, omnia apud praetores gererentur*, 38.2). Ultimately peace reigned when Augustus did (38.2). While the accounts differ in what they emphasize about Pompey's laws, both criticize the disorder of the late Republic and acknowledge its resolution with Augustus.

But like Cicero before him, Tacitus nowhere endorses extreme *libertas*, nor is it clear that Maternus does either, although this has often been assumed based on his (playful?) interjection "make use of ancient outspokenness" (*utere antiqua libertate*, 27.3) and the piquant themes of his tragedies. It is probably Aper who gets the balance right when he praises the fact that the interlocutors can justify their outspokenness ("unreproached outspokenness," *libertas excusata*, 10.8). In quintessentially Ciceronian fashion—and language—Aper remarks that the interlocutors "temper their outspokenness" (*libertatem temperatis*, 23.6). This conception of appropriately restrained *libertas* may underpin Tacitus' famous claim that "Nerva Caesar had mixed together previously irreconcilable things—the principate and liberty" (*Nerva Caesar res olim dissociabiles miscuerit, principatum ac libertatem*, *Agr.* 3.1).[39]

The (Old) Republic and (New) Eloquence

Still, Tacitus repeatedly expresses resignation to the uncomfortable realities of imperial rule while railing against the moral failures and political blunders of those who play a role in the imperial system, whether freedman, senator, or emperor. With this in mind we may also get new purchase on understanding Maternus' adamant (if inscrutable) activities as a poet: he can praise good monarchy as a necessity and expound the peaceful ideal of the poet, but he also may have written plays that criticized the embodiments of tyranny: criticism of Nero or his family and the moral failings of Nero's *scurra* Vatinius (*Domitius, Medea*), for example, or even broader meditations on the nature of tyranny (*Cato, Thyestes*).[40] These are precisely the activities that could make Maternus the talk of the town among a hypercritical elite trained for paranoia by years of turbulent imperial rule, or prove fatal under certain emperors.[41] Yet such attitudes are not irreconcilable with recognizing Vespasian's merits or, if we choose to see some of Tacitus in Maternus,

---

[38] On the importance of Pompey for Cicero in the 50s, see Zarecki (2014), 71–2; Steel (2018).

[39] *Miscere* is part of the vocabulary (with *temperari*) defining the mixed constitution: "these [governments] were mixed in this way" (*haec ... mixta fuerunt*, *Rep.* 2.42.4); see Woodman (2014), 83–4.

[40] See Manuwald (2001a) on the moral rather than anti-Principate content of Maternus' plays; cf. Kragelund (1987). Penwill (2003) offers a staunchly anti-Principate interpretation of Maternus' plays.

[41] The mystery of Maternus' fate remains unsolved. Kragelund (2012) revives the thesis that Domitian killed him in 91 CE for speaking against tyranny. His re-evaluation of the evidence in Cassius Dio increases the probability but cannot clinch an identification with our Maternus. Gallia (2009) discusses whom Maternus may have offended.

grudgingly acknowledging the necessity of a monarchical system when no feasible alternative seemed to exist, considering the broader artistic or political consequences, and hoping for the best.

But did the inevitability of emperors also mean oratorical decline? There are considerable problems in linking the two ideas. Reading Maternus' final speech as Tacitus' ventriloquized condemnation of contemporary oratory is overly simplistic. For all its plausibility, the speech poorly portrays contemporary oratorical venues and possibilities. And, much like Messalla before him, Maternus vastly overstates the universal prevalence of oratory in the Republic.[42] It is undoubtedly true that certain figures, Cicero foremost among them, rode to prominence on the back of legal advocacy and, to a lesser extent, debate before the senate or the people, although his speeches are exceptional in their quality, quantity, and afterlife. Cicero was an exception, not the rule, and only the distorting gaze of nostalgia could make him seem like a normative model.

Further complicating Maternus' picture of contemporary oratory is the other reality, so prominent in Tacitus' historical writings, that the Empire was not defined solely in terms of peace, stability, and oratorical desolation. It is a fitting coincidence that Tacitus' first narrative after his digression on the Roman constitution in the *Annales* is the famous senatorial trial—perhaps the most famous in all of Tacitus' historical writings—of Cremutius Cordus (*Ann.* 4.34–5; see ten Berge on *Annals* 4 in Chapter 12 of this volume). Maternus' penchant for writing poetry and Secundus' praiseworthy biography of his uncle Julius Africanus (*D.* 14.4) suggestively point out that several venues for the exercise of *eloquentia* had emerged, not necessarily against but alongside oratory, and a transgeneric conception of *eloquentia* is developed across the dialogue, especially in the first debate.[43]

Rather than thinking of the *Dialogus* as condemning oratory outright, it may be more fruitful, and historically credible, to see it as part of a broader attempt to document and redefine the ways in which oratorical skill and rhetorical training could find their way into different venues and genres in the public sphere. This also allows us to conceive of Tacitus' writing of history as the continuation or culmination of an oratorical career—not to sever the participants and voices of the *Dialogus* from the Tacitus of the *Histories* and *Annals*, but to read them together. The writing of history, "an alternative venue for political discourse," is not antithetical to oratory but rather an attempt "to situate his historiography as a form of direct political engagement," as Lydia Spielberg remarks.[44] Again, Cicero was one possible model given that he too reconceptualized his writings under Caesar as innovative public and forensic performance: "My writings, confined at home, will undoubtedly match my greatest achievements in the forum and abroad" (*profecto maximis rebus forensibus nostris et externis inclusae et domesticae litterae respondebunt, Orat.* 148).

[42] Scaevola's questioning of oratory's centrality to politics in *De Oratore* should not be discounted; his objections are never refuted. On Maternus' flawed (or at least tendentious) portrayal of oratory, see van den Berg (2014), 186–207. See Roller (2011) on new venues for eloquence in the Empire.

[43] Notice of the biography of Julius Africanus indirectly advertises Tacitus' writing of the *Agricola* (whether completed or planned). On the transgeneric conception of *eloquentia*, see van den Berg (2014), 146–8, 163–4, 299–300.

[44] Spielberg (2019), 175 and 173. See further Woodman (1988) on oratory and historiography.

Tacitus, even after the *Dialogus*, continued his interest in oratory, as Pliny's letters demonstrate.[45] Pliny himself was another example of the attempt to broaden conceptions of *eloquentia* into new genres while still maintaining an active connection to oratory. His letters are both the product of oratorical expertise and a crucial vehicle with which to promote his oratorical exploits. The risk in reading the *Dialogus* as Tacitus' turn away from oratory is that it involves the false division of treating oratory and historiography as career choices, as if they were akin to the modern difference between, say, a lawyer and a novelist.[46] Cicero continued to evolve throughout his lifetime, partly in response to new constraints, and partly to adapt his literary ambitions to the evolving nature of the public sphere. His examinations of statehood and oratorical history were themselves filled with a judicious mix of pessimism about contemporary developments and some hope in future change, resisting the slide into comfortable nostalgia or starry-eyed progress.[47] Tacitus seems partly to share Cicero's resigned optimism, at least insofar as he employed eloquence in an attempt to rectify moral and political failings. That he also evolved as Cicero did—at a different pace and for different reasons, to be sure—is just another way in which he explored new voices and venues for civic and moral engagement, all the while remaining in dialogue with Cicero.

Further Reading

Schofield (2021) discusses the political philosophy of Cicero, who was Rome's most influential political theorist. Steel (2018) and Zetzel (2022) examine Cicero's dialogues of the 50s BCE. Lintott (1997) surveys ideas about the mixed constitution in antiquity, which was a precursor to the American constitution's separation of powers. Noreña (2009) succinctly discusses autocracy. For broad interpretations of the *Dialogus*, see Goldberg (2009) and van den Berg (2014). Marincola (1999) considers Tacitus' self-deprecating pose of the decline of historiography, an article whose insights can also be used fruitfully to think about the *Dialogus*. Spielberg (2019) reads Tacitus' writings as political engagement. Levene (2004) surveys aspects of literary-historical thinking in the *Dialogus*.

Christopher S. van den Berg, Dialogus de oratoribus In: *The Oxford Critical Guide to Tacitus*. Edited by: Salvador Bartera and Kelly E. Shannon-Henderson, Oxford University Press. © Oxford University Press 2025. DOI: 10.1093/9780191915086.003.0004

[45] Goldberg (2009), 79 and 79 n.14 corrects Mayer's (2001), 6 claim that Tacitus subsequently published no speeches (repeated by Keeline (2018), 231). See Griffin (1999) on the similarities between Tacitus and Pliny (and modern prejudices about their biographies).

[46] Goldberg (2002, a review of Mayer (2001)) soberingly reminds us: "Tacitus' intellectual biography cannot be culled from a reading of the *Dialogus*."

[47] See Zetzel (2022) on this foundational tension in *De Oratore* and *De Republica*; van den Berg (2021) for the *Brutus*.

4

Histories 1

Cynthia Damon

Introduction

In the *Histories* Tacitus tells the story of the brief principates of Galba, Otho, and Vitellius, and the longer span of Flavian dominance, twenty-eight years all told (69–96 CE). It was a period that began in the chaos consequent on the collapse of Rome's first dynasty, the Julio-Claudians, and ended with the collapse of Rome's second dynasty, the Flavians. These were also the decades of Tacitus' own youth and early career as one of Rome's public officials; when he wrote the *Histories*, in the first decade of the second century CE, he was well on his way to the top of the senatorial career ladder. But most of the *Histories* is lost, and the extant books treat only the civil wars of 69 CE and the first few months of Vespasian's principate. The year 69 CE in fact gets more narrative space than any other year covered by Tacitus, and fully half of *Histories* 1 is devoted to the first two weeks of that eventful year, a fifth of the book to the day on which Rome saw the violent end of the first of the year's four emperors and the accession of the second, January 15, 69 CE.

With its narrative of conflict among three short-lived emperors and its hints about the off-stage Vespasian, the first of the Flavians, *Histories* 1 is an exciting tale. Highlights are Galba's rationale for adopting a successor (1.15–16), the ill-omened presentation of his heir to the troops (1.18), the small beginnings of Otho's successful coup (1.21–31), an advising scene replete with all the nastiness of court politics (1.32–3), the murder of Galba and his closest associates with the populace looking on as if it were a show (1.40–1), the distress of the senate in the face of rapid changes of rulers (1.45, 1.47), the first description of the year's third emperor, Vitellius, whose character plainly disgusted Tacitus (1.62), and the menacing Vitellian invasion of Italy (1.63–70). The book ends on a tense note, with Vitellius' massive force north of the Po and Otho on his way to confront it. The date is March 14, 69 CE.

Histories 1 also introduces us to the aims, claims, sources, and literary techniques of Tacitean historiography as he embarks on a new genre, moving on from the works in which he found his voice after the repressive years of Domitian (*Agr.* 2.3–3.2).[1] In it he extends his earlier analyses of the Principate as a political system, focusing here on the challenges of writing history under a regime hostile to truth and transparency and the civil war conditions that radically changed the relations between center and periphery, or more particularly between political and military power, in the Roman Empire. In *Histories* 1 Tacitus gives his first demonstration of the power of a historian who looks to posterity.[2]

---

[1] See Audano, Chapter 1 in this volume.   [2] Damon (2017).

The Narrative

The structure of *Histories* 1 is complex but always clear. After a panel introducing the work and its author (1.1–3) and sketching the social hierarchy and geographical extent of the Roman Empire after the death of Nero (1.4–11), the narrative begins on January 1, 69. For most of the book Tacitus is narrating simultaneous events. In its first panel he reports actions of the rivals Galba and Otho in Rome during the first two weeks of the year (1.12–47), then restarts the year in Germany with a legionary mutiny on January 1 and proclamations of a third imperial contender, Vitellius, on January 2–3 (1.51–62). Thereafter he describes Vitellian forces marching simultaneously on separate routes from the Rhineland to northern Italy during the first ten weeks of 69 (1.63–70) before detailing the events of those same weeks in Rome under Otho (1.71–90). The narrative structure reflects the fact that in early 69 the Roman Empire had no center, a situation that revealed a hidden truth about the empire: "An emperor can be made elsewhere than in Rome" (1.4.2: *posse principem alibi quam Romae fieri*).

Preface to the *Histories* (1.1–3)

The first chapter of the *Histories* communicates the work's topic (Rome under the Principate) and chronological scope (Galba to Domitian), the author's credentials and aspirations, and his promises of concern for posterity and fidelity to truth, all in a challenging Latin style that eschews complacency of thought and expression and suits Tacitus' material. "I begin a work rich in events, appalling for its battles, riven with seditions, even in peacetime cruel" (1.2.1: *opus aggredior opimum casibus, atrox proeliis, discors seditionibus, ipsa etiam pace saevum*).[3] Such is the accord between content and expression in this description of the *Histories* that the adjectives are progressively more suited to the era than to the work (see further under Program below). The next two chapters list the *Histories*' particular themes: wars (internal, external, and "often a messy mix of the two," 1.2.1: *plerumque permixta*), natural disasters, the disintegration of the social fabric, and human character (base and admirable). This "table of contents" entices the reader[4] even if its prevailing colors are dark, with references to cruelty, violence, disorder, disease, and destruction. But Tacitus also indicates that histories of this period require thoughtful readers: "Truth is shattered," he says at the outset (1.1.1: *veritas…infracta*), and a reader ought to think about the causes and consequences of this state of affairs. Bias is a worry, for example, in both author and reader: "An author's ambition you could easily discount, but attacks and ill-will are heard with ready ears" (1.1.2: *sed ambitionem scriptoris facile averseris, obtrectatio et livor pronis auribus accipiuntur*). In effect, he demands that the reader scrutinize the historian—himself included—along with the history and be wary of hearing what she wants to hear.

The opening words of the preface—"The beginning of my work will be the year with Servius Galba (for the second time) and Titus Vinius as consuls" (1.1.1: *initium mihi operis Servius Galba iterum Titus Vinius consules erunt*)—look forward to the conclusion of the

---

[3] Wellesley (1989) prints *tempus adgredior dirum*.   [4] So Woodman (1988), 167.

introductory panel as a whole (1.1–11), quoted below, and its contents are fittingly capped by its final word, "punishment" (1.3.2: *ultionem*).

Chronological retrospective and geographical survey (1.4–11)

In *H.* 1.4–11 Tacitus provides a two-part retrospective on the state of the empire in the months following the collapse of the Julio-Claudian dynasty, with 1.4–7 treating the capital city, 1.8–11 the armed provinces. Galba had been *princeps* for more than half a year when the narrative proper begins on January 1, 69, and his principate ends fifteen days into 69 CE, so a retrospective allows Tacitus to bring the reader quickly to the narrative precipice on which the section concludes: "Such was the state of the Roman world when Servius Galba, consul for the second time, and Titus Vinius ushered in the year; their last, and nearly the last for Rome as well" (1.11.3: *hic fuit rerum Romanarum status, cum Servius Galba iterum Titus Vinius consules inchoavere annum sibi ultimum, rei publicae prope supremum*). Content, structure, and style make these chapters a masterly piece of historical writing.

Tacitus begins with reactions to Nero's death (1.4) and traces Rome's increasing familiarity with Galba: in 1.5 Galba is known only by reputation, in 1.6 we follow his march to Rome, in 1.7 his aging physique is a source of ridicule to those who see him. No event is dated, and even relative chronology is left rather fuzzy. As defined by chapters 4–7, the significant elements in the "condition of the City" (1.4.1: *status urbis*) are the attitudes toward Galba in the various groups surveyed and the general instability of a city crowded with the disaffected and the armed.

These two themes are reversed in prominence in chapters 8–11. Galba is mentioned only twice (1.8.2, 1.10.3), but the potential for turbulence is measured province by province, moving roughly clockwise around the Mediterranean: Spain is rated low, Gaul rather higher, the German military zone higher still; by contrast, calm reigns in Britain, Illyricum, and, at least for the moment, the East (1.8–10). Chapter 11 begins with a glance at Egypt (as always a special case) and at Africa, where the potential for turbulence has already been expended. After the provinces garrisoned by legions, the geographical list modulates to a categorical one with Mauretania as the hinge: due west of the province of Africa, it heads the list of provinces administered by imperial procurators, none of which poses any independent threat to the *status quo*. Bringing up the rear are the unarmed provinces governed by senators, none even mentioned by name, and Italy, not a province at all but like the senatorial provinces in its defenselessness before the legions (1.11.3).

The two parts of this diptych draw on and define themselves against different precedents. The temporal retrospective of chapters 4–7 puts the *Histories* in dialogue with the works of a historian of the civil wars of the late Republic, Sallust, who "looks back" near the beginning of each of his works; with the verbal and programmatic echoes of "it seems appropriate to look back" (1.4.1: *repetundum videtur*; cf. Sall. *Cat.* 5.9: *repetere*, *Jug.* 5.3: *repetam*) Tacitus points the reader to Sallust, and more generally to a reading grounded in the Republican past. The geographical survey of chapters 8–11, however, would seem to have more in common with the "overview of the whole empire" that the first emperor, Augustus, wrote for his successor (Suet. *Aug.* 101.4: *breviarium totius imperii*; the document itself does not survive). In other words, Tacitus adopts the perspective of an administrator concerned to explain how the empire works. For him, living as he did under the system created by Augustus, this was a live issue. The catalog format of both parts of the retrospective facilitates brevity and requires attentive reading. The emphatic adjective *permixta*, for example (1.2.1, quoted above), means not just "thoroughly mixed" but, as rendered above, something like "a messy mix." The entanglement of internal and external affairs in this period fed conflict at Rome and in the provinces alike,[5] and a good reader is henceforth on alert.

With the aforementioned reference to Italy Tacitus completes his geographical circuit, and with the following echo of the consular formula with which the work began (1.11.3; cf. 1.1.1, both quoted above) he completes his temporal retrospective and poises the narrative on January 1, 69.

Galba as *princeps* (1.12–20)

By the end of the preface the reader of the *Histories* has learned to read with an eye to the Republican past, the contemporary political system, the vulnerability of truth, and the power of words. The first large panel of the narrative proper focuses on Rome and Galba's efforts to shore up his fast-eroding position. Principal among these was the adoption of a son to succeed him, Piso Licinianus (1.12–19). Galba explains his decision to Piso and his inner circle with a long speech (1.15–16). For Galba, a nostalgic 70-something, the prime consideration was character (1.16.1):

Si immensum imperii corpus stare ac librari sine rectore posset, dignus eram a quo res

publica inciperet: nunc eo necessitatis iam pridem ventum est, ut nec mea senectus conferre

plus populo Romano posset quam bonum successorem, nec tua plus iuventa quam bonum

principem.

If the immense bulk of the empire were able to stand balanced without someone to guide it, I was the right person to restore the Republic. But we long ago reached a state in which my old age can confer nothing better on the Roman people than a good successor, nor your youth anything better than a good ruler.

Dynastic succession gave us Tiberius, Caligula, Claudius, and Nero, he says, but "adoption will find the best successors" (1.16.1: *optimum quemque adoptio inveniet*). Furthermore, the very element of choice represents, if not freedom, exactly, "a substitute for freedom" (1.16.1: *loco libertatis*). Galba's high-minded argument resonates both with past and future conditions—the Julio-Claudian and Flavian dynasties, and the adoptive "dynasty" under which Tacitus was writing—and with a contemporary speech, the public *Panegyricus* in which Pliny the Younger praised Nerva's adoption of Trajan in 97 CE (esp. *Pan.* 7–8). But like the adoption itself, this section as a whole is a story of failure, setting the stage for the violent deaths of Galba and his inner circle, including Piso (1.41–3), and justifying Tacitus' negative assessment of Galba (1.49.4, quoted below). Galba's actual successor, Otho, makes his first appearance in chapter 13, where we learn that Galba considered and

[5] See further Ash (1999b); Master (2016).

rejected Otho as a successor. Character, it is clear, was not the right criterion in 69 CE. The disciplinary action with which Tacitus concludes his discussion of Galba's measures pertains to the praetorians (1.20), which provides an easy transition to Otho's praetorian-backed coup (1.21–6).

Otho's conspiracy (1.21–6)

Otho's principate was as short-lived as it was unexpected; he was dead by March (2.49.2). The seeds of his defection, in Tacitus' analysis, lie in self-interest, both his own and that of the close associates who fostered huge hopes in him (1.21–2). Strikingly, Tacitus gives Otho a soliloquy in which he goads himself to crime, concluding (1.21.2):

> *occidi Othonem posse. Proinde agendum audendumque, dum Galbae auctoritas fluxa,*
>
> *Pisonis nondum coaluisset.…mortem omnibus ex natura aequalem oblivione apud*
>
> *posteros vel gloria distingui; ac si nocentem innocentemque idem exitus maneat, acrioris*
>
> *viri esse merito perire.*

> Otho could be killed. Accordingly, now is the time for action and daring, while Galba's authority is tottering and Piso's has not yet coalesced.…Death, though the natural end for all alike, is differentiated by oblivion or renown among posterity. If the same outcome awaits guilty and innocent, the more vigorous man will make sure he deserves to die.

To the considerations of survival and historical memory mentioned by Otho his associates added enticements that were "his if he dared" (1.22.1: *si auderet,…sua*): "a court like Nero's, luxury, illicit loves, marriages, and the other things royalty lusts after" (1.22.1: *aulam Neronis et luxus adulteria matrimonia ceterasque regnorum libidines*). Otho, it seems, is a puzzling blend, a vigorous voluptuary.

The seeds of defection were planted in the fertile soil of disaffection in the powerful Praetorian Guard (1.23–5), a disaffection that spread to the other military units in Rome with the news of sedition in Germany (1.26). The panel in fact moves from Otho's internal deliberations in the immediate aftermath of the adoption of Piso (1.21–22.1) back to his time in Lusitania and Spain when he hoped and believed that *he* would be Galba's chosen successor and courted favor (1.22.2–24.1), then gradually forward through his march to Rome with Galba (1.24.2) and back to the post-adoption present (1.25.1). Verb tenses and temporal adverbs neatly articulate the various phases: "Many things were simultaneously spurring Otho to action" (1.21.1: *multa simul exstimulabant*) after a soothsayer "had persuaded him" to hope (1.22.2: *persuaserat*); "Otho had long since been seeking the affections of the soldiers" (1.23.1: *studia militum iam pridem … affectaverat*; cf. 1.24.1: *addiderat* "had added") but subsequently "began to intensify" his efforts to win the praetorians over (1.24.2: *intendebat*). The "present" is announced with the first perfect tense in four chapters (1.25.1): "But at present (*tum*) he put one of his freedmen…in charge (*praefecit*) of the upcoming crime." Throughout *Histories* 1 narrative techniques such as this cope handily with the chronological complexity of civil war.

January 15, 69 CE (1.27–43)

The narrative of January 69 moves forward again in chapter 27 with the final clash between Galba and Otho. The work of a single day, 15 January 69, it occupies a long and dramatic two-part panel.

The beginning of Galba's end (1.27–35)

At the outset of this panel Galba and Otho are juxtaposed, with Galba dignified but unrealistic and ineffective, Otho hiding tumultuous emotion. The prosecution of Otho's plans and his proclamation as emperor are noted briefly but develop no momentum as yet (1.27.2–28). In chapter 29 the focus returns to Galba and Piso, who makes his cameo appearance in a speech to a Praetorian Guard unit (1.29.2–30) that shows Piso to be "extremely like" Galba (1.38.1: *simillimus*) and thus utterly unsuitable for the situation, even if his generalization about military coups proves prescient: "No one has ever applied virtue's attainments to exercising a command criminally won" (1.30.1: *nemo…umquam imperium flagitio quaesitum bonis artibus exercuit*). The remainder of the panel is devoted to Galba's response to Otho's challenge (1.31.1–2, 1.32.2–33) and the mood in Rome, both military (1.31.3) and civilian (1.32.1, 1.34–5). As Tacitus' material gets more exciting the narrative's forward progress slows.

Otho's coup d'état (1.36–43)

The scene then returns to the praetorian barracks, where the coup is gathering momentum. After a paragraph illustrating the breakdown of traditional military discipline, which ends with Otho "doing all things in a servile fashion to achieve a master's power" (1.36.3: *omnia serviliter pro dominatione*), comes a speech, again to the Praetorian Guard, in which Otho is held up to Piso's measure (see above) and shown to be pragmatic but also short-sighted or at least disingenuous (1.37–8). "I do not summon you to warfare or danger," he says (1.38.2: *non ad bellum vos nec ad periculum voco*), but warfare and danger will in fact soon engulf not only Galba and Piso but also Otho and his troops. Verbal and contextual contrasts such as those just mentioned hone the reader's understanding even without commentary from the historian. With chapter 39 the focus shifts back to Galba's party, beginning with Piso, until their final frantic discussions end with the arrival of news about Otho. A brief glance back at the praetorian barracks shows Otho dispatching the troops (1.40.1), then the soldiers arrive in the forum to murder first Galba (1.41) then his fellow consul Vinius (1.42) and Piso, the man Galba wanted to succeed him (1.43). Tacitus uses every tool in his narrative kit to convey the horror of the scene, soundscape included: "It was not commotion, not calm, but the silence characteristic of great fear and great wrath" (1.40.1: *non tumultus, non quies, quale magni metus et magnae irae silentium est*).

Interlude (1.44–50)

Galba's principate ends in chapter 43. Otho's begins, effectively, in chapter 71. The intervening chapters set the stage (darkly) for Otho's three-month principate (1.44–50) and describe Vitellius' uprising (1.51–70). In content and pace these two panels are very different: the first stands still in time (January 15th) and place (Rome), the second moves steadily forward from the events in the late spring of 68 that precipitated Nero's downfall to the early spring of 69 and carries Vitellius' legions from their bases along the Rhine to the brink of, and then over, the Alps. Chapters 44–50 thus form an interlude between two sections of great activity. Galba's story ends with obituaries, first his associates' (1.48), then, in more detail, his own (1.49), concluding with its famous summation: "in the common opinion of all, capable of ruling—had he not ruled" (1.49.4: *omnium consensu capax imperii, nisi imperasset*). The rulers and would-be rulers of the *Histories* are all assessed on their capacity for ruling, which is a persistent concern in Tacitus' works (see above for Otho and Piso, and the Program section below), as is ensuring that the dead get their due of memory.[6] Meanwhile the background for Otho's story acquires definition as Rome's various groups reorient themselves around the new *princeps* (1.45–6). The interlude concludes by looking back over a long series of past civil wars (1.50.2: *repetita bellorum civilium memoria*) and ahead to Vespasian, who would soon initiate the year's second war, or rather, the latest instantiation of a dire constant in the history of Rome.[7] Scanty in events, these chapters are lavish in emotion (joy 1.44.1, 1.47.1; fear 1.50.1, 1.50.4; sorrow 1.50.1) and highly stylized, abounding in *sententiae* (12 in 7 chapters; see further in the Writer section below).

Disaffection in Germany and Gaul: Introduction (1.51–4)

Tacitus turns away from the foreboding of chapter 50 to provide background for Vitellius' challenge to first Galba then Otho. In addition to answering the questions "Why here?" and "Why now?" this section characterizes the forces from which Vitellius drew his armies and the men who led them. As in chapters 4–11, providing background takes Tacitus beyond the temporal boundaries of the year 69 CE.

Chapter 51 is devoted to the currents of emotion in the German armies in the aftermath of their easy victory over Vindex, a provincial governor who had declared against Nero in 68:[8] a sense of power and greed for the profits of power clashed with a consciousness of having backed a loser in Nero. Lax discipline facilitated the growth of sedition, ominous rumors added urgency. Chapters 52–53.2 introduce Vitellius, newly arrived in the area, and the men who would become his principal supporters, Fabius Valens and Caecina Alienus. In chapter 54 a small incident illustrates the tinderbox atmosphere of the camp and prompts the generalization "agreeing to go to war is easier for bad people than agreeing to get along in peacetime" (1.54.3: *faciliore inter malos consensu ad bellum quam in pace ad concordiam*).

Acclamation of Vitellius and preparations for war (1.55–62)

Discontent develops into open revolt (1.55). Drawn up to renew their oath of loyalty to Galba on the first day of 69, the four legions of Lower Germany in their three separate

---

[6] On memorializing the dead, cf. *Ann.* 3.65.1, 16.16.1–2; on Tacitus' obituaries see Pomeroy (1991), 192–225. For the idea of being capable of ruling, cf. Pagán, Chapter 9 in this volume.
[7] Joseph (2012a); Ash (2010c) and (2019).   [8] See Brunt (1959); Murison (1993), 1–3.

camps are reluctant and restive. Two legions in Upper Germany abandon Galba, taking an oath of loyalty to the senate and people of Rome instead. Back in Lower Germany a leader, or at least a figurehead, has been found in Vitellius. Momentum then gathers quickly: support accrues first from one, then the other legion of Lower Germany, then from the legions of Upper Germany, and finally from nearby Gallic peoples (1.56–7). The pacing of this snowballing narrative is masterful. How accurately Tacitus reflects the actual events is another question.[9]

In chapters 58–9 Vitellius starts making decisions, with deference to the demands of his soldiers apparent at every turn. Support begins to arrive from more distant parts of the empire: Belgica, Lugdunum, Raetia, Britannia. In chapter 60, on Britain, the narrative again pauses. The province was a standing interest of Tacitus', generously chronicled in the *Annals* as well as the *Agricola*.[10] The episode illustrates the collapse of military discipline in Rome's armies everywhere and ends with a tag generalizable to the civil war as a whole: among commanders equal in rank, one was "more powerful because of his recklessness" (1.60: *audendo potentior*).

By chapter 61 the Vitellians have planned a two-pronged invasion of Italy, with 30,000 men under Caecina's command, 40,000 under Valens'.[11] Chapter 62, which sketches the "amazing difference" between the sluggish Vitellius and his energetic soldiers (1.62.1: *mira…diversitas*), provides an ominous backdrop to an invasion that begins in the falsely bright light of a "favorable omen" (1.62.3: *laetum augurium*).[12]

Invasion of Italy (1.63–70)

Having described Vitellius, the officers on whom he was dependent, and his men, Tacitus now sets two of the three armies in motion toward Rome. The focus is on "the behaviour of men and armies when the restraints of peace are suddenly removed."[13] Valens and Caecina pursue their different routes through Gaul simultaneously; Tacitus accords them sequential panels similar in length but very different in incident. Vitellius himself remains apparently immobile.

Valens' itinerary is given in some detail: Trier, Metz, Toul, Langres, Lyon, Vienne, Luc-en-Diois are the modern names of the towns through which Tacitus tracks him in chapters 63–6. His stated task was to "win over" the inhabitants of these and the many other settlements through which he passed in marching along the now century-old Roman road, "or else to ravage their territory if they resist" (1.61.1: *allicere vel, si abnuerent, vastare*). Resistance is nowhere encountered, but the march to the Alps was not uneventful, owing to the brutality of the men and the greed of both the men and their general. The panel's conclusion shows that winning over Gaul lost out to wringing profit and pleasure from it (1.66.3).

For Caecina Tacitus gives not an itinerary but a profitable and bloody war against the Helvetii, a people sadly diminished since Caesar's day. The narrative displays Caecina's

[9] See Murison (1979).   [10] See chapters 1, 14, and 16 in this volume.
[11] 1.61.2, with 2.87.1 for the 60,000 under Vitellius; but see Murison (1993), 85–6 for the (im)plausibility of these numbers.
[12] On omens in the *Histories*, see Morgan (2000); Shannon (2014).
[13] Syme (1958a), 170; see further Ash (1999b).

military competence: he summons allies (1.67.2), coordinates troop movements (1.68.1), uses his forces efficiently (1.68.2), takes prompt advantage of opportunities that arise (1.70.1), and weighs strategic alternatives (1.70.2–3); the campaign might almost be one of Caesar's—except that the Helvetii were not external enemies but allies (1.67.1). Valens ends his panel poised for the crossing *ad Alpes* (1.66.3); Caecina goes up and over (1.70.3).

Otho as princeps in Rome (1.71–90)

With the Vitellians en route to Italy, Tacitus returns to Otho in Rome in mid-January. This final three-part narrative panel concludes with Otho's departure for war in March.

Otho as head of state (1.71–9)

The panel begins with a section that balances chapters 12–21 on Galba as *princeps*: where Galba failed completely, Otho makes the best of a bad situation. The more positive tone here is set in relief by the violence of the Vitellian advance. The section opens with Otho's first independent acts, a pardon (1.71) and a punishment (1.72), both of which caused "exultation" in the capital (1.72.1: *exsultatio*); he also temporizes (1.73). Chapters 74–5 treat a series of exploratory exchanges between Otho and Vitellius and reveal the inevitability of war. Chapter 76 tracks the various declarations of loyalty: with Otho stands Illyricum (and later Judea, Syria, and Africa), with Vitellius Spain and Gaul. Geography decides (1.76.1). But Otho's attention is not yet on war. Chapters 77–8 describe his benefactions to various civilian groups: the ruling elite in Rome (1.77.2–3), provincials (1.78.1), the urban *plebs* (1.78.2). Though very different from Galba's disciplinary measures (1.20), Otho's conciliatory measures are no more effective. In chapter 79 war resurfaces: the Rhoxolani invade Moesia.[14] The fight against an external enemy is easily won by a general loyal to Otho, and his success forms a striking backdrop to Otho's struggles with the military forces under his command in Rome (see below). As experienced in Rome, the period was a grim one: fear prevailed, even when its causes were well-hidden (1.71.1).

Otho as commander in chief (1.80–6)

For the second section of this panel Tacitus turns from military success against an external enemy to mutinous troops in Rome and "a riot that nearly destroyed the city" (1.80.1: *seditio prope Urbi excidio*). The chain of command in the Praetorian Guard, already undermined by the soldiers' distrust of their officers and a general lawlessness (both amply illustrated in the narrative of Otho's coup), collapses after a miscalculation by a tribune. When his nighttime opening of the arsenal arouses suspicion, the soldiers take up their weapons, kill the tribune and two centurions, and rush through Rome demanding sight of the emperor they had made (1.80). More blood is shed at the Palace, but Otho's pleas appease the soldiers temporarily (1.81–82.1). The next day a large bribe, a salutary demonstration of their officers' disgust, and a speech by Otho restore order, if not calm (1.82.2–85.1; see further in the Writer section below). Fear is again the final note (1.85.2–3), and the following chapter on supernatural phenomena and a natural disaster gives it cosmic scope (1.86).

---

[14] On the episode, see Ash (2010b).

Otho's preparations for war (1.87–90)

Tacitus now begins the account of Otho's military effort. In chapters 87–8 Tacitus mentions only what Otho could initiate with troops available in Rome; the movement of the Danube legions is reserved for *Histories* 2. Tacitus emphasizes the problems besetting Otho's forces, which, despite the military might and loyalty of the men (1.87.1), suffered under a crippling confusion of authority (1.87.1–2). He adds a long tirade on the folly of Rome's "military" aristocracy, now sadly decayed (1.88.2–3) and another on her anxious and misguided populace (1.89.1–2), which gives Otho a send-off worthy of Caesar or Augustus after he entrusts the state first to the senate and then to his own brother (1.90).

Although Otho himself remains in Rome until the end of this panel, events bring many areas of the empire back into the narrative (in 1.76 Illyricum, Spain, Gaul, Judea, Syria, Egypt, Africa; in 1.78 Spain, Cappadocia, Asia; in 1.79 Moesia; cf. 1.8–11). The final chapter's glancing and ironic evocation of Rome's political history and the transformation from Republic to Empire—"the senate...the people...the dictator Caesar...the emperor Augustus" (1.90.1–3: *patribus...populi...dictatorem Caesarem...imperatorem Augustum*; cf. *Ann.* 1.1.1)—provides a foil to the brutal wars that will decide its future, the subject of *Histories* 2–3. *Histories* 1 ends with a concentration of focus: the date is March 14, and Otho sets out for war.

The Historian

Program (1.1.1–1.4.1)

Questions of aim and method appear with particular urgency at the outset of an author's work in a new genre. By starting *Histories* 1 on January 1, 69 and placing the names of the year's consuls in the opening sentence (1.1.1, quoted above), Tacitus evokes a traditional historiographic framework that presumes the significance of the Republican yearly cycle. But by varying the traditional formula—the names appear in the nominative case instead of the ablative—and supplementing it with references to himself and his work, he problematizes the annalistic framework and foregrounds the historian's role.[15] As evidence he adduces the disappointing histories of the period since the battle of Actium: the authors were small talents hampered by political ignorance and by the passions and pressures of life in an autocratic regime. Truth suffered, and so did humankind, for subservience and hatred were selfish indulgences in an historian, incompatible with concern for posterity (1.1.1: *cura posteritatis*).

When Tacitus was writing (*c.* 100 CE), the form of government established after the battle of Actium, the Principate, was on sounder footing than ever, but the genre of historiography was in trouble, at least according to Tacitus (1.1–2, cf. *Ann.* 1.1.2).[16] However, he argues here that the historian, or at least *this* historian, can attain sufficient knowledge and autonomy to reconstruct the "shattered truth" (1.1.1: *veritas...infracta*). First, however, he puts the reader on notice that a historian's entanglements with political power require scrutiny *as one reads*, and that neither self-interest nor malice should pass muster (1.1.2).

---

[15] On the ablative absolute formula for dating purposes in the *Annals*, see Ginsburg (1981).
[16] On Tacitus' prefaces, see Marincola (1999).

His own entanglements come next: none with Galba, Otho, or Vitellius, increasingly substantial with Vespasian, Titus, and Domitian (1.1.3). Can he write a worthwhile history of these Flavians? He gives the reader of the *Histories* three things to bear in mind. First, he represents his political career as an accumulation of political and social prestige (1.3.1: *dignitatem nostram*), prestige that would be forfeit if he wrote abjectly.[17] Second, he enunciates a general principle: integrity requires a historian to present the people who appear in the narrative without favor or hatred (1.1.3: *neque amore...et sine odio*). And third, he lays out the criteria for autonomy: you have to be able to feel what you want and say what you feel (1.1.4). Tacitus' professions of impartiality and autonomy—both here and in the *Annals*—have provoked many readers. Is he so naive as to believe that the causes of bias are limited to past or potential advantage or injury to the historian himself? And how, given the manifestly impassioned character of his narratives and his frequent recourse to insinuation, can he claim autonomy? The *Histories*, it is clear, is a high-stakes venture, and Tacitus expects posterity to hold him accountable using the narrative itself, not his prefatory assertions, as evidence.

However, even a worthwhile history will only benefit posterity if it gets read, so the table of contents provided in chapters 2–3 promises both exciting material (assassinations, civil war, natural disasters, human havoc) and broad coverage (in the empire, provinces from Britain to Parthia; in the natural world, land, sea, and sky; in society, ranks from ennobled to enslaved). The content of the projected work is closer to Thucydides' catalog of suffering in the human and natural spheres (Thuc. 1.23) than to Herodotus' "great and amazing deeds of both Greeks and barbarians" (Herod. 1.1). But if Tacitus' chosen period is not happy, it is significant: even the adulteries are *magna adulteria* (1.2.2). Significant of what? Of moral choices that themselves require the reader's evaluation. The Roman catchword for such choices, *exempla*, duly appears in the preface (1.3.1). In all of Tacitus' work *mala exempla* ("instances of evil") are more numerous than *bona* ("instances of good"), and this is particularly true of *Histories* 1.

Besides assembling the truth, or some portion of the truth—Tacitus' historical research (see below) and political experience (see above) do not always suffice for the full story—and offering an exciting story about a significant (if painful) era, the historian aims to show cause and effect (1.4.1):

> *Ceterum antequam destinata componam, repetendum videtur qualis status Urbis, quae mens exercituum, quis habitus provinciarum, quid in toto terrarum orbe validum, quid aegrum fuerit, ut non modo casus eventusque rerum, quid plerumque fortuiti sunt, sed ratio etiam causaeque noscantur.*

> But before I write what I have planned on, it seems appropriate to look back and ask about the situation in Rome, the attitude of the armies, the disposition of the provinces, and what was sound in the world, what sickly, so that not only occurrences and outcomes, which are generally matters of chance, but also their explanation and causes may be known.

All of the topics mentioned here—Rome, armies, provinces, and more generally the condition of the world, sound or sickly—figure largely not only in the retrospective announced

---

[17] On the "abject" in Tacitus, see Sailor (2008).

here but also in the narrative of the *Histories* 1, as we have seen. Tacitus' confidence in the historian's ability to explain is at a high-water mark here at the outset of the *Histories*; several passages in the *Annals* suggest a significant retreat (e.g. *Ann.* 3.18.4, 6.22.1).[18] He is particularly attentive to success and failure. In essence Tacitus has to tell the stories of fall (Galba, Otho, Vitellius) and rise (Otho, Vitellius, Vespasian) three times each, and the mistakes of Vespasian's predecessors help explain Vespasian's success. The Flavian dynasty does not remain (and perhaps never was) a paragon, but by Tacitus' account it began well, and *Histories* 1's account of the reigns that preceded Vespasian's is crucial for showing how it did so.[19]

Sources and parallel tradition

The events of *Histories* 1 took place when Tacitus was about 13 years old. When he came to write it *c.* 100 CE, he was able to draw upon contemporary documents and some three decades' worth of retellings both oral and written.

Documentary archives would have yielded little toward the narrative of *Histories* 1, since the significant events of January–March 69 did not occur at official meetings. It is more difficult to gauge the importance of oral report. Tacitus cites no oral source, but some of the people named in connection with the book's events were active well into the 90s and at least one, Arrius Antoninus, seems to have survived into the period of the book's composition (1.77.2). It is possible, moreover, that Tacitus owes the story of Otho's naval expedition to Narbonensis (1.87.1–2) to his father-in-law, Agricola, who lost his mother in that campaign and spent time in the area shortly after it (*Agr.* 7.1–2); the expedition is treated by no other source.

As for written sources, Josephus, an older contemporary of Tacitus, tells us that the period from Nero's suicide to Vespasian's accession had been treated by many authors both Greek and Roman (*BJ* 4.492–6). But all indications in *Histories* 1 suggest that Tacitus used a single written source as the basis of his narrative. He does have more material than the authors of the parallel tradition (see below), but his narrative of the events of January 1–March 14 is also the longest. Where the accounts overlap they are generally in agreement on events and they sometimes even share details of language; there are no significant differences in matters of fact. If Tacitus did supplement the common source with documentary evidence or oral testimony or with material from another written source, his supplements are rather small.[20] The identity of the common source remains a matter of scholarly dispute and need not detain us here; as we saw above, Tacitus considered none of his predecessors in the field satisfactory.[21]

The three parallel accounts of the events Tacitus describes in Book 1 are: Plutarch's *Lives* of Galba and Otho; Suetonius' *Lives* of Galba, Otho, and Vitellius; and the excerpts and epitomes of Dio, Book 64. By careful comparison among the four, one is able to see

---

[18] On the passages, see respectively Devillers (Chapter 11) and Shannon-Henderson (Chapter 13) in this volume.
[19] See further Damon (2006).
[20] Damon (2003), 22–3.   [21] 1.1; cf. 2.101.1 and see Syme (1958a), Appendix 29.

more clearly here than anywhere else in Tacitus' historical work the choices he makes in the selection, arrangement, and presentation of his material.[22]

Writer

The subject matter of *Histories* 1 is civil war. For the historian civil war shows a political system pressed to the breaking point, and as one of history's recurrent phenomena it enables connections with the past and the future (see above on 1.50.2). For the literary artist, likewise, civil war offers both a rich mine of material and an opportunity to engage with other writers; for Tacitus these include Thucydides, Sallust, Vergil, and Lucan.[23] This is not the place for discussion of these large-scale affordances, which apply to much of Tacitus' work, but two aspects of Tacitus' literary artistry in *Histories* 1 do warrant mention: speeches and *deinosis*.

There are four substantial speeches in *Histories* 1 (Galba to Piso, 1.15–16, discussed above; Piso to praetorians, 1.29.2–30; Otho to praetorians 1.37–38.2, 1.83.2–84). Even the addressees reflect civil war conditions: not political assemblies or juries but an inner circle and mutinous soldiers. These speeches are absent from the parallel tradition: Plutarch mentions both Piso's address (*Galb.* 26.4) and Otho's second speech (*Oth.* 3.8), but Tacitus makes the men speak for nearly two chapters each, as he does for Otho's first address, which Suetonius summarizes in a few words (*Oth.* 6.3). Galba's adoption speech is not even mentioned elsewhere. In other words, these are all free compositions that, as we have already seen, contribute to the historian's analysis of events and delineation of character.[24] Otho's post-riot speech, for example, is part of a panel on how civil war saps military discipline, and the theme of military discipline dominates it, with manifest irony, since despite its favorable reception (1.85.1) the speech is utterly without effect: Otho's soldiers are quite unruly in *Histories* 2 and the senate is threatened again at 2.52.1. The reader learns along with Otho that "it was impossible for a principate gained by crime to be retained by sudden restraint and old-fashioned severity" (1.83.1: *non posse principatum scelere quaesitum subita modestia et prisca gravitate retineri*).

As is the case in this speech, so more generally Tacitus' literary artistry is used to emphasize the darker aspects of the Roman world in *Histories* 1. Ancient rhetorical theory designates this procedure *deinosis*, or "making terrible," and Quintilian describes it as "style adding force to things that are undeserved, harsh, or hateful" (*Inst.* 6.2.24); its relevant emotions are anger, hatred, fear, jealousy, and grief (6.2.20). *Deinosis* is deployed at moments of special bitterness, where narration and explanation are not enough. In the panel on Vitellius, for example, Tacitus reports his execution of four centurions. Nomen and cognomen are tolled for each. Then comes the explanation: they were "condemned for the crime of loyalty" (1.59.1: *damnatos fidei crimine*).[25] To the question of why they were killed, the neutral answer would have been "because (as proven at 1.56.1) they were loyal to Galba." In Tacitus' answer, style—an oxymoron—weighs in to charge those responsible for the centurions' deaths with a perverse morality in which loyalty is a crime.

---

[22] Damon (2003), 24–30.   [23] See Joseph (2012c).
[24] See further Keitel (1987), (1991); Sailor (2008), ch. 4; Levene (2009a).
[25] On *fides* and the Flavians, see Bartera (2019).

Sententiae, or expressions of conspicuous verbal neatness and often universal relevance (Quint., *Inst.* 8.5.3), represent a particularly prevalent form of *deinosis* in *Histories* 1 and create the impression that the historian is "master of all he surveys."[26] Tacitus uses the *sententia* primarily to enunciate grim truths on civil war themes such as cruelty (1.2.1), crime and punishment (1.30.1, 1.59.1), danger (1.21.2), the breakdown of military discipline (1.36.3, 1.60), and mob behavior (1.54.3).[27] Master he may be, but his domain appalls him.

Further Reading

Histories 1 is accessible in English in a sensitive and stylish translation by W. H. Fyfe (1912), revised and annotated by D. S. Levene (1997). Commentaries by Chilver (1979) and Damon (2003) will help a reader explore historical and literary questions. Useful discussion of the historical events of 69 CE can be found in Morgan (2006), of the historian in Whitton (2012). For the nexus of historiography and politics, good starting points are Sailor (2008) and Devillers (2012). Ash (1999b) is fundamental on the work's military actors, Joseph (2012a) on the civil war theme. Haynes (2012) is an engaging meditation on the insights to be gained from Tacitean historiography.

Cynthia Damon, Histories *1* In: *The Oxford Critical Guide to Tacitus.* Edited by: Salvador Bartera and Kelly E. Shannon-Henderson, Oxford University Press. © Oxford University Press 2025. DOI: 10.1093/9780191915086.003.0005

---

[26] See Sinclair (1995), 147; Damon (2003), 15–16; Keitel (2006).
[27] All of these *sententiae* are quoted above; for more examples, see Damon (2003), Appendix 2.

5

Histories 2

Lydia Spielberg

Histories 2[1] opens "at the other end of the world" from Rome, where "Fortuna was laying the foundations and groundwork for a dynasty that was by turns fruitful for common-wealth or horrific and brought success or destruction to the emperors themselves" (2.1.1: *Struebat iam fortuna in diversa parte terrarum initia causasque imperio, quod varia sorte laetum rei publicae aut atrox, ipsis principibus prosperum vel exitio fuit*). Yet after this sweeping prospect of the Flavian dynasty and its fate spread across the whole of the Mediterranean world, Tacitus takes us not to its founder Vespasian in Jerusalem but to his son Titus, in transit and unsure what to do. Titus had set off for Rome while Galba was still in power, ostensibly to pay his father's respects to the new emperor, and rumor, the fickle crowd, and oracles have already presaged an imperial future for him (2.1.1–2). He has only made it to Corinth when he learns of the events of *Histories* 1: Galba is dead, Otho emperor, Vitellius and his German armies on the march; matters may have changed further by the time he reaches either Rome or Jerusalem. What should he do now?

The "plot" of *Histories* 2 is the war in Italy between Vitellius and Otho, which ends with the latter's defeat and suicide and Vitellius' grotesque march of triumph and entry into Rome. Meanwhile, the Flavian war machine is slowly set in motion. These two main strands are intercut with brief glimpses of minor figures: the death of a heroic Ligurian mother (2.13.2); a conspiracy against the governor of Mauritania (2.58.1–59.1); a Gallic pretender (2.61.1). Such vignettes build delay and tension, as they show the consequences of civil war spreading throughout the empire. The resulting fragmented narrative also highlights the particular historiographical challenge of the subject matter. Important actors are so divided in space that they must act in partial or full ignorance of one other, and unreliable rumors often supersede trustworthy information. Very little of *Histories* 2 takes place in Rome, or even in the major cities of the empire, but neither are we on the frontiers or in uncharted wilderness; rather, the action happens, and, as Titus discovers in the first paragraph, decisions must be made, while "on the way."[2] The same challenges of distance, simultaneity, and unreliable information confront the historian who must weave together a narrative spread over multiple theaters of war.[3]

Agency presents a second problem for the historian. Flavian propaganda portrayed Vespasian as divinely predestined to rule and compelled to assume power against his will.

---

[1] I have relied throughout on the commentaries of Ash (2007b); Chilver (1979); Heubner (1963–76), ii. These, along with Ash (1999b) on Tacitus' portrayal of armies and generals, Haynes (2003) on ideology and imperial fictions, and Joseph (2012c) on poetic allusions in the *Histories*, should be consulted for further discussion of any passage, although they are not cited on each occasion.

[2] On travel and imperial space, see Laurence (2019) and, with reference to the *Histories*, Pomeroy (2003); Master (2016), 84–98.

[3] Cf. *Hist.* 1.4.1, for the global scope of Roman imperial history; cf. Polyb. 1.3.3–4.11. On the historiographical challenges (and opportunities) of temporal muddiness, see Ash (2007b), 8–9.

Fortune and his soldiers assumed agency (and civil war guilt) for a victory that, in retrospect, was inevitable.[4] The horrors of civil strife, too, seem foreordained by fate.[5] Although Tacitus partially concurs with what seems to have been the Flavian presentation of events, his work calls into question this narrative of Vespasian's predestined success, while small episodes show individuals attempting to exercise agency or, more often, avoid the exercise of agency in order to secure their own safety.

Finally, both historian and historical figures must grapple with the past, both proximate and distant. The memory of late Republican civil wars haunts the *Histories*, but in Book 2, generals and armies more frequently swerve away from its lessons and fail to meet even its standard of morality. More distant Roman history, however, is conspicuously forgotten or ignored. Between Vitellius' "barbarian" armies of Gauls and Germans and Vespasian's weakness for "Eastern" divination and superstition, Roman identity, especially as expressed through collective memory of time and place, risks being lost, replaced by spectacular gestures (another running motif of the book).

This chapter explores these three themes—information and the spaces of empire, individual agency, and historical memory—with particular attention to scenes of deliberation and hesitation by those caught between major events and places. When characters try to decide on the best course of action, they entertain multiple possible futures and their consequences. Such "sideshadowing" of possible alternative histories complicates both the predestination implied by *fortuna* and fate and the reader's knowledge of what in fact came to pass.[6] Tacitus thus brings to the foreground the uncertainty of living through events whose outcome and significance has yet to be determined.

Preparing the Ground: 2.1–10

The first ten chapters of *Histories* 2 set up nearly all of the concerns of the book: deliberation and strategic thinking, the distances of the empire, travel and spectacle, the susceptibility of the crowd to rumor, and the Flavian "long game." Titus, a practiced courtier, deftly demonstrates how to anticipate the emotions and strategies of an unknown emperor.[7] If he goes to Rome, he reasons, he may become a hostage to a new emperor unlikely to be impressed by hastily retitled congratulations, but returning to his father could be construed as an act of rebellion, albeit a potentially forgivable one if his father backs the right side. Titus resolves his dilemma by abandoning a courtier's expertise for a would-be dynast's: "Those debating war must forget about causing offense" (2.1.3: *obliviscendum offensarum de bello agitantibus*). Titus' sententious conclusion proves itself over the course of the book, as the decisive action necessary to seize and keep power contrasts with the caution and abdication of responsibility needed to survive under it.

---

[4] Ferrill (1965); Ramage (1983), 209–14.

[5] On this theme in Tacitus, see Keitel (1984); O'Gorman (1995b); Damon (2010); Ash (2010c); Joseph (2012c); Ash (2019); Celotto (2021).

[6] The term "sideshadowing" was coined and theorized by Morson (1994) and Bernstein (1994); it has been fruitfully applied to ancient historiography, see e.g. Hau (2013); Grethlein (2013). Riedl (2010) surveys many types of counterfactual history in the *Histories*. Pagán (2006b); O'Gorman (2006); and Suerbaum (1997) have also written about alternative history in Tacitus' works. On uncertainty in historiography, see Domainko (2018); Greenwood (2016).

[7] Cf. Paterson (2007), 135–6. On Tacitus' Titus, see further Bartera (forthcoming b).

Despite his haste, Titus stops at Paphos to see the temple of Venus. As if imitating Titus'
self-indulgence, Tacitus likewise diverts the narrative into a digression on the temple and
its cult, promising that "it will not take us far out of the way" (2.2.2: *haud fuerit longum*).
Here Titus receives an encouraging private prophecy (2.4.1–2). Omens, and the ease with
which not only the populace but also the Flavian high command believes in them, will be
another important strand in the subsequent narrative; Titus' prophecy has a parallel in
the encouraging prophecies Vespasian receives at Carmel (2.78.3–4) and, later, the temple
of Serapis in Alexandria (4.81–4).[8] The temple's marvels, which Titus' guides proudly
explicate, and the digression itself are presented as diversions not only for Titus, soon to
be given sole command of the siege of Jerusalem (2.82.3), but for Tacitus' readers, soon to
be dragged back to the uninspiring war between Otho and Vitellius. Detours and idle
sightseeing prove to be another leitmotif of *Histories* 2, often in a discordant key. The
same "desire" (2.2.2: *cupido*) that motivates Titus will later spur Vitellius to tour the battlefield at Bedriacum (2.70.1–4) and German soldiers, newly arrived in Rome, to seek the
Lacus Curtius, which they know only as the spot where Galba was brutally murdered
(2.88.3).[9]

Next in this introduction to the Flavians comes the remarkable fact that Vespasian was
the first to wage civil war successfully from the East: in the civil wars of the late Republic,
the strongest armies came from Italy and Gaul, "and for Pompey, Cassius, Brutus, Antony
– all of whom civil war pursued across the sea – things did not end well" (2.6.1: *et Pompeio,
Cassio, Bruto, Antonio, quos omnes trans mare secutum est civile bellum, haud prosperi
exitus fuerant*). *Exitus* can refer to both the "outcomes" of the campaigns and the "ends" of
leaders: Pompey, Brutus and Cassius, and Antony suffered roughly the same sequence
of fates as Galba, Otho, and Vitellius (murder through treachery, suicide in defeat, and
dissipation—although Vitellius will not even manage as noble an end as Antony). Tacitus
dwells on the paradox that the faction that would emerge victorious in 69 shares characteristics not with the winners but with the losers of past cycles of civil war.

Roman historians and moralists traditionally associated the East with the decline of
virtus and discipline, its luxury and wealth ruining commanders and armies alike.[10]
Vespasian was acclaimed emperor in Alexandria and surrounded himself with Eastern
dynasts (2.81.1).[11] Nevertheless he brings a disciplined and experienced army against
Vitellius, whose debauched retinue "intermingled with actors and flocks of eunuchs"
(2.71.1: *immixtis histrionibus et spadonum gregibus*) recalls Horace's abuse of Cleopatra's
train, "a polluted flock of disease-befouled men" (*C.* 1.37.9–10: *contaminato cum grege
turpium/morbo virorum*). Titus has an affair with the Jewish princess Berenice, yet, unlike
Cleopatra to Marc Antony, this Eastern queen aids the Flavian cause apparently without
corrupting it (2.2.1).[12] Vitellius and his German legions, on the other hand, descend from
the Alps, stereotypically the locus of hardened barbarians à la Brennus' Gauls or the
soldiers of Lucan's Caesar, but, once they have won, they reprise in miniature the decline

---

[8]   But see Haynes (2003), 118–47; Shannon (2014) for parallels between the temple-digressions and superstition/
false belief elsewhere in the *Histories*. On Vespasian in Alexandria, see Luke (2010) with further references.
[9]   Cf. Germanicus in the *Annals*, who likewise desires tours of battlefields (*Ann.* 1.61.1) and marvels (*Ann.*
2.69–71); see Pelling (2012), 298 n. 33; both Pagán (Chapter 9) and Damtoft Poulson (Chapter 10) in this volume.
[10]   See Liv. 39.6.7, Sall. *Cat.* 20.8; Earl (1961), 41–59.
[11]   For sinister implications of Vespasian's Eastern allies, see Andrade (2012), 444–51.
[12]   On Berenice and the Eastern Queen tradition, see Anagnostou-Laoutides and Charles (2015).

of Roman morals: "As if without a rival, he and his army erupted into foreign customs with cruelty, lust, rapine" (2.73.2: *tum ipse exercitusque, ut nullo aemulo, saevitia libidine raptu in externos mores proruperant*; cf. 2.69.2).[13] Tacitus' language recalls Sallust's judgment on Rome's moral collapse after the destruction of "rival Carthage" (*Cat.* 10.1, *Carthago aemula*) and the plundering of Asia Minor (Sall. *Cat.* 10.4–8, *Jug.* 41.3).

The Flavian narrative portrayed Vespasian reluctantly taking power to rescue the *res publica* suffering from Vitellius' victory and excesses, and then only when his soldiers forced the role upon him at sword-point (Jos. *BJ* 588–604).[14] By introducing the Flavian plans before the armies of Otho and Vitellius have had their first clash, Tacitus corrects this timeline: charismatic Titus brought about a pragmatic alliance between hardened soldier Vespasian and skilled courtier Mucianus upon the death of Nero (2.5.2), and they began to collect supporters in their armies, both officers and soldiers (2.6.1–2).[15] Vespasian and Mucianus delay their imperial aspirations out of policy, not loyalty: "They decided to wait while others fought [. . .] thinking it made no difference whether fortune favored Vitellius or Otho; in success even exceptional leaders grow arrogant; these had discord, fecklessness, luxury: and through their own faults one would perish in war, the other in victory" (2.7.1: *sed bellantibus aliis placuit exspectare. [...] nec referre Vitellium an Othonem superstitem fortuna faceret. rebus secundis etiam egregios duces insolescere: discordiam his, ignaviam, luxuriem; et suismet vitiis alterum bello, alterum victoria periturum*). A scornful reference to *fortuna*, emphasized by f-alliteration, contrasts with the cynical truism that success leads to arrogance. This also recalls Sallust, who saw in the Republican institution of two consuls an attempt to prevent "human nature growing arrogant when unchecked" (Sall. *Cat.* 6.7: *per licentiam insolescere animum humanum*) and who commented on the inevitability of Roman moral decline since "success wears out the minds of even the wise" (*Cat.* 11.8: *quippe secundae res sapientium animos fatigant*).[16] Tacitus' repeated *sc*-sounds point back through Sallust to Cato the Elder, who warned in a famous speech on behalf of the Rhodians, "I know it is common human practice, when matters are successful and thriving and promising, for the mind to inflate and for one's arrogance and aggression to wax and expand" (*FRHist.* 5 F 87: *scio solere plerisque hominibus rebus secundis atque prolixis atque prosperis animum excellere atque superbiam atque ferociam augescere atque crescere*).[17] That the Flavian leaders have read their history bodes well for them, but these allusions to Republican history and the corruption that caused its civil wars suggest that the Flavians may not escape the moral consequences of success. Moreover, Tacitus has just qualified Vespasian's virtues: "If not for his greed, equal to generals of old" (2.5.1: *si avaritia abesset, antiquis ducibus par*). Greed (*avaritia*) is the vice that Sallust posited as the root of the Republic's decline, since over time it turned into to luxury, arrogance, and cruelty (*Cat.* 10.1–6, 11.1–13.5).[18] Vespasian's *avaritia*, then, prefigures and warns of the eventual end of the Flavian dynasty in the tyrant Domitian.

After this introduction, the Flavians disappear from the narrative for sixty-five chapters, but before returning to the war between Othonians and the Vitellians, which plays out

---

[13] For parallels between Vitellius and Caesar, see Joseph (2012c); Celotto (2021).
[14] On Tacitus' relationship to the Flavian tradition, see Briessmann (1955); Ash (2007b), 32–4.
[15] Cf. Bartera (2019), 263–4.
[16] On the influence of Sallust on Tacitus, see Syme (1958a), 144–50; Syme (1964), 292–6; Galtier (2011), 34–7.
[17] *Insolescere* may also be Catonian: Gell. *NA* 6.3.1.
[18] On Vespasian and his predecessors, see Damon (2006).

much as Vespasian and Mucianus predicted, Tacitus pauses again with the episode of a "False Nero," the first of several low-status pretender figures in the book.[19] This anonymous slave or freedman attracts followers in Asia Minor and Achaea, whose "desire for revolution" confirms what they want to believe. In this, he parodies, in a way, the claims and strategies of more successful "pretenders" such as Otho, Vitellius, and Vespasian.[20] The False Nero lurks in in-between spaces and temporalities: a storm brings him to the island of Cythnus, he co-opts "wandering" (*vagos*) deserters and some soldiers "in transit from the East" (2.8.1: *quosdam ex Oriente commeantium*), and seeks particularly to win the support of a centurion traveling as an emissary of the Syrian armies to the Praetorians in Rome (2.8.2). "Chance" (2.8.2: *fors*) brings a provincial governor and his naval escort to Cythnus, and in the end, this pretender's fate is decided by ship-captains who are loyal to a governor appointed by Galba rather than to the name of Nero.[21] These names of already dead emperors give a slightly disjointed temporality to the whole episode, as if the Eastern Mediterranean has not yet caught up with the latest regime change. Yet when the head of the pretender is sent to Rome, we find that the senate is still consumed with petty feuds from Nero's reign that were reignited in Galba's (2.10.1). The nominal rulers at the center of the empire seem to be nearly as behind the times as the confused soldiers in the provinces.[22]

Armies, Generals, and Battle: 2.11–38

The war between Otho and Vitellius is largely conducted by their subordinate generals. In northern Italy and the region around the Po, Otho's generals Celsus, Spurinna, and Suetonius Paulinus are waiting to intercept the Vitellian Caecina as he brings his army down from the Alps. The classic historiographical conflict between the "rash" general and the "prudent" general plays out during the skirmishes that lead up to the battle of Bedriacum.[23]

The ambitious Caecina exemplifies the rash commander. His attempt to besiege Placentia fails because he has moved too impetuously (2.21.1). Then "with more eagerness than care" (2.24.1: *avidius quam consultius*) he tries to set up an ambush that relies on luring the enemy into "rushing" after cavalry used as bait. But the Othonian Celsus learns about the plan and springs the trap against Caecina's army. This victory of calculation (and intelligence gathering) also displays the limits of caution. Celsus' colleague Suetonius delays his men too long, giving the Vitellian cavalry the opportunity to escape, and once his legions have routed Caecina's infantry, he orders them to fall back rather than pursue the enemy to the end (2.26.1). Although Tacitus upholds Suetonius' prudence (previously on display at 2.23.3–4), he also notes its ambivalent reception. According to some, Paulinus could have destroyed Caecina's army in this battle, had he not prudently ordered his forces to hold back from pursuing them (2.26.2).[24]

---

[19] On False Neros, see Bowersock (1987), 308–10; Champlin (2003), 10–12.
[20] Morgan (1993); on rumor and belief, see Gibson (1998); Haynes (2003), 90–3.
[21] Cf. Bartera (2019), 262–6.   [22] Cf. Keitel (1993).
[23] On this topos in the *Histories*, see Riedl (2010), 94–100; for antecedents in Roman historiography, see Levene (2010a), 186–208; Chaplin (2015), 109–11.
[24] See Morgan (1996).

This could-have-been narrative of alternate history exacerbates the distrust Otho's soldiers feel for their generals, as they interpret Paulinus' reluctance to give battle as political caution aimed at preserving his safety with either victor or even in hopes of being proclaimed emperor himself (2.37.1).[25] Ironically, Paulinus will eventually claim to have deliberately sabotaged Otho in order to gain credit with Vitellius (2.60.2). When it comes to their armies, however, generals on both sides practice self-interested restraint instead of imposing discipline with decisive authority. Troops are given free rein to pillage civilians (2.12.2–13.2, 56.1–2, 87.2–88.2), and mutinies among the Othonians at Placentia (2.17.2–19.2) and the Vitellians at the Ticinus (2.27.2–29.3) show generals coaxing armies that they cannot command.[26]

Nevertheless, with the reluctant cooperation of the rival Vitellian commanders Caecina and Valens, the fortunes of the Vitellians begin to improve, accompanied by better information from scouts, spies, and the large numbers of deserters, "as happens in civil wars" (2.34.1: *ut in civili bello*). Despite this generalization, presumably applicable to both armies, Tacitus previously identified only the Othonians' use of advance knowledge of the enemy's plans; now that the Vitellians are successful, he emphasizes their gathering of military intelligence.

In reverse fashion, Otho's commanders are in disarray as they prepare for the battle of Bedriacum. The accepted wisdom seems to have been that Otho—like Pompey at Pharsalus—ought to have delayed battle, and that the emperor's rashness and inability to restrain his eager army led him to defeat.[27] Tacitus gives Paulinus an extended discourse in which he argues forcefully against committing to a battle; rather, Otho should delay until reinforcements arrive from the East, while Vitellius' weak supply lines and unreliable auxiliaries break down (2.32). The experienced military men agree, but their "inexperienced and rash" (*imperitia properantes*) opponents Titianus and Proculus use an argument that cannot be countered by *ratio*, declaring that "Fortune and the gods and Otho's divine power" support the emperor's plans and will ensure his victory (2.33.1: *fortunam et deos et numen Othonis*). It is a commonplace that flattery destroys the trust between prince and adviser, but here Tacitus shows the pernicious instrumentalization of emperor-adulation in political debate.

This emphasis on the internal dynamics of Otho's *consilium* appears to be unique to his account. Suetonius puts the responsibility on Otho's own "rashness" (*temeritas*) and inability to restrain his overeager army (*Oth.* 9). Plutarch, like Tacitus, narrates the *consilium* in some detail but has Titianus and Proculus present reasoned arguments for hurrying the engagement (*Oth.* 8). By omitting counterarguments to Paulinus' speech, Tacitus implies that Titianus and Proculus resorted to flattery because they had no substantive case (2.33.2).[28] They invoke the imperial *numen* as a kind of "nuclear option" against other members of the *consilium*, who cannot disagree without appearing disloyal. Tacitus shows how effectively imperial flattery closes off deliberation by immediately moving to the next matter: should Otho take part in the battle? This time, Paulinus and Celsus know better than to protest: "[They] gave no more opposition so as not to seem to be exposing the emperor to danger" (2.33.2: *Paulino et Celso iam non adversantibus, ne principem obiectare periculis viderentur*). With his wiser advisers silenced, Otho agrees to retreat to

[25] Keitel (1987).   [26] See in general Ash (1999b), 31–4, 39–48.
[27] For a modern analysis, see Morgan (2006), 123–30 on the dynamics of rashness and caution.
[28] Wellesley (1960), 281–2.

Brixellum. Although Tacitus does not take a position on the initial question of fighting or delaying, he condemns this decision as "the first moment of disaster for Otho's side" (2.33.3: *is primus dies Othonianas partes adflixit*). Tacitus not only shows Otho to be someone who does not deliberate but shows that in a court corrupted by sycophants, deliberation becomes impossible.

With reasoning and forethought closed off, Tacitus now intervenes with a rare first-person verb (2.37.1: *invenio*) to discuss the facticity of the story that the armies of Otho and Vitellius, disgusted with their commanders, debated whether to choose a new emperor together or even hand over the choice to the senate, and that Suetonius Paulinus tried to delay battle because he hoped to be the one chosen (2.37.1).[29] The story gives a self-interested motive to Paulinus' counsel, but its investigation allows Tacitus to display his own reasoning powers as he determines what would have been possible or probable in the past. The historian extrapolates first Paulinus' thoughts—his capacity for prudence would not have led him to rely on a spontaneous desire for peace among hardened civil war soldiers—then examines the plausibility of the very idea that the armies might have decided to conclude a peace and choose an emperor (2.37.2):

> *neque aut exercitus linguis moribusque dissonos in hunc consensum potuisse coalescere, aut legatos ac duces magna ex parte luxus egestatis scelerum sibi conscios nisi pollutum obstrictumque meritis suis principem passuros.*

> Armies with incompatible languages and customs could not have united into such a consensus, nor would their legates and commanders, for the most part accomplices of each other's extravagance, insolvency, and crimes have been prepared to accept an emperor not corrupt and obligated to their services.

In the first place, Tacitus asserts, the changed nature of the Roman military has altered the state of civil war: a truce and return to consensus presumes shared values and a shared identity. But as Tacitus shows throughout, the Roman armies of this civil war, and Vitellius' armies in particular, depend heavily on "barbarian" auxiliaries. Vitellian cohorts go into battle "with savage chant and, in their ancestral manner, nude" (2.22.1: *cantu truci et more patrio nudis corporibus*), and, when Vitellius' army eventually reaches Rome, his soldiers are a terrifying and comic sight: "bristling with animal skins and huge spears" (2.88.3: *tergis ferarum et ingentibus telis horrentes*), they slip and stumble on the cobblestones as they try to navigate the city. Even the general Caecina shocks Italian *municipia* by dressing in barbarian garb after descending from the Alps like an invading Brennus or Hannibal (2.20.1).[30]

As for the self-interest and greed of the generals, Tacitus again turns to Sallust for a digression in which he traces the "ancient vice long since sown in human nature: the desire for power" which "matured and burst forth" concomitant with Rome's empire (2.38.1: *vetus ac iam pridem insita mortalibus potentiae cupido cum imperii magnitudine adolevit erupitque*). Tacitus sets the war between Otho and Vitellius into a long historical cycle of struggles for power (as well as the literary memory of those struggles), but also

---

[29] This tale is presented as fact by Plutarch: *Oth.* 9.3.
[30] On these stereotypes in Tacitus, see Ash (2014); Master (2016), especially 174–93; on ethnographic discourse in general, see Woolf (2011).

suggests that this instantiation is even worse than its predecessors: "Legions of Roman citizens did not abandon their weapons at Pharsalus and Philippi; so much less were Otho's and Vitellius' armies going to lay down war willingly. The same divine wrath, the same human madness, the same causes of wickedness drove them into the state of strife" (2.38.2: *non discessere ab armis in Pharsalia ac Philippis civium legiones, nedum Othonis ac Vitellii exercitus sponte posituri bellum fuerint: eadem illos deum ira, eadem hominum rabies, eaedem scelerum causae in discordiam egere*). The repetition of *eadem* hammers home the sameness of the evils.[31] The final reason why there could never have been a reconciliation between opposing armies is the inevitable repetition of civil war.

Yet in the aftermath of the battle, upon the surrender of Otho's soldiers, Tacitus gives a scene of concord and recognition between the armies of exactly the kind that he previously asserted was impossible (2.45.3):

> *tum victi victoresque in lacrimas effusi, sortem civilium armorum misera laetitia detestantes; iisdem tentoriis alii fratrum, alii propinquorum vulnera fovebant: spes et praemia in ambiguo, certa funera et luctus, nec quisquam adeo mali expers, ut non aliquam mortem maereret.*

> Vanquished and victors overflowed with tears, taking bitter pleasure in cursing the lot of civil war; sharing tents, some tended the wounds of brothers, others of kin: hopes and rewards were up in the air, funerals and grief real and present. No one was sufficiently untouched to have no death to mourn.

The scene evokes both the tragic recognition of enemy dead after Catiline's defeat in Sallust's *Bellum Catilinae* (*Cat.* 61) and the temporary reconciliation between Caesarean and Pompeian soldiers at Ilerda (Caes. *BC* 1.74–6; Luc. 4.169–205).[32] Depending on the rhetorical needs of each episode, Tacitus depicts the same armies sometimes as engaged in a contest between brave Italians and monstrous barbarians and sometimes as victims in a civil war tragedy of Roman kin against kin.

From Bedriacum and Back Again: 2.39–73

After this extended build-up and narrative delay, the battle of Bedriacum starts abruptly, before either side is prepared.[33] Tacitus can thus omit preliminaries like troop dispositions and exhortations. He depicts unconnected moments on the battlefield from the point of view of the soldiers fighting in a varied landscape where "there was no single face of battle" (42.2: *non una pugnae facies*). The scattered and confusing narrative, Ash observes, mirrors the scattered and discordant loyalties of the soldiers.[34] The field of battle itself seems to determine the outcome in each place. The Vitellian legions are aided by trees and brush that keep them out of view of the enemy (2.41.2), while Otho's generals cannot maneuver their battle lines into order because they are on a narrow road with deep ditches

---

[31] Cole (1992), 243; Ash (2010c), 125–6. [32] See Manolaraki (2005), 253–5; Joseph (2012c), 121–5.
[33] For a historical account of the battle, see Morgan (2006), 130–8; for Tacitus' combination of sources Duchêne (2012).
[34] Ash (2007b), 184.

on either side (2.41.3). Where there is an open field, by contrast, Roman legions can meet each other (2.43.1: *patenti campo duae legiones congressae sunt*), and Tacitus can at last narrate a "proper" battle, albeit a disturbingly internecine one, with legions identified by name, captured standards, charges and counter charges, and reported officer deaths—until the intervention of Vitellius' Batavian auxiliaries decisively breaks Otho's army.[35] By the time of this final rout, the landscape has gained a gruesome addition: the roads are filled with corpses that hamper Otho's fleeing army (2.44.1).

It takes eleven chapters for news of Bedriacum to spread through Italy and Gaul (2.46–57). First it reaches Otho, who, in keeping with his anti-deliberative character, has already made his decision: suicide (2.46.1: *consilii certus*). His final hours receive a heroic and expansive treatment reminiscent of accounts of the paradigmatic suicide of Cato the Younger.[36] Otho's final speech challenges Tacitus' sententious conclusions. The historian had stated that the combatants in 69 only laid down their arms out of "fecklessness" (*ignavia*) and that nothing can halt the drive to domination once it has taken root (2.38.2). Rather, Otho asserts that his is a conscious moral act, an *exemplum* that others can imitate: "Not fighting more than once is the example *I* shall set" (2.47.2: *ne plus quam semel certemus, penes me exemplum erit*). This has seemed a troubling inconsistency in Tacitus' portrayal of Otho, but the paradox is the quintessential one of civil war, where military valor means slaughtering fellow citizens and constancy in pursuing the fight means allowing citizens to be slaughtered by each other.[37]

Meanwhile, the senators waiting for news at Mutina find themselves in the same dilemma that Titus faced at the beginning of the book. Caught between reigns, they are pressed by Otho's suspicious soldiers to maintain loyalty to him while knowing that Vitellius may already be the new emperor. When the town council of Mutina spontaneously offers the senate money and troops, calling them "conscript fathers" as if they held official authority, they shrink from the "untimely honor" (2.52.2: *intempestivo honore*). The Mutinan councilors seem to be more than a hundred years out of date: in 43 BCE a senatorial army did take the field at Mutina in the war against Antony.[38] Times have changed since the Republican civil wars, however, and the idea that the senate might take charge of an army seems ludicrously inept. Tacitus' readers knew, moreover, that neither consul of 43 survived the "senatorial" victory at Mutina, and that the armies loyal to Caesar's heir Octavian then demanded that he be allowed to stand for consul. The quickly dismissed sideshadow of a senatorial army in 69, impossible in the world of the Principate, recalls the events that Augustus used to slide into absolute power in the first place.[39]

The news arrives in uncertain dribbles of rumor. One of Otho's freedmen arrives with his last commands (2.53.2), but he is followed by a freedman of Nero named Coenus, bearing the lie that Otho lives and has been victorious in a second battle (2.54.1). Traveling like Vergil's Fama, Coenus has arrived more quickly than any authoritative source.[40] Indeed, Coenus is revealed to have invented his story precisely so that imperial posting

[35] On the conventions of Greco-Roman historiographical battle narrative, see Woodman (1979); Woodman (1988), 168–79; Lendon (1999); Levene (2010a), 261–316; Lendon (2017). Cf. the classic work of Keegan (1976).
[36] Cf. Martial 6.32. On Otho's final speech, see Edwards (2007), 36–9; Schunck (1964); Keitel (1987), 77–80; Neumeister (2000), 201–3. On Cato as the model for heroic suicide, see Griffin (1986a), (1986b).
[37] Joseph (2012c), 153–67; cf. Roller (1996) and Gorman (2001) on heroism and civil war.
[38] For a concise historical overview of these events and their aftermath, see Osgood (2006), 50–60.
[39] For such a narrative, see e.g. *Ann.* 1.10.2 with Pagán, Chapter 9 in this volume.
[40] *Aen.* 4.173–88; see in general Hardie (2012), and, on rumors in Tacitus, Shatzman (1974); Gibson (1998).

stations would honor his pass issued by Otho.[41] Whereas swift couriers should aid in the dissemination of truth against rumors, in the upside-down world of civil war, they assist misinformation. In the end, Coenus' fleetness only hastens his end: within a few days he reaches Rome where he is put to death "on Vitellius' orders" (2.54.2: *iussu Vitellii*).[42] Presumably, this refers to a proxy for the new emperor, as Vitellius is 500 miles away in western Gaul and has not even learned that he has won the war.[43] Nonetheless, orders can be given in his name as soon as he is recognized as emperor, even if he himself does not know of his victory, just as Otho can continue to authorize the use of the posts after his death, as long as people believe he still lives and rules.

Tacitus then moves to Rome where there is "no anxiety" and the Cerialia are in progress "as usual" (2.55.1: *nihil trepidationis…ex more*). The announcement that Otho is dead and the urban cohorts have taken the oath to Vitellius is given in the theater. This is the first appearance of the Roman people in *Histories* 2; while in *Histories* 1 they despaired at making a choice between two vicious *principes*, now they do not seem to distinguish between the dramatic performances and games they watch at the festival and the changes of power going on around them, applauding Vitellius in absentia like a favorite actor (2.55.1).[44]

But the Roman people's incuriosity and addiction to spectacle pales beside their new emperor's.[45] Vitellius is the last person to learn of his own victory, long after the fact.[46] Although in *Histories* 1 Vitellius displayed all the vices of gluttony, apathy, and abdication of responsibility, Tacitus shows him acting somewhat competently before the news arrives, gathering together his forces, conducting a levy in Gaul to restore the numbers of his legions, and summoning another legion from Britain (2.57.1). This makes his change upon learning that he is emperor all the more dramatic. Just as the Flavians predicted at the beginning of the book, however, the news of his victory leads to the "fecklessness and extravagance" that will be Vitellius' downfall (cf. 2.7.1). Over the next few chapters, he sinks into debauchery and apathy amid feasts, troupes of actors, and gladiatorial shows.

Particularly emblematic of Vitellius' unreflective and passive consumption is his visit, between gladiatorial shows, to the battlefield at Bedriacum, where he desires to "survey the traces of fresh victory with his eyes" (2.70.1: *vestigia recentis victoriae lustrare oculis*), as if the sight of unburied corpses is simply another spectacle.[47] In keeping with *lustrare*'s connotations of a ritual circuit, Vitellius' "lustration" of the field, not quite forty days later, completes the spatio-temporal loop of news and rumor that the battle began. But Vitellius' visit and actions are anything but a ritual purification. His religious tourism duplicates and inverts Titus' visit to the shrine of Venus at the beginning of the book. The altars at Paphos were untouched even by rain; the ground of Bedriacum is soaked in human blood. Tacitus describes a scene of progressive decomposition and unrecognizability in high poetic language.[48] The gaze moves from "gouged bodies" and "lopped-off limbs" to "rotting

---

[41] On the imperial *cursus*, see Lemcke and Coşkun (2013).

[42] Coenus' route and death parallel that of the False Nero (see above, p. 66).

[43] Some scholars have been sufficiently disturbed by the impossibility of Vitellius literally giving orders in Rome that they have suggested reading *iussu L. Vitellii*, so that the emperor's brother gives the order; against this proposal, see Ash (2007b), 224.

[44] On this motif, see Keitel (1992).

[45] For these Vitellian traits, see Keitel (2007); Haynes (2003), 71–111.

[46] In reality, he may have received the news not long after it was brought to Rome: Murison (1993), 144–5.

[47] On this famous episode, see Woodman (1979); Funari (1989); Morgan (1992); Keitel (1992); Pagán (2000); Manolaraki (2005); Keitel (2007); Joseph (2012c), 144–52.

[48] Funari (1989) details parallels for each phrase.

shapes of men and horses" to "earth soaked with putrefaction," and, finally, to a panoramic landscape: "trees and crops trampled into a terrifying emptiness" (2.70.1: *lacera corpora, trunci artus, putres virorum equorumque formae, infecta tabo humus, protritis arboribus ac frugibus dira vastitas*). Each of these elements recalls specific moments in Tacitus' narrative of the battle, and so makes even starker the omissions of Vitellius' officers, who exaggerate their exploits into a heroic battle (2.70.3).

Some of Vitellius' soldiers happily go back over the places where they fought, but others are overcome by "the unpredictability of the universe and tears and pity" (2.70.3: *varia sors rerum lacrimaeque et misericordia*), in a reprise of the tears of reconciliation they experienced after the battle that echoes Aeneas' reaction to the reliefs of the Trojan War in Carthage (Verg. *Aen.* 1.461–2).[49] Vitellius, however, appears to feel nothing, and this moment shows him as a monster: "He did not avert his eyes or shudder at so many thousand unburied citizens. He was actually happy and unaware of his looming fate as he renewed a sacrifice to the local gods" (2.70.4: *at non Vitellius flexit oculos nec tot milia insepultorum civium exhorruit: laetus ultro et tam propinquae sortis ignarus instaurabat sacrum dis loci*).[50] The ritual phrase *sacrum instaurare* ("sacrifice anew") mocks the perversity of Vitellius' scrupulous religious observance in a place of human carnage. But there is also a grim joke in the technical meaning of *instaurare*, to repeat a rite from the beginning because it was done incorrectly the first time, as if the coming second battle at Bedriacum, with its second slaughter of Roman citizens (*H.* 3.15–29), will be Vitellius' "renewal" of the bloodshed he has just gazed upon.[51]

Vespasian Sets the *Moles Belli* in Motion (2.74–86)

When Tacitus finally turns to the Flavian party, everyone from soldiers to client kings is ready to declare Vespasian emperor—except for Vespasian himself, who continues to hesitate as he enumerates the risks that a bid for power entails: Vitellius' strength, the unreliability of armies' loyalties in a civil war, and even the possibility of assassination by one of his own men (2.75). Like Titus at the beginning of the book, Vespasian imagines several possible disaster scenarios, and like Titus, he reminds himself that preparing for the contingencies of losing is pointless once he has begun to make a bid for power: "Those who desire imperial power have no middle ground between the summit and the abyss" (2.74.2: *imperium cupientibus nihil medium inter summa et praecipitia*). Vespasian's prudent calculations contrast starkly with the decidedly un-deliberative and un-reflective Otho and Vitellius. In addition, Mucianus urges Vespasian to step forward as emperor in a speech that enumerates Vespasian's advantages both moral and practical.[52]

Mucianus, astute at playing and predicting political games (2.5.1), will subsequently play the crowd at Antioch, where he stirs up outrage with fictitious Vitellian plans to transfer the Syrian legions to Germany (2.80.3). Tacitus hints that his speech to Vespasian is staged as well: a military crowd witnesses Vespasian being "summoned" to power.

---

[49] Joseph (2012c), 149–52.   [50] Keitel (1992), 342–6.

[51] On the repetition, see Manolaraki (2005), 261–5; Joseph (2012c), 113–44; Oakley, Chapter 6 in this volume.

[52] On this speech, see Levene (2009a), 220–1; Keitel (1991), 2786–7. On types of arguments in Tacitean speeches, see Levene (1999).

Although Mucianus bolsters his case with many arguments about his own good faith, the feasibility of the campaign, and a few nods toward the need of the state for a competent and not corrupt emperor (2.76.1–2), his key argument is necessity: Vespasian's military fame has already made him into a perceived usurper in the eyes of any other emperor; therefore, he must seize power to survive (2.76.3). Mucianus ends with a *sententia* that echoes the spirit of Titus' conclusion at 2.1.3 and Vespasian's at 2.74.2: "Our cause is better in wartime than in peace: those considering rebellion have already rebelled" (2.77.3: *meliorem in bello causam quam in pace habemus*: *nam qui deliberant, desciverunt*). The final push comes from the soldiers, who, in a possibly staged scene, acclaim Vespasian as *Imperator* (2.80.1).

Vespasian seems to be moved less by Mucianus' reasoned exhortation than by the urging and enthusiasm of those around him who adduce oracles and portents that predict his rule (2.78.1–4) and by his own recollection of omens that might confirm his ambitions. In a practical sense, these are all signs that he has the support and devotion of his soldiers and that he has begun to be seen as a legitimate, even divinely ordained ruler by the people at large.[53] Tacitus' Vespasian does not come across as a reluctant emperor compelled by his soldiers but rather as a cautious general who does not commit himself until he knows that he can win. Yet the Flavians presented themselves as the restorers of traditional Roman religion and preservers of pristine Italian identity, and the portent that Vespasian takes to heart is a traditional Italic one: a cypress tree that revived from its stump (2.78.2). But Tacitus characterizes this as Vespasian's susceptibility to *superstitio*, excessive or irregular religious practice, and connects it to his employment of and open dependence on the guidance of an astrologer after he becomes emperor.[54]

Once the "unwieldy mass of war" (2.74.2: *in tanta mole belli*) has started to roll, the delays that have pervaded Tacitus' narrative turn to speed. Within two weeks of Vespasian's acclamation, much of the Roman East has sworn allegiance and Eastern kings have lavished their support and wealth on the Flavian cause. "Everything"—conscripting armies, requisitioning arms, minting coins—"begins to happen in a rush" (2.82.1: *cuncta…festinabantur*), including illegal exactions and confiscations, harbingers of future treason trials (2.84.1–2). Swiftness marks the events that follow: defections of legions in Illyria "speed up what Vespasian started" (2.85.1: *accelerata interim Vespasiani coepta*); the Pannonian legions join the Flavians "without hesitation" (2.86.1, *haud cunctanter*), and the vigorous imperial procurator Cornelius Fuscus "set[s] a ferocious torch to the war" (2.86.3: *acerrimam bello facem praetulit*).

Tacitus tempers this seemingly unstoppable forward momentum with the tale of Tettius Julianus, legate of the Seventh Legion stationed in Moesia. After escaping assassination by a rival, Julianus hides in the mountains that border Thrace, a proverbially wild territory that resists imperial knowledge. He then sets off to join Vespasian, but makes sure that he will not have to take part in civil war by "dragging out the trip with assorted delays, traveling slowly or quickly according to the news he received" (2.85.2: *per varias moras susceptum ad Vespasianum iter trahens et ex nuntiis cunctabundus aut properans*). Julianus' delays allow for a late change of sides, should Vespasian prove unsuccessful, but let him maintain

---

[53] Morgan (1992).
[54] Wardle (2012) gives a measured evaluation of Tacitus' portrayal of Vespasian's "religiosity" compared to the parallel tradition.

that he was always Vespasian's partisan, if the Flavians win. He turns the uncertainties of travel and the vagaries of rumor into a shield.

Preparing for the Next Round: 2.87–101

The final section of the book returns to Rome. As the Flavian cause waxes, victory and luxury have enervated Vitellius and his forces. Whether Vitellius attends the games or tries to conciliate the senate, he earns mockery (2.90.1, 91.2–3). His utter ignorance of Roman history and religion is more serious when, as Pontifex Maximus, he declares a religious ceremony on the day that commemorated two catastrophic military defeats of the early Roman Republic, the battles of the Allia and the Cremera (2.91.1).[55] When Vitellius' army finally marches out, it, too, has been ruined by inaction, poor discipline, and the temptations of the city, becoming a mirror of its dissipated commander in chief (2.99.1).[56] Even above his gluttony, however, Vitellius' great failure has consistently been apathy and deliberate ignorance, "transacting even important business with a short audience, incapable of dealing with serious matters" (2.59.1: *brevi auditu quamvis magna transibat, impar curis gravioribus*). As the Flavians advance and governors defect, Vitellius attempts to ignore and then suppress the news, delaying necessary preparations not from caution but simply from unconcern (2.96–8).

Histories 2 began in the Eastern Mediterranean with reactions to and deliberations taken about news from Rome. It ends with information going the opposite direction, but with much more intent and effect. Tacitus describes in some detail how the Flavians use the landscape and space of the empire to control the news: they hold the passes through the Alps, while the Etesian winds make travel from East to West far more difficult than in the other direction (2.98.1–2).[57] As a result, the Flavian party can control information about their own plans and strength, which they selectively disseminate to garner support among governors and legions, while they have easy routes for learning of Vitellius' plans. Their strategy succeeds: when Vitellius finally orders his armies out to meet the Flavian invasion, Caecina, in concert with the fleet commander Lucilius Bassus, defects to Vespasian, possibly after being suborned by Flavian agents in Rome (2.99.2). But the Flavian domination of the narrative extends into historiography. In the book's last chapter, Tacitus confronts and dismisses the victors' version of history: "Historians of this era who wrote accounts of this war while the Flavian dynasty held power reported [Caecina's and Bassus'] motivations as 'concern for peace' and 'love of country' – adulatory distortions" (2.101.1: *scriptores temporum, qui potiente rerum Flavia domo monimenta belli huiusce composuerunt, curam pacis et amorem rei publicae, corruptas in adulationem causas, tradidere*). The subservient Flavian historians parrot the same "empty slogans" Caecina himself previously used in false assurances to Otho's generals (2.20.2: *inrita nomina*), now presumably made to Vespasian's. As Tacitus prepares to move from the victories and reigns of the "bad" imperial claimants Otho and Vitellius to the victory of the dynasty that managed to last, he assures the reader that he will judge Vespasian just as closely as his predecessors.

---

[55] Further discussion at Hardie (2012), 295–7.   [56] Pigoń (2017).
[57] Cf. 2.73.1 where Vitellius too easily believes the report of spies that all is well in the East.

Further Reading

In addition to the commentaries and books cited in footnote 1, the following are good starting points among the many classic articles in English that deal with *Histories* 2: Keitel (1992) and Manolaraki (2005) on spectacles; Pomeroy (2003) and (2006) on space and "staging" in the *Histories* respectively; Damon (2006) on the portrayal of Vespasian. Master (2016) is an important and provocative book on the role of ethnic soldiers in the *Histories*; Morgan (2006) provides a synthetic account of the historical events of 69 CE. For details about individual figures, readers are directed to the *TE*.

Lydia Spielberg, Histories *2* In: *The Oxford Critical Guide to Tacitus*. Edited by: Salvador Bartera and Kelly E. Shannon-Henderson, Oxford University Press. © Oxford University Press 2025. DOI: 10.1093/9780191915086.003.0006

6

Histories 3

S. P. Oakley

Histories Book 3 is the most exciting book that Tacitus wrote.[1] It develops many of the character-descriptions and themes that have appeared already in books 1 and 2 into a narrative that brings the story of 69 CE to a climax at once compelling and shocking. The book starts far from Rome in an obscure corner of what is now Slovenia, with troops that have pledged allegiance to Vespasian uncertain what to do; after reaching its first climax in the sack of Cremona, it ends at Rome with the twin climaxes of the burning of the Capitol and the killing of Vitellius by Vespasian's troops. Two disreputable men dominate: at the book's beginning the dynamic Antonius Primus, who leads the way from Slovenia to Rome; at its end the torpid Vitellius, whose inertia leads only to his ruin. The scenes in which the narrative is set change some eight times, most often with alternation between Vitellius and the Flavian forces. Each return to these Flavians brings them closer to Rome and to the overthrow of Vitellius. Most of this chapter will consist of analysis of the book's main themes and characters; but since thematic analysis does not allow passages to be placed in their full narrative context and cannot evoke the ever tightening noose around Vitellius' neck, we shall start with a brief summary of the narrative, which may be divided into nine sections (A–I below).

* * *

A. (1.1–35.2). At Poetovio, modern Ptuj, commanders of forces fighting for Vespasian discuss whether they should await the arrival of Mucianus, Vespasian's most powerful ally, before advancing into Italy. Antonius urges an advance, and the troops agree. The cavalry rapidly advances west, into what is now Italy: to Aquileia, to Opitergium, to Altinum, to Patavium, to Ateste, and to Forum Alieni, where victory in a skirmish encourages reinforcements to join. Vicetia is then seized as they head for Verona, a town loyal to Vitellius, which they besiege. Meanwhile, news of the defection from Vitellius of the fleet at Ravenna encourages Caecina Alienus, one of the consuls and a Vitellian, actively to try to join his force to the Flavian side; but his troops, appalled at the notion that they, the renowned German legions, should surrender without fighting, rebel, take him captive, and head toward Cremona to join the Vitellian legions there. Antonius, fearful that reinforcements would be brought to the Vitellians from Rome by Fabius Valens and from north of the Alps, advances toward Cremona, ordering his troops to plunder. At Bedriacum the two forces clash in a battle of fluctuating fortunes that is won by the Flavians. Antonius can hardly restrain the Flavian troops from advancing on Cremona, when news of the arrival of Vitellius' legions concentrates their minds.

---

[1] Much of the excitement comes from Tacitus' exceptionally vivid style; here there is space only for passing comment on a few passages that illustrate this.

A grim battle is fought at night in which the Flavians are eventually victorious. They capture the camp that the Vitellian forces had built adjacent to the walls of Cremona and then sack Cremona itself.[2] The beaten Vitellian legions are sent to Illyricum and messengers are sent throughout the empire to announce the Flavian success.

B. (30.1–44). With the introductory phrases *At Vitellius profecto Caecina* ("But Vitellius, when Caecina had set out…") Tacitus' narrative moves to Rome, the reference to Caecina taking us back in time before the events just narrated to his departure from Rome at 2.99–101. We learn that after dispatching Fabius Valens, Vitellius has done almost nothing in response to the threat from Primus. When news of Caecina's attempted defection comes, the senators praise him and abuse Caecina—but are cautious not to insult the Flavian leaders. Vitellius' brother seizes the chance to secure the death of an enemy, the blameless Junius Blaesus. In the meantime, Valens progresses too slowly through Italy, and, after he has heard the result of the battle at Cremona, he goes to Gaul, where he is captured and subsequently killed. News of his capture brings further defections in Spain, Gaul, and Britain.

C. (45.1–48.3). The narrative changes scene once again to describe how the discord in the Empire encouraged unrest among the Britons, Germans, and Dacians, all of which is quelled. The rebellion of the freedman Anicetus in Pontus on what is now the north Turkish coast allows the book its only significant glance at Vespasian himself. His decisive action ends this rebellion, and, uplifted by his campaign's going even better than he has dared to hope, he travels to Alexandria, to crush the Vitellian forces there.

D. (49.1–53.3). Tacitus describes the preparations in Umbria of the Flavians for crossing the Apennines, the only significant physical barrier between them and Rome.

E. (54.1–59.3). With another "But Vitellius," Rome and the inert *princeps* return. At first Vitellius refuses to give credence to bad news, but finally acts, dispatching commanders and himself joining his troops at Mevania in Umbria—only to retreat back to Rome after he hears that the fleet at Misenum has defected and has seized Tarracina and other nearby towns. Sending his brother to deal with this defection, Vitellius holds a levy in Rome; but this proves abortive, and his retreat from Mevania encourages widespread defection in the central Apennines. Tacitus now introduces characters new to Book 3, all domiciled in Rome: Petilius Cerialis (a central character in books 4 and 5), who escapes from the city and is co-opted among the leaders of the Flavian forces; Vespasian's son, the future emperor Domitian (both mentioned in the *Histories* for the first time); and Vespasian's brother Flavius Sabinus (previously mentioned at 1.46.1, 2.55.1, 63.1–2, 99.2).

F. (60.1–63.2). We return to Umbria. Antonius' troops, based now at Carsulae, wish to march on Rome, but Antonius urges caution and suggests that a bloodless victory is possible. On the Vitellian side leaders return to Rome. Then news of the capture of Fabius Valens and his death at Urvinum weakens morale still further and a mass defection of troops at Interamna and Narnia follows. The Flavian forces try to negotiate with Vitellius, who, blind to his predicament, haggles about what he would be allowed in his post-imperial life.

G. (64.1–75.3). In Rome, Sabinus is urged to take an active role in events and himself negotiates with Vitellius, again inconclusively. Vitellius tries to abandon his principate

[2] For more detail on these events, see below, p. 84.

but, when his supporters block his way, he returns to the Palatine. After leading senators and others flock to Sabinus' house, the crowd and some troops begin to fight for Vitellius and Sabinus retreats to the Capitol. Soon Vitellian troops attack the Capitol; Sabinus and other leading Flavians are killed; and the Capitol itself is burned down. Domitian, who had joined Sabinus on the Capitol, manages to escape.

H. (77. 1–4). The actions of Lucius Vitellius, who crushes the rebels at Tarracina without difficulty, make for a brief interlude.

I. (78.1–86.3). Finally, we come to the last stages of the Flavian advance. They move forwards from Narnia to nearby Ocriculum, where, instead of pressing on to Rome, they delay, partly in deference to restraining letters from Mucianus. But news of the destruction of the Capitol impels them to move, and soon they are on the outskirts of Rome at Saxa Rubra. There is some abortive negotiation on the part of those based in Rome. Antonius himself wishes to defer entry into Rome until the following day, but his troops insist upon attacking. Vitellius had thought of trying to escape to his brother's forces at Tarracina, but he changes his mind; he is discovered in a hiding place in the palace, dragged out, and killed at the Gemonian steps. The books ends with Domitian emerging from hiding and being greeted as Caesar.

* * *

Tacitus' dramatic portrayal of the character and actions of Antonius Primus, Vitellius, and others should be placed in the wider context of a historian's need to explain events. Like many other Greek and Roman historians, Tacitus tended to make the behavior and character of the actors in his history an important feature of his explanations. A historian might be expected either to praise character and behavior or to make an adverse judgment, and the Roman habit of viewing notable persons as exemplars of virtue or vice encouraged the moral tone of such judgments.[3] Tacitus is less overtly didactic in tone than, for example, Thucydides, Polybius, or Livy, but both his *Annals* and his *Histories*, whose first three books deal with a year in which civil war shattered many accepted norms of decent conduct, are full of searing criticisms of immoral behavior, and he cannot resist finding (or hinting at) some fault even in characters of whom most approved.[4] Few escape his acid pen, but in *Histories* Book 3 there are two clear exceptions. The first is Vipstanus Messalla, who enters the narrative at 9.3:[5] "Vipstanus Messalla was tribune in command of this legion, a man with famous ancestors, outstanding himself, and the only person who brought praiseworthy principles to this war" (*legioni tribunus Vipstanus Messalla praeerat, claris maioribus, egregius ipse et qui solus ad id bellum artes bonas attulisset*). The second is Junius Blaesus, who never plots against Vitellius and is described at 39.2 as "a good man, no fomenter of disorder, seeking after no hastily gained position, and still less in pursuit of the Principate, he had not escaped sufficiently to prevent his being thought deserving of it" (*sanctus inturbidus, nullius repentini honoris, adeo non principatus adpetens, parum effugerat ne dignus crederetur*).[6]

---

[3] See e.g. Marincola (1997), 158–74; Oakley (1997–2005), iv. 557.

[4] See for example his comments on Flavius Sabinus at 75.1. However, Tacitus' refusal to acquiesce in simple descriptions of character can lead also to surprising compliments; see e.g. the final words of his obituary of Fabius Valens (62.2, quoted below, p. 86) and some of his obituary of Vitellius (86.2).

[5] He is mentioned also at 3.11.3, 18.2, 25.2, 28.1, 4.42.1–2 and is an important interlocutor in the *Dialogus*.

[6] For a similar comment on a senator's being regarded in popular opinion as worthy of the Principate, see 1.49.4.

Antonius Primus enters Tacitus' narrative first at 2.86.1, where in Pannonia he brings the thirteenth and seventh legions over to Vespasian's side.[7] There follows a memorable portrait, which sets the stage for his extraordinary prominence in book 3 (2.86.2):

praepositus a Galba septimae legioni scriptitasse Othoni credebatur, ducem se partibus offerens; a quo neglectus in nullo Othoniani belli usu fuit. labantibus Vitellii rebus Vespasianum secutus grande momentum addidit, strenuus manu, sermone promptus, serendae in alios invidiae artifex, discordiis et seditionibus potens,[8] raptor largitor, pace pessimus, bello non spernendus.

After having been put in command of the seventh legion by Galba, he was believed to have written to Otho and put himself forward as a leader of his faction; but, passed over, he took no part in the war involving Otho. When Vitellius' affairs began to fall apart, he followed Vespasian and added great impetus, being energetic in action, ready with speech, crafty at stirring up hatred against others, a powerful player amidst disharmony and mutinies, a plunderer, a briber, exceptionally wicked in times of peace, but not to be ignored in war.

Book 3 provides many opportunities to observe both the desirable and the less desirable traits of Antonius' character. His dynamism is illustrated by his name appearing thirty times in the nominative case as the subject of verbs, and only four times in oblique cases; he entirely eclipses his fellow commander Arrius Varus.[9] The "great impetus" mentioned in the character sketch begins in chapters 2 and 3, when Antonius tells the counsel of the thirteenth legion that it should move at once against the Vitellians, from whom they had nothing to fear. Energy and violence mark Antonius' initial actions: as the Flavian forces advance on Aquileia, he is said to be (6.1) "snatching (*rapienti*) those in special detachments and part of the cavalry out of their cohorts for the purposes of invading Italy"; Aquileia itself is then "seized" (6.2: *occupata*); and near Verona Antonius makes a "sudden attack" (9.1: *repentino incursu*) on the enemy. "Ready with speech" is illustrated well by the speech just mentioned,[10] but also by his theatrical rescue of Tampius Flavianus from mutinous troops, who listen to him alone among their commanders (10.3) and by his explaining to his troops that they were ill-equipped to attack Cremona (20.1–3). The deviousness described in the initial portrait is hinted at later: Tacitus, using his favored device of referring to real or alleged contemporary opinion or rumor,[11] states that some thought that Antonius had himself stirred up the mutinies that left him as the sole commander with any authority (11.4). Antonius' abilities on the field of battle itself are displayed best at the second battle of Bedriacum: after Arrius Varus makes a headlong and foolish charge that nearly leads to disaster, Antonius retrieves the situation (17.1):

---

[7] For sympathetic assessments of Antonius' character that place Tacitus' evidence in a wider context, see Treu (1948) and Shotter (1977).

[8] On the allusion here to Vergil's Drances (*Aen.* 11.340 *seditionibus potens*), see Ash (2007b), ad loc.

[9] Varus is mentioned at 3.6.1, 6.2, 16.1, 52.3, 61.2, 63.2, and 64.1.

[10] Martial (10.73.1) calls the older Antonius "eloquent" (*facundus*).

[11] The device has been much discussed by scholars; see e.g. Shatzman (1974). Sometimes Tacitus reports rumors because they played an important role in shaping events; see e.g. 3.25.1 (the rumor that Mucianus had arrived leads to Flavian success at the second battle of Bedriacum) and Gibson (1998).

Nullum in illa trepidatione Antonius constantis ducis aut fortissimi militis officium omisit. occursare paventibus, retinere cedentes, ubi plurimus labor, unde aliqua spes, consilio manu voce insignis hosti, conspicuus suis.

In that frightening situation Antonius shirked no duty of either a steadfast commander or a very brave soldier. He blocked the way of those who were frightened, restrained those who were retreating; wherever most effort was needed and from where any hope could be drawn, by his planning, fighting, and speech he was a remarkable figure in the eyes of his opponents, and readily visible to his own men.

Because his troops were exhausted Antonius wisely does not seek to follow up his victory.

Hitherto, apart from the mention of the rumor at 11.4, there has been little in the opening of the book to bear out the less attractive features of Tacitus' character sketch of Antonius. But at 28.2 he reports the view of the elder Pliny that by pointing to Cremona itself (and, by implication, the future opportunity to plunder it) Antonius had encouraged his troops to persevere in their attack on the Vitellian forces outside Cremona.[12] Tacitus tells us that Antonius' behavior got worse after the sack of Cremona (49.1–2): he cultivates his troops since they offered a route to power and promotes the least disciplined to the rank of centurion. This diminishes still further the power of the Flavian leaders over their troops: "Nor were soldiers under the authority of their commanders, but their commanders were dragged along by the violent behavior of the soldiers" (*nec miles in arbitrio ducum, sed duces militari violentia trahebantur*). Tacitus offers alternative explanations of Antonius' motive and characteristically places the more derogatory in second place:[13] "Either he thought that he had done enough for the war and that what followed would be easy, or good fortune, acting on such a character, had revealed greed, arrogance, and other hidden evils" (*satis factum bello ratus et cetera ex facili, seu felicitas in tali ingenio avaritiam superbiam ceteraque occulta mala patefecit*). But Antonius has overreached himself, making light of the imminent arrival of Mucianus, which was "something more deadly than to have spurned Vespasian" (49.2: *quod exitiosius quam Vepasianum sprevisse*). That mistake leads to a feud between the men, further encouraged when Antonius blames Mucianus for Vespasian's not rewarding him as he had hoped. Antonius writes to Vespasian a letter outlining his services and contrasting them with those of Mucianus, a good illustration of Tacitus' initial comment that Antonius knew how to stir up hatred of others. Tacitus tells us that Antonius conducted the feud in a straightforward manner, but Mucianus more cunningly, more relentlessly, and (readers may surmise) to greater effect (52.2–3). All this becomes apparent in Book 4, when Mucianus breaks Antonius' power.

In the final third of the book Antonius appears less often. At 63.1 he gives a kindly reception to surrendering Vitellian troops, and at 63.2 he makes a generous offer to Vitellius. At 60.1 his oratory is still good enough to control troops who, preferring victory to peace, wished to reject negotiations with the Vitellians, and at 80.2 his authority ensures a better reception of the envoys from Rome than was the case with those envoys who had

---

[12] For this fragment of Pliny's continuation of the history of Aufidius Bassus, see "Plinius," *FRHist.* II.1022–3 (B. Levick). Tacitus also says that Vipstanus Messalla had thought that Hormus was responsible and claims to be unable to decide between the two, adding that so disgraceful an utterance was compatible with the behavior and reputation of both.

[13] On this phenomenon, see especially Whitehead (1979).

been sent to other Flavian leaders; but at 82.1, in line with Tacitus' comment at 49.1–2, he fails to restrain his troops in their desire to burst into Rome. In connection with his delaying of the final stage of the march on Rome, Tacitus, who thought that haste could have saved the Capitol from burning and Sabinus from death, reports a rumor that Antonius was negotiating with Vitellius and had been promised Vitellius' daughter in marriage (78.1–2), and he criticizes Antonius' "untimely compliance" (78.3 *praepostero obsequio*) in letting Mucianus come closer.

Already, before Book 3 begins, Tacitus' Vitellius[14] offers an extraordinary spectacle of self-indulgent luxury and gluttony,[15] lack of initiative and thought for future action,[16] ignorance,[17] dithering vacillation,[18] and fearfulness.[19] How Antonius could seize so much narrative space at the beginning of the book is explained by the graphic portrait that accompanies Vitellius' first proper entry into it at 36.1:

> *Vitellius…curis luxum obtendebat: non parare arma, non adloquio exercitioque militem firmare, non in ore vulgi agere, sed umbraculis hortorum abditus, ut ignava animalia, quibus si cibum suggeras, iacent torpentque, praeterita instantia futura pari oblivione dimiserat.*

> Vitellius was using luxurious living as a veil for his worries: he was not equipping his armed forces, nor building the confidence of his troops by encouragement and training, nor carrying out business under the gaze of the crowd; but hidden in the shades of his gardens, like sluggish animals who lie prostrate and inert if you supply them with food, he had cast from his mind with equal forgetfulness events that had taken place, that were pressing on him, and that would occur.

The triple anaphora of *non* negating the three historic infinitives (a form of verb normally used to describe not inertia but a developing situation) forcefully marks Vitellius' failure to respond to the challenge posed by Vespasian. *Torpor* and its cognates (here *torpent*) reappear with the force of a *Leitmotiv* in Tacitus' remarks on Vitellius: first used of him at 1.62.2 and 2.77.3,[20] we meet them again at 3.63.2, in one of the most devastating of all Tacitus' *sententiae*: "Such inertia had gripped his mind that if others had not remembered that he had been emperor, he would forget" (*tanta torpedo invaserat animum, ut, si principem eum fuisse ceteri non meminissent, ipse obliviceretur*).[21] The betrayal of Vitellius by Lucilius Bassus and the defection of the fleet at Ravenna, setbacks that should have induced action at Rome, find him "idling and flaccid" (36.2: *desidem et marcentem*) at Aricia. "In his indolent disposition" (36.2: *apud socordem animum*), the news that Caecina

---

[14] Engel (1977) examines the evidence of Tacitus and others in an attempt to produce a more favorable account of Vitellius.

[15] The most important passage is 1.62.2, where Vitellius' troops demand action, but he "was inert (*torpebat*) and anticipating the rank of Emperor by idle luxury and lavish banquets, tipsy in the middle of the day and weighed down by his stomach"; see also 2.31.1, 62.1 "a disgusting and insatiable delight in feasts" (*epularum foeda et inexplebilis libido*), 67.2, 68.1, 95.2.

[16] See 1.52.4 "idle disposition" (*segne ingenium*), 2.87.1 "more despised and idle as each day passed" (*contemptior in dies segniorque*), 95.3.

[17] See 2.59.1.

[18] See 2.57.2 "inconstancy of character" (*mobilitate ingenii*), 92.2 "changeable" (*mutabilem*).

[19] See 2.68.4.

[20] A chapter earlier (2.76.2) Mucianus had warned Vespasian against displaying this characteristic.

[21] *Obliviceretur* recalls *oblivione* at 36.1.

had both defected and been imprisoned prompts joy rather than diligence. When Vitellius' brother encourages him to kill Blaesus by arguing that there was more danger to the emperor from Blaesus in Rome than from Vespasian, whom so many loyal armies and such distance separated from Rome, and that Vitellius should make Blaesus "realize that [he] was alive and ruling" (38.4: *sentiat vivere Vitellium et imperare*), readers may easily detect the authorial irony in both "alive" and "ruling." After responding with characteristic doubts about how to proceed (39.1 "panicking between crime and fear" [*trepidanti inter scelus metumque*]), Vitellius settles on poison, visits the dying man, and (39.1) "boasted that he had fed his eyes in watching the death of his enemy" (*pavisse oculos spectata inimici morte iactavit*)—a sentiment characteristic of a tyrant.[22] Henceforth, fear will become an ever more prominent part of the portrait:[23] in the following pages we are told that he is "fearful" (56.2: *trepidus*) and "acting from fear" (58.2: *a metu*), makes a "frightened departure" (59.1: *pavidus…discessus*) from his forces, and fears everything (85.4: *omnia metuenti*).

Between 54.1 and 56.3 (part of E above) Tacitus emphasizes more than anywhere else his theme that the Vitellians regularly missed opportunities to win the campaign. Vitellius himself prohibits news of the defeat at Cremona to be spread and kills those who spread it (54.1-2). When Julius Agrestis, after failing to rouse Vitellius to manly action, goes north, views the enemy forces, reports back, and kills himself after Vitellius denies the truth of what he had said, Tacitus gives weight to his final words by reporting them in direct speech (54.2-3). "Aroused as though from slumber" (55.1: *ut e somno excitus*), Vitellius tries to act, but to no good effect, since the forces that he marshalled, easily sufficient to defeat Antonius, needed a different commander to be victorious. Vitellius makes reckless promises and rewards which would have wrecked the empire and which showed no care for the future (55.2). At Mevania he is "dithering" (55.3: *incertus animi*) and clueless about generalship (56.1); his attempt to address his troops is more bizarre than the dire natural omens that greeted the scene (56.1-2); he disperses his forces when a move across the Apennines would have allowed him to defeat the tired and ill-provided enemy (56.3); and centurions and other well-informed people who wish to give advice are warded off by his friends (56.3).

When Sabinus opens negotiations with Vitellius about abdication, his facial expression is "submissive and unworthy of his rank" (*proiectus et degener*) (65.2). His friends argue that he was mistaken to think that he would be treated well by the Flavians and that he should decide whether he was going to die amidst insults or a show of manliness (*virtutem*) (66.4); but deaf to "plans involving bravery" (*fortia consilia*; 67.1) he enacts his farcical attempt at abdication and "bereft of any plan" (*consilii inops*) he returns to the palace (68.3). After Antonius' troops have broken into the city, Tacitus conjures up a memorable scene of fear, squalor, and vacillation as Vitellius flees the palace (absurdly carried in a sedan chair), only to change his mind, return, and die (84.4).[24]

---

[22] See Leigh (1996) and, on food and power in Tacitus, Woodman (2006b) = (2012), 339-60. In the case of Vitellius, feeding is an entirely apt metaphorical usage.

[23] Levene (1997), 136-47 discusses the themes of pity and fear in the latter parts of Book 3.

[24] Tacitus' writing is here as brilliant as anywhere in the book; see e.g. Oakley (2009) 206-11.

Many ancient historians enjoyed describing reversals of fortune, which could evoke both pity and pleasure.[25] Tacitus had already referred to pity for Vitellius, or at least for the office of emperor, at 58.2–3. At 68.1 he describes Vitellius' attempt to abdicate thus:

Nec quisquam adeo rerum humanarum immemor, quem non commoveret illa facies, Romanum principem et generis humani paulo ante dominum relicta fortunae suae sede per populum, per urbem exire de imperio. nihil tale viderant, nihil audierant.

Nor is there anyone so unmindful of the affairs of men whom that scene would not stir—a Roman Emperor, and only shortly before the lord of the human race, had abandoned the abode of his high position and was passing out of his office through the people, through the city. They had seen nothing like it, heard nothing like it.

The power of Tacitus' sentiment is enhanced by its expression: *fortunae* points directly to the theme of the reversal of fortune; *facies* encourages visualization of the scene; the dignity of the office from which Vitellius was falling is underlined by the weighty *Romanum principem et generis humani paulo ante dominum*; the anaphora and balance provided by the repeated *per* evoke the humiliating walk through the crowds in Rome; and the two cola *nihil tale viderant, nihil audierant*, balanced by anaphora of *nihil* and verbs of perception in the pluperfect tense, bring out just how extraordinary was the spectacle. At Vitellius' death we read (84.5):

vinctae pone tergum manus; laniata veste, foedum spectaculum, ducebatur, multis increpantibus, nullo inlacrimante: deformitas exitus misericordiam abstulerat.

His hands were bound behind his back. After his clothing had been ripped he was led away, a disgusting sight, with many people taunting him but no one in tears: the degradation of his end had removed all pity.

Once again he encourages visualization (*spectaculum*) and deploys balance and antithesis (*multis increpantibus, nullo inlacrimante*). One might have expected more compassion to be described but Tacitus' narrative has now taken us beyond pity to ghastly contempt.

By most of Vitellius' more senior supporters Tacitus is unimpressed. They are shown as either actively treacherous (thus Caecina at 9.2 and 13.1, acting on a plan mentioned at 2.93.2, 99.2, 100.1–101.2), lukewarm and disloyal (37.2, 58.2), or incompetent because of their slow movement (Caecina at 9.2, Valens at 40.1–41.2).[26] Twice Tacitus contrasts the willingness of the common soldiers to fight for Vitellius with the treachery of their commanders (13.2–3 [Caecina's troops], 61.3 "there were frequent desertions of tribunes and centurions. For the common soldiers had stayed firmly for Vitellius": *crebra transfugia tribunorum centurionumque; nam gregarius miles induruerat pro Vitellio*). Loyalty mattered to Tacitus, and this explains the final partly complimentary words in his obituary of Valens (62.2, quoted below, p. 86).

---

[25] Classic statements of this are Polyb. 1.1.2 and Cic. *Fam.* 5.12.4; see further e.g. Marincola (1997), 23 and (on this book) Levene (1997).

[26] On fidelity and treachery in the *Histories*, see Bartera (2019), esp. 266–8 on Book 3.

Tacitus was interested as much in the behavior of groups of people as in that of individuals. No one who reads the *Histories* can fail to notice his descriptions of the rapacity and unruliness of Rome's legions and auxiliaries during the civil war. In Book 3, this theme is generally met in connection with the troops led by Antonius. Minicius Justus, a prefect of the seventh legion, is sent to Vespasian because of the troops' anger at his commanding "more strictly than was suitable for a civil war" (7.1: *adductius quam civili bello imperitabat*). When wrongly suspecting betrayal the same legion turns its anger against Tampius Flavianus (10.1–4). As though infected by disease the mutiny then spreads. In the mistaken belief that their commander Aponius Saturninus was planning to betray them to Vitellius, the Moesian legions turn on him, determined not to be outdone by the strength of the mutiny against Tampius. Tacitus acidly comments (11.2) that "there was a contest in license and effrontery, as once there had been in virtue and moderation" (*ut olim virtutis modestiaeque, tunc procacitatis et petulantiae certamen erat*).[27] The other officers can do nothing, and Aponius is rescued only by choice of a good hiding place (11.4).

The attitudes of the troops are well revealed by their role in the sack of Cremona, whose destruction is one of the more heinous crimes of the civil war. After the first significant victory of the Flavians, the troops want to sack Cremona in order to gain booty for themselves; ignoring their centurions and tribunes, they brandish their weapons and demand the order to advance; and with great difficulty Antonius restores some order with the speech already mentioned. Mutiny was still being threatened when the advance of Vitellian legions turns the minds of the troops to battle (19.1–21.1). Victorious in that battle, the Flavian forces had to choose between retreating, fortifying a camp of their own, or attacking the Vitellian camp adjoined to Cremona. Strongly influenced by their greed for booty, the volatile troops reject delay (26.3); therefore Antonius decides to attack the camp; and it is when the tired troops falter that their leaders point to Cremona (27.3). After the camp has been stormed, the outskirts of the town are itself attacked, the crowd of traders contained in it being an inducement to plunder (30.2). After the surrender of the Vitellians, Antonius and the other leaders turn a blind eye to the sacking of Cremona carried out by the troops. At 60.1 the troops wish to march on Rome rather than await reinforcements, lest the reinforcements take some of the booty for themselves. At 80.2–81.1 they molest various ambassadors sent from the city, who include the Stoic philosopher Musonius Rufus, whose sermonizing Tacitus describes as "untimely" (*intempestivam sapientiam*) and whose discomfiture he seems to relish.

Under Tacitus' searching gaze the urban plebs has already in books 1 and 2 been criticized for its fickle insouciance.[28] As Book 3 progresses the theme becomes more insistent: when Vitellius hands out largesse all around the plebs gapes in admiration (55.2); when Vitellius tries to abdicate its utterances are "flattering and untimely" (*blandae et intempestivae*)—while the troops watch with a threatening silence (67.2); when Antonius' forces break into the city and the Vitellians offer some resistance, the crowd watches as though at the gladiatorial games, cheering now one side, now the other, and seizing any spoil from the fallen for themselves (83.1); and when Vitellius has been killed, Tacitus comments, "And the commons harried him after he had been killed with the same perversity with

---

[27] Tacitus may here be ironically recalling Sallust, *Catiline* 9.2.
[28] See e.g. 1.89.1, 2.90.2. On Tacitus' contempt for the populace of Rome, see further Syme (1958a), 531–3.

which they had cultivated him when alive" (*et vulgus eadem pravitate insectabatur interfectum, qua foverat viventem*, 85).

Throughout the book an intermittent and somewhat sinister note is struck by Tacitus' references to Mucianus, king-maker supreme and now moving west with his troops toward Rome.[29] At 8.2–3 Antonius is told in letters from Vespasian to await his arrival, and in frequent letters Mucianus says that the arrival of his legions would lead to a bloodless victory; but the authorial voice claims hypocrisy: Mucianus was "greedy for glory and holding back all renown from the war for himself." After a brief appearance in Moesia (where he makes sensible dispositions) at 46.2–3 and a passing reference at 47.3, Mucianus reappears at 52.1–3, fearful that he might miss out on glory from the war and writing ambiguous letters to Antonius and Varus that both commended their advance and recommended delay; and allies of Mucianus serving with Antonius write letters, sent on to Vespasian, that incriminate Antonius. When Antonius' forces get closer to Rome, Mucianus joins Antonius in offering Vitellius a safe retirement (63.2), but friends persuade Vitellius to trust neither man (66.3). At 75.2 Tacitus states that the killing of Sabinus brought joy to Mucianus, since (we presume) a rival for influence was removed. The explanation for the perverse delay of the Flavian forces in marching on Rome was disputed among Tacitus' sources (78.1–3): some mentioned the rumors about Antonius and Vitellius' daughter; others said that these were false and invented to curry favor with Mucianus; by reporting these speculations, Tacitus is able to cast aspersions on both men. Tacitus then offers his own apportioning of the blame, which includes the delay caused by Mucianus' letters. What has been anticipated in Book 3 finally comes to fruition early in Book 4: Mucianus reaches Rome, takes control of politics, and brings an end to Antonius' period of dominance (4.11.1).

The civil war of 69 offered much else on which Tacitus was able to pass adverse or wry comment: the freedman Hormus' being regarded as a leader of a faction (3.12.3),[30] women fighting (32.2, 69.3), senators and army commanders muting their criticism of the opposition, or support for their own side, lest the opposition should win (3, 9.4, 37.2). Most shocking of all, *Histories* Book 3 offers two contrasting instances of family member killing family member. In the first a son who was serving in Antonius' forces kills his father (who had been serving in a Vitellian legion), begs forgiveness, and buries him. Tacitus states that word spread through the lines of battle and the troops curse civil war, but then comes a stinging *sententia* (25.3): "They say that an evil deed has been done—and they <carry on> do<ing> it" (*factum esse scelus loquuntur faciuntque*). Later, at 51.1–2, a soldier claims a reward from his leaders because he has killed his own brother. Tacitus contrasts his behavior with that of a soldier in an earlier civil war who had committed suicide after performing a similar deed and comments on "such great lack of respect amongst the victors [i.e. the Flavians] for what was right and wrong" (*tantam victoribus adversus fas nesfasque inreverentiam*).

Several of the events in *Histories* 3 are thematically similar to those told in Books 1 and 2.[31] The battle around Bedriacum and Cremona (3.15–29) between the Flavians and Vitellians

[29] For Tacitus' initial character-sketch, see 1.10.1–2; for his decisive galvanizing of Vespasian, see 2.74.1–84.2.
[30] For a similar remark about freedmen, see 1.76.3.
[31] See the further examples and detailed discussions of Joseph (2012c), 95–144.

recalls that at Bedriacum between the Othonians and Vitellians (2.39–45).[32] In the first battle the troops on both sides recognize each other (2.42.2); it is in the second that the son kills his father (3.25.2). The death in Rome of the old and ineffectual *princeps* Galba (1.41–9) is recalled first by the death there of the old Sabinus (74.2), then by the destruction of the old Capitol, and finally by the death of Vitellius, not so old as Galba but even more ineffectual and made to view Galba's place of death before he dies. Like Galba (1.35.1, 41.2), Vitellius (3.85.4) leaves the palace before his death in a sedan chair. The killers of Galba ignore the sight of the Capitol and the temples looming over (*imminentium templorum*) the forum (1.40.2); later, the Vitellians will rush past these temples (3.71.1 *imminentia foro templa*) as their attack on the Capitol leads to its burning. The narrative thus draws attention to both the wearisome repetitiousness of the violence of civil wars and the similar morality of victors and vanquished; often the telling of the episode in Book 3 surpasses a similar narrative earlier in the text in horror and intensity.

Death-notices and obituaries are also a recurring theme, starting with that of Galba (1.49.2–4). These are a regular feature of ancient historiography and gave Tacitus the chance to offer a pithy summation of a dead man's morality.[33] The carnage of *Histories* 3 allowed for many, including those of Junius Blaesus (39.2), Flavius Sabinus (75.1–3), and Vitellius himself (86.1–2), but three deserve special notice. The (mostly) disreputable actions of Fabius Valens draw forth a fine example of Tacitus' pointed style (62.2):

> *Natus erat Valens Anagniae equestri familia. procax moribus neque absurdus ingenio famam urbanitatis per lasciviam petere. ludicro Iuvenalium sub Nerone velut ex necessitate, mox sponte mimos actitavit, scite magis quam probe. legatus legionis et fovit Verginium et infamavit; Fonteium Capitonem corruptum, seu quia corrumpere nequiverat, interfecit, Galbae proditor, Vitellio fidus et aliorum perfidia inlustratus.*

> Valens was born at Anagni into an equestrian family. Licentious in his behavior but not unintelligent, he sought a reputation for refinement through frivolity. Under Nero he performed—cleverly rather than respectably—in farces at the Juvenalia Games, as though under compulsion but soon spontaneously. As legionary legate he both supported Verginius and slandered him. He killed Fonteius Capito either after seducing him or because he had failed to seduce him. A betrayer of Galba, he was faithful to Vitellius and made prominent by the treachery of others.

Antitheses run throughout the passage: "undisciplined in behavior" but not stupid; a reputation for being a wit but in fact dissolute; forced to perform but then doing so willingly; supporter of Verginius and then disloyal to him; and finally, and surprisingly, a betrayer of Galba but loyal to Vitellius and exalted because of the treachery of others. The delayed *scite magis quam probe* is a fine example of the sting that Tacitus could impart to the tail of a sentence; and *et fovit Verginium et infamavit* exhibits a classic formulation for a *sententia*.

More striking, however, than any of these passages are two examples of a feature that Tacitus took over from Livy and others: the obituary of a town or the like. The three-sentence

---

[32] Tacitus draws attention to this at 2.23.2, 3.24.1, and 3.

[33] For the historians in general, see Pomeroy (1991). For Tacitus in particular, see Pomeroy, pp. 192–225; Syme (1958*b*) = (1970), 79–90; and Woodman and Martin (1996), 268–9 (on *Ann.* 3.30.1).

obituary of Cremona, the first of the book's climaxes, culminates in an antithesis that is a withering indictment of civil war (34.1):

igitur numero colonorum, opportunitate fluminum, ubere agri, adnexu conubiisque gentium adolevit floruitque, bellis externis intacta, civilibus infelix.

Therefore it grew and flourished because of the number of the colonists in it, its good position by rivers, the fertility of its land, the inclusion and marriage with foreigners, untouched by foreign wars, unfortunate in civil wars.

The passage anticipates the weightier and longer obituary of the Capitol (72.1–3). Tacitus introduces his reflections on its burning with scathing comment (72.1):[34]

Id facinus post conditam urbem luctuosissimum foedissimumque rei publicae populi Romani accidit, nullo externo hoste, propitiis, si per mores nostros liceret, deis, sedem Iovis Optimi Maximi, auspicato a maioribus pignus imperii conditam, quam non Porsenna dedita urbe neque Galli capta temerare potuissent, furore principum excindi.[35]

The most grievous and shameful crime that had happened to the commonwealth of the Roman people since the founding of the city took place when there was no foreign enemy, when the gods would have been propitious (if our behavior had allowed), namely the destruction by the madness of the imperial contenders of the seat of Jupiter the Best and Greatest, which had been founded with good auspices by our ancestors as a guarantee of empire and which neither Porsenna when the city had surrendered nor the Gauls when they had captured it had been able to violate.

In his preface (1.2.2) Tacitus had drawn attention to the burning of the Capitol as one of the most notable features of the *Histories*. It was the "guarantee of empire," symbolic of Roman power surviving through the centuries.[36] Sallust (*Cat.* 18.8) says that had Catiline not been incompetent, "the worst crime since Rome's foundation would have been committed" (*post conditam urbem Romam pessimum facinus patratum foret*); in a clear allusion, Tacitus shows how those contending for power had surpassed Catiline. They had achieved what no foreign enemy had managed. Manlius Capitolinus had saved the Capitol from the Gauls in 390 BCE; Sabinus and the Flavians had failed to stop the Vitellians from climbing it in 69 CE. The Capitol now stands symbolic of the wanton destruction by the madness of civil war of centuries of hallowed and valued tradition,[37] symbolic of an empire that seems to be on the verge of ruin.[38]

---

[34] Döpp (2003) discusses Tacitus' style as deployed in this chapter.
[35] This sentence has a characteristically Tacitean shape: its main clause (*Id ... accidit*) comes first; then ablatives of attendant circumstances (or absolute) (*nullo ... deis*) introduce a continuation. The fullest discussion of this pattern is Kohl (1959); for further bibliography see e.g. Oakley (2009), 205 n. 35.
[36] See e.g. Liv. 5.54.7, Hor. *Carm.* 3.30.8–9, Verg. *Aen.* 9.448.
[37] For some reflections on this symbolism, see e.g. Edwards (1996), 78–81; Ash (2007c), esp. 229–36 (with remarks on the personification of the temple and Tacitus' portrayal of the topography of Rome in the *Histories*); and Sailor (2008), 205–18.
[38] But in Tacitus matters are rarely simple: the Roman Empire does recover, and the Gauls are wrong to regard the burning of the Capitol as an omen for their own victory (4.54.2).

Passing comment has been made in various places on the flamboyant and mesmerizing language with which Tacitus tells his story. The *Histories* are enriched by many echoes and allusions to Vergil's *Aeneid*;[39] in Book 3, where these are particularly prominent, words recalling the apocalyptic sack of Troy in *Aeneid* 2 are regularly and appropriately deployed as the civil war moves toward its climax.[40] Two examples from many may serve as illustrations: when the Flavian troops burst into the Vitellian camp abutting Cremona Tacitus (28) writes about "diverse shapes of dying men and every representation of deaths" (*varia pereuntium forma et omni imagine mortium*), which recalls *Aeneid* 2.369 "very numerous representation of death" (*plurima mortis imago*); when the Flavians try to stop the Vitellians from advancing on the Capitol they block the way with (71.2) "statues, the adornments of their ancestors" (*statuas, decora maiorum*), which recalls *Aeneid* 2.448 "the adornments of fathers of old" (*veterum decora...parentum*), the evocation of Vergil enhancing the sense of the wanton destruction of tradition mentioned above. But other parts of the *Aeneid* are evoked too: when late in the day Vitellius tries to negotiate Antonius writes back (3.81.2) that "with the slaughter of Sabinus and the burning of the Capitol barterings of the war had been broken off" (*Sabini caede et incendio Capitolii dirempta belli commercia*); similarly, Aeneas tells Magus (*Aen.* 10.532–3) that "Already back then when he had killed Pallas Turnus had removed those barterings of the war" (*belli commercia Turnus | sustulit ista prior iam tum Pallante perempto*).

* * *

The killing of an emperor, the treachery of the upper classes, the frightening insubordination of troops, the pillaging and sacking of an Italian city, Rome's Capitol ablaze, son killing father, and brother killing brother. No other extant book gave Tacitus such scope for the powerful writing and the moralizing that the Romans liked to find in works of history.

Further Reading

General accounts of the *Histories* may be found in e.g. Syme (1958a), 130–216, Martin (1981), 67–101, and Ash (1999b), esp. chapters 5 and 7, which touch on many themes covered in this essay. Heubner (1972) and Wellesley (1972) are commentaries on the Latin text of *Histories* 3.

S. P. Oakley, Histories 3 In: *The Oxford Critical Guide to Tacitus*. Edited by: Salvador Bartera and Kelly E. Shannon-Henderson, Oxford University Press. © Oxford University Press 2025. DOI: 10.1093/9780191915086.003.0007

[39]   See n. 7 for one already noted.

[40]   Many Vergilian passages are cited in the commentaries of Heubner (1972) and Wellesley (1972), but for general discussion see esp. Baxter (1971) and Joseph (2012c) (via his index on p. 215). Vergil avoids any pattern that would allow one side the honor of being associated with Aeneas and his Trojans.

7

Histories 4

Timothy A. Joseph

Summary

The events of Book 4 take place in three centers of action: Rome, the Rhineland, and Alexandria.[1] The book opens in Rome in December 69 (4.1–11), first with an overview of the state of affairs in the aftermath of the Flavian victory and Vitellius' death (4.1.1–4.3.2), then with an account of the first meeting of the senate after that victory and the senatorial debate that it brings (4.3.3–4.10), and finally with the arrival in the city of Vespasian's most significant ally, Mucianus, the recent governor of Syria (4.11). Next (4.12–37) Tacitus turns his attention to the Rhineland and to a detailed account of the revolt of the auxiliary cohorts under the command of the Batavian prince and Roman citizen Julius Civilis, an uprising that had begun much earlier in the year 69 when Vitellius was still emperor (3.46.1) and that had been encouraged by the Flavian generals Antonius Primus and Hordeonius Flaccus, the legionary commander in Germany (4.13.2–3). Civilis, accumulating neighboring tribes as allies in his effort, wages a series of attacks on Roman fortifications along the Rhine, including a number of sieges of Castra Vetera (4.22–3 and 4.28–30). A consequence is mutiny among the pro-Vitellian legionaries, who kill the distrusted Flaccus (4.36.2). Tacitus returns to Rome at 4.38–50 to recount a reprise of senatorial debates and a series of actions by Mucianus, including his planning for the assassination of the distrusted governor of Africa Lucius Calpurnius Piso (4.48–50). After describing Vespasian's reception in Alexandria of the news of his victory and a conversation there with his son Titus (4.51–2), Tacitus revisits Rome to describe the dedication of the restored Capitol (4.53). From here he returns to the Rhineland (4.54–79), where, with Vitellius' death and Vespasian's victory known, the Batavians and a number of Gallic states are now in open rebellion against Rome. At Rome Mucianus directs multiple legions to Gaul (4.68); and the subsequent series of victories over the Treveri and Lingones by the commander of legio XIV Gemina (and son-in-law of Vespasian) Petilius Cerialis (4.71–8) bring resolution to the Gallic rebellion, though not to the conflict with Civilis and the Batavians, an affair that Tacitus will take up again at 5.14–26 (where the text of the *Histories* breaks off; see Bloch, Chapter 8 in this volume). After more on Mucianus' actions in Rome (4.80), Tacitus returns to Alexandria to describe Vespasian's supernatural healing of two men and his visit to the Temple of Serapis (4.81–4). The book concludes with Mucianus and Domitian in Gaul to declare victory over the Gallic rebellion (4.85–6); the former curbs the military ambitions of the latter, but rumors circulate that Domitian had reached out to Cerialis about securing power for himself.

---

[1] I am thankful to the volume's editors, Salvador Bartera and Kelly Shannon-Henderson, as well as Elizabeth Keitel and Thomas Strunk, for reading and commenting on drafts of this chapter.

A wide-angle look at the content and structure of Book 4 seems to show a sense of renewed order to Roman affairs after the multifront civil war, confusion, and chaos of Books 1–3. For one, Tacitus uses the break in books to mark the conclusion of Vitellius' life, told at the end of Book 3, and the beginning of Vespasian's reign, one that readers knew would last ten years and thus stabilize a state that had seen four different *principes* over the previous eighteen months. Further, a first glance at the arrangement of Book 4 as a whole shows what seems to be a fairly clear division among domestic affairs (*res internae*) at Rome and foreign affairs (*res externae*) in the provinces.[2] This is the method of organization that carries through other works of annalistic historiography such as Livy's *History* and through much of the later *Annals*, which, like *Histories* 4, cover years more stable than the discordant year of 69 in *Histories* 1–3. Order, it appears, has come both to Rome and to Tacitus' annalistic endeavor.

But not so fast. From the beginning to the end of Book 4 Tacitus keeps before our eyes a battery of unresolved problems and tensions, both for the Roman state of the years 69–70 and for the system of the Principate generally. The Rome that Tacitus presents here was in a condition of acute precariousness, with power still in the balance, easy distinctions of identity becoming increasingly uncommon, and its center decentered. This chapter will concentrate on Tacitus' exploration in Book 4 of the continuation of Rome's destabilized condition, and on how this condition is reflected in the style and arrangement of the book's material.

"Savage Even in Its Peace"

The failure of Vitellius' and Book 3's end to bring any comfortable resolution to war-torn Rome is made clear in the very first sentence of Book 4 (4.1.1):

> *Interfecto Vitellio bellum magis desierat quam pax coeperat. armati per Urbem victores implacabili odio victos consectabantur: plenae caedibus viae, cruenta fora templaque, passim trucidatis ut quemque fors obtulerat.*

> With Vitellius killed, it was more that war had stopped than that peace had begun. Throughout the city the armed conquerors were chasing down the conquered with implacable hatred. The streets were filled with carnage, the forums and temples were bloody, since whomever chance threw before the victors was slaughtered in passing.

Although Rome's streets and monuments are already bloodstained, the slaughter in the city, we learn, is ongoing, and over the remainder of Book 4's opening tableau Tacitus characterizes postwar Rome with many of the hallmarks of a captured city, employing diction that recalls his cityscape of the captured and looted Cremona at *H.* 3.33.[3] This opening sets the tone for much of what is to come in the book, following through on Tacitus' introductory statement at *H.* 1.2.1 that the part of his work covering the Flavians' reign would be "savage even in its peace" (*ipsa etiam pace saevum*)—just as the Julio-Claudian

---

[2] Sage (1990), 888–9. See Ginsburg (1981) on this method in the Tiberian *Annals*.
[3] See Joseph (2012c), 170–2; and Paul (1982) and the essays in Closs and Keitel (2020) on the motif of the captured city.

period had offered "recent examples of a savage peace" (*recentia saevae pacis exempla*, *H.* 1.50.2; cf. *Ann.* 1.10.4). The Principate during peacetime is itself violent, and, here in 4.1 as elsewhere in Tacitus' writing, a certain assimilation of civil war and political life under the Principate emerges.[4]

Shortly afterwards Tacitus rings what sounds like a fuller note of resolution when writing of the actions of the senate on December 21, 69, the day after Vitellius' death (4.3.3):

> *at Romae senatus cuncta principibus solita Vespasiano decernit, laetus et spei certus: quippe sumpta per Gallias Hispaniasque civilia arma, motis ad bellum Germaniis, mox Illyrico, postquam Aegyptum Iudaeam Syriamque et omnis provincias exercitusque lustraverant, velut expiato terrarum orbe cepisse finem videbantur.*

> But at Rome the senate, happy and full of hope, decrees to Vespasian all the powers usually given to *principes*. Indeed these civil contests taken up in the Gallic and Spanish provinces, with the German provinces and soon Illyricum rising up to war, after they had passed though Egypt, Judea, and Syria, and every province and army—as though the whole world had been expiated—seemed to have come to an end.

The hopefulness of the senate as Vespasian takes power in Alexandria recalls their similar sanguinity the previous year, when, with Nero dead and the new *princeps* Galba still in Hispania, "the senators were cheerful, and they immediately took up freedom more boldly, since it was toward a new and absent *princeps*" (*patres laeti, usurpata statim libertate licentius ut erga principem novum et absentem, H.* 1.4.3). That optimism in June of 68 was of course misplaced. And while Vespasian's rise will not quickly cascade into chaos and civil bloodshed as Galba's had, the senate's cheerful outlook in December 69 is revealed to be similarly blinkered. In a number of ways the civil struggles for Rome only *seemed* (*videbantur*) to be reaching an end, as discord and political contestation will carry on in several arenas—including in the senate itself.

In the following chapters (4.4–10) Tacitus dwells at length on senatorial actions on that first day, applying a microscope to their deliberations on one day in the same way he will at the outset of *Annals* 1 when zooming in on initial senatorial exchanges with Tiberius (see Pagán, Chapter 9 in this volume). In this way the senator-historian with a particular interest in that body's standing[5] gives pride of place to what senators have to say about their personal and collective positions vis-à-vis the new regime.[6] But what becomes immediately clear is that disagreement and rancor will carry the day. A central point of contention is whether the senatorial delegation to Vespasian should be chosen by the senators' votes or by lot. Arguing for senatorial prerogative is the independent minded if vain (so 4.6.1 and 4.7.1) Helvidius Priscus, who is given a character sketch and backstory at 4.5.1–6.2. Arguing for the use of the lot is his bitter enemy Eprius Marcellus, the accuser under Nero in 66 of Helvidius' father-in-law and fellow Stoic Thrasea Paetus.[7] Helvidius' speech encouraging senatorial assertiveness (4.7) is followed in 4.8 by Marcellus' advocating deference and putting forward the credo of "praying for good emperors, tolerating

---

[4] See O'Gorman (1995b), 122–4; Sailor (2008), 191; and Joseph (2012c), 169–89; as well as Keitel (1984) on the *Annals*.

[5] On which see Syme (1970), 1–10.   [6] Keitel (1993), 42–5; Spielberg (2019), 141–2.

[7] An episode Tacitus will narrate at *Ann.* 16.21–35; see Bartera, Chapter 18 in this volume.

whatever kind you get" (*bonos imperatores voto expetere, qualescumque tolerare*, 4.8.2).[8] Tacitus describes the whole exchange with the language of physical combat: it is a "fierce quarrel" (*acre iurgium*, 4.6.3), with the one senator "attacked" (*impugnari*, 4.8.1) by the other, and words "hurled with great animosity on each side" (*magnis utrimque contentionibus iactata*, 4.8.5)—imagery recalling the back-and-forth siege warfare of the *Histories'* earlier books.[9] Eprius' position of senatorial acquiescence prevails in the fight (*vicit*, 4.8.5), just as the later argument by Volcacius Tullinus (again opposed by Helvidius; see below) that the senate should defer to Vespasian on payment for the Capitol's restoration carries the day (4.9.2). The final episode recounted here, in 4.10, is the Stoic Musonius Rufus' attack of Publius Celer for false testimony during the trial of Barea Soranus in 66 (narrated with Thrasea's trial at *Ann.* 16.21–35). And so, this seemingly hopeful day in the senate (recall 4.3.3), marked by Tacitus as an opportunity for new beginnings, is consumed to a great extent with "hatreds renewed" (*odia renovari*, 4.10.1) and "souls stirred toward vengeance" (*motis ad ultionem animis*, 4.10.1).

The senatorial infighting and prevailing penchant for deference expose the abiding weakness of the senate, whose members are more comfortable contesting each other than asserting their position alongside the regime in power, even a new and unsure one. Adding to that sense of fitfulness and uncertainty is that it is not in fact Vespasian or his sons who are wielding power now, as the first sentence after the account of senatorial debates dramatically highlights (4.11.1):

> *Tali rerum statu, cum discordia inter patres, ira apud victos, nulla in victoribus auctoritas, non leges, non princeps in civitate essent, Mucianus Urbem ingressus cuncta simul in se traxit.*

> With this state of affairs—when there was discord in the senate, anger among the conquered, no authority among the conquerors, and no laws, no *princeps* in the state—Mucianus entered the city and pulled everything all at once to himself.

The paratactic sentence, a hallmark of Tacitus' style,[10] builds with an accumulating series of factors that collectively convey the scale of the continuing discord and disorder in Rome. With the arrival of Mucianus at the sentence's end comes a sense of order—but also the threat of further destabilization. While the phrase *Urbem ingressus* may simply mark his arrival in the city, the verb *ingredior* can mean "to attack" (*OLD* 6); and in books 1–3 Tacitus had used the pairing of *ingredior* and *urbs* to characterize the ominous armed arrivals in Rome of Galba (1.37.3), Vitellius (2.89.1), and Antonius Primus (3.82.1). Tacitus thus compels the reader to consider that Mucianus' arrival may be more an act of aggression on Rome than an entrance.[11] Moreover, Tacitus' emphasis on the absence of a *princeps* in the city underscores not only the remoteness of Vespasian, still in Alexandria, but also that there is a noticeable vacuum of power. Mucianus, who "with his appearance, gait,

[8] See Strunk (2017), 124–7, and Spielberg (2019) on the debate; and O'Gorman (2020) on the divergent character-types of Marcellus (118–23) and Helvidius (130–4) and the approaches to senatorial conduct that they represent.
[9] Joseph (2012c), 173–4.
[10] Syme (1958a), 197. Cf. *Ann.* 1.2.1 and 11.5.1, comparable paratactic sentences capturing a usurpation of power (I thank Thomas Strunk for this point).
[11] Joseph (2012c), 175.

and armed guard embraces the power of the *princeps*, though foregoing the name" (*apparatu incessu excubiis vim principis amplecti, nomen remittere*, 4.11.1), swiftly fills this vacuum with his arrival.

After his extended treatment at 4.12–37 of the Batavian revolt and the failures of Roman leadership along the Rhine (to be discussed below), Tacitus returns to affairs in Rome at 4.38–50 and touches on many of the themes explored at 4.1–11. Again, as at 4.3.3, there are notes of resolution and return to order, as when an account of Mucianus' outmaneuvering of the volatile Antonius Primus (4.39.3–4) concludes with: "And so, with everything disordered taken care of, its own appearance returns to the city, as well as its laws and the duties of its magistrates" (*sic egesto quidquid turbidum redit Urbi sua forma legesque et munia magistratuum*, 4.39.4). But again, the appearance (*forma*) of the restoration of order can be deceiving. Once more Tacitus treats at length the sparring in the senate over old feuds, this time on January 1, 70. Musonius now succeeds in condemning Publius Celer for informing against Soranus (4.40.3); and, when the senators agree to swear oaths that they had not acted to harm other senators (4.41), a few parse their words, others perjure themselves, and at least one, Paccius Africanus, is forcibly driven out (*proturbant*, 4.41.3) of the senate house. The central panel at 4.42–3 focuses on Vipstanus Messala's defense of his brother Aquilius Regulus, who under Nero had brought down Cornelius Orfitus and the family of the Crassi; and then Curtius Montanus' long and passionate response, vilifying colleagues such as Regulus who cave to emperors' strongarm tactics and stating that, as a body, "we have grown weak, conscript fathers" (*languimus, patres conscripti*, 4.42.6). Helvidius—brought out by Tacitus once again as the champion of senatorial *libertas*—builds on Montanus' speech with the hopes of "laying low" (*prosterni*, 4.43.1) his rival Eprius Marcellus, who briefly leaves the senate house with Crispus Vibius but soon returns (4.43.1–2). And so "the day is consumed by discord" (*consumptus per discordiam dies*, 4.43.2).

Just as things had played out at 4.1–11, this contentious activity in the senate concludes with the collective surrender of freedom, once again to Mucianus, now one of the year's consuls (4.44.1):

Proximo senatu inchoante Caesare de abolendo dolore iraque et priorum temporum necessitatibus, censuit Mucianus prolixe pro accusatoribus; simul eos, qui coeptam, deinde omissam actionem repeterent, monuit sermone molli et tamquam rogaret. patres coeptatam libertatem, postquam obviam itum, omisere.

At the next meeting of the senate, Caesar [Domitian] began by speaking about forgetting the pain, anger, and drastic measures of former times, and Mucianus weighed in at length on behalf of the informers. And at that time—in a gentle tone, as though he were asking them—he cautioned those who were returning to prosecutions they had begun but then given up. The conscript fathers, after running into this resistance, gave up the freedom they had begun to pursue.

While Domitian begins the process of quelling the senatorial upheaval (*inchoante Caesare*), it is Mucianus who steps in as the subject of the sentence's verbs (*censuit* and *monuit*) and effectively squashes the impetus toward independence, leading the senators themselves to again give up (*omisere*) their push for freedom. The passage exposes in straightforward terms the senate's abiding weakness while also underscoring Mucianus' dominance of the events of Book 4.[12] The coming chapters bear out further his sway and effectiveness as Flavian fixer par excellence: he calms a mutiny of Vitellian loyalists in the praetorian camp (4.46); dispatches the centurion Papirius to assassinate the suspected Lucius Piso in Africa (4.49.2–3); marshals an army to enter Gaul (4.68); orders the assassination of Vitellius' son and neutralizes his rival Antonius Primus (4.80); and simultaneously suppresses both the Gallic threat and Domitian's suspicious aspirations (4.85). Mucianus thus cuts a complicated and curious figure: now an ally of Vespasian but not long ago a rival in the East; not himself a Flavian, and rather frequently a check on the one member of the family in Rome, Domitian (see further below); an effective conveyor of postwar stability but, given his eminent position in the crucial first year of Flavian power, at the same time a threat to challenge Vespasian's hold on power. It may be significant that, as the year 70 advances, Vespasian is still seeking divine confirmation of his fortune from Serapis in Alexandria (4.82.1)—perhaps reflecting his uncertainty about the safety of his position vis-à-vis Mucianus.[13]

The fits and starts of resolution, slowed by threats of renewed and fresh discord and further power struggles, seem at last to find grounding in the ceremony on June 21, 70, for the dedication of the new Capitoline Temple (4.53), whose destruction in December 69 had marked the low point of not just the civil wars but, as Tacitus had put it, all Roman history (3.72.1). The ritual, initiated by Vespasian *per litteras* (he is the subject of *confert* in 4.53.1), is described in detail, with Tacitus noting the use of the temple's original site (4.53.1) and adherence to traditional ritual practice (4.53.2–3) but also that the building's foundation was sprinkled with precious metals that were as yet untouched, "just as they had been born" (*sed ut gignuntur*, 4.53.4). This is a moment of restitution, of rebirth, of a fresh start for Rome. Yet once again Tacitus undercuts the mood of the day in a number of ways. For starters, Vespasian's physical absence from this seminal event itself suggests that all is not stable and secure. Further, Tacitus highlights Helvidius' participation in the ritual (4.53.3), which compels us to recall the senator's unsuccessful advocacy for senatorial control of the restoration (4.9.2); this sequence of episodes may thus serve as backdrop for the account of his trial, exile, and death later in Vespasian's reign.[14] While the physical temple can be rebuilt, Helvidius the failed champion of senatorial *libertas* here may represent the impossibility under the Flavian regime of restoring old ideals.[15] The hopefulness of the passage is also dimmed by the readers' knowledge that this temple, once completed in 75, would stand only another five years, burning down in 80 (Dio 66.24.2). It would be replaced in 82 by Domitian's garish gilded reconstruction (see Pliny *Pan.* 52.3–4; Suet. *Dom.* 13.2; and Plut. *Publicola* 15.3–5), which he inscribed with his own name (Suet. *Dom.* 5). To readers of the *Histories*, published in the aftermath of Domitian's oppressive reign, any consideration of the Capitol was surely colored by the knowledge of further disaster and disgrace to the building in the coming years.[16]

---

[12]   See Haynes (2003), 152–5; De Kleijn (2013); and Altman (2020).

[13]   Chilver and Townend (1985), 4, pointing to Suet., *Vesp.* 7.1–2. Note also the red flag of Mucianus' greater affinity with Titus than with Vespasian (2.5.2 and 2.74.1). See Shannon (2014), 281–92, on the visit to Serapis' temple and the numerous complications the episode may introduce into the narrative of the *Histories*.

[14]   So Sailor (2008), 223–8; see Suet. *Vesp.* 15 on Helvidius' exile and death.

[15]   I thank Salvador Bartera for sharing an unpublished paper on Helvidius in Tacitus' works as an embodiment of the republican tradition of senatorial *libertas*.

[16]   See Sailor (2008), 226–9.

Moreover, this passage ostensibly marking the restoration of concord, and of a new postwar order delivered by Vespasian's victory, is immediately followed by a striking subversion of any sense of peace and Flavian harmony (4.54.1):

Audita interim per Gallias Germaniasque mors Vitellii duplicaverat bellum. nam Civilis omissa dissimulatione in populum Romanum ruere, Vitellianae legiones vel externum servitium quam imperatorem Vespasianum malle.

Meanwhile news of the death of Vitellius throughout Gaul and Germany had doubled the war. For Civilis, putting aside dissimulation, rushed against the Roman people, and the Vitellian legions preferred foreign servitude to Vespasian as emperor.

We see that Tacitus chooses to follow his treatment of the landmark event of restoration and rebirth after the war with a return back in time[17] to the war along the Rhine, which is now expanding (*duplicaverat*). What is more, he chooses to signpost straightaway the Roman legionaries' entrenched *opposition* to Vespasian. To that arena of conflict and its complications in Tacitus' narrative we now turn our focus.

"The Mixed Appearance of Civil and Foreign War"

The promise in the *Histories*' table of contents of not just civil and foreign wars but also "thoroughly mixed" or "entirely confounded" (*permixta*, 1.2.1) wars is met in Tacitus' lengthy, multistage account of the revolt of the allied Batavian cohorts under the leadership of Julius Civilis, the coordinated uprisings of neighboring Germanic and Gallic tribes, and the numerous ways these events and the Roman armies' responses to them are embroiled in the civil war between Vitellius and Vespasian. The complexus of events, which receive only brief mention in other sources (Front. *Str.* 4.3.14; Dio 66.3; and Jos. *BJ* 7.75–88), is indeed confounding;[18] and Tacitus himself has trouble defining the conflict in any neat or consistent way. Earlier in the *Histories* he previews it by calling it "a war that was at the same time domestic and foreign" (*interno simul externoque bello*, 2.69.1) and as a time when "the Roman state was nearly shattered by the sloth of its leaders, the sedition of its legions, the violence of foreigners, and the perfidy of allies" (*socordia ducum, seditione legionum, externa vi, perfidia sociali prope adflicta Romana res*, 3.46.1). At the outset of his account in Book 4, he writes of how the war "blazed with the great movement of foreign and allied nations" (*quanto externarum sociarumque gentium motu flagraverit*, 4.12.1) and then of the Roman legionaries' confusion when seeing in their besiegers "the mixed appearance of civil and foreign war" (*mixta belli civilis externique facie*, 4.22.2).

While characterizing the conflict in these ways, Tacitus also compels the reader to see the interrelation of activity on the Rhine with the ongoing uncertainty at Rome by interspersing the Rhineland narrative with the Roman narrative (at 4.12–37, 4.54–79, and then 5.13–26; the juxtaposition at 4.53–4 discussed above is representative), and also by choosing to narrate much of the content from Germany and Gaul long *after* contemporaneous

---

[17] See Chilver and Townend (1985), 66.
[18] Syme (1958a), 174: "The Batavian revolt is confused and confusing."

events took place in Italy.[19] This is on the one hand a choice of necessity in the annalistic format, as Tacitus tries to present his material in cohesive and readable blocks of *res externae* and *res internae*, a practice used again in the *Annals*, where he blocks events crossing multiple years into the treatment of a single year (e.g. *Ann.* 12.31–40 covers events in Britain in 47–54 under the year 50). But in the case of the "mixed" Batavian revolt and its fallout, "one cannot easily determine whether [the] event falls under the rubric of *res externae* or *res internae*;"[20] and Tacitus' decision to narrate the entirety of this conflict after the civil wars' apparent conclusion at 3.86 and the markers of an ostensible return to postwar order in 4.1–11—and to commit nearly two-thirds of Book 4 to that conflict—certainly contributes to the complication and a certain prolonging of the *Histories*' civil-war narrative.

The figure of the revolt's leader Julius Civilis is a striking embodiment of the internal/external tensions of the war. For one, the Batavians as a group hold an extraordinarily liminal position, in their relationship with Rome, as trusted auxiliary cavalrymen in the German wars (4.12.3), but also as a threat to stability in recent years (1.59.1, 4.13.1), and in their status as boundary-crossing island-dwellers in the modern-day Netherlands.[21] Their leader bears a name that is "almost too good to be true,"[22] with a *nomen* indicating his lineage from the Roman settlers of the Julian *gens* and thus connection to the power signified by the Caesars, and a *cognomen* bringing to mind not only his Roman citizenship but also his capacity as an agent of civil discord. From his introduction as a destabilizing threat at 1.59.1 to his domination of Book 4 and then into the ongoing narration of his seemingly irrepressible campaign when the text of Book 5 breaks off, Civilis emerges as "a prime emblem of the capacity of the hybrid figures inevitably produced by colonialism to throw the orderly workings of its discourses into confusion."[23]

Tacitus makes Civilis self-aware of his liminal status and the threat it posed, writing that "Civilis was by nature shrewd in a way beyond what is common for barbarians, and he fashioned himself as a Sertorius or a Hannibal, due to the similar disfigurement on his face" (*Civilis ultra quam barbaris solitum ingenio sollers et Sertorium se aut Hannibalem ferens simili oris dehonestamento*, 4.13.2). The Batavian leader self-consciously shares with these two famed fighters of the Romans a missing eye; like the one, the Carthaginian general Hannibal (247–183 BCE), he is a foreigner threatening Rome from across the Alps; like the other, the Roman general and usurper of Hispania Sertorius (*c.* 126–73 BCE), he is a Roman citizen turned enterprising provincial enemy.[24] He is happy to play both parts. In a similar way he can play the role of Flavian supporter and confidante (see below) but also grow out and dye his hair red to look the part of a barbarian leader (4.61.1). Further still, Civilis even embraces the confusion of the combat itself, when, for example, he calls on his troops to put out all fires and fight the Romans in the dark of night, relishing in the "dissonant din [and] uncertain outcomes" (*strepitus dissoni, cursus incerti*, 4.29.2) that come with it.

The causes for the Batavian revolt and the resultant widespread disturbances are, like Civilis, not easy to pin down. There were personal reasons: Civilis' brother Claudius

---

[19] Brunt (1960), 512–17 sorts through the dating references.　　[20] Master (2016), 142; see further 133–8.

[21] See Ash (2014), 188–99, on Tacitus' fascination with the liminal Batavians.

[22] Haynes (2003), 148; see too O'Gorman (1995b), 128–9.　　[23] Shumate (2012), 494.

[24] See Ash (2014), 189–90, and Gerrish (2021) on the evocation here of Sallust's Sertorius at *Hist.* 1.88.

Paullus had been executed and Civilis brought in chains to Nero for suspicion of their involvement in Vindex's revolt in 68. After he was released by Galba (4.13.1) and he returned to the Rhineland, the German legions continued to harbor distrust of him. The backdrop of these "causes for anger" as well as the "hope taken from Roman troubles" (*causae irarum spesque ex malis nostris*, 4.13.1) led the opportunistic Civilis to seize the moment, giving as reason for the uprising not these personal grievances but Vitellius' ongoing conscription of troops (4.14.1), which Batavian leaders now agreed to refuse (4.14.2). Civilis' rousing speech and cry for freedom from Roman servitude (4.14.2–4; redoubled at 4.17.2–6) are persuasive, and neighboring German tribes soon join the revolt (4.15–17; by 4.28.1 it is "all Germany," *universa Germania*), participating in the series of attacks on legionary camps. Later events will reveal the complexities of Civilis' rhetoric about freedom—it soon becomes clear that he is seeking for himself a Germanic-Gallic kingdom (*regno*, 4.18.1; cf. Cerialis' words at 4.73.3).[25] But his grievances about the draft and the treatment of provincial soldiers speak to what was surely a real and abiding problem in Tacitus' time: with the expansion of the Empire, the nature of Roman citizenry had changed, power had been decentered, and, as Civilis embodies so vividly, any simplistic dichotomy of Roman and Other had been forever altered. These transformations of identity posed a major threat to any lasting stability, if a greater share of power was not granted to provincials.[26]

Tacitus makes it clear that Civilis has plans for independence from Rome and for his own dominion over Germany and Gaul, and that his show of support for Vespasian is an act of deception (4.13.2).[27] The attacks on the pro-Vitellian German legions, while beneficial to and indeed encouraged by the Flavian commanders Primus and Flaccus (4.13.2, 4.32.1, and 5.26.3), are a separate challenge to Roman stability—and only intensify after the Flavian victory (4.54.1). But the Batavian revolt does touch upon another arena in the civil war between Vitellius and Vespasian: the ferocious infighting in the Rhineland camps. The revolt gets going when—and to an extent because (recall 4.13.1)—the Roman civil war is raging, and "without a doubt the common soldiers were loyal to Vitellius, each of the most decorated was partial to Vespasian" (*haud dubie gregarius miles Vitellio fidus, splendidissimus quisque in Vespasianum proni*, 4.27.3). The battle-lines within the camps are neatly drawn, and things come to a head when the discontented legionaries, suffering repeated attacks from the Batavians and their allies, direct their rage toward the murder of their commander Flaccus, whom they suspect to be in league with Civilis (4.36.2)—an extraordinary act that is repeated when they murder his successor Dillius Vocula (4.59.1). These events are not isolated, and they carry on long after Vespasian's victory (announced at 4.31.1), with fissures so great that, at the end of 69, "statues of Vitellius were still put up in the camp and throughout the neighboring states of the Belgae—even though by now Vitellius had fallen" (*Vitellii tamen imagines in castris et per proximas Belgarum civitates repositae, cum iam Vitellius occidisset*, 4.37.2). The Rhineland camps thus offer another bloody front in the civil wars—complete with its own series of battles and assassinations, and its own inside/outside agitator, Civilis—and a front that Tacitus chooses to narrate entirely after the civil wars' ostensible resolution at the end of Book 3.

[25] Brunt (1960), 504; and Keitel (1993), 48–9.   [26] Master (2016).
[27] See Brunt (1960), responding to the argument by Walser (1951), 86–128, that any characterization of the war as foreign, not strictly civil, is a result of the pro-Flavian bias of Tacitus' source.

Furthermore, Tacitus appears to draw a number of thematic parallels between the uprising on the Rhine and the actions of the claimants for power in books 1–3. Civilis' "manipulation of public misfortune for private gain and to settle old scores" recalls the self-serving behavior of Otho, Aulus Caecina, and other Roman grandees in the year 69.[28] The splintering of Civilis' campaign when similarly ambitious leaders from other tribes join also maps onto the fracturing of leadership and ensuing mayhem in books 1–3.[29] Another factor linking the two accounts is the prominence of rumors and "talk" (*fama*) as movers of action, a favorite device of Tacitus'[30] that he brings out for key moments of Book 4's careening war narrative (see 4.33.3,[31] 4.34.5, 4.54.1, 4.68.1), just as he had for books 1–3.

The actions along the Rhine also have parallels with the events in the senate narrated elsewhere in Book 4. On the most basic level, the fights for freedom by the Germanic and Gallic states fail in the same way that the senate's pushes for independence peter out.[32] In each instance the option of peace is preferred to freedom;[33] and the speech that Tacitus has Petilius Cerialis deliver to the Treveri (4.73–74) echoes Eprius Marcellus' at 4.8, each advocating for acceptance of the imperial order and the unknowns that come with the alternation between "good" and "bad" emperors (4.8.2, 4.74.2). Cerialis points out that the alternative to Roman subjection is not freedom but subjection to other, closer masters in Gaul and Germany (4.74.2–3)—a point demonstrated when we read of the imperial ambitions of not just Civilis (4.18.1) but also Julius Classicus of the Treveri (4.59.2, requiring an oath to the *imperium Galliarum*) and Julius Sabinus of the Lingones (4.67.1, demanding to be hailed as "Caesar").[34] These Romanized provincials/provincial Romans can only conceptualize power in Roman terms.[35] The upshot of this and other parallels is another dissolution of difference between Romans and the others around them.

"The East Growing Strong"

A theme that emerges clearly from Book 4—and into Book 5, with Judea (5.1–13) and once again the Rhineland (5.14–26) as the planes of action—is the "gap in the significance of the city,"[36] a flattening of Roman geography,[37] as Tacitus "implicitly challenges the normative paradigm of Rome as 'home.'"[38] Events on the Rhine not only mirror but come to overshadow events in Rome, while, all the while, the *princeps* himself is off in a completely different arena, Alexandria. Tacitus' memorable bon mot at the outset of the work that "the secret was out that the emperor could be made elsewhere than Rome" (*evulgato imperii arcano, posse principem alibi quam Romae fieri*, 1.4.2), confirmed by the rises of Galba in Hispania, Vitellius in Germany, and Vespasian in Judea, also has a broader application: the Roman story itself has become conspicuously detached from Rome.

---

[28] Keitel (1993), 47.   [29] Ash (2009), 97.
[30] Shatzman (1974); Gibson (1998); Hardie (2012), 284–313.
[31] Which Gibson (1998), 117, compares with 3.25.1.   [32] Sage (1990), 888–90; Keitel (1993), 51–7.
[33] Keitel (1993), 46, on the Gauls at 4.67–9.
[34] See Haynes (2003), 161; Master (2016), 145–6; Gerrish (2021), 484–5, pointing also to the Treviran senate at 5.19.3.
[35] Haynes (2003), 176; Master (2016), 145–52.   [36] Sailor (2008), 189.
[37] Master (2016), 62–5.   [38] Gerrish (2021), 475.

A result of the de-centering of action in Book 4, and also of the domination of action by the ostensibly marginal figures Mucianus and Civilis, is that Vespasian and the Flavian family can seem to emerge from these pages as almost tangential.[39] But at the same time Vespasian, who delivers no speeches in the book, develops a certain mystique, an aura not unlike the one Augustus had cultivated.[40] Crucial to enhancing that mystique in Book 4 are the accounts of Vespasian's miraculous healing of a blind man and a wounded man (4.81) and the validation of his rise by the god Serapis (4.82.1). In Book 5, when describing prodigies in Judea, Tacitus will write (5.13.2):

> *pluribus persuasio inerat antiquis sacerdotum litteris contineri, eo ipso tempore fore ut valesceret Oriens profectique Iudaea rerum potirentur. quae ambages Vespasianum ac Titum praedixerat.*

> Among more [Jews] there was a conviction that it was contained in their priests' ancient writings that the East would grow strong at that very time, and that men setting forth from Judea would become powerful over all things. This puzzling prophecy had predicted Vespasian and Titus.

Tacitus goes on to note the incorrect interpretation of this prophecy by those in Judea at the time; with hindsight, he gets it right: a dynasty emerging from the East, with many of the associations and religious aura of an Eastern monarchy,[41] comes to dominate Rome.

Tacitus and his readers also knew that this dynasty would lead to, and conclude with, the "savagery" of Domitian (so *Agr.* 2.1, 3.2; cf. 45.1–2 and Suet. *Dom.* 10–11). The young Domitian is present for much of the action of Book 4, straightaway assuming the name of Caesar (4.2.1; cf. 3.86.3) and the position of praetor with consular power (4.3.4), even though he is overshadowed or outmaneuvered by Mucianus time and again (4.39.2–3, 4.44.1, on which see above; 4.68.2–3, 4.80.1, 4.85). However, for all of the strength and possible danger that Mucianus poses in Book 4, he does not mobilize against Vespasian. It may be more apt to read Mucianus' ascendancy as a red herring, distracting the reader— albeit temporarily—from the threat of Domitian.[42] After all, concerns about the younger Flavian son's behavior (see 4.2.1) are cause for a conference between Vespasian and Titus (4.51–2), and Mucianus' play in 4.85 to manage Domitian's ambitions, while successful, is followed by rumors that the young prince had plans to usurp his father or brother (4.86). It is with the uneasy image of Domitian on the move that Book 4, like Book 3 (3.86.3), comes to a close—a final destabilizing and unsettling blow to Tacitus' already unstable, uncertain postwar narrative.

Further Reading

Chilver and Townend (1985) is an historical commentary on Book 4, as well as Book 5. Keitel (1993) provides an insightful overview of many of the themes that run across the book. Brunt (1960) helpfully sorts through the complications of Tacitus' treatment of the Batavian revolt. The work by

---

[39] Sage (1990), 889.   [40] Haynes (2003), 171–4.
[41] Haynes (2003), 140–7; Feldherr (2009a), 308–9; Joseph (2018), 74–81.   [42] Levene (2009a), 223.

Haynes (2003), 148–77, Master (2016), and Gerrish (2021) explores the significance of Civilis and his revolt for our understanding of the Principate and the Roman world of Tacitus' time, while Ash (2006b), 99–116 considers the reception of Civilis in the Netherlands in the sixteenth and seventeenth centuries. The political dynamics of senatorial action in Book 4 are explored by Strunk (2017), 122–31, Spielberg (2019), and O'Gorman (2020); and the prime place of Mucianus in the book by De Kleijn (2013) and Altman (2020).

Timothy A. Joseph, Histories 4 In: *The Oxford Critical Guide to Tacitus*. Edited by: Salvador Bartera and Kelly E. Shannon-Henderson, Oxford University Press. © Oxford University Press 2025. DOI: 10.1093/9780191915086.003.0008

8

Histories 5

René Bloch

With Book 5 the transmission of the *Histories* comes to an abrupt end. As if fate had wanted to distribute the surviving text (ch. 1–26) fairly, two subjects receive discussion in equal length: thirteen chapters on the Jews and the Jewish–Roman war (5.1–13) and thirteen chapters on the final developments of the Batavian uprising along the northern Rhine (5.14–26). The transmission breaks off in the middle of a speech by Civilis, the leader of the Batavians.

Jews and Batavians in the *Histories*

In the introduction to the *Histories*, Tacitus prominently summarizes the events he will be discussing as *prosperae in Oriente, adversae in Occidente res* (1.2.1). With the "success in the East" Tacitus most probably refers to the victory over the Jews, and with the "adverse circumstances in the West" to the Batavian revolt. With this statement, the topics of the fragmentary remains of Book 5 (and also parts of Book 4, in the case of the Batavians) are on the table from the beginning of the work. At the outset of Book 5 Tacitus returns to where he has led his reader earlier in the *Histories*: to the beginning of the year 70 (cf. *H.* 4.39.1) and the siege of Jerusalem. In 2.4.3 Tacitus stated that Vespasian "had brought the war against the Jews to a successful end with only the assault on Jerusalem remaining" (*profligaverat bellum Iudaicum Vespasianus, obpugnatione Hierosolymorum reliqua*). The capture of Jerusalem, however, Tacitus adds, would be hard work for the Romans because of the "nature of the mountain and the stubborn superstition" of the besieged (*ob ingenium montis et pervicaciam superstitionis*). These are some of the keywords that will later be central to Tacitus' presentation of Judea and the Jews: Jerusalem is described as a city standing on a height (5.11.3: *urbem arduam*), its population as most stubborn (5.12.2: *pervicacissimus*) and subservient to superstition (5.13.1: *gens superstitioni obnoxia*). Yet it must be stressed that the Jews and Judea are hardly a topic before Book 5. As a matter of fact, the Jews are nowhere mentioned explicitly in the first four books of the *Histories*. Tacitus' focus is very much on Rome and the gradual rise to power of the Flavians. The provinces are on the horizon early on, but they are of interest mainly with regard to the Roman legions stationed there and their role in the Roman power game.[1] In 1.10.1 Tacitus states that in the spring of 69 "the East was not yet in uproar" (*Oriens adhuc immotus*), a surprising observation at first sight, given that by then the Jewish revolt

---

[1] Jonathan Master acutely notes that the "tour of the periphery" at the beginning of the *Histories* "offers readers a glimpse of a future in which the center of power in the Roman world is wherever the most powerful army is" (Master (2016), 98).

(and civil war) had been going on for several years (the revolt broke out in 66). But Tacitus' focus is on Rome. Even in his survey of Jewish history in Book 5, when it comes to the year 69, Tacitus states, "The next year, occupied with civil war, proceeded quietly inasmuch as it pertained to the Jews" (*H.* 5.10.2: *proximus annus civili bello intentus quantum ad Iudaeos per otium transiit*). From Josephus we know that the *Jewish* civil war continued throughout the year 69.[2] Tacitus' relative silence about the Judean revolt in the first four books of the *Histories* coincides with remarks that anticipate Roman victory. The victory over the Jews is already mentioned in Book 2 (2.78.2: *Iudaicae victoriae*), and Vespasian's soldiers are described as victorious before they have actually won (2.76.5: *belli domitor externi*, "conqueror[s] in a foreign war"). The opposite can be said about the Jewish historian Josephus and his *Bellum Iudaicum*: the Year of the Four Emperors and the rise of the Flavians is merely the backdrop for Josephus' main interest, the Jewish–Roman war and the destiny of Jerusalem. In light of the long history of reception of Tacitus' digression on the Jews from late antiquity to modern times,[3] it is important to note that Judea and the Jews were by no means of central importance in the first four books of the *Histories*. We also need to keep this relative silence in mind with regard to the lost parts of Book 5 and the rest of the *Histories* (see below).

As for the Batavians and their presence in the first four books of the *Histories*, things are a bit different. What we have noted about Judea is in principle also true for Germania: what happens in the provinces is of importance first and foremost with regard to the developments in Rome. Moreover, Tacitus emphasizes from the beginning of his work that civil and foreign wars are bleeding into each other.[4] Yet the revolt of the Batavians is much more present in the first four books of the *Histories* than the Jewish–Roman war. This stems in part from the fact that the Batavian revolt under the leadership of Civilis was very much homegrown. The revolt could only break out, as Donald Dudley notes, "against the background of the unprecedented demoralisation of the Rhine armies after they had been defeated by the departure of the best troops to win the throne of Vitellius."[5] Civilis himself is a former Roman auxiliary officer. The contexts of the two uprisings discussed in Book 5 are thus quite different: here the revolt in the provincial East, there a mutiny that very much involved provincial soldiers before turning into a "full-fledged revolution seeking independence for a collection of Germanic and Gallic peoples."[6]

Tacitus' thirteen chapters on the Batavian revolt in Book 5 follow up on two earlier reports in the *Histories*. The first, *H.* 4.12–37, starts out with a historical sketch of the Batavi (4.12.2). Before they were expelled by a civil war, they formed part of the Chatti and lived across the Rhine; then "they occupied the end of the Gallic shore, empty of inhabitants, and likewise an island situated between shallow places" (*extrema Gallicae orae vacua cultoribus simulque insulam inter vada sitam occupavere*). Some of the ethnographic material on the Batavians mentioned later in Book 5 is already referred to in Book 4: they are excellent swimmers and of great height, and even their children are taller than those of

---

[2] Josephus, too, states that Vespasian and Titus were preoccupied with what was going on in Rome and that they, for the time being, left the campaign against the Jews aside (*BJ* 4.502: ὑπερεώρων τὴν ἐπὶ Ἰουδαίους στρατείαν).

[3] Cf. Bloch (2012b).

[4] In *H.* 1.2.1 Tacitus programmatically states: *trina bella civilia, plura externa ac plerumque permixta* ("there were three civil wars, more foreign wars, and often they were intermingled").

[5] Dudley (1968), 181. Cf. Master (2016).   [6] Master (2016), 30.

others (4.12.3, 14.1). Tacitus then goes on to explain how under Civilis the Batavians began to revolt against the Romans, "for whom they had often fought; but they were tired of their prolonged and pointless soldiering" (4.20.1: *pro quibus totiens bellantes: longa atque inrita militia fessis*), at first with glorious victory (4.17.1: *clara ea victoria*) but later with great losses (4.33.4). Later in Book 4, Tacitus returns to the Batavian revolt in an equally long section (4.54–79—again twenty-six chapters). The burning of the Capitol had given hope to the people that Roman power would come to an end, and was interpreted as a sign of divine wrath (4.54.2: *caelestis irae*) that the sovereignty of the world would now pass to the people beyond the Alps. "Such were the vain and superstitious prophecies of the Druids" (*superstitione vana Druidae*), Tacitus comments. In 5.13.1–2, he expresses dismay about the Jews' interpretation of prodigies in the skies of Jerusalem in very similar language: the superstitious people misinterpreted them as the fulfillment of an old prophecy and believed that the East would rise to power and that men starting from Judea should take possession of the world (*ut valesceret Oriens profectique Iudaea rerum potirentur*). In the Batavian revolt, as narrated by Tacitus in his second report, the Romans continued to suffer losses, while Civilis' strength grew enormously (4.66.3: *ingens rerum*). But as in the first report on the revolt, so also in the second eventually things turn around in favor of the Romans (4.71–9). The second report ends with the Roman victory in Trier. This is where the third report on the Batavians in Book 5 (ch. 14–26) will resume: once more with setbacks for the Romans at first, before the pendulum swings once more in their favor.

Histories 5.1–13: Jews and Judea

Book 5 of the *Histories* begins with a sympathetic portrait of Titus, who "showed himself seemly and energetic in arms" and who "mixed with the common soldiers with the honor of his generalship unstained" (5.1.1: *decorum se promptumque in armis ostendebat…in agmine gregario militi mixtus, incorrupto ducis honore*). With this, Tacitus sets Titus in contrast to Domitian (4.86.2: *disparem*), whose tendency to dissimulation was highlighted at the end of Book 4. Overall, Tacitus speaks highly of the Flavians (especially Vespasian and Titus), and the negative portrait of the Jews which follows contributes to his favorable description of the new dynasty.[7] At the end of the first chapter of Book 5 the narrative tension is at its peak—the fall of Jerusalem is imminent—but Tacitus, following a long historiographical tradition, interrupts his military report to insert an ethnographic excursus: "But because I am to recount the last day of a well-known city, it seems fitting to lay bare its beginnings" (5.2.1: *Sed quoniam famosae urbis supremum diem tradituri sumus, congruens videtur primordia eius aperire*). Tacitus' excursus on Judea reads like an "epilogue" *avant la lettre*.[8] His use of the word *famosus* may be intentionally ambiguous here. In Tacitus the word can also mean "notorious," "infamous" (*H.* 2.97.2, 4.41.2).

---

[7] Tacitus' portrait of Titus is, however, not positive throughout: it was because Titus had the wealth and pleasures of Rome on his mind that he wanted to attack Jerusalem instead of waiting for the Jews to surrender: *H.* 5.11.2, cf. Gruen (2016), 278. On Tacitus' Titus, see Bartera (forthcoming b).

[8] Lewy (1969), 140. In the case of the destruction of the city of Cremona (*H.* 3.34) and the burning of the Capitol (*H.* 3.72), Tacitus summarizes the history of these places *after* their destructions.

In the excursus Tacitus condemns the Jews in very strong language: the Jews are referred to as "the most loathsome people" (5.8.2: *taeterrimam gentem*), "the most contemptible of the subjects" (*despectissima pars servientium*), and "a people most prone to lust" (5.5.2: *proiectissima ad libidinem gens*). Tacitus' defamation of the Jews and Judea goes beyond that of the Egyptians or other peoples.[9] His aggressive language against the Jews was not without predecessors: already Seneca, writing long before the Jewish–Roman war, refers to the Jews as "the most accursed people" (*sceleratissima gens*).[10] We know from Josephus' apologetic treatise *Contra Apionem* that a number of accusations against the Jews were circulating among Hellenistic authors such as Lysimachus, Chairemon, and Apion. Tacitus may have had access, possibly through an indirect source, to some of these authors.[11] In any case, Tacitus clearly shared the negative stereotypes on the Jews. It has been argued that Tacitus had a political agenda in this excursus and that he wanted to warn the reader of the Jews.[12] However, when Tacitus wrote the *Histories*, c. 105–10 CE, neither Judea nor the Jews were of any particular concern to the Roman authorities.[13] The digression has more of a literary and ethnographic function than an immediate political one. It is also noteworthy that nowhere in the *Histories* (or the *Annals*) does Tacitus point out Jewish figures as such: neither Queen Berenice (for whom Titus, Tacitus says, had strong feelings: *H.* 2.2.1, 81.2), nor her brother Agrippa II or her father Agrippa I (*H.* 5.1.2; *Ann.* 12.23.1, 13.7.1) are identified as Jews. Tiberius Julius Alexander, the nephew of Philo of Alexandria, who according to Josephus did not remain loyal to the ancestral customs (*AJ* 20.100) and later played an important role in Vespasian's rise to power, is labeled as an Egyptian and a Roman (*H.* 1.11.1; cf. *Ann.* 15.28.3: "the famous Roman knight," *illustris eques Romanus*), but not as a Jew.

The general question of Tacitus' sources for his detailed excursus on Judea and the Jews has been raised often in scholarship, with no clear result.[14] It is safe to say that Tacitus relied on more than one source. As a matter of fact, there is no other passage in his oeuvre where Tacitus presents a greater variety of sources, albeit unnamed, than when he discusses the origin of the Jews (5.2–3; see below).[15]

The twelve chapters of the digression cover much more than what Tacitus announces at the beginning of the book, and go far beyond the early history of Jerusalem. It is in fact the most detailed ethnographic survey on Jews and Judea in pagan literature.[16] Tacitus inserts it at a point in his narrative where his "history stops being an account of civil war."[17] This was a fitting moment for an ethnographic digression, preparing the reader for the final days of Jerusalem and the great victory of the Flavians. Ethnographic digressions are indeed, as Karl Trüdinger wrote, "the pauses in the mighty dramatic structure of history, the choruses of historical tragedy."[18] The excursus on the Jews is a mixture of highly stylized

---

[9] Cf. *H.* 1.11.1 where Tacitus lashes out against the Egyptians, calling the province "on account of superstition and lasciviousness prone to discord and instability, ignorant of laws, having no experience of magistrates" (*superstitione ac lascivia discordem et mobilem, insciam legum, ignaram magistratuum*).

[10] Seneca, *De Superst.* apud August. *Civ.* 6.11.   [11] Cf. Siegert (2008) on Josephus' *Contra Apionem*.

[12] Rosen (1996).

[13] Bloch (2002), 129–37; Gruen (2016), 268–9. The so-called Diaspora riots only broke out in 115 CE.

[14] Cf. the discussion of scholarship in Bloch (2002), 19–21.   [15] Aubrion (1985), 119.

[16] Detailed commentaries on the excursus are provided by Stern (1980); Heubner and Fauth (1982); Bloch (2002).

[17] Feldherr (2009a), 302.   [18] Trüdinger (1918), 116.

language (see the discussion of Vergilian innuendos below) and aggressive content.[19] The text is not devoid of genuine ethnographic interest, but it is also not simply ethnography for its own sake. What we encounter is, as Erich Gruen rightly notes, "the familiar Tacitus, the historian fond of paradox and antinomies, prone to irony and incongruity."[20]

The structure of the excursus is somewhat unusual as it does not start out with the geographic setting (as in the *Germania* and the excursus on Britain in the *Agricola*), but with a detailed discussion of the Jews' origins followed by two chapters on laws and institutions. Only then, in the middle of the digression, does Tacitus present the peculiarities of Judean geography. The last section covers the history of Judea up to the fall of Jerusalem.

Tacitus lists no fewer than six possibilities for an origin of the Jews. In all six versions, the Jews are described as an ancient people, even reaching back to mythical times. A great variety of geographical origins throughout the Mediterranean is listed, as if to underline the widespread diaspora of the Jews. According to the first theory, the Jews migrated as exiles from Crete to Libya "at the time when Saturn, driven away by the power of Jove, had ceased from ruling" (5.2.1: *qua tempestate Saturnus vi Iovis pulsus cesserit regnis*). A second version has the "superfluous" (*exundantem*) Jewish population under the leadership of Hierosolymus and Juda in the reign of Isis move from Egypt into neighboring lands. Many believe, Tacitus continues, that the Jews were forced to leave Ethiopia under the kingship of Cepheus. According to a fourth source, which comes close to the biblical narrative, the Jews were Assyrian refugees who first gained control of a part of Egypt and later had their own "Hebrew" land. The fifth theory Tacitus introduces as "illustrious" (5.2.3: *clara*), thereby classifying those previously mentioned as unimpressive: some say that the Jews are identical with the Solymi, known from Homer's epics, and that the name of Jerusalem goes back to those who founded the city. The sixth and final explanation of the origin of the Jews is presented as the one that is shared by "most authors" (5.2.3: *plurimi auctores*). It is indeed an origin that is known in different versions from several Greco-Egyptian authors cited in Josephus' treatise *Against Apion*, and which can be traced all the way back to Hecataeus of Abdera (*c.* 300 BCE), who wrote the earliest ethnographic text on Jews in Greek literature.[21] The Jews, the story goes, are responsible for a plague that broke out in Egypt and therefore were expelled from that country. Under the guidance of Moses, "one of the exiles," the people marched for six days and on the seventh reached a country, expelled the inhabitants, and founded a city with a temple.

After this extraordinary outline of the possible origins of the Jews (all of which emphasize that the Jews are not autochthonous), Tacitus goes on to explain Jewish rites and customs. These are introduced as being in opposition to those of all other peoples: "There everything is profane that is sacred to us, and then again what is impure to us is allowed with them" (5.4.1: *profana illic omnia quae apud nos sacra, rursum concessa apud illos quae nobis incesta*). In what follows, however, the contrast is rather with Egyptian than with Roman rituals: the Jews sacrifice ox and ram in mockery of the Egyptian gods Ammon and Apis; in their temple they dedicate a statue of the donkey because it was that animal which led the Jews to water resources during their journey in the desert (5.3.2, 4.2–4—a striking contradiction to Tacitus' subsequent statement in the excursus that the

---

[19] Cf. Bernays (1861), 56: "the most adventurous absurdities in magnificent language" ("die abenteuerlichsten Verkehrtheiten in prächtiger Sprache").

[20] Gruen (2016), 280.   [21] Diod. 40.3.1–3; cf. Aziza (1987).

Jews erect no statues in their temples, 5.5.4, 9.1). Furthermore, Tacitus provides explanations for the Jewish abstention from pork, "frequent fasts," the "Jewish bread" (5.4.3: *crebris...ieiuniis...panis Iudaicus*),[22] and the Sabbath. All of these rituals are brought into relationship with the exodus from Egypt. While Tacitus is not exactly sympathetic to the first set of customs, they can, he says, at least be "justified by their antiquity" (5.5.1: *antiquitate defenduntur*). The other *instituta* of the Jews, however, "prevailed because of their depravity" (*pravitate valuere*). Here Tacitus lashes out against the Jews' proselytism, their loyalty among each other, and their misanthropy—the oldest *topos* of Greco-Roman ethnography on the Jews.[23] Tacitus inadvertently admits that historical reality looked quite a bit different and that Jews by no means simply stayed apart or always were in harmony with each other by referring to the love affair between Berenice and Titus (2.2.1, 81.2) and to the Jewish civil war (5.12.4). Jews, Tacitus continues in the excursus, introduced circumcision "in order to be recognizably different" (5.5.2: *ut diversitate noscantur*). It is noteworthy that Tacitus—who, by contrast, comments elsewhere on the reddish hair of the Britons (*Agr.* 11.2) and the blue eyes of the Germans (*G.* 4)—otherwise does not comment on the Jews' looks. He only makes a general statement on their "healthy bodies able to withstand hard work" (5.6.1: *corpora hominum salubria et ferentia laborum*), an almost literal copy of a Sallustian note on the Africans (*Jug.* 17.6: *genus hominum salubri corpore, velox, patiens laborum*, "a race of men with healthy bodies, swift, and able to withstand hard work"). Tacitus is no exception in this regard: Greco-Roman ethnography has nothing to say about a particular Jewish look.[24] Jewish monotheism and aniconism are highlighted, but summarized negatively as flattery (*adulatio*) and put into contrast to the Jews' not honoring kings or Caesars (*H.* 5.5.4: *non regibus haec adulatio, non Caesaribus honor*, "this flattery is not given to their kings, nor this honor to the Caesars"). The Jews' customs, Tacitus sums up at the end of his survey on Jewish customs, are "ridiculous and shabby" (5.5.5: *absurdus sordidusque*). Again, Tacitus does not hide his thorough contempt for the Jews.

Only now, in the middle of the excursus, does Tacitus come to mention geography. He leads the reader from north to south in the direction of the city that will eventually be at the center of his interest: from Mount Lebanon via the river Jordan and the Dead Sea to Jerusalem, "the capital of the Jews" (5.8.1: *Hierosolyma genti caput*). For the geographic features of Judea, Tacitus could draw on his predecessors (such as Strabo):[25] he describes the balsam and palm tree and, more extensively, the *paradoxon* of the Dead Sea.[26] As in the chapters on the Jews' origins and customs here, too, the information conveyed is more than simply ethnographic. The Dead Sea with its offensive odor and its surrounding wasteland are described in gloomy language. As Eduard Norden has incisively suggested, Tacitus here seems to take up Vergilian language from the *Aeneid*'s "mourning fields" (*lugentes campi*).[27] The description of the burned area of Sodom and Gomorrah at the

---

[22] Tacitus is the only pagan source for the Jewish bread (*mazza*). He explains the custom with the *raptae fruges*, that is, "the haste with which they seized the grain," which comes close to the Biblical (and Jewish) explanation for eating unleavened bread. Cf. *Exod.* 12:39: "The dough they had brought out of Egypt they baked into unleavened loaves. It was not leavened, because they had been driven out of Egypt and could not wait. They did not even prepare food for the journey" (trans. *New American Bible*).

[23] Berthelot (2003); Bloch (2012a); Schäfer (2014).   [24] Cohen (1993); Bloch (2000).

[25] Strabo 16.2.34, 41–5.   [26] Cf. on this passage Shannon-Henderson (2022), 29–31.

[27] *Haud procul inde campi, quos ferunt olim uberes magnisque urbibus habitatos fulminum iactu arsisse; sed manere vestigia* (*H.* 5.7.1: "Not far from here are plains which they say were once fertile and settled with great

Dead Sea, where "all the plants, whether emerging spontaneously or sown by hand…vanish, black and rotten, into a kind of dust" (5.7.1: *nam cuncta sponte edita aut manu sata…atra et inania velut in cinerem vanescunt*), not only continues the unpleasant portrait of the preceding chapters but also anticipates the landscape of the destroyed city of Jerusalem.

The fourth block of the digression (5.8–10) is a brief sketch of Judean history, reaching from the Seleucids to contemporary Roman times. As in the chapters on the origins of the Jews, it is a history of banishment and exile. Once more, the Jews are placed in a negative light.[28] Towards the end of the chapters on the Jews, Tacitus leads the reader back to Jerusalem and its temple: under Pompey (63 BCE) "the walls of Jerusalem were razed, but the temple remained standing" (5.9.1: *muri Hierosolymorum diruti, delubrum mansit*). Not forever, as the reader knows. With chapter 11 Tacitus returns to where he took off at the beginning of Book 5: Titus pitched his camp before the walls of Jerusalem. Now, Jerusalem had to fall immediately (5.11.2). But as mentioned early on in the *Histories* (2.4.3), the elevated city of Jerusalem as well as the Jewish temple with its citadel-like walls would be very difficult to conquer. Tacitus here projects his reading of Jewish customs onto the very founders of Jerusalem: the Jews knew that "their different customs" (5.12.2: *ex diversitate morum*) would lead to many wars, and this is why the city's structure was prepared for long sieges.

The section on the Jews and the Jewish–Roman war ends with the dramatic scene of prodigies in the sky over Jerusalem: contending armies were seen, and "weapons glowing with a bright red color" (5.13.1 *rutilantia arma*). Tacitus' description of the omen (also mentioned by Josephus and Suetonius)[29] quite openly echoes a scene in Vergil. In Book 8 of the *Aeneid*, Venus, before presenting Aeneas with a shield depicting the glorious future of Rome, sends celestial signs to her son: "In the calm region of heaven, between clouds, they behold arms flashing red (*arma…rutilare*) in the brightness and clashing in thunder."[30] Aeneas immediately recognizes that these omens relate to him (*ego poscor Olympo*: "It is I who am summoned by Olympus") and to the Trojans' victory over the Rutulians (*heu quantae miseris caedes Laurentibus instant*: "Alas, how much slaughter awaits the wretched Laurentines!").[31] Similarly, in Tacitus the Flavians interpret the portents over Jerusalem as predicting their victory. The divinities leave the temple of Jerusalem (5.13.1: *excedere deos*).[32] The narrative leaves no doubt that Jerusalem will fall. But not yet: at the end of this long section on the Jews and Judea Tacitus reiterates the picture of a dramatic conquest: "Until everything invented for conquering cities, with old methods or with new ones, was brought together" (5.13.4: *donec cuncta expugnandis urbibus reperta apud veteres aut novis ingeniis struerentur*). And then follows one more report on the Batavian revolt.

---

cities but then burned up under a rain of thunderbolts—but the traces remain") echoes *nec procul hinc partem fusi monstrantur in omnem/lugentes campi* (*Aen*. 6.440–1: "And not far from here are shown the mourning plains spread in every direction"). Cf. Norden (1913), 663. Norden rejects, with good reason, the possibility that Tacitus drew here (or elsewhere) from Josephus.

[28] Yavetz (1998), 94: "Every phenomenon in Jewish history which might be positively evaluated is deliberately omitted and every reprehensible one is overemphasized and condemned out of all proportion."

[29] Josephus, *BJ* 6.312–13 and Suetonius, *Vesp*. 4.5.

[30] Vergil, *Aen*. 8.528–9. Heubner and Fauth (1982), ad loc.   [31] Vergil, *Aen*. 8.533, 537.

[32] The use of the plural in this *evocatio* is somewhat puzzling after Tacitus has insisted on the singularity of the Jewish god. *Excedere deos* may be another allusion to Vergil, cf. *Aen*. 2.351–2: *excessere omnes adytis arisque relictis/di quibus imperium hoc steterat* (Aeneas recalling the fall of Troy: "Leaving behind their sanctuaries and altars, the gods because of whom this empire had stood all departed"). But see also Josephus *BJ* 6.300: a voice was heard in the temple of Jerusalem saying "μεταβαίνωμεν ἐντεῦθεν" ("Let us leave this place").

Histories 5.14–26: The Third Report on the Batavian Revolt

Chilver and Townend in their commentary on Book 5 label these last chapters as "disappointing:" Chronological and geographical information is incomplete and "the sudden collapse of the Batavians, and Civilis with them, comes as a surprise."[33] It is indeed not very easy to follow Tacitus' narrative in these chapters. The Batavians are called *Germani*, but then we also hear of the Cugerni (16), the Bructeri (18), and Chauci (19). With chapter 14 Tacitus returns to where he had left the reader at *Histories* 4.78, that is, the unfortunate battle the Batavians had fought at Trier (5.14.1: *post malam in Treveris pugnam*). Now the Batavians under the leadership of Civilis are encamped at Xanten (Vetera). As in the digression on the Jews, Tacitus draws a sharp dichotomy: this time between the tall Batavians (5.14.2: *proceritas corporum*), good swimmers, on one side, and the water-shy Romans (*nandi pavidus*) with their heavy armor on the other.[34] However, as in the previous chapters on the Batavian revolt, Tacitus narrates the conflict not so much as one between two different peoples, but rather as the revolt of provincial soldiers trying to "destabilize the empire"[35] and as a duel between the Roman general Cerialis and the (Romanized) Batavian leader Civilis.

As in the two previous reports on the revolt, the Batavians are at first victorious, but then they are forced to give in, this time for good and (as criticized by Chilver and Townend) a bit suddenly. The common people of the Batavians, Tacitus reports in chapter 25, tired more and more of this war. But as Tacitus rushes to the end of his report, he suggests this sentiment perhaps extends to the Batavian leadership as well. Book 5, as it has come down to us, ends with a fine portrait of internal Batavian opinions: the common people are mindful of the great power of Rome and that "they, the Batavians, are just a small fraction of mankind" (5.25.1: *quotam partem generis humani Batavos esse!*). The leaders then turn their anger against Civilis: the revolt was a mistake from the beginning, the gods were against the attacks on Roman legions (5.25.1–3). The difference between the Batavians' willingness to give in on the one side, and the Jews' continuous, stubborn revolts on the other side (5.10.2: *quod soli Iudaei non cessissent*, "only the Jews had failed to surrender"), cannot have escaped the reader's attention. While there are some parallels between Tacitus' presentation of the Batavians and that of the Jews, the differences prevail. The Batavians are presented as strong fighters, a people of the kind the Roman Empire needs,[36] while the Jewish fighters are described as a great nuisance. Book 5 breaks off in the middle of Civilis' response to this change of mind among the Batavians (ch. 26). What happened to Civilis in the end is not reported by any ancient source.

The Lost Part of Book 5

What did Tacitus write in the lost part of Book 5?[37] It is, of course, impossible to say with any degree of certainty. Yet we do have some indications that allow us to make some

[33] Chilver and Townend (1985), 97.

[34] Cf. Roymans (2004), 221–34 on the image and self-image of the Batavians. The latter can be tracked on Batavian gravestones. According to Roymans, "It was precisely through interaction with the Roman empire that the Batavian self-image was forged. Batavian identity was partly defined by the Romans in terms of a set of clichés, to which the Batavians then responded" (234).

[35] Master (2016), 3.   [36] Master (2016), 172.

[37] Cf. Syme (1958a), 211–16; Wille (1983), 319–20. There is no reason to assume that the loss of the report on the fall of Jerusalem is the result of a Christian disagreement with what Tacitus wrote (*pace* S. Borzsák,

legitimate hypotheses. There is hardly any doubt that Tacitus returned to the siege of Jerusalem. He would have described the fall of the city and the destruction of the Jewish temple. It is very likely that he would have come to mention the triumph of Vespasian and Titus in the summer of 71.[38] As a matter of fact, there "was enough material to carry book V down to the end of 73," including the closing of the Temple of Janus and the censorship of Vespasian and Titus.[39] But how much space did Tacitus dedicate to the final scenes of the Jewish–Roman war? He surely said more on the topic than Suetonius and certainly much less than Josephus.[40] It is tempting to suspect that Tacitus contrasted the rebuilding of the Capitol, which he surely mentioned,[41] with the destruction of the Jewish temple. The Flavian emperors made use of their victory over the Jews as ostentatiously as possible. Their success, very much needed after the civil war of 69 CE, was visibly present throughout Rome: at the Arch of Titus where the spoils from Jerusalem were (and still are) depicted and in the newly built temple of Peace (*templum Pacis*) where the booty was displayed. The Flavian amphitheater (Colosseum) was at least partly financed from "the spoils of the war," as an inscription from the site has it.[42] Moreover, *Iudaea Capta* coins commemorating the Roman victory over the Jews were struck throughout the Flavian emperorship.[43] Still, in spite of the Flavian propaganda and in light of Tacitus' rather limited interest in the topic in the first four books of the *Histories*, one should not assume that Tacitus dedicated too much space to the final days of the Jewish–Roman war. What Ronald Syme phrased in somewhat dramatic language remains a convincing assessment: "The preliminaries, it is true, are narrated at some length; but it would have been a sin against history and proportion to allow Jerusalem and the Jewish triumph to occupy almost a whole book."[44] Tacitus shows remarkable interest in the Jews and Judea in the digression, but that interest was probably limited to that section of the book. Moreover, while Tacitus often speaks rather highly of Vespasian and Titus (Vespasian: *H.* 2.5.1, 2.80.1, 2.82.1; Titus: 5.1.1), he is of course far from being a partisan of the first two Flavian emperors, not to mention the third (Domitian: *Agr.* 2–3, 45).[45] As a matter of fact, Tacitus openly criticizes those historians who at the time of the Flavians were steered more by flattery (*adulatio*) than truth (*H.* 2.101.1). Tacitus was no court historian and hardly felt compelled to follow the Flavian propaganda machine with regard to the Roman victory over the Jews.

Two late antique Christian historians, Orosius and Sulpicius (both writing around 400 CE), provide us with some hints of what Tacitus said in the lost part of the *Histories*, and in particular the lost part of Book 5. Orosius, in his polemical *Historiae adversum paganos*, actually cites Tacitus (*ut verbis Cornelii Taciti loquar*). This is the only real fragment (or rather excerpt) from the lost part of the *Histories* (Orosius, *Hist.* 7.3.7 = Tac. *H.* Test. 4):[46]

"P. Cornelius Tacitus," *RE* Suppl. 11: 446). As the late antique and medieval Christian reception of Josephus shows, Christians very eagerly related the fall of Jerusalem as a divine punishment for the Jews' unwillingness to accept Jesus Christ (even if Tacitus' version might have differed from Josephus'). On the lost part of the book, see also Shannon-Henderson (forthcoming).

[38] Cf. Suetonius, *Vesp.* 8.1; *Tit.* 6.1; Josephus, *BJ* 7.121–57.   [39] Syme (1958a), 211.

[40] Suetonius, *Tit.* 5.2 (not even mentioning explicitly the destruction of the Jewish temple); Josephus, *Bell. Jud.*, all of Book 6.

[41] As did Suetonius, *Vesp.* 8.5.   [42] *CIL* 6.40454a.   [43] Cf. the good survey in Millar (2005).

[44] Syme (1958a), 211 n. 5. For a different view cf. Damon (2003), 84–5: "T. must have devoted a large part of book 5 [to the Flavian triumph over the Jews]."

[45] On Tacitus' presentation of the Flavians cf. Ash (1999b), 127–46.

[46] On the "fragments" of the *Histories* as they are listed in the standard editions of the *Histories* cf. Barnes (1977). Ronald Syme, in a playful moment, invented a Tacitean fragment on Titus and Berenice as a proof-text of sorts for textual forgery: Syme (1991).

deinde, ut verbis Cornelii Taciti loquar, sene Augusto Ianus patefactus, dum apud extremos terrarum terminos novae gentes saepe ex usu et aliquando cum damno quaeruntur, usque ad Vespasiani duravit imperium. hucusque Cornelius.

Next, to quote the words of Cornelius Tacitus: "Janus was opened in Augustus' old age and remained so until the rule of Vespasian, while on the boundaries of the world new peoples were sought, often with gain and sometimes at a loss." Thus far Cornelius.

Vespasian closed the temple of Janus in the year 71. When Tacitus came to describe this (most probably in Book 5), he apparently added a digression on the temple of Janus from which Orosius then drew.[47] Orosius also refers to Tacitus (as well as Suetonius) for the number of Jewish victims over the Jewish–Roman war: "That six hundred thousand Jews were killed in that war is stated by Cornelius and Suetonius" (Orosius, *Hist.* 7.9.7 = Tac. *H.* Test. 3: *sexcenta milia Iudaeorum eo bello interfecta Cornelius et Suetonius referunt*). This is the only secure information about Tacitus' lost report on the Flavian victory over the Jews. Yet there is more. Some 160 years ago, Jacob Bernays, in a fundamental study, convincingly showed that Sulpicius Severus in his comments on the final days of Jerusalem drew from Tacitus.[48] Severus does not cite Tacitus explicitly here (he is generally reluctant in citing his sources), but Tacitean vocabulary and the fact that his description differs from that of Josephus are strong indicators that he indeed relies on Tacitus. In the two brief paragraphs from Severus, we hear how the streets of Jerusalem were covered with bodies and how desperate Jews, suffering from terrible hunger, "dared to do every abominable thing for the sake of food and did not refrain even from human bodies" (Sulpicius Severus, *Chron.* 2.30.3 = Tacitus, *H.* Test. 1, *quin omnia nefanda esca super ausi ne humanis quidem corporibus perpercerunt*). As for Titus, he deliberated with his advisors (Sulpicius Severus, *Chron.* 2.30.6 = Tacitus, *H.* Test. 2)

an templum tanti operis everteret. etenim nonnullis videbatur aedem sacratam ultra omnia mortalia illustrem non oportere deleri, quae servata modestiae Romanae testimonium, diruta perennem crudelitatis notam praeberet.

whether he should destroy a temple of such workmanship. For it seemed to some that a consecrated shrine, famous beyond all works of men, ought not to be destroyed, whose preservation would display a testament to Roman moderation, while its demolition would be a perennial marker of Roman cruelty.

Titus did not share that point of view. Rather he and others argued that (Sulpicius Severus, *Chron.* 2.30.6 = Tacitus, *H.* Test. 2)

evertendum in primis templum censebant, quo plenius Iudaeorum et Christianorum religio tolleretur: quippe has religiones, licet contrarias sibi, isdem tamen ab auctoribus profectas; Christianos ex Iudaeis extitisse: radice sublata stirpem facile perituram.

the destruction of this temple would be a primary means in order to wipe out more fully the religion of the Jews and the Christians; for they said that these religions, while at odds with

[47] Barnes (1977), 229. Orosius returns to Tacitus' comments on the temple of Janus in *H.* 7.19.4.
[48] Cf. Bernays (1861), 51–61; Barnes (1977). Laupot (2000) is critical of Bernays.

one another, nevertheless were originated from the same progenitors; that the Christians had sprung from the Jews: if the root were removed, the stock would easily perish.

That Tacitus had Titus link Judaism with Christianity is very unlikely. The Christians are not mentioned in the excursus on the Jews: they only become (briefly) a topic in the *Annals* in the context of the fire in Rome (*Ann.* 15.44.2–5). There Tacitus refers to Christianity "as if he had not mentioned it before in his writings."[49] Severus most likely used Tacitus and gave his account a Christian dress.[50] The Christian agenda becomes even stronger in Severus' theological interpretation of the destruction of the Temple:

> Thus, by the assent of God, the souls of everyone incensed, the temple was torn down, three hundred thirty-one years hence. And this was the ultimate destruction of the temple and final captivity of the Jews (*haec ultima templi eversio et postrema Iudaeorum captivitas*), through which, banished from their native country, they are seen to have been dispersed through the entire world; they are a daily testament to the world that they have been punished on account of no other thing than for the impious hands that they placed upon Christ.[51]

One can assume that Tacitus only reported Titus' decision to destroy the temple and to bring the war to an end.[52] In Severus' rewriting of Tacitus one catches exactly the difference between pagan and Christian antisemitism.[53] For Severus the Jews are a daily challenge (*cotidie*), for Tacitus one nuisance among others.

Further Reading

Bloch (2022a); Feldherr (2009a); Gruen (2016); Master (2016); Roymans (2004).

René Bloch, Histories 5 In: *The Oxford Critical Guide to Tacitus*. Edited by: Salvador Bartera and Kelly E. Shannon-Henderson, Oxford University Press. © Oxford University Press 2025. DOI: 10.1093/9780191915086.003.0009

---

[49] Barnes (1977), 228.   [50] Bernays (1861).   [51] Sulp. Sev. *Hist.* 2.30.8.
[52] According to Josephus, who was very much dependent on Flavian goodwill, Titus wanted to spare the temple (*BJ* 6.241). In Josephus' version, the fall of the temple was an accident, triggered by a Roman soldier "awaiting no orders." Titus not only did not give the order to set fire to the temple, but even "ran to the temple to arrest the conflagration" (*BJ* 6.252, 254).
[53] Cf. Bloch (2022b).

9

Annals 1

Victoria Emma Pagán

In true programmatic fashion, *Annals* 1 introduces the temporal framework, the Julio-Claudian dynasty, and the most salient theme of the *Annals*, the distinction between liberty and autocracy.[1] Book 1 begins with the death of Augustus and the accession of Tiberius in the year 14 CE (*Ann.* 1.1–15). Tacitus narrates the mutinies of the Pannonian and German legions on the Rhine and the subsequent campaigns of legions under Germanicus (*Ann.* 1.16–52). His account of the year closes with the obituary of Julia the Elder, daughter of Augustus, and a disturbance at games held in honor of Augustus (*Ann.* 1.53–4). The rest of *Annals* 1 is taken up with the events of the year 15, with foreign affairs again appearing before domestic ones.[2] During the German campaigns (*Ann.* 1.55–71), Arminius and Segestes vie for power among the Chatti and Cherusci; Germanicus makes an expedition and discovers the remains of the army of Varus; Caecina retreats; Agrippina the Elder prevents the destruction of the bridge over the Rhine. The book closes with events at Rome, *inter alia*: Tiberius' revival of the law of *maiestas* (treason); his generosity to impoverished senators; the flood of the Tiber and debate on proposals to deal with flooding; disturbances at the theater; a temple to Augustus in Spain; and provincial administration (*Ann.* 1.72–80). The book—and the year—closes with a notice regarding Tiberius' method of conducting the election of consuls (*Ann.* 1.81).

History writing captivates in part because it has the potential to mitigate and even overcome the powerful grip that time has on the human experience. Historians can bring the past to life; explain causation; wield praise and blame of individuals and communities to create and maintain identities. Narratives of the past can be written in such a way as to reflect present circumstances, a concept known as metahistory.[3] No doubt a metahistorical perspective suffuses the works of Tacitus, but for Syme it was "a pervasive influence" on Tacitus' treatment of the accession of Tiberius, which was influenced by contemporary events surrounding death of Trajan and succession of Hadrian.[4] Tacitus' treatment of time is at the heart of this analysis of *Annals* 1, which begins with problem of Augustus before assessing the middle chapters 16–51, where the revolts of the legions in Pannonia and Germany form the bulk of Book 1. The third section considers treason trials and concludes with an examination of the penultimate paragraph, 80, to observe Tacitus' method and mindset toward history writing. Embedded at the end of Book 1 is a passing reference with repercussions felt in the Neronian Principate. Before surveying Book 1, however, the opening gambit demands attention.

---

[1] See Wirszubski (1950) for an early study of *libertas*; Lavan (2013) on the ever-changing concept of *libertas*; Strunk (2017), 23–37 on the two types of freedom, from domination and of political participation.
[2] On the traditional form of the annalistic year in the Tiberian hexad, see Ginsburg (1981).
[3] White (1973) provides the seminal formulation, which Haynes (2012), 285 brings to Tacitus.
[4] Syme (1958a), 498.

The Preface

The enunciation of the subject matter is exceedingly brief: *inde consilium mihi pauca de Augusto et extrema tradere, mox Tiberii principatum et cetera* ("So it's my plan to hand down a few things about Augustus and his final days, then the Principate of Tiberius and the rest," *Ann.* 1.1.3). As Syme puts it, "The *Annales* from the opening words go to the limit of brevity"; and Woodman too, finds "from this laconic statement the reader is left to draw what further conclusions he can about the narrative which begins with the very next sentence."[5] Yet even before this concise statement, the first three sentences of the *Annals* display complexity and elegance. *Urbem Romam a principio reges habuere*; *libertatem et consulatum L. Brutus instituit* ("From the outset, kings held the city of Rome; Lucius Brutus established freedom and the consulship," *Ann.* 1.1.1). These two declarative, transitive sentences are bound all the more tightly by asyndeton (the lack of a conjunction) and the repeated pattern of object, subject, verb, but with chiasmus of number: singular object, plural subject; plural objects, singular subject. The effect achieves (at least) three things simultaneously. In terms of content, Tacitus announces the subject matter of the *Annals* as the city of Rome and his organizing principle for the *Annals* according to center and periphery, which will be manifest not only in Book 1 in his narratives of the mutinies in Pannonia (*Ann.* 1.16–30) and in Germany (*Ann.* 1.31–51), but throughout the *Annals* in his narratives of provinces, client kingdoms, and the buffer zones between Rome and the East. However, center and periphery apply to more than geography.[6] The *Annals* are about centers of power and peripheries inhabited by the powerless: *princeps* and senate; general and soldiers; governor and provincials; Roman and non-Roman; all of which are expressions of the dichotomy between freedom and servitude—implied in this first sentence by contrast with *libertas*, but with servitude not yet named, and thereby conspicuous by its absence.[7]

Formally, the first sentence begins with a dactylic hexameter that raises the generic expectations of epic poetry and the shared subject matter of heroes and wars, affinities recognized even in antiquity. Quintilian defined history as *proxima poetis, et quodam modo carmen solutum* ("closest to poetry, and in a certain sense a poem freed <from the constraints of meter>," *Inst.* 10.1.31), although by beginning with a dactylic hexameter Tacitus upends Quintilian's definition and imposes, momentarily, the constraints of meter on his subject. Tacitus was not the only historian to use meter; Livy begins his preface with a half-hexameter and an allusion to Ennius.[8] Allusions to Lucan and Vergil in the *Annals* and *Histories* have long been recognized; more recently Rhiannon Ash has explored Tacitus' presentation of poets, both famous and obscure, in the *Annals*.[9] But the opening hexameter briefly casts the *Annals* as an epic. The first two words of the *Aeneid*, *arma virumque*, announce the subjects of the epic poem in chiasmus ("arms," the subject of books 7–12, and "the man," subject of books 1–6). The first two words of the *Annals* on the other hand, *urbem Romam*, which artfully condense the *Aeneid*'s opening dactyls into weightier spondees, are semantically pleonastic and metrically insistent.

---

[5] Syme (1958a), 304; Woodman (1988), 168.   [6] Pomeroy (2003).
[7] For the Tacitean phrase, see Mellor (1993), 133.   [8] Wiseman (2002), 331–8.
[9] Lucan: Robbert (1917) and Marshall (2011); Vergil: Baxter (1972); Epic poets: Joseph (2012b) and Ash (2016b).

Furthermore, the elision of *Romam a principio* that glides the second spondee into the next dactyl is a mimesis of the inextricable political-historical bond between Rome, the city, and the Principate. For with the prepositional phrase *a principio* Tacitus engages in poetic etymologizing, since, given that the subject matter of the *Annals* will be the Julio-Claudian Principate, it is difficult not to hear in the temporal phrase a nod to the *princeps*. Rome and the Principate are thus inseparable.[10] Over and against this implicit hint of the Principate in *a principio* is the explicit description of the Republic, expressed using hendiadys (*libertatem et consulatum*, "liberty and the consulship") that refuses to subordinate one idea to the other.

Thirdly, the sentence provides a temporal starting point and a window into Tacitus' thinking; as N. P. Miller comments, "It implies a conception of historical development, of the place of the Principate in Roman History as a whole."[11] Tacitus' starting point is measurable in relation to other extant Roman historians. For Sallust, *urbem Romam* (*Cat.* 6.1) is the vanishing horizon of his first historical work, the *Bellum Catilinae*, in which *urbs Roma* is a point of retreat at the start of a literary career. For Tacitus, *urbs Roma* becomes a point of departure in what is, to the best of our knowledge, the last of his literary endeavors.[12] By setting aside legendary kings and even the somewhat more historical stories about the foundation of the consulship, Tacitus dispenses with concerns about the boundary between myth and history.[13] As Tacitus' full hexameter expands and even completes Livy's opening dactylic half line (*facturusne operae pretium sim*, praef. 1, "Whether I am about to undertake something worthwhile"), it condenses Livy's content. Kings occupy the whole of Livy Book 1, which ends with the establishment of the consulship, and so with the hendiadys *libertatem et consulatum*, Tacitus telescopes all of pre-Republican history.

The second sentence of the *Annals* then continues to shrink the content of Livy's entire first pentad into one paratactic tricolon: *dictaturae ad tempus sumebantur; neque decemviralis potestas ultra biennium neque tribunorum militum consulare ius diu valuit* ("dictatorships were assumed for the occasion, the power of the decemviri did not last more than two years, and the consular power of the military tribunes did not prevail for long," *Ann.* 1.1.1). The third sentence summarily dismisses the Republic's most notorious potentates in pairs that yield to one. The sentence structure itself appears to erode the consulship that rested on two men, as the civil wars of the late Republic result in the rise of one man alone: *non Cinnae, non Sullae longa dominatio; et Pompei Crassique potentia cito in Caesarem, Lepidi atque Antonii arma in Augustum cessere, qui cuncta discordiis civilibus fessa nomine principis sub imperium accepit* ("The despotism of neither Cinna nor Sulla lasted for long, and the power of Pompey and Crassus quickly yielded to Caesar, the arms of Lepidus and Antony to Augustus, who inherited the whole world weary with civil war under the name of *princeps*," *Ann.* 1.1.1). As Ellen O'Gorman notes, "The same process is repeated in the second chapter, revealing the eliminations made necessary by this absorption"; similarly, Christina Kraus speaks of "a proliferation of *nomina* that will rapidly yield

---

[10] On the unusual formulation *a principio*, see Joseph (2012b), 382.   [11] Miller (1992), 97.
[12] In addition to this commonly recognized allusion to Sallust, Woodman (1992b), 567–8 has identified a second point of contact. The two historians are the only ones to use the expression *procul habere* metaphorically and in contexts that describe their political careers; see also Krebs (2012) on connections between Sallust and the *Agricola*.
[13] Feeney (2007), 86–107.

to *Augustum*."[14] The reader who picks up the *Annals* learns quickly that Tacitus presses few words to much work.

Augustus

The title of the first Medicean manuscript is *P. Cornelii Taciti Ab Excessu Divi Aug.*: "Of P. Cornelius Tacitus, From the death of the divine Augustus."[15] For an author writing under the Principate of Trajan, the year 14 CE and the accession of Tiberius can seem a reasonable starting point. For Syme, however, the choice of year causes problems for Tacitus: "The historian betrays, repeatedly, a preoccupation with Augustus," and just two pages later the preoccupation becomes a suspicion, "nascent or by now corroborated, that he had made a bad start with Tiberius Caesar."[16] Syme proposes the year 4 CE as a more suitable starting point, since foreign and domestic policy, treason trials, the condition of the armies, and disputes with Armenia were already underway.[17] Actions, decisions, and programs which in the *Annals* appear to be distinctly Tiberian likely derived from Augustan precedents. However, by beginning in 14, Tacitus makes Tiberius appear independent and autonomous. Then there is the description of the battle of the Teutoburg Forest in 9 CE at *Ann.* 1.61–2, which so noticeably interrupts the temporal sequence of Book 1 that the starting date appears to be incontrovertibly mistaken. Syme believes that had Tacitus started in 4 CE, "…the Varian disaster having been narrated, the subsequent operations would be seen in their true light—and it would scarcely have been possible to give Germanicus so much space."[18] Elsewhere I have argued that Germanicus' return to the Teutoburg Forest is an artful digression in which Tacitus explores themes of transgression and transformation, victory and defeat.[19] Similarly, attention to the artistic play between narrative and historical time adds another dimension to our understanding of the inauguration of the *Annals* with the death of Augustus.

Death usually signals closure in a narrative, often signaled in literature by images of nightfall, winter, old age, journey's end. Tacitus upends this convention twice in the extant *Annals*, in twin passages that inaugurate the reigns of Tiberius and Nero: *primum facinus novi principatus fuit Postumi Agrippae caedes* ("The first deed of the new Principate was the murder of Agrippa Postumus," *Ann.* 1.6.1) and *prima novo principatu mors Iunii Silani* ("The death of Junius Silanus was the first in the new Principate," *Ann.* 13.1.1).[20] These sly verbal echoes ought to be considered in the larger context of the *Annals*, which begin with the death of Augustus, a move that challenges preconceptions about the conventions of narrative unity that assume death as an ending, not a starting point. In his discussion of closure in Plutarch's *Lives*, Christopher Pelling reminds us of two relevant passages of Aristotle.[21] In the *Poetics*, Aristotle declares that "unity of the plot does not, as some persons think, consist in the unity of the hero" (8.1451a16), and in the *Nicomachean Ethics* Aristotle questions whether we can truly count no man happy until he is dead, since "the notion that the dead are not touched at all by the fortunes of their descendants or any of their

[14] O'Gorman (1995a), 97; Kraus (2009), 101.
[15] Mendell (1957), 295; see also the catalog of editions and commentaries, Ulery (1986).
[16] Syme (1958a), 372, 374.
[17] Syme (1974), 484, (1978), 197–8, (1984a); see also Goodyear (1972), 99–100.
[18] Syme (1958a), 370 n. 3.   [19] Pagán (1999).   [20] Woodman (1995a).   [21] Pelling (1997), 250.

friends has a chilling effect on us and is generally repudiated" (1.11, 1101a16). Tacitus would seem to adhere to these Aristotelian principles. Although Tiberius is the subject of the first hexad, Tacitus does not narrate his birth or early life. Furthermore, Tiberius' self-imposed retirement on Rhodes from 6 BCE to 2 CE is recounted at *Ann.* 6.20 under the year 33 CE. The Tacitean Tiberius is a unified character not because of the artificial constraints imposed by the genre of biography but because of the artistry of plot that allows Tacitus to break free from the constraints of time. Although the *Annals* begin with the death of Augustus, his fortunes continue beyond his death, which is not a conclusion but a catalyst with implications for all those descendants and friends—and enemies—contained within the *Annals*. In short, even if Tacitus had begun in 4 CE, the Augustan achievement still could not be measured upon his death in 14 CE. By beginning with his death, Tacitus sets the stage for an examination of the posthumous legacy.[22]

At the beginning of the *Histories*, Tacitus tells us that if he lived long enough, he would compose a history of Nerva and Trajan (*H.* 1.1.4). A less specific promise was made in the preface to the *Agricola*: *non tamen pigebit vel incondita ac rudi voce memoriam prioris servitutis ac testimonium praesentium bonorum composuisse* ("I shall not regret, even if in language unskilled and plain, recounting the history of our earlier servitude and the testimony of our present happiness," *Agr.* 3.3). The earlier servitude was delivered in the *Histories*, as Tacitus himself states in the *Annals*: *libris quibus res imperatoris Domitiani composui* ("in the books I composed on the history of the emperor Domitian," *Ann.* 11.11.1). But the testimony of his present happiness never materialized. Twice, then, Tacitus contemplates writing a history of Nerva and Trajan, but as far as we know, he never fulfilled the promise. Instead, he retreated, going further back into history and not forward in time, despite his promise to narrate the post-Flavian period. Rather, he makes one final promise, to write about the age of Augustus: *sed aliorum exitus, simul cetera illius aetatis memorabo, si effectis in quae <te>tendi plures ad curas vitam produxero* ("As for the deaths of others, I will relate the rest of their age, if, after finishing what I have begun, I should prolong my life to yet more work," *Ann.* 3.24.3). For Syme, this promise is the most damning evidence of a miscalculated starting point; Tacitus acknowledges the mistake of not beginning with Augustus. More recently, however, O'Gorman considers the refusal to write about Augustus and argues that when Tacitus elects to begin with the reign of Tiberius and not Augustus, his refusal has political implications.[23]

Tacitus' most overt engagement with Augustus comes at *Annals* 1.9–10, with the *Totengericht*, or judgment of the dead (a more accurate term than "obituary," since these two paragraphs record the opinions about Augustus held by different groups of people). *Annals* 1.9–10 is framed in diametrically opposed categories of praise and blame. Tacitus rapidly dismisses the vapid observations of the majority, who are overly impressed with nothing more than mere coincidences: Augustus died on the same day he received his first command, in the same bedroom of the house at Nola where his father died; his consulships equaled those of Valerius Corvus and Gaius Marius together, and so on (*aliaque honorum multiplicata aut nova*, "and other honors, whether multiplied or new," *Ann.* 1.9.2).

---

[22] Similarly, the *Histories* begin after the death of Nero, who although seldom present in the text (and then only posthumously) provides the impetus for the narrative as a present absence without which the *Histories* could not have been written; see Haynes (2003), 34–70.

[23] O'Gorman (1995a), 102; Woodman (1975), 288 downplays the significance of such promises.

Tacitus then moves on to the more balanced assessment of the insightful (*prudentes*, 1.9.3), and at this point Tacitus could not have ignored the *Res Gestae*, Augustus' own widely published record of his achievements.[24] Some extol Augustus' actions (1.9.3–5), others criticize them in the longer, more detailed paragraph 1.10. Olivier Devillers has argued that *Ann.* 1.9–10, constructed on an axis of approval and disapproval, should be regarded as demonstrating the relevant and irrelevant categories for the writing of history. The items in paragraph 9 do not matter as much as the items in paragraph 10, and these distinctions would have guided Tacitus in the construction of the promised history of the Augustan age.[25]

The second sentence (1.10.2) provides a salient example of the approach that Tacitus takes to writing history. Critics assert that Augustus was not motivated by filial piety and political exigency (*pietatem erga parentem et tempora rei publicae*) but by a desire for rule (*cupidine dominandi*, *Ann.* 1.10.1). Thereupon, by decree of the senate, he took up the consulship and rights of the praetor (1.10.2). An ablative absolute describes the circumstances that opened this opportunity for Augustus: *caesis Hirtio et Pansa*, "once Hirtius and Pansa were cut down." However, Tacitus follows this with alternative explanations for their deaths (*Ann.* 1.10.2):

> *sive hostis illos, seu Pansam venenum vulneri adfusum, sui milites Hirtium et machinator doli Caesar abstulerat…*

> whether the enemy took them, or whether poison poured in a wound took Pansa and the soldiers and Caesar, orchestrator of the treachery, took Hirtius…

Shotter has attempted to show that "by putting the *sive…seu* part of the sentence in the indicative, Tacitus assumes responsibility for it, and in this way gives the suggestion of foul play less credence than did those whose views he was reporting."[26] But opinions in the *Annals* are notoriously difficult to pinpoint, for one can never be quite sure whether the opinions expressed are those of the times narrated, or those of Tacitus' own day, or indeed of Tacitus himself. History and metahistory are inextricable. Instead, let us compare how Suetonius narrates the same material (*Suet. Aug.* 11.1):

> *hoc bello cum Hirtius in acie, Pansa paulo post ex vulnere perissent, rumor increbruit ambos opera eius occisos…*

> In that war, when Hirtius died in battle, Pansa a little later from a wound, rumor grew that both deaths were his doing….

To express the deaths of the consuls, Tacitus uses an ablative absolute (*caesis Hirtio et Pansa*) where Suetonius uses a circumstantial clause (*cum Hirtius…Pansa…perissent*). But Tacitus distributes what Suetonius reports as rumor over two balanced alternatives: either they died in battle (*hostes illos…abstulerat*) or by foul play (poison, *venenum*, and the treachery of Augustus, *machinator doli Caesar*). Tacitus dissects the explanations into rational categories ("either…or") rather than identify them as founded in rumor.[27] And with the loaded alternative, Tacitus points the reader to the second, more sinister

---

[24] Pagán (2020), 379–81.   [25] Devillers (2009b).   [26] Shotter (1967), 173.
[27] On rumor in Tacitus, see Ryberg (1942); Shatzman (1974); Gibson (1998); Cogitore (2012).

explanation.[28] Tacitus couches the deaths of Hirtius and Pansa in implied rumor, in distinct contrast to the rumors, clearly indicated as such through use of the word *rumor*, that circulated in Augustus' old age regarding possible successors (*variis rumoribus*, 1.4.2); or his secret visit to the island of Planasia to ascertain whether the exiled Agrippa Postumus might be a suitable candidate (*rumor incesserat*, 1.5.1); or when Tiberius transferred elections from the Campus Martius to the senate, which caused some hollow rumor among the populace (*inani rumore*, 1.15.1). When faced with the dilemma of extracting Tacitus' opinion from speeches, rumors, and views attributed to others, Luce prudently turned toward a more fruitful approach. Tacitean opinions are difficult to extract because they are not meant to be extracted; rather, more is to be gained by preserving the contexts in which such information is delivered. Luce encourages us to consider the possibility that for Tacitus, the particular carries more weight than any universal that might be abstracted.[29] And so in the case of the deaths of Hirtius and Pansa, the second explanation of foul play, although couched in rumor, prevails.

Although the life of Augustus does not fall within the temporal framework of any of Tacitus' extant works, nevertheless he dominates. Augustus appears in every single extant book of the *Annals* and *Histories* (even in the incomplete *Annals* Books 5, 6, 11, 16 and *Histories* Book 5), and in the *opera minora* as well. In his sole mention in the *Agricola*, Tiberius observes his precept regarding the limits of Empire (*Agr.* 13);[30] Augustus cannot be ignored in a discussion of the politics of oratory (*D.* 13, 17, 28, 38). Even in the *Germania*, although Augustus is not identified by that name, the reference is unmistakable: *Varum trisque cum eo legiones etiam Caesari abstulerunt* ("[the Germans] took from a Caesar Varus and the three legions with him," *G.* 37.4). Tacitus turns this measured reference ("a Caesar," "three legions") into one of his most expansive digressions in the *Annals*, the return to the Teutoburg Forest (1.61–2).

Mutiny

Tacitus expands and condenses material with equal originality. The late Republic and the rise and reign of Augustus were treated by Asinius Pollio, Cremutius Cordus, Nicolaus of Damascus, and Livy. Tacitus abbreviates them all into two succinct paragraphs, which stand in sharp contrast to the protracted narrative given to the mutinies of the legions in Pannonia and Lower Germany that occupy nearly half (45 percent) of *Annals* 1, for which Tacitus would have had to rely on memoirs, *commentarii*, and other less comprehensive sources.[31] Whether they had access to the same, or to even fuller sources, the accounts of Velleius (2.125), Suetonius (*Tib.* 25.1–2), and Cassius Dio (57.4–5) are much less thorough.[32]

Tacitus' expansiveness on the mutinies has caused some skepticism. Goodyear questions whether "the very generous scale of treatment" can "adequately be explained by supposing that he regarded them [the mutinies] as exceptionally important historically."[33]

---

[28] Whitehead (1979), 493: "When…Tacitus did wish to load the choice one way or the other, it was virtually always toward the second (or last) alternative."

[29] Luce (1986), 144–50.   [30] On Tiberius' observance of Augustan precedent, see Cowan (2009).

[31] On Tacitus' sources generally, see Potter (2012); for the *Annals*, Devillers (2003).

[32] On Cassius' Dio's account, see Parat (2021).   [33] Goodyear (1972), 194–5.

Subsequent studies of the episodes have shown that regardless of whether the mutinies posed a tangible threat to the emerging authority of Tiberius, Tacitus elaborates for purposes beyond historical accuracy. Even if the historical import of the mutinies is questionable, their narrative function is paramount, especially when seen in comparison to the *Histories*, a similarly "top-heavy narrative," in the words of Rhiannon Ash.[34] The *Histories* were designed to cover twenty-seven years (69–96 CE), but the extant books 1–5 bring the reader only to the year 70. The details lavished on the Year of the Four Emperors was warranted because those events would have resonated with Tacitus' contemporary audience: "The civil wars of 69 had clear links with more recent history." Nerva's successful adoption of Trajan only narrowly forestalled another civil war. For Ash, the extensive coverage of the mutinies in *Annals* 1 likewise "activates this possibility," and "raises the spectre of civil war by pointed formulation."[35]

In part the narratives of the mutinies are so long because Tacitus names so many non-elites with active roles, men who appear nowhere else in the historical record. Percennius, the ringleader, led a theatrical group before becoming a common foot soldier (*Ann.* 1.16.3). Aufidienus Rufus, mocked by the mutineers, rose through the ranks from private to centurion to prefect (*Ann.* 1.20.1). Vibulenus was a recruit who suffered the same fate as Percennius—capital punishment on Drusus' command (*Ann.* 1.22.1, 1.29.4). Sirpicius was a centurion (*Ann.* 1.23.5); Lucilius a centurion also unattested elsewhere, who earned a second name: the soldiers called him "Bring Another" (*cedo alteram*), since after breaking his rod on the back of a soldier while administering beatings, he would demand in a loud voice that they bring him another, and yet another (*Ann.* 1.23.3). Similarly, a preponderance of non-elites unknown but for Tacitus is a striking feature of the narrative of the Pisonian conspiracy. Tacitus lists by name the victims of Nero's purge, men and women with no connections and therefore no safeguards, the rank and file, as he calls them (*Ann.* 15.71.4): Cluvidienus Quietus, Blitius Catulinus, Julius Altinus, Caedicia, Artoria Flaccilla, all named only upon banishment, exiles never to be heard from again. Throughout *Histories* 1–3, the civil wars provide ample opportunity for non-elites to emerge; for example, Otho relied on two junior officers, Veturius and Barbius Proculus, to circulate the daily watchword (*H.* 1.25.1).[36] Mutiny, conspiracy, and civil war are arenas for displays by non-elites.

Above all, the mutinies are just the first of many chances in the *Annals* to drive home the often repeated idea that only a few men are *capax imperii*, capable of ruling the Empire, and these men run a risk hardly worth taking. Before he died, Augustus described three men who might rise in his place: Asinius Gallus was ambitious but inferior; Lucius Arruntius was not only up to the task but daring as well; Marcus Lepidus was *capax* but indifferent (*Ann.* 1.13). The first two met with violent ends on charges concocted by Tiberius. For his ability to survive with integrity, Lepidus earns high praise from Tacitus (*Ann.* 4.20.2).[37] This theme of *capax imperii* is echoed in the account of the Pannonian revolt. Drusus, son of Tiberius, is only able to restore order after the mutinous soldiers are frightened by an eclipse of the moon. Taking advantage of their superstition and fear,

---

[34] Ash (2009), 88.   [35] Ash (2009), 90, earlier observations by Kotzé (1996), 127–8.
[36] Even when their names are unknown, Tacitus still includes them. In a battle between Vitellians and Flavians, two soldiers disguised themselves and cut the ropes of the siege engines. "They were immediately run through and for that reason their names have been lost, but the deed is scarcely doubted" (*statim confossi sunt eoque intercidere nomina, de facto haud ambigitur, H.* 3.23.2).
[37] See ten Berge, Chapter 12 in this volume.

he sends out a general message rebuking the soldiers and questioning their judgment: do they really think it prudent to entrust rule to the likes of a Percennius or a Vibulenus? "In short, will they take charge of the Empire of the Roman people instead of men like Nero and Drusus?" (*denique pro Neronibus et Drusis imperium populi Romani capessent? Ann.* 1.28.4). Initially the rhetorical questions pertain directly to the mutiny at hand, calling the instigators by name. However, the final question, *imperium…capessent*, although semantically and grammatically distinct, is nevertheless etymologically connected to the phrase *capax imperii*. Thus, into the hyperbolic rebuke of the mutinous soldiers Tacitus subtly inserts the question of who is fit to rule. The accession of Tiberius and the military challenges to that accession compel a reflection on the nature of power and those capable of wielding it. In the end, the soldiers resign; however, the anticlimactic outcome matters less than the fact that they took their chances in the face of a new imperial regime. The soldiers' reaction to the accession of Tiberius may have escalated the emperor's tyrannical tendencies, since in the future he will have to exert power to prevent a more damaging revolt and ensure steadfast allegiance. It should be clear that Tacitus uses the mutinies as an opportunity to meditate on the nature of power and the morality of dissent, two themes that pursue the *Annals* to their bitter end.[38]

Treason and Poppaeus Sabinus

A year into his principate, Tiberius revived the *lex maiestatis* ("law of treason," *Ann.* 1.72), a rather vague law that criminalized offences that diminished the majesty (*maiestas*) of the Roman people. Rather than define the term, however, Tacitus provides instead a sort of genealogy. Although the name of the law was the same, the cases that came before the courts were different. In the past, cases were argued based on deeds; for example, if a soldier betrayed the army, citizens caused riots, or magistrates conducted business improperly: "words went unpunished" (*dicta impune erant, Ann.* 1.72.2), says Tacitus. Even so, the vagueness of the charge and its metamorphoses over the course of centuries from the end of the Republic into the Julio-Claudian age made it a malleable and potent weapon in the hands of politicians seeking influence. Under Augustus, as the interests of the general welfare and good of the state increasingly converged on the person of the Emperor, the scope of the *lex maiestatis* expanded to include offenses against the Emperor or his family. Tacitus pins this novelty squarely on Augustus, "the first to handle a case about libellous pamphlets under the guise of this law" (*primus Augustus cognitionem de famosis libellis specie legis eius tractavit, Ann.* 1.72.3). Augustus was prompted by the especially vigorous attacks of Cassius Severus on noble men and women. Thus for Tiberius there was precedent for invoking the law; however, procedures and outcomes remained highly irregular, with the result that *maiestas* continued to conceal political wrangling and even personal animus under the guise of law. Trials were highly irregular, ad hoc affairs, and punishments included banishment, exile, relegation, and confiscation of property. Some defendants who anticipated conviction under the shifty law took their own lives before verdicts could be rendered, thus further complicating the ability to

---

[38] See Pagán (2005) for a fuller treatment of this thesis.

understand procedures and outcomes clearly. Of the prosecutors, on the other hand, we have a very good picture. Known as *delatores*, these "informants" are a stock character type in Tacitus, negatively portrayed.[39]

Tacitus proceeds to narrate three *maiestas* trials.[40] Equestrians Faianius and Rubrius (two men who are not mentioned anywhere else in the historical record) served as test cases. Faianius was accused of including among his home's worshippers of Augustus (who were apparently maintained in the homes of those who could support such groups) a mime named Cassius. Mimes, like actors, were socially and legally stigmatized, making them inappropriate persons for the worship of the emperor; however, Cassius was particularly scandalous because of his "bodily" reputation (*corpore infamem, Ann.* 1.73.2), from which we might infer that he engaged in prostitution. Furthermore, when selling his garden, Faianius also disposed of a statue of Augustus. Rubrius was accused of violating the divinity of Augustus by perjury. The cases were advanced by Pompeius Macer, the praetor for the year 15 CE. Tiberius, reluctant to engage in such seemingly paltry litigation, exercised impartiality. While Tacitus' narrative makes it seem as though Tiberius was acquitting the men, in fact he was merely providing his own opinion to the consuls. This first instance of *maiestas* in the *Annals* thus brings into sharp relief the more pernicious prosecutions that would come to characterize the latter part of Tiberius' reign.

Third is the case of Granius Marcellus, governor of Bithynia, accused under the law of *maiestas* by a member of his own staff, the otherwise unknown Caepio Crispinus. The charge seems to have stemmed from a combination of provincial maladministration and verbal disapproval of Tiberius. The prosecutors were clever enough to allege that Granius made disrespectful remarks about Tiberius that could not be ignored because they were grounded in fact; by virtue of their truth, they were believed to have been said (*Ann.* 1.74.4). Nonetheless, the case was dismissed, except for the charges of provincial maladministration.

The case is notable for two reasons. First, Caepio was assisted in the case by Romanius Hispo, a well-known rhetorician of the age whom Seneca the Elder portrays as a vehement and combative orator (*Contr.* 1.2.16), and whom Quintilian reports was charged with outrageous crimes himself (*Inst.* 6.3.100). Second, Hispo added a charge of *impietas*, since Granius had placed a statue of himself higher than those of members of the imperial house, and because he had replaced an image of Augustus with that of Tiberius. Clearly the case of Granius Marcellus provided opportunity for jockeying and political maneuvering, all of which angered Tiberius: "At this, he blazed forth" (*ad quod exarsit, Ann.* 1.74.4). Even if he later repented the outburst (*paenitentiae patiens, Ann.* 1.74.6), he had demonstrated the incipient power of *maiestas* to ruin lives.

Poppaeus Sabinus provides a fitting coda. In the penultimate paragraph of Book 1, we are told that Tiberius extended Sabinus' governorship of Moesia and added the provinces of Macedonia and Achaia. This extension is indicative of Tiberius' policy: *id quoque morum Tiberii fuit, continuare imperia ac plerosque ad finem vitae in isdem exercitibus aut iurisdictionibus habere* ("This was also Tiberius' custom, to continue commands and keep most men in the same armies and jurisdictions until the end of their lives," *Ann.*1.80.1).

---

[39] First identified by Walker (1952), 215–18; fully explored by Rutledge (2001).
[40] For a study of all the trials in the *Annals*, see Bablitz (2015).

The rest of the paragraph is sheer editorializing: *causae variae traduntur* ("Various reasons are given," *Ann.* 1.80.2). Tiberius retained governors either because of inertia, or out of a preference for mediocrity; regardless, the practice pinched opportunities from other senators. Tiberius' hesitation (*haesitatione*, 1.80.3) contributes to the portrait of his hesitancy to rule as sketched in Book 1 and his latent tendency towards tyranny as developed in the remaining books of the first hexad.[41]

In addition to commenting on administrative policy and adding further dimensions to Tiberius' character, the paragraph introduces a figure whose reach extends from the beginnings of the Julio-Claudian dynasty to its bitter end—and beyond. Sabinus, a *novus homo*, entered the senate under Augustus, who appointed him governor of Moesia, which he governed for an unprecedented twenty years. Sabinus thus falls into the category of men singled out by Tacitus who execute their duties inconspicuously, like Marcus Lepidus, and even Agricola. In 26 CE Sabinus was granted a triumph for his actions in Thrace (*Ann.* 4.46); in 31 CE he is mentioned as having sent letters to Tiberius (*Ann.* 5.10.2–3); in 35 CE he died, his life summed up in one sentence: "At the end of the year Poppaeus Sabinus departed from life, a man of modest origin who gained the consulship and triumphal honor through his friendship with emperors and who governed the greatest provinces for twenty-four years, not on account of any great skill but because he was equal to the work and nothing more" (*Fine anni Poppaeus Sabinus concessit vita, modicus originis, principum amicitia consulatum ac triumphale decus adeptus maximisque provinciis per quattuor et viginti annos impositus, nullam ob eximiam artem, sed quod par negotiis neque supra erat, Ann.* 6.39.3).[42] This brief but pointed obituary, however, is not the last mention of Sabinus in the extant *Annals*. He appears once more in the character sketch of his granddaughter: "There was in the city one Poppaea Sabina, her father Titus Ollius, but she took the name of her maternal grandfather, Poppaeus Sabinus, of illustrious memory and distinguished for his consulship and triumph" (*Ann.* 13.45.1: *erat in civitate Sabina Poppaea, T. Ollio patre genita, sed nomen avi materni sumpserat, inlustri memoria Poppaei Sabini consularis et triumphali decore praefulgentis*). Poppaea is of course the scandalous mistress, then wife, of Nero, whose first husband was in fact Otho, long before his rise to power. Book 4 ends with the marriage of Agrippina the Younger and Domitius Ahenobarbus, the parents of Nero. Yet even before this overt foreshadowing of the union that would produce the future *princeps*, as Book 1 draws to a close, with the drop of a name while explaining Tiberius' policy regarding provincial administration, Tacitus prefigures one of the most notorious women of the Neronian age and establishes unity across the *Annals*.

The book closes with the first consular elections (the bedrock of any free and open society) conducted under Tiberius, but their exact procedure eludes the historical record. Tacitus suggests some sort of pre-selection of candidates, but avers only that the more the process looked like freedom, the more potential it had for erupting into servitude (*Ann.* 1.81.4). Of its many artistic achievements, *Annals* Book 1 forecloses any possibility of a return to liberty or retreat from tyranny.

---

[41] O'Gorman (1995a); *pace* Goodyear (1981), 182.

[42] In fact he governed for only twenty years, and the superlative *maximis provinciis* is questionable.

Further Reading

Kraus (2009) is a comprehensible introduction to *Annals* 1; Benario (2012) situates Book 1 in the broader context of the *Annals*. O'Gorman (1995a) analyzes the problem of Augustus in *Annals* 1; these ideas are expanded in O'Gorman (2000), 23–45. Fulkerson (2006) analyzes the theatrical nature of the mutinies, Woodman (2006a) the imagery of madness. Bhatt (2016) explores the reception of Percennius in mid-20th-century European thought. Marincola (1999) puts the preface into the larger context of Tacitus' works. Levene (2010b) takes *Annals* Book 1 as a starting point for his investigation of comparisons between Tacitus and Pompeius Trogus.

Victoria Emma Pagán, Annals *1* In: *The Oxford Critical Guide to Tacitus*. Edited by: Salvador Bartera and Kelly E. Shannon-Henderson, Oxford University Press. © Oxford University Press 2025. DOI: 10.1093/9780191915086.003.0010

10

Annals 2

Aske Damtoft Poulsen

Annals 2 is, above all, the book of Germanicus. Each of the four narrative years of the book (16–19 CE) has something to say about the man who for years seemed destined to succeed Tiberius as emperor before his untimely and suspicious death. The account of his campaign in Germania is the main narrative event of 16 CE. In 17 CE he celebrates a triumph in Rome and is entrusted with a special command in the East. The year 18 CE is devoted entirely to his travel eastwards to take up this command. And in 19 CE he visits Egypt before succumbing to an illness, or poison, on his way back to Syria.[1] However, *Annals* 2 is much more than an account of Germanicus' final years and death. In this book, Tacitus' storyworld expands dramatically to incorporate almost the entire Roman world. While *Annals* 1 alternates between Rome and Germania (and Pannonia), *Annals* 2—in addition to affording a whopping twenty-one chapters to Germanicus' final campaign in Germania (2.5–25)[2]—also brings the reader to the Eastern kingdoms of Parthia and Armenia, to the Roman provinces of Syria and Africa, to Cappadocia, to Thrace, to Actium and Athens, to the islands of Euboea, Lesbos, and Rhodes, to Troy and the oracle of Clarian Apollo at Colophon in Asia, to the imperial province of Egypt, and to Antioch in Syria. No other Tacitean book boasts such an impressive geographical scope.

Deceit and Deception in Rome and Beyond

Despite the variety of venues, *Annals* 2 exhibits an impressive coherence of theme. As noted already in 1989 by Bronwyn Williams, "[f]alse friendship and internal treachery pervade the subject matter of *Annals* 2."[3] Although word counting should not be confused with philology, it bears noting that with forty-one occurrences the book has the highest number of words that designate deceit and/or deception in the *Annals*: *decipere*, "to deceive, mislead" (2.46.1); *dissimulare*, "to disguise, conceal" (2.42.3); *dissimulatio*, "dissimulation, concealment" (2.57.3); *dolus*, "deception, trickery" (2.3.2, 5.1, 42.3, 64.3 [*subdolus*], 65.2, 88.2); *ementiri*, "to lie, fabricate" (2.66.1); *fallere*, "to deceive, trick" (2.66.2); *falsum*, "falsehood" (2.39.4, 57.2, 82.5); *falsus*, "false, forged" (2.55.2, 80.2); *fictus*, "made up, false, deceitful" (2.65.2, 67.3); *fingere* (in the sense *OLD* 9–10), "to fabricate, make false"

---

[1] Scholarship on Taciteus' Germanicus is daunting: see esp. Shotter (1968); Borzsák (1970); Ross (1973); Rutland (1987); Williams (1989), 141–6; Pelling (1993); O'Gorman (2000), 46–69; Pigoń (2008); Kraus (2009); Williams (2009b); Kelly (2010); Manolaraki and Augoustakis (2012); Shannon-Henderson (2019), 69–120.

[2] The city of Rome is absent from the narrative from 2.2.1 to 2.34.1, making this the longest stretch of narrative without mention of Rome (whether in the form *Roma* or *urbs*, "the City") in the *Annals*. On the significant amount of space given to Germanicus' ultimately rather insignificant Germanic wars, see Pigoń (2008), 288.

[3] Williams (1989), 147. For an alternative take on the main theme of the book, see Baxter (1972), who focuses on the problem of succession. As noted by Ginsburg (1981), 26, however, the succession theme is prominent throughout *Annals* 1–6: "Eleven out of twenty-one years open with entries relevant to the succession theme."

(2.26.5, 42.3, 71.4); *fraus*, "deceit, trickery" (2.17.5, 39.1, 46.1, 65.2 and 5, 71.2, 88.1); *insidiae*, "ambush, plot, treacherous attack" (2.5.3, 65.4 [*insidias* and *insidiator*], 71.1, 73.2); *perfidia*, "faithlessness, treachery" (2.8.4, 13.1 [*perfidus*], 46.1); *proditor*, "betrayer, traitor" (2.10.1, 45.3); and *simulare* (in the sense *OLD* 1–2, 5), "to pretend, simulate" (2.11.2, 29.2, 40.2).[4]

Many of these examples occur in the narrative of the endgame of Tiberius' rivalry with Germanicus, as the bitter old uncle seeks to get rid of his young and likeable nephew. At the beginning of the book, Tiberius uses the outbreak of turmoil in the east as a pretext to recall Germanicus from his loyal legions in Germania and expose him to "deceit and hazards" (*dolo simul et casibus*, 2.5.1) in new provinces. The emperor's scheming bears fruit at 2.69–72, when Germanicus succumbs to a mysterious illness on the way back to Syria from Egypt. Although Tacitus shies away from stating outright that the young prince was poisoned by Piso on Tiberius' orders, the reader would be excused for connecting the dots that lead to such a conclusion. Tiberius' hatred of his nephew (and the latter's awareness thereof) is mentioned already at 1.33.1, Piso certainly believes that he has been installed as governor of Syria "to restrain Germanicus' hopes" (*ad spes Germanici coercendas*, 2.43.4), and Germanicus—when he speaks from his deathbed about being "surrounded by treacherous plots" (*insidiis circumventus*, 2.71.1) and falling to "a womanly trick" (*muliebri fraude*, 2.71.2)—explicitly blames Piso while also showing dread of Tiberius. Finally, those attending the funeral in Antioch note that he, like Alexander the Great, had fallen to "the plots of his own people" (*suorum insidiis*, 2.73.2).[5]

However, not only the major narrative strand of the book but also its various other accounts revolve around the theme of deceit and deception. From treachery at the Parthian court (2.1–2) to underhanded Roman involvement in Armenia (2.3), from ambushes and oath-breakers in Germania (2.5–17) to a plan to seize the banished Agrippa "by either trick or force" (*fraude aut vi*, 2.39.1), from a Cappadocian king tricked by Tiberius (2.42.2–4) to accusations of treachery among Germanic chieftains (2.46.1), the book is littered with examples of deceit and deception. As such the treatment of deceit and deception in *Annals* 2 illustrates a characteristic element of Tacitus' historiographical mode, namely the interweaving of the main Roman narrative with accounts of events along and beyond the borders.[6]

Where occurrences of deceit and deception come thickest and fastest is in the account of events in Thrace at 2.64–7, which narrates Thracian affairs from 12 to 19 CE. Upon the death of king Rhoemetalces in 12 CE, Augustus had divided the kingdom between his brother Rhescuporis and son Cotys. At first, they act with "deceitful harmony" (*subdola concordia*, 2.64.3), but Rhescuporis merely "fabricates restraint" (*ficta modestia*, 2.65.2) and negotiates with a mind set on "deceit" (*fraude*, 2.65.2). Cotys realizes the "trick" (*dolum*, 2.65.3) too late and is put in chains, whereupon Rhescuporis writes to Tiberius that an "ambush" (*insidias*, 2.65.4) had been laid for him, but that the "ambusher"

---

[4] My search words include also *adsimulare* (*OLD* 1–2, 5b), *dissimulator, fallacia, fallax, fraudator, insidiari, mendacium, mendax, perfidiosus, prodere* (*OLD* 7–8), *proditio, simulatio*, and *simulator*. In terms of frequency of deception-words, *Annals* 2 (approx. 1/251) is superseded only by *Annals* 6 (approx. 1/200), which brings Tiberius' deceitful rule to its climax, as well as *Histories* 2–4 (approx. 1/227, 1/207, and 1/228 respectively), which narrate the breakdown of military *fides* during the year of four emperors (cf. Bartera (2019)).

[5] All translations of *Annals* are my own, though heavily indebted to Woodman (2004).

[6] On Tacitus' use of foreigners to frame the main Roman narrative, see Walker (1952), 225–9; Keitel (1978); Damtoft Poulsen (2018); cf. Laruccia (1980); O'Gorman (1993); (2014); Clarke (2001); Krebs (2011a); Rutherford (2010). For a postcolonial approach to Tacitus, see Shumate (2012).

(*insidiatorem*, 2.65.4) has been forestalled. Tiberius replies gently—but with an undertone of menace—that "if there had been no trick" (*si fraus abesset*, 2.65.5), Rhescuporis would have no qualms about coming to Rome to defend himself. With Roman soldiers arriving to bring Cotys to Rome, Rhescuporis, starting to feel the heat, orders the execution of his nephew and "lies" (*ementitur*, 2.66.1) that he has committed suicide. Tiberius is not fooled, however, and appoints an old friend of Rhescuporis as governor of neighboring Moesia "for the purpose of deceiving him" (*ad fallendum*, 2.66.2). Rhescuporis is lured into the Roman garrison, where he is surrounded by soldiers and dragged to Rome. Accused in the senate by Cotys' wife, he is banished to Alexandria and killed shortly thereafter "either because he tried to escape or on some trumped-up charge" (*fugam temptans an ficto crimine*, 2.67.3). The account of the troublesome succession in Thrace is particularly pertinent to the main Roman narrative, since Rhescuporis and Cotys—like Tiberius and Germanicus—are uncle and nephew.

The theme of deceit and deception makes a final, bookend appearance in the account of the death of the Germanic leader Arminius. Having earlier been deserted by his uncle Inguiomerus—those uncles!—on the eve of battle against Maroboduus (2.45.1), he becomes a victim of "the deceit of his kinsmen" (*dolo propinquorum*, 2.88.2) shortly after Tiberius, in ironic contrast to his use of trickery to get rid of Germanicus, declines an offer from a Germanic chief to poison Arminius with the claim that "the Roman people extracted vengeance from their enemies not through deceit and secrecy but openly and armed" (*non fraude neque occultis, sed palam et armatum populum Romanum hostes suos ulcisci*, 2.88.1).[7] *Annals* 2, then, exhibits three accounts of a deceitful uncle pitted against a (more or less) innocent nephew: Tiberius versus Germanicus, Rhescuporis versus Cotys, and Inguiomerus versus Arminius. At the end of the book all three nephews are dead. The theme of avuncular deceit, in short, is a pivotal element in the intratextual tapestry of *Annals* 2, connecting events in Rome with those in Thrace and Germania.

Tampering with the Annalistic Structure

Tacitus' employment of the annalistic structure in the *Annals* is flexible.[8] The historian is not averse to tampering with chronology for literary and rhetorical effect, and Book 2 has its fair share of examples. Most notably, Germanicus' eastern tour at 2.53–8 is the only theme of the remarkably brief treatment of 18 CE; not a single event in Rome or elsewhere from this year is deemed worthy of mention by the historian. As Goodyear has noted, such extreme selectivity is surely to be attributed to the purposes of plot and the construction of a captivating dramatic arc: "[A]s the tragedy of Germanicus draws to its climax attention must increasingly focus on him, and so it does, with only one break (62–8)."[9]

[7] Rome had refused a similar offer to poison king Pyrrhus of Epirus (Plut. *Pyrrh.* 21; Liv. *Per.* 13). On the irony at play here, see Walker (1952), 124; Syme (1958a), 266–7; Baxter (1972), 269; Ginsburg (1981), 45; Williams (1989), 151, who notes that Tiberius uses treachery also against Agrippa Postumus (1.6), the false Agrippa Postumus (2.39–40), King Archelaus (2.42.2–5), Maroboduus (2.63), and Rhescuporis (2.64–7); Grethlein (2013), 147; Low (2013), 24–8, 65–75. On Tacitus' Tiberius as the archetypical hypocritical tyrant, see Griffin (1995), 33–43; cf. Sailor (2019), 104–5.
[8] On the structure of *Annals* 1–6, see Ginsburg (1981).   [9] Goodyear (1981), 352.

Another illustrative example occurs at 2.84, in the narrative of 19 CE. Livia, the wife of Tiberius' biological son Drusus, gives birth to male twins. The timing is poignant, with Rome still in the grip of sorrow (*maestitia*, 2.84.1) after the recent death of Germanicus earlier in the same year. Not only does this coincidence add to the pain of those mourning his loss, but Tiberius' demonstrable happiness—to the point of "boasting in front of the senators" (*iactaret apud patres*, 2.84.1)—comes off as wildly inappropriate. So far so good, but Tacitus has tampered with chronology. As Hirschfeld noted already in 1913, a date of birth for the twins in 19 CE is incompatible with several other pieces of evidence, not least *Ann.* 6.46.1.[10] Building on Hirschfeld's claim, Goodyear argues that the twins were born at least one and probably two years or more later, but that Tacitus "for purposes of dramatic juxtaposition…anticipates an event which really occurred later."[11] In this way Tacitus highlights the sorrow of those mourning Germanicus through contrast with Tiberius' joy, and stresses the rivalry between the Claudian (Tiberius, Drusus) and Julian (Germanicus, Agrippina the Elder) wings of the ruling house. Moreover, the historian has made sure that what is to the joy of Tiberius is to the sorrow of his fellow Romans and to the discomfort of the readers of *Annals*, thus underlining the emotional fissure separating the emperor from his subjects.[12]

While the tampering with chronology at 2.84 may strike a modern reader as unsettlingly unscientific, it is a trifle compared with the much greater license taken by Tacitus in his narration of Drusus' activities in Germania and the troublesome succession in Thrace at 2.62–7.[13] Placed in 19 CE, these events probably occurred primarily in 18 CE, although they may have stretched into and ended in the following year.[14] Foreign wars, of course, are problematic for annalistic historians, as they tend to bridge two or more years. That said, Tacitus has no qualms about dividing his narrative of foreign wars into smaller parts when that suits him. The war against Tacfarinas, for example, starts at 2.52 (17 CE) and then reappears at 3.20–1 (20 CE), 3.32 (21 CE), 3.73–4 (22 CE), and 4.23–6 (24 CE). In Devillers' compelling analysis, the intermittent intrusion of Tacfarinas and Africa into the narrative allows Tacitus to comment on the gradual deterioration of Tiberius' character.[15] Literary and rhetorical aims trump a consistent procedure when dealing with events that span several years.

The bookend account of Arminius' death and obituary is yet another example of Tacitus eschewing chronology for literary purposes, as the Germanic leader probably did not die until two years later.[16] This anticipation of Arminius' death allows Tacitus to draw together the narrative strands of *Annals* 2 in its final chapter.[17] After Tiberius declines an offer to

---

[10] Hirschfeld (1913), 857, who also musters Dio 59.1.2 and Philo *Leg.* 26 as evidence.

[11] Goodyear (1981), 438.   [12] Cf. Goodyear (1981), 438.

[13] Cf. Goodyear (1981), 438: "After swallowing that camel [2.62–7] let us not strain at this gnat [2.84]."

[14] Goodyear (1981), 395.   [15] Devillers (1991); cf. Strunk (2017), 47–9.

[16] The claim that Tacitus moves Arminius' death forward from 21 to 19 CE rests on the interpretation of *duodecim [annos] potentiae explevit* ("he completed twelve years in power," 2.88.3) as taking the Battle of Teutoburg Forest in 9 CE as the point of departure; cf. Furneaux (1896), 384–5; Walker (1952), 124; Syme (1958a), 266; Koestermann (1963–8), i, 415; Goodyear (1981), 447 ad loc. 2.88.2–3; Woodman (2004), 82 n. 151; Grethlein (2013), 138.

[17] Cf. Ginsburg (1981), 41: "One of the ways Tacitus ties the end chapters in with the Tiberian narrative as a whole is to select items for the close of the year which take up themes the historian has already introduced." On the remarkableness of *Annals* 2 ending with an obituary of Arminius rather than Germanicus, see Ginsburg (1981), 45. While Tacitus frequently ends a year with an obituary—eight out of eighteen in *Annals* 1–6 (Ginsburg (1981), 32)—no other barbarian receives an obituary in the extant part of his corpus. On obituaries in the *Annals*, see Syme (1958b), whose list of twelve obituaries (embracing twenty persons) is incomplete, lacking, among

poison the Germanic leader (see above on 2.88.1), Arminius is killed by his own kinsmen: "But Arminius, with the Romans withdrawing and Maroboduus expelled, sought kingship and thus met with opposition from his freedom-loving compatriots. Under armed attack and struggling with varying success, he fell to the cunning of his kinsmen" (*ceterum Arminius, abscedentibus Romanis et pulso Maroboduo regnum adfectans, libertatem popularium adversam habuit, petitusque armis cum varia fortuna certaret, dolo propinquorum cecidit*, 2.88.2). Tiberius' refusal to use poison against the Germanic leader stands in ironic contrast to his use of underhanded means against his own nephew and adopted son, who (so Tacitus suggests) was poisoned on his orders, and Arminius—who has already been betrayed by his uncle Inguiomerus (2.45.1)—instead becomes the victim of deceit at the hands of his own family. Tacitus' tampering with the annalistic structure, then, purposely accentuates the major theme of the book: deceit and deception. Finally, the obituary of Arminius that follows the notice of his death further accentuates the parallel with Germanicus, as the Germanic leader is designated "undoubtedly the liberator of Germania" (*liberator hau<d> dubie Germaniae*, 2.88.2); for Germanicus, as we shall see in the third and final section, personified the hopes for a return to freedom (*libertas*) in Rome.[18]

From Hope and Hopelessness to Helplessness and Regret

Reading Tacitus' *Annals* can be a miserable experience: year after year, emperor after emperor, Rome sinks ever deeper into a quagmire of moral decay, political incompetence, and overt authoritarianism. In the words of Sir Ronald Syme, "The *Annales* convey the traveller through a bleak land without light or hope."[19] Syme's remark, however, is only partially true, for *Annals* 1–2 is in fact full of hopes: dashed hopes. The main narrative strand of the book relates the extinction of Germanicus and the hopes placed on him by various segments of Roman society. A quick look at the word count for *spes* ("hope") and *sperare* ("to hope") reveals that the frequency is higher in *Annals* 1–2 than 3–16.[20] What is more, seven of the thirty-two occurrences of *spes* and *sperare* in *Annals* 1–2 refer to Germanicus.

Whereas the Roman people, believing that Germanicus' father, Drusus the Elder, would have restored the Republic (*libertatem redditurus*, 1.33.2), attach "the same hope" (*spes eadem*, 1.33.2) to his son, the mutinous soldiers in Germania entertain "a great hope" (*magna spe*, 1.31.1) that Germanicus will lead them in a bid for the purple.[21] However, even though he has both reasonable cause to rebel (cf. 1.33.1 on his awareness of Tiberius' animosity) and

---

others, that of Arminius; cf. "Obituary", *TE* 754–6 (Pomeroy), who *does* mention Arminius; on death notices in ancient historiography more generally, see Pomeroy (1991).

[18] The phrase *liberator...Germaniae* recalls Arminius' introduction into the narrative at 1.55.2 as *turbator Germaniae*; cf. Pelling (1993), 81; Sinclair (1995), 23; cf. Syme (1958a), 530–1. On Tacitus' verdict on Arminius and his legacy, see Damtoft Poulsen (2018), 63–6, with further bibliography.

[19] Syme (1958a), 545; cf. Trilling (1976) = Ash (2012), 435: "We are aware of him [Tacitus] as one of the few great writers who are utterly without hope." See also Griffin (2009), 168–72. For a more detailed treatment of the reader's experience of *Annals* 2, see Damtoft Poulsen (2020). On the arousal of emotions in ancient historiography more generally, see Levene (1997); Marincola (2003).

[20] There are 32 occurrences out of approximately 21,050 words (for a frequency of 1/658) in *Annals* 1–2 vs. 84 occurrences out of approximately 67,410 words (for a frequency of 1/803) in *Annals* 3–16.

[21] The broad political spectrum of the hopes embodied by Germanicus mirrors the diverging political beliefs of his past and future family members: his grandfather Mark Antony, a would-be king in the Eastern mold; his great-uncle Augustus, a dynast turned princeps; his father Drusus, a republican; and his son Caligula and grandson Nero, authoritarian emperors. On Drusus' alleged desire to reinstate the Republic and its rumored role in his

Rome's most powerful army within his grasp (cf. 1.34.1 on his proximity to "the highest of hopes," *summae spei*), Germanicus opts out. Despite his nephew's consistent loyalty, Tiberius is delighted when disturbances in the East afford him a pretext to remove Germanicus from his legions in Germania (2.5.1).[22] When he is finally dispatched to the East—after another reminder of the emperor's animosity (2.42.1)—Tiberius simultaneously appoints Cn. Piso as governor of Syria. While Tiberius' motives remain shrouded in rumor, Piso assumes that he has been appointed "to restrain Germanicus' hopes" (*ad spes Germanici coercendas*, 2.43.4). While the dispatch of Piso and the seriousness with which he embraces his task suggest a belief that these hopes are of a substantial (and dangerous) nature, they are left wholly unspecified. Indeed, the *spes Germanici* have taken on a life of their own to the point that Piso can hardly know if he is supposed to oppose Germanicus' own hopes (subjective genitive) or the hopes others had placed on him (objective genitive).

Germanicus' embodiment of hope is underlined yet again when, before setting off for the East, he consecrates a shrine to *Spes*, the goddess of hope (2.49.2).[23] These hopes, of course, come to naught. Germanicus falls sick at 2.69.2 and—after having been "briefly roused to hope" (*paulisper ad spem erectus*, 2.71.1)—soon finds himself on his deathbed giving final instructions to family and friends. Although he finally acknowledges the potential power of these hopes in his final speech, their nature and parentage remain ambiguous: "If anyone was affected by my hopes [or 'the hopes placed on me'], my kindred blood, even resentment toward me while I lived, they will shed tears that a once flourishing survivor of so many wars has fallen to a womanly trick" (*si quos spes meae, si quos propinquus sanguis, etiam quos invidia erga viventem movebat, inlacrimabunt quondam florentem et tot bellorum superstitem muliebri fraude cecidisse*, 2.71.2). As in the mention of Piso's belief that he has been appointed to oppose *spes Germanici* at 2.43.4, *spes meae* may here be understood both/either subjectively ("my hopes") and/or objectively ("hopes placed on me").[24] By leaving the substance of the hopes unspecified and the identity of those who entertain them ambiguous, Germanicus allows his listeners (and Tacitus' readers) to draw their own conclusions. Neither those who had imagined him a champion of freedom nor those who had wanted him to make a bid for the purple need restrain their pity or renounce their anger at his alleged murder. Clarification would only risk alienating possible avengers.

The contradictory hopes attached to Germanicus are underlined again when Tacitus relates the reactions to his death.[25] At the funeral in Antioch he is seen as a would-be emperor, as illustrated by the comparison with Alexander the Great and the explicit counterfactual with which it climaxes: "If he had been the sole arbiter of affairs, with kingly prerogative and name, he would have obtained military glory more readily, just as he surpassed [Alexander] in clemency, moderation, and the other good qualities" (*quod si solus arbiter rerum, si iure et nomine regio fuisset, tanto promptius adsecuturum gloriam militiae, quantum clementia temperantia, ceteris bonis artibus praestitisset*, 2.73.3).

---

death, see Suet. *Tib.* 50.1, *Claud.* 1.4–5. On Tacitus' tendency to represent Germanicus from the perspective of the potential futures that he embodies, see Williams (2009b), 118–19.

[22] On Germanicus' loyalty to Tiberius despite being aware of his animosity, see also 2.22.1, 26.5, 43.6, 55.6. On Tiberius' distrust of Germanicus, see also 1.7.6, 52.1 (with Pelling (1993), 71), 62.2, 69; cf. Low (2013), 44.

[23] On the Tacitean Germanicus as an embodiment of hope (of every sort), see O'Gorman (2000), 47–9.

[24] On the objective use of the possessive pronoun, see Kühner and Stegmann (1955), §116.2.5; cf. Menge (1965), §71.

[25] Cf. Pelling (1993), 78.

When news of his faltering health reach the City, however, the Roman people reaffirm their belief that Germanicus, like his father, had intended to restore the Republic (2.82). Finally, when Agrippina the Elder returns to Rome with her husband's ashes at the beginning of *Annals* 3, soldiers, magistrates, and people—seemingly oblivious to the fact that the hopes they had pinned on him were not the same—unanimously lament their lost savior: "They kept crying out that the commonwealth had fallen, and that no vestige of hope remained" (*concidisse rem publicam, nihil spei reliquum clamitabant*, 3.4.1).[26]

The emotional spectrum of the characters, then, includes both hope and hopelessness, but what about helplessness? Unlike hope and hopelessness, helplessness—the sensation that you are, in the words of Ash, "watching a disaster narrative unfold"[27]—requires two characteristics that are as inaccessible to characters as they are inescapable for readers: prescience and impotence. Where characters face an open future, readers of historiography are positioned as helpless spectators whose knowledge of the past is offset by their inability to interfere.[28] Tacitus exploits this distinct position of the reader to the maximum in *Annals* 1–2. Consider, for example, how a sense of impending doom is generated by the description of Germanicus' triumph in 17 CE, as the celebratory tone is undercut by the spectators' anxious reflection that the good fortunes of his father Drusus and the young Marcellus—both equally popular among the people—had come to premature ends: "short-lived and ill-fated," they observe, "are the darlings of the Roman people" (*breves et infaustos populi Romani amores*, 2.41.3).[29] Where the characters experience a mixture of fear and hope, the reader—knowing full well where things are headed—feels helpless as the extinction of Germanicus and the hopes placed on him draw nearer.

Not only is the reader repeatedly reminded of Germanicus' pitiful end, but Tacitus consistently highlights moments when the young prince could have acted differently and thus changed the course of his story, perhaps even Roman history. For while Germanicus is energetic to the point of recklessness as a general in Germany, he is frustratingly passive when faced with the increasingly paranoid Tiberius and the aggressive insubordination of Piso.[30] In *Annals* 1, as we have seen, he rejects the offer made by the mutinous legions in Germania to put him on the throne. In *Annals* 2 the road not taken by Germanicus becomes a veritable leitmotif, not least in the account of his Eastern travels.[31] When he visits Actium to pay his respects to his ancestors, Tacitus reminds us about his civil war ancestry (2.53.2),[32] and when he enters the strategically important province of Egypt without permission (but also without ill intent), a jittery Tiberius rebukes him (2.59–61).[33]

---

[26] On this passage, see also Devillers at Chapter 11 in this volume.

[27] Ash (2006b), 89: "Entering Tacitus' world is not straightforwardly pleasurable, but it does have a certain compulsion and fascination to it, as the audience becomes steeped in the guilty pleasures of watching a disaster narrative unfold."

[28] Cf. Kelly (2010), 233: "Yet this hope [that Germanicus would restore *libertas*] is increasingly undercut by the fact of which every Roman reader would have been perfectly aware: Germanicus' impending extinction."

[29] Cf. O'Gorman (2000), 56–7: "the overwhelming sense of Germanicus' mortality…turns the triumph into a funeral procession."

[30] On the contrast between Germanicus' vigorous activity during the Germanic campaign and his passivity and dependence on others during the mutiny, see Pigoń (2008). On Tiberius' paranoia about potential rivals, see Kraus (2009), 104–5. On Agricola as another Tacitean character who declines to challenge the emperor (and dies a suspicious death), see Haynes (2004), 41; see also Audano, Chapter 1 in this volume.

[31] On the incongruities between Tacitus' representation of Germanicus' Eastern travels and the material evidence, see Damon and Palazzolo (2019), 203; cf. Low (2016a).

[32] On Germanicus' stopover at Actium, see O'Gorman (2000), 62–9.

[33] Kraus (2009), 112; cf. Pelling (1993), 71–2; Kelly (2010). The historical authenticity of the hopes placed in Germanicus is hinted at in one of the Oxyrhyncus papyri (*P. Oxy* 2435), whose record of a speech delivered in Alexandria notes the crowd's emotional interruptions. On the papyrus, see Sherk (1988), 60.

Sandwiched between these two passages, Germanicus is presented with several chances to confront Cn. Piso, at whose hands he will allegedly be murdered.[34] Shortly after learning about his "early," or perhaps "timely," death—the meaning of *maturum* (2.54.4) is notoriously ambiguous[35]—from the Oracle at Colophon, he saves his future assassin from shipwreck (2.55.3). He then thrice refuses to deal with Piso despite his blatantly threatening transgressions: stirring up soldiers and provincials (2.55.4–6), refusing to obey orders (2.57.1–3), and making insults during a dinner party (2.57.4). In short, the characterization of Germanicus reaffirms both his potential danger and his unswerving loyalty to Tiberius, his opportunities to change the course of his story as well as his consistent refusal to do so.

By envisaging Germanicus as a lost opportunity to break the downward trajectory of Rome and forcing the reader to witness the unrealized futures imagined by his contemporaries, the narrative harnesses the emotional potential inherent in the knowledge disparity between characters and reader to devastating effect. Since only the reader knows from the start that Germanicus and the hopes placed in him will die prematurely, only the reader can appreciate the significance of his repeated refusal to challenge Tiberius. While the experiences of characters and readers converge briefly in the aftermath of Germanicus' death, Tacitus restores the knowledge disparity by introducing a new hope already during his funeral in Rome: "Turning to heaven and the gods, they prayed that her [Agrippina's] progeny would remain untouched and that they would outlive those who were hostile toward them" (*versique ad caelum ac deos integram illi subolem ac superstitem iniquorum precarentur*, 3.4.2). This prayer will admittedly be partially granted, but the reader's knowledge of the past immediately serves to re-establish the experiential dissonance between characters and reader. Where the characters pray for a better future, the reader is already dreading the pitiful end of Agrippina (cf. 6.25, Suet. *Tib.* 53) and the gradual extinction of her line—Nero Julius Caesar (d. 30/31 CE), Drusus the Younger (d. 33 CE), Julia Drusilla (d. 38 CE), Caligula (d. 41/42 CE), Julia Livilla (d. 41/42 CE), and Agrippina the Younger (d. 59 CE), as well as the brutal reigns of her son Caligula and grandson Nero.[36] By continuously introducing and dashing the hopes of his characters in this way, Tacitus maintains a dissonance between the experiences of characters and readers, and confines the reader to a state of helplessness.

Although the contrast between ignorant characters and omniscient audience in historiography mirrors that of other kinds of ancient literature where the finale is known in advance by the audience (most notably epic and tragedy), the position of Tacitus' contemporary readers as inheritors of the textual world of the *Annals* adds further emotional complexity, facilitating the stimulation of regret. For contrary to the comfort of distance enjoyed by spectators of tragedies (at least those plots that deal in myth), whose helplessness as witnesses to a tragedy is mitigated by their knowledge that the events portrayed happened a long time ago, almost in a different world, Tacitus' contemporaries have a personal stake in the outcome of the narrative.[37] Since they must live with the consequences

[34] Cf. Sailor (2019), 104. On the ambiguity of Piso's character as both enemy of Germanicus and champion of freedom, see Williams (1989), 146; Pelling (1993), 83–4; Low (2013), 97. On the conflict between Germanicus and Piso in *Annals* 2, see also Andrade (2012), 459–69.

[35] Shannon-Henderson (2019), 104.

[36] On the sense of foreboding generated by Tacitus' focus on Agrippina's fecundity and children after Germanicus' death, see O'Gorman (2000), 74–7.

[37] Cf. Damtoft Poulsen (2020). On Germanicus' ignorance and lack of self-awareness as reminiscent of tragic heroes, see Santoro L'Hoir (2006), 92–7; cf. Manolaraki and Augoustakis (2012).

of the decisions made by the characters, they are eminently well-positioned to feel regret. "If only Germanicus had acted!" might have been a typical reaction to *Annals* 2 from Tacitus' contemporary readers.

That said, Germanicus' contradictory character and the ambiguity of the hopes placed on him mean that this counterfactual past remains ambiguous: Would his "citizenlike disposition" and "remarkable affability" (*civile ingenium, mira comitas*, 1.33.2) have facilitated a restoration of the Republic, or would his impetuosity (cf. his amateurish handling of the mutiny in Germany at 1.31–51), disregard for proper boundaries (cf. his spontaneous trip to Egypt at 2.59), love of the East (cf. his grand tour at 2.53–.61, including the donning of Greek attire at 2.59.1), and flair for the theatrical (cf. his attempted suicides at 1.35.4 and 2.24.2) have turned him into an emperor in the mold of his grandson Nero?[38] The parallel with Arminius might be illuminating, as the dichotomy between Arminius the liberator and Arminius the would-be king suggests that Germanicus too incorporates both possibilities.[39] Given that the Principate changed (or uncovered hidden traits of) those who held supreme power (Tiberius, 6.51.3; Nero, 14.52.1; Galba, *H.* 1.49.4; Vespasian, *H.* 1.50.4), it seems that a final verdict on Germanicus as would-be liberator/emperor must remain elusive.[40] In *Annals* 2, that is, hope is kindled and put out without its potential being made clear—leaving readers to contemplate what might have been and to rue an unrealized opportunity to reassert freedom in Tiberian Rome.

Further Reading

While examples of deceit and deception are ubiquitous in the Tacitean corpus, their predominance in *Histories* 3, which relates a breakdown of military *fides*, is well analyzed by Bartera (2019.) On Tacitus' employment of the annalistic structure, Ginsburg (1981) remains essential. The interpretive fruitfulness of reading non-Roman narratives contextually, that is, side-by-side with the main Roman narrative, is incisively demonstrated by Sailor (2019), which takes its cue from Arminius' meeting with his brother Flavus at the Weser (2.9–10). On the character of Germanicus, on whom so much has been written (see footnote 1 above), Pelling (1993) is still the place to start and continues to drive scholarship, although his idea of the young prince as a blast from the past ("brilliant, yes, but brilliantly anachronistic", p. 78) is being increasingly challenged by studies that focus on his relationship with the future: O'Gorman (2000) explores the *spes Germanici*, Williams (2009b) points out that Germanicus is represented from the perspective of the various, unrealized futures that he embodies, and Daly (2020) notes that he may be read as a template for how to avoid civil war. For the Tiberian hexad in its entirety, Williams (1989) and Kraus (2009) are excellent and accessible.

Aske Damtoft Poulsen, Annals *2* In: *The Oxford Critical Guide to Tacitus*. Edited by: Salvador Bartera and Kelly E. Shannon-Henderson, Oxford University Press. © Oxford University Press 2025. DOI: 10.1093/9780191915086.003.0011

[38] For reflections on what Germanicus might have been like as emperor, see Ross (1973); Williams (1989), 141–4; Pelling (1993), 64–7; Kelly (2010), 231–7; Andrade (2012); Low (2013), 25–6, 71–2, 92–127. On Tacitus' Germanicus as a reminder that civil war is not inevitable, see Daly (2020).

[39] For a more detailed analysis of the parallel between Germanicus and Arminius and its interpretive implications, see Damtoft Poulsen (2018), 81–90; (2020). On the freedom/tyranny parallel between Rome and Germany, see also Walker (1952), 225–9; Williams (1989), 143–4; Low (2013), 68–75. On counterfactual thinking and alternative pasts in ancient historiography, see Suerbaum (1997); Morello (2002); O'Gorman (2006); Pagán (2006b); Grethlein (2013); Pelling (2013); Tordoff (2014); Damtoft Poulsen (forthcoming).

[40] Cf. Williams (2009b), 118–19, 129–30. On 6.51.3, see Shannon-Henderson, Chapter 13 in this volume. For a similar argument about Tacitus' Titus, see Bartera (forthcoming b).

11

Annals 3

Olivier Devillers

Book 3 of the *Annals* is not considered to be the most emblematic of Tacitus. It is, however, the most "senatorial," in terms of the number and variety of matters addressed that concern the Senate. Reflection on this assembly is indeed a significant element of the book (see section below on The Senate), but this aspect cannot be dissociated from the image of the emperor Tiberius (see section below on Tiberius). These two features are themselves determined by the historian's use of documents (see section below on Sources) as well as by his recourse to various compositional devices (see section on Composition). The result is a complex narrative that only makes sense insofar as it can also be read as an echo of the historian's own experience of the Principate (see section on Self-representation).

Composition

Book 3 covers the years 20, 21, and 22 CE. A first section (3.1–19), in continuity with Book 2, describes the arrival of the ashes of Germanicus (dead in October 19 CE) and the trial of Cn. Piso. Thereafter, no single event detains Tacitus for long until the death of Drusus, son of Tiberius, in 23, with which he begins Book 4 and the second half of the Tiberian hexad. The end of the year 20 as well as the years 21 and 22 are then presented as a succession of events treated more or less briefly, and the only markers which structure the narrative are the mentions of the consuls at the opening of each new year. The traditional ordering of material—*res internae/externae/internae*—is basically respected, most clearly for the year 21, with the lengthy evocation of the revolt of Florus and Sacrovir (see section on External affairs below).

Obituaries

Obituaries, a traditional rubric of annalistic history, have been identified as a structuring item in Book 3.[1] The first such passage concerns Vipsania, whose death provides an opportunity to recall, through the fate of Agrippa's children, the vicissitudes of the imperial *domus* (3.19.3). As for the other obituaries, some evoke men whose careers are characterized by a limited number of interactions with the imperial family, such as L. Volusius (3.30) and Asinius Saloninus (3.75.1). Others concern personalities whose prominence is due to their closeness to the rulers; undoubtedly that leads them to the top, but their

---

[1] Gingras (1992).

power is unstable, and they hardly enjoy popularity. Examples of this type include Sallustius Crispus (3.30), Sulpicius Quirinius (3.48), and Ateius Capito (3.75.2).

Ateius in particular had his accession to the consulship (in 5 CE) accelerated by Augustus. Tacitus somewhat artificially parallels his career with that of another jurist, Labeo, who had died a few years earlier; while Labeo was an example of *incorrupta libertas* ("uncompromising independence"), Capito was notable for his "obedience to the rulers" (*obsequium dominantibus*) and seems to have lacked *libertas*; he had admittedly opposed Tiberius in a previous trial for *maiestas*, but in this Tacitus sees only a pretense of freedom (3.70.1: *quasi per libertatem*, "as a show of independence").

All these obituaries show the appearance, alongside traditional careers, of new types of successful careers based on service to the emperor. Thus a new era seems to be emerging. In this same perspective, Book 3 ends with the mention—echoing the funeral of Germanicus at the beginning of the book—of the funeral of Junia Tertulla (3.76). She was sister of Brutus, wife of C. Cassius and niece of Cato, and her death is significantly dated relative to the battle of Philippi, which Tacitus considers a key moment in the disappearance of the Republic.[2] With Junia, a last vestige of the Republican era dies. The tyranny whose development is chronicled in books 4–6 can begin.

External affairs

The revolt of Florus and Sacrovir (3.40–7) is the external affair to which Tacitus pays the most attention. In the account he provides, the number of events reported seems too large for an episode which would have occurred within just a few months; the historian condensed into his account of the year 21 CE events which would have occurred over a longer period beginning in 20 CE, and possibly even including some from the end of 19 CE. In any case, Tacitus does not linger on the chronology, nor on the details of the military operations, but focuses on a few themes: the motives of the Gauls, the reactions in Rome, and the attitude of Tiberius. The speech that Tacitus makes the Gauls deliver highlights the theme of *libertas* (3.40.3: *resumendae libertati tempus*, "a chance to regain freedom"). This could also refer to the situation in Rome, especially since in evoking the reactions in the city, Tacitus makes the citizens mention their "miserable peace" (3.44.3: *miseram pacem*) as well as *maiestas*. Tiberius, for his part, appears mysterious and inscrutable,[3] as befits his usual dissimulation. Through these traits—some of which are found, for example, in the later account of Boudicca's revolt under Nero (see Whitton, Chapter 16 in this volume, on Book 14)—Tacitus shows a way of dealing with external affairs by echoing internal ones, which is a frequent feature of his writings.

Sources

The dominant view since Ronald Syme is that of a well-documented Tacitus, carefully selecting his sources and reelaborating them in accordance with the imperatives of the

---

[2] Cf. 1.2.1: *Postquam Bruto et Cassio caesis nulla iam publica arma...* ("After the killing of Brutus and Cassius had left the republic disarmed...").

[3] e.g. in 3.44.4: *neque loco neque vultu mutato* ("without having moved or changed his countenance").

narrative.[4] But as far as the reign of Tiberius is concerned, at least until the death of Sejanus, the comparison with Cassius Dio suggests the existence of a common source which would have provided both authors with the framework of their narrative. From this framework—most likely Aufidius Bassus—each historian would have made choices to omit or minimize certain events, or to seek additional information from other sources that can be termed subsidiary.[5] In the case of Book 3, these subsidiary sources mainly concern the Senate. Some of them may be part of the so-called Julio-Claudian historiography; for example, for the trial of Aemilia Lepida (3.22–3), Tacitus would have found details in Servilius Nonianus, a historian and senator who was particularly interested in the fate of members of the senatorial class. However, other documents would also have been used, namely the *senatus consulta* and the *acta senatus*, which provided information on the activity of the Senate.[6]

In this respect, Book 3 is noteworthy for the comparison that can be made between the Tacitean account of the trial of Piso and a document of this type, the *senatus consultum de Cn. Pisone patre* (*SCPP*, "Decree of the Senate concerning Cn. Piso the father"). This long inscription (176 lines), discovered at the end of the 1980s near Seville, exposes the outcome of the trial. It offers a rare opportunity to examine Tacitus' account in comparison with a contemporary documentary source.[7]

The *SCPP* is dated to December 10, 20 CE; in the *Annals*, the trial's mention at the beginning of year 20 is immediately followed by the ovation of Drusus (3.19.3), which is dated to May 28 by the *Fasti Ostienses* (a calendar of Roman magistrates and significant events from 49 BCE to 175 CE found at Ostia). There are two ways to explain the delay between the trial and the *SCPP*. Either the trial took place in November–December, but Tacitus placed it earlier in his narrative to achieve a specific effect; or the trial took place in May, and the time spent on writing the *SCPP* indicates the care with which it was prepared. In any case, the *SCPP* reveals to what extent literary elaboration and self-representation, whether imperial or senatorial, played a part in this type of document.[8] This could not but arouse the skepticism of a politician as astute as Tacitus. His approach was therefore not to construct his narrative from the *SCPP* alone, but to combine it with other sources and reconsider it from his own interpretation of the events. In this way, Tacitus integrates the *SCPP* into his global vision of the trial, and even if he diverges from it, he cannot be accused of having deliberately or mischievously distorted the facts; on the contrary, he may have considered that he was restoring a truth that the document did not allow to be perceived.[9]

The same critical approach is applied to other parts of the trial. Concerning Piso's last message, which Tiberius reads aloud (3.16.3–4),[10] Tacitus reports not only what was contained in it but also what was not contained in it, namely that Piso said nothing about Plancina (3.16.4). Further on, the initial omission of Claudius from a motion, also possibly

[4] Syme (1958a), 271–303; Devillers (2003).
[5] For example, Drusus' illness during the year 21 is reported only incidentally; Bellemore (2003), 280–1. See further Devillers (2020).
[6] This view, supported by Syme and largely adopted, has however been tempered by other researchers; e.g. Momigliano (1961); Townend (1961); Levick (1976), 222.
[7] Damon (1999).   [8] So Damon (1999), 147: "It is no less carefully crafted than Tacitus' own narrative."
[9] A parallel is offered by Tacitus' use of the famous speech of Claudius on the admission to the Senate of the notables of Gaul (11.23–5; see Gillespie, Chapter 14 in this volume).
[10] Such a document could also have been found in the *acta senatus*.

known from the *acta senatus*, leads to an authorial comment on destiny (3.18.3–4). As a further example, the text of Tiberius' speech at the beginning of Piso's trial (3.12) was probably known to Tacitus, but the historian re-elaborated it in order to integrate it into his *Annals*: in particular, there are lexical similarities with the last words of Germanicus on his deathbed,[11] and the way Tiberius criticizes the display of Germanicus' corpse recalls his criticism of Germanicus' treatment of the remains of Varus' legions.[12]

The *acta senatus* were probably Tacitus' source for other trials and debates in the Senate. In these cases, too, there is evidence of a responsive approach to these documents. Thus, although Tacitus probably reflects the words of Tiberius after the execution of Clutorius Priscus (3.51.1), the comment with which he accompanies these words, *solitis sibi ambagibus* ("with his usual ambiguity"), is of his own making. As another example, when Caecina's speech on the wives of provincial governors mentions women's interference in military affairs (3.33.3), Tacitus' words refer to Plancina (echoing 2.55.6), but at the same time it seems possible that Caecina had in mind Agrippina the Elder, who had intervened at the time when the legions he led were coming back from Germany (echoing 1.69.4).

As for other documentary sources, Tacitus evokes in 3.3.2 an investigation that he made using not only the *acta diurna* but also the works of other historians;[13] this investigation, on the absence of Antonia, the mother of Germanicus, at the funeral of her son (3.3.2), again leads Tacitus to make an interpretation in his own voice; it is moreover echoed, at the end of the book, when another absence is signaled, that of the *imagines* of Cassius and Brutus at the funeral of Junia (3.76.2). This is indicative of the fact that, in *Annals* 3, reflection on oblivion and memory is an underlying theme.

Finally, it does not seem that Tacitus and Cassius Dio, who are both often referred to as senatorial historians and use some of the same sources, were interested in the Senate in a similar way. Dio's approach is rather an institutional one; the Senate as a whole has his attention, and the relationship with this assembly is a significant criterion in his assessment of each reign. Tacitus, who reinterprets and transforms the *exempla* tradition,[14] is more attentive to senators as individuals. This more individualized approach may be the reason why many of the senators' speeches that appear in the *Annals* do not appear in Dio. For example, in his account of the trial of Clutorius Priscus (3.49–50), Tacitus introduces a speech that allows him to showcase Lepidus, in his view an exemplary character.[15]

Tiberius

The first hexad of the *Annals* has received considerable attention for how Tacitus uses various techniques of innuendo in elaborating the figure of Tiberius. These techniques are used throughout Book 3,[16] particularly in the first section, up to the end of Piso's trial. Speeches, such as the one in which Tacitus evokes the indignation of the Romans at the impunity enjoyed by Plancina (3.17.1–2), are one of these techniques. Another category,

---

[11] 3.12.4 and 2.71.1: *interceptus*; 3.12.6 and 2.71.2: *propinquus sanguis*; 3.12.7, *finguntur*, and 2.71.4, *fingentibus*.
[12] 3.12.4: *contrectandum vulgi oculis* ("[why had a corpse] to be exposed to the eyes of the crowd"); cf. 1.62.2: *adtrectare feralia* ("handle dead remains"). See Shannon-Henderson (2019), 131.
[13] On the *acta diurnal*, see *BNP* 1.115–17 (C. Gizewski).   [14] See Turpin (2008).
[15] See Strunk (2010) and (2017).   [16] Cf. Carpentieri (2007).

similar to speeches, is the opinions and feelings attributed to various characters, either individually or in groups. Several of these "attributions of thoughts" convey an insinuation against the emperor: for example, the conviction of the Romans that the death of Germanicus was welcome to Tiberius (3.2.3), his irritation because of the popularity of Agrippina (3.4.2), the impression on Piso that the emperor's impassivity produced (3.15.1), and Tiberius' shame at having to absolve Plancina (3.18.1). As another example, at the time of Germanicus' funeral, the prevailing feeling was that in death he had not received the honors considered typical for anyone of his rank (3.5.1); similarly, at the end of Piso's trial, the feeling is expressed that Germanicus had not received the justice due to every man (3.17.1). The recurrence of this trait unifies the two parts (return of the ashes and trial) which form the first section of the book. Moreover, the popular reactions to the return of Germanicus' ashes (3.1–2) recall the soldiers' pity when Agrippina left their camp (1.40–1) and contrast with the ambiguous attitude that is attributed to Tiberius and Livia at the time. The section is also characterized by many rumors, for example about the poisoner Martina (3.7) or about Piso's attitude on his return to Rome (3.9.1). These rumors not only tell an alternative "truth" compared to the official versions; they also show that the Romans were not satisfied with the versions produced by the emperor and his entourage.[17]

In the following parts of the book, Tacitus reports a number of trials (more than any other historian of this period) which also serve to reveal Tiberius' behavior. Concealment is a major theme. The trial of Lepida (3.22–3) at the end of the year 20 shows the emperor as unreadable.[18] In 3.72, the restoration of the theater of Pompey by Tiberius (3.72.2) is set alongside Lepidus' request to restore the Basilica of Paulus (3.72.1). This successive appearance of Lepidus and of the theater of Pompey recalls the trial of Lepida, a relative of Lepidus who had invoked the pity of the crowd precisely at the theater of Pompey (3.23.1). In the very theater where Lepida had tried to resist her condemnation, the emperor was placing a statue of his minister Sejanus.[19]

For the year 21, the trial of Considius Aequus and Caelius Cursor (3.37) gives Tacitus the opportunity to underline, by words attributed to the people, Tiberius' "secrecies" (*secreta*). In the same year, the trial of Priscus sees Tiberius again reacting to the sentence pronounced by the Senate "with his usual ambiguities" (3.51.1: *solitis sibi ambagibus*). This trial also includes an allusion to that of Libo Drusus (2.50.2), the only other one before that time to have resulted in a conviction under the charge of *maiestas* and during which Tiberius had already acted in a deceitful way.

In the year 22, while C. Silanus is hardly able to defend himself, Tiberius cannot help putting him under pressure (3.67.2). At the end of this trial, although Tiberius softens the punishment of the accused, Tacitus adds that the emperor only manages to be moderate when he is not motivated by personal enmity (3.70.5). The historian thus reaffirms one of the usual vices of the tyrant: his anger (*ira*).[20]

The character of Tiberius is also revealed through his relationship with his relatives. In his account of the trial of Piso, Tacitus uses insinuation to show Tiberius' hostility towards

---

[17]   On rumors in Tacitus, see Shatzman (1974); Gibson (1998); Autin (2019).

[18]   3.22.2: *Haud facile quis dispexerit illa in cognitione mentem principis; adeo vertit ac miscuit irae et clementiae signa* ("One would hardly have distinguished, in this trial, the mood of the emperor, so much did he alternate and mix the signs of anger and clemency").

[19]   Gowing (2009), 100.   [20]   On the vices of the tyrant, see e.g. Dunkle (1967).

Germanicus. Thereafter, Agrippina the Elder, the widow of Germanicus, catches the historian's attention. She is depicted in action only in the *Annals*, and Book 3 begins a process of "complexification" in her portrait which will intensify in Book 4.[21] No doubt she has the historian's sympathy for having been a victim of Tiberius, and Book 3 contains no critical or ambiguous discussion about her. It is nevertheless not hard to see that, as a woman of the Julio-Claudian dynasty, in the event that her husband had come to power she could have become an abusive empress, as Livia was before her and as her own daughter, Agrippina the Younger, will be after her.[22] The presence of these female figures in the *Annals* is a consequence of the consolidation of the dynasty. Such is the paradox of the portrait of Agrippina: It is a woman of the imperial house who embodies the sort of opposition to the emperor which one might have expected to have arisen among the senators.

In Book 3, more attention is paid to Drusus, the son of Tiberius, consul for the second time with the emperor in 21. After the departure of his father for Campania, he is in charge of affairs and appears to be well received by the Romans (3.31.2). In 3.37.2, statements attributed to the people seem to credit him with a decision that in fact came from Tiberius; in this passage, Tacitus, who usually sees the bad side of the qualities of his characters, shows on the contrary that certain vices of Drusus could be given a positive spin; the historian moreover uses this opportunity for a comparison with the emperor, whose gloomy mood he mentions once again (3.37.2: *maestam vigilantiam et malas curas*, "gloomy vigilance and evil concerns"). This more positive portrait of Drusus would be justified narratively by the fact that his death at the beginning of Book 4 is linked to a deterioration of Tiberius' reign (see ten Berge, Chapter 12 in this volume).

Another significant actor is Livia. The relationship of Tiberius with his mother seems to have deteriorated. Because of her poor health, the emperor hastens his return to Rome, and in the view of some, as Tacitus states, one of the reasons for his haste is to conceal the dislike he had for her;[23] but if he had delayed, the same persons would not have failed to see in this a sign of neglect. As we can see, Tiberius' dissimulative nature continues to force those around him to make assumptions.

Last but not least, Augustus is omnipresent in Book 3. In particular, he is mentioned in all the affairs dealt with in the section relating to the end of the year 20 (3.20–30), where Tacitus expresses his intention to write about Augustus once the *Annals* are completed (3.24.3). Three main themes can be identified in the references to Augustus. First, Augustus is often associated with the formation and consolidation of his dynasty. Such mentions are found especially at the beginning of the book in relation to Agrippina,[24] but Lepida too reminds us that she had been destined to become Augustus' daughter-in-law (3.23.1). Unlike Germanicus and his descendants, Tiberius is not related to Augustus by blood; this can be a source of concern for the emperor. Second, Augustus can be invoked for the purposes of legitimization. Tiberius especially (and also, by extension, his son Drusus; cf. 3.34.6) resorts to Augustus to settle a debate, assume a position, or justify his own

---

[21] Adam (2015).   [22] Cf. McHugh (2012), 75–6.

[23] 3.64.1: *sincera adhuc inter matrem filiumque concordia sive occultis odiis* ("either there was still a sincere harmony between the mother and the son, or their antagonisms were concealed").

[24] 3.4.2: *solum Augusti sanguinem* ("the only blood of Augustus"); cf. 1.40.3: *se divo Augusto ortam* ("she had sprung from the divine Augustus"); 1.41.2: *Augusti avi memoria* ("memory of her grandfather Augustus"); 4.52.2: *imaginem veram* ("his true image"); 4.67.4: *effigiem divi Augusti* ("the statue of divine Augustus").

actions (e.g. 3.54.2, 3.56.3, 3.68.1, 3.71.2).[25] This use of Augustus as a political precedent distinguishes Tiberius from Agrippina the Elder, who only refers to Augustus in terms of dynastic legitimacy.[26] Finally, the assessment of Augustus' political achievements provides Tacitus with the material for a reflection on the regime. In Book 3, we note, for example, that Augustus is associated with a more coercive type of legislative activity (3.24.2, *maiestas*; 3.25.1, *lex Papia Poppaea*), wields the tribunician power (3.56.2), and gives support to the more obedient senators (3.75.1, Capito and Labeo). Tacitus' digression on the laws shows not only the pacifying action of the constitution Augustus established,[27] but also the shortcomings of these laws, even the oppressive abuses to which they could lead. This section on laws is supplemented for the year 22 by the debate on luxury at 3.52–5, which illustrates the same problem.[28]

The Senate

In Book 3, reference to tradition is no less pervasive than reference to Augustus: for example, in the comments of the people on Agrippina, described as the "sole example of antiquity" (3.4.2: *unicum antiquitatis specimen*); in Tiberius' plea for restrictions on the honors to Germanicus (3.6.3) or to Drusus, said to be "contrary to Roman tradition" (3.59.2: *contra patrium morem*); in Tacitus' account of the decimation of a cohort, "an act of antique memory" (3.21.1: *e vetere memoria facinore*); in the emphasis on the ancestors of Lepida (3.22.1, 3.23.1); in Tacitus' observation that the law of *maiestas* as applied by Augustus went beyond the "clemency of our ancestors" (3.24.2: *clementiam maiorum*); in the digression on the laws going back to the origins of the city (3.25–8); in the invocation of ancestral custom during a debate in the Senate in 21 (3.31.4: *memorabantur exempla maiorum*, "they noted the lessons of our ancestors"); in comments on the parsimony of Tiberius (3.52.1) or of Vespasian (3.55.4); in the emperor's speech on luxury (3.53.4: *priscum ad morem*, "to ancient custom"); in the debates on the *flamen* of Jupiter (3.58, 71.2–3) and the sanctuaries in Asia (3.60–3); at the time of the trial of C. Silanus (3.69.3: *sic a maioribus institutum*, "so it was established by our ancestors"); and with regard to the Vestal Torquata (3.69.6). Yet Rome, and especially the Senate, find themselves living under a relatively new regime. Certain remarks attributed to Lepidus[29] or to Tiberius[30] associating the emperors with tradition show a consciousness of this duality on the part of one senator and on the part of the emperor himself. This situation was a source of tensions that Tiberius may have tried to ease, as when he referred the trial of Piso to the Senate, which in a way made the assembly a guardian of imperial *maiestas*.[31] But if an attempt was made to establish the foundations of a mutually advantageous political collaboration,

---

[25] On Tacitus' depiction of Tiberius' use of the precedent of Augustus, see Cowan (2009).

[26] Gillespie (2020a).

[27] 3.28.2: *dedit iura quis pace et principe uteremur* ("he gave a constitution of such a nature as to provide us peace under an emperor").

[28] See also 3.69.3–4; Mastrorosa (2009), 157–9.

[29] 3.50.2: *principis moderatio maiorumque et vestra exempla* ("the moderation of the emperor and the precedents of your ancestors as well as yours").

[30] 3.54.2: *tot a maioribus repertae leges, tot quas divus Augustus tulit* ("so many laws devised by the ancestors, so many others passed by the divine Augustus").

[31] Cf. Suspène (2010), 863–5.

Tacitus certainly does not allow us to perceive it clearly. In the *Annals*, most senators do not act in a constructive way but out of ambition or fear, within a relationship whose inegalitarian character the historian does not ignore.[32] Thus, in the aftermath of the trial of Piso, several affairs show that *maiestas*—which from 21 CE onwards seems to intervene in every legal case[33]—becomes an obstacle to the free decision-making of the senators and generates a deleterious atmosphere in Rome. We can see it in particular in 3.36, when the senator Cestius complains that a woman condemned for fraud at his request can insult him without consequence by seeking the protection of statues of the emperor.

Two phenomena closely related to *maiestas* are emphasized: *delatio* and *adulatio*. *Delatio*, linked to the activity of the accusers, is said to be relentless: "For neither Tiberius nor the accusers got tired" (3.38.1: *Non enim Tiberius, non accusatores fatiscebant*). The trial of C. Silanus thus features various accusers from several social classes, providing Tacitus the opportunity to show, in the person of Bruttedius Niger, something of an archetype of these men (3.66.4). *Adulatio* develops particularly after the dignity of the emperor or his family has been saved from a perceived threat; the senators then compete to offer proposals aimed to prove their concern for the emperor. This adulation is not limited to trials, as can be seen, for example, at the time of the election of a governor in Africa (3.35.3), after the extinction of the revolt of Florus and Sacrovir (3.47.3–4), or when Drusus is given the tribunician power (3.57.1).

Adulatio, "flattery," according to Tacitus, became widespread in Rome in this period (3.65.2: *tempora illa adeo infecta et adulatione sordida fuere*, "so infected and soiled with adulation were those times "), and it becomes the object of a digression in which Tacitus reports these words attributed to Tiberius: "These men!—how ready they are for slavery!" (3.65.3 *O homines ad servitutem paratos!*). This statement also indicates that *adulatio* is a key element in the *libertas/servitus* theme that is prominent in the book. As a result, Book 3, by insisting so much on *delatio* and *adulatio*, in no way shows a Senate which is capable of reinventing itself under the Principate, but becomes the chronicle of a toxic relationship,[34] underlining the factors of tension and division, the risk of abuses and ruptures and the lack of freedom.[35]

In this context, an element common to various affairs dealt with in the year 21 is the difficulty the Senate has in acting and deciding by itself. For example, the affairs mentioned in 3.31 and 3.36 are settled by Drusus, and it is the same for the debate on the wives of governors (3.33–4); two knights are punished "at the behest of the emperor" (3.37.1: *auctore principe*); the Senate does not dare to go against the opinion of the *princeps* in the case of Caesius Cordus (3.38); and a public funeral is decreed to Sulpicius Quirinius at Tiberius' request (3.48). The same tendency to defer to the emperor can be noticed in Tacitus' account of the year 22 (3.52–76). For the question of luxury,[36] it is the desire to imitate the emperor and to please him, rather than the actual laws, which puts an end to sumptuary excesses: "After having been consulted, the senators had given all this affair

---

[32] For a different view, see O'Gorman (2020).

[33] Cf. 3.38.1: *addito maiestatis crimine, quod tum omnium accusationum complementum erat* ("after adding the charge of maiestas, which then complemented all the accusations").

[34] So Shannon-Henderson (2019), 133: "The toxic relationship between ruler and ruled in Imperial Rome."

[35] e.g. 3.51.2: *non senatui libertas ad paenitendum erat* ("The senate lacked freedom to change its decision"); 3.65.3: *illum* [= Tiberium], *qui libertatem publicam nollet* ("he who denied public freedom").

[36] 3.52.2: *consulti patres integrum id negotium ad principem distulerant* ("after having been consulted, the senators had given all this affair to the emperor").

to the emperor" (3.52.2: *consulti patres integrum id negotium ad principem distulerant*; cf. 3.55.4). In the trial of C. Silanus, whereas the accusers come up with Republican precedents, Tiberius settles the case with an Augustan precedent (3.68.1). The emperor also has a decisive part in the trial of L. Ennius (3.70.3). Moreover, the narrative of the year combines religious issues (on the *flamen*, on the right of asylum) and dynastic ones (tribunician power to Drusus, Livia's illness), in such a way as to reveal the growing impact of the imperial family in public affairs.[37] In the case of the absence of the *flamen* of Jupiter from Rome (3.59.1, 3.71.2–3), which involves continuity with Republican tradition, Tiberius again settles the issue by referring to Augustus (3.71.2); a Republican precedent is cited (3.71.3), but secondarily, and Tacitus, by using the passive *memorabatur* ("it was noted"), leaves it unclear whether Tiberius himself raised it. The debate in the Senate on the sanctuaries in the cities of Asia[38]—a debate marked by Republican tradition even as Tiberius is consolidating the Principate[39]—is left to the initiative of the senators but is characterized by many confusions, hesitations, and errors, which contrast with the rapidity with which Drusus reacts to the abusive use of the emperor's images (3.36.4). The connection between the two passages[40] suggests the extent to which issues related to the new regime overlap with more traditional ones. In the same sense, the book ends with the statement that Tiberius "did not prohibit" (*neque prohibuit*) the eulogy of Junia (3.76.2), which means that he had the power to do so.

Another significant theme of Book 3 concerns *clementia* and the sanctions pronounced at the ends of trials.[41] During the trial of Lepida, the emperor exempts his son Drusus from being the first to speak upon the verdict, which gives rise to various interpretations: Is Tiberius trying not to subject the senators to the influence of the initial opinion of the imperial family? Or is he deliberately leaving them the responsibility for the most severe sentence (3.22.4)? The question arises in an even more obvious way during the trial of Clutorius Priscus. Tacitus makes clear that, in a case assimilated to a trial of *maiestas*, the Senate does not have the freedom to exercise *clementia* (3.51.2: *non senatui libertas* [...] *erat*, "the senate lacked freedom..."), so that the ten-day delay established between the decrees of the Senate and their registration in the treasury is irrelevant as long as the emperor remains inflexible. *In* this way, the trial reveals a tendency of the emperor to reserve the exercise of *clementia* for himself, a tendency which has a counterpart in Book 14 with the trial of Antistius Sosianus (14.48–9; see Whitton, Chapter 16 in this volume). It does seem that this debate on *clementia* did indeed occur, as other sources (Velleius Paterculus) and documents (*SCPP*) suggest, and as can also be seen in the trial of C. Silanus (3.68–9). But it also appears that Tacitus organized Book 3, which precedes the turning point of the Tiberian principate, in such a way as to emphasize this matter.

In sum, even if the book multiplies echoes of the past, it is obvious that a new reality has been imposed. This is also reflected, for example, in the way the consuls of the year 21 are introduced, as if in a parenthesis, as a fact secondary to the death of Germanicus and

---

[37] Shannon-Henderson (2019), 140–60.   [38] On the episode, see also Poulle (2010).

[39] 3.60.1: *Sed Tiberius vim principatus sibi firmans, imaginem antiquitatis senatui praebebat* ("Tiberius, as he strengthened the power of the principate, was offering the senate a façade of tradition").

[40] 3.60.1: *licentia atque impunitas* ("license and impunity"); cf. 3.36.1: *licentia impune* ("license with impunity").

[41] See Cowan (2016).

the return of his ashes.[42] Against this background, the death of Junia at the end of the book appears as a symbolic event which prepares the coming of a more "imperial" era with the emergence of Sejanus.

Book 3 thus stands out as a book of transition, and it is in this sense that one of its paradoxes can be explained. Indeed, while Book 3 is part of a process of deterioration of the reign of Tiberius, examples drawn from its second part give the impression that this emperor had a certain moderation, in particular in the use of the laws—for example, as regards the repression of luxury (3.52–5) or the designation of the governors of provinces.[43] But, in fact, the idea is that "the worm is in the fruit." It is thus not surprising to see that the historian shows at the same time the worm (*adulatio, delatio*) and the fruit (the persistence of "a traditional façade" [3.60.1: *imaginem antiquitatis*]).

Self-representation

Tacitus opts for an annalistic mode of exposition, strongly structured and accompanied by traditional subject matter. The difficulties in following this pattern that he encounters as early as the first hexad, as well as the adaptations he is compelled to make to it,[44] cannot escape his readers. This illustrates how much the Principate no longer has anything to do with the Republic, despite the myth of the *res publica restituta* to which Tiberius was still referring.

Intertextuality in Tacitus is often similarly meaningful: in many instances the comparison between the Tacitean text and the reference text points to a historical change. For example, the trial of Clutorius, which places a party in favor of capital punishment in opposition to a minority in favor of a more lenient sentence (3.50–1), is reminiscent of the debate in Sallust on the fate of the Catilinarian conspirators (Sall. *Cat.* 51–2). The allusion is ironic and suggests a decline of the assembly, with the Senate of 21 CE making its decisions only to please the emperor, whereas the Senate of 63 BCE had acted vigorously for the sake of the Republic.[45] As another example, Tiberius, while discussing the honors to Germanicus, says, "Princes are mortal, the republic is eternal" (3.6.3: *Principes mortales, rem publicam aeternam esse*). A similar association between his own mortality and the immortality of the Republic is found in Scipio's speech in Livy 28.28.11. However, in the speech attributed to Tiberius by Tacitus, the emperor had just alluded to Caesar and Augustus as *divi* (3.6.2), which perhaps leads the reader to question how the notion of mortality can be applied to them. The discrepancy between the imperial context and the Republican allusion highlights the alterations made to the tradition by the Principate.[46]

Such allusions are intended to show how much the Principate penetrated and transformed Rome. This is also the case when Tacitus superimposes the imperial voice onto his own authorial discourse. At the end of the excursus on the laws, it is stated that the imitation of the ancients has been replaced by the imitation of the emperor, but with the added

[42] 3.2.3: *consules M. Valerius et M. Aurelius (iam enim magistratum occeperant) et senatus ac magna pars populi viam complevere* ("The consuls M. Valerius and M. Aurelius—for they had already commenced their magistracy—as well as the senate and most of the people filled the roads"). See Gingras (1992), 243.

[43] See especially 3.69.4: *nec utendum imperio ubi legibus agi possit* ("There is no need to resort to power when you can use laws").

[44] Ginsburg (1981).   [45] Ginsburg (1986), esp. 528–30.   [46] Shannon-Henderson (2019), 127.

observation that the imperial times themselves have produced their own *exempla* (3.55.5: *nostra quoque aetas multa laudis et artium imitanda posteris tulit*, "Our age too has produced many virtues and talents worthy of imitation by prosperity"), according to a formulation which might be reminiscent of the *Res Gestae*.[47]

Tacitus also alludes implicitly to his own works to prepare for the deterioration of Tiberius' reign, which will be a major feature of the narrative from Book 4 onwards. Such is the case for the mentions of Sejanus (3.16.1, 3.66.3, 3.72.4). Likewise, the remark on the unforeseeability of *fortuna* in 3.18.4 is perhaps echoed by the opening of Book 4.[48] Furthermore, the mention of a statue representing Sejanus in the theater of Pompey (3.72.3) announces the way in which this man will occupy Rome after the emperor retires to Capri.[49] Sallustius Crispus (3.30) can also be seen as a prefiguration of the powerful Sejanus. Other hints suggest the fateful end of the house of Germanicus (cf. Shannon-Henderson, Chapter 13 in this volume): the fears for the family of Germanicus (3.17.2), the fact that Vipsania would be the only child of Agrippa who would not suffer a violent death (3.19.3). In a more allusive way, the reference to the absence of the *imagines* of Cassius and Brutus at the funeral of Junia (3.76.2) could be thought to prefigure the episode in Book 4 when Cremutius Cordus is accused of having praised the two men in his annals (4.34–5; cf. Chapter 12 on Book 4 in this volume). There is finally an explicit reference to the accession to power of Claudius in 3.18.4.

Returning to the question of Tacitus' historical method, the trial of Piso exemplifies an actual "crisis of information," insofar as the ability to reconstruct the past is constantly jeopardized by rumors and suspicions. It is with precisely this observation that Tacitus concludes his account of the case.[50] This shows the difficult task of the historian, who has to describe a time when the ruling power has sole control of the channels of communication. By displaying the problems he faces as a historian of the Principate, Tacitus reveals the autocratic nature of the regime. The same can be said of the passages where he attributes a feeling, a motivation or a reaction to someone (see section on Tiberius above); their frequency suggests that under the Principate, it was not safe to express one's feelings openly, that opinions were kept secret, and that the role of the historian was to recreate them.

It is also in Book 3, in a context of *adulatio*, that Tacitus exposes his project of providing an exemplary history: "The main function of the annals, in my opinion, is that virtues are not ignored and that the fear of infamy and posterity come to evil words and deeds" (3.65.1: *praecipuum munus annalium reor ne virtutes sileantur utque pravis dictis factisque*

---

[47] Cf. *Res Gestae* 8: *exempla imitanda posteris tradidi* ("I handed precedents worthy of imitation by posterity").

[48] 4.1.1: *repente turbare fortuna coepit* ("suddenly fortune began to disturb everything"). See Shannon-Henderson (2019): 137–40.

[49] See also 3.31.2: *longam et continuam absentiam paulatim meditans* ("he gradually began to think about leaving for a long time and with no interruption").

[50] 3.19.2: *Is finis fuit ulciscenda Germanici morte, non modo apud illos homines qui tum agebant, etiam secutis temporibus vario rumore iactata. Adeo maxima quaeque ambigua sunt, dum alii quoquo modo audita pro compertis habent, alii vera in contrarium vertunt, et gliscit utrumque posteritate* ("This was the end of the vengeance for the death of Germanicus. It has been variously commented on not only by contemporaries but also in the following times. So many ambiguities are present in the greatest events, while some consider what they have heard in any way to be certain, others convert truth in its opposite and both attitudes grow stronger among posterity").

ex posteritate et infamia metus sit).[51] The words *ne* [...] *sileantur*[52] put the historian, who does not want to conceal, in opposition to the dissimulator Tiberius. There is moreover some similarity between this statement in Tacitus' own voice and the last words he attributes to Germanicus.[53] This similarity links the historian with the senators who were friends of Germanicus, and thus expresses something of an association between the historian and the senator, which seems to have driven Tacitus' historical approach.

Conclusion: *Libertas* as a Common Denominator

Book 3 is illustrative of the ambiguities of the regime, which are expressed first through Tiberius' ambiguity, but also through the senators' position between the appearance of freedom and the reality of monarchy, and even through the position of the historian himself, facing sources whose credibility is corrupted by the imperial context. There are also the larger ambiguities of the three years of transition between the death of Germanicus, who would have represented in the view of some a last hope of freedom,[54] and the ineluctable deterioration of the reign, if not of the regime, which the first words of Book 4 announce.

So Book 3 is definitely the book of *libertas*, but it is most of all the book of *libertas* in danger: for the emperor, for the Senate, for Tacitus himself, on both the political and the historiographical level. The way the historian uses the figure of Augustus as a tool to reveal certain salient features of the regime is representative of the need he felt as an historian both to contextualize the emergence of this regime and to reflect on how a new form of *libertas* might actually exist under it—the type of *libertas* that Tacitus chose for himself, an individual *libertas* which, as an ultimate paradox, only exists because the collective *libertas* of the senatorial class has disappeared.[55]

Further Reading

The best commentary in English on Book 3 is by Woodman and Martin (1996). As for Tacitus' description of Tiberius and the processes at work in the first hexad, a seminal work is Walker (1952). In addition to the articles relating to one episode or one character in particular (cf. works cited), some contributions offer global or very complete readings of Book 3: Gingras (1992), Bellemore (2003), or the chapter on Book 3 in Shannon-Henderson (2019), 121–66.

As for the *SCPP*, there are two complementary and similar editions of the inscription, the Spanish one favoring the archaeological context (Caballos, Eck, and Fernández [1996]), the German one favoring the commentary (Eck, Caballos, and Fernández [1996]). For an edition with English translation, Potter and Damon (1999); with a commentary, Cooley (2023).

Olivier Devillers, Annals 3 In: *The Oxford Critical Guide to Tacitus*. Edited by: Salvador Bartera and Kelly E. Shannon-Henderson, Oxford University Press. © Oxford University Press 2025. DOI: 10.1093/9780191915086.003.0012

[51] On this passage, see Luce (1991); Woodman (1995b); Turpin (2008).

[52] A similar expression also appears in the account of trial of Piso, 3.16.1: *neque tamen occulere debui* ("yet I should not have concealed").

[53] 2.71.3: *non hoc praecipuum amicorum munus est, prosequi defunctum ignavo questu, sed quae voluerit meminisse* ("the main duty of friends is not to escort a corpse with vain complaints, but to remember his wishes").

[54] See Damtoft Poulsen, Chapter 10 in this volume.

[55] On *libertas*, see Wirszubski (1950); Cogitore (2011). On Tacitus and *libertas*, see Liebeschuetz (1966); Ducos (1977); Leake (1987); Morford (1991).

12

Annals 4

Bram ten Berge

This chapter surveys the book that Sir Ronald Syme once called "the best that Tacitus ever wrote."[1] Covering 23–8 CE, the third of the five periods into which Tacitus divided Tiberius' life (*Ann.* 6.51), it chronicles the decisive turning point in that emperor's reign: the murder of his son Drusus in 23 by his wicked minister and later virtual co-emperor Sejanus and, under the latter's influence, his withdrawal to Capri in 27. The book also contains important chapters about Tacitus' historical methods and memorable descriptions of treason trials and of military campaigns in northern Africa, Thrace, and Germany. Readers of Book 4 are spoiled with a recent Cambridge commentary by Woodman (2018, complementing Martin and Woodman (1989)), which explicates, in characteristic fashion, Tacitus' stylistic virtuosity and his engagement with his literary predecessors. My focus here is on how Tacitus engages with his *own* texts, especially (though not exclusively) with selected episodes in the *Agricola* and with the preface to the *Histories*, which help to elucidate the nature and development of Tiberius' reign and of the Principate as an institution. Tacitus used his earlier texts as productive sources, and it is my principal aim to demonstrate the necessity of reading his different texts in conjunction to properly understand his aims and historical vision.[2]

There is a longstanding tendency in Tacitean studies to read Tacitus' texts in isolation—there is no standard edition containing all five texts—and to focus chiefly on his engagement with the literary tradition. This (natural) approach fails to recognize Tacitus' prolific use of his own oeuvre[3] and encourages misguided assumptions about the immaturity of his earlier texts and the ostensible disjunction between the latter and the later historical narratives. Reading Tacitus' texts in conjunction shows not only that the historian continued to explore many of the themes and concerns that had occupied him in the immediate post-Domitianic period, but also that his outlook on the imperial system of government and Rome's empire, while gradually becoming more intricate, largely remained consistent throughout.[4] Tacitus' experience under Domitian shaped his historical outlook, and the figures of Agricola and Domitian—whose portraits encapsulate a set of senatorial/imperial virtues and vices against which Tacitus continued to measure other people's character and conduct—would remain some of his chief intertextual targets. As we shall see, unpacking the intertextual interactions with these programmatic figures, and with other salient episodes in Tacitus' earlier works, is essential for properly understanding the account of Tiberius' reign and the Principate, for whose development the years 23–8 constituted a critical juncture.

---

[1] Syme (1984), 1031.

[2] Tacitus variously clarifies that he composed his oeuvre as an integrated whole and that we should read each of his works alongside its predecessors: ten Berge (2023).

[3] "The author T. engages with most is himself": Goodyear (1981), 90.

[4] See ten Berge (2023), 7–8 with nn. 26–7, for a summary of scholarship on this issue.

Preface: 4.1–3

Book 4 opens, pointedly, with a second preface that signals the turning point in Tiberius' reign. Coming at the midpoint of the Tiberian hexad, it engages productively with Sallust and Velleius and with Tacitus' own oeuvre. The historian writes that the first nine years of Tiberius' reign were peaceful and prosperous—in part the result of the emperor's adherence to Augustan precedent (*Agr.* 13.2; *Ann.* 1.54.2, 1.77.3, 3.68, 4.37.3, 6.32.1)—but that Fortune now intervened. Under the growing influence of Sejanus—whose power was virtually unchecked after his murder of Drusus, and whose position as Tiberius' "partner in labor" (*socius laborum*, 4.2.3) and "assistant in power" (*adiutor imperii*, 4.7.1) resembles the position (*socius imperii*, *H.* 2.77.1, 2.83.1) of another self-serving and manipulative "helper" figure, Vespasian's associate Mucianus in the *Histories*—the reign takes a turn for the worse: Tiberius begins to be savage or to abet other people's savagery (4.1.1: more below).

Next follows a portrait of Sejanus that stresses his extraordinary power as a mere knight (*eques*), his ability to gain the confidence of the otherwise careful and inscrutable Tiberius,[5] his ultimate aim (*dominatio* and *regnum*), and his methods of obtaining it (by stealthily eliminating Drusus and other members of the imperial household and by attempting to marry Drusus' wife Livi(ll)a).[6] Tacitus both describes Sejanus' destructive influence on Tiberius with a verb (*devincire*, "to bind" someone) used across the *Annals* to mark the vulnerability of emperors to their intimates (*devinxit*, 4.1.2; cf. 1.3.4, 11.28.2, 12.64.3, 13.46.2),[7] and emphasizes that it reflects "divine anger toward Rome" (*deum ira in rem Romanam*, 4.1.2).[8] Characteristically, Tacitus foreshadows what lies ahead: many will be destroyed when Sejanus is powerful, and equally many after he falls from grace.

That Tacitus modeled his Sejanus on Sallust's Catiline and Velleius' Sejanus is well known and elucidated by Woodman.[9] The interactions with Sallust are especially powerful, connecting Sejanus and Catiline both in their ambition for *dominatio/regnum* and in their character and criminal methods, and signaling the importance of these years for the trajectory of both Tiberius' reign and the Principate. So, Tacitus' claim that "[the imperial household was flourishing] when Fortune suddenly began to be disruptive, and Tiberius himself began to be savage or to offer power to savage men" (*cum repente turbare*[A] *fortuna*[B] *coepit*,[C] *saevire*[D] *ipse aut saevientibus*[D] *vires praebere*, 4.1.1) evokes Sallust's description of the destruction of Carthage: "Carthage, the rival of Rome's power, was eliminated root and branch, all seas and lands became accessible, and Fortune began to be savage and to disrupt everything" (*Carthago aemula imperi Romani ab stirpe interiit, cuncta maria terraeque patebant, saevire*[D] *fortuna*[B] *ac miscere omnia*[A] *coepit*,[C] *Cat.* 10.1). Just as the victory over Carthage altered the course of the Republic, so the Principate now changes course.

The significance of this turning point is reinforced by echoes of the preface to the *Histories*, where *saevitia* likewise is a main theme (*H.* 1.2.1, 1.2.3) and where Tacitus likewise ascribes the violence and oppression of an entire period (viz., the Flavian era) to divine anger: "the gods cared not about our security but about vengeance" (*non esse curae deis securitatem nostram, esse ultionem*, *H.* 1.3.2; the notion recurs at *H.* 1.18.1, 2.38.2, 4.3.3, 4.54.2).[10]

---

[5] See Seager (2005) for the biography of Tiberius.
[6] On Sejanus, see Birley (2007); Champlin (2012). The name Livi(ll)a (which is not in Tacitus' text) serves to distinguish Drusus' wife Claudia Livia from Livia Drusilla, wife of Augustus and mother of Tiberius.
[7] Malloch (2013), 417–18.   [8] Shannon-Henderson (2019), 168–73.
[9] Woodman (2018), 4–9, 59, 62–3, 66–7, 70–1, 77.
[10] Cf. Shannon-Henderson (2019), 16–17, 170–1, 215 and n. 18.

Tacitus extends the *saevitia* of the civil wars of 68–70 to the Flavian era, describing his subject as one period "horrible in disasters, dreadful in its wars, rent with sedition, savage even in peace" (*dirum casibus*, **atrox** *proeliis, discors seditionibus, ipsa etiam* **pace saevum**, *H.* 1.2.1; cf. the very different description of this period by the imperial loyalist Marcus Aper: *D.* 17.3).[11] This image is echoed in the opening of Book 2, where the adjective **atrox** is repeated with reference to the whole of the Flavian dynasty. The notion that the Flavian era was savage even in peace recurs later in the preface (**atrocius** *in urbe* **saevitum**, *H.* 1.2.3), where Tacitus foreshadows the enduring influence of the *delatores*, who were protected by Domitian and Mucianus after the second battle of Bedriacum (*H.* 4.44) and who (despite Titus' measures: Suet. *Tit.* 8.3) remained powerful throughout the Flavian period (*Agr.* 2.2, 45.1; *D.* 8). Tacitus, as many have noted,[12] assimilates the Principate to civil war, stressing the violence against fellow Romans perpetrated by emperors and lethal informers.

That oppression was a systemic feature of the Principate is underlined by several intra- and intertextual links connecting the Julio-Claudian and Flavian eras and pointing out the dubious nature of the alleged state of "peace" they represented: **pace saevum** at *H.* 1.2.1 (of the Flavian principate) is recalled by **saevae pacis** at *H.* 1.50.2 (probably of the whole of the Julio-Claudian principate)[13] and by *sub Tiberio et Gaio tantum* **pacis** *adversa ad rem publicam pertinuere* ("under Tiberius and Gaius only the misfortunes of peace affected the state") at *H.* 1.89.2. The notion of systemic oppression appeared already in the preface to the *Agricola*, where the destruction of Arulenus Rusticus and Herennius Senecio under Domitian is described as follows: "Savagery was inflicted not only on the authors themselves but also on their books" (*neque in ipsos modo auctores, sed in libros quoque eorum* **saevitum**, *Agr.* 2.1 ~ *atrocius in urbe* **saevitum**, *H.* 1.2.3). These impersonal passive verbs (cf. the force of *licebat* at *Agr.* 17.2, of Vespasian's reign) suggest that such violence was due to institutional forces, just as the subject *fortuna* at *Ann.* 4.1.1 and *annus* at *Ann.* 4.6.1—both non-personal agents that are made the subjects of the sentences in which they appear— suggest that "Tib[erius]'s deterioration is attributed to an external agency."[14] When Tacitus, then, introduces Book 4 of the *Annals* by writing that Tiberius began to **saevire** and **saevientibus** *vires praebere*, he evokes a nexus of verbal links that, taken together, suggest that the *saevitia* that that emperor began to exhibit and facilitate[15] continued throughout the century (it persisted from 23 to 70)[16] and so constituted a real crossroads. It is thus appropriate that the prefaces to the *Histories* and to Book 4 of the *Annals* should stress the gods' anger, "casting a baleful shadow over everything that follows."[17]

23 CE: 4.4–16

The narrative of 23 likewise engages productively with Tacitus' earlier texts. Tiberius' announced trip abroad on the pretext that the armies needed fresh levies (4.4.2), and his

---

[11] Damon (2003), 82–4, 287; Ash (2007b), 329; Levick (2016), 235.

[12] Keitel (1984); Sailor (2008), 183–249; Joseph (2012c); Ash (2019).

[13] Damon (2003), 201.   [14] Woodman (2018), 89–90.

[15] Tacitus implies, rather unfairly, that *delatio* rose steeply under Tiberius: Walker (1960), 84–6; Rutledge (2001), 88–9.

[16] *H.* 1.68.2, 1.87.1, 2.31.1, 2.73, 2.77.3; *Ann.* 6.20.1, 6.46.4, 6.48.2, 13.43.2, 14.4.4, 14.11.3, 15.36.4, 15.62.2, 16.10.1, 16.13.2, 16.18.3, 16.25.2, 16.26.3.

[17] Woodman (2018), 66.

enumeration of the legions (4.4.3), prompt Tacitus to summarize the state of the Empire (4.5)—a crucial chapter for the modern historian as it records where the now twenty-five legions are stationed, and another concern that the opening of *Annals* 4 shares with the opening of the *Histories* (*H.* 1.4)—and then the first nine years of Tiberius' principate (4.6). This last chapter, which recalls some of the language used at 4.1.1, underlines the change in Tiberius' reign and offers valuable testimony to his merits as *princeps*, which Tacitus records in greater detail than one might anticipate.

The chapter stresses administrative principles and practices that Tacitus commends across his oeuvre as marking good imperial rule: the proper functioning of the senate, and freedom for its most distinguished members to speak their mind (4.6.2); checks on sycophancy (4.6.2); imperial decision-making enjoying senatorial consent (4.6.2); the appointment of magistrates based on merit instead of nepotism (4.6.2); the proper functioning of the laws (the treason law excepted) under an emperor executing his legal duties and resolving disputes in the courts (4.6.2, 4.6.4); few slaves and freedmen in the imperial household (4.6.4; the implied contrast is with Tiberius' later regime (6.38.2) and especially with those of Claudius and Nero); extended terms abroad for competent equestrian officials (4.6.3; cf. 1.80 for extended senatorial posts); and fair treatment of provincial populations (4.6.4). In most of these principles, Tiberius follows Augustan precedent.[18] Others, like extended appointments abroad, were a novelty and have yielded different explanations from both ancient and modern observers.[19]

Several of the above virtues—the consideration of merit in official appointments (*Agr.* 19.2–3, 22.4), the limited influence of slaves and freedmen (*Agr.* 19.3), the importance of judicial balance (*Agr.* 9.2–3), and the absence of provincial mismanagement (*Agr.* 9, 19–20.1)—appeared in the idealized portrait of Tacitus' father-in-law Agricola, whose example Tacitus continually recalls across his oeuvre.[20] The *Germania* provides further intertextual background: in Germany, chiefs are chosen based on proven merit (*Germ.* 7.1), freedmen have little influence (*Germ.* 25.2; cf. *D.* 7.1, 13.4), and public deliberation is preferred to one-man decision making (*Germ.* 11.2 is echoed, in places, at *Ann.* 4.6.2).

Likewise, Tacitus' claim that Tiberius "saw to it that the provinces were not disturbed by new burdens and that they might endure old ones without the greed and cruelty of Roman officials" (*et ne provinciae **novis oneribus turbarentur** utque vetera sine **avaritia** aut **crudelitate** magistratuum **tolerarent**, providebat*, 4.6.4) re-employs (traditional) vocabulary used in the *Agricola* (and re-used in the *Histories* and *Annals*) to articulate the provincial outlook on Rome's empire.[21] *Agr.* 13.1 expresses the fundamental point that provincial subjects tolerate a certain threshold of burdens but see excessive demands or violence as constituting enslavement and as meriting revolt (*ipsi Britanni dilectum ac tributa et iniuncta imperii munia impigre obeunt, si **iniuriae** absint: has aegre **tolerant**, iam domiti ut pareant, nondum ut **serviant***, "The Britons themselves readily endure the conscription, the tribute, and the obligations imposed by the Empire, as long as there are no abuses: these they are unwilling to tolerate; they have now been reduced to subjection, not yet to slavery"). The vices said to be absent under early Tiberian governors mirror those

---

[18] Woodman (2018), 89–95. On Tiberius' evolving relationship with Augustan precedent, see Cowan (2009).

[19] Ancient: *Ann.* 1.80, 3.32.1, 3.56, 4.6.2–3; note Tiberius' views at *Ann.* 2.36.2–3, 3.69.2–3; examples at *H.* 2.65.2; *Ann.* 6.27.3, 13.22.1. Modern: Syme (1958a), 441; Griffin (1995), 44–9; Seager (2005), 147.

[20] See ten Berge (2023).   [21] On barbarian speeches in Roman historiography, see Adler (2011).

that pushed Boudicca (see Whitton on Book 14, Chapter 16 in this volume) to revolt (*Agr.* 15.1–4; *Ann.* 14.31.1, 14.35.1) and that Calgacus decried when rousing his Caledonians (*Agr.* 31.1). They are also the vices that Agricola's administration is said to have lacked or eliminated (*Agr.* 9, 19–20.1); early Tiberian governors, then, operate like the idealized Agricola. Reflecting the deterioration of Tiberius' reign are three later examples of gubernatorial abuse—the excessive severity toward the Termestini (4.45.3), the Thracians' anticipation of new burdens (4.46.2), and the impossible demands made of the Frisii (4.71–2)—that are described with the above language[22] and that suggest a departure from the "Agricolan" standard of earlier governors. Such verbal correspondences allow us to reconstruct a narrative that reflects Tacitus' enduring concerns and that elucidates the broader change in Tiberius' principate.

That change, according to Tacitus, was triggered not by Germanicus' death in 19 (as Suetonius (*Cal.* 6.2) and Dio (57.7.1, 57.13.6, 57.19.1) had it), for he still had Drusus to assist and check him,[23] but by Drusus' death in 23, which removed the chief restraint on Sejanus' ambitions and wholly changed Tiberius (4.7.1). Tacitus seems to believe that the elimination of rivals removes anxiety and gives free rein to malicious tendencies—Tiberius had an innate propensity for *saevitia* (1.4.3) that now erupted, similar to the influence of Livia's death on Tiberius and Sejanus (5.1.1). This conception likely was shaped under Domitian, who, he claimed, had accelerated his oppressions after Agricola's death in 93 (*Agr.* 44.5; the reign of terror recounted at *Agr.* 2 and 45.1–2 followed Agricola's demise). We may also note, in this regard, the alleged effect of L. Calpurnius Piso's elimination on Otho (*H.* 1.44.1–2), and of Otho's removal to Lusitania (*Ann.* 13.47.1) and the elimination of Agrippina the Younger (*Ann.* 14.13.2), Afranius Burrus (*Ann.* 14.52.1), Faustus Sulla (*Ann.* 14.57.4), and Rubellius Plautus (*Ann.* 14.58–9) on Nero. Domitian the tyrant created Tacitus the historian; that emperor, and his treatment of Agricola, shaped Tacitus' view of the Principate and its *principes*.[24]

Following Tacitus' claims at 4.7.1, the subsequent narrative is dominated by Sejanus' attacks against Agrippina the Elder and her sons, the account of which is elucidated, again, by intertextual correspondences with earlier Tacitean episodes. Sejanus, having eliminated Drusus with impunity, begins plotting against Agrippina (4.12). Since (unlike in Drusus' case) poison was impracticable, he resolves to attack Agrippina's "obstinacy" (***contumacia***), urging Livia and Livi(ll)a to complain to Tiberius about her arrogance, popular support, and desire for *dominatio*. He also sends "cunning" (***callidi***) accusers against her and urges others to incite her in "twisted conversations" (***pravis*** *sermonibus*). The vocabulary, again, is precise. Tacitus had used the noun *contumacia* in his programmatic description of Agricola's conduct as marking a "middle path" between the extremes of stubborn defiance and gross sycophancy (*Agr.* 42.3).[25] The noun recurs at *Ann.* 4.20.3, where Tacitus praises Marcus Lepidus, who mirrors Agricola in walking a path between ***contumacia*** and *deforme obsequium* ("disgraceful compliance"). Throughout, Tacitus

---

[22] The most explicit example is *si nullo **novo onere** temptarentur*, "if they were tried by no new burden" (4.46.2) ~ *ne provinciae **novis oneribus** turbarentur*, "[he saw to it] that the provinces were not disturbed by new burdens" (4.6.4).

[23] Cf. *donec Germanicus ac Drusus superfuere*, "while Germanicus and Drusus were alive" (6.51.3): see Shannon-Henderson on Books 5–6, Chapter 13 in this volume.

[24] See ten Berge (2023), especially chapters 1, 4, and 5.

[25] See ten Berge (2023), 36–7, 326–9. Strunk (2017), 3–37, summarizes scholarship on the "middle path" paradigm.

ascribes *contumacia* and its cognates to individuals who act beyond their station and defy the limits imposed on them by the imperial dispensation.[26] The fate of men like Thrasea Paetus and Helvidius Priscus the Elder would show that cunning accusers could capitalize on behavior that might be construed as being anti-imperial. Just as Nero's henchmen Cossutianus Capito and Eprius Marcellus would accuse Thrasea of ***contumacia*** (*Ann.* 16.22.2, 16.28.1)[27] to intensify Nero's hostility, so Sejanus' creatures reminded Tiberius that Agrippina refused to show the kind of behavior suitable for an imperial subject.

That Sejanus' accomplices will succeed in framing Agrippina is suggested by their depiction as ***callidi*** and ***pravi***. Tacitus frequently ascribes *calliditas* ("cunning") and *pravitas* ("viciousness") to individuals who maliciously misrepresent others: the "malicious men" (*maligni*) who put a "negative spin" on Maternus' *Cato* (***prava*** *interpretatio*, *D.* 3.2); the ***pravus et callidus*** Licinius Proculus, Otho's Praetorian Prefect, who denounced the generals Paulinus, Celsus, and Gallus to him and urged him to demote them ahead of the first battle of Bedriacum (*H.* 1.87.2); Titus Vinius, who displayed similar behavior (*H.* 1.64.4) and who is the only other individual in the extant corpus who combines ***calliditas*** and ***pravitas*** (*H.* 1.48.4); and other ***callidi*** or ***pravi***.[28] Sejanus' *callidi*, then, are part of a line of individuals who craftily attack their own and their emperor's rivals. That they successfully manipulated Tiberius is confirmed at *Ann.* 5.3.2, where the emperor, no longer hiding his resentment after the emotional release of his mother's death (5.3.1), openly condemns Agrippina and her son Nero Caesar, charging the former with ***contumacia*** (see Shannon-Henderson on Books 5–6, Chapter 13 in this volume). Reading Tacitus' works in conjunction shows Sejanus' attacks against Agrippina and her family to be part of a longer pattern of emperors and their henchmen destroying (perceived) rivals.

The year 23 ends with several chapters relating Tiberius' personal involvement in senatorial business (4.13–16). Two points stand out. First, the emperor's focus on work reveals his "Agricolan" way of handling personal loss (4.13.1, 4.15.1 ~ *Agr.* 6.2, 7.1, 29.1). More significant is what these chapters show about the scope of senatorial activity and the developing role of the emperor in it. Tiberius' wishes govern the trial of Lucilius Capito (4.15.2–3), as they had C. Silanus' trial the previous year (3.67). Tiberius, moreover, by allowing the province of Asia to dedicate a temple to him, Livia, and the senate in recognition of the convictions of Capito and Silanus (4.15.3)—he had prohibited the dedication of statues and altars after Cn. Piso's conviction (3.18.2)—publicly gratifies the province's desire for vengeance, thus "setting a worrying precedent for future *ultio*-related dedications."[29] While Tiberius' involvement foreshadows both the senate's increasingly limited capacity to influence judicial and political matters[30] and the increasing *saevitia* that marks Tiberian and post-Tiberian Rome, Tacitus stresses that public business was still left largely to the senate, signifying Tiberius' continued adherence to Augustan precedent. Tacitus' claim that "*even then* all things were handled by [the senate]" (*apud quos etiam tum cuncta* *tractabantur*, 4.15.2) echoes *publica negotia et privatorum maxima apud patres* ***tractabantur*** ("public business and the most important of private affairs were handled by the senate")

[26] *H.* 2.77.3, 3.63.1, 4.74.4; *Ann.* 1.24.3, 2.57.3, 3.12.1, 4.29.3, 4.60.1, 5.3.2, 16.22.2, 16.28.1.
[27] See Bartera, Chapter 18 in this volume.
[28] *H.* 1.14.1, 1.25.1, 3.53.3; *Ann.* 2.30.3, 2.57.2, 3.65.1, 6.5.2, 11.3.2, 11.33.1, 12.41.3, 13.47.1, 14.22.3.
[29] Shannon-Henderson (2019), 176.
[30] This development is also explicated in Tacitus' earlier texts: ten Berge (2023), chapters 1–3. For a more positive assessment of senatorial agency and efficacy as presented in Tacitus' *Annals*, see O'Gorman (2020).

at 4.6.2 and suggests that not much had changed *yet*, but that change for the worse was on the horizon (Tacitus here may be thinking of private trials before the emperor, which soon came into vogue: *D.* 7.1; *Ann.* 6.10.2).[31] The use of the "temporal innuendo" *etiam tum*[32] recalls 3.72.1 and 3.74.4,[33] which, together with 4.15.2, reflect the growing restrictions on the senatorial aristocracy, restrictions that, in many cases, were established late in Augustus' reign but that intensified in the second half of Tiberius' principate.

24 CE: 4.17–33

The narrative of 24 resumes Sejanus' attacks against Germanicus' friends and family and records important developments in the scope and application of the "treason law" (*lex maiestatis*). Sejanus continues to plot against Agrippina, feeding Tiberius' suspicion that there is a "faction of Agrippina" (*partes Agrippinae*) and looming civil war (4.17.3) and engineering the first of many trials against her family's supporters.

C. Silius and his wife Sosia are condemned for treason (on various pretexts), while Titius Sabinus' trial is postponed. As often happened in such trials, Silius preemptively commits suicide, and Sosia is exiled.[34] Contrary to expectation, "violence was done to Silius' property" (*saevitum tamen in bona*), and Tacitus accentuates the occasion's significance: "That was the first time Tiberius was attentive to another's money" (*ea prima Tiberio erga pecuniam alienam diligentia fuit*, 4.20.1). *Saevitum* recalls *saevire* and *saevientibus* vires praebere at 4.1.1, marking this as a concrete manifestation of Tiberius' decline, standing in contrast to his earlier responses in analogous contexts (2.48.2, 3.18.1, 3.23.2, 3.68.2).

Asinius Gallus' and Marcus Lepidus' different proposals about the handling of Sosia's property (4.20.1) prompts Tacitus to digress on Lepidus' character, which, as noted above, recalls *Agr.* 42.3–4 and confirms the historian's endorsement of the "middle path" paradigm (it is further endorsed at 5.11.1, 6.10.3, 14.47.1).[35] Three more cases follow (4.21–2), the last of which—Cassius Severus' relegation from Crete (his erstwhile place of exile) to Seriphos (4.21.3)—connects with earlier Tacitean contexts elucidating the man's aggressive oratorical style (and its importance in the history of oratory) and its consequences under Augustus (*D.* 26.4; *Ann.* 1.72.3).

Tacitus now interrupts the domestic narrative to record the closure of the nearly ten-year war against the Numidian deserter Tacfarinas (2.52, 3.20.1, 3.72.4–74). These chapters (4.24–6), in addition to engaging with Sallust,[36] take up enduring Tacitean themes that explain the war's persistence. Tacitus stresses that the triviality of the *ornamenta triumphalia*[37]—a concern first enunciated at *Agr.* 40.1—saw Roman commanders merely do enough to earn this award and then leave Tacfarinas to recover (4.23.1). In 24 CE, Tacfarinas—one of several auxiliary chiefs who exploit their knowledge of Rome's armies

---

[31] Woodman (2018), 126 (citing Furneaux).   [32] Woodman (2018), 126.
[33] Woodman and Martin (1996), 477–8, 489.
[34] Scholarship on *maiestas* trials is vast. Rutledge (2001) remains excellent; see also Further Reading.
[35] It also found contemporary endorsement: Pliny playfully echoes Tacitus' *Agricola* to suggest that Pliny's Verginius was the chief example of one who earned glory though self-effacement (*Ep.* 9.10): Whitton (2019), 108–10.
[36] Woodman (2018), 153–8.
[37] These were among the few military distinctions left to generals under the early Principate. For their ready distribution, even for non-military purposes, cf. *Ann.* 3.72.4–73.1, 11.20.3, 13.53.1, 15.72.1.

and expose its dangerous reliance on *auxilia* (another enduring Tacitean theme)—is decisively defeated. The account of this final campaign ends with the denial of due honors to the victorious general, Publius Dolabella, lest the glory of Junius Blaesus, Sejanus' uncle, be diminished (4.26.1). Following his concern to rectify the distorted circulation of glory under the Principate, Tacitus notes that, despite Tiberius' interference, Dolabella's fame surpassed that of Blaesus.

The year's final chapters return to the treason law, focusing on Vibius Serenus' case against his father, which is introduced with language that (again) recalls the Book's preface and that marks it as another significant episode in Tiberius' decline: "The same year saw a dreadful example of misery and savagery" (*isdem consulibus, miseriarum ac **saevitiae** exemplum atrox*, 4.28.1). Reflecting the nature of the Principate at this juncture is the claim that Caecilius Cornutus, falsely accused by Serenus of being one of his father's accomplices, commits suicide "because being accused was considered equivalent to ruin" (*quia periculum pro exitio habebatur*, 4.28.2). This phrase is similar in sentiment to *inter damnatos magis quam inter reos Anteius Ostoriusque habebantur* ("Anteius and Ostorius were considered as being among the condemned rather than among the defendants") at *Ann.* 16.14.3, suggesting the enduring lethality of the *delatores*. What initiated this dark development was Tiberius' quashing of a senatorial vote (in response to Cornutus' death) in favor of eliminating rewards for *delatores* when a defendant commits suicide (4.30.2–3). Tacitus, again, accentuates the moment's significance: informers, who were barely checked by punishments,[38] were now encouraged by rewards. The moment is also marked by changes in Tiberius' behavior: his customary clemency—toward the elder Serenus and afterward toward C. Cominius—is presented as a momentary reprieve from "the string of horrors" (*his tam adsiduis tamque maestis*, 4.31.1) of which his "uncharacteristically harsh and open" (*durius contraque morem suum palam*, 4.30.2) opposition to the senatorial vote is but one symptom.

After two further cases—against P. Suillius Rufus (whose bloody record under Claudius is foreshadowed here) and Catus Firmius (4.31)—Tacitus digresses to comment on the monotony and bleakness of his material (4.32–3). Typically considered a "second preface" in Book 4, the digression underlines the deterioration of Tiberius' reign announced in the opening chapters. Tacitus contrasts his material with that of his republican predecessors: while *they* had enjoyed the freedom to explore momentous wars and internal disputes— the destructive influence of the Principate on the quality and scope of literature and ora- tory had already been explored in the *Dialogus de oratoribus* and in the prefaces to the *Agricola*, *Histories*, and *Annals*—Tacitus' field is "narrow and inglorious" (*nobis in arto et inglorius labor*, 4.32.2), consisting of undisturbed peace in Rome, its "sorry affairs" (***maestae** urbis res*, recalling *his tam adsiduis tamque **maestis***, 4.31.1), and an emperor uninterested in military expansion (cf. *Agr.* 13.2; *Ann.* 2.26). Not only is Tacitus' material narrow, it is also monotonous and disturbing: "Savage orders, continuous accusations, false friendships, the ruin of blameless people, and the same causes for their destruction" (*saeva iussa, contin- uas accusationes, fallaces amicitias, perniciem innocentium et easdem exitii causas*, 4.33.3; analogous comments about his material appear at 6.38.1 and 16.16.1).

---

[38] "*Poenis* almost certainly alludes to the successive measures taken against *delatores* by Titus (Suet. *Tit.* 8.5), Nerva (Dio 68.1.2) and Trajan (Plin. *Pan.* 34–5)": Woodman (2018), 168.

Still, Tacitus avers, recording these things is useful, helping readers see how ostensible trivialities can have major consequences (4.32.2; cf. 6.7.5) and offering insight into life under the Principate, which is important since "few have the foresight to distinguish the honorable from the baser, and the expedient from the destructive, and most learn from other people's experiences" (*pauci **prudentia honesta** ab deterioribus, **utilia** ab noxiis discernunt, plures aliorum eventis docentur*, 4.33.2). Elsewhere, Tacitus combines the adjectives *honesta* and *utilia* only at *Agr.* 8.1, where the *prudens* Agricola (*Agr.* 9.2) is described as one who "knew how to obey and had learned to combine expediency with honor" (*peritus obsequi eruditusque **utilia honestis** miscere*). Agricola exemplifies the *pauci* who know how to operate honorably under the strictures of the Principate. This intertext, and an analogous digression in the Neronian books (16.16; cf. *homines **amicitiae fallaces**, 16.32.2 ~ **fallaces amicitias**, 4.33.3), suggests the digression's broader application both within the *Annals* and across the corpus.[39]

The utility of Tacitus' "monotonous" material lies in part in his description of the Principate as being marked by systemic oppression, and of the emperors as displaying broadly similar behavior, which means that the account of any of them bears on the others, including the emperor under whom the reader himself lives, whom he can therefore "read" more accurately.[40] As Clarke puts it, "If one of Tacitus's concerns is the static scenario of the Principate, this might support the idea of learning by example how to deal with an ongoing situation."[41] That a narrative about specific individuals could, by implicit comparison or contrast, apply to others and make the latter feel criticized is emphasized at 4.33.4, and Tacitus had already commented on literary works (Arulenus Rusticus' and Herennius Senecio's *vitae* of Thrasea Paetus and Helvidius Priscus the Elder: *Agr.* 2.1) and dramatic productions (Maternus' *Cato* in the *Dialogus*) that were construed as reflecting poorly on the emperor and/or the Principate.

25 CE: 4.34–45

Another example immediately follows the digression: the trial against the "blameless" (*innocens*, 4.34.2 ~ *perniciem **innocentium***, 4.33.3; *innocentem* Cornutum, 4.28.3) Cremutius Cordus. The old man had provoked Sejanus in 22 CE (Sen. *Dial.* 6.1.3, 6.22.4; Tac. *Ann.* 3.72.3; Dio 57.24.2–4) and was now accused of treason on the ground that in his *Annales*, a history produced under Augustus that seems to have treated the civil wars of the 40s and 30s and part of that emperor's reign, he had glorified Caesar's assassins Brutus and Cassius and called the latter "the last of the Romans" (*Romanorum ultimus*, 4.34.1; cf. Suet. *Tib.* 61.3).[42] Under Augustus not only actions but also words had become liable to charges of treason.[43] But the treason law did not yet cover historical works, and Augustus had raised no objections when encountering Cremutius' text (Tac. *Ann.* 4.34.3–5; Suet. *Tib.* 61.3;

---

[39] See Woodman (2018), 171–4, for the scholarly debate. See also Bartera, Chapter 18 in this volume.
[40] Sailor (2008), 253–68.   [41] Clarke (2002), 98–9.
[42] For an introduction to Cremutius' *Annales*, see "A. Cremutius Cordus," *FRHist.* 1.497–501 (B. Levick); Lentano (2021).
[43] On the development of the treason law under Augustus, see Peachin (2015). Cf. Sen. *Ben.* 3.27.1 and Dio 53.19.3–4, 56.27.1 on Augustus; Sen. *Con.* 10 pr. 5 ff. on the case against T. Labienus; Tac. *Ann.* 1.72.3–4 on that against Cassius Severus. See also Pagán, Chapter 9 in this volume.

Dio 57.24.3). According to Tacitus, a history now for the first time became the target of a *maiestas* charge (*Ann.* 4.34.1; cf. Suet. *Tib.* 61.3; Dio 57.24.2–4).[44] The historian is concerned to stress that attempts to destroy Cremutius' books had the opposite effect of making them more desirable and the author's fame greater (4.35.4–5; cf. Sen. *Dial.* 6.1.3; Dio 57.24.4), claims that evoke his comments about the analogous fate of Rusticus and Senecio and their books (*Agr.* 2.1–2).

Much has been written about these chapters, which plainly are self-reflective and methodologically significant, but perhaps the most important point (in addition to the development of the treason law) is that Cremutius' fate illustrates the challenge for imperial historians, including Tacitus himself, to tell their truth in the face of the Principate's restrictions on (authorial) *libertas*.[45] The narration of Cremutius' fate serves, among other things, to suggest that Tacitus' *Annals* are similarly "dangerous" (read: relevant), and it may further serve as an implicit exhortation to the Trajanic government not to constrain Tacitus' *libertas*, which, if that reading is correct, reinforces the analogous cautionary (and cautious) signaling to the regime in the prefaces to the *Agricola*, *Histories*, and *Annals*.[46]

The image of endless accusations—introduced at 4.31.1 and 4.32.2—continues at 4.36. Two cases are selected to exemplify the general atmosphere: in the first, a magistrate is interrupted during a religious ceremony to hear an accusation (4.36.1), while the second— involving another false accusation made with impunity by Serenus (cf. 4.28.2)—demonstrates the notion that the more hated and relentless an informer was, the more "protected" (*tutior*) and "inviolable" (*sacrosanctus*) he became (4.36.3). This fundamental point about imperial *delatio* runs through the *Annals*. It was enunciated at 1.74, where Tacitus foreshadows the current "reign of terror" and offers a stereotypical portrait of the hated but powerful *delator*,[47] and examples of virtually immune informers abound, most prominently P. Suillius Rufus (11.5–7, 13.42–3), Cossutianus Capito (11.6.3, 13.33.2, 14.48.1–2, 16.21–2, 16.26, 16.33), and Eprius Marcellus (13.33.3, 16.22.5, 16.26.2, 16.28.1, 16.33.2; *H.* 4.6.1, 4.7.3, 4.43). Already in the *Dialogus* Tacitus had Aper stress the extraordinary power of the "morally corrupt" (*neuter moribus egregius*) Marcellus and Vibius Crispus (cf. *H.* 2.10), calling them "the state's most powerful men" (*potentissimi civitatis*) and "princes of the court" (*principes fori*, *D.* 8.3). Catullus Messalinus, Mettius Carus, and Baebius Massa, whose future lethality is foreshadowed at *Agr.* 45.1 and *H.* 1.2.3, 4.50.2, would have featured prominently in the final books of the *Histories*.

After recording a request from Further Spain to build a temple to Tiberius and Livia and the emperor's speech to the senate denying the request (4.37–8),[48] we reach the pivotal chapters of Book 4: Tiberius' crafty denial of Sejanus' request to marry Livi(ll)a, and Sejanus' subsequent attempts to get Tiberius to leave Rome (4.39–41). Notably, Tiberius cites Agrippina's antagonism as a reason *not* to grant Sejanus' request (4.40.3)—which is ironic since this was the basis of Sejanus' attempts to frame her. Also notable are Sejanus'

---

[44] On whether the charge against Cremutius was in fact novel, see Peachin (2015), 17–46.
[45] Moles (1998); Sailor (2008), 250–313; Wisse (2013).
[46] Sailor (2008), 119–82; Strunk (2017), 29–30, 179; ten Berge (2023), 28–31, 198–205, 304–6.
[47] Rutledge (2001), 18, 322 n. 14.
[48] On these chapters, see Pelling (2010); Woodman (2018), 207–15; Shannon-Henderson (2019), 184–92.

complaints to Tiberius about life in Rome (4.41.3), which constitute a recurring motif across Tacitus' oeuvre.[49]

Crucial for the ongoing theme of Tiberius' decline is that, while Sejanus is urging him to leave Rome, there happens to be a trial against the Narbonese orator Votienus Montanus for insults against the emperor (4.42.1). At the pre-trial arraignment, an impetuous soldier (another stereotype: cf. *Agr.* 9.2) publicly repeats the insults. Hearing what people were saying behind his back shocked Tiberius, and this had two consequences. First, it convinced the "already delaying" (*iam cunctans*) emperor to avoid the senate. These words suggest that Sejanus' attempts had been successful, that Tiberius' "innate caution" (*insita cunctatio*, 4.11.1) soon set in, but that he now changed his mind again.[50] Second, Tiberius now becomes more merciless against defendants (4.42.3), exacerbating the ongoing pattern of *saevitia*.

26 CE: 4.46–61

After recounting Poppaeus Sabinus' campaign against the Thracians (4.46–51)—a highly stylized[51] account that both reflects Tacitus' concern to restore to successful generals their due distinction[52] and that implicitly affirms his complaints about his material at 4.32— Tacitus resumes his narrative of Sejanus' attacks against Agrippina. First, her cousin Claudia Pulchra is destroyed by Domitius Afer (4.52; cf. 4.66, 14.19), an odious character who exemplifies the stereotypical characteristics of the imperial *delator* as articulated in the *Dialogus*, *Histories*, and *Annals* (*D.* 8; *H.* 1.2.3, 2.10, 4.7, 4.41–2; *Ann.* 1.74). Pulchra's destruction, mirroring that of Sosia (4.19), continues the theme of violence against friends of Germanicus' family. Tensions between Agrippina and Tiberius now intensify, first when she accosts him while he is sacrificing to Augustus (4.52.2–3; her point that he ought not simultaneously slay victims for his adopted father *and* slay the latter's descendants is expressed with great virtuosity),[53] next when she asks him, in vain, to find her a new husband (4.53).

Tacitus' organization of Book 4 remains sophisticated: the three-chapter section describing the increasing tensions between Agrippina and Tiberius (4.52–4) variously mirrors the three-chapter section on Sejanus and Tiberius at 4.39–41, with Agrippina's request for a husband mirroring Sejanus' request to marry Livi(ll)a (4.39). Likewise, Sejanus' "warning" to Agrippina (via individuals "posing as friends," *per speciem* **amicitiae**, 4.54.1 ~ *fallaces* **amicitiae**, 4.33.3) that Tiberius is planning to poison her (4.54) evokes (and verbally recalls) his maneuvers in 23, when he had tried to convince Tiberius to poison Drusus after circulating a rumor that his son was planning to poison him (4.10.2–3). The result of Sejanus' schemes—which made Agrippina act suspicious of Tiberius at a banquet,

---

[49] *Agr.* 40.3; *D.* 9.5, 13; *Ann.* 2.34.1, 4.28.3, 4.41.3, 6.26.1–2, 14.53–4, 14.56.
[50] Woodman (2018), 229–30.   [51] Woodman (2018), 240–1.
[52] Note the similarly belabored, and extraordinarily lengthy, accounts of the campaigns of Agricola, Germanicus, and Corbulo: Syme (1958a), 492–6, 579. On Agricola, Germanicus, and Corbulo, see chapters 1, 10, and 17 in this volume.
[53] Woodman (2018), 258–9; Shannon-Henderson (2019), 194–6.

which in turn offended the emperor (4.54.2)—was the generation of *another* rumor, namely that Tiberius was in fact secretly planning her destruction.[54]

Tacitus now reaches the crucial moment in Book 4: Tiberius' departure from Rome. The emperor, says Tacitus, "having considered the matter for a long time and having often postponed the plan, left for Campania, on the pretext of dedicating a temple to Jupiter at Capua and another to Augustus at Nola, but really to live away from Rome" (*inter quae diu meditato prolatoque saepius consilio tandem Caesar in Campaniam, specie dedicandi templa apud Capuam Iovi, apud Nolam Augusto, sed certus **procul**[A] **urbe**[B] **degere**,[C] 4.57.1).* Tiberius had contemplated leaving since at least 21 (3.31.2), and he had changed his mind several times. Tacitus writes that, although he follows the *communis opinio* in ascribing Tiberius' decision to Sejanus' influence (cf. *huc flexit, ut Tiberium ad vitam **procul Roma**[A,B] amoenis locis **degendam**[C] impelleret* at 4.41.1: "he had determined to encourage Tiberius to live in a charming place away from Rome"), the fact that the emperor stayed on Capri for another six years after Sejanus' demise and had shown a similar penchant for seclusion on Rhodes (4.67.2) made it seem *more* accurate (*verius*) to ascribe it to Tiberius himself (4.57.1–2). These ostensibly incompatible explanations have caused some controversy, but Woodman (following Luce) is right to see them as complementary.[55] Indeed, the notion, emphasized at 4.1.2 (*devinxit*: see above), that an emperor's intimates knew his predilections and thus could steer him in certain directions runs across the corpus (*Agr.* 41.1; *H.* 2.63.1, 3.38.2; *Ann.* 16.18.3).

Like the trial of Montanus, another chance event (viz., the incident at Sperlonga) further increases Sejanus' influence with Tiberius (4.59.1–2)—the interplay between design and chance in Sejanus' rise is notable—and he capitalizes on it to begin plotting against Agrippina's sons Nero and Drusus Caesar, partly by manipulating the latter and inflaming him against his brother (4.59.3–60). Not only does the master puppeteer Sejanus—the imagery of deception and role playing at 4.59.3–60 is striking—methodically engineer the boys' destruction, but he will also soon succeed in getting Tiberius out of Rome.

27 CE: 4.62–7

Reflecting Sejanus' extraordinary position, and the increasing *saevitia* it engenders, is "the ever greater, more savage, and uninterrupted violence" of the *delatores* (*ita accusatorum maior in dies et infestior vis sine levamento grassabatur,* 4.66.1) that, on Tacitus' account, now marks Tiberian Rome. The historian selects for mention Afer's attack on Quintilius Varus (4.66.2), son of the ill-fated general and Afer's earlier victim Pulchra (4.52), and another friend of Germanicus' family. The senate voted to suspend the case and wait for Tiberius, "which," according to Tacitus, "was the only way to escape temporarily any impending horrors" (*quod unum urgentium malorum suffugium in tempus erat,* 4.66.2). Tacitus' description is suspect,[56] reflecting both his cynical historical outlook and his "classic technique of creating an 'impression' which fails to be supported by the 'facts' provided."[57]

---

[54] On rumor in Tacitus, see Shatzman (1974); Gibson (1998).
[55] Woodman (2018), 271.   [56] Rutledge (2001), 143–4.
[57] Woodman (2018), 302 (citing Walker).

One impression Tacitus creates here is of the senate's anxiety and incapacity when the *princeps* is absent[58]—something that will worsen when Tiberius abandons Rome (4.67).

The transition from 4.66.2 to 4.67.1 is pointed: when Rome needs its emperor most, he is off in Campania and soon on Capri, creating for his constituents a *solitudo* as he himself seeks it on the island (4.67.2; cf. 4.41.3). As the ethnographic nature of the chapter suggests, Tacitus accentuates Tiberius' self-imposed "exile" by depicting Capri as a foreign country,[59] and its remoteness intensifies the decline in the emperor that Tacitus has traced throughout Book 4: "Once intent on the cares of the state [cf. 2.34.3, 3.54.5, 6.2–4], he now focuses on secret luxuries and an evil leisure" (*quanto intentus olim publicas ad curas, tanto occultior<es> in luxus et malum otium resolutus*, 4.67.3).

The change of abode, however, did not change one fundamental aspect of Tiberius' character—his "rashness in suspecting and believing things" (*suspicionum et credendi temeritas*, 4.67.3)—which Sejanus further exacerbated through his now open attacks against Agrippina and Nero. The end of Agrippina, Nero, and Drusus—all were dead by 31—must have been recorded in the now missing sections of Book 5 (see Shannon-Henderson, Chapter 13 in this volume).

28 CE: 4.68–75

The final year opens with the postponed (cf. 4.19.1) attack on Titius Sabinus (4.69–71.1), another loyal friend of Germanicus' family, whose entrapment by one of Sejanus' henchmen pretending to be his confidant typifies the dark image of imperial Rome described at 4.33.3.[60] The way that Sabinus is urged to reveal his "treason," his immediate condemnation by Tiberius and execution (reflecting the emperor's *suspicionum et credendi temeritas* and his increasing, and increasingly open, *saevitia*), his depiction as a sacrificial victim to Sejanus (4.70.1),[61] his being misrepresented to the senate as having been a real threat to the state (4.70.4), and the terror and suspicion that his case inspired in others (4.69.3) continue various narrative strands throughout the *Annals*.

The terror spread by the *delatores* is presented as debilitating Rome's government, causing the alarmed senate both to be indifferent to military failure in Germany (and to imperial attempts to cover it up: 4.72–74.1) and to engage in gross sycophancy (cf. the senate's emotional response to Domitian's oppressions: *Agr.* 2.3–3.1). Access to Tiberius, and safety and success in Rome, now depended on Sejanus, with whom many senators and knights tried to ingratiate themselves through flattery, canvassing, or complicity (cf. *Agr.* 45.1). Tacitus now foreshadows the imminent destruction of Sejanus himself (recorded in the lost portions of Book 5) and his associates (cf. 6.7.2, 6.8.1–2, 6.14.1, 6.29.3), suggesting that the *fallaces amicitiae* that had (allegedly) destroyed so many Romans will rebound on Sejanus and his supporters.

Book 4 closes with a final foreshadowing: the marriage, arranged by the emperor himself, of Agrippina's daughter to Cn. Domitius. The name of their son, whose reign would variously resemble that of Tiberius, did not require mention.

---

[58] Woodman (2018), 303.

[59] On Capri as being an ambiguous and wondrous place, see Christoforou (2022), 207–8 and the references there.

[60] For the trial, see Rutledge (2001), 144–6.   [61] Shannon-Henderson (2019), 205–8.

Further Reading

In addition to Rutledge (2001) and Peachin (2015), see Rogers (1935) and Bauman (1974) on the development of the treason law under Tiberius. On the structure, language, and themes of *Annals* 1–6, see Ginsburg (1981). Talbert (1984) remains crucial for our understanding of the nature and development of the senate under the Principate. Levick (1999a) and Seager (2005)—who also discuss the treason law—offer the authoritative modern biographies of Tiberius. On Agrippina the Elder, finally, consult Barrett (1996), Chapter 3.

Bram ten Berge, Annals 4 In: *The Oxford Critical Guide to Tacitus*. Edited by: Salvador Bartera and Kelly E. Shannon-Henderson, Oxford University Press. © Oxford University Press 2025. DOI: 10.1093/9780191915086.003.0013

13

Annals 5 and 6

The End of the Beginning

Kelly E. Shannon-Henderson

How to end a reign?[1] With *Annals* 5–6, Tacitus' account of the principate of Tiberius draws to a close. The books are marked by deaths: of the emperor's mother, relatives, friends, and finally of Tiberius himself. These are books, then, full of endings—but not *just* endings; for while Tiberius' reign lurches toward its grim conclusion, Tacitus also prepares the way for his account of the (even grimmer) Julio-Claudians who would follow.

Scholars have hotly debated where these two books themselves begin and end. The Medicean manuscript that is our sole witness to this part of the *Annals* does not mark a division between Book 5 and Book 6, although it does for the other books. We are also missing something after *Annals* 5.5: although the manuscript marks no break, we find ourselves in a completely different context in 5.6, which begins with a sentence fragment.[2] This lacuna has also swallowed up the remainder of Tacitus' account of the year 29 CE (with which Book 5 began), the entirety of 30 CE, and the beginning of the account of 31 CE. The next date we find in our text is the consulship of Cn. Domitius and Camillus Scribonianus, 32 CE (6.1.1). This means that we have lost Tacitus' (no doubt masterful) description of Sejanus' downfall and execution in 31 CE; the reasons why Tiberius turned against his former favorite still remain obscure.[3]

This loss has made it difficult for scholars to figure out how Tacitus arranged all this material across the book-division. Justus Lipsius in the sixteenth century proposed that Tacitus originally ended Book 5 with the strife between consuls Trio and Regulus (5.11), and that Book 6 began in 32 CE with 6.1.1;[4] the lost material, including Sejanus' execution, would then all have fallen within Book 5. In 1848, however, Friedrich Haase argued that Tacitus, who structured his book beginnings and endings so as to achieve the maximum possible impact, was more likely to have concluded Book 5 with a description of Sejanus' execution, and that 5.6–5.11 actually belonged to Book 6. This explains the otherwise confusing layout of many editions and translations of the *Annals*, which sometimes insert a heading for "Book 6" before 5.6–11 (which are sometimes designated 6[5].6–11). More recently, Clifford Ando has urged a return to Lipsius' view.[5] In what follows, I will operate on the assumption that *Annals* 6 originally began at 6.1.

[1] In addition to thanking all three for their comments and suggestions on this chapter, I am also grateful to Rhiannon Ash for sharing her forthcoming essay; to Salvador Bartera, for his excellence as co-editor of this volume; and to A. J. Woodman for his continuous instruction and guidance throughout my two decades as a reader of ancient historiography. I dedicate this chapter to the memory of my father, James A. Shannon, Jr.
[2] Ando (1997) summarizes the controversy. Woodman (2017), 3 provides an image of the manuscript at this crucial moment.
[3] Birley (2007) surveys possible motivations and actors behind the scenes.
[4] For Lipsius' views on book-beginnings in the *Annals*, see Bartera (2016), 117–18.
[5] Ando is followed by Woodman (2004), 163; Woodman (2017), 3–9.

Less widely accepted has been Ando's suggestion, which even he describes as "radical,"[6] that 6.51 is not actually the original end of *Annals* 6. It is true that Tiberius' funeral and Caligula's succession are not narrated here, but we do not have any reason to believe that they must have been.[7] As we shall see, the obituary of Tiberius at *Annals* 6.51 provides an exceptionally fitting end to the book, the hexad, and Tiberius' life, forcing us to think retrospectively about the entire account that has preceded and to consolidate our assessment of Tiberius and his principate before reading onward to Caligula. In fact, Tacitus elicits this sort of careful thinking and re-thinking throughout *Annals* 5 and 6. In writing about this final phase of Tiberius' rule, he interweaves executions and suicides with themes of truth and discernment. The project of *Annals* 5–6, in other words, is not just the project of how to dispatch an emperor; it is a master class in the difficulties a historian faces in attempting to impose order and meaning on the chaotic and catastrophic events of the past.

Death and Dynasty (29 CE: *Annals* 5.1–5)

At the beginning of *Annals* 5 and Tacitus' account of 29 CE, Livia dies. The placement of her obituary notice is striking: Tacitus more often places such obituaries at the *end* of the narrative of a year rather than the beginning.[8] This attention-grabbing placement puts Livia's death notice in close proximity to Tacitus' report of the marriage of Agrippina the Younger to Domitius (4.75), forming a sort of hinge that connects Book 5 to Book 4. Like Livia's first marriage to Ti. Claudius Nero, that of Agrippina the Younger would produce one emperor (Nero) who would be adopted by another (Claudius), with disastrous results. Livia's obituary reminds us that the marriage of Agrippina the Elder and Germanicus, which produced Agrippina the Younger, was the only biological link between Augustus and his wife: "She brought forth no offspring after [her marriage to Augustus], but had grandchildren in common with him, connected as she was to the blood of Augustus through the union of Agrippina and Germanicus" (5.1.2: *nullam posthac subolem edidit, sed sanguini Augusti per coniunctionem Agrippinae et Germanici adnexa communes pronepotes habuit*). This impacts Tiberius, too, who did not possess that all-important blood connection to the first emperor. And when Tacitus notes that Caligula, "who took control of affairs in due course" (5.1.4: *qui mox rerum potitus est*), was the one to deliver Livia's funeral oration, he reminds us that Livia's involvement in the imperial succession was not positive, since it resulted ultimately in the reign of the horrible Caligula.[9]

Indeed, it is not only the significant placement of Livia's obituary, but also its content, that Tacitus uses to blacken her reputation and remind the reader of the dark consequences of her meddling. Although Tacitus must admit Livia conducted herself with blameless chastity, her relationships with her husband and son are described with

[6] Ando (1997), 285.
[7] Woodman (2017), 288 compares the death/funeral of Claudius and accession of Nero, which are split across books 12–13. The death of Germanicus (Book 2) and its aftermath (Book 3) also straddle a book division.
[8] Compare Junia's death, related at the end of Book 3 and 22 CE (3.76), and Julia's, described near the end of the account of 14 CE (1.53). On Tacitus' deployment of obituary notices, see Ginsburg (1981), 39–40.
[9] Barrett (2003), 59.

unconcealed hostility:[10] "She was charming beyond what was considered appropriate for ancient women, she was uncontrolled as a mother and complaisant as a wife, well suited to her husband's skills and her son's pretense" (5.1.3: *comis ultra quam antiquis feminis probatum, mater impotens, uxor facilis et cum artibus mariti, simulatione filii bene composita*). Even the observations that Livia was "charming" (*comis*) and "complaisant" (*facilis*) have their dark sides: these descriptors may imply that she was more interested in being likable than in being genuine, or that she turned a blind eye to Augustus' affairs.[11] But the phrase "uncontrolled mother" (*mater impotens*) is particularly damning. It recalls Tacitus' observation that one of the reasons transmitted (*traditur*) for Tiberius' self-imposed exile on Capri was that "he was thrust out by his mother's lack of restraint, for whom he felt aversion as an ally of his dominion but whom he could not get rid of, since he had received that very dominion as a gift from her" (4.57.3: *matris impotentia extrusum, quam dominationis sociam aspernabatur neque depellere poterat, cum dominationem ipsam donum eius accepisset*). Some gifts, evidently, are so big they can never be repaid.[12] Even Livia's death will not completely eliminate this mother–son rivalry. Tiberius, although he had rushed back to Rome during her illness in 22 CE (3.64.1), now fails to attend her funeral (5.2.1) and refuses honors decreed to her by the senate "as though out of modesty" (*quasi per modestiam*) but perhaps actually out of personal animus.[13]

The obituary also recalls Tacitus' description of popular opinion toward the end of Augustus' life, when some people deplored Livia's "womanly lack of restraint" (*muliebri impotentia*), which ensured that after Tiberius' succession he, or all of Rome, would "have to be slave(s) to a woman" (1.4.5: *serviendum feminae*).[14] Tacitus also impugns Livia's marriage to Augustus. Whereas parallel accounts suggest that her first husband, Tiberius Nero, was happy for Livia to divorce him, and even describe him playing the role a father would normally fulfill in the wedding ceremony when she married Octavian (Velleius Paterculus 2.79.2, 94.1; Dio 48.44.3), Tacitus focuses on the marriage's haste and notes that "it is uncertain whether she was unwilling" (5.1.2: *incertum an invitam*) for Octavian to "snatch her away" (*aufert*) from her first husband. This not only reprises the grousing by Augustus' critics that Livia had been "abducted" (1.10.5: *abducta*), gossip which now apparently "has become accepted historical fact," but also casts aspersions on Livia's own motives, implying that even early in Livia's life "there already existed an embryonic lust for power."[15]

Livia's oppressive motherhood is now at an end, but these intratextual references remind us that the unrestrained domination of one woman, who controlled her son the emperor and therefore Rome, has done its part in establishing a miserable state of affairs in Rome that will continue to the end of the Julio-Claudian dynasty she helped to establish.[16] And in the short term, too, her death has disastrous consequences, unleashing

[10] See further Barrett (2003), 45–9.   [11] Barrett (2003), 54–5; Woodman (2017), 55.
[12] Lendon (1997), 66–9, 72–3 nicely articulates the dishonorable state of clientage to which a man would be reduced in Roman culture if unable to repay a favor. This was particularly problematic for an emperor (Lendon (1997), 126–8).
[13] Cf. Woodman (2017), 56–7. Velleius, by contrast, suggests Tiberius was truly sad and Livia truly modest (2.130.5).
[14] Woodman (1998), 237–9 points out the ambiguity of the subject of *serviendum*, which he understands to be Tiberius, and most commentators assume is the Roman people collectively. On these passages, see further Santoro L'Hoir (1992), 122–3, 133–4.
[15] Flory (1988), 350, 357.
[16] The ascendancy of Agrippina the Younger will similarly be characterized as "almost manlike slavery" (12.7.3: *quasi virile servitium*), and she will also be accused of "womanly lack of restraint" (12.57.2: *impotentiam muliebrem*). See further Gillespie, Chapter 14 in this volume.

a period of "sheer and oppressive domination" (5.3.1: *praerupta iam et urgens dominatio*): while she was alive "Sejanus did not dare to surpass a parent's authority" (*neque Seianus audebat auctoritati parentis antire*), but after her death he and Tiberius "burst forth as though released from their reins, and letters were sent against Agrippina and Nero" (*tunc velut frenis exsoluti proruperunt, missaeque in Agrippinam ac Neronem litterae*). Tacitus compares Tiberius and Sejanus to raging beasts[17] released from their restraints now that the mitigating influence of Livia has been removed. This anticipates an observation Tacitus will make in his obituary of Tiberius, where he says that Tiberius "burst forth" (6.51.3: *prorupit*) into vice after Sejanus' death and notes that there was still some good in him "while his mother was unharmed" (6.51.3: *incolumi matre*). While Agrippina's supporters chant dramatically outside the senate house (5.4.2), it is only Tiberius' failure to specify a punishment (5.3.3) and the uncharacteristic interference of Junius Rusticus (5.4.1) that delays the implementation of the accusations against Agrippina and Nero (5.4.3). So even though Livia is dead, dynastic rivalries persist.

Friendship and Suicide (31 CE: *Annals* 5.6–11)

When the narrative resumes after the lacuna, we find ourselves wading through the aftermath of Sejanus' fall, in the midst of a defense speech delivered by an unnamed erstwhile supporter of Sejanus. He complains that Tiberius apparently "has pardoned himself" (*sibi ignoscit*) for his own association with Sejanus—which apparently went all the way to letting him marry into the imperial family (5.6.2)[18]—but is now allowing Sejanus' other supporters to be persecuted. The fact that friendship has become a liability precipitates, for the speaker, a crisis of values: "I could not make a distinction as to whether it is more miserable to be accused because of a friendship or to make an accusation against a friend" (5.6.3: *miserius sit ob amicitiam accusari an amicum accusare, haud discreverim*).[19] The lapidary quality of this *sententia* is striking; that Tacitus should place this universally applicable dictum about fidelity to friends in the mouth of a devotee of the horrific Sejanus is more striking still.

The speaker chooses to take his own life to preserve his freedom of action and avoid being forced to accuse his friend Sejanus to save his own skin:[20] "Free and acceptable to my own self, I will forestall danger" (5.6.3: *liber et mihi ipsi probatus antibo periculum*). He calls upon his friends to remember him as one of "those who have escaped public evils through an excellent end" (*iis qui fine egregio publica mala effugerunt*), marking himself as part of a growing trend of political suicides under the principate.[21] Tacitus' attitude to such suicides elsewhere is somewhat ambivalent,[22] but here Tacitus' description of the

---

[17] Probably horses, but perhaps lions according to Woodman (2017), 61.

[18] Possibly Sejanus was allowed to marry Julia Livi(ll)a, something Tiberius had previously forbidden (*Ann.* 4.39–41); see Bellemore (1995) and Birley (2007), 141.

[19] For the principate's impact on the institution of aristocratic friendship, see Seager (1977); Winterling (2008). The Latin *amicitia* connotes not only personal friendship but also patronage relationships and political alliances; see Powell (1995), 41–4. On Roman friendship generally, see Konstan (1997), chapter 4.

[20] So Woodman (2017), 70.

[21] On the phenomenon of suicide-as-resistance, formulaic and modeled on the deaths of Socrates and Cato the Younger, see Griffin (1986a); Griffin (1986b); van Hooff (1990), esp. 52–3; Hill (2004), esp. 183–8.

[22] See *Agr.* 42.4, *Ann.* 16.16.2.

unnamed speaker's death is remarkably balanced. He remarks on the man's "fearless expression" (5.7.1: *intrepidum vultum*) in his final moments; describes the manner of death ("he fell upon his sword," *gladio...incubuit*, considered the noblest method of suicide);[23] and takes care to remark that Tiberius "did not assail the deceased with any accusations or reproaches" (5.7.2: *neque Caesar ullis criminibus aut probris defunctum insectatus est*).[24] This is a far cry from the pathetic suicide of Vitellius, who "finished his life in mental distress" (5.8.2: *vitamque aegritudine animi finivit*) trying to open his veins with a penknife.[25] So the fact that Tacitus accords such even-handed treatment to our unnamed orator of 5.6 shows that, despite Tacitus' clear identification of Sejanus as a problematic and destructive force within Tiberius' principate, this does not mean the historian will always be hostile to his supporters. In fact, Tacitus seems to be implicitly criticizing the kind of society where the rise and fall of individuals in the imperial court have made traditional friendship a dangerous proposition.

Adding to the atmosphere of danger and menace at the end of the book are Tacitus' pathetic description of the execution of Sejanus' children (5.9) and the ominous appearance in the East of an impostor pretending to be Drusus (son of Agrippina the Elder and Germanicus), who has been imprisoned in Rome for the last year (5.10).[26] In addition to highlighting the tenseness of the general atmosphere, where rumors swirl and small children are considered a potential threat, these episodes both highlight Tacitus' difficulties in figuring out the truth of what happened. The rape of Sejanus' daughter is so horrific that Tacitus must appeal to unnamed "authors of that period" (5.9.2: *temporis eius auctores*) to authenticate the report. Yet for the false Drusus, all of Tacitus' attempts to find out the affair's conclusion are ultimately fruitless (5.10.3: *neque nos originem finemve eius rei ultra comperimus*, "Nor have I ascertained the beginning or end of this affair any further"), in contrast to the similar stories of the false Agrippa Postumus (2.39–40), Germanicus (2.82.4–5), and Nero (*H.* 2.8–9), where Tacitus is able to say how things ended, and to Dio's brief discussion of the same episode in which the false Drusus is captured and brought before Tiberius (58.25.1). Such was the period immediately after Sejanus' downfall, an event so significant that it not only devastates contemporary society but also impedes the historian's fact-finding abilities and forces him to authenticate reports of horrific violence.

Sex and Tyranny (32 CE: *Annals* 6.1–14)

Tacitus' opening of his account of the year 32, perhaps "the most brilliant of all" his year-beginnings,[27] shows us how things have changed now that Sejanus is dead. In his obituary of Tiberius at the end of the book, Tacitus will remind us that Tiberius kept "his lusts covered up" (6.51.3: *obtectis libidinibus*) until Sejanus' death ushered in the final phase of his life, in which "he finally burst forth simultaneously into crimes and disgraces" (6.51.3: *postremo in scelera simul ac dedecora prorupit*). Tiberius' critics had previously complained

[23] Grisé (1982), 96; van Hooff (1990), 51.
[24] Accusations of *maiestas* could still be made posthumously: Hill (2004), 190–1.
[25] See Grisé (1982), 55–6.
[26] Cf. Suet. *Tib.* 54.2 and Dio 58.3.8; Tacitus' account of Drusus' imprisonment has been lost. On the false Drusus, see further Tuplin (1987); Devillers and Hurlet (2007).
[27] Woodman (2017), 83.

that he had spent his entire exile on Rhodes in his earlier life "practicing...secret lusts" (1.4.4 *secretas libidines meditatum*);[28] so perhaps he is now able to revert to type.

Tiberius, who has been on the Italian mainland and even at times appeared to be approaching Rome, now returns to Capri[29] "out of shame at his crimes and his untamed lusts, with which he had become so inflamed that in a kingly manner he polluted freeborn youth with illicit sex" (6.1.1: *pudore scelerum et libidinum, quibus adeo indomitis exarserat, ut more regio pubem ingenuam stupris pollueret*). So depraved were Tiberius' tastes that new words had to be found to describe them: *sellaria* and *spintriae*, whose exact meanings have been debated but which probably refer respectively to brothels and sex workers/erotic performers.[30] Noting the inventions of new things is something of a "preoccupation" of ancient historians,[31] and new words are particularly significant: ever since Thucydides' memorable discussion of how civil conflict in Corcyra warped the use of political terminology (3.82.4), historians' discussions of linguistic change had been charged. Whereas Thucydides deplored how intense political competition destabilizes language, Tacitus' general view seems to be that it is the *lack* of competition operating in the principate that allows for "top-down linguistic façades [to be] imposed," as Lydia Spielberg has recently observed.[32] Claudius will also innovate in the Latin language by adding new letters to its alphabet (11.13.2), but Tiberius' linguistic contributions are of a much more disreputable kind, "provid[ing] a further mark of degradation" wrought upon Roman society by his principate.[33] We are told that, in addition to assessing his victims' physical attractiveness, Tiberius "regarded the decorous boyhood of some, the ancestors' images of others, as incitements for desire" (6.1.2: *in his modestiam pueritiam, in aliis imagines maiorum incitamentum cupidinis habebat*). The pedigree that should traditionally be a criterion for office-holding (cf. 4.6.2: *nobilitatem maiorum*, "ancestors' nobility") is now a criterion for sex with the emperor.[34]

Tacitus' observation that Tiberius acted "in a kingly manner" (*more regio*) evokes the stereotype of the foreign (especially Greek) tyrant as someone who exercised violence and lust without restraint, which had become a *topos* in Roman literature.[35] The description here of Tiberius enticing, badgering, and even forcibly abducting young freeborn men for sexual purposes (6.1.2) ticks all of those boxes, with children being taken from their parents' very arms (*et si retinerent propinquus aut parens*) serving as a particular (and particularly distressing) hallmark of tyrannical behavior.[36] The slaves Tiberius dispatched to find these young targets are instructed, if they resist, to rape them, "as they would in the

---

[28] Cf. Galtier (2011), 186 and n. 238.

[29] For Tiberius' time on Capri, see Houston (1985); Parker (2009). See also Ash (2024), 54–5 for a spatial reading of this passage.

[30] See Champlin (2011), who rejects the traditional interpretation that the terms have to do with anal intercourse. The words also appear in Suetonius (*Tib.* 43).

[31] Oakley (1997–2005), ii, 94; see examples there cited.

[32] Spielberg (2017), 364, 360–4 on Tacitus. See also Walker (1952), 241.   [33] Woodman (2017), 90.

[34] Woodman (2017), 89. In addition to the parallels there cited, cf. also *Anacreontea* 29.5 γένος οὐδὲν εἰς ἔρωτα, "Lineage is nothing to love" (a reference I owe to A. J. Woodman), although in the erotic context of the poem the comparison seems to be with money, the only thing love *does* value. On *imagines*, see Flower (1996).

[35] See recently the contributions in Panou and Schadee (2018), especially Baraz (2018). Cf. 4.35.5, where Tacitus, speaking of Cremutius Cordus (on whom see ten Berge, Chapter 12 in this volume), notes the futility of attempts to censure literature by "foreign kings or those who practiced the same savagery" (*externi reges aut qui eadem saevitia usi sunt*).

[36] Woodman (2017), 93 with parallels there cited. For other "tyrannical" crimes of Tiberius, see Galtier (2011), 216–18.

case of war-captives" (6.1.2: *velut in captos*). For rape and child abduction are also a common element of the *urbs capta* ("captured city") motif; Tiberius and his henchmen are therefore also like an enemy army attacking their own people.[37] The tyrannical Tiberius may not have physically entered Rome, but he is morally and metaphorically destroying it.

The accusation and acquittal of Cotta Messalinus (6.5–7) show that Tiberius' power and control continue despite his slide into sexual depravity. Universally hated as the "originator of all the most savage proposals" in the senate (6.5.1: *saevissimae cuiusque sententiae auctor*), Cotta is accused of questioning Caligula's masculinity and making a macabre joke at Livia's expense,[38] and when involved in a financial dispute with Lepidus and Arruntius (whom Augustus had identified as capable of rule; cf. 1.13.2), blithely notes, "The senate will protect them, but my little Tiberius will protect me" (6.5.1: *illos quidem senatus, me autem tuebitur Tiberiolus meus*). The diminutive form of the emperor's name may simply imply Cotta's affection for him, but could also suggest excessive familiarity or even mockery and contempt.[39] And Cotta turns out to be right: after Tiberius' intervention by letter (6.6), Cotta is let off despite his manifest guilt—and even though Sextus Vistilius, who lacks the all-important connection with Tiberius, is punished with formal withdrawal of the emperor's friendship and commits suicide when similarly accused of denigrating Caligula's manhood, an accusation Tacitus says may have been false (6.9.2: *sive ficto habita fides*, "or perhaps credibility was given to something made-up").[40] After Cotta's acquittal, his accusers are actually punished for prosecuting him. Tacitus says that "nothing more honorable than this ever happened to Cotta" (6.7.1: *quo non aliud honorificentius Cottae evenit*); the fact that punishment of one's enemies is apparently now the best way of conferring honor in Tiberian Rome speaks volumes.

The friendship (with Tiberius) that saves Cotta also forms a sharp contrast with the friendship (with Sejanus) that puts the equestrian M. Terentius (unknown outside Tacitus) in the emperor's crosshairs. Like the unnamed speaker of 5.6–7, Terentius delivers a rousing oration[41] defending his own connection with Sejanus on the grounds that Tiberius himself had elevated him: "It is not our task to judge whom you raise up above the rest and for what reasons. To you the gods have given the highest power of judgment over affairs; to us is left only the glory of obedience" (6.8.4: *non est nostrum aestimare, quem supra ceteros et quibus de causis extollas: tibi summum rerum iudicium di dedere, nobis obsequii gloria relicta est*). Terentius, however, is saved "by the constancy of his speech, and because a man had been found who would express what everybody was pondering in their hearts" (6.9.1: *constantia orationis, et quia repertus erat, qui efferet quae omnes animo agitabant*). The notion that forthrightness should be rewarded comes as something of a surprise, given not only Terentius' relationship with Sejanus[42] but also the

---

[37] Paul (1982), 147. See also Keitel (1984) and Joseph, Chapter 7 in this volume, n. 3.

[38] See Shannon-Henderson (2019), 213 on the significance of the "nine-day funeral banquet" (6.5.1: *novendialem...cenam*).

[39] Familiarity is especially implied by the possessive adjective (*meus*), which Biville (2006) has identified as an assertion of membership within a family or shared social group. For diminutives as potentially insulting, see Hanssen (1952), 114, 234, 241.

[40] Whitehead (1979), 484 notes, "There is no way...of telling whether Vistilius had indeed done this or was simply alleged to have done this." For the withdrawal of the emperor's friendship, see Rogers (1959); Kierdorf (1987); Winterling (2008), 309.

[41] Ash (2021b) explicates the speech's significant intertextual references. Dio 58.19.3–5 has a shorter version of the same affair, where he seems to have used Tacitus as a source.

[42] Cf. Woodman (2017), 122.

general atmosphere of these books of the *Annals* (for example the punishment of Cremutius Cordus for "free speech" in *Annals* 4), and we are left wondering whether something else is at play in Terentius' success—perhaps the tinge of obsequiousness in his words implying that Tiberius has a divine right to rule is what has actually won him his pardon.[43] The morality and rewards of friendship, therefore, remain ambiguous, further contributing to the destabilized atmosphere.

Fate and Food (33 CE: *Annals* 6.15–27)

Grimness continues. Book 6 is the book of the *Annals* with the highest concentration of deaths, and the year 33 CE has the highest concentration within Book 6.[44] Tiberius' handling of a financial crisis is the closest thing we get to a bright spot, and even this ends with a senatorial decree characterized by "keen beginnings, as frequently happens in such cases, but a lack of concern for the conclusion" (6.17.4: *acribus, ut ferme talia, initiis, incurioso fine*).[45] We have the first mention in the extant text of Macro (who will have been initially introduced in the now-lost portion of *Annals* 5), Sejanus' successor as prefect of the Praetorian Guard, who will be a central figure in Tiberius' death (6.15.2; cf. 6.50.5).[46] Executions escalate when Tiberius, "roused by punishments" (6.19.2: *inritatusque suppliciis*) as though his appetite has been whetted for more blood,[47] orders the execution of all remaining prisoners accused of friendship with Sejanus. The consequences are immense and repulsive: "There lay a huge slaughter, [bodies of] every sex, every age, illustrious and ignoble, scattered about or in piles" (6.19.2: *iacuit immensa strages omnis sexus omnis aetas, inlustres ignobiles, dispersi aut aggerati*).[48] Tacitus' wording recalls the indiscriminate destruction of Germans regardless of age or sex by the Roman army (1.51.1), and anticipates a similar destruction from a deadly whirlwind that hits Campania in 65 CE (16.13.2);[49] but here Tiberius, not military zeal or natural disaster, is solely responsible for Roman deaths. In a pathetic scene, friends and relatives are prevented from weeping for the dead (a crime that had already been fatal for the old woman Vitia, 6.10.1) or cremating the bodies of their loved ones, which bob putridly in the Tiber:[50] "Thanks to the strength of their fear, the connection that characterizes the human condition had perished, and pity was avoided to the degree that savagery increased" (6.19.3: *interciderat sortis humanae commercium vi metus, quantumque saevitia glisceret, miseratio arcebatur*). The disruption to typical funeral customs is another historiographical motif pointing back to Thucydides: in his famous account of the plague that attacked Athens in 429 BCE, bodies of the dead and dying pile up in the streets, near public fountains, and in temples, and the sheer magnitude makes it impossible for people to bury their family

---

[43] Shannon-Henderson (2019), 218–19.   [44] Woodman (2017), 149.
[45] On the financial crisis, see Elliott (2015), with an excellent survey of previous scholarship.
[46] On Macro, see the references in Absil (1997), 127–8.
[47] For this interpretation of *inritatus*, see Woodman (2017), 165.
[48] On the implications of denial of burial in Roman culture, see Hope (2000), 116–20, esp. 116.
[49] Cf. also the widespread destruction caused by the fire of 64 (15.38), although it is described with different wording.
[50] The Tiber had a history of being used as a place of disposal for the bodies of criminals and the victims of political violence: Kyle (1998), 218–24. For the motif of ideologically motivated prohibitions on mourning, cf. Lucan 2.38–45 (I owe this parallel to Rhiannon Ash).

members (Thucydides 2.52.2–4). But here the *saevitia* of the tyrannical Tiberius, not an epidemic, leads to putrid rot in Rome's streets.[51]

Against this horrific background, Tacitus deploys a careful sequence of chapters that shifts our attention to the (equally horrific) future, for which Tiberius will also bear some responsibility. In reporting Caligula's marriage, Tacitus describes the future emperor as "covering his monstrous spirit in a deceitful modesty" (6.20.1: *immanem animum subdola modestia tegens*), keeping silent about the punishments of his mother and brother, and imitating Tiberius' behavior so closely that it was said "there had never been a better slave or a worse master" (*neque meliorem umquam servum neque deteriorem dominum fuisse*). This look to the future inspires another: Tiberius predicts to Galba (whose only connection to these events is the fact that he happens to be consul that year, 6.20.2: *tum consule*), that he "too will one day taste power" (*et tu, Galba, quandoque degustabis imperium*). We have, then, two predictions about future emperors—both bad ones—who will afflict Rome in the short term (after Tiberius' death) and the long term (after the end of the Julio-Claudian dynasty has plunged Rome into civil war).

Tiberius makes his prediction using skills learned from his astrologer Thrasyllus,[52] which prompts Tacitus to consider "whether mortals' affairs are turned by fate and immutable necessity, or by chance" (6.22.1: *fatone res mortalium et necessitate immutabili an forte volvantur*). Tacitus rehearses the Epicurean and Stoic positions for and against the role of fate in human affairs, and ultimately fails to come to a firm conclusion. But given that other astrological predictions described in the *Annals* have a tendency to come true, we might be meant to think that the third viewpoint Tacitus expresses in 6.22 is the one to which the historian is guiding his reader: astrology is a generally valid science, but individual practitioners sometimes deceive. On a larger timescale that extends beyond Tiberius' principate, then, astrology can provide readers with some answers about what is going to happen. This raises potentially uncomfortable questions about the role of fate, a force that in this case is far from providential; if the stars predicted that Caligula and Galba would rule, could Tiberius (or anyone else in Rome) have done anything to prevent them?

Tiberius' prediction of Galba's "taste of power" sets the tone for the succeeding chapters—for, apart from fate, the other overwhelming theme of 33 CE is food, as A. J. Woodman has shown.[53] Following close on the heels of Tacitus' digression on fate come four deaths by starvation. Some are suicides. The first is Asinius Gallus, a man Augustus had thought was possibly interested in ruling (1.13.2) who has clashed with Tiberius several times.[54] In this case, death by starvation is perhaps a convenient way for an antagonist to be eliminated without Tiberius having to get his hands dirty.[55] But the last of the four deaths by starvation—that of legal expert Cocceius Nerva (6.26.1–2), grandfather of the future emperor and the only senator to follow Tiberius to Capri (4.58.1)—is somewhat different. Tacitus' choice of the wording *abstinentiam cibi coniunxit* to describe the action identifies Cocceius' death very much as part of a sequence: as Woodman notes,

---

[51] Yet Tacitus has also built up a complex metaphor of disease and the body politic throughout the Tiberian hexad: see Woodman (2010b), esp. 43–7.

[52] On 6.21, see Shannon-Henderson (2019), 224–9 with further bibliography there cited. On Thrasyllus, see Tarrant (1993), 8–11.

[53] See Woodman (2006b).   [54] On Asinius Gallus, see Devillers (2009a).

[55] Van Hooff (1990), 46.

the words "suggest that Nerva has deliberately 'joined his starvation'" to the previous ones, "and hence that he has chosen this manner of death as an eloquent comment on theirs."[56] Self-starvation, after all, is by necessity premeditated, a drawn-out type of death that provokes a reaction or sends a message; as Tiberius himself recognizes (6.26.1), and as Nerva's intimates confirm (6.26.2), it is clear that Nerva has chosen suicide as a way of opting out of the horrors of the regime.[57]

But the most interesting of the deaths is that of Drusus, son of Agrippina the Elder and Germanicus, who expires after nine days deprived of food when he finally runs out of "pitiable nourishment" (6.23.2: *miserandis alimentis*)—a rather elevated way to describe what turns out to be his mattress-stuffing, which he has been reduced to eating. The pathos of the situation is increased all the more when we learn for the first time that Tiberius had once instructed Macro to remove Drusus from custody and set him up in a position of leadership in the event of a revolt by Sejanus.[58] This brief glimpse of an alternative history in which Drusus is reconciled with Tiberius and rises to prominence is a stark contrast with the treatment he has actually received. We are perhaps reminded of Junius Rusticus' prediction that Tiberius might not welcome any rash actions against Agrippina and Nero (5.4.1 "the old man could one day regret the destruction of Germanicus' offspring," *posse quandoque Germanici st<irpis ex>itium paenitentiae <esse> seni*). But now there is no sign Tiberius regrets what might have been.

Tacitus again deploys the theme of verification and believability when he describes a public recitation of Drusus' words and his mistreatment at the hands of his captors, who not only physically abused him but also kept a day-by-day account of his minutest movements. We have seen such spying before (e.g. on Titius Sabinus, 4.69.1), but the fact that in Drusus' case the surveillance was done openly, and that Tiberius has no shame about revealing it now, truly strains credibility: "It was scarcely believable that for so many years men had stood by to receive his expressions, groans, even his secret murmuring, and that the grandfather could bring himself to hear of it, read of it, and divulge it in public" (6.24.1: *adstitisse tot per annos, qui vultum gemitus, occultum etiam murmur exciperent, et potuisse avum audire legere, in publicum promere vix fides*). The senators listening are also struck with "fear and wonderment" (6.24.3: *pavor et admiratio*) at this extreme revelation from an emperor "formerly clever and secretive in concealing crimes" (*callidum olim et tegendis sceleribus obscurum*). Similarly, upon the death of Agrippina, reported in the next chapter, Tiberius tastelessly boasts that she was not strangled (6.25.3), publicizing his real attitude to her death in a way that parallels his revelation of Drusus' shocking treatment.

Another part of what sparks the senators' reaction is the report of Drusus' dying words. He shifts from pretended madness (6.24.2: *alienationem mentis simulans*) to premeditated curses (*meditatas compositasque diras*) once he believes he has nothing left to lose, perhaps mirroring Tiberius' own rejection of concealment. This also plays into ancient conceptions about curses, which were thought to have more power when spoken by someone at death's door. Drusus' words show hallmarks of the formulae found on curse tablets: the *quid pro quo* structure, expressing the hope that the target of the curse will suffer the same thing he has inflicted on others (*quem ad modum...ita*), and the idea that the descendants

---

[56] Woodman (2017), 197.   [57] Grisé (1982), 82–3; van Hooff (1990), 33, 38, 40, 45–6.
[58] See further Pigoń (1993).

of the accursed should also be affected (*posteris*).[59] But this is not just standard-issue curse language. The motif of Tiberius' house filled with bloodshed (6.24.2: *quem ad modum nurum filiumque fratris et nepotes domumque omnem caedibus complevisset*, "in the same way that he had destroyed his daughter-in-law, brother's son, grandchildren, and filled his entire house with slaughter") looks both backward to the recent horrific description of a Tiber choked with corpses (6.19.3)[60] and forward to the equally grim familial murders that will be perpetrated by Tiberius' successors Claudius and Nero.[61] And Tiberius' descendants here are not the ones who will be punished, but the ones to whom (along with his ancestors) the emperor owes satisfaction: "He should pay the penalty to the name and race of his ancestors, and to posterity" (*ita poenas nomini generique maiorum et posteris exsolveret*). Tiberius has already shown himself to be obsessed with avoiding a negative posthumous reputation (see e.g. *Ann.* 4.38), and it is possibly this to which Drusus refers; but we may also be meant to think of the issues raised in the astrological digression (6.20–2), where we were invited to consider the question of who is responsible for future grim moments in the principate. Drusus' curse appears to tap into the idea that Tiberius' actions will shape subsequent history in a way that makes it impossible for him to avoid its negative judgment.

Drusus' hope that Tiberius would pay a penalty to future generations later shows hints of coming true, in the sense that Tiberius seems, at the end of his life, to be considering his own posthumous reputation differently. Fulcinius Trio (the pro-Sejanus consul of 5.11), in a display of defiance that is at odds with these frightening times, reveals in his will bold accusations against Macro and some of Tiberius' freedmen, and openly calls Tiberius senile (6.38.2: *ipsi fluxam senio mentem…obiectando*, "accusing the man himself of a mind feeble with old age").[62] Tiberius unexpectedly wants this read out publicly, "either showing off his tolerance for the free speech of others and disregarding his own disgrace, or, long ignorant of Sejanus' crimes, he later preferred them, however they were said, to be publicized, and to become knowledgeable of the truth (which flattery impedes) even via disgrace" (6.38.3: *patientiam libertatis alienae ostentans et contemptor suae infamiae, an scelerum Seiani diu nescius mox quoquo modo dicta vulgari malebat veritatisque, cui adulatio officit, per probra saltem gnarus fieri*). This is not the Tiberius we have previously been shown. In 25 CE the public revelation of secret insults against him (4.42) needled Tiberius so much that they precipitated his withdrawal from Rome. And as far back as 14 CE Tacitus had described him as always speaking in "vague and obscure words even in affairs he was not covering up, whether this was because of his nature or because he had become used to doing so" (1.11.2: *Tiberioque etiam in rebus quas non occuleret, seu natura sive adsuetudine, suspensa semper et obscura verba*). Publicizing Trio's will is the culmination of Tiberius' new tendency toward openness and revelation toward the end of his life,[63] beginning with an apparent *cri de coeur* in the letter to the Senate about Cotta (6.6.2)[64]

---

[59] Strubbe (1991), 43.

[60] For the motif cf. the Sibyl's gruesome prediction of "the Tiber foaming with much blood" at Vergil *Aen.* 6.87 (*Thybrim multo spumantem sanguine*, with thanks to Rhiannon Ash for the parallel).

[61] Cf. e.g. 12.1.1: *caede Messalinae convulsa principis domus*, "The emperor's house was violently shaken by the slaughter of Messalina."

[62] Dio 58.25.2 explicitly states that Trio took his own life. On wills as a place to give free expression to abuse, see Champlin (1991), 16. For Roman ideas on loss of mental acuity in old age, see Parkin (2003), 228–30.

[63] Woodman (2017), 249.

[64] See further Levick (1978) and Shannon-Henderson (2019), 214–17.

and escalating in his publicization of his foul treatment of Drusus (6.24). But the idea of Tiberius' disregard for his own reputation (*contemptor suae infamiae*) is an even more sudden shift; as recently as 6.30.4 he has appeared to acknowledge that in old age *fama* may be all that is left to prop up his position. Is Tacitus showing the reader a leopard who has changed his spots at the eleventh hour, an arch-dissimulator veering sharply toward the disclosure of even the worst things he has done, and discarding any concern for post-humous reputation?

From here, we accelerate. The year 34 CE is the second shortest narrative year in the *Annals* and consists of "continuous slaughter in Rome" (6.29.1: *at Romae caede continua*). The majority of the account of 35 CE is taken up with a digression on affairs in Parthia, which will also feature heavily in 36 CE (6.41–4).[65] Tacitus states explicitly that he has included this "so the mind" of the reader "can have a rest from evils at home" (6.38.1: *quo requiesceret animus a domesticis malis*). For very little has changed. Tacitus describes Tiberius, who has advanced closer to Rome than usual, "watching, so to speak, the blood moving in waves through each house[66] or the hands of the executioners" (6.39.2: *quasi aspiciens undantem per domos sanguinem aut manus carnificum*). The image of waves of blood vividly recalls both the multitude of floating bodies in the Tiber (6.19.3: *fluitantia*) and also Drusus' curse against Tiberius for filling his own house with slaughter (6.24.2).

The End (37 CE: *Annals* 6.45.3–51)

In the last chapters of Tiberius' life, Tacitus weaves together into a masterful web the themes that he has introduced throughout the book: dissimulation, foreboding, hunger, and the difficulty of arriving at the truth. Tacitus' account of 37 CE, inaugurated by what are ominously described as "the last consuls for Tiberius" (6.45.3: *supremi Tiberio consules*), opens with a callback to 6.20–2. Caligula is single again after the death of Claudia, whom he married at 6.20.1, and Macro attempts to develop a hold over the man he assumes will be the next emperor by throwing at Caligula his own wife Ennia, who is evidently supposed to seduce Caligula with the false promise that she will get Macro to ensure Caligula's succession, then murder Macro and marry Caligula instead.[67] Unlike other authors,[68] Tacitus constructs a version of their relationship that has Caligula deceiving Ennia just as much as she is deceiving him: "Although he was disturbed in his mind, nevertheless he had learned the falsehoods of pretense in his grandfather's lap" (6.45.3: *etsi commotus ingenio, simulationum tamen falsa in sinu avi perdidicerat*). This, too, makes us recall 6.20.1, where we were told that when he followed Tiberius to Capri, Caligula had made it his business to modulate his words and behavior precisely to suit whatever type of day Tiberius seemed to be having (*qualem diem Tiberius induisset*). So at the moment when Tiberius himself seems to be abandoning his dissimulative ways, Caligula is marking himself out as the next deceiver-in-chief.[69]

---

[65] On this Parthian digression, see Ash (1999a). On Parthian sections in the *Annals* in general, see Keitel (1978); Gowing (1990).

[66] See Woodman (2017), 251 for this translation of *per domos*.

[67] Woodman (2017), 270–1 explicates the situation and compares the parallel traditions.

[68] See further Birley (2007), 144–7.   [69] Cf. Devillers (2021), 74–5.

Yet the student has not quite yet become the master, for "all this was known to Tiberius" (6.46.1: *gnarum hoc principi*), and it makes him hesitate about naming Caligula as his successor. Other factors against Caligula include "the common people's enthusiasm" for him, which "was a cause of hatred with his grandfather" (*vulgi studia, eaque apud avum odii causa*). Popularity has always been ill-fated for other members of this family line, as the onlookers at Germanicus' triumph in 17 CE had noted: "Brief and ill-omened were the loves of the Roman people" (2.41.3: *breves et infaustos populi Romani amores*).[70] Caligula's popularity will also be ill-fated, for the entire city of Rome just as much as for himself, given the nature of his reign, the disastrousness and brevity of which Tiberius can already predict. For Tiberius again, as in 6.20–2, indulges in his favorite hobby of prophecy, "throwing out words through which it could be understood that he was able to predict the future" (6.46.3: *iactis tamen vocibus per quas intellegeretur providus futurorum*). He predicts that Caligula will be like the worst possible version of Sulla (known for plunging republican Rome into a bloody civil war) and will murder Tiberius Gemellus (grandson of the emperor) before eventually being assassinated himself. Yet Tiberius' grim prescience[71] is at odds with his fear that "if a successor were sought outside the house, he was afraid that the memory of Augustus and the name of the Caesars would turn to laughingstock and scorn; for his concern was not the favor of people in the present so much as currying favor with future generations" (6.46.2: *sin extra domum successor quaereretur, ne memoria Augusti, ne nomen Caesarum in ludibria et contumelias verterent, metuebat: quippe illi non perinde curae gratia praesentium quam in posteros ambitio*). We appear here to be witnessing a last gasp of Tiberius' concern for his posthumous reputation—albeit a misguided one, for in what sense does he believe that the principate of the awful Caligula will not tarnish the name of the Caesars? Throwing up his hands, Tiberius leaves the decision to fate (6.46.3: *consilium, cui impar erat, fato permisit*, "he left to fate a decision to which he was unequal").[72]

That fate will turn out to be hostile, as Tacitus hints in observing that, with the incidents involving Acutia, Junius Otho, and Albucilla and her alleged affair-partners, "the seeds were sown even for future slaughters after Tiberius" (6.47.1: *futuris etiam post Tiberium caedibus semina iaciebantur*). The statement recalls Tacitus' similarly allusive observation that "the first crime of the new principate was the slaughter of Agrippa Postumus" (1.6.1: *primum facinus novi principatus fuit Postumi Agrippae caedes*); Tiberius' successor will begin a similar track record of death. And, importantly, Tiberius is not the only one who realizes this. One of Albucilla's alleged paramours is L. Arruntius, a reminder of Book 1, one of those whom Augustus had judged capable of ruling (1.13.2). Despite his friends' pleas, Arruntius commits suicide rather than waiting to try his luck under Caligula after Tiberius dies. Arruntius' warnings about Caligula are likened explicitly to prophecy (6.48.3: *haec vatis in modum dictitans*, "repeating these things in the manner of a prophet"); so it is not only the emperor-astrologer Tiberius who can make predictions about the future. Arruntius' decision to act on his predictions is explicitly endorsed by Tacitus as the correct course of action: "Subsequent events will serve as proof that Arruntius used his death well"

[70] See Shannon-Henderson (2019), 63–5 on this episode. See also Devillers (2021), 75.
[71] Woodman (2017), 274 suspects that Tacitus is deliberately subverting the real-life Tiberius' claim to *providentia*, a virtue he advertised on coinage.
[72] See further Shannon-Henderson (2019), 233–5.

(*documento sequentia erunt bene Arruntium morte usum*). What is less clear, but suggestive, is the question of whether Tacitus also endorses Arruntius' idea that Tiberius' behavior changed for the worse during his time as emperor (6.48.2: *Tiberius post tantam rerum experientiam vi dominationis convulsus et mutatus sit*, "Tiberius had been torn apart and changed by the force of sole rule even after so much experience of affairs"), a judgment which the reader may soon compare with Tacitus' own analysis of the phases of the emperor's life in his upcoming obituary (6.51).[73]

The authorial voice's twofold endorsement of Arruntius' predictions therefore sets the stage perfectly for the death to follow. Tacitus tells us that "now his body, now his strength, deserted Tiberius—but not yet his dissimulation" (6.50.1 *iam Tiberium corpus, iam vires, nondum dissimulatio deserebat*), and that "he hid his decline although it was obvious" (*quamvis manifestam defectionem tegebat*), to the extent that his doctor Charicles must resort to duplicity to discover that the emperor is actually dying. During a feast, Charicles pretends to leave early and grasps the emperor's hand, ostensibly as a gesture of farewell but really to take his pulse, "but he did not deceive him; for Tiberius, perhaps offended and therefore suppressing his anger all the more," continues the banquet to cover up his weakness (6.50.3: *neque fefellit: nam Tiberius, incertum an offensus tantoque magis iram premensa*), thereby "literalising the metaphor" of the taste of power, "capitalizing on his hold on the banquet to prove his hold on life."[74] But Charicles has the information he needs to inform Macro that Tiberius will die within days. In Tiberius' final moments the lavish banquet gives way to the pathetic spectacle of a dying old man crying out for food just as Drusus had done;[75] is the joke (cf. 6.46.5: *eludere*) now on Tiberius? Perhaps not. In the murky atmosphere of the difficulty of proof that Tacitus has created throughout the last part of *Annals* 6, it should perhaps come as no surprise that the exact moment of Tiberius' death is somewhat difficult to pin down: "He is believed," but not known, "to have fulfilled his mortality on March 16 when his breath was cut off" (6.50.4: *XVII kal. Apriles interclusa anima creditus est mortalitatem explevisse*), much as "it was not sufficiently ascertained whether Tiberius had found Augustus still breathing or dead" (1.5.3: *neque satis compertum est, spirantem adhuc Augustum…an exanimem reppererit*) when he rushed to Nola during his predecessor's final illness. Both Macro and Caligula are surprised when Tiberius briefly returns to life and has to be smothered with a pile of clothes (6.50.5). Tiberius' pathetic end shows how hard it is to arrive at the truth where the deaths of emperors are concerned, particularly ones who are deliberately deceptive.

How to end a reign—and a life? Enigmatically; for one of the most hotly debated chapters of Tacitus is the final obituary of Tiberius delivered in 6.51. Obituary notices are a common feature of historical prose, and Tacitus himself includes death-notices for important men and women throughout the *Annals*,[76] but the one for Tiberius is long and unusually involved. We might expect this for an emperor, but Tiberius' might be meant to be striking even by comparison with the other Julio-Claudians; we do not possess Tacitus' account of the deaths of Caligula or Nero, but Claudius receives no similar paragraph

---

[73] Woodman (2017), 279–80 is more positive, Martin (2001), 188 more hesitant.

[74] Woodman (2017), 285. Tacitus has already told us that Tiberius "was accustomed to make fun of doctors' skills" (6.46.5: *solitusque eludere medicorum artes*) and those who used them. See also Ash (2024), 49–52 for an excellent reading of this episode.

[75] Woodman (2017), 286.   [76] On obituaries in Tacitus, see Syme (1958b); Pomeroy (1991), ch. 9.

when he dies at the end of *Annals* 12. One thing Tacitus is doing is to round off the hexad, for there are reminiscences of the start of the *Annals* here. The obituary's note that Tiberius' "origin on both sides was from the Claudian line" (6.51.1: *utrimque origo gentis Claudiae*) might make the reader recall observations at the end of Augustus' life that Tiberius had "the old, deep-seated haughtiness of the Claudian family" (1.4.3: *vetere atque insita Claudiae familiae superbia*), and the list of rivals by whom he was "tormented" (6.51.1: *conflictatus est*) recalls Augustus' doomed succession plans described in 1.13.1–3. True enough, then, the claim that "from his earliest infancy his situation was unsettled" (6.51.1: *casus prima ab infantia ancipites*), tossed about upon the stormy seas of politics that favored others.[77]

The obituary's final sentence (6.51.3), which seeks to divide Tiberius' life into phases based on his behavior, is exceptionally difficult to interpret.[78] It has often been misunderstood as though Tacitus were saying that Tiberius kept his character hidden, and gradually "unmasked" his true nature as various people who exercised a moderating influence on his behavior—Germanicus, Drusus, Livia, Sejanus—died off.[79] This interpretation is hard to sustain, for Tacitus' language does not suggest revelation so much as actual change in Tiberius' behavior.[80] What the obituary does, as Woodman perceptively describes it, is to "periodise…the deterioration of Tiberius and his principate according to the loss of his successive helpers, until, in the final period, he experiences the isolation of power which he so dreaded in 14 CE."[81] It might come as something of a surprise to the reader who is just emerging from the disasters of *Annals* 6 to be suddenly reminded that Tiberius started off well, and could actually be described as "excellent in his life and in his reputation" (*egregium vita famaque*) before he became emperor. Tacitus thus explicitly contradicts the rumors of Tiberius' bad character that were swirling at the time of his succession (1.4.3–4):[82] although people at the time wanted to see Tiberius as wicked from the start, we now see that this was mostly malice, since we have been given no evidence that he did anything wicked during this period (an impression Tacitus has strengthened by choosing to avoid describing events prior to 14 CE in detail). It should also be noted that for the first three periods described, "the common thread is goodness";[83] even in the period between his accession and the deaths of Germanicus (19 CE) and Drusus (23 CE) there are virtues even if they are accompanied by a certain disingenuousness (*occultum ac subdolum fingendis virtutibus*, "secretive and clever at fashioning his virtues"),[84] and in the period between 23 CE and Livia's death in 29 Tiberius does have some genuine good (*bona*) about him even if it is tempered with evil (*mala*). That middle period appears to be something of a tipping-point, since what follows is worse: the period (29–31 CE) when Tiberius' behavior deteriorated into *saevitia* as he wavered between positive and negative attitudes to Sejanus, and the period after Sejanus' death (31–7 CE) when the *saevitia* continued and the only change was that Tiberius felt able to act freely on his sexual desires (*libidinibus*).

---

[77] On the nautical metaphor, see Woodman (2017), 288–9.

[78] My reading is indebted to Woodman (1989).

[79] Martin (1990), 1550: "He discarded one mask after another; only at the end was the true Tiberius revealed." See also Martin (1990), 1514.

[80] Martin (2001), 192 sees "five phases mark[ing] a progressive deterioration in Tiberius' behaviour." Gill (1983) disproved the long-held belief that ancients believed people's essential character was fixed and immutable; but see also Hands (1974). Cf. Luce (1986), 152–7.

[81] Woodman (2017), 310.   [82] Woodman (2017), 295.   [83] Woodman (2017), 294.

[84] I follow the interpretation of Woodman (2017), 296 on *fingendis virtutibus*. See also Martin (2001), 200–2.

The final phrase, "once shame and fear were removed and he used only his own talents" (*postquam remoto pudore et metu suo tantum ingenio utebatur*), is exceptionally prone to misinterpretation by translators.[85] The Latin word *ingenium* can mean either "intellect" or "character, nature," and many readers of this sentence have inclined to the latter, interpreting Tacitus to be saying that Tiberius "used only his own true nature." But it is more likely that the phrase means something like "after he had only his own wits to rely on"—that is, once Tiberius has no one left to help him bear the heavy burden of the principate that he claimed he never wanted in the first place (1.11.1), he gave in to his own basest instincts.

What the obituary gives the reader, in other words, is a moment to think back over everything in the preceding hexad. For the periods which Tacitus identifies also correspond to important structural moments of the Tiberian books: *Annals* 4 becomes the transitional period. The moment after Drusus' and Germanicus' deaths when Sejanus becomes dominant comes at the beginning of *Annals* 4, when *saevitia* in Tiberius caused by Sejanus is explicitly identified as a new trend (4.1.1) and we are told that "Tiberius' principate changed for the worse" (4.6.1: *Tiberio mutati in deterius principatus*). But the mitigating influence of Livia was still present, as we realize once it has been withdrawn following her death at the start of *Annals* 5 and we are told that "after that there was headlong and pressing domination—for while Augusta was unharmed there was still a refuge…" (5.3.1: *ex eo praerupta iam et urgens dominatio. nam incolumi Augusta erat adhuc perfugium*). In other words, the reader now realizes that the successive loss of each of his helpers has been the major structuring factor not only of Tiberius' own behavior but also of the history of Rome that was so inextricably connected with it, and of Tacitus' literary retelling of that history. What *Annals* 5–6 have shown us is the period when Tiberius, using only his own *ingenium*, paved the way for even darker days to come.[86]

Further Reading

The commentary of Woodman (2017), to which much of my essay is indebted, should be any reader's first port of call to learn more about *Annals* 5 and 6. Previous commentaries include Furneaux (1896), Koestermann (1963–8), ii, and Martin (2001). Birley (2007) is a perceptive analysis of the fall of Sejanus.

Kelly E. Shannon-Henderson, Annals *5 and 6: The End of the Beginning* In: *The Oxford Critical Guide to Tacitus.*
Edited by: Salvador Bartera and Kelly E. Shannon-Henderson, Oxford University Press. © Oxford University Press 2025.
DOI: 10.1093/9780191915086.003.0014

[85] See the summary of Woodman (2017), 300–1.
[86] See Devillers (2021), 85–7 for the "prospective dimension" of the end of Book 6.

14

Annals 11 and 12

Caitlin Gillespie

Annals 11 and 12 are all that remain of the Claudian books of the *Annals*, affording only a partial view of Claudius' thirteen-year reign and the events of 47–54 CE. In this narrative, Tacitus largely conforms to the overwhelmingly hostile literary tradition about Claudius. The historian records Claudius' fulfillment of his censorial duties, his attention to anti-quarian concerns, and his interest in foreign events, providing glimpses into positive moments in the emperor's career. Domestic affairs, however, become political and eclipse all other aspects of Claudius' reign, from the fall of Messalina to the rise of Agrippina the Younger and the concomitant advance of Nero. Claudius remains largely unaware of his domestic situation, and Tacitus' account wavers between dark comedy and domestic tragedy. Alongside the drama within the imperial household, foreign matters provide thematic parallels with, and commentary upon, events in Rome. By chronicling Claudius' ignorance and passivity, Tacitus critiques a regime that allowed women and freedmen to wield excessive political power.

Introducing Messalina

Although not the original opening of *Annals* 11, our modern entry point into the Claudian Principate *in mediis rebus* confirms Messalina's power and demarcates the *cubiculum* ("bedchamber") as a place of politics as well as transgression.[1] After a lengthy lacuna in the surviving text, the extant narrative covers the end of the year 47 CE and part of the year 48 CE.[2] After the death of Tiberius in Book 6, the missing books detailed the events of the years from 37 CE to the beginning of 47 CE and included the entirety of Caligula's Principate, Caligula's murder in 41 CE and the unlikely advance of his uncle Claudius,[3] and the beginning of Claudius' rule, including the conquest of Britain in 43 CE and the assumption of the censorship by Claudius and Lucius Vitellius in 47 CE. By the time the extant portion of *Annals* 11 begins, his wife Messalina has given birth to two children, Britannicus and Octavia, and the imperial dynasty appears firm.

The surviving text of *Annals* 11 begins mid-sentence with the trial of Decimus Valerius Asiaticus in 47 CE. Asiaticus served twice as consul and was chiefly responsible for the murder of Caligula. His trial showcases Claudius' weaknesses as a ruler and the authority of Messalina.[4] Messalina harbors ill will towards both Asiaticus and his rumored partner in adultery, Poppaea Sabina (mother of Nero's future wife), and covets the gardens of

---

[1] On the connection between landscape and memory in Tacitus' account of Messalina, see Gillespie (2020b).
[2] On the manuscript of *Annals* 11–16, see Malloch (2013), 9–21.
[3] Tacitus refers to this previously at *Annals* 3.18.4. See Devillers, Chapter 11 in this volume.
[4] On Asiaticus' downfall, see Osgood (2011), 147–9. Compare the account of Cassius Dio (60.29.4–6).

Lucullus (11.1.1), which are under the care of Asiaticus.[5] She works through Publius Suillius Rufus and Britannicus' tutor Sosibius to convince Claudius that Asiaticus might be preparing a political coup (11.1.2). Without ascertaining the truth, Claudius orders Asiaticus shackled and brought to Rome (11.1.3). A trial is held in the imperial *cubiculum* ("bedchamber") rather than the senate, with Claudius presiding, and the charges include corruption of Roman soldiers, adultery with Poppaea, and a soft body, implying effeminacy and perhaps pathic homosexuality (11.2.1).[6] Messalina is present, and she orders Vitellius to ensure a conviction. Poppaea dies by suicide at the urging of Messalina's agents, and Claudius is so unaware that at his next dinner party he asks Poppaea's husband Publius Cornelius Lentulus Scipio where she is (11.2.2). Claudius allows Asiaticus to choose his mode of death; Asiaticus opens his veins, "stating that it would have been more honorable to die through the cunning of Tiberius or an attack of Gaius Caesar, than to fall because of womanly treachery and the shameful mouth of Vitellius" (*cum se honestius calliditate Tiberii vel impetu C. Caesaris periturum dixisset, quam quod fraude muliebri et impudico Vitellii ore caderet*, 11.3.2). By eliding the emperor's role in his conviction, Asiaticus implicitly condemns the emperor for his dependence on his wife and her degenerate agent.[7] His trial establishes the difference between appearance and reality in the imperial household: Claudius presides, but the freedmen and Messalina exert control.

Claudius the Antiquarian

Claudius' rule is characterized by his proclaimed adherence to Augustus as his model and his attention to tradition. He stages Secular Games (*ludi saeculares*) 800 years after their founding and 64 years after Augustus' celebration (11.11.1). Tacitus has an insider's knowledge of these games as part of his own position as quindecimvir.[8] The historian uses the games as an excuse to introduce the young Nero: Nero and Britannicus both perform in the "Game of Troy" (*lusus Troiae*), and Nero has the people's favor in part because they pity him and his mother Agrippina the Younger as targets of Messalina's brutality (11.11.2–12.1). Claudius fails to notice the tension within his own household, and Tacitus implicitly criticizes his misplaced attentions. The emperor is busy with censorial acts, including a law concerning creditors, the construction of three new aqueducts, and adding three new letters to the Latin alphabet (11.13). The first two actions are laudable, and the third provides Tacitus with an opportunity to digress on the history of the alphabet and showcase his own interest in origins (11.14).[9] Claudius demonstrates continued interest in antiquarian practices when he consults the senate about the haruspical priesthood, an ancient Etruscan practice, which was falling out of use (11.15).[10] This episode subtly acknowledges

[5] On gardens in Roman literature, see Beard (1998); Boatwright (1998); Pagán (2006a); see further von Stackelberg (2009) on Messalina and the gardens of Lucullus.
[6] On the *cubiculum* as a space that varies between public and private, see Riggsby (1997); see further Nissinen (2009). On this episode, see Tagliafico (1996); de Vivo (2009). On *mollitiam corporis* as a reference to effeminacy and the implication of pathic homosexuality, see Malloch (2013), 69.
[7] I.e. By calling Vitellius' mouth "shameful," he suggests that he performed oral sex, a marker of sexual degeneracy and effeminacy (Malloch (2013), 81).
[8] See Shannon-Henderson (2019), 10–17.
[9] See especially Malloch (2013), 216–31 on the history of the alphabet and Tacitus' sources; Malloch (2013), 217 notes that Claudius himself wrote in the alphabet.
[10] On Claudius and the haruspical priesthood, see Shannon-Henderson (2019), 247–50.

Claudius as a historian himself. Although Tacitus does not mention it, Claudius wrote a history of the Etruscans.[11]

Claudius' interest in the development of the Empire and the political involvement of its constituents is showcased in a proposal of 48 CE. Claudius consults a senatorial committee concerning whether the leading men of the part of Gaul called Gallia Comata should be allowed to hold public office in Rome (11.23.1–25.4). The emperor supports the measure and speaks before the senate, celebrating traditional Roman openness towards the best non-Romans, contrasting Rome with Athens and Sparta, celebrating the potential for Gallic wealth to be used in Rome, and emphasizing Rome's history of innovation (11.24.1–7). The following *senatus consultum* ("senatorial decree") allows the Aedui the right to hold office. Claudius' speech survives on an inscription known as the Lyon Tablet (*CIL* 13.1668 = *ILS* 212).[12] This inscription provides a rare opportunity to compare Tacitus with contemporary documentary sources.[13] The historian has adapted the style of the original speech to match the tone of the *Annals*, transforming an original that was "long-winded, meandering, and pedantic" into a sophisticated speech with an effective argument.[14] Malloch notes a shift in content from the original speech's "emphasis on constitutional innovation to Rome's history of openness to foreigners."[15] Tacitus' Claudius uses his own Sabine ancestor Clausus and the citizenship and patrician status that he received in Rome as his inspiration for a policy of acceptance (11.24.1). The strong rhetorical performance Tacitus gives Claudius suggests the historian (a provincial himself) approved of the measure and supported Claudius' "openness to the participation of provincials in the Roman political process."[16] To round out his censorial activities, Claudius increases the number of patricians and revises the list of senators. In the census, 5,984,072 citizens were counted.[17]

Messalina's Fall

The remainder of *Annals* 11 traces the fall of Messalina (11.26–38). The lengthy episode confronts the emperor with the reality of political rivals, while illustrating the power of his freedmen as compared to his own submissiveness. Claudius emerges as ill-suited for the position of *princeps*, allowing those closest to him to exert power, destabilize his household, and threaten the security of the state. In Tacitus' account, domestic disharmony and immorality symbolize political disruption, and Messalina's sexual and moral disgrace is translated into a political threat. Messalina burns with desire for the superlatively handsome consul designate Gaius Silius, forcing him to divorce his wife Junia Silana and become her lover (11.12.2).[18] Tacitus marvels at the public nature of their relationship (11.12.3):

---

[11] As is noted by Malloch (2013), 231, 362; cf. Suet. *Claud.* 42.2.

[12] See Malloch's edition in his commentary on *Annals* 11 (Malloch (2013), 469–71), and his more recent edition with commentary (Malloch (2020)).

[13] Cf. The *Senatus Consultum de Cn. Pisone Patre* and the trial of Piso in *Annals* 3 (see Chapter 11 in this volume).

[14] Malloch (2013), 340–1.   [15] Malloch (2013), 341.   [16] Malloch (2013), 7.

[17] On Tacitus' record of the census, see Kron (2005); Scheidel (2008); Launaro (2011).

[18] See Panoussi (2019b) on Messalina and Agrippina the Younger as sexual aggressors in the *Annals*.

illa non furtim, sed multo comitatu ventitare domum, egressibus adhaerescere, largiri opes honores; postremo, velut translata iam fortuna, servi liberti paratus principis apud adulterum visebantur.

She, not secretly but with a great retinue, frequented his house, attached herself to his outings, lavished wealth and honors; finally, just as though fortune had already been transferred, enslaved people, freedmen, paraphernalia of the emperor were seen at the home of the adulterer.

Messalina moves objects from the imperial household that seem to denote imperial power, and her action suggests a symbolic transfer of that power. Tacitus then alternates scenes between the adulterous lovers with depictions of the emperor and his freedmen, building tension in his detailed drama of Messalina's end. The parallel narratives present two different power structures contending for control: Messalina and her lover, and an emperor ruled by his freedmen. Messalina and Silius establish their position as a potential new imperial couple by legitimizing their relationship. Silius proposes and the couple celebrates all the traditional aspects of a marriage ceremony while Claudius is away at Ostia to make a sacrifice.[19] Tacitus admits that their performance of the marriage ritual seems incredible (*fabulosum*), "but nothing has been composed to excite wonder; in fact I record the reports and writings of the older generation" (*sed nihil compositum miraculi causa, verum audita scriptaque senioribus trado*, 11.27). Tacitus does not specify whether Messalina divorced Claudius and a formal legal marriage took place, or remarried without divorcing Claudius.[20] Scholars have debated whether Messalina's marriage to Silius was politically motivated or emerged as a result of her uncontrolled desire.[21] Whatever her motivations, the impact is political. Tacitus uses the episode to distill Claudius' reign into a rivalry for power between his freedmen and his wives. As a result of Messalina's marriage, the freedmen Callistus, Narcissus, and Pallas fear for their own authority, and the emperor's mistresses Calpurnia and Cleopatra inform Claudius of Messalina's actions. Claudius panics, wonders if he is still emperor, and allows Narcissus to guide his response upon his return to Rome.

Silius and Messalina's marriage serves as a reminder that the hereditary dynasty cannot be assumed to continue indefinitely. Tacitus finds the system of a hereditary Principate problematic and critiques the excessive political influence it gives imperial women as the mothers of potential heirs. The marriage exemplifies Tacitus' narrative of moral decline and an imperial household in crisis. The historian highlights the interplay between political power and considerations of gender and status, as readers witness the freedman Narcissus wrest control from the emperor's wife. The emperor shows himself easily manipulated, and his wife's self-destructive behavior comes to a dramatic, bloody end. Tacitus' genre-bending account verges on tragedy. Messalina learns of Claudius' approach while celebrating a mock vintage with Silius and a chorus of women dressed as Bacchants (11.31.2–3).[22] Messalina attempts to approach Claudius on the road from Ostia and is prevented by

[19] On the Roman marriage ceremony, see Hersch (2010); Treggiari (1991); Panoussi (2019a), 17–21. On the marriage of Messalina and Silius, see Cenerini (2010).
[20] Cf. Suet. *Claud.* 26.2.
[21] See e.g. Malloch (2013), 392–8; Fagan (2002) with bibliography; Questa (1995); Osgood (2011), 209–13; Nappa (2010) on Tacitus and Juvenal. See further Joshel (1995) and Santoro L'Hoir (1994).
[22] On this episode and the *Bacchae* of Euripides, see La Penna (1975); Henrichs (1978).

Narcissus, and returns to the gardens of Lucullus. Once Claudius is in Rome, the executions begin: Silius and his associates, the actor Mnester (one of Messalina's lovers), and several others are killed (11.35–6). Messalina remains in the gardens with her mother Domitia Lepida, and Narcissus orders her assassination; she fails to die by suicide, and Tacitus explains, "there was nothing honorable in a mind destroyed by wantonness" (*animo per libidines corrupto nihil honestum inerat*, 11.37.4). She is dispatched by an officer and the body is given to her mother for burial (11.37). The murder is reported to Claudius, who has no reaction, even when he observes the mourning of his children; the senate condemns Messalina's memory, and Narcissus is presented with an honorary quaestorship (11.38).[23]

Messalina's end is engineered by Narcissus rather than Claudius, showcasing the power dynamic between the insecure emperor and his authoritative freedmen. The aftermath of her death shows various actors vying to control Messalina's memory. Tacitus states, "The senate helped [Claudius'] forgetting by decreeing that her name and image must be removed from public and private places" (*iuvitque oblivionem eius senatus censendo nomen et effigies privatis ac publicis locis demovendas*, 11.38.3). The erasure of Messalina's memory follows a senatorial decree called a *damnatio memoriae* ("condemnation of memory") in modern scholarship.[24] Although Claudius is the primary audience, the implication is that the Roman populace should also forget Messalina when her image disappears from view. Tacitus rejects the concept that the senate or imperial family should be able to control collective memory. Claudius demonstrates the desired reaction to the death of his wife through his seemingly immediate forgetfulness, while Tacitus restores Messalina to memory and the history of the Julio-Claudian dynasty through his extensive narration.

The Rise of Agrippina the Younger

Annals 12 continues the account of 48 CE. Although the book does not open with a new year, nevertheless a new era is dawning. Agrippina the Younger propels the narrative and the influence of the freedmen wanes. As the book opens, a contest for Claudius' next wife ensues. Tacitus characterizes the emperor as "impatient with unmarried life and obedient to the commands of his wives" (*caelibis vitae into<le>ranti et coniugum imperiis obnoxio*, 12.1.1). Freedmen guide the emperor's choices, and the contestants are judged on their ancestry, beauty, and wealth, with the freedman Callistus promoting Lollia Paulina, Pallas speaking for Agrippina the Younger, and Narcissus supporting Aelia Paetina. Agrippina succeeds because she and her son are descended from the Julio-Claudian line (her father Germanicus was Claudius' brother), and the imperial house should not be divided (12.2.3); she visits her uncle to make her case personally (12.3.1). Agrippina's aspirations for power are boundless, but her advancement depends upon her marriage and that of her son. She plots Nero's marriage to Claudius' daughter Octavia, who is already betrothed to Lucius Silanus (12.3.2); accordingly, Silanus is accused of incest with his sister Junia Calvina by Vitellius and removed from the office of praetor (12.4.1–3). Nero and Octavia marry in 53 CE, when the future emperor is sixteen (12.58.1).

---

[23] On the death of Messalina, see Major (1993); Mastellone (2004).
[24] On the *damnatio memoriae*, see Varner (2001), (2004) and Flower (1998), (2006).

In 49 CE, Vitellius speaks in the senate on Claudius' behalf concerning the impending marriage of the emperor to his niece. He identifies several qualities sought after in a wife: someone who is noble, of proven fertility, and without a husband. The law forbidding incest is changed and the marriage allowed (12.7.2). The results alter the course of Roman history (12.7.3):

> *versa ex eo civitas, et cuncta feminae oboediebant, non per lasciviam, ut Messalina, rebus Romanis inludenti. adductum et quasi virile servitium: palam severitas ac saepius super-bia; nihil domi impudicum, nisi dominationi expediret. cupido auri immensa obtentum habebat, quasi subsidium regno pararetur.*

From that point the state was transformed and all things served a woman who did not make sport of Roman affairs through licentiousness, as with Messalina. It was a strict and almost manly servitude. In public, there was austerity and very often arrogance; at home nothing unchaste unless it contributed to power. Her vast desire for gold had the excuse that she was preparing protection for her royal power.

Tacitus contrasts the wives of Claudius in intention more than morality: both wives commit adultery, but Messalina's recklessness was sportive, while Agrippina's actions are calculated to increase her power. Tacitus suggests that Messalina's attempt to replace Claudius was motivated by her unbridled sexual desire, and he juxtaposes her with Agrippina, who poses a very real and very dangerous political threat. He condemns Agrippina's actions as immoral, un-Roman, and un-womanly, and her masculine character as comparable to that of her mother.[25] Although women could not hold official political positions, Agrippina consistently challenges that boundary.

Agrippina's role in the *Annals* wavers between the stereotypes of the "harsh stepmother" (*saeva noverca*), "commander woman" (*dux femina*), and sexual transgressor.[26] Her rule begins inauspiciously, as Silius dies by suicide on her wedding day, and Calvina is banished from Italy. Agrippina attempts to regain a positive reputation by recalling the philosopher and writer Seneca from exile as a tutor for Nero (12.8.2).[27] Nero is engaged to Octavia and becomes equal to Britannicus as a potential imperial heir (12.9.2). Tacitus confirms Agrippina's increasing authority via a catalog of her victims, including Lollia Paulina and Claudius' mistress Calpurnia (12.22.1–3). In 50 CE, Agrippina engineers Claudius' adoption of Nero and receives the honorific title of Augusta, which had been granted only to Livia before her (12.25–6).[28] Tacitus draws explicit parallels between Agrippina and Augustus' wife, from their promotions of their sons to their receipt of similar honors. Agrippina also advertises her independent authority and wealth outside of Rome, paying tribute to her mother and Rome's allies by bringing about the founding of a veteran colony in the Ubian capital, where she was born; the colony was named Colonia Claudia Augusta Ara Agrippinensis (modern day Cologne) (12.27.1).

---

[25] After Agrippina the Elder's death, Tiberius condemns her as follows: "Agrippina, intolerant of equality, greedy for rule, had shed the vices of women for manly concerns" (*sed Agrippina aequi impatiens, dominandi avida, virilibus curis feminarum vitia exuerat, Ann.* 6.25.2).

[26] See Ginsburg (2006), 106–32.

[27] Seneca's role in the *Annals* is discussed more fully by Gowing in Chapter 15 in this volume.

[28] On the meaning of *Augusta*, see Kolb (2010).

Agrippina schemes for Nero's accession from his marriage to Octavia to his adoption by Claudius. Tacitus' account of 51 CE begins with a celebration of Nero's early promotion into adulthood at the age of thirteen and other honors; circus games are held, during which Nero dons triumphal garb, though he had not served in a military campaign, while Britannicus wears a purple-edged toga (12.41.1–2). The occasion provides an opportunity for Agrippina's subterfuge, and Britannicus' supporters are removed from view. She consolidates her power by contriving to have Britannicus' tutors exiled and killed, and taking charge of Britannicus' custody herself (12.41.3). She removes the remaining supporters of Messalina and advertises her own venerable position by ascending the Capitoline in a *carpentum*, a specialized carriage employed for sacred objects and occasionally sanctioned for use by Roman matrons (12.42.2):[29]

> *suum quoque fastigium Agrippina extollere altius: carpento Capitolium ingredi, qui <ho>nos sacerdotibus et sacris antiquitus concessus venerationem augebat feminae, quam imperatore genitam, sororem eius, qui rerum potitus sit, et coniugem et matrem fuisse unicum ad hunc diem exemplum est.*

> Agrippina heightened her own eminence as well: she went up the Capitoline in a carriage, an honor yielded of old to priests and sacred objects that increased veneration of the woman, who, as the daughter of a general, sister and wife and mother of a man who ruled the state, is a unique example to this day.

Agrippina uses the *carpentum* in order to liken herself to a sacred object such as a statue of a goddess and achieves her aim of increasing her veneration by the populace. Tacitus' Agrippina takes an active role in augmenting her image of power, and seems to consider herself worthy of cultic attention and honors appropriate to the gods. Tacitus recognizes Agrippina's unique position in the imperial family via her descent from the general Germanicus and relationship to three successive emperors as sister of Caligula, wife to Claudius, and mother of Nero.[30] He follows her triumphant display with portents indicating impending doom (12.43). His juxtaposition suggests that Agrippina has gone too far in her claims to power and cultic attention, and that her actions have jeopardized the safety of the state.[31]

Claudius' Demise

Annals 12 pivots around Agrippina and Claudius remains a background emperor. He continues his penchant for antiquarianism, and Tacitus includes one of his major contributions to the Roman state to end the year 49 CE. Claudius expanded the city limits, and Tacitus digresses on the history of the *pomerium* and its extensions under Sulla and Augustus (12.23.2–24.2).[32] The historian emperor places himself as the successor to these

---

[29] On the *carpentum* and its use by matrons portrayed as problematic or threatening, see Hudson (2016) and (2021), 208–47. Hudson argues that Tacitus portrays Agrippina's *carpentum* privileges, "as a mark of her excessive power, and of Claudius' role as henpecked husband" (Hudson (2021), 247).

[30] On Agrippina as an *unicum exemplum*, see Gillespie (2014a).

[31] See Shannon-Henderson (2019), 267–9 for this reading of the *carpentum* episode.

[32] See Boatwright (1984). The *pomerium* was the religious boundary that separated the city from the surrounding land; see "*pomerium*," *BNP* 11: 542 (H. Galsterer).

political giants. He maintains a blissful ignorance about his wife's domineering power plays, and his failure to rein in Agrippina is showcased to the public in 52 CE. A public works project at Lake Fucinus ends in disaster when Claudius stages a naval battle as part of the celebrations of opening a new waterway between Lake Fucinus and the Liris (12.56.1). Claudius presides over the spectacle in a military cloak (*paludamentum*) with Agrippina in a mantle of gold (*chlamys*), a Greek garment suggestive of a monarch (12.56.3). The carelessness of the project manifests immediately, as the water overflows; Agrippina blames Narcissus, and he charges her with "womanly unruliness and excessive hopes" (*impotentiam muliebrem nimiasque spes*, 12.57.2). Tacitus employs the spectacle to emphasize that Agrippina presented herself as a co-ruler with Claudius on the model of a foreign queen, and to demonstrate the power struggle between Agrippina and the freedman. One episode shows a parallel with Messalina's uncontrolled desires. In 53 CE, Agrippina drove Claudius to extreme brutality in order to gain the gardens of Statilius Taurus: Taurus was falsely accused of extortion and magical beliefs and died by suicide before waiting for a conviction (12.59.1–2). The narrative recalls Messalina, the trial of Asiaticus, and the possession of the gardens of Lucullus. Messalina's and Agrippina's intense longing is characterized by the same participle (*inhians*; cf. 11.1.1), tying the episodes together.

Tacitus' account of 54 CE is overtaken by the death sequence of Claudius, beginning with ominous portents and a drunken remark of Claudius that suggests he is fated to punish Agrippina (12.64.1). Panicked by his utterance, Agrippina resolves on murder, but first destroys her perceived imperial rival, Domitia Lepida. As the daughter of Antonia and mother of Messalina (cf. 11.37–8), Lepida could claim an illustrious birth almost equal to Agrippina's, and the emperor's wife considers her a powerful rival for Nero's favor. Agrippina charges Lepida with attacking her via curse tablets and not controlling her enslaved people in Calabria, crimes deserving capital punishment (12.65.1). Narcissus offers strong opposition and considers Domitia's downfall as a sign of his own ruin (12.65.2). He departs for Sinuessa, marking the end of his power struggle with Agrippina. Agrippina controls both history and narrative for the remainder of *Annals* 12. She employs Locusta as poisoner and the eunuch Halotus as her agents for the murder of Claudius (12.66.2). The emperor ingests a poisoned mushroom and is finished off by the doctor Xenophon, who sends a poison-coated feather down his throat as if to assist in his vomiting up the mushroom (12.67.1–2). The senate is summoned and although Claudius is already dead, Agrippina withholds that information until preparations are readied for Nero's accession (12.68).

On the 13th of October, the dual announcement goes public: Claudius is dead and Nero is the new emperor. Tacitus closes *Annals* 12 with the following comparison (12.69.3):

> *caelestesque honores Claudio decernuntur et funeris sollemne perinde ac divo Augusto celebratur, aemulante Agrippina proaviae Liviae magnificentiam.*

> Divine honors were decreed for Claudius and his funeral rite was celebrated in the same manner as the divine Augustus', since Agrippina rivaled her great- grandmother Livia's magnificence.

The image of Claudius' funeral echoes that of Augustus, and Tacitus subtly invites readers to consider whether Livia had a role in the death of Augustus, given the actions of

Agrippina (cf. *Ann.* 1.5.1).[33] Claudius' will is not read, and, in complete contrast to the extensive obituary of Tiberius at the end of *Annals* 6, Tacitus denies him even a brief obituary (12.69.3). Thus *Annals* 12 opens with a wedding and closes with a funeral, and the imperial *domus* is shaken once more. Agrippina seems in control of her 16-year-old son, Nero, and the stage is set for a new regime, presented by Tacitus as a co-rulership between mother and son reminiscent of Livia and Tiberius.

External Affairs in *Annals* 11 and 12

Tacitus balances his account of internal affairs within Rome with external affairs, including the year's campaigning, in accordance with the expectations of annalistic history; however, the historian also shows variation in his selection and arrangement of his material, abandons the traditional year by year framework of the genre after the Tiberian books, and manipulates the form in ways that connect the wars outside of Rome to broader thematic concerns.[34] Foreign affairs provide a mirror to Rome and subtle commentary on her own power struggles. Claudius showcases an interest in foreign affairs and is generally adept at appointing suitable men to foreign posts. He dispatches kings to Armenia and to the Cherusci (11.8.1, 11.16.1), instructs client kings of Armenia and the Aorsi (11.9.2, 12.20.2), and sends provincial governors to Pannonia, Britain, and Syria (e.g. 12.29.2, 12.40.1, 12.54.4); however, he fails to provide advice to his subordinates, recalls the Roman general Domitius Corbulo to limit the success of this potential rival (11.19.3),[35] and depends upon others to guide his judgments and resolve threats.[36]

Claudius' successful campaign into Britain under the leadership of Aulus Plautius in 43 CE became the defining moment in his foreign policy: although not a military man, Claudius accomplished the imperial aspiration to expand the Empire. The campaign would have been covered in the missing books of the *Annals*. As a result of his victories, Plautius celebrated an *ovatio*, a type of minor triumph, and served as the first governor of Britain.[37] The extant *Annals* resume in 50 CE, when the governor Publius Ostorius faces rebellion (12.31–2). Under the leadership of Caratacus, the Silures and their allies revolt. Caratacus exemplifies the historian's use of non-Romans to comment upon affairs in Rome and embodies values prized by the Romans themselves, and even recognizes Claudius' own desire to be remembered for his clemency.

Prior to a decisive battle in the ninth year of the war (51 or 52 CE) Caratacus exhorts his army to yield at nothing (12.34.1):[38]

---

[33] For a comparison of Agrippina and Livia in the *Annals*, see Foubert (2010). See further Pagán, Chapter 9 in this volume.

[34] See Ginsburg (1981) on the form of Tacitus' annalistic history. Livy sets the narrative pattern of following internal events with external events, closing with internal affairs at the end of the narrative of each year; Tacitus includes both internal and external affairs, but varies the Livian framework (Ginsburg (1981), especially 53–79).

[35] On Corbulo, see Gowing, Chapter 15 in this volume. On his campaigns against the Chauci and his recall under Claudius (*A.* 11.18–20), compare the account of Dio/Xiph. (60.30.4–6).

[36] See Malloch (2013), 8–9.

[37] See Cassius Dio (60.19.1–23.6). On affairs in Britain see further Audano, Chapter 1 in this volume.

[38] Webster (1981) provides a history of the campaign against Caratacus.

enimvero Caratacus huc illuc volitans illum diem, illam aciem testabatur aut recuperandae libertatis aut servitutis aeternae initium fore; vocabatque nomina maiorum, qui dictatorem Caesarem pepulissent, quorum virtute vacui a securibus et tributis intemerata coniugum et liberorum corpora retinerent.

Moreover Caratacus circulating here and there testified that that day, that battle would be the beginning of either the recovery of freedom or of eternal servitude. He called out the names of their ancestors who had repelled the dictator Caesar, by whose courage they themselves, free from axes and taxes, kept the bodies of their wives and children undefiled.

Non-Roman speeches are a common feature of Roman historiography, particularly in military contexts.[39] Caratacus condemns the Roman imperialist strategy that subjugated local peoples through military might and excessive taxes, and allowed Roman soldiers to violate the bodies of even women and children. These are traditional topoi of pre-battle speeches, as well as the promise to win or die trying; this sentiment is present in the speeches of other rebels in Britain, including the Caledonian Calgacus (*Agr.* 32.4; see Audano, Chapter 1 in this volume), and Boudica, leader of the Iceni (*Ann.* 14.35.2; see Whitton, Chapter 16 in this volume). Caratacus is willing to fight for freedom at any cost. This drive is absent from the Roman senate, whose acceptance of ill-suited emperors and their influential wives is compared by Tacitus to a state of servitude.

Despite Caratacus' powerful words, the Romans defeat the rebels and capture Caratacus' wife and daughter, and his brothers surrender (12.35.3). Caratacus seeks the aid of Cartimandua, client queen of the Brigantes, but she betrays him to the Romans and he is brought to Rome and paraded in front of the populace. He speaks before Claudius and Agrippina, extols the value of clemency, and receives a pardon for himself and his family.[40] They give equal thanks to Claudius and Agrippina, and Tacitus observes, "that was new and unlike customs of old, that a woman preside over Roman standards: but she carried herself as a partner in power in an Empire secured by her ancestors" (*novum sane et moribus veterum insolitum, feminam signis Romanis praesidere: ipsa semet parti a maioribus suis imperii sociam ferebat*, 12.37.4). Tacitus' Britons assume Agrippina is Claudius' equal, and Tacitus uses the occasion to highlight the theme of dissimulation in images of authority. Although not an official ruler, Agrippina has continually usurped official functions and continues to go unchecked. Tacitus' narrative of Britain illuminates the dangers of female rule, highlighting the disloyalty and violence of Cartimandua. Cartimandua is viewed as a traitor by her own people for allying herself with Rome, and her Brigantes prefer her former husband, Venutius. He gains power, and Cartimandua seeks the aid of the Romans.[41] While the Britons resist succumbing to the rule of a woman, Caesius Nasica and his army assist the client queen and persevere (12.40.3). The Brigantes provide an alternate response to female leadership, rejecting the rule of a woman, while the Romans accept Agrippina as their quasi-regent.

While provincial governors attempt to control affairs in Britain at the western edge of the Empire, events in Parthia and Armenia present Rome with new challenges and

---

[39] On which, see especially Adler (2011).   [40] Cf. Cass. Dio. 60.33.3c.
[41] On Cartimandua's divorce and brutal treatment of Venutius' family, see Tac. *H.* 3.45.

opportunities. Tacitus evinces his own interest in Parthia in his extensive eastern narrative, spread throughout the *Annals*. Augustus had established peace with Parthia, and his
successors generally followed suit. However, Roman–Parthian relations remained complex, with Armenia caught in the middle both geographically and politically; both empires
made a claim to Armenia, but tensions were managed without resorting to all-out war.[42]
During the reign of Claudius, Parthia is embroiled in civil conflict, and Rome takes
advantage. Caligula had summoned King Mithridates I of Armenia to Rome, and Armenia
became a Parthian possession; Claudius restores Mithridates I to the throne in Armenia
while Parthian entities vie for power (11.8.1–9.2). The violent, luxury-loving Gotarzes II
eventually emerges victorious, but his Parthians seek the assistance of Claudius in install-
ing Meherdates as their ruler instead (11.10.4). Gotarzes captures Meherdates and removes
his ears but allows him to live, mocking him for acting Roman (12.14.3). Gotarzes sickens
and dies, Vonones is summoned to be king, and reigns briefly before his son Vologaeses
takes the reins (12.14.4). Mithridates of Bosporus (not to be confused with Mithridates of
Armenia) musters an army and seizes power, but is captured by Eunones and his Aorsi,
allies of the Romans; Eunones requests Claudius' clemency for his captive, and Mithridates
is brought to Rome and displayed before the Roman people (12.15, 19.3, 21.1). Claudius
follows a similar pattern to his predecessors in his diplomatic dealings with Parthia and
Armenia, intervening when his assistance is requested and showing himself a relatively
competent heir to Augustus and Tiberius.

The eastern narrative has thematic importance as a story of political infighting, deception, and murder. Keitel identifies parallels between the dynastic struggles in Armenia and
Parthia and those within the imperial household in Rome, and argues that these parallels
lend coherence to the Claudian books on the whole.[43] The narrative of Radamistus offers
several points of contact that cast Tacitus' condemnatory portraits of Messalina and
Agrippina the Younger in sharp relief. In 51 CE, the Parthians are ruled by Vologaeses, the
Iberians by Pharasmanes, and the Armenians by his brother Mithridates. Pharasmanes'
son Radamistus desires power. His aptitude for rule is suggested by his character:
Radamistus is "handsome in stature, remarkable in bodily strength, learned in traditional
skills, and with a brilliant reputation among locals" (*decora proceritate, vi corporis insignis
et patrias artes edoctus, claraque inter accolas fama*, 12.44.3). Pharasmanes convinces him
to attack Mithridates, his uncle and father-in-law. Radamistus approaches his uncle, feigning
strife with his father, and is welcomed affably. He then entices the leading men of Armenia
to revolution (12.44.5). Pharasmanes sends troops to his son, and Radamistus forces
Mithridates to flee. A treaty is proposed, and Radamistus tricks his uncle into a meeting.
Radamistus leads him to a grove where he is captured and killed. His wife, children, sister,
and uncle are killed as well (12.47.4–5).

Radamistus, now a hated murderer, rules over his ill-gotten gains, and invades Armenia
in 53 CE. The Armenians revolt and beset the palace. Radamistus escapes with his wife
Zenobia, and Tacitus recounts their journey to close his narrative of the year (12.51.1–4):

*Nec aliud Radamisto subsidium fuit quam pernicitas equorum, quis seque et coniugem
abstulit. [2] sed coniunx gravida primam utcumque fugam ob metum hostilem et mariti*

---

[42] For a brief history of Roman–Parthian relations and the control of Armenia, see Malloch (2013), 119–26.
[43] Keitel (1978), 462.

caritatem toleravit; post festinatione continua ubi quati uterus et viscera vibrantur, orare ut morte honesta contumeliis captivitatis eximeretur. [3] ille primo amplecti adlevare adhortari, modo virtutem admirans, modo timore aeger, ne quis relicta poteretur. postremo violentia amoris et facinorum non rudis destringit acinacen vulneratamque ripam ad Araxis trahit, flumini tradit, ut corpus etiam auferretur: ipse praeceps Hiberos ad patrium regnum pervadit. [4] interim Zenobiam (id mulieri nomen) placida in <e>luvie spirantem ac vitae manifestam advertere pastores, et dignitate formae haud degenerem reputantes obligant vulnus, agrestia medicamina adhibent cognitoque nomine et casu in urbem Artaxata ferunt: unde publica cura deducta ad Tiridaten comiterque excepta cultu regio habita est.

Radamistus had no aid other than the fleetness of his horses, by which he got himself and his wife away. But his pregnant wife tolerated the first part of the flight one way or another out of fear of the enemy and fondness for her husband; after uninterrupted hurry, when her womb was shaking and innards quivered, she asked to be prevented from the insults of captivity through an honorable death. He at first embraced, comforted, and encouraged her, now admiring her courage, now sick with fear lest anyone seize her after she was left behind. Finally, with the impetuosity of love and not inexperienced in crime, he drew his short sword and dragged her, wounded, to the bank of the Araxis, gave her to the river, so that even her body might be removed. He himself went headlong to the Iberi, the kingdom of his ancestors. Meanwhile shepherds noticed Zenobia (that was the woman's name) in a calm overflow, breathing and giving manifest signs of life, and from the dignity of her appearance, thinking her not ignoble, bandaged her wound, applied rustic medicines, and after learning her name and case brought her to the city Artaxata. From there she was taken under the care of the state to Tiridates, received affably, and maintained in royal style.

Zenobia provides a stark contrast to the immoral, power-hungry Julio-Claudian wives. This ruler's wife is an unexpected role model of fearless uxorial dutifulness. Tacitus is the only source for the escape of Zenobia, and the historian creates a pathos-laden scene between a pregnant wife and her husband. Zenobia's strength of character is ascertained by her willingness to die to protect her husband. Radamistus admires Zenobia's courage, but fails to give her an honorable death. Rather, Zenobia is brought to Tiridates, Radamistus' enemy; rather than punish her, Tiridates recognizes her bravery and nobility and keeps her in royal style. In creating an emotional scene between Radamistus and Zenobia, Tacitus humanizes the traitorous Radamistus and ennobles his wife, celebrating Zenobia for her exemplary courage. The vignette gains significance through comparison with Rome. Radamistus and Zenobia display a marital devotion lacking in the relationship of Agrippina the Younger and Claudius, providing an ironic contrast. Radamistus is comparable to both Nero (as heir) and Agrippina the Younger (as plotter).[44] His end confirms that his wife was the real positive model: Radamistus returns to the court of his father in Iberia, but continues to plague the Armenians (13.6.1). In 58 CE, his father Pharasmanes orders his death as a traitor in order to demonstrate loyalty to the Romans (13.37.3).

---

[44] Keitel (1978), 469–70.

Conclusion

Intrigue and murder within ruling households dominate *Annals* 11 and 12. Although they are the "Claudian" books, the emperor rarely controls the narrative. Claudius is a liminal character in his own history, displaced by the licentious Messalina, the imperial freedmen, and the power-hungry Agrippina the Younger. Tacitus denigrates the emperor for his dependence on his subordinates, complementing other hostile literary sources on the emperor. Foreign affairs provide commentary on and comparisons with the situation within the Roman imperial household. Despite Claudius' flaws, Tacitus records with interest the emperor's antiquarian concerns and forward-thinking proposals, including the admission of select Gauls into the senate, the extension of the *pomerium*, and censorial duties that offer relief from the narrative of the instability of the imperial *domus*. At the opening of *Annals* 13, the young emperor Nero provides a potential guide to interpretation in his funeral laudation for his adoptive father.[45] In a speech written by Seneca, Nero praises Claudius' lineage and the accomplishments of his ancestors, his intellectual achievements, and his foreign policy, but fails to mention Claudius' famed conquest of Britain and causes his audience to laugh when he turns to Claudius' foresight and wisdom (*Ann.* 13.3.1). Although a historian himself, Claudius failed to foresee how history would remember him.

Further Reading

For *Annals* 11, see the authoritative commentary of Malloch (2013); on *Annals* 11 and 12, see Benario (1983). For biographies, see Osgood (2011) and Levick (1990) on Claudius, and Barrett (1996) and Ginsburg (2006) on Agrippina the Younger. Milnor (2005) and Severy (2003) remain requisite reading on the imperial family, morality, and gender, while Santoro L'Hoir (1994), Hälikkä (2002), and Rutland (1978) focus on Tacitus, women, and power in the *Annals*. Joshel (1995) and Gillespie (2020b) address Messalina's characterization; Gillespie (2014a) focuses on Agrippina the Younger as a unique model; Panoussi (2019b) compares them. On the revolt of Caratacus, see Webster (1981); on Parthia and Armenia, see Keitel (1978).

Caitlin Gillespie, Annals *11 and 12* In: *The Oxford Critical Guide to Tacitus*. Edited by: Salvador Bartera and Kelly E. Shannon-Henderson, Oxford University Press. © Oxford University Press 2025. DOI: 10.1093/9780191915086.003.0015

---

[45] On the opening of Book 13, see Gowing, Chapter 13 in this volume.

15

Annals 13

Mentors, Murder, Mother, and Mayhem

Alain M. Gowing

Book 13 of Tacitus' *Annals* opens with a long, delightfully periodic, and highly informative sentence that lays out some of the book's chief topics and concerns (*Ann.* 13.1.1):

> *Prima novo principatu mors Iunii Silani proconsulis Asiae ignaro Nerone per dolum Agrippinae paratur, non quia ingenii violentia exitium inritaverat, segnis et dominationibus aliis fastiditus, adeo ut C. Caesar pecudem auream eum appellare solitus sit: verum Agrippina fratri eius L. Silano necem molita ultorem metuebat, crebra vulgi fama anteponendum esse vixdum pueritiam egresso Neroni et imperium per scelus adepto virum aetate composita, insontem, nobilem et, quod tunc spectaretur, e Caesarum posteris: quippe et Silanus divi Augusti abnepos erat.*

First to die under the new principate was Junius Silanus, proconsul of Asia, a death orchestrated through a plot of Agrippina's and without Nero's knowledge—not because Silanus had caused his demise through any viciousness of temperament (he was lazy and disdained by other regimes to such an extent that C. Caesar used to call him "the golden sheep"). Rather, Agrippina, having devised the death of his brother L. Silanus, feared an avenger, in light of frequent popular rumors that preferable to Nero, who had scarcely left boyhood and had acquired rule through a crime, would be a man of stable age, blameless, noble, and from among the descendants of the Caesars (a respected quality at the time): indeed, Silanus was also the great-grandson of Augustus.

What do we learn from this? The opening words tell us that Nero's reign begins with a murder—the "first," the clear implication being that there will be more. Nero's ignorance of the matter is noted, as is his innocence—along with Agrippina's deceit. In sum: murder, a ruthless mother, and a blameless (for the moment) boy-emperor. Tacitus also gestures toward the legacy and shadow of Augustus and, more broadly, Julio-Claudian family intrigue: the victim here, Junius Silanus, was the proconsul of Asia and direct descendant of Augustus, and this, combined with an apparently blameless character and competence, made him a viable candidate for the principate. *Haec causa necis*, as Tacitus pithily puts it— "this was why he had to die" (13.1.2). These are, to be sure, by now familiar themes to anyone who has read the previous twelve books. For Tacitus the reign of Nero is a continuation of the mostly disastrous, scandal-filled Julio-Claudian dynasty. But this time there is a tantalizing twist: Nero, as every reader knows, will be the last of the Julio-Claudian emperors.

It does not take Tacitus long (the second sentence, in fact) to hint at the dark side of Nero's character—vices that were as yet hidden, but which he shared with Narcissus, the malevolent and troublesome freedman of Claudius with whom readers will be quite familiar: *cuius (sc. Neronis) abditis adhuc vitiis per avaritiam ac prodigentiam mire congruebat*, "with whose [i.e. Nero's] as yet hidden vices Narcissus was in marvelous harmony in terms of his greed and extravagance" (13.1.3). In rather short order Narcissus is compelled to take his own life, the second of many deaths soon to come. In some sense this part of the opening of Book 13 may ironically hint at Nero's own end, with which the now-lost final Book 18 may have concluded, himself a victim of his own greed and excess.[1]

But readers will have to wait for Nero's vices to come into full view, for in chapter 2 we meet two crucial characters who will serve as a check on Nero's worst tendencies, Burrus and Seneca. The chronological range of Book 13, 54–8 CE, is relevant and significant here: these are the first four years of the well-known Neronian *quinquennium* or five-year period during which Nero's reign, closely controlled by Seneca, Burrus, and his mother, was mostly successful. The "uneventful annals of good government," as Syme puts it.[2] As becomes clear, however, left to his own devices, and as the restraints on his behavior gradually fall away (usually the result of murder or suicide), Nero's real character comes into full and horrific view.

Book 13, like the other surviving books of the *Annals*, is immensely rich and complex; the full range of Tacitus' talent is in evidence on every page. In this brief chapter, however, I wish to focus on three key aspects of Book 13 touched on in the opening two chapters that lay the groundwork for much of what will transpire in books 14–16 (and were presumably present in the concluding two books of the *Annals*): Nero's mentors as well as other individuals against whom Tacitus invites us to measure the emperor; the women in his life, especially his mother Agrippina; and Nero's increasingly bad behavior and deterioration, especially as they play out at or are associated with various locales in the city of Rome. Tacitus interweaves other issues, themes, and events into the narrative of Book 13, but usually connects them in one way or another with these three overarching concerns.

Mentors and Models

Throughout his account of the Julio-Claudian emperors Tacitus parades before us individuals who either aid and abet the emperor's worst tendencies or serve as foils that throw his vices into relief. In the Tiberian books, for instance, Livia and Sejanus fulfill the former role, while Germanicus, although not an entirely positive role model, nonetheless emerges as a preferable alternative to the paranoid Tiberius.[3] In Book 13 we encounter a similar, if broader, cast of characters, with Nero's mother Agrippina and Pallas serving as the controlling mother and meddlesome freedman respectively; we shall also encounter for the first time Poppaea, who will eventually prove central to Nero's downfall, while Seneca and Burrus play the role of "wise advisors." We will also meet the fully competent general

---

[1] For the notion that *Annals* 18 may have concluded with the death of Nero, see Syme (1958a), 265; Martin (1981), 162–3, however, is skeptical that in the case of Nero Tacitus adhered to a hexadic structure and suggests that Tacitus could have brought his account of Nero's reign to a close in the lost half of Book 16. See further Bartera, Chapter 18 in this volume.
[2] Syme (1958a), 262. For assessments of the *quinquennium*, see Griffin (1976), 37–8, 83–4. See further below with n. 21.
[3] See Damtoft Poulsen, Chapter 10 in this volume.

Corbulo and the senator Thrasea Paetus, who will play a pivotal role in the "Stoic opposition" that develops in response to Nero in subsequent books.[4]

At least in Book 13, other than his mother Agrippina, who plays a special part in the Neronian narrative, the most prominent restraints or influences on the young emperor are Seneca and Burrus. The former would be well known to Tacitus' readers, not only for his political career but perhaps even more so for his fame as a writer and philosopher. Appointed by Agrippina as Nero's tutor in 49 CE after being recalled from exile, he continued his tutelage of Nero well into his principate. Seneca's partner in this endeavor, Sextus Afranius Burrus, was a less familiar character, though by virtue of his position perhaps no less powerful. Appointed by Claudius as prefect of the praetorian guard in 51 CE, Burrus was suitable for the post, according to Tacitus, because of his "exceptional military reputation" (*egregiae militaris famae*, *Ann.* 12.42.1); in this capacity he had been present at and evidently supported the accession of Nero upon the death of Claudius (*Ann.* 12.69.1–2).[5]

From the outset Tacitus is explicit about both their individual competence and their crucial role in keeping Nero in check (*Ann.* 13.2.1):

> *Ibaturque in caedes, nisi Afranius Burrus et Annaeus Seneca obviam issent. hi rectores imperatoriae iuventae et, rarum in societate potentiae, concordes, diversa arte ex aequo pollebant, Burrus militaribus curis et severitate morum, Seneca praeceptis eloquentiae et comitate honesta, iuvantes in vicem, quo facilius lubricam principis aetatem, si virtutem aspernaretur, voluptatibus concessis retinerent.*

> And events were heading toward slaughter, had not Afranius Burrus and Annaeus Seneca intervened. These mentors of the emperor's youth were in agreement (unusual in a pact of power) and equally influential in different ways, Burrus in military matters and the sternness of his behavior, Seneca in his instruction in eloquence and a creditable cordiality, each helping the other in order to more easily keep their hold on the slipperiness of the emperor's youth by conceding pleasures if he scorned virtue.

Straightaway Tacitus furnishes evidence, noting that the 17-year-old Nero's well received eulogy of Claudius was composed by Seneca (13.3.1); the following year, according to Tacitus, Seneca also prepared speeches for Nero vaunting his "clemency," *clementia*, specifically in the case of Plautius Lateranus, restored to senatorial rank by the emperor (13.11.1; on Nero's clemency, see further below). Shortly after his eulogy for Claudius, Nero's competence is tested by the necessity of appointing someone to deal with the Parthian incursion into Armenia. This results in the appointment of the very capable Corbulo, thus signaling some hope that "a place had apparently been cleared for virtues" (*videbatur...locus virtutibus patefactus*, 13.8.1), although Tacitus clearly implies that this

---

[4] In Syme's phrase, these characters provide "dramatic contrast" with Nero, perhaps not commensurate with their historical significance (Syme (1958a), 579). To Walker (1952), Seneca and Burrus are "Collaborators" (222–5), Thrasea an "Intransigent" (229–30) (both exemplars of her "type-characters" in Tacitus).

[5] The scholarship on Seneca is of course immense, but for his role in Tacitus in particular, see Dyson (1970); Griffin (1976), 441–2 and passim; "Seneca," *TE*: 985–8 (B. Demiriş). For Burrus, see Koestermann (1963–8), iii on 13.2.1; "Afranius Burrus, Sextus," *TE*: 23–4 (A. Mancini). The way this pair is introduced here, with full names, and the opening chapter in general have been noted by Syme (1958a), 743 as a marker that Book 13 represents a fresh start within the *Annals* as a whole; cf. Koestermann (1963–8), iii on 13.1.1 and 2.1.

was at the urging of Burrus and Seneca who were "known for their substantial experience of affairs" (*multa rerum experientia cognitos*, 13.6.3).

Initially, at least, Nero gravitates away from his domineering mother to Seneca and Burrus, there being at no point any love lost between these two and Agrippina (e.g. 13.14.3). Seneca seems to collude in gratifying the emperor's youthful passions and indiscretions (13.13.1); and when Nero receives information against his mother to the effect that she was planning some sort of coup—a charge which leads Nero to contemplate murdering his mother (as he will eventually do)—Burrus lends his support, traveling with Seneca to confront Agrippina with the charge, eliciting a memorable outburst from the emperor's mother and recorded by Tacitus (13.21).[6]

If in these few instances Seneca and Burrus are seen to steer Nero in the right direction or at least to control him, to shield him from his own worst tendencies and the pernicious influence of others, their influence rapidly wanes or is called into question as Nero's own personality and predilections come to the fore. Thus, notably, after their contretemps with Agrippina recorded at 13.21, for all intents and purposes Seneca and Burrus disappear from Book 13, though they will re-emerge early in Book 14 in connection with Agrippina's demise.

In addition to Nero's mentors Seneca and Burrus, in Book 13 Tacitus also draws attention to two individuals in particular who serve as foils to the emperor. Not, that is, necessarily as sources of influence, but rather to throw the emperor's own failings into relief. One of these is Domitius Corbulo, the other, Thrasea Paetus.

As noted above, Corbulo first arrives on the scene in Book 13 at 13.8.1, as Nero, much to his credit, places him in charge of the campaign in Armenia. Thereafter, as Tacitus weaves from domestic to foreign affairs, as he characteristically does throughout the *Annals*, Corbulo's activities in the East receive regular mention.[7] Tacitus' admiration of Corbulo is readily apparent from the outset; he instantly secures respect by his physical appearance, experience, and character: "[Corbulo was] powerful in physique…a man of great eloquence and, beyond his experience and wisdom, imposing even in the display of inanities" (*corpore ingens, verbis magnificis et super experientiam sapientiamque etiam specie inanium validus*, 13.8.3). In each of his appearances in Book 13, Corbulo emerges as extraordinarily competent and successful (see esp. 13.35); as Tacitus pointedly notes with his use of the loaded word *exemplum*, he was an "example to all," *exemplum omnibus* (13.35.4). Tacitus devotes a substantial stretch of Book 13 (13.34.2–41.3) to an extended narrative of Corbulo's successful campaign in Armenia, which culminates with the destruction of its capital, Artaxata (13.41.2–3). Although this is the last mention of Corbulo in the book, he will play a prominent role in subsequent books, where his function as a foil to Nero is made still more explicit (see e.g. 14.22.4–23.1, where Tacitus juxtaposes Nero's decadence with Corbulo's continued military success).[8] There can be no doubt that Tacitus would have dramatically highlighted his fall from Nero's favor and subsequent suicide in 67 CE, which Corbulo was ordered to commit in suspicion of his involvement in conspiracies against the emperor.[9]

---

[6] For the unusualness of this speech, see Levene (2009a), 213–14; Koestermann (1963–8), iii, ad loc. ("ein rhetorisches Meisterwerk").

[7] For Tacitus' technique in handling domestic and foreign affairs, see Ginsburg (1981), 53–79 and passim.

[8] See Whitton, Chapter 16 in this volume.

[9] For Corbulo's suicide, evidently a notable event, see Dio 63(62).17.5–6. On Corbulo generally, see Gilmartin (1973); and in Tacitus, Tresch (1965), 139–47 and esp. Ash (2006a).

One measure of how Tacitus might have handled Corbulo's suicide may be gleaned from the way he dramatizes the similarly enforced suicide of one of the foremost figures of the so-called "Stoic opposition," Thrasea Paetus. Ironically, in fact, the extant *Annals* break off precisely at the dramatic moment when the outspoken senator takes his own life (16.35), surely one of the most poignant scenes in the entire work. This concludes a long stretch of narrative in Book 16 devoted to the end of Thrasea, a stretch that opens with Tacitus' remark that in ordering Thrasea's death Nero aimed to "kill Virtue itself" (*virtutem ipsam exscindere*, 16.21.1). However, despite the prominent part he plays in the Neronian books, only once do we meet Thrasea in Book 13, and late in the book at that, as he opposes a senatorial dispensation to allow Syracusans to exceed the number of allotted gladiatorial shows (13.49). Although Tacitus concedes that this is a seemingly trivial episode, the fact that the famous Paetus is at the center of the event is given as the historian's reason for its inclusion: it hints at Paetus' future outspokenness, contrary nature, and defense of "senatorial freedom" (13.49.2: *libertate senatoria*). It is perhaps worth noting, as a mark of Paetus' notoriety, that although this is his first appearance in the *Annals*, he is not given a lengthy or formal introduction. Most likely Tacitus felt his readers need only read his name to understand this was the well-known senatorial adversary of Nero.[10]

Mother Agrippina *et aliae*

Whereas Burrus and Seneca appear for the most part to exert—or try to exert—a positive influence on Nero, and the characters of Corbulo and Thrasea contrast markedly with that of the emperor, Nero's mother Agrippina serves a contrary purpose.[11] The infamous and murderous daughter of Germanicus is by this point well known to Tacitus' readers from her part in previous books, not least for orchestrating the death of her husband, the emperor Claudius (12.66–7).[12] We have also been braced for something that becomes abundantly clear as the Neronian narrative progresses and the relationship with his mother becomes increasingly strained: "[Agrippina] could not give orders to her son...but neither could she tolerate being given orders by him" (*[Agrippina] filio dare imperium, tolerare imperitantem nequibat*, 12.64.3). So it comes as no surprise that Tacitus pulls out all the rhetorical stops in introducing her in Book 13, noting her fierce opposition to Burrus and Seneca: "They both shared in struggle against the ferocity of Agrippina, who, ablaze with all the desires of her malevolent supremacy, had Pallas on her side..." (*certamen utrique unum erat contra ferociam Agrippinae, quae cunctis malae dominationis cupidinibus flagrans habebat in partibus Pallantem...*, 13.2.2). Early on she shows signs of these "desires of her malevolent supremacy" by attempting to wheedle a place next to Nero when he meets with Armenian legates, a "disgraceful" act averted by the intervention of Seneca (13.5).

Tacitus marks Nero's dalliance with the freedwoman Acte as the beginning of his break with Agrippina, when "the power of his mother was gradually broken" (*infracta paulatim*

---

[10]   For Thrasea Paetus, see Bartera, Chapter 18 in this volume. See also Wirszubski (1950), 138–43; Turpin (2008), esp. 378–89 and passim.

[11]   With respect to the substantial body of scholarly work on Agrippina the Younger in Tacitus, a good place to start is Ginsburg (2006). See also Tresch (1965), 76–111; Barrett (2017), esp. 64–71; Gillespie (2014a); Gillespie (in preparation). For a good historical overview, see Drinkwater (2019), 32–55.

[12]   See Gillespie, Chapter 14 in this volume.

potentia matris, 13.12.1) and Nero gravitated toward Seneca (13.13.1). When Agrippina's notorious attempts at placating her son fail (most notably at 13.13.2), she turns to "terror and threats" (*ad terrorem et minas*), hinting that she would attempt to replace Nero with Britannicus (13.14.2–3). Nero's response is to poison his stepbrother during a dinner party, an act that leads Agrippina to believe (rightly) her own life to be in danger (13.16.4).[13]

These events set off Agrippina's rapid fall from favor, the stages of which are narrated in some detail in Book 13 and set the stage for her demise in Book 14. They also underscore a further leitmotif evident in Book 13 and all the Neronian books, Nero's poor relations with his dysfunctional family and more specifically with female family members, a trait that he seems to share with every other emperor of the Julio-Claudians.

While Agrippina plays an outsized role in Book 13, the brief appearances of Octavia, the daughter of Claudius and Messalina and the sister of Britannicus, are distinctly more poignant in light of the gruesome manner of her death at 14.64. Nero's marriage to Octavia in 53 CE, just prior to his accession, is recorded at 12.58 (he was 16, she was 14). Although Octavia is to this point and generally a colorless character in Tacitus, at 13.12.2 he is more forthcoming: she was a "noble" young woman and of "proven probity" (*nobili quidem et probitatis spectatae*). This remark is made, however, in the context of the report of Nero's increasingly lustful, wandering ways and his marked dislike of his wife. Oddly enough, Agrippina, following her falling out with Nero, will eventually seek out an alliance of sorts with Octavia (13.18.2), thus conjoining one of Tacitus' least likable characters with one of his most sympathetic. Octavia comes to serve, like Thrasea and Corbulo, as an antithesis, another foil, to the emperor. Tellingly, Octavia is even credited with a distinctly Stoic attitude toward her husband's misbehavior (13.16.4), an association underscored by the manner of her death at 14.64.[14]

But certainly the other female character who looms large in Book 13 but who, like Octavia, makes only a brief appearance, is Poppaea. Given her subsequent importance, and the fact that she will displace Agrippina to become the most influential female presence in the emperor's life, Tacitus equips Poppaea with a lengthy introduction in Book 13, which he dramatically prefaces with the remark: "No less notable in that year was the shamelessness that marked the beginning of massive disasters for the state" (*Non minus insignis eo anno impudicitia magnorum rei publicae malorum initium fecit*, *Ann.* 13.45.1). The "shamelessness" that precipitates such "massive disasters" is the seduction of Nero by Poppaea. Drawing on Sallust's memorable description of Sempronia (Sall. *Cat.* 25), the historian leaves no doubt as to his views on Poppaea's character (*Ann.* 13.45.2–3):[15]

(2) huic mulieri cuncta alia fuere praeter honestum animum. quippe mater eius, aetatis suae feminas pulchritudine supergressa, gloriam pariter et formam dederat; opes claritudini generis sufficiebant. (3) sermo comis nec absurdum ingenium: modestiam praeferre et lascivia uti; rarus in publicum egressus, idque velata parte oris, ne satiaret aspectum, vel

---

[13] In narrating this event, Tacitus evokes a parallel between Nero and legendary instances of fraternal strife (*antiquas fratrum discordias*, 13.17.2), an instance of how Tacitus deliberately colors the Neronian narrative in particular with quasi-mythical—and theatrical—elements. See Furneaux (1907), ad loc.; Shannon-Henderson (2019), 287–8.

[14] Octavia assumes far greater prominence in Book 14. See O'Gorman (2000), 142–3; Keitel (2009), 130–2; Whitton, Chapter 16 in this volume.

[15] For the allusion to Sallust, see Syme (1958a), 353; Koestermann (1963–8), iii, 325. On this and on Poppaea generally, see also Holtztrattner (1995), 12–17; Barrett (2017), 73–5.

quia sic decebat. famae numquam pepercit, maritos et adulteros non distinguens; neque adfectui suo aut alieno obnoxia, unde utilitas ostenderetur, illuc libidinem transferebat.

(2) This woman had everything else except honorable intentions. Her mother, surpassing in beauty the women of her age, had equipped her with both fame and good looks; her wealth was sufficient for the luster of her ancestry. (3) In speech she was affable; her talent, not disagreeable. She exhibited modesty and practiced rashness; her appearances in public were rare, and even then with part of her face veiled, either to deny people the satisfaction of a glimpse or because it was becoming. Never did she spare her reputation, drawing no distinction between husbands and adulterers; impervious to either her own or another's emotion, she would direct her lust wherever advantage was apparent.

Tacitus dates the emergence of Poppaea to the year 58 CE, as a sort of grim harbinger (among others) of the looming termination of the *quinquennium Neronis*.[16] Following this introduction, Tacitus briefly sketches her seduction of Nero, who dispatches her husband Otho to govern Lusitania (where he will remain for ten years until his successful coup to become emperor in 68 CE) in order to clear the way for his affair with and subsequent marriage to Poppaea (13.46).

Tacitus' interest in women in power has often been noted and continues to be the focus of much first-rate scholarship on the historian.[17] The Neronian narrative, however, is distinguished by the sheer number of women, both "good" and "bad," who play both major and minor roles.[18] Agrippina and Poppaea may loom large, but often it is the "minor" characters who prove equally intriguing but whose appearances are restricted to one or two brief scenes. In Book 13 examples of such characters are the poisoner Locusta, who provides Nero with the means to do away with Britannicus (13.15.2), or Pomponia, one of the more curious minor characters in Book 13. Though he deals with her in just a few sentences, Tacitus manages to conjure in Pomponia a poignant picture of spousal devotion, a life filled with long-suffering sadness, and under Nero an unjust prosecution for "foreign superstition" ("Pomponia Graecina, a distinguished woman…, was brought up on a charge of foreign superstition and entrusted to the arbitration of her husband. In accordance with ancient custom, in the presence of their relatives he investigated his wife's culpability and repute and declared her innocent. This Pomponia had a long and ceaselessly sad life," *Pomponia Graecina insignis femina…superstitionis externae rea, mariti iudicio permissa. isque prisco instituto propinquis coram de capite famaque coniugis cognovit et insontem nuntiavit. longa huic Pomponiae aetas et continua tristitia fuit,* 13.32.2–3).[19] In this seemingly minor episode and with this minor character—and through these female characters generally—Tacitus captures and anticipates the impact of Nero's reign.

---

[16] On Tacitus' powerful introduction of Poppaea here, see Koestermann (1963–8), iii, 324–2, on 13.45–6. For her displacement of Agrippina, Walker (1952), 24.

[17] Especially pertinent here is Barrett (2017); see also Gillespie (in preparation).

[18] Milnor (2009), 285, notes that in the *Annals* women are given "far greater prominence" than in Tacitus' other works, most likely for reasons of history and source material, but also symbolically as well. She astutely observes: "The domestic sphere, and the women who inhabit it, appear in the *Annals* as a shadowy but frighteningly powerful presence, lurking and manipulating from beyond the wall separating public from private life" (Milnor (2009), 286).

[19] This is not Locusta's first appearance in the *Annals*: see 12.6.1, where she is said to be among the "instruments of rule", *inter instrumenta regni*, a clear reference to her later role in the demise of Britannicus. For Pomponia, see esp. Gillespie (in preparation).

Mayhem and Madness

Covering as it does the *quinquennium Neronis*, Book 13, it should be stressed, does give Nero his due on more than one occasion, albeit usually as a consequence of firm guidance by others. There are some notable instances of Nero's early competence and attentiveness: his appointment of Corbulo, for instance (13.8, discussed above); displays of "mercy" or *clementia*, a quintessential imperial virtue in which Nero had been well schooled by Seneca's essay for him entitled *De Clementia*, which must be behind the emperor's repeated pledges to exercise *clementia* (13.11);[20] his early attempts at granting the Senate some degree of autonomy (e.g. 13.28, with the famous line, "There persisted nonetheless some semblance of the Republic," *Manebat nihilo minus quaedam imago rei publicae*); his efforts in the direction of tax relief (13.50); or in his handling of the Frisian envoys at 13.54, which reveals a certain sensitivity to the need for prudent diplomacy with Rome's allies.[21]

But readers know full well that this "good behavior" will not last, that whatever "good" things Nero might have done early in his reign are not characteristic. Book 13 features ample glimpses of Nero's fundamentally (in Tacitus' view) evil character. As noted above, Tacitus early on makes note of Nero's "greed and extravagance" (*avaritiam ac prodigentiam*, 13.1.2). Certainly, the most horrific illustration of this is the murder of his stepbrother Britannicus. Nero's malevolence toward the young man is hinted at early in the book at 13.10.2, but when his mother Agrippina begins to show a marked preference for Britannicus, by way of a punishment for Nero's snub of her, Nero decides the 14-year-old brother of his wife Octavia has to be gotten out of the way. But this is merely the opening act of Nero's lengthy descent into, if not madness, then certainly unchecked eccentricity.

One of the more intriguing aspects of Tacitus' account of Nero's increasing debauchery is the way he often maps these experiences onto the topography of Rome, sometimes quite specifically. The full role of the city of Rome in the Neronian narrative (and in the *Annals* generally) is beyond the scope of this chapter,[22] but Nero's first forays out into the city in Book 13 offer useful examples.

The first significant occurrence, two years into his reign in 56 CE, comes toward the middle of Book 13, when Nero takes to the streets at night, in disguise, for a bit of fun (13.25.1–2):

(1)...*otium foris, foeda domi lascivia, qua Nero itinera urbis et lupanaria et deverticula veste servili in dissimulationem sui compositus pererrabat, comitantibus qui raperent venditioni exposita et obviis vulnera inferrent, adversus ignaros adeo, ut ipse quoque exciperet ictus et ore praeferret. (2) deinde ubi Caesarem esse, qui grassaretur, pernotuit augebanturque iniuriae adversus viros feminasque insignes, et quidam permissa semel licentia sub nomine Neronis inulti propriis cum globis eadem exercebant, in modum captivitatis nox agebatur.*

(1) Abroad there was inactivity, but at home foul debauchery, as Nero wandered through the streets of Rome and its brothels and side streets dressed as a slave in order to conceal

---

[20] See O'Gorman (2000), 149–50. For Seneca's *De Clementia*, see Braund (2009).
[21] For Nero's successes during the *quinquennium*, see Griffin (1984), 51–66.
[22] I explore this topic via the Tiberian books in Gowing (2009), much influenced by Rouveret (1991), among others.

his identity and in the company of men who would seize items displayed for sale and inflict blows on passers-by so unwitting that Nero too received and displayed bruises on his face. (2) Later—when it became known that it was the emperor who was prowling about, and injuries against distinguished men and women were increasing and some people, now that license was granted, went unpunished under cover of Nero's name, as they carried on the same behavior with their own groups—nights were passed as if in a state of captivity.

The distinction drawn between "foreign" and "domestic," a common annalistic feature (see n. 7), is marked by the words *fora* and *domus*. Tacitus' use of the latter gestures back to a point made early on in Book 13, as he underscores the necessity to keep the emperor's private and public lives separate. Tacitus puts this in concrete terms: *discretam domum et rem publicam*, "the emperor's house was separate from the state" (13.4.2). As with the opening words of the *Annals*, urbs Roma (*Ann*. 1.1.1), which may also be both figurative and literal, we might not initially imagine that *domum* here at 13.4.2 refers to Nero's physical home. But the line between emperor's real and metaphorical "house" will gradually become blurred over the course of the Neronian books. Indeed, by the time Tacitus is done, the city—which comes to be identified with the *res publica* or the state and where the emperor's first *foeda lascivia* will be acted out in public rather than in private—will become precisely Nero's *domus* with the construction of his sprawling *Domus Aurea* or Golden House, as suggested by the memorable epigram quoted by Suetonius ("Rome will become a house," *Roma domus fiet*, *Nero* 39.2). We have no real idea of *where* these scenes in 13.25.1–2 occur, merely unspecified streets, brothels, and hangouts in the city. What matters is that this event marks the beginning of Nero's "performances," where he exchanges his role as emperor for a disguise, acting out in ways he never would or should have as princeps. This is our first glimpse of the fantasy world into which Nero will increasingly retreat, a world where nothing and no one seems real.[23]

The next occurrence, however, Tacitus pinpoints rather precisely, topographically speaking. It is two years later, in 58 CE, when Nero travels well outside of the city, to the Milvian Bridge two miles to the north and across which the Via Flaminia passes into Etruria (13.47.1–2):

(1) Hactenus Nero flagitiis et sceleribus velamenta quaesivit... (2) pons Mulvius in eo tempore celebris nocturnis inlecebris erat; ven<ti>tabatque illuc Nero, quo solutus urbem extra lasciviret. igitur regredienti per viam Flaminiam compositas insidias fatoque evitatas, quoniam diverso itinere Sallustianos in hortos remeaverit...

(1) To this extent Nero veiled his outrages and crimes .... (2) The Milvian Bridge at that time was well known for its nighttime allurements; and Nero went there often, so he might practice his debauchery more freely outside the city. Therefore the traps that had been laid were fatefully evaded by Nero as he returned along the Via Flaminia, since he had taken a different route to the Gardens of Sallust...

---

[23] On this passage, see Bartera (2011), 166–7.

Nero evidently frequented this well-known pickup spot at night. On this occasion he is duped into believing that he was going to be ambushed but evaded the trap by taking a different route home, which takes him through the *Horti Sallustiani*, the Gardens of Sallust. Such specificity may derive from Tacitus' source, but it nonetheless makes the point that Nero is apparently attempting to keep himself out of the public eye. There may be more to this: Tacitus' reader would probably know that the original version of this bridge had been built in 206 BCE by a distant relative of the emperor's, at least by adoption: Gaius Claudius Nero, famous for his defeat of the Carthaginian army at the Metaurus River, whose memory Nero here defiles by his behavior. More recently, of course, the bridge figures in the story of the Catilinarian Conspiracy of 63 BCE, for it was here that conspirators were prevented from leaving Rome with incriminating evidence. That story is known not only from Cicero (*Cat.* 3.5–6) but also from Sallust (*Cat.* 45.1), Tacitus' great model, through whose gardens Nero ironically makes his escape.[24]

A notably inconspicuous observation in Book 13 alerts us to Tacitus' sensitivity to Nero's defiling of (and eventual damage to) the city of Rome. At 13.31.1 he opens his account of the year 57 CE with the observation that really, nothing much happened that year. With one possible exception:

> *Nerone iterum L. Pisone consulibus pauca memoria digna evenere, nisi cui libeat laudandis fundamentis et trabibus, quis molem amphitheatri apud campum Martis Caesar exstruxerat, volumina implere, cum ex dignitate populi Romani repertum sit res inlustres annalibus, talia diurnis urbis actis mandare.*

> With Nero (for the second time) and L. Piso as consuls, few events worthy of memory occurred—unless ones finds it pleasing to fill volumes with praises of the foundations and beams with which the emperor had erected a mammoth amphitheater on the Plain of Mars, although it has been revealed that, in accord with the dignity of the Roman people, famous events should be entrusted to annals but actions such as these to the daily record of Rome.

Dripping with Tacitean cynicism, this passage captures a good deal: the absence of much of genuine historical interest in this year and in the *quinquennium* generally (in Tacitus' view), a sardonic reference to a structure that symbolizes Nero's penchant for games and performance, and the way Nero's actions sully the dignity of the Roman people…and Tacitus' *Annals*. The amphitheater, notorious for its extravagance, is a physical reminder of the emperor's eccentricities and the mark he will leave on the city, as Tacitus will make abundantly clear in Book 15.[25]

---

[24] Various locales in the city continue to figure in the Neronian narrative in connection with the emperor's escapades, e.g. *Ann.* 14.14.1–2 (Nero's performance in the Vatican Valley); 14.15.1–2 (Nero holds the Ludi Iuvenales in a grove near the Naumachia Augusti); 15.37 (his notorious party in the Stagnum Agrippae). The fire of 64 CE and its destruction of much of Rome will of course play a central role in Tacitus' account, as will the subsequent construction of the Domus Aurea. On Book 15 and the fire, see Ash, Chapter 17 in this volume.

[25] For this amphitheater, see Richardson (1992), 10–11. The lavish description in Calpurnius Siculus *Ecl.* 7.23–72 is likely of this structure.

Conclusion

Although perhaps an obvious point, it must be stressed that the Nero we meet in the pages of Tacitus is in large part a literary creation. Recent historical studies of Nero have gone out of their way to stress precisely this point.[26] There is little doubt, however, that the Nero Tacitus conjures in Book 13 and beyond is not meant to impress us as a nice man and an exemplary emperor. But for all of Tacitus' unflattering portrait of the emperor, even he is not above injecting a note of uncertainty and ambiguity into his narrative. As we have seen, he is willing to give Nero credit when credit is due, especially in Book 13 and its coverage of the first four years of the *quinquennium Neronis*.

There remains, however, the year 59—the final year of the five. This Tacitus postpones until Book 14. But as if to taunt his readers with the possibility that by the end of 58 CE— and of Book 13—all is not lost, he concludes this opening book of the Neronian narrative with a tantalizing event (13.58):

> *Eodem anno Ruminalem arborem in comitio, quae octingentos et triginta ante annos Remi Romulique infantiam texerat, mortuis ramalibus et arescente trunco deminutam prodigii loco habitum est, donec in novos fetus revivesceret.*

> In the same year, the tree in the Comitium, known as the Ruminalis, which eight hundred and thirty years previously had provided shelter to the infants Remus and Romulus, through the death of its limbs and the wilting of its trunk, reached a stage of decay that was considered a portent, until it revived with fresh shoots.

The message strikes me as a bit ambiguous. There seems to be little doubt that this reference to the tree under which Romulus and Remus were nursed is meant to conjure memories of fratricide and thus of Nero's murder of Britannicus.[27] But why does the tree put out fresh shoots? Is the implication that despite Nero's debased character and mismanagement, Rome, like the tree, will revive and survive, as it always has, with the tree a symbol of the *aeternitas imperii* ("eternity of empire")? A sign of renewed hope that Nero will somehow recover himself and prove to be a "good" emperor after all? Or simply that the withering of the tree mirrors the degradation Nero has inflicted (and will inflict) on Rome? The ambiguity is quintessential Tacitus. Whatever the meaning of this cryptic conclusion to Book 13, it achieves Tacitus' main goal: it makes us want to turn the page and find out what happens next.

Further Reading

Although there is no single book or article devoted exclusively to Book 13 as a whole, discussions of the Neronian books and related issues, historical and otherwise, abound. At present, the most accessible commentaries on Book 13 remain those of Furneaux (1907), in English, and Koestermann (1963–8), in German. For those who read German, Tresch's 1965 monograph on the Neronian books usefully explores various issues associated with Tacitus' account, though organized by theme

---

[26] See summary and discussion of Nero's reputation in Drinkwater (2019), 7–31.
[27] See Shannon-Henderson (2019), 229–30, 290–2 with references.

or character rather than by book; Lindl (2020) similarly examines the narrative order of the Neronian books with a focus on their themes and Tacitus' devices for engaging the reader. Keitel (2009), one of Tacitus' most observant readers, is an excellent examination of the Neronian books; Martin (1981), 162–88, offers a succinct survey. For those interested in historical overviews that also have much to say about Tacitus and the events and characters covered in Book 13, we have several superlative biographies in English: Griffin (1984), Champlin (2003), and Drinkwater (2019).

Alain M. Gowing, Annals *13: Mentors, Murder, Mother, and Mayhem* In: *The Oxford Critical Guide to Tacitus*.
Edited by: Salvador Bartera and Kelly E. Shannon-Henderson, Oxford University Press. © Oxford University Press 2025.
DOI: 10.1093/9780191915086.003.0016

16

Annals 14

Christopher Whitton

Book 14 is one of the most exciting books of the *Annals*, and the most ostentatiously structured of them all. Agrippina's murder launches it, Octavia's seals it, and Boudica holds the center: this second book of Nero's reign turns on three queens destroyed. Within that frame Tacitus fits the rest of his chosen material for the years 59, 60, 61, and (in part) 62 CE, including Nero's debut as stage artist, Seneca's fall from grace, and the deaths of Burrus, Plautus, and Sulla. It's a customary annalistic blend, customary too in its gestures at biographical narrative, as Nero consolidates his reign through emancipation (from Agrippina, Burrus, Seneca)—or, it might be said, succumbs to new seduction and corruption (by Poppaea, Tigellinus, the stage). This chapter reads the book with an eye to its finely tuned modes of narration, organization, and historical explanation, and a particular focus on its intense self-referentiality (a.k.a. intratextuality). Abundant parallels resonate across and beyond Book 14, posing interesting and sometimes unsettling questions about repetition and difference in Tacitus' historical world.

1–13. Queen Drama (1): Agrippina

Gaio Vips<t>ano <C.> Fonteio consulibus diu meditatum scelus non ultra Nero distulit…

In the consulships of Gaius Vipstanus and Gaius Fonteius, Nero put off no further the crime he had long considered…(*Ann.* 14.1.1)

The first sentence sets the tone, grim and familiar: *scelus* ("crime"). Readers of the *Annals* know well enough by now that Principate and Murder are an indivisible couple; death inaugurated Nero's reign (13.1.1) as it did Tiberius' (1.6.1). Book 14 is duly suspended between two zeniths of criminality—Nero's assassination of his mother Agrippina in 59, and a run of imperial murders alleged or actual (Burrus, Cornelius Sulla, Rubellius Plautus and, most outrageous of all, Octavia) in 62—which Tacitus thereby picks out as two pivots in Nero's perverse maturation as emperor.

That maturation is already on display in the opening words. In 13.1.1 Agrippina had Junius Silanus murdered, "Nero unawares" (*ignaro Nerone*, ablative absolute); now, four-and-a-half years on, Nero (*Nero*, nominative) looks more like a man in control, and Agrippina has become the target. So at least we surmise: Tacitus leaves the *scelus* unspecified, tantalizing us for a moment—or leaving us to fill in a very obvious blank. What Neronian crime needs less introduction than the murder of his own mother?[1] Matricide

---

[1] Already notorious (Mart. 4.63, Stat. *Silv.* 2.7.118–19). Suetonius gives it exceptional coverage in his *Life of Nero* (34).

marks a special low, and Agrippina, a Dowager Empress of unparalleled dynastic and public power, is an ultimate victim.[2]

As for "a man in control," here—as so often and so tellingly in Tacitus—first impressions deceive. Nero was emboldened, we learn, in part by "the old age of his rule" (*vetustate imperii*, acerbic words for a 21-year-old), but mainly by his lover Poppaea (14.1.1):[3]

> ...*et flagrantior in dies amore Poppaeae, quae sibi matrimonium et discidium Octaviae incolumi Agrippina haud sperans...incusare principem et pupillum vocare...*

> ...and he being daily more ardent in his love for Poppaea, who, not expecting her marriage and Octavia's divorce while Agrippina was safe and well,...took to attacking the emperor and calling him a little boy...

The decisive pace is aborted, Nero's decisiveness qualified, by a characteristic "appendix sentence" purporting to read his mind—and revealing Poppaea's control over it.[4] The syntax is eloquent: slipping in late and obliquely (*Poppaeae*, objective genitive), she hijacks the sentence in a word (*quae...*), relegating Nero to puny object (*principem et pupillum*), before taking over the narrative voice too, in a long indirect speech. Whether Tacitus is right to credit her with such influence at this point is an open question.[5] The structural force of *Annals* 14, driving towards Poppaea's marriage at its end, must be one factor; there's also the myth-making pull of the plotline "man passes from mother's control to wife's/lover's." Certainly the effect of his account is as insidious as Poppaea allegedly is: a Neronian match and more for the Sejanus of the Tiberian *Annals*.[6]

From there the murder takes its course (14.2–9): alleged attempts at incest (Tacitus cites sources; professes dispassion; but flagrantly assassinates Agrippina's character); the council of murder, at which the freedman Anicetus proposes a collapsing boat; Agrippina lured to dinner at Baiae; the collapse of the boat and Agrippina's escape; her knowing strategy for survival (feign ignorance); Nero, terrified, frames her freedman Agermus as would-be assassin;[7] the murder itself, vivid and brutal; the cremation and obituary; Nero racked with guilt but piled with flattery; his letter to the senate, penned by Seneca, denouncing Agrippina's supposed treason; the senate craven in its response, decreeing thanksgivings— but Thrasea Paetus, bastion of independence, walks out.

These are famous pages, celebrated and faulted for their dramatic flair.[8] A conveniently restricted cast keeps things simple: four principals (Nero the tyrant, Poppaea the counselor, Anicetus the henchman, Agrippina the victim), select supporting roles (Seneca and Burrus, Agermus, the unspeaking assassins), and even a Chorus (local folk holding vigil

---

[2] On Agrippina see Eck (1993); Barrett (1996); and Ginsburg (2006). Dynastically unique: 12.42.2.
[3] Griffin (1984), 100–3; Holztrattner (1995).
[4] On Tacitus' "appendix sentences," see first Damon (2003) 16–19.
[5] Many doubt it: see e.g. Martin (1990) 1563.
[6] In *Annals* 4 (see ten Berge, Chapter 12 in this volume) Sejanus burrows into Tiberius' affections, and tries to marry into the imperial family. Poppaea does both at once.
[7] "Agerinus" is a Renaissance error. On the historical Agermus, see Eck (2022).
[8] Morris (1969), 79–120 is an acute reading, Marchetta (2004) a prodigious one (500 pages); see also Quinn (1963), 11–29; Scott (1974); Ginsburg (2006), 46–53; Keitel (2009), 127–30; and Glendinning (2010), 98–103. Attempts to read against Tacitus' grain include Dawson (1969); Luke (2013); and Drinkwater (2019), 179–87. Keppie (2011) charts the topography. "Dramatic" is an *idée fixe* of the scholarship: see Ash (2021a), with e.g. Monteleone (1975) and (1990) (intertexuality with Seneca); Muller (1994) (Aristotelian tragedy); Foucher (2000), 792–9 (tragicomedy); and Marchetta (2004), 97–186 (Seneca's *Thyestes* refashioned).

after Agrippina's shipwreck, 14.8.1). There's the black comedy of the collapsing boat (14.5):[9] Crepereius abruptly squashed; farcical confusion as conspirators and non-conspirators cancel out each others' efforts; the "carelessness" (*imprudentia*), as Tacitus drily puts it, with which Acerronia, less schooled than her mistress in imperial dealings (and quick to forget her loyalty), claims to be Agrippina in the hope of being rescued—and is clubbed to death. The murder itself (14.8.2–5), by contrast, is tragic, both loosely (the narrated pathos of a death scene; the inexorable tightening of the narrative net around its victim) and specifically in her last words, *ventrem feri* ("strike the belly!", powerful in its dynastic symbolism),[10] which activate a rich chain of resonances including Euripides' Clytemnestra, Seneca's Jocasta (another queen with incest on her CV), and, most proximately, the pseudo-Senecan *Octavia*, where Agrippina makes the same gesture in *its* narrative of her death.[11] No wonder that, when Nero drops a sword to frame Agermus, Tacitus drops a loud hint about performativity (14.7.6: *Ipse...scaenam ultro criminis parat*, "he himself actively laid the scene for a charge"): the emperor's amateur dramatics are in full swing, and so are Tacitus' literary dramatics.[12]

At the same time, this is an "interested" (i.e. far from impartial) narrative worthy of an expert advocate, brimming with the skillful insinuation and stirring *enargeia* or "experientiality" that a prosecutor might deploy in a murder case.[13] Not that Agrippina is a straightforward victim. *Annals* 12 and 13 have hardly endeared her to us;[14] in Book 14 the barbs on her sexual history (14.2.2) are followed by unkind words on female credulity (14.4.1) and sardonic comment on her greed, constant to the last (14.6.3). The quotation that ends her obituary—*"Occidat," inquit, "dum imperet"* ("'Let him kill [me],' she said, 'provided he rule'," 14.9.3)—leaves a sour aftertaste not just of more tragedy, but of a villainous lust for power (for Nero) at any price.[15] And yet she is one of several Tacitean characters of whom Malcolm's epitaph holds true: "Nothing in his life became him, like the leaving it."[16] In part that's because her unpleasantness is matched and more by Nero's inhumanity in killing her; in part it reflects the ennobling force in Tacitus' world of taking your own life or, next best, facing murder bravely. The Otho of the *Histories* is the salient example, transformed in 69 CE from insidious plotter to Stoic suicide (*H.* 2.49); it's no accident that Agrippina's aftermath ten years earlier echoes his.[17]

---

[9] Read as tragicomic *peripeteia* by Foucher (2000), 797–8. Baldwin (1977) pans the whole matricide (and Book 14 at large) for humor.

[10] O'Gorman (2000), 138–41; Ihrig (2007), 337–426.

[11] Euripides: Baltussen (2002); Seneca: Hind (1972). *Octavia* 368–72 "...'This, this is what the blade must strike,' she says, 'which bore such a monster!'" (itself reworking Jocasta in Seneca *Oedipus* 1038–9). Boyle (2008) (whose translation I use here) is an excellent point of access to the *Octavia*, of which more below.

[12] "Amateur dramatics": Woodman (1993); Bartsch (1994), 1–62; Edwards (1994); Champlin (2003), 53–83. The echo when Nero literally treads the boards (14.15.4: *ipse scaenam incedit*, "he himself proceeded onto the stage") joins the dots.

[13] Tacitus' prowess as advocate: Pliny *Epistles* 2.1.6, 2.11.17, 9.23. *Enargeia*: Lausberg (1998), §§810–19 gathers ancient theory; Huitink (2019) is a refreshing introduction.

[14] See Chapters 14 and 15 in this volume.

[15] It appropriates a notorious line of the stage tyrant Atreus, *Oderint, dum metuant* ("Let them hate [me], provided they fear," Accius *Atreus* 203–4 Ribbeck).

[16] *Macbeth* I iv.

[17] 14.9.2 "The pyre (*rogo*) lit, a freedmen of hers by the name of Mnester ran himself through with the steel (<*se*> *ipse ferro transegit*), whether through affection (*caritate*) for his patron or out of fear (*metu*) of destruction. This end of hers (*Hunc sui finem*)..." ~ *H.* 2.49.4 "Some of the soldiers killed themselves beside the pyre (*iuxta rogum interfecere se*), not out of guilt or for fear (*ob metum*), but in emulation of his fine behavior and affection (*caritate*) for the emperor. This end of his life (*Hunc uitae finem*)..."

Which takes me to a third layer of this tale. Not just dramatic and oratorical, it oudoes even Vergil in its intense self-referentiality:[18] Agrippina's death exorcises a host of imperial ghosts through echoes and inversions.[19] There's her own murder of Claudius (12.66–8), a crime for which she now pays indirect penance (like mother, like son),[20] and it's no surprise if Britannicus, Nero's first shot at domestic murder (13.15–17), is also in the air;[21] we can add Claudius' previous wife Messalina, whose fantastical fall and death (11.26–38) seal his penultimate book as Agrippina's launches this second of Nero's.[22] More surprisingly, perhaps, there is Tiberius. In his last social act (6.50) he dines with Charicles, a doctor who has irritated him, at a villa on the promontory of Misenum, in March 37. Agrippina's last social act (14.4) is to dine with Nero at a villa near Misenum, in March 59. For all Tacitus' professed cynicism about coincidences of place and time (1.9.1), this one evidently caught his eye: the subject, the geography, even the month conspire to make Agrippina's last supper a curious, inverted re-run of Tiberius' (more hypocritical hosting, but this time the guest will die).[23]

While we're on male models, we might add the lonely death of Vitellius late in *Histories* 3.[24] But two others loom larger still. One is Germanicus, the emperor who never was.[25] Small but insistent echoes of his life, (allegedly foul) death, and aftermath in *Annals* 1–3 repeatedly invite comparison with the fate of his daughter Agrippina and the foul doings of his grandson Nero, marking this matricide as a climax of the whole *Annals* so far, the ultimate self-evisceration of the house of Germanicus.[26] The other is Galba, the first emperor to die in Tacitus' historical works. In one account of his death he "actively presented his neck to the assassins" (*obtulisse ultro percussoribus iugulum*), telling them to "get on and strike" (*agerent ac ferirent*, *H.* 1.41.2). When the assassins (*percussores*) surrounded Agrippina, "holding out her womb, she exclaimed, 'Strike the belly!'" (*protendens uterum "ventrem feri" exclamavit*, 14.8.5). Her defiant gesture, we saw, has good tragic precedent;

---

[18] I tread behind Henderson (1989), 172 ("monumental energy of concentrated writing in self-responsion"); see already Walker (1960), 69–71 on "parallelism" between episodes as a form of "allusiveness." Four significant studies of Tacitean intratextuality, variously described, are Brakman (1925), 190–7; Woodman (1979); Joseph (2012c), 115–27, 145–7, and 169–72; and ten Berge (2023).

[19] Set out in Whitton (forthcoming d).

[20] e.g. 14.1.1: *diu meditatum scelus* ("the crime he had long considered") ~ 12.66.1: *sceleris olim certa* ("long sure of crime"); 14.7.2: *Tum pavore exanimis* ("Then, lifeless with fear") ~ 12.67.2: *Igitur exterrita* ("Therefore, terrified"), each following a failed first attempt.

[21] Minutely, in 14.5.1: *reclinis* ("reclining," of Acerronia, lulled into false unconcern) ~ 13.16.3: *reclinis* (Nero, falsely exuding unconcern); also the swift and modest funerals (14.9.1 ~ 13.17.1).

[22] Most strikingly, 11.32.3: *tribus omnino comitantibus (id repente solitudinis erat)* ("accompanied by only three people, such was her sudden solitude") is echoed across 14.5.1: *duobus e numero familiarium...comitantibus* ("accompanied by two people from the (whole) number of her intimates") on the boat and 14.8.3: *nunc solitudinem ac repentinos strepitus* ("now there was solitude, and sudden noises"), in Agrippina's bedroom.

[23] 14.4.2: *excepit manu et complexu* ("received her with hand and embrace") ~ 6.50.2: *manum complexus* ("embracing his hand"), both deceptive; 14.4.3: *tamquam id quoque honori matris daretur* ("as if this too were being granted to his mother's honor") ~ 6.50.3: *quasi honori abeuntis amici tribueret* ("as if he were paying it to his departing friend's honor").

[24] Including 14.8.4: *abeunte...ancilla* ("as her maidservant left") ~ *H.* 3.84.4: *dilapsis etiam infimis servitiorum* ("with even the lowliest of his slaves slipping away"): the same telling detail (and syntax).

[25] On Germanicus' own death, see Damtoft Poulsen, Chapter 10 in this volume.

[26] e.g. Nero chooses murder by shipwreck because poison "could not be put down to chance" (*referri ad casum non poterat*, 14.3.2); contrast Germanicus, who saved his supposed enemy Piso from shipwreck, even though Piso's death "could have been put down to chance" (*posset...ad casum referri*, 2.55.3). Anicetus cynically attributes the intended drowning to personified nature (14.3.3: *quod venti et fluctus deliquerint*, "the crime that winds and waves committed"); compare Tiberius on the naval disaster actually suffered by Germanicus (2.26.2: *quae venti et fluctus...damna intulissent*, "the losses that winds and waves had inflicted").

but it also bears close comparison with Galba's in January 69: the anatomy differs, and with it the metaphorical weight (decapitation for a head of state; matricide with a blow to the womb), but this and other echoes also pinpoint a likeness between Nero's murderous plot against her and Otho's against Galba.[27] In narrating Agrippina's death, Tacitus circles back to the inaugural crime of the *Histories*—a remarkable fact not just in terms of his literary career but for its historical implications: Nero's mother, the woman who came closer than any other to holding the reins of power at Rome, is assimilated to his actual successor; and her murder is framed as a climax, not just of Nero's moral abominations, or indeed of the *Annals* as we have it, but of the perverted imperial statecraft that scars *Histories* and *Annals* alike.

14–28. Interlude: Emperor of the Stage

Agrippina's death and its aftermath fill almost a quarter of Book 14, an extreme instance of Tacitus' penchant for elaborating a few events while drastically compressing others, and (especially in the later books) for privileging the world of the Palace over the business of SPQR ("the Senate and People of Rome"): in a world where *l'état, c'est moi* (the king is the state), history turns ever more biographical. Witness the rest of 59 CE, squeezed into miniature compass (14.14–19), even that mostly taken up with Nero's peccadilloes. Emboldened by reactions to his matricide, the emperor enters Rome as if in triumph (14.13.2):

> *Hinc superbus ac publici servitii victor Capitolium adît, grates exsolvit, seque in omnes libidines effudit quas male coercitas qualiscumque matris reverentia tardaverat.*

> Then proud, a conqueror of public slavery, he approached the Capitol, paid thanks, and abandoned himself to all the urges, barely checked, that respect for his mother (such as it was) had restrained.

Safely dead, Agrippina almost looks like she was a good influence (and another death enters the echo-chamber, as Nero, freed from Agrippina, replays Tiberius, freed from Livia).[28] Meanwhile Nero, his own man at last (we are allowed to forget Poppaea for a couple of years), is more directly damned: killing his mother was bad enough, but now he descends to singing and dancing.[29] This first sentence inscribes bathos of a particular sort, as the emperor mounts the Capitoline, performs vows, then—a *-que* is all it takes—tumbles into depravity.

Nero has been associated with public spectacle from his debut in the text (11.11); now his career as "emperor of the stage" is launched.[30] After the arch entertainment of the

---

[27] e.g. 14.2.2 (assassinating Agrippina's character) ~ *H.* 1.42 (assassinating Titus Vinius' character), 14.4.4 (Nero's hesitation at killing his mother) ~ *H.* 1.44.1 (Otho's compunction at killing Galba and Vinius), and 14.8.1 ~ *H.* 1.36.2 and 1.40.2 (pre-death crowd scenes), each with echoes in diction and syntax.

[28] Cf. 5.3.1 (breaking free from filial obedience). The parallel of Livia and Agrippina, scheming empress step-mothers, is the most prominent responsion in the *Annals*; see e.g. Martin (1990), 1551; Santoro-L'Hoir (2006), 129–30; and the repetition of *novercalibus odiis* ("with stepmotherly hatred") across 1.6.2 and 12.2.1.

[29] Cf. Juv. 8.220. Subrius Flavus ranks "charioteer and artist" equal to "murderer" and "arsonist" in his Neronian charge-sheet (15.67.2).

[30] Heldmann (2013), 337–45. "Emperor of the stage": Pliny *Panegyricus* 46.4 (*scaenici imperatoris*), echoed in *Ann.* 15.59.2 and often since (e.g. Griffin (1984), 160–3).

Agrippina affair, Tacitus switches to moralizing invective: Nero's charioteering and lyre-playing are a "disgusting pastime" (14.14.1: *foedum studium*), his hangers-on a "heap of filth" (*colluvies*, 14.15.3); a milder but bitter epigram captures the impossible position of the put-upon praetorian prefect Burrus: *accesserat…maerens Burrus ac laudans* ("there was in attendance…Burrus, mourning and praising," 14.15.4). A swipe at Nero's poetry, not even his own work,[31] and his philosophizing (14.16) brings this first panel of "Nero the Artist" to a mordant close.

That leaves barely a page for all other events—which is to say, all public business—of 59.[32] Tacitus picks out one, the calamitous brawl at a gladiatorial show in Campania (14.17). The transition from Nero is deadpan (14.17.1: *Sub idem tempus*, "Around the same time"), but narrative juxtaposition does its work in sowing hints of "sentimental" caus-ation, as if Nero's sports were to blame for disaster in a related arena. The briefest of bul-letins on senatorial affairs (14.18, two matters involving Cyrene) and a contrasting pair of death notices bring the year to an abrupt close.

60 CE gets equally short shrift (14.20–8). Here too theater dominates, with the inaugur-ation of a new festival, the Neronia (but Tacitus damns the name to silence), heading the year (14.20–1). This time Tacitus moralizes by way of a set-piece debate between critics of Nero's Grecizing innovation and its defenders; no prizes for guessing where he sides. Then the succession theme flares up. A comet is taken to portend change; Rubellius Plautus is on the lips of all, and earns warm words from Tacitus as a man of high morals who won fame in spite of himself (we are left to contrast Nero). Excitement is caused by a coinci-dence involving Nero and a storm: "The rumors were fuelled by the interpretation of a lightning-strike, no less vacuous in its origin (*Auxit rumorem pari vanitate*)…" (14.22.2). Once again Tiberian shadows loom, this time the rockfall at Sperlonga that helped Sejanus on his way to influence ("the vacuities of rumor were increased by (*auxit vana rumoris*)…," 4.59.1): coincidence of idea (act of nature prompts talk) and place (villas in Latium) produces another historical echo and inversion (Sejanus' rise becomes Plautus' fall), duly annotated. Plautus is packed off to Asia but lives to die another day: Nero instead takes a swim in an aqueduct, a taboo for which he pays with illness (14.23.3–4)—rather mild retribution, it might seem, from the gods who left Agrippina's murder unpunished (14.12.2).

At Corbulo… ("But Corbulo…," 14.23.1): while Nero is splashing about, his general wages war. Corbulo's campaigns in the East, the major foreign affair of the Neronian books,[33] get only brief mention in this one (14.23–6),[34] leaving the stage largely clear for Britannia. But brevity only broadens the gulf, and thins the line, between the *imperator* (commander) Corbulo, marching hundreds of miles within a couple of pages, and *imper-ator* (emperor) Nero, stationary in Rome.[35] The point is delicately underlined when Corbulo escapes assassination (14.24.3), echoing and varying the fictive assassination attempt on Nero by Agrippina's freedman Agermus (14.10.3). A third monarch-figure ends the segment, Tigranes arriving to be installed as client king of Armenia, soaked in the "slavish passivity" (14.26.1: *servilem patientiam*) he has been taught at Rome—a taster for his tribulations in Book 15, and for the slavery theme about to burst out in Britannia.

---

[31] Suetonius begs to differ (*Nero* 52 with Syme (1958a), 782).   [32] Murgatroyd (2006).

[33] See Gilmartin (1973); Chapters 15 and 17 in this volume.

[34] Gilmartin (1973), 599–604; Ash (2006a), 369–71; also Pfordt (1998), 150–5; Geiser (2007), 70–9.

[35] Motion: Hutchinson (2020), 118–20. Corbulo ~ Nero: Morris (1969), 139–41, with Ash (2018), 19–20 on the limits to such "foiling."

The brief end-of-year miscellany (14.27–8) includes salutary interventions by Nero in senatorial practice (blink and you miss them), in a lull which only serves to emphasize the disaster around the corner –

29–39. Queen Drama (2): Boudica

– in Britannia, where the Boudican revolt (14.29–39) dominates the narrative for 61 CE and, through its central position, reigns over the whole book.[36] In the broader run of the *Annals*, it constitutes a belated appendix to the Claudian books, which must have featured the invasion of 43 (in Book 10?), and do include Ostorius Scapula's campaigns of 49 and 50 (*Annals* 12.31–40). Within Book 14, it supplies strong contrast in location and theme to the palace intrigues that begin and end the book. But Tacitus also, as ever, invites reflection on similarities. One concerns slavery and slavishness. The other involves queens or, more precisely, empresses.

At one level it's a familiar tale: Roman greed prompts (justified) rebellion, which in turn prompts (justified) reprisal.[37] While the governor (i.e. military commander) Suetonius Paulinus is busy invading Mona (Anglesey), the procurator (i.e. fiscal administrator) Catus Decianus mistreats the Iceni, a client kingdom in modern Norfolk: the deceased king Prasutagus' property is confiscated, his wife Boudica (a.k.a. Boudicca or Boadicea)[38] beaten, his daughters raped. Hence revolt, costing a legion, three major towns, and tens of thousands of lives. Paulinus defeats Boudica and inflicts reprisals. But conflict simmers, fanned by Decianus' successor, and Nero sends his freedman Polyclitus to arbitrate between governor and procurator. Later on a pretext is found to remove Suetonius from his command, and inglorious peace—or "idle inactivity" (*segni otio*, 14.39.3)—is restored.[39]

At another level, it's an equally familiar exercise in "compare and contrast."[40] We may find Britannia "othered," a place defined by the female and irrational (not just Boudica, doomed to failure, but the whirling Druids on Mona and the raving prophetesses of doom at Camulodunum). But its subjugation can also be paralleled with the experience of the Roman elite: the Britons enslaved by empire, the Romans enslaved by an emperor. Tacitus had explored that uncomfortable parallel in the *Agricola*, where the Boudican revolt (*Agr.* 15–16) serves as prelude to Agricola's conquest of Calgacus under another Bad Emperor, Domitian; now he hints at a parable of slavery to Nero.[41] The story begins with the Iceni, their property plundered "by means of slaves" (14.31.1: *per servos*, i.e. Decianus' agents), the king's family "treated like slaves" (*inter mancipia habebantur*), and climaxes in the

---

[36] The revolt is now generally dated to 60 (Birley (2005), 48–9), against an explicit statement by Tacitus (14.29.1): a signal error, or signal artistic license.

[37] The Frisii in 4.72–3 are paradigmatic.

[38] "Boudica" is linguistically correct. Tacitus probably wrote *Boudicca*; the folk name "Boadicea" arose from corruptions in the text of the *Annals*. See Woodman (2014), 172.

[39] On 14.29–39, see Pfordt (1998), 156–69; Levene (2009b), 230–2; and the work of Roberts and Lavan cited below. Among modern historical accounts of the revolt, see e.g. Frere (1987), 70–4 and Mattingly (2006), 106–13. On Boudica, see first Braund (1996), 118–46, with Webster (1993) and Gillespie (2018); on her reception as constructed founding figure of British "nationhood," see Williams (2009a) and Vandrei (2018). More and less scholarly biographies of her proliferate, despite the paucity of source material (beyond Tacitus, only Dio 62.1–12).

[40] Roberts (1988).

[41] Lavan (2011); Lavan (2013), 12–17 and 147–55.

grotesque power of Polyclitus: terrifying to the Roman soldiers, he is a joke to the Britons, "among whom the flame of freedom (*libertate*) even then still burned, and the power of freedmen (*libertinorum*) was not yet known" (14.39.2). The wordplay, unusually bald for Tacitus, captures an artificial but pregnant paradox: the Britons are free, while Nero has freedmen—to whom senators are as good as enslaved.

More prominent still is the gender theme. Boudica is the only female "barbarian" to challenge Rome in the *Annals*, a *femina dux* ("woman general," *Agr.* 16.1 and 31.4) to stir the same blend of curiosity, horror, and admiration as Vergil's Dido (*Aeneid* 1.364: "*dux femina facti*," "'a woman led the deed'")[42] and her historical counterpart Cleopatra.[43] But powerful women weren't confined to the edges of the Julio-Claudian Empire. Boudica is not a queen in her own right,[44] but a queen consort—in Roman terms, an empress; directly analogous, then, to Agrippina, whose death begins this book, and to Octavia, who ends it, as well as more broadly to the whole line of dominating imperial women who stud the *Annals*.[45]

Boudica's stirring battle oration[46] ends on her gender: "This [i.e. victory or death], she said, was a woman's resolve; let men live and be slaves!" (*Id mulieri destinatum; viverent viri et servirent*, 14.35.2); the wicked sound-play, pinning *vir* ("man") to *servire* ("be a slave"), points the paradox (in ancient terms) of a world where women can show greater resolve than men.[47] She opens with gender too (14.35.1):

Boudicca curru filias prae se vehens, ut quamque nationem accesserat, solitum quidem Britannis feminarum ductu bellare testabatur, sed tunc non ut tantis maioribus ortam regnum et opes, verum ut unam e vulgo libertatem amissam, confectum verberibus corpus, contrectatam filiarum pudicitiam ulcisci.

Boudica, carrying her daughters before her on her chariot, as she reached each tribe, attested that it was to be sure customary for the Britons to wage war under the generalship of women, but that now she was not, as a woman born of such great ancestors, avenging kingdom and wealth, but rather, as one of the commons, avenging liberty lost, a body exhausted by beatings, and the mishandled chastity of her daughters.

The iconic image of Boudica carrying her daughters[48] recalls an equally iconic scene in Book 1, Agrippina the Elder "carrying her baby son in her lap" (*parvulum sinu filium gerens*, 1.40.4) out of a mutinous camp in Germania: another masculine woman (differently) wronged by the Roman army.[49] But it's hard not to think of Agrippina the Younger too—as Tacitus for one did.

[42] Echoed again in 14.35.1 *feminarum ductu* ("the leadership of women"), quoted below.
[43] On the *dux femina* in Tacitus, see Santoro L'Hoir (1994), expanded in Santoro L'Hoir (2006), 111–57; Ginsburg (2006), 112–16 (Agrippina); Gillespie (2018), 91–104 (Boudica).
[44] Unlike the canny Cartimandua, queen of the Brigantes further north (12.36.1, 12.40.2–3).
[45] On Agrippina the Younger, see also Gillespie, Chapter 14 in this volume.
[46] Adler (2011), 117–61; Gillespie (2018), 55–68.
[47] Others are Octavia's slave and Epicharis, both impervious to torture (14.60.3, 15.57).
[48] Memorialized in Thornycroft's statue *Boadicea and Her Daughters* (1856–c. 1885), beside Westminster Bridge in London (Ward-Jackson (2011), 340–4).
[49] For a different view of Agrippina the Elder and Boudica as usurpers of male power, see Santoro L'Hoir (1994), 8–11 and (2006), 116, 130, and 139–41.

Boudica's words on female leadership and her noble ancestry strike an interesting chord. In a vivid scene back in 50 CE, the captured British king Caratacus and his family pay public homage to Claudius in Rome (12.37).[50] Then they do the same to Agrippina. Tacitus pauses on this outrage (12.37.4):

> *Novum sane et moribus veterum insolitum, feminam signis Romanis praesidere; ipsa semet parti a maioribus suis imperii sociam ferebat.*

> Without doubt, it was new and uncustomary in the manners of the ancients for a woman to preside over Roman standards; she for her part spoke of herself as an ally in the imperial power born of her ancestors.

Echoes of diction and idea point the parallel,[51] and the contrast: a Roman empress playing general beside her husband, and justifying it with her own ancestry; a British empress serving as general after her husband's death, and justifying it not by ancestry, well though she could, but with moral outrage. If Boudica's abused body (*confectum verberibus corpus*) has a whiff of Agrippina's brutal death (*multisque vulneribus confecta est*, "and she was finished off with many wounds," 14.8.5), then, it's no accident; and we might sit up when (for instance) the failure to defend Camulodunum (14.32.2: *impedientibus qui occulti rebellionis conscii consilia turbabant*, "hindered by those who, secretly party to the rebellion, were throwing their plans into confusion") recalls the jostling aboard Agrippina's collapsing boat (14.5.2: *turbatis omnibus et quod plerique ignari etiam conscios impediebant*, "with all in confusion, and because the many who were unaware were hindering even those who were party to it")— with the stakes raised from a handful of lives aboard ship to an entire urban population. Not only is Boudica another (and othered) Agrippina, Nero's plot against his mother is replayed both in the British revolt (we might say plot) against Rome, and in Boudica's own fate at Roman hands. It's an interesting and provocative double parallel, blending "sentimental" causation (foul deeds at the heart of Empire prompt disaster at its edge) with a kind of "sideshadowing," as events in the provinces refract those at home.[52]

All that only makes the plainness of Boudica's death the more striking. In battle the Romans prevail; the Britons are slaughtered; "Boudica ended her life with poison" (*Boudicca vitam veneno finivit*, 14.37.3), cruelly deflating her call to arms (*viverent viri et servirent*) in somber anticlimax. Or is it muted admiration? Here is a suicide—the ultimate form of "taking back control," in Stoic terms—noble in its simplicity, Cleopatran in both mode (poison) and outcome: unlike Caratacus, Boudica will not be paraded in triumph.[53] Tacitus characteristically denies us an explicit verdict, but the episode as a whole has cast a kinder light on her than it easily might have done.[54] Meanwhile we are positively obliged,

---

[50]   Discussed for different reasons by Gillespie, Chapter 14 in this volume.

[51]   *Solitum quidem* (~ *novum sane et…insolitum*) *Britannis feminarum ductu bellare testabatur* (~ *feminam signis Romanis praesidere*)…*tantis maioribus ortam regnum* (blending the idea in *parti a maioribus suis imperii* with Caratacus' words in the same scene, 12.37.1: *claris maioribus ortum*, "born of illustrious ancestors").

[52]   I adapt the "foreshadowing" of Keitel (1978). Fuller treatment of the Agrippina/Britannia responsions in Whitton (forthcoming a).

[53]   Cf. Horace *Odes* 1.37.21–32; Braund (1996), 143.

[54]   Outrage at her mistreatment (14.31.1), not Boudica herself, stirs the rebellion, and she is not mentioned again until her heroizing battle speech. That keeps her at a distance from the Britons' atrocities, and holds the focus on her as a woman wronged (in that measure, more an Octavia than an Agrippina). In *Agr.* 16.1 and 31.4, by contrast, she actually leads the uprising (so too in Dio 62.1–2, 7).

not just by the echoes we have heard, but by the power of structure, to compare this death at the center of the book with Agrippina's at the start, and Octavia's at the end. Two empresses at Rome are accused of plotting against Nero and murdered. Here is a foreign empress who actually does revolt, and dies a nobler death—another, similar yet different, victim of Neronian Empire.

40–59. Of Slaves and Senators

Eodem anno Romae insignia scelera… ("In the same year at Rome, notable crimes…," 14.40.1). Domestic matters for 61 and 62 infuse the rest of Book 14 with a steadily increasing sense of suffocation, as one man after the next, and an empress too, falls or dies. If *insignia scelera* suggests more of the depressing same (cf. 14.1.1: *scelus*), these opening outrages, for once, are not Nero's. First, the falsification of a will, a high misdemeanor in a society obsessed with testamentary law;[55] a full seven senators and equestrians are named and shamed (14.40–1). Second, the murder of Pedanius Secundus, prefect of the city, by one of his slaves (14.42–6). Master-murder in imperial Rome triggered a ruthless statutory response, the execution of the entire slave-household—in this case around 400 men, women, and children. That was too much even for contemporary tastes, prompting a popular uprising and a debate in the senate. The senate upheld the law, but it took the praetorian guard, under Nero's orders, to ensure that the crucifixions were carried out. Tacitus characteristically spends little time on the murder and less on the executions; instead he focuses the episode on the senatorial debate, more specifically on a single speech—one of the longest in the *Annals*—by the eminent jurist Cassius Longinus, upholding the law.[56]

Taken as a whole, the episode constitutes an unusual instance of the senate and Nero working in tandem and in defense of the law, if also showing the senate's inability to enforce that law unaided. But it poses two dilemmas for the reader: should all those innocent slaves be pitied; and should their penalty have been waived? Both questions were live in Tacitus' day: as recently as 105 CE, the senate had debated a similar case, reaffirming the law again, and almost voting to execute the victim's freedmen too.[57] Here he is typically equivocal (and reader responses vary accordingly), but seems to err toward "no" on both questions. A clue to that, and a complication to the "senate and emperor" tale, lies in the speaker, Cassius Longinus: not just a fierce paragon of antique severity (hence suitably Sallustian tones),[58] but another future victim of Nero.[59] Another lies in the fact that his speech contains yet more aftershocks of Agrippina's murder.[60]

Cassius' most graphic argument involves a miniature narrative of the crime, which, he claims, could not have been carried out without accomplices or witnesses. Suppose the slave in question managed to plan it and acquire a weapon on his own (14.44.1):

---

[55] Champlin (1991), 86–7.
[56] Crook (1970); Bauman (1989), 92–102; and Ginsburg (1993), 96–102; also Bellen (1982); Nörr (1983); Wolf (1988); and Petersen (2019), 492–526.
[57] Pliny *Epistles* 8.14; cf. Harries (2013).   [58] Martin (1990), 1558–9.
[59] 16.7–9; see Bartera, Chapter 18 in this volume.   [60] Whitton (forthcoming a).

num excubias transire, cubiculi fores recludere, lumen inferre, caedem patrare <poterat>
omnibus nesciis?

was he really able to get past the guards, open the doors of the bedroom, carry in a light,
perpetrate the murder—all without anyone's knowledge?

Compare the vivid narrative of Agrippina's death (14.8.2–5). Anicetus surrounds the villa
with guards (*statione*), smashes open the front door (*refractaque ianua*), comes to the
doors of the bedroom (*ad fores cubiculi*), enters the dimly lit room (*modicum lumen
inerat*); if he has come to perform a crime (*facinus patraturus*), says Agrippina, she does
not believe Nero ordered it. The clutch of echoes is surely not chance: this "slavish plot,
which no one prevented" (*insidias serviles, quas nemo prohibuit*, 14.43.2) is an oblique
double of the "plot" (*insidias*, 14.3.2) against Agrippina, stirred up by wily words of
Poppaea which "no one prevented" (*nemo prohibebat*, 14.1.3). The image of Rome as slave-
household, with Agrippina as master (*sic*), was firmly established in Book 12;[61] recall that
Anicetus, the agent of her death, was a freedman—a quarter-step away from a slave in
Tacitus' book—and the glove fits still better. All of which gives special depth to Longinus'
incredulous question about complicity (*...omnibus nesciis?*). When soldiers, senate, and
people meekly swallowed Nero's claims about his matricide (14.11–12), that was surely
complaisance, not credence: in that measure, all Rome was complicit in Agrippina's death.
    Cassius' meditation on master-murder doubles, then, as a meditation on mother-
murder: Agrippina's long shadow continues to fall across the book, posing further dilemmas. If Secundus' slaves were rightly crucified, should that affect our judgment of a society
which stood by when Agrippina died? "No," we might legitimately reply; but then there's
the *Annals'* greatest plot of all, the Pisonian conspiracy (15.48–74).[62] There Rome's senator-
slaves turn on their master, triggering another ruthless response, now in the form of serial
executions and forced suicides. Of course, Tacitus does not draw the parallel explicitly
(again subtle echoes do the work);[63] but Cassius' words turn out to resonate far beyond
the Secundus case, and even beyond Agrippina's. A master, he sharply notes, can never be
legally murdered (14.43.4). What about an emperor?
    The year ends with a brief senatorial miscellany (14.46: a senator found guilty of pro-
vincial extortion; jostling over a census in Gaul) and a weighty death notice. Memmius
Regulus had won a shining reputation, and was even named by Nero as a potential successor. A dangerous accolade (cf. 1.13.2–3) for a dangerous name ("Little King"), as the mordant continuation reminds us: *Vixit tamen...* ("And yet he lived...," 14.47.1). But Regulus
receives a special and bitter honor from Tacitus too, the last formal obituary to end a year
in the extant *Annals*: from here on, the deaths flow too thick and fast for such niceties.[64]
Well, nearly to end the year. With a straight but tart face, Tacitus adds that Nero dedicated
a gymnasium and distributed oil: senatorial business and noble deaths hardly merit prime
billing when the emperor has a philhellenic itch to scratch.
    The year 62 CE opens with a seminal moment, the return of the treason trials that stain
the Tiberian *Annals*,[65] and so broaches a theme lightly touched thus far in Nero's books:
the relationship between emperor and ruling class. A praetor, Antistius Sosianus, stands

---

[61] 12.7.3: *cuncta feminae oboediebant* ("all was slave to a woman").
[62] Discussed by Ash, Chapter 17 in this volume.   [63] See again Whitton (forthcoming a).
[64] Martin (1981), 175–6; Keitel (2009), 132–3.   [65] See Pagán, Chapter 9 in this volume.

accused of mocking the emperor in poetry.[66] The charge is brought by Cossutianus Capito, son-in-law of Tigellinus, two dark names to inaugurate the year; Thrasea Paetus dares to speak against the death penalty, in equally dark anticipation of his own fate.[67] After Agrippina's death he kept intransigent silence (14.12.1); now he speaks, producing an unusually direct confrontation of senator and emperor.[68] Nero (it was believed) wanted Antistius condemned to death, so that he could then commute the sentence in a show of imperial *clementia*.[69] Thrasea's attack is scrupulously indirect, unassailable in its insincerity: "safe criticism" to a T.[70] There was no need, he said, for "a senate under an excellent emperor and bound by no obligation" (*egregio sub principe et nulla necessitate obstricto senatui*, 14.48.3) to impose the death penalty. Let Antistius be exiled instead, as living proof of "public clemency" (*publicae clementiae*)—a grand phrase, but a wry one too, in appropriating for the senate a virtue which Nero claimed for his own.

With this display of "freedom" (*libertas*) Thrasea casts off metaphorical chains (*servitium aliorum rupit*, "broke the others' slavery," 14.49.1), but not for long. Nero expresses fury in a letter of equal indirection: of course the senate was free to judge as it saw fit. Thrasea sticks to his guns, the other senators dare not change their vote (that would be to admit that they perceived Nero's anger),[71] and Antistius gets off with exile: a rare victory of right over might—for which Thrasea will pay. Delicate contrasts come in the case of Fabricius Veiento, accused of calumny against senators rather than the emperor (14.50), but referred to Nero, who banishes him too, and decrees that his books be burned, that powerful symbol of tyranny.[72]

This prelude over, the state slips further into sickness, *gravescentibus in dies publicis malis* ("as public ills became daily more severe," 14.51.1). First, the death of Burrus (14.52), perhaps natural, but laced with rumors of poisoning which recall another quasi-victim of tyranny, Agricola (*Agr.* 43.2); his post as prefect of the praetorian guard is split between the sheepish Faenius Rufus and the vulpine Ofonius Tigellinus.[73] That leaves only Seneca from the awkward triumvirate of Agrippina, Burrus, and Seneca, guardians of Nero's first years in power; his great death scene is still a book away (15.60–4), but the fall begins now.[74] Unnamed detractors urge Nero to shed his old tutor (14.52), as Poppaea had urged him to shed his mother (14.1.1–2). Then comes the encounter. We have seen Nero crossing swords with Thrasea indirectly in the senate; now he and Seneca speak in private and face to face, in a unique pair of speeches (14.53–6). Seneca requests leave to retire; Nero—delivering his only direct speech of the extant *Annals*—declines.

---

[66] Bradley (1973); Ginsburg (1986); Petersen (2019), 384–9.

[67] Tacitus' Thrasea has been much written about (see Bartera's "Further Reading" in Chapter 18 in this volume). Capito takes a leading role in his fall (16.21–2, again with Bartera in this volume).

[68] Ronning (2006), 336–9 gives a shrewd and sceptical reading. Thrasea spoke at 13.49 too, but there the confrontation was oblique.

[69] A virtue publicly associated with Nero in Seneca's *De Clementia* (below). The tussle over *clementia* was not new: see Cowan (2016) (especially p. 98) and Devillers, Chapter 11 in this volume.

[70] Turpin (2008), 382–4. For "safe criticism," see Ahl (1984); see also O'Gorman (2020), 99–106 on "counter-speech."

[71] Being seen to understand the emperor is axiomatically dangerous in the *Annals* (1.11.2, 14.6.1).

[72] *Agr.* 2.1, *Ann.* 4.35.4–5; see further ten Berge, Chapter 12 in this volume.

[73] Rufus will join the Pisonian conspiracy. Tigellinus will join Poppaea in Nero's inner council of evil (15.61.2).

[74] On Tacitus' Seneca, see first Ker (2012); Wildberger (2015); and Pliotis (2023), 116–79. The fullest reading of 14.53–6 is Brinkmann (2002), 14–90.

It's another masterclass in courtly indirection, a match and more for the letters of Sejanus and Tiberius in 4.39–40.[75] On the face of it, the encounter is friendly. Making no reference to his danger, Seneca begs retirement as a benefaction and offers to return his wealth to Nero. In reply, Nero insists that he still depends on Seneca's help, and refuses the money. He then embraces and kisses Seneca, who thanks him—at which point Tacitus pierces the façade with an acidic epigram on thank-yous (*qui finis omnium cum dominante sermonum*, "which is how all conversations with a master end," 14.56.3). That quip recalls Agricola again, another senator hypocritically shepherded into retirement;[76] it also aptly invokes Seneca's own literary voice, since the witticism is his.[77] But the speeches themselves form a peculiar sort of Senecan dialogue, responding in particular to the *De Clementia* of 55/56 CE.[78] That work had staged a lecture to Nero on clemency, exhorting the new emperor to continue in his impeccable ways. Tacitus reshapes it into a real confrontation in which Nero has right of reply—and shows himself, seven years on, far from the ideal monarch than Seneca had tried to shape.

Perculso Seneca… ("With Seneca struck down…," 14.57.1): two words slice through the verbal dance, brusquely summarize the scene, and extend an implied chain of causation from Burrus' death through Seneca's fall to the murders of Rubellius Plautus and Cornelius Sulla (14.57–9). Both dangerously well connected, they had had their cards marked early in Nero's reign and had both suffered *de facto* exile.[79] Yet again poisonous whisperings in Nero's ear, this time by Tigellinus, precipitate their fall (14.57.1–3). Death follows, told swiftly for Sulla, fully in Plautus' case, a miniature *exitus*[80] which doubles as a smuggled-in dash of "foreign affairs" (the scene is Asia): false rumors that Plautus might fight back; his Stoic calm; a brutal end, hacked down by a centurion while Nero's eunuch Pelago supervises (14.59.2).[81]

That's as much relief as we get from the gloom at home. The narrative travels with Plautus' head back to the capital, where the senate not only thanks Nero for taking steps against these two dangerous elements, but expels them—too late, Tacitus archly remarks, to do them harm.

60–5. Queen Drama (3): Octavia

The grim litany of 62 CE reaches its paradoxical climax in the murder of a mere "girl,"[82] Nero's wife and almost-sister Octavia (14.60–4).[83] She also completes the trio of queenly

---

[75] Another emperor politely refuses a request from a privileged adviser (there a request for marriage). There, however, Sejanus ends up with greater influence, and it is Tiberius who retires (to Capri).

[76] *Agr.* 42.2 *agi sibi gratias passus est*, "he [i.e. Domitian] allowed himself to be thanked" (*sc.* for refusing Agricola a post).

[77] *De Beneficiis* 4.17.3 and *De Ira* 2.33.2, combined already in *Agr.* 42.2 (Griffin (1976), 442); also *De Tranquillitate* 14.5 on saying "thank you" after your children have been murdered (cf. *Ann.* 15.71.1).

[78] Braund (2009), 160 and Pliotis (2023), 134–9; also Brinkmann (2002), 25–35; Griffin (2013), 83–7; and Pliotis (2023), 138 on shades of *De Beneficiis*. Woodman (2010a) emphasizes un-Senecan aspects of the speeches.

[79] 13.19–23, 13.47.3, 14.22.3. A family tree in Griffin (1984), 12–13.

[80] On Tacitus and *exitus* literature, see Bartera, Chapter 18 in this volume.

[81] Another flash of Agrippina, killed by a trierarch and a centurion while Anicetus supervised (14.8.4–5).

[82] 14.64.1: *puella*, used loosely: she was 22 or 23 (Gallivan (1974)).

[83] Octavia was Claudius' daughter, Nero (adopted in 50 CE) his son. To avoid a marriage between siblings, Octavia had been adopted into another family.

destruction that studs the book. If the deaths of Agrippina, the dowager empress who lusted after Roman domination, and Boudica, the empress widow who fought Rome for freedom, provoke equivocal responses, Octavia's drips with pathos: an innocent creature falls prey to Poppaea's machinations and suffers divorce, imprisonment, and an agonizing end (steamed to death), falsely accused of adultery and sedition. Once again Tacitus' dramatic and oratorical art is on prominent display.[84]

As with Agrippina's murder, the historicity of his account is moot.[85] The smooth linearity of a narrative which makes Octavia's divorce follow consequentially on the deaths of Sulla and Plautus, then foreshortens events of several months into a single "act," makes good reading but questionable chronology.[86] Tacitus again keeps the cast conveniently small and tells a simple tale of villains and victim (was there really no pro-Octavia faction at court?); his vivid portrait of individual power-play and suffering leaves limited space for the fact of Nero's marriage to Poppaea, over in an instant (14.60.1: *exim Poppaea coniungitur*, "Forthwith he married Poppaea;" cf. 14.59.3) and plays down the dynastic stakes (any husband or child of Octavia's would have had a strong claim on the throne).[87] To be sure, the plain fact that these events end the book asserts their political as well as their moral significance; but the narrative presents first and foremost a tragedy.

More than that, it recalls a specific play. Octavia's divorce and death had already been dramatized in the *Octavia*.[88] Written in the style of Seneca, it portrays Octavia as a Roman Electra, the innocent victim of a scheming (step-)mother, and Nero as a tyrant in the mold of Atreus, spurning Seneca's calls to clemency, ordering the deaths of Plautus and Sulla, raging at popular riots against Poppaea, and condemning Octavia to death; it also features the vivid account of Agrippina's death that we met earlier. If the material sounds familiar from *Annals* 14, that may not just reflect their shared subject matter. As his Octavia boards ship, Tacitus stirs pathos through "audience pity":[89] observers recall other Julio-Claudian women exiled to the same island (Pandateria, near Naples), but reflect that Octavia's fate is the cruellest of all: even her short life thus far has been all misery. Pathetic stuff, but also pointed in literary terms: these words echo both Octavia's opening laments and the Chorus' final consolation from the *Octavia*, digesting that play into a few lines.[90] We might even wonder whether the whole framing of *Annals* 14, from Agrippina's death through to the sorry trio of Plautus, Sulla, and Octavia, the termination of Seneca's influence too, found inspiration in it. Certainly here at the end, where the *Octavia* turns Roman history to tragedy, Tacitus recasts that as (tragic) history.

The loudest artifice of all, though, is the ring-composition of Book 14.[91] As with Agrippina, so here Poppaea's weasel words prompt the crime (14.61.2–4); a supportive crowd is violently dispersed (14.61.1); Anicetus returns as agent of death (14.62.2–4); verbal echoes abound. Of course there are manifold differences, above all in the contrast between scheming, mature Agrippina and innocent, young Octavia; but we have learned by now that Tacitean parallels point to difference as well as similarity—and we can easily

[84] Drama: Batomsky (1992); Murgatroyd (2008).   [85] Meise (1969), 196–215.   [86] Rogers (1964).
[87] Not elided: this is the point of Poppaea's climactic "warning" to Nero, that, if he left Octavia single and alive, "people would give her a husband" (14.61.4: *illi maritum daturos*).
[88] See n. 11.   [89] Levene (1997).   [90] Ferri (1998); Billot (2003); Whitton (forthcoming b).
[91] e.g. Morris (1969), 185–9 and 192–3; Martin (1990), 1562–4.

see why matricide might be paired with uxoricide, meditated acts of murder on Nero's two nearest female kin.[92]

Senatorial votes of thanks come thick and fast, prompting a rare outburst from Tacitus: *Dona ob haec templis decreta que<m> ad finem memorabimus?* ("How long will we keep relating gifts decreed to the temples for such things?," 14.64.3). We are left to infer that Octavia was treated as a public enemy, her death presented as a moment of salvation for Rome, like those of Agrippina, Plautus, and Sulla before her, and like the mass of Pisonian conspirators in Book 15.[93] Finally, an annalistic notice with a twist: three last deaths (as if there had not been enough), but not ending a year, and not senatorial; rather, three imperial freedmen murdered by Nero. That further affirms Nero's emancipation from the legacy of Claudius,[94] and confirms his (or someone's) grip on power—but not without a teaser of the challenge to come. Plots have defined *Annals* 14, and the book ends with gloomy anticipation of the conspiracy against Nero himself that will occupy so much of the next one, "great – and ill-starred" (*magna...et improspera*, 14.65.2). A grim cycle closes, and another begins.[95]

Further Reading

Other readings of Book 14 include Martin (1981), 170–9 and (1990), 1557–69; Morford (1990), 1604–11; and Rudich (1993), 35–74. Among commentaries Woodcock (1939), aimed at students, remains useful on language and style; Koestermann (1963–8), iv (in German) sets the scholarly standard; Whitton (forthcoming e) pursues suggestions made here. Two more are available online: Morris (1969), 81–200, with acute remarks on 14.1–26 and 14.40–64, and Adams (1970), a technical treatment of Tacitus' language. The most recent monographs on the Neronian *Annals* (both in German) are Tresch (1965) and Lindl (2020). Benario (1995), 143–6 and (2005), 318–20 summarizes bibliography on Book 14 from 1984 to 2003; later work can be traced through Lindl (2020).

Christopher Whitton, Annals *14* In: *The Oxford Critical Guide to Tacitus*. Edited by: Salvador Bartera and Kelly E. Shannon-Henderson, Oxford University Press. © Oxford University Press 2025. DOI: 10.1093/9780191915086.003.0017

[92] He will kill Poppaea too, but spontaneously (16.6.1): see Bartera, Chapter 18 in this volume.

[93] Hence matching outrage in 15.74.1 *Tum dona et grates deis decernuntur* ("Then gifts and thanks were decreed to the gods").

[94] Contrast 11.38.4, three freedmen flourishing (one of whom, Pallas, dies here).

[95] I am grateful to John Henderson, Myles Lavan, and Tony Woodman for their comments on a draft of this chapter.

17

Annals 15

Rhiannon Ash

Introduction

At the finale of the previous book, *Annals* 14, Tacitus displays a shocking scene: the young Octavia is forced to commit suicide, but she does so with quiet dignity and delivers a death which coheres with Roman perceptions of idealized masculine bravery. Her poignant exit has some overlap with Seneca's extended "showcase" suicide in *Annals* 15, encouraging comparisons with the high-profile Stoic philosopher. Yet Octavia's suicide is not the final episode of the previous book. In a grubby coda (*Ann.* 14.65), Nero is last seen engaging in an activity traditionally associated with women—poisoning—as he eliminates a succession of prominent freedmen who are now an inconvenience to him.[1] This juxtaposition of Octavia and Nero conducting themselves in these ways subverts the audience's usual expectations about gender roles in Roman culture, further undercutting the emperor's already dubious standing as *princeps*. Where will Tacitus take us from here? Can the atmosphere of Nero's principate deteriorate any further?

In *Annals* 15 (the third book of the *Annals* devoted to Nero's principate), the "bird's-eye view" of the historical terrain covered spans the Empire and takes us all the way from looming military trouble in the East in Parthia and Armenia (15.1–17), way back west to senatorial business in Rome (15.18–22), where we then stay for the birth and death of Nero's short-lived daughter (15.23) and a surprising diplomatic solution to the trouble in the East, despite considerable military posturing from the Romans (15.23–32). This is then followed by a sequence of acting and orgies (15.33–7), a devastating fire, the scapegoating of the Christians, and deviant reconstruction of the city as Nero's vanity project, the Golden House, comes to fruition (15.38–47). The book culminates in a conspiracy, which, despite its spectacular failure, dominates the remainder of the book's narrative as its bloody aftermath unfolds in a sequence of deaths and suicides (15.48–74) that continues in *Annals* 16.

The spatial dynamic of this book is thus initially centrifugal and then markedly centripetal. It moves a long way from (what is often thought of as) the traditional annalistic structure of the year (namely, sections on *res internae*, "internal affairs," sandwiching *res externae*, "external affairs," in the middle).[2] So, after the opening scenes in the East, we are relentlessly pulled back to Italy and the claustrophobic environment of Rome, where the narrative focus (unusually, within books of the *Annals*) stays for the remainder of the book and also all that survives of *Annals* 16, rather like an adverse weather system which

---

[1] Cf. Tac. *Agr.* 43.2 (and Woodman (2014), 305) for the possibility of another emperor, Domitian, being a poisoner. See further on *Ann.* 14, Chapter 16 in this volume.

[2] See Ginsburg (1981) on such issues in the first hexad of the *Annals*.

refuses to budge. Even Nero's planned tour of Greece (15.33.2) gets abandoned for reasons that Tacitus cannot fathom (15.36.1), and although the emperor whimsically contemplates going to Egypt, a mysterious panic attack in Vesta's temple keeps him in Rome (15.36.2–3). Yet despite the dominance of the city as the setting, *res externae* (as Woodman argues) are still creatively embedded in this narrative metahistorically as Nero "transforms" Rome into Alexandria.[3] It also seems likely that Tacitus intended the Romanocentric pull of *Annals* 15 to set up a geographical contrast with the missing final books, which would have been dominated by locations outside Italy (Nero [belatedly] in Greece; Vindex in Gaul; Galba in Spain).

In terms of chronology and coverage, the book (unevenly) encompasses four years (62–65 CE). Two massive annalistic units (14.48–15.22, comprising forty chapters for 62 CE; 15.48–16.13, comprising forty chapters for 65 CE) incorporate the two longest years of this principate in terms of their narrative extent, giving them an impressive scale which highlights their significance in Tacitus' interpretation of Nero's regime (and beyond). For Syme, the importance for Tacitus of the "long year" 62 CE lies in the fact that "Seneca's power snapped," allowing the new joint praetorian prefect Tigellinus to rise to prominence as a second Sejanus.[4] This was also the year which saw the charismatic general Corbulo's successful activity in the east, maintaining the prominence of a military man who would later be invited to Greece by Nero in late 66 or early 67 CE—only to be forced to commit suicide (Dio 63.17.5–6). The significance of the other "long year," 65 CE, lies in the failed conspiracy and its consequences, including the death of Nero's former tutor and adviser Seneca. Various potential alternative emperors were opportunistically eliminated in the aftermath of the plot (whether or not they had been involved in it).

Structurally, *Annals* 15 is a messy and boundary-breaking book, since these two substantial annalistic sections sprawl and spill over the book's beginning and end. They sandwich between them and showcase two much more lean and compact years (15.23–32, ten chapters for 63 CE; 15.33–47, fifteen chapters for 64 CE).[5] The practical impact of this narrative arrangement—whereby the end of the book does not coincide with the end of the year—is to propel readers forward and to keep people reading into the next book. The strategy recalls Ovid's pointed structural arrangement in the *Metamorphoses*, where he makes some stories straddle the boundaries between book-divisions and encourages readers' forward momentum through the text. We can compare here the chronology and coverage of an earlier book, the much more self-contained *Annals* 4, which contains six years (4.1–16 = 23 CE; 4.17–33 = 24 CE; 4.34–45 = 25 CE; 4.46–61 = 26 CE; 4.62–7 = 27 CE; 4.68–75 = 28 CE), where the beginning and end of the book neatly coincide with the beginning and end of the annalistic year. In contrast, the arc of *Annals* 15 propels readers onward toward Nero's end (even if that end is itself the focus of narrative delay, since it seems very likely that *Annals* 15 sits as the third book within its own hexad within a work of eighteen books).[6] The emotional and dramatic high point of this book coincides with

---

[3] Woodman (1998), 181.

[4] Syme (1958a), 263 quoting *mors Burri infregit Senecae potentiam*, "the death of Burrus smashed the power of Seneca" (*Ann.* 14.52.1).

[5] See Higbie (2010) on book divisions, first used by Ephorus in the fourth century BCE as an organizing principle, and used structurally by Tacitus to reflect his conception of history.

[6] See Ando (1997) for a discussion of the beginning and end of *Annals* 6, touching upon a whole range of issues pertinent to the structure of the entire *Annals* and arguing that we do not possess the original end of

its final phase, as the bloody finale of the conspiracy litters the text with bodies. The conspiracy itself can be seen as an instance of false closure, since if it had succeeded, then Nero's principate would have ended in 65 CE (and *Annals* 15 would have been the last book of the work).[7]

The (End of the) Year 62 CE: Trouble in the East (15.1–17) and Senatorial Business in Rome (15.18–22)

The beginning of *Annals* 15 is relatively low-key compared with some other extant books in the work—for example, *Annals* 3 (a particularly relevant book to compare with this one, since it is also the third within its hexad), has a much more arresting start, with Agrippina's spectacular journey by ship back to Italy with Germanicus' ashes.[8] By opening with the bridging word *interea* ("meanwhile"), Tacitus signals an overspill of historical material from the previous book, whereby his extensive narrative for the year 62 CE (14.48–15.22) spans the book-division (thus contrasting with the start of the previous book, *Annals* 14).[9] Tacitus now picks up again on events in the East, which were last in the frame at *Annals* 14.23–6 and which (as so often in the *Annals*) are driven by tensions over which of the two imperial powers, Rome or Parthia, will secure the throne of Armenia for its tame nominee.[10] The first historical figure we encounter in *Annals* 15 is the *rex Parthorum* (15.1.1), Vologaeses I.[11] This puts an eastern king, and indeed, the concept of kingship—*rex* is the second word of the book—center stage, reprising the powerful focus at the start of the *Annals* (*Vrbem Roman a principio reges habuere*, "As for the city of Rome, kings ruled it from the very start," 1.1.1).[12] The opening focus on this king also forms a striking bookend with the figure of Nero at the close.[13] By that point, the emperor is being treated by some senators as if he were a god, including the proposal that a temple

Book 6; see also Shannon-Henderson, Chapter 13 in this volume, and Bartera, Chapter 18 in this volume, "Post Scriptum."

[7] There is clearly creative interplay here with Ennius' *Annales*, where fifteen books were extended by three books to create an eighteen-book work. On such issues, see further Elliott (2013), 38–40.

[8] See Devillers, Chapter 11 in this volume for further discussion of *Ann.* 3.

[9] *Interea* ("meanwhile") may also have epic resonances. Three books of Vergil's *Aeneid* (5, 10, 11) have it in the opening line.

[10] On Corbulo's campaigns in the East, see Gilmartin (1973) and Keitel (1978) for the role of Parthia and Armenia earlier in *Annals* 11 and 12. On the chronology, see Wheeler (1997). Malloch (2013), 114–74 is tremendously helpful on the eastern narratives in the *Annals* and the wider Parthian context.

[11] See *OCD*⁴ (M. S. Drower, E. W. Gray, and B. M. Levick) for this charismatic king, who ruled Parthia from c. 51/52 CE to 79/80 CE. In 51 CE he had tried to make his younger brother Tiridates king of Armenia (*Ann.* 12.50), although inadequate planning let the Iberian adventurer Radamistus seize control briefly. After the Parthians had expelled Radamistus (*Ann.* 13.6.1), rumors reached Rome that Armenia was being ransacked, and so Nero dispatched his general Corbulo to the area (54 CE). The Roman nominee for Armenia was Tigranes V (formerly a hostage in Rome). Chapter 14 in this volume also discusses affairs in Parthia and Armenia in *Ann.* 11–12.

[12] See Leigh (2013), 453 arguing that Tacitus' opening sentence plays with the opening of Aristotle's *Ath. Pol.*: Aristotle describes "the historical evolution of the world's first democracy," whereas Tacitus "sketches the movement from kingship back to kingship with scarcely a mention of the Republican institutions which came in between." Malloch (2022) deconstructs cyclical readings of this opening sentence which often link it back to the regal period.

[13] For similarly expressive "bookending," see *Annals* 3, which opens with Agrippina the Elder bringing Germanicus' ashes to Italy and closes with the funeral of the formidable Junia (Cato's niece, Cassius' widow, and Brutus' sister), thus placing two impressive women at the book's boundaries. Woodman and Martin (1996), 11 compare this presentation to Vergil *Aeneid* 7, which opens with Aeneas' dead nurse Caieta and closes with the warrior Camilla ("No other book of the extant *Annals* is framed by women, yet the frame is an apt reflection of the female presence which pervades Book 3").

to *Divus Nero* (15.74.3) should be founded. Nero rejected that grandiose idea, but it is a troubling marker of the times that such a suggestion could even be made about a living *princeps*.[14] So, a book which opens with a king in the East closes with a potential god in Rome.

One of the most striking aspects of this opening section of *Annals* 15 in the East is that Nero himself has such a low profile: he is certainly the distant recipient of letters from his representatives (15.3.2, 15.8.2), but as events unfold he is not directly named until the point when Corbulo's colleague, the hapless general Caesennius Paetus, has reached a humiliating agreement with Vologaeses (15.14.3), thus associating Nero with a low point for Rome in the handling of international affairs.

Another surprise is that Tacitus opens the narrative by focalizing through the Parthian king Vologaeses, allowing us to understand his irritations and concerns (15.1.1–2). His short but impressive speech to the Parthian nobles is marked by Ciceronian (*in integro*, "in an intact state," 15.2.3) and archaizing (*non ibo infitias*, "I will not embark on denial," 15.2.3) touches.[15] And Vologaeses can be wry and self-aware, as when he concludes his speech by telling his audience of Parthians (traditionally considered arrogant by Romans) why a reputation for restraint is desirable. He flatters his listeners by calling them *summi mortalium*, "the highest mortals" (15.2.3), a gracious compliment from one bearing the *summum nomen*, "king of kings."[16] Throughout the whole eastern narrative, Vologaeses is cast as subtle, artful, and sensitive towards the impression which he creates on those around him (unlike Nero, one might add). There is an engaging elegance about him, which goes against the grain of readers' expectations, given Roman authors' tendencies to tarnish their portraits of enemy leaders.

On the other side of the equation is the heavyweight Roman general Domitius Corbulo, whose memoirs Tacitus used (cautiously) as a source.[17] Although one possible narrative strategy for Tacitus would have been to present polarized portraits of a slippery Parthian Vologaeses and an impressive Roman Corbulo, that sort of unsubtle foiling is not something which he generally favors, and he pointedly rejects that model here (just as he does in portraying Tiberius and Germanicus in *Ann.* 1–2, where Germanicus is far from a straightforward hero). Instead, Corbulo is portrayed as unattractively ambitious, self-seeking, and entirely prepared to boost his own reputation at the expense of his subordinates (particularly Caesennius Paetus, who mistakenly thinks that the way to make progress in the area is to engage in fighting) and even at the expense of Roman soldiers' lives.[18] When the reckless Paetus' bullish leadership leads him and his men into danger, he has to ask Corbulo for help—twice (15.10.4, 15.11.3), because Corbulo does not intervene at first. Corbulo's deliberately slow rescue effort (15.10.4: *nec a Corbulone properatum*, "nor was there any hurried response from Corbulo")—a travesty of how Romans were ideally supposed to behave in a war zone when their compatriots' lives were at risk—compromises

[14] On emperor cult, see further Price (1984) and Gradel (2002). Shannon-Henderson (2019), 285–349 discusses Nero's attitude to religion.
[15] Ash (2018), 65 (*in integro*) and (2018), 64 (*non ibo infitias*).   [16] Ash (2018), 66.
[17] Ash (2018), 108; "Cn. Domitius Corbulo," *FRHist.* I.538–45 (B. Levick) lays out Corbulo's life and works. Tacitus' lexical choices *expostularent* (15.5.1) and *infirmaverat* (15.9.2) have been thought to derive from Corbulo's memoirs. See further Devillers (2003), 37–9.
[18] See further Ash (2006a) on Tacitus' ambivalent portrait of Corbulo.

his moral credibility, as Paetus humiliatingly surrenders to the Parthians (15.14.3).[19] Later in the narrative, Corbulo (to glorify himself) ruthlessly treats Paetus as a scapegoat (15.26.3), even sending Paetus' son to bury the remains of the Roman dead (15.28.2).[20] This is not an attractive or uplifting portrait: it depicts an arrogant and self-serving general whose efficiency is made more complex by the impact of his ambition on those around him.

Tacitus' decision not to put Corbulo on a pedestal (quite the opposite) reflects his strong desire to assert his historiographical independence, particularly given that Corbulo's daughter, Domitia Longina, married Domitian (Suet. *Dom.* 1.3, Dio 66.3.4). In 96 CE, she crucially kept quiet about the palace plot, which led to his assassination in a sequence of events that would have been narrated in the missing finale of Tacitus' *Histories*. Given Tacitus' hostile view of Domitian elsewhere (e.g. *Agr.* 44.5, 45.2), it seems likely that he would have had positive feelings about Domitia, the woman who helped remove him from power (and life). One might also have expected Tacitus to offer a positive portrait of her father (especially since Corbulo was a victim of Nero). Yet Tacitus as a historian is often strongly counter-suggestible and keen not to be seen uncritically absorbing the dominant viewpoint of his sources.[21] Domitia Longina was still alive when Tacitus was writing the *Annals* (assuming that some brick-stamps from the 120s found in Rome refer to her) and so this too might have nudged him not to construct a portrait of her father which was overly positive.[22] Tacitus needed to be seen to assert his independence as a historian to bolster his credibility.

In many ways, Vologaeses and Corbulo have much in common, and make ideal sparring partners, because (unlike Caesennius Paetus) they both understand the implicit rules of the game in the East. So, Corbulo's campaigning more often involves posturing rather than pitched battles (15.3.1: *bellum habere quam gerere malebat*, "he preferred to have a war on hand rather than actually to wage one"), a strategy which was effective on the ground, but which undercuts the traditional image of an idealized general. Yet engaging in a mode of mock "warfare" without committing Rome to a costly and difficult campaign was exactly the right move for the circumstances. Similarly, Vologaeses may "talk the talk" and deliver a feisty anti-Roman speech to the council of Parthian nobles in support of his brother Tiridates, King of Armenia (15.2.1–3), but as Tacitus reveals, underneath that palatable façade he actually has a long-standing and deep-rooted desire to avoid warfare with Rome (*arma Romana*, 15.5.3).[23] And curiously enough, too, such techniques of posturing and play-acting in the East recall the prevailing ideology of the Neronian principate and the geographically far-distant emperor back in Rome. Perhaps there is, after all, more overlap between the dominant atmosphere of this opening section of *Annals* 15 and the current ethos in Rome than first seems apparent.

In a twist which typifies Tacitus' heightened awareness of the gulf between appearance and reality, he draws the eastern narrative to a close by putting the spotlight on the

---

[19] For a positive example of altruistic conduct cf. Fabius Maximus' speedy and selfless rescue of his arrogant colleague Minucius (Livy 22.27–30). This is the sort of model which Corbulo could have followed, but did not.

[20] Cf. Germanicus, who himself takes the lead in burying the remains of Varus' troops at *Ann.* 1.62.1 rather than sending a subordinate.

[21] See Levick (2002) ventriloquizing Domitia Longina and including (211) a subtle discussion of where to locate her actions along the spectrum of "partner to the tyrant or assassin of my husband."

[22] *CIL* XV 548–58; Levick (2002), 199 n. 2. It is entirely possible that Corbulo may have redeemed himself during his (missing) death-scene (cf. Tacitus' portrait of Otho in the *Histories* and his suicide scene at *H.* 2.49).

[23] See further Ash (2015b) on such "shadow-boxing" in the East.

celebratory trophies and arches on the Capitol, which the senate had decreed even though in practice the "war was still undecided" (15.18.1: *integro adhuc bello*). As Waddell puts it, "the sudden contrast between the actual outcome of the war and its overblown representation in Rome highlights the irony of false memorialization."[24] As well as false memorialization, this is also an example of false closure, since the situation in the east is currently at the point of a hiatus as winter sets in: the action has been suspended, but the Armenian question has not yet been resolved, and it is clearly going to return.

Meanwhile, however, the play-acting of Vologaeses and Corbulo in the East appears to have spread to the senators in Rome, whose jingoistic measures (trophies and arches), decreed while the war was still ongoing (15.18.1), bear absolutely no relation to the reality of the situation in the East but are designed for feel-good public consumption in Rome. That superficially glitzy outward-facing stance of triumphalism is then juxtaposed with some rather grubby miscellaneous business conducted within the senate, as Tacitus concludes the year's narrative. The endemic problem of "simulated adoption" is confronted, whereby opportunistic individuals acquire privileges by adopting and then relinquishing their new (and often adult) "children" (15.19). Then the senators address an individual case which raises wider issues, namely the problem of a haughty provincial, the otherwise unknown Cretan Claudius Timarchus, who insults and dishonors the senate by boasting that it is in his power to award votes of thanks to proconsular governors in Crete after their term of office (15.20–2).[25]

This dispiriting combination of mercenary Romans out to promote their own interests and a powerful provincial who has absolutely no respect for the institutions of the Roman state raises important questions about the caliber of prominent men in Roman society and suggests a tarnished reality, which may even indicate that Timarchus' scorn is understandable. The only silver lining is the speech in *oratio recta* of the senator Thrasea Paetus, proposing Timarchus' exile from Crete and a general policy that all provincials should be banned from delivering formal speeches of thanks to the senate after a governor leaves.[26] This leads to a rare moment of consensus, and even Nero has his moment in the sun when he intervenes constructively after the consuls almost stall the process by objecting on a technicality (15.22.1). This unusual image of *princeps* and senate pulling together for the greater good of the state is all too fleeting, but it shows that even the wayward Nero has some potential to make a positive contribution.

The Year 63 CE: An Imperial Birth and Death (15.23) and a Diplomatic Solution in the East (15.24–32)

If there is one chapter which eloquently showcases the malaise at the heart of Nero's principate (and Tacitus' nuanced techniques of conveying it), it is the opening one for the

---

[24] Waddell (2013), 480.

[25] He has a "speaking name", apt in the current context, evoking the concepts of τιμή = "honor" and ἀρχή = "power" (Ash (2018), 121).

[26] Thrasea Paetus (or Paetus Thrasea as Tacitus calls him at 15.20.2, with anastrophe of names) also has a "speaking name": Paetus = "squinting" [Lat.] and Thrasea = "boldness" [Greek]. The speech itself is not particularly outspoken, but failing to keep a low profile in Nero's principate was potentially dangerous and his intervention might be considered as a kind of lopsided boldness.

following year (15.23). Although this is not a "purple passage" (like the description of the Great Fire), there is still a lot going on here historiographically. As Tacitus explains, early in 63 CE, Nero "welcomed with joy beyond mortal" (*ultra mortale gaudium accepit*, 15.23.1) a daughter, Claudia Augusta, born to him and Poppaea. Tacitus' snapshot of the emperor's hyperbolic reaction deftly suggests Nero's complete lack of emotional control, which contravenes standard positive expectations about Roman masculinity—which were normally predicated on a man's ability to keep his emotions in check.[27] Tacitus' precise lexical formulation, with its focus on normal mortal reactions being transgressed, subtly and crisply hints at the basic dynastic problem at the heart of the imperial *domus*, namely that Nero is in fact mortal, and if he were to die, then he currently has no successor. This lack of clarity about the future means that the stability of the Principate is highly vulnerable in the event of anything unexpected taking place.

While Nero's own delight at the birth of his daughter is classed as exceptional, Tacitus then moves the focus to the reaction of the senate and lists the sequence of extravagant measures which the senators enacted: polysyndeton reflects the lavish scale of the proposals, and verbs in the pluperfect tense (*commendaverat*; *susceperat*) show that the sycophancy had started even before the child's birth (15.23.2). Tacitus then brutally moves to the *peripeteia* in pithy alliterative language: "it was all for nothing, since the infant died within four months" (*quae fluxa fuere, quartum intra mensem defuncta infante*, 15.23.3). As often, Tacitus includes the crucial point in an appended ablative absolute after the main clause.[28] And by calling the child *infans* rather than using her name, he quietly suggests that the hyperbole of the reaction from Nero and the senate was misplaced. Yet this does not break the now-entrenched behavior patterns. Using an elegant overarching chiastic arrangement within the chapter (reactions of Nero/senate—senate/Nero), Tacitus illuminates further excessive measures from the histrionic senate (including the proposal that the dead infant should be made a goddess: as Lozano observes, between Augustus' principate and the Antonine dynasty only twenty-five members of the imperial family were granted this distinction).[29] Then, in a pithy formulation, Tacitus observes that the emperor "behaved as immoderately in grief as he had in happiness" (*ut laetitiae, ita maeroris immodicus egit*, 15.23.3). It is a wry touch that by not giving details here, the narrator manifests a restraint not being displayed by Nero himself.

Finally, the chapter ends with a flashback, recalling that, when the whole senate rushed out to Antium where the child was born to offer their congratulations, Thrasea Paetus was banned from coming, in an "insult presaging his impending murder" (*praenuntiam imminentis caedis contumeliam*), which he tolerated "with spirit unmoved" (*immoto animo*, 15.23.4), thus showing an impressive calmness compared with the emperor's fluctuating emotions described earlier in the chapter. And when Nero subsequently boasted to Seneca that he had been reconciled with Thrasea, Seneca congratulated him, which implies that Thrasea's friendship was (or should be considered) sufficiently valuable to Nero that he needed to do anything to retrieve it. Tacitus thus signals that the morally robust dealings of Thrasea Paetus and Seneca with Nero in 64 CE have a direct causal relationship with their subsequent suicides forced upon them by the emperor in 65 CE (Seneca) and 66 CE

[27] Späth (2012) offers a useful discussion of constructions of masculinity in Tacitus.
[28] See Damon (2003), 16–19 on such "appendix sentences."
[29] Lozano (2007), 141. Gradel (2002), 355–6 usefully discusses the number of *Divi* in the imperial family.

(Thrasea Paetus).[30] His sources for these interactions (or "duel of insults," as Lendon puts it) are conveniently masked by a verb in the passive voice (*adnotatum est* "it was noted") and an anonymized collective oral report (*ferunt*, "they say").[31] Yet the final impression created is that any failure to join in with Nero's hyperbolic register and the affirming chorus of "performed" collective emotions mirroring the emperor's own can have deadly consequences.

In the narrative for the remainder of the year, the military posturing between Rome and Parthia resumes as Vologaeses sends legates to deliver some artfully insulting instructions to Nero in Rome, which reveal Caesennius Paetus' humiliating withdrawal from Armenia in a way which adds further humiliation to the Romans (15.24). The emperor is stung by this insult, which triggers him indignantly to begin a war to retrieve Roman honor (15.25). Whether Tacitus intends us to compare Nero in the domestic sphere delivering insults to Thrasea Paetus (whose scope for retaliation is limited) and Vologaeses' snub of Nero (who can call on the Roman army to respond) is uncertain. Yet there is certainly some tension and complexity for Tacitus' readers if they do feel a flash of satisfaction in seeing Nero being wrong-footed by the Parthian king's games. At the very least, the satisfying sense of "us" and "them" which often permeates such narratives of foreign warfare is undercut.[32] What is also striking about this whole narrative is how Nero's "leadership" in Rome is almost completely sidelined, so that it is Corbulo who calls the shots and manages the campaign more or less as he likes. So, after redistributing some legions between Syria and Armenia and grandiloquently addressing his troops, he crosses the Euphrates (15.26), deliberately following the same route of his illustrious republican predecessor Lucullus back in 69 BCE and thereby engaging in self-conscious *aemulatio* (15.27.1). Despite all this posturing, when legates arrive from Vologaeses and Tiridates seeking peace, Corbulo sends back a conciliatory reply enabling both sides to draw back from the brink (15.27). The ousted king of Armenia Tiridates then asks to meet Corbulo (15.28) and does so in a cordial atmosphere, agreeing to lay his diadem before Nero's image in the east before eventually receiving it back from the real *princeps* in Rome (which would have been narrated in the missing part of the *Annals*: cf. 16.23.2). The initial capitulation takes place before Parthian cavalry and Roman legionaries (15.29.1–2) and the sequence ends with an affable banquet and Tiridates' preparations for the long journey to Rome (15.30–1). Thus, Nero's aggressive warmongering gets majestically undercut in a choreographed performance which allows both sides to retreat from a destructive conflict with their honor intact. A "phantom" war quickly evaporates, saving both Parthian and Roman lives. The fact that this ingenious face-saving solution is delivered by Corbulo, whose posthumous reputation is that of a supremely talented general, without a single battle being fought is just one of many surprises in this book.[33] Perhaps, after all, there is a time and a place for play-acting.

---

[30] Tacitus' Thrasea Paetus delivers "an intertextual re-enactment of Seneca's death-scene" (Connors (1994), 228).

[31] Lendon (1997), 145.

[32] See Marincola (1997), 287–8 for a useful appendix discussion of the Roman conventions of *nos* and *nostri* in such settings.

[33] On this section, see Ash (2006a) and (2015b), 152–5, and Geiser (2007), 117–32.

The Year 64 CE: Acting and Orgies (15.33–7) and
the Great Fire (15.38–47)

After the unexpectedly positive resolution of the eastern problem, the mood of the book darkens dramatically as Tacitus delivers for 64 CE one of the most creative and memorable annalistic units of the whole surviving work. The narrative is suddenly dominated (overwhelmed, even) by a tsunami of physical destruction and moral degradation, opening with the spontaneous collapse of the amphitheater at Naples (15.33), then presenting the Great Fire in Rome as the centerpiece (15.38–41), before moving to the deviant rebuilding of the city (15.42–5) and the finale of the attempted escape of some gladiators at Praeneste, which (despite its modest scale) prompts grandiose rumors of history repeating itself through comparison with the republican bête noire, Spartacus, and his slave revolt (15.46). This is the sort of rumor which reflects the mood of the times, but through its hyperbole it also displays the general penchant within Neronian society for melodrama and mirage over substance.[34] As if this is not already bad enough, prodigies concluding the year warn of further destruction (15.47).

It is no coincidence that (finally) this is the section of the book's narrative where Nero's name really starts to come to prominence.[35] His name is immediately conspicuous in the opening sentence for the year (*C. Laecanio M. Licinio consulibus acriore in dies cupidine adigebatur Nero promiscas scaenas frequentandi*, "With Gaius Laecanius and Marcus Licinius as consuls, Nero was being driven by the desire, sharper each day, to appear on public stages," 15.33.1). The cumulative and constant emotional pressure on him is captured in the imperfect tense of the verb; and a striking lexical choice (only here in extant Latin does the adjective *promisca* modify *scaena*) draws attention to the transgression of a Roman emperor actually stepping onto the public stage to perform, while the plural form of the noun (*scaenae*) and selection of verb (*frequentandi*) even suggests potential repetition of the degrading act.[36] His name is also "up in lights" in the final chapter of the year where Tacitus highlights the appearance of a comet, "something always expiated by Nero with illustrious blood" (*sanguine illustri semper Neroni expiatum*, 15.47.1).[37] Even by Tacitus' normal standards this is a caustic gloss, as the generalizing *semper* captures Nero's habitual warped response in sacrificing noble victims (rather than animals) to the gods, but the (misleading) implication that the prophetic comets just keep on appearing suggests that the sacrifices are not working.[38] As Shannon-Henderson observes, "the gods manifest their anger…by sending continual prodigies, but the divine wrath they express

---

[34] On Tacitean rumors (and beyond), see Shatzman (1974); Laurence (1994); Gibson (1998); and Feldherr (2009c).

[35] Forms of the name *Nero* appear 9 times (15.1–32; 17 *OCT* pages; 0.52 appearances of the name per *OCT* page), 13 times (15.33–47; 9 *OCT* pages; 1.44 appearances of the name per *OCT* page), and 41 times (15.48–75; 17 *OCT* pages; 2.41 appearances of the name per *OCT* page), and in the same three sections, forms of *Caesar* appear 8 times, 1 time, and 7 times. This is fairly broad-brush overview, but it shows that from 15.33 onwards, Nero becomes increasingly prominent.

[36] Ash (2018), 159. In the *OLD frequento* (7b) suggests that there is little or no idea of repetition in this instance, but the plural noun *scaenae* implies otherwise. Comparison with Suetonius' less elaborate formulation (*prodire in scaenam concupiit*, *Nero*, 20.1) underlines the stylistic flourishes of Tacitus' Latin.

[37] Heubner (1994) in his Teubner follows Ernesti in deleting the name, but the *OCT* retains it. Cf. Suet. *Nero* 36.1.

[38] In the extant narrative Tacitus records only one other comet for Nero's principate in 60 CE (14.22.1). Pliny describes it shining *adsiduum prope ac saevum*, "almost constantly and with ferocity" (*NH* 2.92). It was supposedly visible for six months (Sen. *NQ* 7.21.3). See Shannon-Henderson (2019), 325 for the violation implicit in Nero's human rather than animal sacrifices and Donovan Ginsberg (2020) on the allusive resonances of this particular comet.

seems by now incapable of expiation even when humans are able to recognize it."[39] There is also a witty touch, as the light which is naturally associated with the comet is transferred lexically to the disgrace of the "illustrious" blood used for its atonement. As Lendon notes, Latin words associated with honor often rely upon the metaphor of shining, but *illustris* is here used in a dark context which accentuates dishonor.[40]

In the narrative of this annalistic year, Tacitus continues to make expressive use of the imagery of light and heat, as when he describes Nero's observation about the Roman people being "rekindled" (*refoveri*, 15.36.3) by the sight of their *princeps*—it is hard not to see caustic wit here in this choice of verb casting the emperor as a fire-starter given that the narrative of the Great Fire is just around the corner.[41] Then there is Tigellinus' infamous banquet, artfully introduced as an example "so that the same kind of monstrous behavior should not have to be narrated repeatedly" (*ne saepius eadem prodigentia narranda sit*, 15.37.1). The vivid description of various kinds of deviant behavior at the banquet is put on display on and around Agrippa's Lake (a location associated with Augustus' right-hand man, the great general Marcus Vipsanius Agrippa, and thus being degraded by this grubby party). The action reaches a climax after darkness falls and every nearby grove and the surrounding houses "shone with lights" (*luminibus clarescere*, 15.37.3). It is bad enough that such transgression is taking in place in Rome, but even worse that it is so visible (and vividly preserved for condemnation by posterity in Tacitus' elaborate scene-painting). Yet just when it looks as if things cannot deteriorate further, Tacitus showcases the mock marriage of Nero and a man called Pythagoras, complete with all of the paraphernalia of a real ceremony, including wedding torches, in a scene where the contrast between light and dark is used powerfully to trigger a collective sense of shame: "everything, in short, was observed which even in the case of a woman is covered by night" (*cuncta denique spectata, quae etiam in femina nox operit*, 15.37.4).[42] Tacitus' caustic comparison with the experience of a real woman at an actual wedding (Roman marriages were consummated in darkness) might also illuminate the point that Nero is still without an heir after his daughter's death. At any rate, the causal link between the torches used in this polluted wedding and the real fire which breaks out in the city is already tangible, but Tacitus accentuates it crisply in his introduction to the conflagration ("Disaster followed...," 15.38.1: *sequitur clades*). As elsewhere in the narrative, an expressive nexus of imagery is used to deliver caustic moralism and to suggest impressionistically causal connections between certain events.

Tacitus' account of the huge fire which broke out in Rome on July 19th is a prolonged purple passage which has understandably been the focus of much scholarly attention.[43]

---

[39] Shannon-Henderson (2019), 285. She also discusses (2019, 285–349) the religious transgressions of Tacitus' Neronian narrative more widely.

[40] Lendon (1997), 274. Tacitus also plays with the etymological link of *illustris* with *lux* to capture disgrace during Tigellinus' banquet when he showcases the garish nighttime "brothels filled with illustrious [*illustribus*] ladies" (15.37.3).

[41] See Plass (1988) for a brilliant discussion of such issues. Tacitus uses *refoveo* 7 times (2 times in *Histories*; 5 times in *Annals*; not in the minor works). Cf. the depiction of Antonius Primus, grumbling about his cold bath-water and saying that it will soon "heat up," interpreted negatively by critics as a quip about setting fire to Cremona (*H.* 3.32.2).

[42] On the mock wedding, see Woodman (1998), 168–89 and Champlin (2003), 153–77.

[43] See for example Newbold (1974); Holson (1976); Champlin (2003), 178–200; Dando-Collins (2010); Shannon (2012); Shaw (2015); Walsh (2019), 42–72; Closs (2016) and (2020); Barrett (2020), 57–113; and Ash (2022).

Roman historiography relished disaster narratives, such as the pivotal sack of Rome by the Gauls in 390 BCE (represented in historical accounts as a low-point from which the Roman people eventually recovered to become the dominant global imperial power).[44] Such depictions also had rich scope for being infused with epic touches and evoking the archetypal sack of Troy.[45] Yet this particular disaster is self-inflicted, rather than being unleashed by foreign enemies, and sets up the dubious circumstances necessary for a land-grab by the incumbent emperor appropriating the public space of the city for his own private playground, the Golden House. Tacitus only describes this lavish imperial palace in a brief and impressionistic way, almost as if he is engaging in a form of censorship (15.42.1).

Historiographically, there is much at stake in how Tacitus handles his account of the fire. In terms of anti-Neronian bias, it is almost a test case of a historian's claim to impartiality and credibility. Tacitus is at pains to embed in his version an expression of equivocation ("Disaster followed—whether by chance or by the cunning of the *princeps* is uncertain," 15.38.1: *sequitur clades, forte an dolo principis incertum*), to emphasize that Nero himself was at Antium when the fire broke out (15.39.1), to stress that the story of Nero's performance about the destruction of Troy was a rumor (15.39.3; other sources report it as fact, Suet. *Nero* 38.2, Dio 62.18.1), and to convey that (whatever the truth) people certainly believed that the fire was arson (15.44.2). Such touches are all designed to project an impression of a writer who is not pre-judging the issue of responsibility and who is looking at events from multiple angles.

The version of the fire which Tacitus constructs is compelling, without being sensational, and where he does introduce touches evocative of the fall of Troy, he resists laying it on too thickly, such as when he reports that although some victims of the fire could have escaped, they opted not to do so (15.38.6). His readers here would naturally think of Vergil's Anchises, stubbornly refusing to leave his beloved city (*Aen.* 2.634–49), but Tacitus leaves the association hovering, rather than actively drawing the comparison. Moreover, overt comparison with the Gallic sack is made by unnamed sources in the text (15.41.2), rather than by Tacitus himself, who implies that the efforts to align the two fires by significant numbers have been a little too ingenious.[46] In comparison with Tacitus, Suetonius' account (*Nero* 38) is skeletal and paratactic, with virtually no focus on the victims, foregrounding instead Nero's malice aforethought, while what Shaw calls Dio's "rhetorically exaggerated" version (62.16–18) likewise squarely blames Nero as the mastermind.[47] This is not to say that Tacitus is uncritical of Nero. He certainly acknowledges the public relations disaster of how badly he mishandles the aftermath by selfishly building the Golden House (15.42.1). Perhaps most strikingly of all, Tacitus shows how Nero's attempt to defuse the hostile rumor that he had started the fire totally backfires when he targets the Christians and has them crucified on burning crosses in his gardens—so much so that people predisposed to hostility towards members of this strange sect even feel pity for them (15.44.5).[48]

---

[44] See Keitel (2010) on disaster narratives in Tacitus. Kraus (1994a), 87–8 illuminates the language of rebirth used by Livy at the start of Book 6. Livy 5.39–55 describes the Gallic sack and the now fragmentary historian Claudius Quadrigarius started his work with that disaster.

[45] Kraus (1994b); Woodman (2012), 387–92.

[46] Edwards (2011) offers a rich discussion of the relationship to Vergil and Livy in Tacitus' narrative of the fire.

[47] Shaw (2015), 82.

[48] See Shaw (2015) on the possibility that Christian persecution under Nero is a backwards projection of later Roman attitudes. Barrett (2020), 143–74 offers a useful overview of Tacitus' Christians and the Great Fire.

The (Start of the) Year 65 CE: The Pisonian Conspiracy and its Aftermath (15.48–74)

Another surprise in this book is that Tacitus devotes such lavish attention to a conspiracy which failed. That said, his decision to do so makes sense artistically, since a set of events by definition shrouded in secrecy and speculation offers considerable latitude for exciting treatment and for suggestive alignment with previous historical events, such as the Catilinarian conspiracy narrated by Sallust (amongst others).[49] It makes even more sense historiographically, since the unsuccessful plot still had serious consequences, even if it did not secure Nero's removal—indeed, that in itself may be the single most significant outcome of the botched plot.[50] If Nero had been assassinated in 65 CE, or even in 62 CE, when the first glimmer of trouble is highlighted (14.65.2), then other potential contenders for the role of *princeps* would have survived. If we think counterfactually, this conspiracy is important because its failure eliminated founding members of alternative dynasties to the Flavians. So we see removed in quick succession the possibility of a "Pisonian" dynasty under Piso, an "Annaean" dynasty under Seneca, or a "Junian" dynasty under Silanus, or indeed any other dynasty potentially set up by the kingmaker consul Vestinus.[51] Ultimately, the Flavian dynasty (and the civil wars of 69 CE) might never have materialized.

As so often in Tacitus' historical conception of events, this whole sequence is marked by a sense of deterioration from the standards of the past, since it suffers by comparison with previous conspiracy narratives (already a dubious yardstick!). For one thing, its leader (or figurehead) is a lightweight. The affable and good-looking Gaius Calpurnius Piso, despite his family pedigree, is not an obvious imperial candidate; and he has no plan. Tacitus wryly invests his character-sketch of Piso (15.48.2–3) with echoes of the panegyrical poem about Piso, the anonymous hexameter poem *Laus Pisonis*.[52] In addition, Tacitus adds distinctively Sallustian notes here: the prominent position of the character-sketch, separated from the plot's start (15.49.1), recalls Catiline's prominent introduction by Sallust (*Cat.* 5). Yet Piso, lacking drive and determination, is much less formidable than Catiline ever was. Instead, Catiline's traits are refracted amongst many of Piso's followers (15.49–50.3), who themselves are rather a shambolic and disparate group. This introduction of the "supporting cast" recalls Sallust's catalog of Catiline's supporters (*Cat.* 17), but Tacitus incorporates more detail about motives and personalities. The most vibrant participant is the freedwoman Epicharis (15.51), recalling Sallust's noblewoman Sempronia (*Cat.* 25) but outdoing her in virtues—and Epicharis also conspicuously surpasses her aristocratic male colleagues in bravery, once the conspiracy is discovered and she kills herself ingeniously while being brought back for a second day of torture (15.57). Such dialogue with Sallust's Catilinarian conspiracy emphasizes this current plot's "headlessness." Imperial history is often presented by Tacitus as implicitly failing to adhere to the standards of the Republican past—even in the dubious area of conspiracies.[53]

---

[49] See Pagán (2004) for conspiracy narratives (including the Pisonian one) and the various tropes associated with them. Woodman (1993) is the key discussion of Tacitus' "staging" of the plot.

[50] The mutinies in *Annals* 1 offer another example of something which failed, but still mattered. See further Low (2016b).

[51] See O'Gorman (2006) for the "virtual" Pisonian dynasty across the *Annals* and for counterfactual history.

[52] Champlin (1989), 104; Ash (2018), 222–3.

[53] Cf the bemused internal commentators comparing contenders for imperial power in 69 CE with the civil wars of the past (*H.* 1.50).

When Tacitus narrates the conspiracy's unravelling (15.54–9), he sets up a miniature tragedy emanating from the household of the conspirator Scaevinus. Touches such as regular focus on the "stage-prop" of the dagger which would have been used to kill Nero (15.53.2) and the "messenger" Milichus (15.55.1) all contribute to the staginess of this section, which has the feel of a *fabula praetexta* (Roman drama on a historical subject).[54] Nero himself, *ille scaenicus*, "that stage-performer," as Tacitus scornfully calls him (15.59.2), contributes grimly to the action from the sidelines, whether through his ghoulish presence at interrogations by torture (15.58.3) or through placing the personified city into custody ("as it were," 15.58.2).[55] This latter snapshot recalls Seneca's archetypal tyrant king Atreus in Argos (*Thyestes* 180–9), placing "the whole city and its environs under extravagant military arrest."[56] These "stage features" of the conspiracy also foreshadow the first official appearance of Nero on the stage in Rome in Book 16 (*Ann.* 16.4).[57]

Such associations with Senecan tragedy are especially apt, since Seneca himself is one of the many people caught up in the conspiracy's bloody aftermath (even though there is little evidence that he was involved in the plot). The book's closing stages catalog multiple deaths (a warped *aristeia*). Some are impressive, but many are not. In a grim sequence manifesting *variatio* and vivid detail (15.60–70), Tacitus describes ten deaths (following Piso's), with Seneca's suicide being relayed most lavishly. This gives Tacitus the chance to pepper his account with telling verbal echoes from Seneca's own works.[58] Yet despite the prominence and performative aspect of Seneca's ostentatious and slow death, the one which sticks in the memory is that of the military tribune, Subrius Flavus, quoted by Tacitus verbatim during his interrogation when he confronted and denounced Nero face-to-face: "I hated you, and yet none of your soldiers was more loyal to you for the time that you deserved to be loved. I began to hate after you became the murderer of your mother and wife, a charioteer and actor and fire-starter" ("*oderam te…nec quisquam tibi fidelior militum fuit, dum amari meruisti: odisse coepi, postquam parricida matris et uxoris, auriga et histrio et incendiarius extitisti*," 15.67.2). What the blunt, straight-talking Flavus believes about his emperor matters much more than the truth, and his words signal a slow narrative arc towards the military rebellions which would eventually terminate Nero's principate. *Annals* 15 may begin with an extensive spotlight on the showmanship of the flashy general Corbulo, but towards its end, the words of another military man signal the death-knell for this most unusual of emperors. The conspiracy failed, but it still had consequences, and its dominance of this extraordinary book *Annals* 15 reflects this paradox.

Further Reading

On Tacitus' narrative of events in Parthia and Armenia, see Keitel (1978), Ash (2006a) (Corbulo), and Ash (2015b) (Romano-Parthian conflict in Tacitus, with further bibliography). On the narrative

---

[54] See Flower (1995) and Manuwald (2001b) on the *fabula praetexta*. Tacitus knew the pseudo-Senecan *Octavia*, the only example of the genre that survives in its entirety, and used it in his portrayal of Octavia's death (Ferri (1998); Donovan Ginsberg (2016)). On Tacitus' Octavia, see further Whitton, Chapter 16 in this volume.

[55] See Cogitore (2002) on Rome in the conspiracy.   [56] Woodman (1993), 123.

[57] On this episode, see Bartera, Chapter 18 in this volume.

[58] See Ash (2018), 274 for further details. On the deaths of Seneca and others, see Dyson (1970); Griffin (1976), 367–83, 427–44, Batomsky (1992); Hutchinson (1993), 263–8; Edwards (2007), 110–13, 156–7; and Ker (2009), 20–34.

of the fire, see Closs (2020) and Barrett (2020). On the great conspiracy against Nero and its bloody aftermath, see Woodman (1993), Connors (1994), Pagán (2004), and Edwards (2007). Ker (2012) is a good starting point for Tacitus' portrait of Seneca (discussed more extensively in Ker (2009)). Even for Latinless readers, the introduction to the commentary of Ash (2018) gives an accessible overview of the main issues raised by *Annals* 15, and Owen and Gildenhard (2013) is also useful.

Rhiannon Ash, Annals *15* In: *The Oxford Critical Guide to Tacitus*. Edited by: Salvador Bartera and Kelly E. Shannon-Henderson, Oxford University Press. © Oxford University Press 2025. DOI: 10.1093/9780191915086.003.0018

18

Annals 16

Salvador Bartera

Introduction

Tacitus' *Annals* and *Histories* are both incomplete: their two main manuscripts, Laurentianus Mediceus 68.1 (= M1), which contains *Annals* 1–6, and Laurentianus Mediceus 68.2 (= M2), which contains *Annals* 11–16 and *Histories* 1–5, are fragmentary. Nothing has survived of the principates of Caligula, Titus, or Domitian.[1] Book 16 is the last surviving book of the *Annals*. M2 breaks off in the middle of the narrative for the year 66 CE, at the climactic point of Thrasea Paetus' dramatic suicide (chapter 35 in modern editions), mid-sentence: *post lentitudine exitus graves cruciatus adferente, obversis in Demetrium* ***, "Then, as the slowness of death was causing excruciating pain, turning his [sc. eyes] to Demetrius…" In the manuscript, there follows a half blank page. On the next page, the text begins with the opening words of what is, in modern editions, *Histories* 1, but is *Liber XVII* in the second Medicean (M2), which was written in Montecassino in the eleventh century,[2] for the *Annals* and *Histories* were transmitted as one work, in thirty books, covering the period 14–96 CE (Jerome *Comm. ad Zach.* 3.14): "Cornelius Tacitus, who penned the lives of the Caesars in thirty volumes, (from) after Augustus up to the death of Domitian" (*Cornelius Tacitus, qui post Augustum usque ad mortem Domitiani vitas Caesarum triginta voluminibus exaravit*). Since the sudden break in the middle of Book 16 in the manuscript tradition is a probable sign of physical damage to a late-antique archetype (that is, the "original" manuscript from which all subsequent copies, including M2, derive), and since the *Histories*, too, break off in the middle of Book 5, it is impossible to establish with certainty how many books of *Histories* and *Annals* Tacitus wrote.[3]

Nero

The events narrated in Book 16 are carefully prepared for in the preceding narrative, where Tacitus introduces and develops themes and characters that will become central in the events of 66. Such a progress characterizes first and foremost Nero, who gradually

* I would like to thank R. Ash, C. P. Craig, A. J. Woodman, and my co-editor for reading early drafts of this paper. All remaining errors are mine.

[1] On the "missing" parts of Tacitus' oeuvre, see Christoforou and ten Berge (forthcoming).

[2] All surviving manuscripts derive from M2. See Martin (2009); Murgia (2012); Malloch (2013), 9–21; Malloch (forthcoming b). The conventional titles *Annals* and *Histories* did not become regular before the Renaissance. See e.g. Bartera (2016), 113–20.

[3] See the *Post Scriptum* below.

displays all the traits that Tacitus has developed in the earlier books. His characterization of Nero in *Annals* 13–16 conforms to the stereotypical idea of tyrants and shows all the features expected in such a character, from cruelty to incest, from matricide to madness, from megalomania to extreme egocentrism.[4] Since Tacitus is our main source for Nero's principate, and the other relevant sources, Suetonius and Cassius Dio, may be dependent on Tacitus or on common source(s),[5] it is difficult to get rid of Tacitus' extremely rhetorical portrait, which has become part of the historical tradition and has contributed to the widespread image of the emperor who "fiddled while Rome burned."[6] It did not help that Nero suffered posthumous condemnation and that the early Christian writers used Tacitus' account of the aftermath of the Great Fire to identify Nero as the first persecutor of Christians (15.38–44), in fact as the Antichrist himself.[7] The widespread view of Nero as the quintessential monster who killed his mother, burned the city of Rome, and persecuted Christians is due mainly to Tacitus' account.

Tacitus, however, is the only ancient author who doubts Nero's culpability in the Great Fire, and he also provides alternatives for details that the other ancient sources never question, as for example in the case of Poppaea's cause of death (see below). This does not mean that Tacitus' history is "scientific" in a modern sense: his characterization of Nero remains an essentially literary construction, in accordance with the canons of ancient historiography, for which historical truth had a different meaning from what it has today. Indeed, although most scholars accept Tacitus' negative portrait of Nero to some degree, some recent biographers have argued that Nero was bad only on a personal level; in fact he was a good emperor who maintained peace and passed sensible laws.[8] In Tacitus' narrative, Nero's "good years" are the first five (the so-called *quinquennium Neronis*, 54–9),[9] from his accession until the death of his mother Agrippina, when the young *princeps* could rely on the expert guidance of his tutor Seneca and his prefect Burrus. But even in this early phase, Tacitus is clearly setting the scene for the "real" Nero who will gradually emerge as each of his advisers is eliminated. A similar arc of decline can also be observed in the Tiberian and Claudian narratives,[10] but it reaches its climax with Nero, the last of the Julio-Claudians, whose behavior embodies the worst qualities of his ancestors, especially Augustus, whom Nero purported to imitate. Nero's last years are therefore not only an epilogue of his own principate, but of the whole Julio-Claudian dynasty.

The Structure of the Book

The surviving narrative of Book 16 opens in the middle of the year 65 and focuses exclusively on "domestic affairs" (*res internae*). It follows the uncovering of the Pisonian

---

[4] On the rhetorical tyrant, see esp. Dunkle (1971); Tabacco (1985); Cazzuffi (2013); Panou and Schadee (2018). On these features in Tiberius, see Shannon-Henderson, Chapter 13 in this volume.

[5] On Tacitus' sources, see esp. Questa (1967) and Devillers (2003). On Dio's Nero, see Gowing (1997) and Malik (2021); on Dio's sources, see Letta (2021); on Tacitus and Suetonius, see Power (2014).

[6] See Barrett (2021). Cf. also Closs (2020). On the Great Fire, see now Ash (2022).

[7] On Nero the Antichrist, see esp. Malik (2020). It should be noted that Shaw (2015) has questioned Tacitus' account of Nero's persecution of the Christians. See the response by Jones (2017) and Malloch's (2021) review of Barrett (2020).

[8] See e.g. Barrett (2020); Opper (2021); and especially Drinkwater (2019).

[9] See Gowing, Chapter 15 in this volume.

[10] Cf. Tiberius' obituary at 6.51.3. See Shannon-Henderson, Chapter 13 in this volume.

conspiracy (April of 65), to which the second half of Book 15 (48–74) is devoted.[11] Whether the first event that Tacitus records in Book 16, Bassus' gold, happened after the conspiracy is impossible to determine, for it is essentially timeless. Book 16 is structured into three main units: the gold of Bassus (chapters 1–3); the deaths of illustrious senators (7–20); and the trials and deaths of Barea Soranus and Thrasea Paetus (21–35). Sandwiched between the first two units are two significant events: the second *Neronia* (4–5), which is thematically prepared for by the "mythical" story of Bassus' gold, and the death of Nero's second wife Poppaea (6), which introduces the theme of "innocent death" which will characterize chapters 7–20. The second unit of the book also includes one of the most memorable passages of Tacitus' oeuvre: the suicide of Petronius (18–19), Nero's "arbiter of elegance" (*elegantiae arbiter*), which is in obvious contrast with the suicide scenes of the two famous Stoics of the Neronian age, the Younger Seneca and Thrasea Paetus, which respectively precede and follow Petronius.[12] All three men fall shortly after the discovery of the Pisonian conspiracy, although both Seneca's and Thrasea's relationship with Nero had already deteriorated, whereas Petronius' death comes unexpectedly (see below).

Death is a constant theme in the *Annals*, but its presence is especially manifest in Book 16, where the victims frequently die tragically and ostentatiously. The reasons for their deaths are often political and probably due to the recently attempted conspiracy, although a direct link between the conspirators and the victims of Book 16 is often impossible to establish. Many of these victims, especially some illustrious members of the senate, were Stoics. Although the relationship between Nero and the senate began to deteriorate after the death of Agrippina (14.8.5), many of Nero's most vocal opponents, including Thrasea Paetus, continued to be engaged in senatorial activities, at least temporarily. With the removal of Agrippina the Younger, the death of Burrus, and Seneca's retirement, however, Nero felt freer to pursue his artistic interests. He was perhaps encouraged by the rising influence of his second wife Poppaea and his prefect Tigellinus. Several key events point to a growing rift between Nero and the most traditional senate members: his public performance in Naples (15.33), Tigellinus' infamous banquet (15.37), the Great Fire (15.38–44), and eventually the conspiracy of 65. The people continued to support Nero (cf. e.g. their support at the *Neronia*: below), but a growing opposition emerged. Although many of Nero's most vocal opponents happened to be Stoics, there was not an organized "Stoic opposition." Yet many of the victims that Tacitus records in Book 16 were either openly Stoics or had close ties with known Stoics, as I will point out. Among them one must mention the general Corbulo, who also fell victim to Nero in 67, at the height of his power.[13]

Narrative Unit 1

At the opening of Book 16, Nero's disconnection from reality is underlined by the "unreal" story of Bassus, which plays a trick on the *princeps* through the agency of Fortune.[14]

---

[11] Tacitus opens the year 65 at 15.48.1, with the famous character-sketch of C. Piso. The conspiracy, which may have started as early as 62 (cf. 14.65.2), was discovered in mid-April (cf. 15.53.1: Tacitus refers to the Festival of Ceres, which was held on April 12–19). Tacitus, if he wishes to emphasize a significant event such as the Pisonian conspiracy, is not bound by chronology. On the conspiracy, see further Ash, Chapter 17 in this volume.

[12] Seneca's death is narrated at 15.61.2–64 (cf. Lucan's at 15.70.1, Mela's—Lucan's father and Seneca's younger brother—at 16.17).

[13] Corbulo is last mentioned in the extant *Annals* at 15.31. His death was probably recorded in the missing narrative (see the *Post Scriptum* below).

[14] See Shannon-Henderson (2019), 332–6.

The first sentence, "next, Fortune made sport of Nero" (16.1.1: *inlusit dehinc Neroni Fortuna*), underlines a further stage in Nero's behavior, triggered by the dangers he had encountered during the Pisonian conspiracy. Before plunging into the dreadful narrative of illustrious deaths, however, readers are "entertained" by a mythological account: a Carthaginian named Caesellius Bassus tells Nero of a dream in which he saw an enormous amount of gold hidden in a cave. This, Bassus conjectures, must be the gold Dido brought with her when she fled from her brother. The allusion is to the story of Dido that Vergil tells in the *Aeneid*. To make the reference more pointed, the entire passage is loaded with Vergilian language, with a cluster of words that any reader familiar with Vergil would not have missed.[15] Tacitus is adamant about the untrustworthiness of Bassus' account: the man was deranged and could only be believed by an equally deranged emperor.[16] Not only did Nero trust Bassus without checking his reliability, but he was even emboldened by the certainty of the treasure trove. Thus, supported by the court poets who celebrated the event as a new Golden Age, he began to spend the treasury money to build his new palace, only to find himself in hardship once the gold failed to materialize. Nero wanted to be seen as a new founder, a new Aeneas,[17] and, in emulation of Augustus, a harbinger of a new Golden Age. He failed on all counts. Tacitus' narrative subtly underlines Nero's failures, contrasting the emperor's vanity and desires with hard reality: Dido's gold, which Bassus conjectured the queen had hidden to keep the local kings from lascivious behavior, indirectly nurtured Nero's lasciviousness.[18] Unlike Aeneas, who had left the Carthaginian Dido to found what would become Rome, Nero blindly trusted a Phoenician and almost destroyed Rome. Since Nero's destiny was to end the Julian dynasty, the irony of this episode is significant.[19]

Nero found an escape in the timeless world of the past, where the distinction between reality (the aftermath of the conspiracy) and myth (Dido and Aeneas) was blurred. While Bassus' story is not Tacitus' invention (Suetonius briefly mentions it at *Nero* 31.4), its placement at the book-beginning is not coincidental. Since each book-beginning in the Neronian *Annals* features a momentous shift in the principate (the "first death" of Book 13, Agrippina's death at 14, Corbulo's campaigns in Book 15), the story of Bassus, too, is more than a mere interlude.[20] On the contrary, it must be seen as exemplary, for it underlines a further stage in the development of Nero's principate. Tacitus is preparing his readers for Nero's debut on the stage in Rome, which coincided with the second *Neronia*, narrated in the following chapters (4–5).

---

[15] On Bassus' episode and its Vergilian flavor, see esp. Murgatroyd (2002); Hardie (2012), 307–13; Rimell (2015), 66–72; Ash (2015a). On the relationships between Tacitus' text and Vergil, see Geisthardt and Gildenhard (2019), 265–82, with bibliography at 265 n. 78.

[16] Phoenicians were characterized as notoriously untrustworthy. On *Punica fides*, see e.g. Isaac (2004), 329–34; Gruen (2010), 108–28.

[17] Aeneas, son of Venus and father of Iulus (Ascanius), was the mythical ancestor of the Julian dynasty, which could therefore boast a divine origin.

[18] Cf. 16.1.2: "However, as Bassus conjectured, the Phoenician Dido, an exile from Tyre, after founding Carthage, had hidden those treasures lest her new people should become reckless with too much money, or the Numidian kings, already hostile for other reasons, should be enticed to war by the desire for the gold" (*ceterum, ut coniectura demonstrat, Dido Phoenissam Tyro profugam condita Carthagine illas opes abdidisse, ne novus populus nimia pecunia lasciviret aut reges Numidarum, et alias infensi, cupidine auri ad bellum accenderentur*).

[19] From his first appearance in the *Annals* at the *lusus Troiae* (11.11.2), Nero is ominously linked to the foundation myth of Rome. The *lusus* evoked the founder of the family that Nero would extinguish. See O'Gorman (2000), 162–75.

[20] E.g. Syme (1958a), 310, "a light interlude after the Pisonian conspiracy, before the next murders begin." Cf. Woodman (1998), 217.

Nero's love for spectacles is well known.[21] Several scholars have pointed out the theatrical nature of Nero's principate, and his obsession with all forms of art cannot be denied.[22] Yet Nero had so far refrained from appearing on the stage in Rome. His debut at the *Neronia*, therefore, is strongly emphasized by Tacitus, who appears to concentrate here many of the rumors that our other sources, Suetonius and Dio, assign to a variety of events: women giving birth in mid-performance, people suffering seizures, the presence of the *Augustiani* clapping rhythmically to support the emperor's performance (5.1–3). Not everyone approved of Nero's performance: Tacitus singles out two groups, the senate (4.1) and the austere Italians (5.1), and one individual, the future emperor Vespasian, who fell asleep (5.3).[23] From the mythical setting of Bassus to the theatricality of the *Neronia* to Vespasian's destiny, Tacitus appears to mirror the development of Roman history, from the founder Aeneas to the Julio-Claudians to the destiny that awaited the Flavians' rise to power (5.3): "They said that Vespasian...then had escaped imminent destruction because of his greater destiny" (*ferebantque Vespasianum...mox imminentem perniciem maiore fato effugisse*).[24]

The Death of Poppaea

There follows the death of Poppaea, whom Nero killed with a kick while she was pregnant (chapter 6). Tacitus also offers another report, which he does not believe: that Poppaea was poisoned. Both manners of killing her, however, make Nero guilty, and conform to the stereotype of the cruel tyrant.[25] Suetonius (*Nero* 35.3) adds that Nero's rage was caused by Poppaea complaining that he had returned home late from driving his chariot. The circumstances of Poppaea's death are so conventional, and paralleled in stories about other tyrants, that modern scholars have doubted Tacitus' and Suetonius' accounts: less remarkably, she may have died from miscarriage.[26] The most extraordinary point of Tacitus' account, however, is Poppaea's funeral. After Nero delivered a heartfelt "funeral eulogy" (*laudatio funebris*), her body was embalmed, not cremated, as was customary for upper-class Romans of this period, and then buried in the Mausoleum of Augustus. Tacitus does not elaborate much on these details, yet they allude, quite openly, to Nero's and Poppaea's obsession with the East, especially Egypt.[27] Her embalming, which recalled Egyptian practices, brought to mind another eastern queen, Cleopatra, whose relationship with Mark Antony, Nero's great-grandfather, was criticized by Augustus to emphasize his own "Romanness." And the Mausoleum was a key element of his propaganda, for it

[21] See e.g. Pliny *NH* 30.14–15, Suet. *Nero* 20–5, Philostr. *VA* 5.7.
[22] See e.g. Edwards (1994); Bartsch (1994), 1–62; Woodman (1998), 190–217; Beacham (1999), 197–254; Santoro L'Hoir (2006). Theatricality is not limited to Tacitus, of course. See e.g. Ash (2016a) on the theatricality of emperors' death scenes in Suetonius.
[23] Suetonius and Dio, e.g., place the story of Vespasian during Nero's Greek Tour. And some of the details that Tacitus assigns to Nero's appearance at the *Neronia* are used by Suetonius and Dio in more general contexts.
[24] On the Flavians' divine destiny and their attempt to be seen as Augustus' successors, see Bartera (forthcoming b).
[25] See e.g. Champlin (2003), 107–10; Cazzuffi (2013).
[26] See Mayer (1982); Amheling (1986). Poppaea's first child had died within months (15.23). Since Poppaea disappears from the Tacitean narrative for a long time, it is possible that she had problematic pregnancies: the first resulted in the birth of an unhealthy child; the second killed her.
[27] On Roman burial practices and Poppaea, see Counts (1996). On the connections between Poppaea and Cleopatra, see Vout (2007), 157–61. On Poppaea's special connection with Egypt, see e.g. Gillespie (2014b). See also Russo, Guarneri, Borghini, and Pozzi (2023). There is a famous papyrus from Egypt on Poppaea's apotheosis, which was probably sent to Nero as a consolation for her untimely death. Besides Gillespie (2014b), see Boggio (2023) and Audano (2023).

was conceived as a glorification of Augustus' power and dominance over his "eastern" adversary (the building was begun soon after the disclosure of Antony's will, in which he expressed a wish to be buried in Alexandria).[28] Every element in Tacitus' account points to the ironic contrast of the inappropriateness of a public Roman funeral and burial in the Julian-Claudian family tomb for a queen who recalled the quintessential Egyptian enemy (and her lover). The murder of Poppaea, who was pregnant, further underlines Nero's responsibility in extinguishing the Julian line, undermining his wish to be seen as a new founder (see above).

Narrative Unit 2

The second larger narrative unit includes a long list of deaths and/or exiles (chapters 7–20). The first to fall are the illustrious senators L. Silanus and the renowned jurist C. Cassius (7–9), both of whom were probably Stoics. Cassius' daughter was possibly the wife of Corbulo, who had links to L. Vetus, the former governor of Asia and the next victim of Book 16. Tacitus records the forced suicide of Vetus, along with his daughter Pollitta and his mother-in-law, in a memorable and vivid scene (10–11). Vetus' son-in-law Rubellius Plautus, a renowned Stoic, was killed in 62 (14.59.2–3).

After a brief mention of a sycophantic proposal to rename months in Nero's honor (12), Tacitus switches to more typical annalistic material for the end-of-year narrative, recording a devastating storm that swept through Campania and a plague that killed thousands all the way up to Rome's suburbs (13). These natural disasters, which were common occurrences in antiquity, and which Tacitus records with conventional language, are nevertheless interpreted as signs of divine displeasure: "The gods too made a year foul with so many crimes noteworthy by storms and plagues" (*tot facinoribus foedum annum etiam dii tempestatibus et morbis insignivere*). The pestilence, in particular, causes havoc, killing without distinction of gender, class, or age. And yet, Tacitus wryly adds, their deaths were less lamentable, as if in this way they anticipated Nero's cruelty, which the following narrative would reveal.[29] The year 65 ends with the record of a military levy and a fire that destroyed Lyon (13).

When the new year, introduced by the typical formula "with x and y as consuls" (*x y consulibus*), begins, the death notices resume with the suicide of P. Anteius, who may have been the father of the younger Helvidius' wife.[30] Next came the execution of Ostorius Scapula, implicated in an accusation of magic promoted by the notorious informer Antistius Sosianus, an apparently secondary character whose vicissitudes Tacitus follows closely throughout books 14 and 15. There is no direct link between Ostorius and the "Stoic opposition," but it was at his house that Antistius had recited slanderous poems against Nero (14.48), for which he was only exiled (rather than killed) thanks to the intervention of Thrasea Paetus. Moreover, Ostorius' consular colleague had been Suillius Rufus, a brother of Corbulo.

---

[28] On the Mausoleum and the mixed signals it sent, see Zanker (1988), 72–7.
[29] On Tacitus' disaster narratives, see e.g. Keitel (2010); Closs and Keitel (2020).
[30] Helvidius Priscus the Younger, a friend of Tacitus and Pliny, was killed by Domitian in the purge of 93 CE. His father, Helvidius Priscus (the Elder), was Thrasea's son-in-law (see below).

Chapter 16 is one of the most discussed and debated sections of the book, whose difficulty is also amplified by textual problems. Tacitus appears to seek his readers' forgiveness for writing an endless list of deaths, with its risk of causing boredom. The reason for recording these deaths, he adds, is to prevent their being forgotten, even if these men did not die heroically in battles (16.2): "Let this be granted to the posterity of illustrious men, so that, just as by their funerals they are separated from indiscriminate burial, likewise in the transmission of their last moments may they receive and preserve an individual memory" (*Detur hoc inlustrium virorum posteritati, ut, quomodo exsequiis a promiscua sepultura separantur, ita in traditione supremorum accipiant habeantque propriam memoriam*).[31] Next comes the death of some illustrious men, among whom Seneca's younger brother Mela (Lucan's father), and Petronius, stand out for their importance. Mela receives a remarkably negative portrayal: unlike his brothers Gallio and Seneca, who had distinguished senatorial careers, he had abstained from pursuing political honors and had instead sought personal wealth. It was his wealth, which Nero desired, that cost him his life.

Petronius

The death of Petronius, whose identity remains uncertain but who is probably the author of the famous *Satyrica*, deserves special attention. Only Seneca's suicide before him, and Thrasea Paetus' after, receive a comparable treatment. Indeed Petronius' suicide is clearly emulating those of the two famous Stoics. Whether these death scenes, which share many features, are the product of Tacitus' artistry or his source's, is difficult to establish. It seems likely that Tacitus, especially in the latest books of the *Annals*, made use of a particular genre, the so-called *exitus illustrium virorum et feminarum* ("deaths of illustrious men and women"), which became particularly popular in his times, although nothing has survived.[32] Both Seneca's and Thrasea's death scenes—which are not simply similar to, but in dialogue with, each other—ultimately draw inspiration from the famous suicide of Socrates, as narrated in Plato's *Phaedo*, and of Cato the Younger.[33] Both Stoics retire to their houses among a select circle of friends, with whom they converse on philosophical issues, especially on the immortality of the soul. Both face death most heroically, with the typical detachment that was expected of Stoics, setting up an example for surviving family members and their followers. Given Seneca's importance both as politician and as man of letters, and Thrasea's equally important political activity (see below), it is not surprising that Tacitus gave them such prominence in the *Annals*. Tacitus may not have shared Seneca's or Thrasea's political views, but he admired them as men. The two chapters that he devotes to Petronius, however, are as eccentric as the character they describe. Petronius' staged suicide recalls Seneca's and Thrasea's only in appearance; in fact, it completely subverts the Stoics' philosophical principles, in line with the exceptional life of the man. Tacitus emphasizes Petronius' uniqueness by means of an unparalleled description that is meant to mirror the

---

[31]   Cf. *Agr.* 46.4. See also ten Berge, Chapter 12 in this volume.
[32]   For an introduction to the *exitus* literature, see *BNP* 5: 270 (U. Eigler).
[33]   Thrasea had written a life of Cato (cf. Plutarch *Cato Min.* 25.1, 37.1). On Stoic suicide, see the section "Further Reading" below.

unpredictability of his character, since he achieved notoriety and political power by doing the very opposite of what was expected of men of his rank:

> 18.1: "For his day was spent sleeping, his night on duties and the pleasures of life; and just as industriousness had brought fame to others, sluggishness had brought fame to him, and he was not considered a glutton or spendthrift, as most of those who consume their resources, but a man of refined taste. And as for his words and deeds, the more lax they were and displaying a certain indifference to self, the more easily were they interpreted as an example of his candor"…18.3: "Hence the hatred of Tigellinus, as if facing a rival who was more expert in the science of pleasures".

> 18.1: *Nam illi dies per somnum, nox officiis et oblectamentis vitae transigebatur; utque alios industria, ita hunc ignavia ad famam protulerat, habebaturque non ganeo et profligator, ut plerique sua haurientium, sed erudito luxu. Ac dicta factaque eius quanto solutiora et quandam sui neglegentiam praeferentia, tanto gratius in speciem simplicitatis accipiebantur…18.3: Unde invidia Tigellini quasi adversus aemulum et scientia voluptatum potiorem.*

Given such an exceptional character sketch for a man who was governor and consul, and, for a time, Nero's most trusted confidant, it is astonishing that his identity remains doubtful. The fact that the true identity of Silia (chapter 20), a senator's wife and intimate of Petronius, is also unknown, is perhaps a sign of Tacitus' deliberate choice to withhold information, either to protect the reputation of these characters or their families.

Narrative Unit 3

Thrasea Paetus

Annals 16 ends with the last words of Thrasea Paetus, as he opens up his veins during his Socratic suicide (chapter 35). Although Tacitus and Thrasea, as has been suggested, may have been related,[34] this alone does not explain his relevance in the *Annals*. Thrasea embodied the Republican past, the traditional values of the senate, of whose *libertas* ("independence") he was a staunch defender. His account in the *Annals* is perhaps due to Tacitus' personal experience under the Flavians, when several of Thrasea's spiritual successors, whom Tacitus personally knew, were murdered for their political views. After Thrasea's suicide, his son-in-law Helvidius Priscus the Elder was exiled (33.2). He returned under Galba and continued defiantly to uphold the moral views of his father-in-law. Tacitus records his fierce attacks on Eprius Marcellus, one of Thrasea's accusers, at the beginning of *Histories* 4. At first, Vespasian tolerated Helvidius' behavior, but after the latter showed little enthusiasm for Vespasian's choice of Titus as his successor, their relationship quickly deteriorated. Helvidius was eventually exiled and later executed (c. 75). Suetonius says that Vespasian even tried to recall the assassins, and perhaps would have

---

[34] See Birley (2000), 232.

saved him if it had not been wrongly reported that he was already dead (*Vesp.* 15).[35] The Stoics continued to honor the memory of Thrasea and Helvidius under Titus and Domitian, until the latter decided to punish them once and for all in 93. Tacitus immortalized these men in his first work, the *Agricola*, published soon after the death of Domitian, where he recalls that Arulenus Rusticus and Herennius Senecio were killed for having written biographies of Thrasea and Helvidius, respectively (*Agr.* 2.1).[36] It is significant that the subject of Tacitus' first work was his father-in-law. Agricola, a renowned general, had chosen to live his life in complete obedience and loyalty to the emperor, even when it had become obvious that Domitian could not tolerate his success. Whether or not Agricola was poisoned did not matter to Tacitus, who could have made Agricola's death more suspicious than he does (*Agr.* 43.2). What Tacitus admired in Agricola was his loyalty, and the example that he left to his family. Tacitus, in his own way, had chosen a similar course of action. The preeminence that Tacitus assigns to Thrasea in the *Annals*, therefore, is likely focalized through Tacitus' personal experience under the Flavians.

Thrasea and his followers, as well as Seneca, did not oppose the principate because of their philosophical beliefs. Stoicism and principate were not incompatible. In fact, many Stoics, including Seneca and Thrasea, worked within the Neronian government. But once the *princeps* descended into extreme tyrannical behavior, then the Stoic sage was supposed to withdraw his services and retire. To no avail, both Seneca and Thrasea chose, at some point, to withdraw from public life. After the death of Seneca, Thrasea, who had not entered the senate for at least three years (22.1), became Nero's main target. First, Nero got rid of all the "minor" characters. Once Thrasea was virtually isolated, two famous *delatores* ("prosecutors") launched their attack on him and Barea Soranus. Tacitus treats their trials as one narrative unit (21.1): "After butchering so many distinguished men, Nero finally desired to extirpate virtue itself by killing Thrasea Paetus and Barea Soranus" (21.1: *Trucidatis tot insignibus viris ad postremum Nero virtutem ipsam exscindere concupivit, interfecto Thrasea Paeto et Barea Sorano*). Yet the focus is on Thrasea's accusations, of which Tacitus provides a detailed account, recalling point by point what he had already narrated in the previous books. He also adds that what had offended Nero the most was Thrasea's lack of enthusiasm at Nero's *Iuvenalia* games, especially since Thrasea himself had appeared on the stage at local games in his native Patavium.

The leading prosecutors were Cossutianus Capito and Eprius Marcellus. The former was Tigellinus' son-in-law; the latter had a distinguished political career that continued into Vespasian's reign, but eventually he fell from favor under Titus and committed suicide following an attempted conspiracy. Capito is the main accuser against Thrasea: in a fierce speech, both direct and indirect (21–2), he accuses Thrasea of neglecting his senatorial and priestly duties; of honoring Caesar's murderers, Cassius and Brutus; and, more seriously, of planning revolution.[37] Tacitus makes it explicit that these accusations are politically motivated, and their timing is no chance occurrence. Nero wants to act

---

[35] Epictetus, a Stoic philosopher who lived in Rome under the Flavians, recorded a famous exchange between Vespasian and Helvidius, who asserted his right to freedom of speech.

[36] See Audano, Chapter 1 in this volume.

[37] When later Marcellus resumes the attack against Thrasea (28–9), he characterizes Thrasea in terms which, according to Damtoft Poulsen (2021), recall the famous British chieftain Calgacus at *Agr.* 30.5 (but cf. Woodman (2014), ad loc.).

while Tiridates is visiting Rome to receive the kingdom of Armenia (23.2). This allows him both to distract the people with the show of the coronation and to impress the foreign king with the greatness of his own power.

Thrasea had two options before him: to face the charges in the senate before his fellow senators, and perhaps hope for an act of clemency from Nero, or wait for the final verdict at home, surrounded by friends and family. The two courses of action are presented by Tacitus as advice from groups of Thrasea's "intimate friends" (25.1: *proximos*). Both groups have "no doubt about his [sc. Thrasea's] steadfastness" (25.1: *securos de constantia eius*), yet the first, perhaps more idealistic group, hopes that his quasi-divine presence could move even Nero; and even if this were not the case, at least he would achieve an "honorable death" (25.2: *honesti exitus*). Even though Tacitus does not say it, this position appears to be the uncompromising Stoic attitude whose only outcome, an "ostentatious death" (*ambitiosa mors*) that benefited no one, Tacitus had criticized in the *Agricola* (42.4). The second, more practical group, which receives a much longer narrative, realizes that facing the senators would only expose Thrasea to insult and perhaps physical violence. The outcome was not in doubt; moreover, if he chose voluntary suicide instead of waiting for a formal sentence, he would at least preserve some property for his daughter and wife, and spare the senators a shameful decision (26.1–2).[38] Tacitus also takes the opportunity to introduce in this debate Arulenus Rusticus, at the time a "fiery youth" (*flagrans iuvenis*), who would pursue a brilliant career under the Flavians before being put to death by Domitian in 93 (26.4–5; see above). Thrasea's decision to await the verdict at home was in the end sounder, for Barea Soranus, who chose to attend the trial in person, ended up also causing the ruin of his daughter Servilia, accused of magic and dragged into the senate. The prosecution is led by Capito and Marcellus, whose flaming rhetoric Tacitus reproduces in a long indirect speech, counterbalanced by the direct speech of Servilia, young, widowed, isolated, whose only fault was her father's and her husband's disgrace.[39] Servilia's impassioned appeal emphasizes her *pietas* towards her father, which is perhaps meant to contrast with Nero's lack of *pietas* towards his dead mother.[40] In accordance with the recurrent theme of subversion of traditional values that characterizes the Neronian principate, sincere *pietas* thus becomes a cause of destruction. The trial ends with two contrasting examples of friendship (32–3). The first, P. Egnatius, is deceptive: a former friend of Barea turned accuser through bribes. The second, Cassius Asclepiodotus, is a Bithynian who did not abandon his former friend in this dire moment. Barea and Servilia are condemned to commit suicide; the accusers are rewarded with huge sums of money.

The suicide of Thrasea, which marks the end of the extant narrative, is loaded with dramatic details. Just like Seneca, Thrasea is surrounded by a group of friends, while conversing on philosophical matters in his gardens, as the sun is setting (34.1). Only a few of these friends are named: Demetrius, a famous philosopher, with whom Thrasea is

---

[38] Unlike execution, voluntary suicide allowed the victim's heirs to keep at least part of the property. See Plass (1995), 96–7.

[39] Her husband, Annius Pollio, was the brother of Corbulo's son-in-law Annius Vinicianus and was one of the men exiled after the Pisonian conspiracy (cf. 15.71.3). Direct speeches by women are extremely rare in the *Annals*. In the extant Neronian books, the only other case is Agrippina's at 13.21.2–5.

[40] One may also compare the case of Octavia, another of Nero's victims, or Vetus' daughter Pollitta at 10.4 (see above), with whom Servilia shares many traits.

discussing the nature of the soul and the dissociation of spirit and body, and Domitius Caecilianus, an intimate friend. When the death sentence is announced, Thrasea's wife Arria would like to join her husband in death but is prevented for the sake of their daughter.[41] Only Demetrius and Helvidius, in addition to the quaestor who brought the sentence, are allowed to enter Thrasea's bedroom, where the suicide takes place. If the *Annals* ended, as is probable (see the *Post Scriptum*), with Nero's suicide, it is especially ironic that what survives of the *Annals* ends with the perfectly staged suicide of one of the most illustrious of Nero's victims, whose past acting role had angered Nero (see above).[42] Whereas Nero's suicide was a "botched" performance (cf. Suetonius, *Nero* 49) which he failed to properly execute, Thrasea died successfully like a true tragic hero.

Further Reading

The best biographies of Nero in English are those of Griffin (1984), Champlin (2003), and Drinkwater (2019), but many more exist in German, French, or Italian. The companions of Buckley and Dinter (2013) and Bartsch, Freudenburg, and Littlewood (2017) are useful for introductions to various aspects of Nero's reign. One should also consult the guide of Barrett, Fantham, and Yardley (2016), as well as Cooley (2011), which collects and translates the main historical sources, including those found in Smallwood (1967). For more specialized works on Nero, see Rudich (1993) and (1997), and Elsner and Masters (1994). On the characterization of Nero in Tacitus, Suetonius, and Dio, see Schulz (2019). Opper (2021) provides a beautiful introduction to Nero's principate (with a revisionist approach), with high-quality images of all the best-preserved artifacts related to Nero. Tacitus' two chapters on Petronius have received enormous scholarly attention: among the most recent contributions in English, see Haynes (2010). On the identity of Petronius, Courtney (2001) and Schmeling (2011) offer valuable introductions; Rose (1971) remains fundamental. The bibliography on Thrasea and the "Stoic Opposition" is likewise extensive. Important works in English are Brunt (1975), Wistrand (1979), Pigoń (1992), Bauman (1996), Brunt (2013), Geiger (1979), Vervaet (2002), Pigoń (2003), Sailor (2008), Kearns (2011), Strunk (2017). On the concept of *libertas*, Wirszubski (1950) remains a standard reference. On suicide, esp. Stoic suicide, see Griffin (1986a) and (1986b) and Turpin (2008). For individual characters, as well as themes, the recently published *Tacitus Encyclopedia* (*TE*, ed. Pagán (2023)) offers a convenient starting point.

Post Scriptum

The Number of Books

The dominant theory, mainly relying on Jerome (see above)—assuming his information is correct— is that Tacitus wrote eighteen books of *Annals* and twelve of *Histories*.[43] There is strong evidence for this assumption, for the *Annals* appear to be structured in hexads, the first devoted to Tiberius, the second to Caligula and Claudius, and the third to Nero.[44] Yet not everyone agrees on such a hexadic

---

[41] The story of Arria's mother, also named Arria (the Elder), who committed suicide together with her husband Caecina Paetus in 42, is memorably told at Plin. *Ep.* 3.16.

[42] The metaphor of the world viewed as a stage, "in which each man had to play a part," was particularly dear to the Stoics. See Brunt (2013), 28 and Appendix 5–9, 12.

[43] Corruption with numerals, however, is common: see e.g. Oakley (1997–2005), iv, 330–2.

[44] On the hexadic structure of the *Annals*, see esp. Syme (1958a), 253–70, 686–7; *contra*, Goodyear (1970), 17–18. Cf. also Ando (1997). Hendry (2017) suggested two "ogdoads": books 1–8 for Tiberius and Caligula, 9–16 for Claudius and Nero.

structure, especially given the unpredictability of Tacitus' narrative patterns.[45] Moreover, since Tacitus' death is unknown, and since there are no certain references in later writers to the "missing books" of the *Annals*,[46] there is also the possibility that Tacitus died before completing his work.[47]

The almost complete Tiberian books provide the best evidence for Tacitus' general pattern of composition. Each complete book (1–4) is about 10,000 words (see Table 1),[48] but covers an unequal number of years: about two years in Book 1, four years in Book 2, three years in Book 3, six years in Book 4, three years in Book 5, and less than six years in Book 6. In other words, Tacitus' narrative strategy is highly unpredictable, although he seems to reserve particularly significant events for the opening of a new book, independently of its "natural" chronology. Leaving aside Book 1, which prefaces the entire work, Book 2 opens with Germanicus' campaigns, Book 3 with Germanicus' funeral, Book 4 with the rise of Sejanus, Book 5 with the death of Livia, Book 6 with Tiberius' licentious life in Capri.[49]

Six books are devoted to Tiberius' 23-year rule. According to the hexadic theory, six books would then cover Caligula and Claudius. (Since the former was emperor for four years and the latter for thirteen, one can reasonably assume books 7–8 for Caligula and 9–12 for Claudius.) The third hexad would deal with Nero's reign, which lasted about fourteen years (October 54–June 68), only slightly longer than Claudius'. If we look at the structure of books 11–16 (see Table 2), two things stand out: first, the complete books (12–15) are shorter (*c.* 8,000 words, compared with *c.* 10,000 words for 1–6); second, the three complete Neronian books (13–15) gradually increase in length.[50] Yet there is no significant difference as regards the number of years each book covers: both books 2–4 and 12–15 average four narrative years each.

If Book 16, which starts in the middle of the year 65, originally covered four narrative years too, Book 16 could theoretically have covered the rest of Nero's reign (i.e. up to June 68), especially if the book followed the pattern of the previous Neronian books, which gradually increase in length (see above). In this case, what survives of Book 16 would be about half, or perhaps as little as one-third, of its original length. What would the missing part have covered? The most notable domestic event of 66 was the visit of Tiridates, whom Nero had met at Neapolis and escorted to Rome, but part of this is already mentioned in the extant portion (23.2). Then, at the end of the year, Nero began his Greek Tour, which occupied him for the whole of 67, and which included the narrative of Corbulo's death, until he returned to Italy in the first months of 68.[51] Among the most notable foreign events,

---

[45] There are instances where Tacitus combines events that took place over several years, as for example at 6.38.1, "I have combined these achievements of two summers so that the mind might get some respite from domestic evils" (*quae duabus aestatibus gesta coniunxi quo requiesceret animus a domesticis malis*), or where his narrative is extremely compressed because "few events worth recording happened" (13.31.1: *pauca memoria digna evenere*, describing the year 57). On the other hand, Tacitus can also stretch the narrative out, as for example in the years 58 and 65, the only two year-beginnings in books 13–16 for which he departs from the traditionally annalistic "with x and y as consuls" (*x y consulibus*) formula (Bartera 2011, 175–9). The year of the Pisonian Conspiracy, 65, takes up almost half of Book 15.

[46] But see Shannon-Henderson (forthcoming).

[47] See esp. Syme (1958a), 742–5, who detected signs of lack of revision in the later books; *contra*, Goodyear (1970), 18–21; Adams (1974). Tacitus could have finished all the books of the *Annals* he had originally planned but died before revising the last books; or else, *Annals* 16 may be the last book he wrote before dying, whether his original plan was to write sixteen or eighteen books.

[48] On the problematic status of books 5–6, see Shannon-Henderson, Chapter 13 in this volume.

[49] It should also be noted that the event that Tacitus selects for the opening of a new book is often ominous, marking a shift in Tiberius' principate. To open a book with a death defies "natural structure." See Pagán on Book 1 and Gowing on Book 3, in Chapters 9 and 15, respectively, in this volume.

[50] A significant difference between the Neronian and the Tiberian books is the fact that the latter are normally self-contained and each book begins with a new year (apart from the special Book 1; on the problems with Book 3, see Woodman and Martin (1996), 87–8), while each Neronian book continues the narrative year from the previous book, except for Book 14, which opens with the murder of Agrippina (see Whitton, Chapter 16 in this volume). See Ando (1997), 288.

[51] The Greek Tour is one of those events to which Tacitus could have devoted a whole book or dealt with in a few chapters. It is perhaps significant that some episodes that other sources record as happened in the Greek Tour are narrated by Tacitus in relation to Nero's performance at the second *Neronia*. See above.

Table 1 *Annals* 1–6

Book	Number of years covered	Total word count for each book[52]	Narrative years (CE)	Word count for each narrative year
1	<2	10,840	14	740 (preface) + 6,540
			15	3,560
2	4	10,360	16	4,800
			17	1,570
			18	810
			19	3,180
3	3	9,350	20	3,750
			21	2,400
			22	3,200
4	6	10,080	23	2,240
			24	2,090
			25	1,850
			26	2,080
			27	720
			28	1,100
5[53]	3	1,040	29–31	1,040
6	5.5[54]	6,940	32	1,870
			33	1,600
			34	530
			35	1,230
			36	770
			37	940

Tacitus would have narrated the beginnings of the Jewish revolt in 66, and perhaps the military operations that took place in 67 and 68,[55] and then the revolt of Vindex in Gaul, news of which reached Rome in March 68. The rest of the year until Nero's death (June) included Verginius Rufus' military activity in Gaul and the news from Spain that Galba had been proclaimed emperor. Despite Verginius' defeat of Vindex and his unwillingness to be proclaimed emperor, Nero lost hope, perhaps because the praetorians, led by Tigellinus and Nymphidius Sabinus, declared for Galba and withdrew their support. Nero fled; the senate proclaimed Galba emperor and declared Nero a public enemy. The rest of the narrative is mainly known from Suetonius, who gives a memorable account of Nero's death (*Nero* 48–9). Since both the Tiberian and the Claudian books end with the death of the emperor, one can assume that the same happened with Nero, although it is still possible that Tacitus' narrative could have extended as far as the end of the year, so as to reach the starting point of the *Histories* (January 1, 69).[56]

The surviving portion of the *Histories* (1–4 and 5.1–26) may provide a useful comparison. Their narrative covers about two years (69–70).[57] Did Tacitus need seven or nine more books for the reigns of Vespasian, Titus, and Domitian? And how would he have divided them? Syme (1958a),

---

[52] The word count is based on the Latin text downloaded from the PHI database. I have rounded the numbers up to the nearest ten.

[53] I am following Lipsius' book division, adopted by Woodman (2017). Cf. also Ando (1997).

[54] The narrative for the year 37 stops with Tiberius' death, which occurred in March.

[55] One cannot, however, rule out that Tacitus had already dealt with these events in the missing books 5–6 of the *Histories* as background information on Titus' Jewish campaign.

[56] See e.g. Goodyear (1970), 18 n. 1. Ando (1997), 299 raised doubts that *Annals* 6 ended with Tiberius' death.

[57] See Damon (2003), 78. The books of the *Histories* are, on average, 11,000–12,000 words, i.e. longer than the longest book of the *Annals* (1), which is less than 11,000 words.

Table 2 *Annals* 11–16

Book	Number of years covered	Total word count for each book	Narrative years (CE)	Word count for each narrative year
11*	<2	6,750	47*	4,730
			48 (part of)	2,020
12	6	7,450	48 (part of)	360
			49	2,050
			50	1,770
			51	1,420
			52	660
			53	560
			54 (part of)	630
13	4	7,640	54 (part of)	1,190
			55	1,840
			56	720
			57	320
			58	3,570
14	3.5	8,090	59	2,420
			60	1,170
			61	2,090
			62 (part of)	2,410
15	4	9,210	62 (part of)	2,620
			63	1,030
			64	1,880
			65 (part of)	3,680
16	1.5	3,860	65 (part of)	1,370
			66	2,490

686–7, who proposed a total of twelve books, believed that, since very little happened between 71 and 81, Tacitus did not need more than one book for the end of Vespasian and one for the reign of Titus, thus books 1–7 for the years 69–81, and books 8–12 for Domitian.[58] Yet given Tacitus' interest in the Jewish revolt,[59] the internal problems that Vespasian faced in the mid-70s, the disaster of Vesuvius, about which we know Tacitus directly inquired from his friend Pliny (*Ep.* 6.16, 20),[60] a plague that struck Rome, perhaps following the fire of 80, and also the inauguration of the Colosseum and its magnificent spectacles, one wonders if Syme's dismissal of the years 71–81 is justifiable. If Tacitus, as Syme thought, could pack so many events into books 5–7 of the *Histories*, why could *Annals* 16 not suffice for the rest of Nero's reign? On the other hand, if two more books had been devoted to the years 67–8, their narrative would have been extraordinarily detailed. This would not be impossible, of course, because it dealt with the end of Rome's first dynasty, especially if Tacitus had chosen to detail the revolt in Gaul in such a way as to mirror the mutinies of Book 1.[61]

[58] I agree with Goodyear (1970), 18, who pointed out that Syme's assumption that Tacitus crammed almost ten narrative years into two books is problematic.

[59] On Tacitus' missing narrative of the destruction of the Jewish Temple, see Shannon-Henderson (forthcoming).

[60] See Whitton (forthcoming c).

[61] Consider, e.g., the exceptional narrative of the Pisonian conspiracy (almost 3700 words), which Ash (2023) uses as evidence for the hexadic structure of the Neronian books. Ash sees in the conspiracy a most significant turning point, functioning as a "proem in the middle" of a sort, which has a considerable impact on the following narrative, thus breaking the narrative between books 13–15 and 16–18. By comparison, e.g., the Great Fire of 64 (15.38–44) is dealt with in 1,000 words; the fire of the Capitol at *Histories* 3.71–3 in 500; the Jewish excursus (5.2–10) in almost 1,300 words.

In conclusion: although a hexadic structure for the *Annals* remains a compelling theory, mainly because of Syme's authority, it should not be taken for granted. Hexadic structures can be paralleled in epic poetry: Ennius' *Annals* were in eighteen books, Vergil's *Aeneid* in twelve, as well as Statius' *Thebaid*; and Silius' *Punica* were perhaps meant to be in eighteen books. Of the earlier historians, however, as far as we know, only the *Histories* of Cornelius Sisenna were perhaps in twelve books, but some propose eighteen, or even twenty-five.[62]

Salvador Bartera, Annals *16* In: *The Oxford Critical Guide to Tacitus*. Edited by: Salvador Bartera and Kelly E. Shannon-Henderson, Oxford University Press. © Oxford University Press 2025. DOI: 10.1093/9780191915086.003.0019

[62] On the earliest historians, *see FRHist*. Vol. I. On book structure in possible earlier models for Tacitus, see also Ash (2023).

Bibliography

Abbreviations for standard reference works are as follows:

BNP = *Brill's New Pauly: Encyclopedia of the Ancient World*. H. Cancik, H. Schneider, C. F. Salazar and D. E. Orton (eds.). Leiden. 2002–10.

CIL = *Corpus Inscriptionum Latinarum*. Berlin. 1873–.

FRHist. = *The Fragments of the Roman Historians*. T. J. Cornell (ed.). Oxford. 2013. [*FRHist*]

OCD⁴ = *The Oxford Classical Dictionary*. 4th edn. A. Spawforth and E. Eidenow (eds.). Oxford. 2012.

OCT = *Oxford Classical Texts*.

OLD = *Oxford Latin Dictionary*. 2nd edn. P. G. W. Glare and C. Stray (eds.). Oxford. 2012.

RE = *Paulys Real-Encyclopädie der classischen Altertumswissenschaft*. A. F. Pauly, G. Wissowa, and W. Kroll (eds.). Stuttgart. 1903–78.

TE = *The Tacitus Encyclopedia*. V. Pagán (ed.). Hoboken, NJ. 2023.

Abbreviations for journal titles follow the usage of *L'Année philologique*.

References

Abbamonte, G. (2009) "Allocuzioni alle truppe: documenti, origine e struttura retorica," in G. Abbamonte, L. Miletti, and L. Spina (eds.), *Discorsi alla prova. Discorsi pronunciati, discorsi ascoltati: contesti di eloquenza tra Grecia, Roma ed Europa*. Naples: 29–46.

Absil, M. (1997) *Les préfets du prétoire d'Auguste à Commode: 2 avant Jésus-Christ–192 après Jésus-Christ*. Paris.

Adam, A. (2015) "Agrippine l'Aînée ou le paradoxe. Les femmes de la *domus Augusta* et le pouvoir dans les *Annales* de Tacite (livres I à IV)," *Pallas* 99: 111–31.

Adams, J. N. (1970) *A Philological Commentary on Tacitus, Annals 14, 1–54*, DPhil thesis, University of Oxford.

Adams, J. N. (1974) "Were the Later Books of the *Annals* Revised?," *RhM* 117: 323–33.

Adler, E. (2011) *Valorizing the Barbarians: Enemy Speeches in Roman Historiography*. Austin.

Ahl, F. M. (1984) "The Art of Safe Criticism in Greece and Rome," *AJPh* 105: 174–208.

Altman, W. (2020) "Tacitus and C. Licinius Mucianus," *Calíope* 39: 4–36.

Amheling, W. (1986) "Tyrannen und schwangere Frauen," *Historia* 35: 507–8.

Anagnostou-Laoutides, E. and Charles, M. B. (2015) "Titus and Berenice: The Elegaic Aura of a Historical Affair," *Arethusa* 48: 17–46.

Anderson, J. C. G. (1938) *Cornelii Taciti De origine et situ Germanorum*. Oxford.

Ando, C. (1997) "Tacitus, *Annales* VI: Beginning and End," *AJPh* 118: 285–303.

Andrade, N. (2012) "Seducing Autocracy: Tacitus and the Dynasts of the Near East," *AJPh* 133: 441–75.

Ash, R. (1999a) "An Exemplary Conflict: Tacitus' Parthian Battle Narrative ("Annals" 6.34–35)," *Phoenix* 53: 114–35.

Ash, R. (1999b) *Ordering Anarchy: Armies and Leaders in Tacitus' Histories*. Ann Arbor.

Ash, R. (2006a) "Following in the Footsteps of Lucullus? Tacitus' Characterisation of Corbulo," *Arethusa* 39: 355–75.

Ash, R. (2006b) *Tacitus*. London.

Ash, R. (2007a) "Tacitus and the Battle of Mons Graupius: A Historiographical Route Map?," in J. Marincola (ed.), *A Companion to Greek and Roman Historiography*. Chichester and Malden, MA: 434–40.

Ash, R. (ed.) (2007b) *Tacitus. Histories. Book 2*. Cambridge.

Ash, R. (2007c) "Victim and Voyeur: Rome as a Character in Tacitus' *Histories* 3," in D. H. J. Larmour and D. Spencer (eds.), *The Sites of Rome: Time, Space, Memory*. Oxford: 211–37.

Ash, R. (2009) "Fission and Fusion: Shifting Roman Identities in the *Histories*," in A. J. Woodman (ed.), *The Cambridge Companion to Tacitus*. Cambridge: 85–99.

Ash, R. (2010a) "The Great Escape: Tacitus on the Mutiny of the Usipi (*Agricola* 28)," in C. S. Kraus, J. Marincola, and C. B. R. Pelling (eds.), *Ancient Historiography and its Contexts: Studies in Honour of A. J. Woodman*. Oxford: 275–93.

Ash, R. (2010b) "Rhoxolani Blues (Tacitus, *Histories* 1.79): Virgil's Scythian Ethnography Revisited," in J. F. Miller and A. J. Woodman (eds.), *Latin Historiography and Poetry in the Early Empire.* Leiden: 141–54.

Ash, R. (2010c) "*Tarda moles ciuilis belli*: The Weight of the Past in Tacitus' *Histories*," in B. Breed, C. Damon and A. Rossi (eds.), *Citizens of Discord: Rome and its Civil Wars.* Oxford and New York: 119–31.

Ash, R. (ed.) (2012) *Tacitus. Oxford Readings in Classical Studies.* Oxford.

Ash, R. (2014) "Act like a German! Tacitus' *Germania* and National Characterisation in the Historical Works," in O. Devillers (ed.), *Les opera minora et le développement de l'historiograpie tacitéenne.* Bordeaux: 185–200.

Ash, R. (2015a) "At the End of the Rainbow: Nero and Dido's Gold (Tacitus, *Annals* 16.1–3)," in R. Ash, J. Mossman and F. B. Titchener (eds.), *Fame and Infamy: Essays for Christopher Pelling on Characterization in Greek and Roman Biography and Historiography.* Oxford: 269–84.

Ash, R. (2015b) "Shadow-Boxing in the East: the Spectacle of Romano-Parthian Conflict in Tacitus," in V. Hope and A. Bakogianni (eds.), *War as Spectacle.* London: 139–56.

Ash, R. (2016a) "Never Say Die! Assassinating Emperors in Suetonius' *Lives of the Caesars*," in K. de Temmerman and K. Demoen (eds.), *Writing Biography in Greece and Rome: Narrative Technique and Fictionalization.* Cambridge: 200–16.

Ash, R. (2016b) "Tacitus and the Poets: *In nemora et lucos…secedendum est* (*Dialogus* 9.6)?" in P. Mitsis and I. Ziogas (eds.), *Wordplay and Powerplay in Latin Poetry.* Berlin: 13–35.

Ash, R. (ed.) (2018) *Tacitus. Annals Book XV.* Cambridge.

Ash, R. (2019) "*Civilis rabies usque in exitium* (*Histories* 3.80.2): Tacitus and the Evolving Trope of Republican Civil War during the Principate," in C. H. Lange and F. J. Vervaet (eds.), *The Historiography of Late Republican Civil War.* Leiden: 351–75.

Ash, R. (2021a) "The Staging of Death: Tacitus' Agrippina the Younger and the Dramatic Turn," in A. Damtoft Poulsen and A. Jönsson (eds.), *Usages of the Past in Roman Historiography.* Leiden: 197–224.

Ash, R. (2021b) "A Stylish Exit: Marcus Terentius' Swansong (Tacitus, Annals 6.8), Curtius Rufus and Vergil," *CQ* 71: 330–46.

Ash, R. (2022) "'Burn Baby Burn (*disco* in Furneaux)': Tacitean Authority, Innovation, and the Neronian Fire (*Annals* 15.38–39)," in G. Monti, K. S. Kingsley and T. Rood (eds.), *The Authoritative Historian. Tradition and Innovation in Ancient Historiography. Essays in Honour of John Marincola.* Cambridge: 353–72.

Ash, R. (2023) "'Heralding a 'Proem in the Middle'? Tacitus' Pisonian Conspiracy and the End of Nero," in C. Buongiovanni, V. E. Pagán, and C. Renda (eds.), *Political Crisis and Transitions in Roman Historiography of the Imperial Age. ICS* 48: 45–70.

Ash, R. (2024) "Tiberius in Space: Proxemics and the Portrayal of the Princeps," in C. Davenport and S. Malik (eds.), Representing Rome's Emperors. Oxford: 40–62.

Aubrion, E. (1985) *Rhétorique et histoire chez Tacite.* Metz.

Audano, S. (2015) "Sopravvivere senza l'aldilà: la *consolatio* laica di Tacito nell'*Agricola*," in C. Pepe and G. Moretti (eds.), *Le parole dopo la morte: forme e funzioni della retorica funeraria nella tradizione greca e romana.* Trento: 245–88.

Audano, S. (ed.) (2017) *Tacito. Agricola.* Santarcangelo di Romagna.

Audano, S. (ed.) (2020) *Tacito. La Germania.* Santarcangelo di Romagna.

Audano, S. (2023) "Forme e riusi della *consolatio* nell'apoteosi di Poppea (P. Oxy. LXXVII 5105)," *Analecta Papyrologica* 36: 137–47.

Autin, L. (2019) *Voix de la foule chez Tacite. Perspectives littéraires et historiques sur la communication collective au début de l'Empire,* Doctoral Thesis, University of Grenoble.

Aziza, C. (1987) "L'utilisation polémique du récit de l'Exode chez les écrivains alexandrins (IVème siècle av.J.-C.–Ier siècle ap.J.-C.)," *ANRW* II.20.1: 41–65.

Bablitz, L. (2015) "Tacitus on Trial(s)," in L. L. Brice and D. Slootjes (eds.), *Aspects of Ancient Institutions and Geography: Studies in Honor of Richard J. A. Talbert.* Leiden: 65–83.

Baldwin, B. (1977) "Tacitean Humour," *WS* 90 [= NS 11]: 128–44.

Baltussen, H. (2002) "Matricide Revisited: Dramatic and Rhetorical Allusion in Tacitus, Suetonius and Cassius Dio," *Antichthon* 36: 30–40.

Baraz, Y. (2018) "Discourse of Kingship in Late Republican Invective," in N. Panou and H. Schadee (eds.), *Evil Lords: Theories and Representations of Tyranny from Antiquity to the Renaissance.* Oxford: 43–60.

Barnes, T. D. (1977) "The Fragments of Tacitus' Histories," *CPh* 72: 224–31.

Barrett, A. A. (1996) *Agrippina: Mother of Nero.* London [= *Agrippina: Sex, Power, and Politics in the Early Empire.* New Haven].

Barrett, A. A. (2003) "Damned with Faint Praise: Tacitus' Obituary of Livia," in T. Hantos (ed.), *Laurea internationalis: Festschrift für Jochen Bleicken zum 75. Geburtstag*. Stuttgart: 45–60.

Barrett, A. A. (2017) "Nero's Women," in S. Bartsch, K. Freudenburg, and C. Littlewood (eds.), *The Cambridge Companion to the Age of Nero*. Cambridge: 63–76.

Barrett, A. A. (2020) *Rome Is Burning: Nero and the Fire that Ended a Dynasty*. Princeton.

Barrett, A. A. (2021) "Fiddling while Rome Burns: The Aetiology of a Familiar English Expression," *G&R* 68: 173–82.

Barrett, A. A., Fantham, E., and Yardley, J. C. (eds.) (2016) *The Emperor Nero: A Guide to the Ancient Sources*. Princeton.

Bartera, S. (2011) "Year-Beginnings in the Neronian Books of Tacitus' *Annals*," *MH* 68: 161–81.

Bartera, S. (2016) "Commentary Writing on the Annals of Tacitus: Different Approaches for Different Audiences," in C. S. Kraus and C. Stray (eds.), *Classical Commentaries: Explorations in a Scholarly Genre*. Oxford: 113–35.

Bartera, S. (2019) "Flavian *fides* in Tacitus' *Histories*," in A. Augoustakis, E. Buckley, and C. Stocks (eds.), *Fides in Flavian Literature* [= *Phoenix* Suppl. Vol. 55]. Toronto: 257–77.

Bartera, S. (ed.) (forthcoming a) *Tacitus Annals 16*. Cambridge.

Bartera, S. (forthcoming b) "Tacitus' Titus," in P. Christoforou and B. L. H. ten Berge, (eds.) *Tacitus and the Incomplete*. Ann Arbor.

Bartsch, S. (1994) *Actors in the Audience: Theatricality and Doublespeak from Nero to Hadrian*. Cambridge, MA.

Bartsch, S., Freudenburg, K., and Littlewood, C. (eds) (2017) *The Cambridge Companion to the Age of Nero*. Cambridge.

Batomsky, S. J. (1992) "Tacitus, *Annals* 14, 64, 1: Octavia's Pathetic Plea," *Latomus* 51: 606–10.

Bauman, R. A. (1974) *Impietas in principem: A Study of Treason Against the Roman Emperor with Special Reference to the First Century A.D.* Munich.

Bauman, R. A. (1989) *Lawyers and Politics in the Early Roman Empire*. Munich.

Bauman, R. A. (1996) *Crime and Punishment in Ancient Rome*. London.

Baxter, R. T. S. (1971) "Virgil's Influence on Tacitus in Book 3 of the *Histories*," *CPh* 66: 93–107.

Baxter, R. T. S. (1972) "Virgil's Influence on Tacitus in Books 1 and 2 of the *Annals*," *CPh* 67: 246–69.

Beacham, R. (1999) *Spectacle Entertainments of Early Imperial Rome*. New Haven.

Beard, M. (1998) "Imaginary *Horti*: Or up the Garden Path," in M. Cima and E. La Rocca (eds.), *Horti Romani. Atti del convegno internazionale Roma, 4–6 maggio 1995*. Rome: 23–32.

Bellemore, J. (1995) "The Wife of Sejanus," *ZPE* 109: 255–66.

Bellemore, J. (2003) "Cassius Dio and the Chronology of A.D. 21," *CQ* 53: 268–85.

Bellen, H. (1982) "Antike Staatsräson. Die Hinrichtung der 400 Sklaven des römischen Stadtpräfekten L. Pedanius Secundus im Jahre 61 n. Chr.," *Gymnasium* 89: 449–67 [repr. in H. Bellen (1997) *Politik–Recht–Gesellschaft. Studien zur alten Geschichte*. Stuttgart: 283–97].

Benario, H. W. (ed.) (1983) *Tacitus: Annals 11 and 12*. Lanham, MD.

Benario, H. W. (1995) "Recent work on Tacitus (1984–1993)," *CW* 89: 91–162.

Benario, H. W. (tr.) (1999) *Tacitus. Germany*. Warminster.

Benario, H. W. (2005) "Recent work on Tacitus (1994–2003)," *CW* 98: 251–336.

Benario, H. W. (2012) "The *Annals*," in V. E. Pagán, (ed.), *A Companion to Tacitus*. Chichester and Malden, MA: 101–22.

Bernays, J. (1861) *Über die Chronik des Sulpicius Severus, ein Beitrag zur Geschichte der classischen und biblischen Studien*. Berlin.

Bernstein, M. A. (1994) *Foregone Conclusions: Against Apocalyptic History*. Berkeley.

Berthelot, K. (2003) *Philanthrôpia Judaica: Le débat autour de la "misanthropie" des lois juives dans l'antiquité*. Leiden.

Bettini, M. (2015) "La morte e il suo doppio. Il funerale gentilizio romano fra *imagines, ridiculum* e *honos*," in C. Pepe and G. Moretti (eds.), *Le parole dopo la morte: forme e funzioni della retorica funeraria nella tradizione greca e romana*. Trento: 47–178.

Bhatt, S. (2016) "Rhetoric and Truth: Tacitus's Percennius and Democratic Historiography," *Helios* 43: 163–89.

Billot, F. (2003) "Tacitus Responds: *Annals* 14 and the *Octavia*," in M. Wilson (ed.), *The Tragedy of Nero's Wife: Studies on the Octavia Praetexta*. Auckland: 126–41.

Birley, A. R. (tr.) (1999) *Tacitus. Agricola and Germany*. Oxford.

Birley, A. R. (2000) "The Life and Death of Cornelius Tacitus," *Historia* 49: 230–47.

Birley, A. R. (2005) *The Roman Government of Britain*. Oxford.

Birley, A. R. (2007) "Sejanus: His Fall," in N. V. Sekunda (ed.), *Corolla Cosmo Rodewald* 2. Gdańsk: 121–50.

Birley, A. R. (2009) "The *Agricola*," in A. J. Woodman (ed.), *The Cambridge Companion to Tacitus*. Cambridge: 47–58.

Biville, F. (2006) "The Qualification of Personal Names by Possessive Adjectives in Cicero's Letters," in J. Booth, R. Maltby, and F. Biville (eds.), *What's in a Name? The Significance of Proper Names in Classical Latin Literature*. Swansea: 1–11.

Bloch, R. (2000) "Geography without Territory: Tacitus' Digression on the Jews and its Ethnographic Context," in J. U. Kalms (ed.), *Internationales Josephus-Kolloquium Aarhus 1999*. Münster: 38–54 [repr. in Bloch (2022a): 83–100].

Bloch, R. (2002) *Antike Vorstellungen vom Judentum. Der Judenexkurs des Tacitus im Rahmen der griechisch-römischen Ethnographie*. Stuttgart.

Bloch, R. (2012a) "Misanthropia," *Reallexikon für Antike und Christentum* 24: 828–45.

Bloch, R. (2012b) "Tacitus' Excursus on the Jews over the Centuries: an Overview of the History of its Reception," in R. Ash (ed.), *Tacitus. Oxford Readings in Classical Studies*. Oxford: 377–409.

Bloch, R. (2022a) *Ancient Jewish Diaspora: Essays on Hellenism*. Leiden.

Bloch, R. (2022b) "Antisemitism and the Study of Ancient Antisemitism," in A. F. Bakker, R. Bloch, Y. Fisch, P. Fredriksen, and H. Naiman (eds.), *Protestant Bible Scholarship: Antisemitism, Philosemitism, and Anti-Judaism*. Leiden: 41–62.

Boatwright, M. T. (1984) "Tacitus on Claudius and the Pomerium, *Annals* 12.23.2–24," *CJ* 80: 36–44.

Boatwright, M. T. (1998) "Luxuriant Gardens and Extravagant Women: The *Horti* of Rome between Republic and Empire," in M. Cima and E. La Rocca (eds.), *Horti Romani. Atti del convegno internazionale Roma, 4–6 maggio 1995*. Rome: 71–82.

Boggio, T. (2023) "P.Oxy. 77.5105.1–7 (Leonidas of Alexandria): A Dionysiac Procession?," *BASP* 60: 239–54.

Borca, F. (2004) "I Britanni visti dai Romani: questioni di guerra e di antropologia," *Aufidus* 54: 147–75.

Borzsák, S. (1970) "Zum Verständnis der Darstellungskunst des Tacitus: Die Veränderungen der Germanicus-Bildes," *AAntHung* 18: 279–92.

Bowersock, G. W. (1987) "The Mechanics of Subversion in the Roman Provinces," in A. Giovannini (ed.), *Opposition et résistances a l'empire d'Auguste à Trajan*. Vandoeuvres: 291–320.

Boyle, A. J. (ed.) (2008) *Octavia. Attributed to Seneca*. Oxford.

Bradley, K. R. (1973) "*Tum primum revocata ea lex*," *AJPh* 94: 172–82.

Brakman, C. (1925) "Tacitea," *Mnemosyne* 53: 177–200.

Braund, D. (1996) *Ruling Roman Britain: Kings, Queens, Governors and Emperors from Julius Caesar to Agricola*. London.

Braund, S. (ed.) (2009) *Seneca. De Clementia*. Oxford.

Briessmann, A. (1955) *Tacitus und das flavische Geschichtsbild*. Wiesbaden.

Brinkmann, M. (2002) *Seneca in den Annalen des Tacitus*, PhD dissertation, University of Bonn.

van Broeck, L. (2018) *People, Place and Power in Tacitus' Germany*, PhD thesis, Royal Holloway, University of London.

Brunt, P. A. (1959) "The Revolt of Vindex and the Fall of Nero," *Latomus* 18: 531–59.

Brunt, P. A. (1960) "Tacitus on the Batavian Revolt," *Latomus* 19: 494–517.

Brunt, P. A. (1975) "Stoicism and the Principate," *PBSR* 43: 7–35 [repr. in P. A. Brunt (2013) *Studies in Stoicism*, Oxford: 275–309].

Brunt, P. A. (1988) *The Fall of the Roman Republic*. Oxford.

Brunt, P. A. (2013) "High-Ranking Roman Stoics under the Principate [Appendix: Tacitus and the Stoics]," in P. A. Brunt, *Studies in Stoicism*, eds. M. T. Griffin, A. Samuels, and M. Crawford. Oxford: 310–30.

Buckley, E. and Dinter, M. T. (eds.) (2013) *A Companion to the Neronian Age*. Chichester and Malden, MA.

Caballos, A., Eck, W., and Fernandez, F. (eds.) (1996) *El senadoconsulto de Gneo Pisón padre*. Seville.

Campbell, D. B. (2010) *Mons Graupius AD 83*. Oxford.

Canfora, L. (ed., tr.) (1999) *Tucidide. Il dialogo dei Melii e degli Ateniesi*. 3rd edn. Venice.

Carpentieri, A. (2007) "Intratestualità in Tacito: Le Parole di Tiberio ed i *codicilli a Pisone compositi* ('Ann.' 3.12.1 e 16.3–4)," *Lexis* 25: 381–98.

Cazzuffi, E. (2013) "Uxoricidio, necrofilia, incesto e altri aneddoti della leggenda tirannica da Periandro a Nerone," *Eikasmos* 24: 255–73.

Celotto, G. (2021) "The Escalating Repetitiveness of Civil War: Lucanian Allusions in Tacitus' Account of the Conflict between Otho and Vitellius in *Historiae* 1–2," *CW* 114: 171–99.

Cenerini, F. (2010) "Messalina e il suo matrimonio con C. Silio," in A. Kolb (ed.), *Augustae: Machtbewusste Frauen am römischen Kaiserhof?* Berlin: 179–91.

Champion, C. (1994) "'*Dialogus*' 5.3–10.8: A Reconsideration of the Character of Marcus Aper," *Phoenix* 48: 152–63.

Champlin, E. J. (1989) "The Life and Times of Calpurnius Piso," *MH* 46: 101–24.

Champlin, E. J. (1991) *Final Judgments: Duty and Emotion in Roman Wills, 200 B.C.–A.D. 250*. Berkeley.

Champlin, E. J. (2003) *Nero*. Cambridge, MA.

Champlin, E. J. (2011) "Sex on Capri," *TAPhA* 141: 315–32.

Champlin, E. J. (2012) "Seianus Augustus," *Chiron* 42: 361–88.

Chaplin, J. (2015) "Livy's Use of Exempla," in B. Mineo (ed.), *A Companion to Livy*. Chichester and Malden, MA: 102–13.

Chilver, G. E. F. (ed.) (1979) *A Historical Commentary on Tacitus' Histories I and II*. Oxford.

Chilver, G. E. F. and Townend, G. B. (eds.) (1985) *A Historical Commentary on Tacitus' Histories IV and V*. Oxford.

Christoforou, P. (2022) "*Qualem diem Tiberius induisset*. Tiberius' Absences on Capri as an Inspiration for Wonder and Uncertainty," in J. McNamara and V. E. Pagán (eds.), *Tacitus' Wonders*. London: 197–220.

Christoforou, P. and ten Berge, B. L. H. (eds.) (forthcoming) *Tacitus and the Incomplete*. Ann Arbor.

Clarke, K. J. (1999) *Between Geography and History. Hellenistic Constructions of the Roman World*. Oxford.

Clarke, K. J. (2001) "An Island Nation: Re-reading Tacitus' *Agricola*," *JRS* 91: 94–112.

Clarke, K. J. (2002) "*In arto et inglorius labor*: Tacitus' Anti-history," in A. K. Bowman, H. M. Cotton, M. Goodman, and S. Price (eds.), *Representations of Empire: Rome and the Mediterranean World*. Oxford: 83–104.

Clarke, K. J. (2018) *Shaping the Geography of Empire: Man and Nature in Herodotus' Histories*. Oxford.

Closs, V. M. (2016) "*Neronianis Temporibus*: The So-Called *arae incendii Neroniani* and the Fire of A.D. 64 in Rome's Monumental Landscape," *JRS* 106: 102–23.

Closs, V. M. (2020) *While Rome Burned: Fire, Leadership, and Urban Disaster in the Roman Cultural Imagination*. Ann Arbor.

Closs, V. M. and Keitel, E. E. (eds.) (2020) *Urban Disasters and the Roman Imagination*. Berlin.

Cogitore, I. (2002) "Rome dans la conspiration de Pison," in J.-M. Croisille and Y. Perrin (eds.), *Neronia VI: Rome à l'époque néronienne*. Collection Latomus 268. Brussels: 261–72.

Cogitore, I. (2011) *Le doux nom de liberté*. Bordeaux.

Cogitore, I. (2012) "Les rumeurs politiques sont-elles des bruits dans les *Annales* de Tacite?," in M. T. Schettino and S. Pittia (eds.), *Les sons du pouvoir dans les mondes anciens*. Besançon: 399–425.

Cohen, S. J. D. (1993) "'Those Who Say They Are Jews and Are Not': How Do You Know a Jew in Antiquity When You See One?," in S. J. D. Cohen and E. S. Frerichs (eds.), *Diasporas in Antiquity*. Atlanta: 1–45.

Cole, S. (2013) *Cicero and the Rise of Deification at Rome*. Cambridge.

Cole, T. (1992) "'Initium mihi operis Servius Galba iterum T. Vinius consules…'," in F. M. Dunn and T. Cole (eds.), *Beginnings in Classical Literature*. Cambridge: 231–48.

Connors, C. (1994) "Famous Last Words: Authorship and Death in the *Satyricon* and Neronian Rome," in J. Elsner and J. Masters (eds.), *Reflections of Nero: Culture, History, and Representation*. London: 225–35.

Cooley, A. E. (ed.) (2023) *The Senatus Consultum de Cn. Pisone Patre, Text, Translation, and Commentary*. Cambridge.

Cooley, M. G. L. (ed.) (2011) *Tiberius to Nero*. London.

Counts, D. B. (1996) "*Regum externorum consuetudine*: The Nature and Function of Embalming in Rome," *ClAnt* 15: 189–202.

Courtney, E. (ed.) (2001) *A Companion to Petronius*. Oxford.

Cowan, E. (2009) "Tacitus, Tiberius and Augustus," *ClAnt* 28: 179–210.

Cowan, E. (2016) "Contesting *clementia*: The Rhetoric of *severitas* in Tiberian Rome before and after the Trial of Clutorius Priscus," *JRS* 106: 77–101.

Crook, J. A. (1970) "*Strictum et aequum*. Law in the Time of Nero," *Irish Jurist* 5: 357–68.

Daly, M. M. (2020) "Seeing the Caesar in Germanicus: Reading Tacitus' *Annals* with Lucan's *Bellum Civile*," *JAH* 8: 103–26.

Damon, C. (1999) "The Trial of Cn. Piso in Tacitus' *Annals* and the *Senatus Consultum de Cn. Pisone Patre*: New Light on Narrative Technique," in C. Damon and S. Takács (eds.), *The Senatus Consultum de Cn. Pisone Patre. Text, Translation, Discussion*. Baltimore [= *AJP* 120.1]: 143–62.

Damon, C. (ed.) (2003) *Tacitus: Histories Book 1*. Cambridge.

Damon, C. (2006) "*Potior utroque Vespasianus*: Vespasian and his Predecessors in Tacitus' *Histories*," *Arethusa* 39: 245–79.

Damon, C. (2010) "*Intestinum scelus*: Preemptive Execution in Tacitus' *Annals*," in B. Breed, C. Damon and A. Rossi (eds.), *Citizens of Discord: Rome and Its Civil Wars*. Oxford and New York: 261–72.

Damon, C. (tr.) (2012) *Tacitus. Annals*. London.

Damon, C. (2017) "Writing with Posterity in Mind: Thucydides and Tacitus on Secession," in R. K. Balot, S. Forsdyke, and E. Foster (eds.), *Oxford Handbook of Thucydides*. Oxford: 677–90.

Damon, C. and Palazzolo, E. (2019) "Defining Home, Defining Rome: Germanicus' Eastern Tour," in T. Biggs and J. Blum (eds.), *The Epic Journey in Greek and Roman Literature*. Cambridge: 194–210.

Damtoft Poulsen, A. (2017) "The Language of Freedom and Slavery in Tacitus' *Agricola*," *Mnemosyne* 70: 834–58.

Damtoft Poulsen, A. (2018) *Accounts of Northern Barbarians in Tacitus' Annales*. Doctoral thesis, Lund.

Damtoft Poulsen, A. (2020) "Teleology with a Human Face: Side-shadowing and its Effects in Tacitus' Treatment of Germanicus (*Annals* 1–2)," in A. Turner (ed.), *Reconciling Ancient and Modern Philosophies of History*. Berlin and Boston: 149–82.

Damtoft Poulsen, A. (2021) "From Thrasea Paetus to Calgacus–or Was It the Other Way Around? An Example of Tacitean Intratextuality," in A. Damtoft Poulsen and A. Jönsson (eds.), *Usages of the Past in Roman Historiography*. Leiden: 169–93.

Damtoft Poulsen, A. (forthcoming) "All Roads Lead to Ruin: Sallust's Idea(s) of History and Futurity," in A. Krebs (ed.), *The Cambridge Companion to Sallust*. Cambridge.

Dando-Collins, S. (2010) *The Great Fire of Rome*. Cambridge, MA.

Dawson, A. (1969) "Whatever Happened to Lady Agrippina?," *CJ* 64: 253–67.

Devillers, O. (1991) "Le rôle des passages relatifs à Tacfarinas dans les *Annales* de Tacite," *L'Africa Romana* 8: 203–11.

Devillers, O. (2003) *Tacite et les sources des Annales: Enquêtes sur la méthode historique*. Louvain.

Devillers, O. (2009a) "Les passages relatifs à Asinius Gallus dans les *Annales* de Tacite," *REL* 87: 154–65.

Devillers, O. (2009b) "*Sed aliorum exitus, simul cetera illius aetatis, memorabo (Ann.* III, 24, 2). Le règne d'Auguste et le projet historiographique de Tacite," in F. Hurlet and B. Mineo (eds.), *Le Principat d'Auguste: Réalités et représentations du pouvoir autour de la Res Publica Restituta*. Rennes: 309–324.

Devillers, O. (2012) "The Concentration of Power and Writing History: Forms of Historical Persuasion in the *Histories* (1.1–49)," in V. E. Pagán (ed.), *A Companion to Tacitus*. Chichester and Malden, MA: 162–86.

Devillers, O. (2020) "La place de Sénèque le Père parmi les sources possibles des *Annales* 1–6," in M. C. Scappaticcio (ed.), *Seneca the Elder and His Rediscovered Historiae ab initio bellorum ciuilium. New Perspectives on Early-Imperial Roman Historiography*. Berlin and Boston: 235–57.

Devillers, O. (2021) "La dernière année du règne de Tibère dans les *Annales* de Tacite (6.45.3–51)," in P. Duchêne and M. Bellissime (eds.), *Veni, vidi, scripsi: écrire l'histoire dans l'Antiquité*. Actes du séminaire Historiographies antiques 2014–2019, 7. Bordeaux: 73–90.

Devillers, O. and Hurlet, F. (2007) "La portée des impostures dans les *Annales* de Tacite: la légitimité impériale à l'épreuve," in M. A. Giua (ed.), *Ripensando Tacito (e Ronald Syme): storia e storiografia*. Pisa: 133–51.

De Vivo, A. (2009) "Oratoria da camera: il processo *intra cubiculum* di Valerio Asiatico (Tac. *Ann*. XI 1–3)," in G. Abbamonte, L. Miletti, and L. Spina (eds.), *Discorsi alla prova. Discorsi pronunciati, discorsi ascoltati: contesti di eloquenza tra Grecia, Roma ed Europa*. Naples: 15–25.

Dobesch, G. (1995) *Das Europäische "Barbaricum" und die Zone der Mediterrankultur. Ihre Wechselwirkung und das Geschichtsbild des Poseidonios*. Vienna.

Domainko, A. (2018) *Uncertainty in Livy and Velleius: Time, Hermeneutics and Roman Historiography*. Munich.

Donovan Ginsberg, L. (2016) *Staging Memory, Staging Strife: Empire and Civil War in the Octavia*. Oxford.

Donovan Ginsberg, L. (2020) "Allusive *prodigia*: Caesar's Comets in Neronian Rome," *TAPhA* 150: 231–49.

Döpp, S. (2003) "L'incendio del Campidoglio. Sullo stile di Tacito, *Hist*. III 72," *Eikasmos* 14: 231–41.

Drinkwater, J. F. (2019) *Nero: Emperor and Court*. Cambridge.

Duchêne, P. (2012) "Vaincre grâce à une ruse ? La première bataille de Bédriac," *BAGB* 1: 113–31.

Ducos, M. (1977) "La liberté chez Tacite : droits de l'individu ou conduite individuelle," *BAGB*, 194–217.

Dudley, D. R. (1968) *The World of Tacitus*. London.

Dueck, D. (2012) *Geography in Classical Antiquity. Key Themes in Ancient History*. Cambridge.

Dunkle, J. R. (1967) "The Greek Tyrant and Roman Political Invective of the Late Republic," *TAPhA* 98: 151–71.

Dunkle, J. R. (1971) "The Rhetorical Tyrant in Roman Historiography: Sallust, Livy and Tacitus," *CW* 65: 12–20.

Dyson, S. L. (1970) "The Portrait of Seneca in Tacitus," *Arethusa* 3: 71–83.

Earl, D. C. (1961) *The Political Thought of Sallust*. Cambridge.

Eck, W. (1993) *Agrippina die Stadtgründerin Kölns. Eine Frau in der frühkaiserzeitlichen Politik*. Cologne.

Eck, W. (2022) "Das angebliche Praenomen Lucius des Agermus, des Freigelassenen von Agrippina Augusta," *RhM* 165: 429–32.

Eck, W., Caballos, A., and Fernández, F. (eds.) (1996) *Das Senatus Consultum de Cn. Pisone Patre*, Munich.

Edelstein, L. and Kidd, I. G. (eds.) (1989) *Posidonius I. The Fragments*. 2nd edn. Cambridge.

Edwards, C. (1994) "Beware of Imitations: Theatre and the Subversion of Imperial Identity," in J. Elsner and J. Masters (eds.), *Reflections of Nero: Culture, History, and Representation*. London: 83–97.

Edwards, C. (1996) *Writing Rome. Textual Approaches to the City*. Cambridge.

Edwards, C. (2007) *Death in Ancient Rome*. New Haven.

Edwards, C. (2011) "Imagining Ruins in Ancient Rome," *European Review of History/Revue européenne d'histoire* 18: 645–61.

Elliott, C. P. (2015) "The Crisis of A.D. 33: Past and Present," *JAH* 3: 267–81.

Elliott, J. (2013) *Ennius and the Architecture of the* Annales. Cambridge.

Elsner, J. and Masters, J. (eds.) (1994) *Reflections of Nero: Culture, History, and Representation*. London.

Engel, R. (1977) "Das Characterbild des Kaisers A. Vitellius bei Tacitus und sein historischen Kern," *Athenaeum* 55: 345–68.

Fagan, G. G. (2002) "Messalina's Folly," *CQ* 52: 566–79.

Feeney, D. (2007) *Caesar's Calendar: Ancient Time and the Beginnings of History*. Berkeley.

Feldherr, A. (2009a) "Barbarians II: Tacitus' Jews," in A. Feldherr (ed.), *The Cambridge Companion to the Roman Historians*. Cambridge: 301–16.

Feldherr, A. (ed.) (2009b) *The Cambridge Companion to the Roman Historians*. Cambridge.

Feldherr, A. (2009c) "The Poisoned Chalice: Rumor and Historiography in Tacitus' Account of the Death of Drusus," *MD* 61: 175–89.

Ferri, R. (1998) "Octavia's Heroines: Tacitus *Annales* 14.63–64 and the *praetexta Octavia*," *HSCPh* 98: 339–56.

Ferrill, A. (1965) "Otho, Vitellius, and the Propaganda of Vespasian," *CJ* 60: 267–9.

Fick, N. (1994) "Calgacus, héros breton," in D. Conso, N. Fick, and B. Poulle (eds.), *Mélanges François Kerlouégan*. Paris: 235–48.

Flory, M. (1988) "*Abducta Neroni uxor*: The Historiographical Tradition on the Marriage of Octavian and Livia," *TAPhA* 118: 343–59.

Flower, H. I. (1995) "*Fabulae praetextae* in Context: When Were Plays on Contemporary Subjects Performed in Republican Rome?," *CQ* 45: 170–90.

Flower, H. I. (1996) *Ancestor Masks and Aristocratic Power in Roman Culture*. Oxford.

Flower, H. I. (1998) "Rethinking '*Damnatio memoriae*': The Case of Cn. Calpurnius Piso pater in AD 20," *ClAnt* 17: 155–86.

Flower, H. I. (2006) *The Art of Forgetting: Disgrace & Oblivion in Roman Political Culture*. Chapel Hill.

Foubert, L. (2010) "Literary Constructions of Female Identities: The Parallel Lives of Julio-Claudian Women in Tacitus' *Annals*," in C. Deroux (ed.), *Studies in Latin Literature and Roman History* XV. Brussels: 344–365.

Foucher, A. (2000) "Nature et formes de l'"histoire tragique" à Rome," *Latomus* 59: 773–801.

Fratantuono, L. (ed.) (2018) *Tacitus Annals XVI*. London.

Frere, S. (1987) *Britannia: A History of Roman Britain*. 3rd edn. London.

Fulkerson, L. (2006) "Staging a Mutiny: Competitive Roleplaying on the Rhine (*Annals* 1.31–51)," *Ramus* 35: 169–92.

Funari, R. (1989) "Tacito e il linguaggio 'espressionistico': un saggio di commento a 'Hist.' 2,70," *Athenaeum* 67: 584–94.

Furneaux, H. (ed.) (1896) *The Annals of Tacitus. Vol. I: Books I–VI*. 2nd edn. Oxford.

Furneaux, H. (ed.) (1907) *The Annals of Tacitus. Vol. II: Books XI–XVI*. Rev. 2nd edn., eds. H. F. Pelham and C. D. Fisher. Oxford.

Fyfe, W. H. (tr.) (1997; orig. edn. 1912). *Tacitus, The Histories*. Rev. edn., ed. D. S. Levene. Oxford.

Gallia, A. (2009) "*Potentes* and *potentia* in Tacitus's *Dialogus de oratoribus*," *TAPhA* 139: 169–206.

Gallivan, P. A. (1974) "Confusion Concerning the Age of Octavia," *Latomus* 33: 116–17.

Galtier, F. (2011) *L'image tragique de l'Histoire chez Tacite: étude des schèmes tragiques dans les Histoires et les Annales*. Brussels.

Geiger, J. (1979) "Munatius Rufus and Thrasea Paetus on Cato the Younger," *Athenaeum* 67: 48–72.

Geiser, M. (2007) *Personendarstellung bei Tacitus am Beispiel von Cn. Domitius Corbulo und Ser. Sulpicius Galba*. Remscheid.

Geisthardt, J. M. (2015) *Zwischen Princeps und Res Publica: Tacitus, Plinius und die senatorische Selbstdarstellung in der Hohen Kaiserzeit*. Stuttgart.

Geisthardt, J. M. and Gildenhard, I. (2019) "Trojan Plots: Conceptions of History in Catullus, Virgil and Tacitus," in I. Gildenhard, U. Gotter, W. Havener, and L. Hodgson (eds.), *Augustus and the Destruction of History: The Politics of the Past in Early Imperial Rome*. Cambridge: 241–82.

Gerrish, J. (2021) "Sertorius, Civilis, Rome and Exile in Tacitus' *Histories*," *CJ* 116: 473–98.

Giannotti, F. (2018) "L'*imperium* e la *pax*. La celebre *sententia* di Calgaco (Tac. *Agr.* 30,5) tra modelli e fortuna," *SIFC* 16: 213–32.

Gibson, B. J. (1998) "Rumours as Causes of Events in Tacitus," *MD* 40: 111–29.

Gildenhard, I. (2011) *Creative Eloquence: The Construction of Reality in Cicero's Speeches*. Cambridge.

Gill, C. (1983) "The Question of Character-Development: Plutarch and Tacitus," *CQ* 33: 469–87.

Gillespie, C. (2014a) "Agrippina the Younger: Tacitus' *Unicum Exemplum*," in J. Ker and C. Pieper (eds.), *Valuing the Past in the Greco-Roman World*. Proceedings from the Penn-Leiden Colloquia on Ancient Values, 7. Leiden: 269–93.

Gillespie, C. (2014b) "Poppaea Venus and the Ptolemaic Queens: An Alternative Biography," *Histos* 8: 122–45.

Gillespie, C. (2018) *Boudica: Warrior Woman of Roman Britain*. Oxford.

Gillespie, C. (2020a) "Agrippina the Elder and the Memory of Augustus in Tacitus' *Annals*," *CW* 114: 59–84.

Gillespie, C. (2020b) "Messalina's Moveable *Domus*: Landscape and Memory in *Annals* 11," *NECJ*, I believe. 47: 15–50.

Gillespie, C. (in preparation). *Inglorious Labors: Women's Movements in Tacitus' Annals*.

Gilmartin, K. (1973) "Corbulo's Campaigns in the East: An Analysis of Tacitus' Account," *Historia* 22: 583–626.

Gingras, M. T. (1992) "Annalistic Format, Tacitean Themes and the Obituaries of *Annals* 3," *CJ* 87: 241–56.

Ginsburg, J. (1981) *Tradition and Theme in the Annals of Tacitus*. New York.

Ginsburg, J. (1986) "Speech and Allusion in Tacitus, *Annals* 3.49–51 and 14.48–49," *AJPh* 107: 525–41.

Ginsburg, J. (1993) "*In maiores certamina*: Past and Present in the *Annales*," in T. J. Luce and A. J. Woodman (eds.), *Tacitus and the Tacitean Tradition*. Princeton: 86–103.

Ginsburg, J. (2006) *Representing Agrippina: Constructions of Female Power in the Early Roman Empire*. Oxford.

Glendinning, E. (2010) "Heroic Female Death in Tacitus' *Annals* 14 and 15," in L. Langerwerf and C. Ryan (eds.), *Zero to Hero, Hero to Zero: in Search of the Classical Hero*. Newcastle: 96–119.

Goldberg, S. M. (1999) "Appreciating Aper: the Defence of Modernity in Tacitus' *Dialogus de oratoribus*," *CQ* 49: 224–37.

Goldberg, S. M. (2002) "Review of: R. Mayer, *Tacitus: Dialogus de Oratoribus*," *BMCR*.

Goldberg, S. M. (2009) "The Faces of Eloquence: the *Dialogus de oratoribus*," in A. J. Woodman (ed.), *The Cambridge Companion to Tacitus*. Cambridge: 73–84.

Goodyear, F. R. D. (1970) *Tacitus*. Oxford.

Goodyear, F. R. D. (ed.) (1972) *The Annals of Tacitus Books 1–6*. Vol. 1. Cambridge.

Goodyear, F. R. D. (ed.) (1982) *The Annals of Tacitus Books 1–6*. Vol. 2. Cambridge.

Gorman, V. B. (2001) "Lucan's Epic *Aristeia* and the Hero of the *Bellum Civile*," *CJ* 9: 263–90.

Gowing, A. M. (1990) "Tacitus and the Client Kings," *TAPhA* 120: 315–31.

Gowing, A. M. (1997) "Cassius Dio on the Reign of Nero," *ANRW* II.34.3: 2558–90.

Gowing, A. M. (2005) *Empire and Memory: The Representation of the Roman Republic in Imperial Culture*. Cambridge.

Gowing, A. M. (2009) "Urbs Roma: Tacitus on Tiberius and the city," in P. B. Harvey, Jr. and C. Conybeare (eds.), *Maxima debetur magistro reverentia. Essays on Rome and the Roman Tradition in Honor of Russell T. Scott*. Como: 93–106.

Gradel, I. (2002) *Emperor Worship and Roman Religion*. Oxford.

Greenwood, E. (2016) "Futures Real and Unreal in Greek Historiography," in A. Lianeri (ed.), *Knowing Future Time in and through Greek Historiography*. Berlin: 79–100.

Grethlein, J. (2013) *Experience and Teleology in Ancient Historiography: Futures Past from Herodotus to Augustine*. Cambridge.

Griffin, M. T. (1976) *Seneca. A Philosopher in Politics*. Oxford.

Griffin, M. T. (1984) *Nero: The End of a Dynasty*. New Haven.

Griffin, M. T. (1986a) "Philosophy, Cato, and Roman Suicide I," *G&R* 33: 64–77.

Griffin, M. T. (1986b) "Philosophy, Cato, and Roman Suicide II," *G&R* 33: 192–202.

Griffin, M. T. (1995) "Tacitus, Tiberius and the Principate," in I. Malkin and Z. W. Rubinsohn (eds.), *Leaders and Masses in the Roman World*. Leiden: 33–57.

Griffin, M. T. (1999) "Pliny and Tacitus," *SCI* 18: 139–58.

Griffin, M. T. (2009) "Tacitus as a Historian," in A. J. Woodman (ed.), *The Cambridge Companion to Tacitus*. Cambridge: 168–83.

Griffin, M. T. (2013) *Seneca on Society: A Guide to* De Beneficiis. Oxford.

Grisé, Y. (1982) *Le suicide dans la Rome antique*. Montréal.

Gruen, E. S. (2010) *Rethinking the Other in Antiquity*. Princeton.

Gruen, E. S. (2016) "Tacitus and the Defamation of the Jews," in E. S. Gruen (ed.), *The Construct of Identity in Hellenistic Judaism: Essays on Early Jewish Literature and History*. Berlin: 265–80.

Gudeman, A. (1900) "The Sources of the *Germania* of Tacitus," *TAPhA* 31: 93–111.

Gudeman, A. (ed.) (1914) *P. Cornelii Taciti Dialogus de oratoribus*. 2nd edn. Leipzig.

Güngerich, R. (ed.) (1980) *Kommentar zum Dialogus des Tacitus*, ed. H. Heubner. Göttingen.

Hälikkä, R. (2002) "Discourses of Body, Gender and Power in Tacitus," in P. Setälä, R. Berg, R. Hälikkä, M. Keltanen, J. Pölönen, and V. Vuolanto (eds.), *Women, Wealth and Power in the Roman Empire*. Rome: 75–104.

Hands, A. R. (1974) "*Postremo suo tantum ingenio utebatur*," *CQ* 24: 312–17.

Hanssen, J. S. T. (1952) *Latin Diminutives: A Semantic Study*. Bergen.

Hardie, P. (2012) *Rumour and Renown: Representations of Fama in Western Literature*. Cambridge.

Harries, J. D. (2013) "The *senatus consultum Silanianum*: Court Decisions and Judicial Severity in the Early Roman Empire," in P. du Plessis (ed.), *New Frontiers: Law and Society in the Roman World*. Edinburgh: 51–70.

Hartog, F. (1988) *The Mirror of Herodotus. The Representation of the Other in the Writing of History*. Trans. J. Lloyd. Berkeley [orig. published 1980 as *Le miroir d'Hérodote*].

Hau, L. I. (2013) "The Shadow of What Might Have Been: Sideshadowing in Thucydides and Xenophon," in A. Powell and E. Baragwanath (eds.), *Hindsight in Greek and Roman History*. Swansea: 71–90.

Haynes, H. (2003) *The History of Make-Believe: Tacitus on Imperial Rome*. Berkeley.

Haynes, H. (2004) "Tacitus' Dangerous Word," *ClAnt* 23: 33–61.

Haynes, H. (2010) "The Tyrant Lists: Tacitus' Obituary of Petronius," *AJPh* 131: 69–99.

Haynes, H. (2012) "Tacitus' History and Mine," in V. E. Pagán (ed.), *A Companion to Tacitus*. Chichester and Malden, MA: 282–304.

Heldmann, K. (2013) "Der Kaiser singt zur Kithara. Tacitus über Neros Künstlerkarriere und den Gang der Geschichte," in B. Dunsch, A. Schmitt, and T. Schmitz (eds.), *Epos, Lyrik, Drama: Genese und Ausformung der literarischen Gattungen*. Heidelberg: 315–58.

Henderson, J. G. (1989) "Tacitus/The World in Pieces," *Ramus* 18: 167–210 [rev. version in J. G. Henderson (1998) *Fighting for Rome. Poets and Caesars, History and Civil War*. Cambridge: 257–300].

Hendry, M. (2017) "The Structure of Tacitus' *Annals*: Three Hexads or Two 'Ogdoads'?" Unpublished paper; https://www.curculio.org/VOP/Tacitus-Ogdoads.pdf, accessed July 4, 2024.

Henrichs, A. (1978) "Greek Maenadism from Olympias to Messalina," *HSPh* 82: 121–60.

Hersch, K. K. (2010) *Roman Wedding: Ritual and Meaning in Antiquity*. Cambridge.

Heubner, H. (ed.) (1963–82) *P. Cornelius Tacitus, die Historien. Kommentar, Bücher I–V*. 4 vols. Heidelberg.

Heubner, H. (ed.) (1984) *Kommentar zum Agricola der Tacitus*. Göttingen.

Heubner, H. (ed.) (1994) *P. Cornelii Taciti. Tom. I: Annales*. 2nd edn. Stuttgart.

Higbie, C. (2010) "Divide and Edit: A Brief History of Book Divisions," *HSPh* 105: 1–31.

Hill, T. (2004) Ambitiosa mors: *Suicide and Self in Roman Thought and Literature*. New York.

Hind, J. G. F. (1972) "The Death of Agrippina and the Finale of the *Oedipus* of Seneca," *AUMLA* 38: 204–11.

Hirschfeld, O. (1913) *Kleine Schriften*. Berlin.

Holson, P. (1976) "Nero and the Fire of Rome. Fact and Fiction," *Pegasus* 19: 37–44.

Holztrattner, F. (1995) Poppaea Neronis potens: *Die Gestalt der Poppaea Sabina in den Nerobüchern des Tacitus. Mit einem Anhang zu Claudia Acte*. Graz.

van Hooff, A. J. L. (1990) *From Autothanasia to Suicide: Self Killing in Classical Antiquity*. London.

Hope, V. M. (2000) "Contempt and Respect: The Treatment of the Corpse in Ancient Rome," in V. M. Hope and E. Marshall (eds.), *Death and Disease in the Ancient City*. London: 104–27.

Houston, G. (1985) "Tiberius on Capri," *G&R* 32: 79–96.

Hudson, J. (2016) "*Carpento certe*: Conveying Gender in Roman Transportation," *CA* 35: 215–46.

Hudson, J. (2021) *The Rhetoric of Roman Transportation: Vehicles in Latin Literature*. Cambridge.

Huitink, L. (2019) "Enargeia, Enactivism and the Ancient Readerly Imagination," in M. Anderson and D. Cairns (eds.), *Distributed Cognition in Classical Antiquity*. Cambridge: 169–89.

Hutchinson, G. O. (1993) *Latin Literature from Seneca to Juvenal*. Oxford.

Hutchinson, G. O. (2020) *Motion in Classical Literature: Homer, Parmenides, Sophocles, Ovid, Seneca, Tacitus, Art*. Oxford.

Ihrig, M. A. (2007) *Sermone ac vultu intentus: Körper, Kommunikation und Politik in den Werken des Cornelius Tacitus*. Munich.

Isaac, B. (2004) *The Invention of Racism in Classical Antiquity*. Princeton.

Jones, C. P. (2017) "The Historicity of the Neronian Persecution: A Response to Brent Shaw," *NTS* 63: 146–52.

Joseph, T. A. (2012a) "*Repetita bellorum ciuilium memoria*: The Remembrance of Civil War and its Literature in Tacitus, *Histories* 1.50," in J. Grethlein and C. B. Krebs (eds.), *Time and Narrative in Ancient Historiography: The "Plupast" from Herodotus to Appian*. Cambridge: 156–74.

Joseph, T. A. (2012b) "Tacitus and Epic," in V. E. Pagán (ed.), *A Companion to Tacitus*. Chichester and Malden, MA: 369–85.

Joseph, T. A. (2012c) *Tacitus the Epic Successor. Virgil, Lucan, and the Narrative of Civil War in the Histories.* Leiden.

Joseph, T. A. (2018) "East and West in the *Histories* of Herodotus and Tacitus," in M. English and L. Fratantuono (eds.), *Pushing the Boundaries of Historia.* New York: 69–85.

Joshel, S. R. (1995) "Female Desire and the Discourse of Empire: Tacitus' Messalina," *Signs* 21: 50–82.

Kearns, E. (2011) "The Death of Thrasea. Towards a Reconstruction and Interpretation," *Athenaeum* 99: 41–79.

Keegan, J. (1976) *The Face of Battle.* New York.

Keeline, T. (2018) *The Reception of Cicero in the Early Roman Empire.* Cambridge.

Keitel, E. E. (1978) "The Role of Parthia and Armenia in Tacitus *Annals* 11 and 12," *AJPh* 99: 462–73.

Keitel, E. E. (1984) "Principate and Civil War in the *Annals* of Tacitus," *AJPh* 105: 306–25.

Keitel, E. E. (1987) "Otho's Exhortations in Tacitus' *Histories*," *G&R* 34: 73–82.

Keitel, E. E. (1991) "The Structure and Function of Speeches in Tacitus' *Histories* I–III," *ANRW* II.33.4: 2772–94.

Keitel, E. E. (1992) "*Foedum spectaculum* and Related Motifs in Tacitus' *Histories* II–III," *RhM* 135: 342–51.

Keitel, E. E. (1993) "Speech and Narrative in *Histories* 4," in T. J. Luce and A. J. Woodman (eds.), *Tacitus and the Tacitean Tradition.* Princeton: 39–58.

Keitel, E. E. (2006) "*Sententia* and Structure in Tacitus, *Histories* 1.12–49," *Arethusa* 39: 219–44.

Keitel, E. E. (2007) "Feast Your Eyes on This: Vitellius as a Stock Tyrant (Tac. *Hist.* 3.36–39)," in J. Marincola (ed.), *A Companion to Greek and Roman Historiography.* Chichester and Malden, MA: 441–6.

Keitel, E. E. (2009) "'Is Dying So Very Terrible?' The Neronian *Annals*," in A. J. Woodman (ed.), *The Cambridge Companion to Tacitus.* Cambridge: 127–43.

Keitel, E. E. (2010) "The Art of Losing: Tacitus and the Disaster Narrative," in C. S. Kraus, J. Marincola, and C. B. R. Pelling (eds.), *Ancient Historiography and its Contexts: Studies in Honour of A. J. Woodman.* Oxford: 331–52.

Kelly, B. (2010) "Tacitus, Germanicus and the Kings of Egypt (Tac. *Ann.* 2.59–61)," *CQ* 60: 221–37.

Keppie, L. (2011) "'Guess Who's Coming to Dinner': The Murder of Nero's Mother Agrippina in Its Topographical Setting," *G&R* 58: 33–41.

Ker, J. (2009) *The Deaths of Seneca.* Oxford.

Ker, J. (2012) "Seneca in Tacitus," in V. E. Pagán (ed.), *A Companion to Tacitus.* Chichester and Malden, MA: 305–30.

Kierdorf, W. (1987) "Freundschaft und Freundschaftskündigung von der Republik zum Prinzipat," in G. Binder (ed.), *Saeculum Augustum, I: Herrschaft und Gesselschaft.* Darmstadt: 223–45.

de Kleijn, G. (2013) "C. Licinius Mucianus: Vespasian's Co-ruler in Rome," *Mnemosyne* 66: 433–59.

Klodt, C. (2015) "Das Grabmal des Verginius Rufus (Plinius, epist. 2,1, 6,10 und 9,19)," *Gymnasium* 122: 339–87.

Koestermann, E. (1930) "Der taciteische *Dialogus* und Ciceros Schrift *De republica*," *Hermes* 65: 396–421.

Koestermann, E. (ed.) (1963–8) *P. Cornelius Tacitus: Annalen.* 4 vols. Heidelberg.

Kohl, A. (1959) *Der Satznachtrag bei Tacitus.* Würzburg.

Kolb, A. (2010) "*Augustae*: Zielsetzung, Definition, prosopographischer Überblick," in A. Kolb (ed.), *Augustae: Machtbewusste Frauen am römischen Kaiserhof?* Berlin: 11–35.

Konstan, D. (1997) *Friendship in the Classical World.* Cambridge.

Kotzé, A. (1996) "Tacitus' Account of the Pannonian Revolt (*Ann.* 1.16–30)," *Akroterion* 41: 124–32.

Kragelund, P. (1987) "Vatinius, Nero and Curiatius Maternus," *CQ* 37: 197–202.

Kragelund, P. (2012) "Tacitus, Dio, and the 'Sophist' Maternus," *Historia* 61: 495–506.

Kraus, C. S. (ed.) (1994a) *Livy: Ab urbe condita VI.* Cambridge.

Kraus, C. S. (1994b) "'No second Troy': Topoi and Refoundation in Livy book V," *TAPhA* 164: 267–89.

Kraus, C. S. (2009) "The Tiberian Hexad," in A. J. Woodman (ed.), *The Cambridge Companion to Tacitus.* Cambridge: 100–15.

Kraus, C. S. and Woodman, A. J. (1997) *Latin Historians.* Oxford.

Krebs, C. B. (2009) "A Dangerous Book: The Reception of the *Germania*," in A. J. Woodman (ed.), *The Cambridge Companion to Tacitus.* Cambridge: 280–99.

Krebs, C. B. (2011a) "Borealism: Caesar, Seneca, Tacitus, and the Roman Discourse about the Germanic North," in E. S. Gruen (ed.), *Cultural Identity in the Ancient Mediterranean.* Los Angeles: 202–21.

Krebs, C. B. (2011b) *A Most Dangerous Book: Tacitus's Germania from the Roman Empire to the Third Reich.* New York.

Krebs, C. B. (2012) "*Annum quiete et otio transit.* Tacitus (*Ag.* 6.3) and Sallust on Liberty, Tyranny, and Human Dignity," in V. E. Pagán (ed.), *A Companion to Tacitus.* Chichester and Malden, MA: 333–44.

Krebs, C. B. (ed.) (2023) *Caesar: Bellum Gallicum Book VII*. Cambridge.

Kron, G. (2005) "The Augustan Census Figures and the Population of Italy," *Athenaeum* 93: 441–95.

Kühner, R. and Stegmann, C. (1955) *Ausführliche Grammatik der lateinischen Sprache: Satzlehere, Erster Teil*. Leverkusen.

Kyle, D. G. (1998) *Spectacles of Death in Ancient Rome*. London.

La Penna, A. (1975) "I Baccanali di Messalina e le Baccanti di Euripide (nota a Tacito, *Ann.* XI 31, 4–6)," *Maia* 27: 121–3.

Laruccia, S. D. (1980) "The Wasteland of Peace: A Tacitean Evaluation of Pax Romana," in C. Deroux (ed.), *Studies in Latin Literature and Roman History* II. Brussels: 407–11.

Launaro, A. (2011) *Peasants and Slaves: The Rural Population of Roman Italy (200 BC to AD 100)*. Cambridge.

Laupot, E. (2000) "Tacitus' Fragment 2: The Anti-Roman Movement of the Christiani and the Nazoreans," *VChr* 54: 233–47.

Laurence, R. (1994) "Rumour and Communication in Roman Politics," *G&R* 41: 62–74.

Laurence, R. (2019) "The Meaning of Roads: A Reinterpretation of the Roman Empire," in J. Kuuliala and J. Rantala (eds.), *Travel, Pilgrimage and Social Interaction from Antiquity to the Middle Ages*. London: 37–63.

Lausberg, H. (1998) *Handbook of Literary Rhetoric: A Foundation for Literary Study*. Ed. and tr. M. T. Bliss, D. E. Orton, and R. D. Anderson. Leiden [orig. publ. 1960 as *Handbuch der literarischen Rhetorik: eine Grundlegung der Literaturwissenschaft*].

Lavan, M. (2011) "Slavishness in Britain and Rome in Tacitus' *Agricola*," *CQ* 61: 294–305.

Lavan, M. (2013) *Slaves to Rome: Paradigms of Empire in Roman Culture*. Cambridge.

Leake, J. C. (1987) "Tacitus' Teaching and the Decline of Liberty at Rome," *Interpretation* 15: 55–96, 195–308.

Leigh, M. (1996) "Varius Rufus, *Thyestes*, and the appetites of Antony," *PCPS* 42: 171–95.

Leigh, M. (2013) "Tacitus *Annals* 1.1.1 and Aristotle," *CQ* 63: 452–4.

Lemcke, L. and Coşkun, A. (2013) "Users and Issuers of Permits of the Imperial Information and Transportation System in the 1st Century AD," *Latomus* 72: 1034–54.

Lendon, J. E. (1997) *Empire of Honour: The Art of Government in the Roman World*. Oxford.

Lendon, J. E. (1999) "The Rhetoric of Combat: Greek Military Theory and Roman Culture in Julius Caesar's Battle Descriptions," *ClAnt* 18: 273–329.

Lendon, J. E. (2017) "Battle Description in the Ancient Historians Part I: Structure, Array, and Fighting," *G&R* 64: 39–64.

Lentano, M. (ed.) (2021) *Cremuzio Cordo: Gli Annali. Testimonianze e frammenti*. Milan.

Letta, C. (2021) "Literary and Documentary Sources in Dio's Narrative of the Roman Emperors," in C. Davenport and C. Mallan (eds.), *Emperors and Political Culture in Cassius Dio's Roman History*. Cambridge: 74–87.

Levene, D. S. (1997) "Pity, Fear and the Historical Audience: Tacitus on the Fall of Vitellius," in S. M. Braund and D. Gill (eds.), *The Passions in Roman Thought and Literature*. Cambridge: 128–49 [repr. in Ash (2012): 209–33].

Levene, D. S. (1999) "Tacitus' *Histories* and the Theory of Deliberative Oratory," in C. S. Kraus (ed.), *The Limits of Historiography: Genre and Narrative in Ancient Historical Texts*. Leiden: 197–216.

Levene, D. S. (2004) "Tacitus' '*Dialogus*' as Literary History," *TAPhA* 134: 157–200.

Levene, D. S. (2009a) "Speeches in the *Histories*," in A. J. Woodman (ed.), *The Cambridge Companion to Tacitus*. Cambridge: 212–24.

Levene, D. S. (2009b) "Warfare in the *Annals*," in A. J. Woodman (ed.), *The Cambridge Companion to Tacitus*. Cambridge: 225–38.

Levene, D. S. (2010a) *Livy on the Hannibalic War*. Oxford.

Levene, D. S. (2010b) "Pompeius Trogus in Tacitus' *Annals*," in C. S. Kraus, J. Marincola, and C. B. R. Pelling (eds.), *Ancient Historiography and its Contexts: Studies in Honour of A. J. Woodman*. Oxford: 294–311.

Levick, B. (1978) "A Cry from the Heart of Tiberius Caesar?" *Historia* 27: 95–101.

Levick, B. (1990) *Claudius*. London.

Levick, B. (1999a) *Tiberius the Politician*, 2nd edn. London

Levick, B. (1999b; 2nd edn. 2016) *Vespasian*. London.

Levick, B. (2002) "Corbulo's daughter," *G&R* 49: 199–211.

Lewy, J. H. (1969) "Tacitus on the Origin and Manners of the Jews," in J. H. Lewy (ed.), *Studies in Jewish Hellenism*. Jerusalem: 115–89.

Liebeschuetz, W. (1966) "The Theme of Liberty in the *Agricola* of Tacitus," *CQ* 16: 126–39.

Lightfoot, J. (2020) "Tacitus' *Germania* and the Limits of Fantastic Geography," *Histos* 14: 116–51.

Lindl, A. (2020) *Narrative Technik und Leseraktivierung. Tacitus' Annalen XIII–XVI*. Stuttgart.

Lintott, A. (1997) "The Theory of the Mixed Constitution at Rome," in J. Barnes and M. T. Griffin (eds.), *Philosophia Togata 2: Plato and Aristotle at Rome*. Oxford: 70–85.

Lintott, A. (1999) *The Constitution of the Roman Republic*. Oxford.

Low, K. (2013) "The Mirror of Tacitus? Selves and Others in the Tiberian Books of the *Annals*," DPhil thesis, University of Oxford.

Low, K. (2016a) "Germanicus on Tour: History, Diplomacy and the Promotion of a Dynasty," *CQ* 66: 222–38.

Low, K. (2016b) "*Histories* Repeated? The Mutinies in *Annals* 1 and Tacitean Self-Allusion," in V. Liotsakis and S. Farrington (eds.), *The Art of History: Literary Perspectives on Greek and Roman Historiography*. Berlin: 253–69.

Lozano, F. (2007) "*Diui Augusti* and *Theoi Sebastoi*: Roman Initiatives and Greek Answers," *CQ* 57: 139–52.

Luce, T. J. (1986) "Tacitus' Conception of Historical Change: The Problem of Discovering the Historian's Opinions," in I. S. Moxon, J. D. Smart, and A. J. Woodman (eds.), *Past Perspectives: Studies in Greek and Roman Historical Writing*. Cambridge: 143–58.

Luce, T. J. (1991) "Tacitus on History's Highest Function: *praecipuum munus annalium* (*Ann.* 3.65)," *ANRW* II.33.4: 2904–27.

Luce, T. J. (1993) "Reading and Response in the *Dialogus*," in T. J. Luce and A. J. Woodman (eds.), *Tacitus and the Tacitean Tradition*. Princeton: 11–38.

Luke, T. S. (2010) "A Healing Touch for Empire: Vespasian's Wonders in Domitianic Rome," *G&R* 57: 77–106.

Luke, T. S. (2013) "From Crisis to Consensus: Salutary Ideology and the Murder of Agrippina," *ICS* 38: 207–28.

Lund, A. A. (ed.) (1988) *P. Cornelius Tacitus Germania*. Heidelberg.

McHugh, M. R. (2012) "*Ferox Femina*: Agrippina Maior in Tacitus's *Annales*," *Helios* 39: 73–96.

McNamara, J. (2021) "Lost in *Germania*: The Absence of History in Tacitus' Ethnography," in T. Geue and E. Giusti (eds.), *Unspoken Rome: Absence in Latin Literature and Its Reception*. Cambridge: 201–18.

McNamara, J. (2022) "Interpreting Wonders in the *Agricola* and *Germania*," in J. McNamara and V. E. Pagán (eds.), *Tacitus' Wonders*. London: 170–92.

McNamara, J. and Pagán, V. E. (eds.) (2022) *Tacitus' Wonders*. London.

Major, A. (1993) "Claudius and the Death of Messalina: Jealousy or 'Realpolitik'?" *AH* 23: 30–8.

Malik, S. (2020) *The Nero-Antichrist: Founding and Fashioning a Paradigm*. Cambridge.

Malik, S. (2021) "An Emperor's War on Greece: Cassius Dio's Nero," in C. Davenport and C. Mallan (eds.), *Emperors and Political Culture in Cassius Dio's Roman History*. Cambridge: 158–76.

Malloch, S. J. V. (ed.) (2013) *The Annals of Tacitus, Book 11*. Cambridge.

Malloch, S. J. V. (ed.) (2020) *The Tabula Lugdunensis: A Critical Edition with Translation and Commentary*. Cambridge.

Malloch, S. J. V. (2021) Review of Barrett (2020). *Literary Review* 493: 36–7.

Malloch, S. J. V. (2022) 'The Return of the King: Tacitus on the Principate of Augustus', *Hermes* 150: 82–100'.

Malloch, S. J. V. (ed.) (forthcoming a) *Tacitus Annals 12*. Cambridge.

Malloch, S. J. V. (forthcoming b) "Tacitus' *Opera maiora*," in J. Stover (ed.), *The Oxford Guide to the Transmission of the Latin Classics*. Oxford.

Mambwini Kivuila-Kiaku, J. and Nsuka Nkoko, J. B. (2017) *L'Afrique vue par les Romains. Les écrits de Salluste et de Lucain*. Paris.

Manolaraki, E. (2005) "A Picture Worth a Thousand Words: Revisiting Bedriacum (Tacitus *Histories* 2.70)," *CPh* 100: 243–67.

Manolaraki, E. and Augoustakis, A. (2012) "Silius Italicus and Tacitus on the Tragic Hero," in V. E. Pagán (ed.), *A Companion to Tacitus*. Chichester and Malden, MA: 386–402.

Manuwald, G. (2001a) "Der Dichter Curiatius Maternus in Tacitus' *Dialogus de oratoribus*," *GFA* 4: 1–20.

Manuwald, G. (2001b) *Fabulae praetextae. Spuren einer literarischen Gattung der Römer*. Munich.

Marchesi, I. (2008) *The Art of Pliny's Letters: A Poetics of Allusion in the Private Correspondence*. Cambridge.

Marchetta, A. (2004) "La 'rappresentazione' della morte di Agrippina in *Annales* XIV 1–10," in A. Marchetta, *Studi tacitiani*. Rome: 97–596.

Marincola, J. (1997) *Authority and Tradition in Ancient Historiography*. Cambridge.

Marincola, J. (1999) "Tacitus' Prefaces and the Decline of Imperial Historiography," *Latomus* 58: 391–404.

Marincola, J. (2003) "Beyond Pity and Fear: the Emotions of History," *AncSoc* 33: 285–315.

Marshall, M. (2011) *Tacitus and Lucan on Civil War*, DPhil thesis, University of Oxford.

Martin, R. H. (1981; repr. 1994) *Tacitus*. London.

Martin, R. H. (1990) "Structure and Interpretation in the *Annals* of Tacitus," *ANRW* II.33.2: 1500–81.

Martin, R. H. (ed.) (2001) *Annals, V & VI*. Warminster.

Martin, R. H. (2009) "From Manuscript to Print," in A. J. Woodman (ed.), *The Cambridge Companion to Tacitus*. Cambridge: 241–52.

Martin, R. H. and Woodman, A. J. (eds.) (1989) *The Annals of Tacitus Book 4*. Cambridge.

Mastellone, E. (2004) "La fine di Messalina in Tacito. Una morte 'tragica' a rovescio," *BStudLat* 34: 531–57.

Master, J. (2016) *Provincial Soldiers and Imperial Instability in the Histories of Tacitus*. Ann Arbor.

Mastrorosa, I. G. (2009) "*Leges maluerunt*: origine del diritto ed evoluzione giuspolitica in Tac. *Ann*. III, 25–28," *Euphrosyne* 37: 145–62.

Mattingly, D. (2006) *Britain in the Roman Empire: An Imperial Perspective, 54 BC–AD 409*. London.

Mayer, R. (1982) "What Caused Poppaea's Death?," *Historia* 31: 248–9.

Mayer, R. (ed.) (2001) *Tacitus: Dialogus*. Cambridge.

Meise, E. (1969) *Untersuchungen zur Geschichte der Julisch-Claudischen Dynastie*. Munich.

Mellor, R. (1993) *Tacitus*. London.

Mendell, C. W. (1957) *Tacitus: The Man and his Work*. New Haven.

Menge, H. (1965) *Repetitorium der lateinischen Syntax und Stilistik*. Munich.

Millband, E. (2022) *A Commentary on Selected Chapters of Tacitus Annales 13*, PhD thesis, University of Cambridge.

Millar, F. (2005) "Last Year in Jerusalem: Monuments of the Jewish War in Rome," in J. Edmondson, S. Mason, and J.B. Rives (eds.), *Flavius Josephus and Flavian Rome*. Oxford: 101–28.

Miller, J. F. and Woodman, A. J. (eds.) (2010) *Latin Historiography and Poetry in the Early Empire*. Leiden.

Miller, N. P. (ed.) (1959; repr. 1992) *Tacitus. Annals, Book I*. London.

Miller, N. P. (ed.) (1973) *Tacitus. Annals 15*. London.

Milnor, K. (2005) *Gender, Domesticity, and the Age of Augustus: Inventing Private Life*. Oxford.

Milnor, K. (2009) "Women in Roman Historiography," in A. Feldherr (ed.), *The Cambridge Companion to the Roman Historians*. Cambridge: 276–87.

Moles, J. (1998) "Cry Freedom: Tacitus *Annals* 4.32–35," *Histos* 2: 95–184.

Momigliano, A. (1961) Review of Syme (1958a), *Gnomon* 33: 55–58.

Monteleone, C. (1975) "Un procedimento stilistico in Tacito, *Annali* 14, 8–9," *RFIC* 103: 302–6.

Monteleone, C. (1990) "Un modello per Tacito, *Annali* 14, 1–13," *Orpheus* 11: 320–5.

Morello, R. (2002) "Livy's Alexander Digression (9.17–19): Counterfactuals and Apologetics," *JRS* 92: 62–85.

Morford, M. P. O. (1990) "Tacitus' Historical Methods in the Neronian Books of the 'Annals'," *ANRW* II.33.2: 1582–627.

Morford, M. P. O. (1991) "How Tacitus Defined Liberty," *ANRW* II.33.4: 3420–50.

Morgan, M. G. (1992) "The Smell of Victory: Vitellius at Bedriacum (Tac. *Hist*. 2.70)," *CPh* 87: 14–29.

Morgan, M. G. (1993) "The Three Minor Pretenders in Tacitus, *Histories* II," *Latomus* 52: 769–96.

Morgan, M. G. (1996) "Recriminations after Ad Castores: Tacitus, *Histories* 2.30," *CPh* 91: 359–6.

Morgan, M. G. (2000) "Omens in Tacitus' *Histories* I–III," in R. L. Wildfang and J. Isager (eds.), *Divination and Portents in the Roman World*. Odense: 25–42.

Morgan, M. G. (2006) *69 AD: The Year of Four Emperors*. Oxford.

Morris, J. M. (1969) *Compositional Techniques in Annales XIII–XVI*, PhD dissertation, Yale University.

Morson, G. S. (1994) *Narrative and Freedom: The Shadows of Time*. New Haven.

Much, R. (ed.) (1967) *Die Germania des Tacitus*. 3rd edn. Heidelberg.

Muller, L. (1994) "La mort d'Agrippine (Tacite, *Annales*, 14,1–13). Quelques éléments tragiques de la composition du récit," *LEC* 62: 27–43.

Murgatroyd, P. (2002) "Dido's Treasure at *Annals* 16.1–3," in P. McKechnie (ed.), *Thinking like a Lawyer*. Leiden: 131–3.

Murgatroyd, P. (2006) "Tacitus, *Annals* 14.17–19," *Latomus* 65: 115–18.

Murgatroyd, P. (2008) "Tacitus on the Death of Octavia," *G&R* 55: 263–73.

Murgia, C. E. (2012) "The Textual Transmission," in V. E. Pagán (ed.), *A Companion to Tacitus*. Chichester and Malden, MA: 15–22.

Murison, C. L. (1979) "Some Vitellian Dates: An Exercise in Methodology," *TAPhA* 109: 187–97.

Murison, C. L. (1993) *Galba, Otho, and Vitellius: Careers and Controversies*. Hildesheim.

Murphy T. M. (2004) *Pliny the Elder's Natural History: The Empire in the Encyclopedia*. Oxford.

Nappa, C. (2010) "The Unfortunate Marriage of Gaius Silius: Tacitus and Juvenal on the Fall of Messalina," in J. F. Miller and A. J. Woodman (eds.), *Latin Historiography and Poetry in the Early Empire*. Leiden: 189–204.

Neumeister, C. (2000) "Otho: Demagoge–Staatsmann–stoischer Held. Seine drei Reden in den Historien des Tacitus," in C. Neumeister and W. Raeck (eds.), *Rede und Redner: Bewertung und Darstellung in den antiken Kulturen*. Möhnesee: 191–205.

Newbold, R. F. (1974) "Some Social and Economic Consequences of the AD 64 Fire at Rome," *Latomus* 33: 858–69.

Nissinen, L. (2009) "*Cubicula diurna, nocturna*: Revisiting Roman *cubicula* and Sleeping Arrangements," *Arctos* 43: 85–107.

Norden, E. (1913) "Josephus und Tacitus über Jesus Christus und eine messianische Prophetie," *Neue Jahrbücher für das klassische Altertum* 31: 636–66.

Noreña, C. F. (2009) "The Ethics of Autocracy in the Roman world," in R. Balot (ed.), *A Companion to Greek and Roman Political Thought*. Chichester and Malden, MA: 266–79.

Nörr, D. (1983) "C. Cassius Longinus: Der Jurist als Rhetor (Bemerkungen zu Tacitus, ann. 14, 42 ff.)," in H. Heine (ed.), *Althistorische Studien. Hermann Bengtson zum 70. Geburtstag*. Wiesbaden: 187–222.

Oakley, S. P. (ed.) (1997–2005) *A Commentary on Livy, Books VI–X*. 4 vols. Oxford.

Oakley, S. P. (2009) "Style and Language," in A. J. Woodman (ed.), *The Cambridge Companion to Tacitus*. Cambridge: 195–211.

Ogilvie, R. M. and Richmond, J. (eds.) (1967) *Cornelii Taciti de vita Agricolae*. Oxford.

O'Gorman, E. C. (1993) "No Place like Rome: Identity and Difference in the *Germania* of Tacitus," *Ramus* 22: 135–54 [repr. in Ash (2012): 95–118].

O'Gorman, E. C. (1995a) "On Not Writing about Augustus: Tacitus' '*Annals*' Book 1," *MD* 35: 91–114.

O'Gorman, E. C. (1995b) "Shifting Ground: Lucan, Tacitus and the Landscape of Civil War," *Hermathena* 158: 117–31.

O'Gorman, E. C. (2000) *Irony and Misreading in the Annals of Tacitus*. Cambridge.

O'Gorman, E. C. (2006) "Alternative Empires: Tacitus' Virtual History of the Pisonian Principate," *Arethusa* 39: 281–301.

O'Gorman, E. C. (2014) "A Barbarian Is Being Spoken," in O. Devillers (ed.), *Les opera minora et le développement de l'historiograpie tacitéenne*. Bordeaux: 175–84.

O'Gorman, E. C. (2020) *Tacitus' History of Politically Effective Speech: Truth to Power*. London.

Oniga, R. (1995) *Sallustio e l'etnografia*. Pisa.

Oniga, R. (ed.) (2003) *Tacito. Opera omnia. 1*. Turin.

Opper, T. (2021) *Nero: The Man behind the Myth*. London.

Osgood, J. (2006) *Caesar's Legacy. Civil War and the Emergence of the Roman Empire*. Cambridge.

Osgood, J. (2011) *Claudius Caesar: Image and Power in the Early Roman Empire*. Cambridge.

Owen, M. and Gildenhard, I. (eds.) (2013) *Tacitus Annals 15.20–23, 33–45*. Cambridge.

Pagán, V. E. (1999) "Beyond Teutoburg: Transgression and Transformation in Tacitus *Annales* 1.61–62," *CPh* 94: 302–20.

Pagán, V. E. (2000) "The Mourning After: Statius *Thebaid* 12," *AJPh* 121: 423–52.

Pagán, V. E. (2004) *Conspiracy Narratives in Roman History*. Austin.

Pagán, V. E. (2005) "The Pannonian Revolt in the *Annals* of Tacitus," in C. Deroux (ed.), *Studies in Latin Literature and Roman History* XII. Brussels: 414–22.

Pagán, V. E. (2006a) *Rome and the Literature of Gardens*. London.

Pagán, V. E. (2006b) "Shadows and Assassinations: Forms of Time in Tacitus and Appian," *Arethusa* 39: 193–218.

Pagán, V. E. (ed.) (2012) *A Companion to Tacitus*. Chichester and Malden, MA.

Pagán, V. E. (2017) *Tacitus*. London.

Pagán, V. E. (2020) "The Obituary of Augustus in Tacitus, *Annals* 1.9–10," in M. C. Pimentel, A. M. Lóio, N. S. Rodrigues, and R. Furtado (eds.), *Augustan Papers: New Approaches to the Age of Augustus on the Bimillenium of his Death*. Hildesheim: i.377–93.

Panou, N. and Schadee, H. (eds.) (2018) *Evil Lords: Theories and Representations of Tyranny from Antiquity to the Renaissance*. New York.

Panoussi, V. (2019a) *Brides, Mourners, Bacchae: Women's Rituals in Roman Literature*. Baltimore.

Panoussi, V. (2019b) "From Adultery to Incest: Messalina and Agrippina as Sexual Aggressors in Tacitus' *Annals*," in S. Matzner and S. J. Harrison (eds.), *Complex Inferiorities: The Poetics of the Weaker Voice in Latin Literature*. Oxford: 205–23.

Paparazzo, E. (2005) "The Elder Pliny, Posidonius and Surfaces," *British Journal for Philosophy of Science* 56: 363–76.

Paparazzo, E. (2011) "Philosophy and Science in the Elder Pliny's *Naturalis Historia*," in R. Gibson and R. Morello (eds.), *Pliny the Elder: Themes and Contexts*. Leiden: 89–112.

Parat, J. (2021) "The Revolt of the Pannonian Legions and the Working Method of Cassius Dio," in J. M. Madsen and C. H. Lange (eds.), *Cassius Dio the Historian: Methods and Approaches*, Leiden: 130–48.

Parker, G. (2009) "Highways into Byways: The Travels of Tiberius," *Antichthon* 43: 64–78.

Parkin, T. G. (2003) *Old Age in the Roman World: A Cultural and Social History*. Baltimore.

Paterson, J. (2007) "Friends in High Places: The Creation of the Court of the Roman Emperor," in A. Spawforth (ed.), *The Court and Court Society in Ancient Monarchies*. Cambridge: 121–56.

Paul, G. M. (1982) "*Urbs Capta*: Sketch of an Ancient Literary Motif," *Phoenix* 36: 144–55.

Peachin, M. (2015) "Augustus' Emergent Judicial Powers, the *crimen maiestatis*, and the Second Cyrene Edict," in J.-L. Ferrary and J. Scheid (eds.), *Il princeps romano: autocrate o magistrato? Fattori giuridici e fattori sociali del potere imperiale da Augusto a Commodo*. Pavia: 497–554.

Pelling, C. B. R. (1993) "Tacitus and Germanicus," in T. J. Luce and A. J. Woodman (eds.), *Tacitus and the Tacitean Tradition*. Princeton: 59–85 [repr. Ash (2012): 281–313].

Pelling, C. B. R. (1997) "Is Death the End? Closure in Plutarch's *Lives*," in D. H. Roberts, F. M. Dunn, and D. Fowler (eds.), *Classical Closure: Reading the End in Greek and Latin Literature*. Princeton: 228–50.

Pelling, C. B. R. (2010) "The Spur of Fame: *Annals* 4.37–8," in C. S. Kraus, J. Marincola, and C. B. R. Pelling (eds.), *Ancient Historiography and its Contexts: Studies in Honour of A. J. Woodman*. Oxford: 364–84.

Pelling, C. B. R. (2013) "Historical Explanation and What Didn't Happen: The Virtues of Virtual History," in A. Powell (ed.), *Hindsight in Greek and Roman History*. Swansea: 1–24.

Penwill, J. L. (2003) "What's Hecuba to Him…? Reflections on Poetry and Politics in Tacitus' *Dialogue on Orators*," *Ramus* 32: 122–47.

Pepe, C. (2015) *Morire da donna. Ritratti esemplari di* bonae feminae *nella* laudatio funebris *romana*. Pisa.

Perl, G. (2005) "Tacitus *Germania* 37.2 und 4," *Philologus* 149: 170–4.

Petersen, J. (2019) *Recht bei Tacitus*. Berlin.

Pfordt, M. (1998) *Studien zur Darstellung der Außenpolitik in den Annalen des Tacitus*. Frankfurt.

Pigoń, J. (1987) "Some Remarks on Tacitus' *Agricola* 2.1," *Eos* 75: 323–33.

Pigoń, J. (1992) "Helvidius Priscus, Eprius Marcellus, and *iudicium senatus*: Observations on Tacitus, *Histories* 4.7–8," *CQ* 42: 235–46.

Pigoń, J. (1993) "Drusus *imperator*? An Episode in the Fall of Sejanus in Tacitus, Suetonius, and Cassius Dio," *Antiquitas* 18: 183–90.

Pigoń, J. (2003) "Thrasea Paetus, *libertas senatoria*, and Tacitus' Narrative Methods," *Electrum* 9: 143–53.

Pigoń, J. (2008) "The Passive Voice of the Hero: Some Peculiarities of Tacitus' Portrayal of Germanicus in *Annals* 1.31–49," in J. Pigoń (ed.), *The Children of Herodotus: Greek and Roman Historiography and Related Genres*. Newcastle: 287–303.

Pigoń, J. (2017) "Der Kaiser und sein Heer. Zum Bild des Vitellius in den *Historien* des Tacitus," *Hermes* 145: 210–23.

Plass, P. (1988) *Wit and the Writing of History: The Rhetoric of Historiography in Imperial Rome*. Madison.

Plass, P. (1995) *The Game of Death in Ancient Rome*. Madison.

Pliotis, G. (2023) *Studies in the Ancient Reception of Seneca the Younger*, PhD thesis, University of Cambridge.

Pomeroy, A. J. (1991) *The Appropriate Comment: Death Notices in the Ancient Historians*. Frankfurt.

Pomeroy, A. J. (2003) "Center and Periphery in Tacitus' *Histories*," *Arethusa* 36: 361–74.

Pomeroy, A. J. (2006) "Theatricality in Tacitus' *Histories*," *Arethusa* 39: 171–91.

Potter, D. S. (2012) "Tacitus' Sources," in V. E. Pagán (ed.), *A Companion to Tacitus*. Chichester and Malden, MA: 125–40.

Potter, D. S. and Damon, C. (1999) "The *Senatus Consultum de Cn. Pisone Patre*," in C. Damon and S. Takács (eds.), *The Senatus Consultum de Cn. Pisone Patre. Text, Translation, Discussion*. Baltimore [= *AJP* 120.1]: 13–41.

Poulle, B. (2010) "Religion et récit historique: les ambassades des sanctuaires grecs sous Tibère (Tacite, *Annales* III.60–63)," *DHA*, suppl.4.2: 343–50.

Powell, J. G. F. (1994) "The *rector rei publicae* of Cicero's *De Republica*," *SCI* 13: 19–29.

Powell, J. G. F. (1995) "Friendship and Its Problems in Greek and Roman Thought," in D. C. Innes, H. M. Hine, and C. B. R. Pelling (eds.), *Ethics and Rhetoric: Classical Essays for Donald Russell on His Seventy-Fifth Birthday*. New York: 31–45.

Power, T. (2014) "Suetonius' Tacitus," *JRS* 104: 205–25.

Price, S. R. F. (1984) *Rituals and Power: The Roman Imperial Cult in Asia Minor*. Cambridge.

Purves, A. C. (2006) "The Plot Unravels: Darius' Outnumbered Days in Scythia (Herodotus 4.98)," *Helios* 34: 1–26.

Questa, C. (1967) *Studi sulle fonti degli* Annales *di Tacito*. 2nd edn. Rome.

Questa, C. (1995) "Messalina *meretrix augusta*," in R. Raffaelli (ed.), *Vicende e figure femminili in Grecia e a Roma*. Ancona: 399–423.

Quinn, K. (1963) *Latin Explorations. Critical Studies in Latin Literature*. London.

Ramage, E. S. (1983) "Denigration of Predecessor under Claudius, Galba, and Vespasian," *Historia* 32: 201–14.

Ribbeck, O. (ed.) (1897) *Tragicorum Romanorum fragmenta*. 3rd edn. Leipzig.

Richardson, L., Jr. (1992) *A New Topographical Dictionary of Ancient Rome*. Baltimore.

Riedl, P. (2010) "Alternatives Geschehen in Tacitus' Historien," *Millenium: Jahrbuch zu Kultur und Geschichte des ersten Jahrtausends n. Chr.* 7: 87–132.

Riggsby, A. M. (1997) "'Public' and 'Private' in Roman Culture: The Case of the *cubiculum*," *JRA* 10: 36–56.

Rimell, V. (2015) *The Closure of Space in Roman Poetics: Empire's Inward Turn.* Cambridge.

Rives, J. (ed.) (1999) *Tacitus Germania.* Oxford.

Rives, J. (2002) "Structure and History in the *Germania* of Tacitus," in J. F. Miller, C. Damon, and K. S. Myers (eds.), *Vertis in usum: Studies in Honor of Edward Courtney.* Leipzig: 164–73.

Rives, J. (2012) "*Germania*," in V. E. Pagán (ed.), *A Companion to Tacitus.* Chichester and Malden, MA: 45–61.

Robbert, L. (1917) *De Tacito Lucani Imitatore.* Göttingen.

Roberts, M. (1988) "The Revolt of Boudicca (Tacitus, *Annals* 14.29–39) and the Assertion of *libertas* in Neronian Rome," *AJPh* 109: 118–32.

Rogers, R. S. (1935) *Criminal Trials and Criminal Legislation under Tiberius.* Middletown, CT.

Rogers, R. S. (1959) "The Emperor's Displeasure–*amicitiam renuntiare*," *TAPhA* 90: 224–37.

Rogers, R. S. (1964) "Five Over-Crowded Months? A.D. 62," in C. Henderson, Jr. (ed.), *Classical Mediaeval and Renaissance Studies in Honor of Berthold Louis Ullman.* Rome: i. 217–22.

Roller, M. B. (1996) "Ethical Contradiction and the Fractured Community in Lucan's *Bellum Civile*," *ClAnt* 15: 319–47.

Roller, M. B. (2011) "To Whom am I Speaking? The Changing Venues of Competitive Eloquence in the Early Empire," in W. Blösel and K.-J. Hölkeskamp (eds.), *Von der militia equestris zur militia urbana: Prominenzrollen und Karrierefelder im antiken Rom.* Stuttgart: 197–221.

Romm, J. S. (1992) *The Edges of the Earth in Ancient Thought: Geography, Exploration, and Fiction.* Princeton.

Ronconi, A. (2013) "*Exitus illustrium virorum*," in A. L. Trombetti Budriesi (ed.), *Un gallo ad Asclepio. Morte, morti e società tra antichità e prima età moderna.* Bologna: 389–406.

Ronning, C. (2006) "Der Konflikt zwischen Kaiser Nero und P. Clodius Thrasea Paetus: Rituelle Strategien in der frühen Römischen Kaiserzeit," *Chiron* 36: 329–55.

Rose, K. F. C. (1971) *The Date and Author of the Satyricon.* Leiden.

Rosen, K. (1996) "Der Historiker als Prophet: Tacitus und die Juden," *Gymnasium* 103: 107–26.

Ross, D. O. (1973) "The Tacitean Germanicus," *YClS* 23: 209–87.

Rouveret, A. (1991) "Tacite et les monuments," *ANRW* II.33.4: 3051–99.

Roymans, N. (2004) *Ethnic Identity and Imperial Power: The Batavians in the Early Roman Empire.* Amsterdam.

Rudich, V. (1993) *Political Dissidence under Nero: The Price of Dissimulation.* London.

Rudich, V. (1997) *Dissidence and Literature under Nero.* London.

Russo, A., Guarneri, F., Borghini, S., and Pozzi, M. (eds.) (2023) *L'Amato di Iside. Nerone, la Domus Aurea e l'Egitto.* Rome.

Rutherford, R. B. (2010) "Voices of Resistance," in C. S. Kraus, J. Marincola, and C. B. R. Pelling (eds.), *Ancient Historiography and its Contexts: Studies in Honour of A. J. Woodman.* Oxford: 312–30.

Rutland, L. W. (1978) "Women as Makers of Kings in Tacitus' *Annals*," *CW* 72: 15–29.

Rutland, L. W. (1987) "The Tacitean Germanicus: Suggestions for a Re-evaluation," *RhM* 130: 153–64.

Rutledge, S. H. (2000) "Plato, Tacitus, and the *Dialogus de oratoribus*," *Latomus* 254: 345–57.

Rutledge, S. H. (2001) *Imperial Inquisitions: Prosecutors and Informants from Tiberius to Domitian.* London.

Rutledge, S. H. (2013) "Pearls, Gold, Slaves? The Slow Annexation of Britain," in B. D. Hoyos (ed.), *A Companion to Roman Imperialism.* Leiden: 225–36.

Ryberg, I. S. (1942) "Tacitus' Art of Innuendo," *TAPhA* 73: 383–404.

Sage, M. M. (1990) "Tacitus' Historical Works: A Survey and Appraisal," *ANRW* II.33.2: 851–1030.

Sailor, D. (2004) "Significance and Inconsequentiality in the Prologue of *Agricola*," *ClAnt* 23: 139–77.

Sailor, D. (2008) *Writing and Empire in Tacitus.* Cambridge.

Sailor, D. (2012) "The Agricola," in V. E. Pagán (ed.), *A Companion to Tacitus.* Chichester and Malden, MA: 23–44.

Sailor, D. (2019) "Arminius and Flavus across the Weser," *TAPhA* 149: 77–126.

Santangelo, F. (2013) *Divination, Prediction and the End of the Roman Republic.* Cambridge.

Santangelo, F. (2020) "Cicero on Divine and Human Foresight," in C. Beltrão da Rosa and F. Santangelo (eds.), *Cicero and Roman Religion: Eight Studies.* Stuttgart: 105–16.

Santoro L'Hoir, F. (1992) *The Rhetoric of Gender Terms: "Man," "Woman," and the Portrayal of Character in Latin Prose.* Leiden.

Santoro L'Hoir, F. (1994) "Tacitus and Women's Usurpation of Power," *CW* 88: 5–25.

Santoro L'Hoir, F. (2006) *Tragedy, Rhetoric, and the Historiography of Tacitus'* Annales. Ann Arbor.

Schäfer, P. (2014) *Judeophobia: Attitudes Toward the Jews in the Ancient World.* Cambridge, MA.

Scheidel, W. (2008) "Roman Population Size: The Logic of the Debate," in L. de Ligt and S. Northwood (eds.), *People, Land, and Politics: Demographic Developments and the Transformation of Roman Italy 300 BC–AD 14.* Leiden: 17–70.

Schmeling, G. (ed.) (2011) *A Commentary on The Satyrica of Petronius.* Oxford.

Schofield, M. (2021) *Cicero: Political Philosophy.* Oxford.

Schulz, V. (2019) *Deconstructing Imperial Representation: Tacitus, Cassius Dio, and Suetonius on Nero and Domitian.* Leiden.

Schunck, P. (1964) "Studien zur Darstellung des Endes von Galba, Otho und Vitellius in den Historien des Tacitus," *SO* 39: 38–82.

Scott, R. D. (1974) "The Death of Nero's Mother (Tacitus, *Annals*, xiv, 1–13)," *Latomus* 33: 105–15.

Seager, R. (1977) "*Amicitia* in Tacitus and Juvenal," *AJAH* 2: 40–50.

Seager, R. (2005) *Tiberius.* 2nd edn. Malden, MA.

Severy, B. (2003) *Augustus and the Family at the Birth of the Roman Empire.* New York.

Shannon, K. E. (2012) "Memory, Religion, and History in Nero's Great Fire: Tacitus *Annals* 15.41–7," *CQ* 62: 749–65.

Shannon, K. E. (2014) "Aetiology of the Other: Foreign Religion in Tacitus' *Histories*," in C. Reitz and A. Walter (eds.), *Von Ursachen sprechen: Eine aitiologische Spurensuche. Telling Origins: On the Lookout for Aetiology.* Hildesheim: 271–300.

Shannon-Henderson, K. E. (2019) *Religion and Memory in Tacitus' Annals.* Oxford.

Shannon-Henderson, K. E. (2022) "Tacitus and Paradoxography," in J. McNamara and V. E. Pagán (eds.), *Tacitus' Wonders.* London: 17–51.

Shannon-Henderson, K. E. (forthcoming) "Completing Tacitus with Fragments: The Destruction of the Jewish Temple," in P. Christoforou and B. L. H. ten Berge (eds.), *Tacitus and the Incomplete.* Ann Arbor.

Shatzman, I. (1974) "Tacitean Rumours," *Latomus* 33: 549–78.

Shaw, B. D. (2015) "The Myth of the Neronian Persecution," *JRS* 105: 73–100.

Sherk, R. K. (ed., tr.) (1988) *The Roman Empire: Augustus to Hadrian.* Translated Documents of Greece & Rome, 6. Cambridge.

Shotter, D. C. A. (1967) "The Debate on Augustus (Tacitus, "Annals" 1 9–10)," *Mnemosyne* 20: 171–4.

Shotter, D. C. A. (1968) "Tacitus, Tiberius and Germanicus," *Historia* 18: 194–214.

Shotter, D. C. A. (1977) "Tacitus and Antonius Primus," *LCM* 2: 23–7.

Shotter, D. C. A. (ed.) (1989) *Tacitus. Annals IV.* Warminster.

Shumate, N. (2012) "Postcolonial Approaches to Tacitus," in V. E. Pagán (ed.), *A Companion to Tacitus.* Chichester and Malden, MA: 476–503.

Siegert, F. (ed., tr.) (2008) *Flavius Josephus. Über die Ursprünglichkeit des Judentums (Contra Apionem).* Göttingen.

Sinclair, P. (1995) *Tacitus the Sententious Historian: A Sociology of Rhetoric in* Annales *1–6.* University Park, PA.

Smallwood, E. M. (1967) *Documents Illustrating the Principates of Gaius, Claudius and Nero.* Cambridge.

Smith, I. G. (2015) "A Chronology for Agricola, Mons Graupius and Domitian's Triumph in the Chattan War," *Historia* 64: 156–204.

Soverini, P. (ed., tr.) (2004) *Cornelio Tacito. Agricola.* Alessandria.

Späth, T. (2012) "Masculinity and Gender Performance in Tacitus," in V. E. Pagán (ed.), *A Companion to Tacitus.* Chichester and Malden, MA: 431–57.

Spielberg, L. (2017) "Language, Stasis and the Role of the Historian in Thucydides, Sallust and Tacitus," *AJPh* 138: 331–73.

Spielberg, L. (2019) "Fairy Tales and Hard Truths in Tacitus's *Histories* 4.6–10," *ClAnt* 38: 141–83.

von Stackelberg, K. T. (2009) "Performative Space and Garden Transgressions in Tacitus' Death of Messalina," *AJPh* 130: 595–624.

Steel, C. (2018) "*Re publica nihil desperatius*: Salvaging the State in Cicero's Pre-Civil War Philosophical Works," in G. Müller and F. Mariani-Zini (eds.), *Philosophie in Rom—römische Philosophie?* Berlin: 269–82.

Steinmetz, P. (2000) "Die literarische Form des *Agricola* des Tacitus," in P. Steinmetz, *Kleine Schriften.* Stuttgart: 361–73.

Stern, M. (1980) *Greek and Latin Authors on Jews and Judaism.* Vol. 2. Jerusalem.

Strubbe, J. H. M. (1991) "Cursed Be He That Moves My Bones," in C. A. Faraone and D. D. Obbink (eds.), *Magika Hiera: Ancient Greek Magic and Religion.* New York: 33–59.

Strunk, T. E. (2010) "Saving the Life of a Foolish Poet: Tacitus on Marcus Lepidus, Thrasea Paetus, and Political Action under the Principate," *SyllClas* 21: 119–39.

Strunk, T. E. (2017) *History after Liberty. Tacitus on Tyrants, Sycophants, and Republicans*. Ann Arbor.

Suerbaum, W. (1997) "An Scheideweg zur Zukunft. Alternative Geschensverläufe bei römischen Historikern," *Gymnasium* 104: 36–54.

Suspène, A. (2010) "Un 'procès politique' au début de l'Empire romain : le cas de Pison Père," *RH* 650: 845–71.

Syme, R. (1958a) *Tacitus*. Oxford.

Syme, R. (1958b) "Obituaries in Tacitus," *AJPh* 79: 18–31 [repr. in R. Syme (1970), *Ten studies in Tacitus*. Oxford: 79–90].

Syme, R. (1964) *Sallust*. Berkeley.

Syme, R. (1970) "The Senator as Historian," in R. Syme, *Ten studies in Tacitus*. Oxford: 1–10.

Syme, R. (1974) "History or Biography: The Case of Tiberius Caesar," *Historia* 23: 481–96.

Syme, R. (1978) *History in Ovid*. Oxford.

Syme, R. (1984) "How Tacitus Wrote Annals 1–3," in R. Syme, *Roman Papers*. Ed. A. Birley. Vol. 3. Oxford: 1014–42.

Syme, R. (1991) "Titus et Berenice: A Tacitean Fragment," in R. Syme, *Roman Papers*. Ed. A. Birley. Vol. 7. Oxford: 647–62.

Szoke, M. (2019) "Condemning Domitian or Un-damning Themselves? Tacitus and Pliny on the Domitianic 'Reign of Terror'," *BICS* 44: 430–52.

Tabacco, R. (1985) *Il tiranno nelle declamazioni di scuola in lingua latina*. Turin.

Tagliafico, M. (1996) "I processi *intra cubiculum*: il caso di Valerio Asiatico," in M. Sordi (ed.), *Processi e politica nel mondo antico*. Milan: 249–59.

Talbert, R. J. A. (1984) *The Senate of Imperial Rome*. Princeton.

Tan, Z. M. (2014) "Subversive Geography in Tacitus' *Germania*," *JRS* 104: 181–204.

Tarrant, H. (1993) *Thrasyllan Platonism*. Ithaca, NY.

ten Berge, B. L. H. (2023) *Writing Imperial History: Tacitus from* Agricola *to* Annales. Ann Arbor.

Thomas, R. F. (1982) *Lands and Peoples in Roman Poetry: The Ethnographic Tradition*. Cambridge.

Thomas, R. F. (2009) "The *Germania* as literary text," in A. J. Woodman (ed.), *The Cambridge Companion to Tacitus*. Cambridge: 59–72.

Tordoff, R. (2014) "Counterfactual History and Thucydides," in V. Wohl (ed.), *Probabilities, Hypotheticals, and Counterfactuals in Ancient Greek Thought*, Cambridge: 101–21.

Toswell M. J. (2010) "Quid Tacitus…? The *Germania* and the Study of Anglo-Saxon England," *Florilegium* 27: 27–62.

Townend, G. B. (1961) "Traces in Dio Cassius of Cluvius, Aufidius and Pliny," *Hermes* 89: 227–48.

Traversa, L. (2015) "*Prudentia* e *providentia* in Cicerone: il 'ritorno al futuro' dal *de inventione* al *de officiis*," *Historia* 64: 306–35.

Treggiari, S. (1991) *Roman Marriage*: Iusti Coniuges *from the Time of Cicero to the Time of Ulpian*. Oxford.

Tresch, J. (1965) *Die Nerobücher in den Annalen des Tacitus: Tradition und Leistung*. Heidelberg.

Treu, M. (1948) "M. Antonius Primus in der taciteischen Darstellung," *WJA* 3: 241–62.

Trilling, L. (1976) "Tacitus Now," in L. Trilling (ed.), *The Liberal Imagination: Essays on Literature and Society*. New York: 198–206 [repr. in Ash (2012): 435–40].

Trüdinger, K. (1918) *Studien zur Geschichte der griechisch-römischen Ethnographie*. Basel.

Tuplin, C. J. (1987) "The False Drusus of A.D. 31 and the Fall of Sejanus," *Latomus* 46: 781–805.

Turpin, W. (2008) "Tacitus, Stoic *exempla*, and the *praecipuum munus annalium*," *ClAnt* 27: 359–404.

Ulery, R. W. (1986) "Cornelius Tacitus," in F. E. Cranz, V. Brown, and P. O. Kristeller (eds.), *Catalogus translationum et commentariorum: Mediaeval and Renaissance Latin Translations and Commentaries*. Washington, DC: vi. 87–174.

van den Berg, C. S. (2014) *The World of Tacitus' Dialogus de Oratoribus: Aesthetics and Empire in Ancient Rome*. Cambridge.

van den Berg, C. S. (2021) *The Politics and Poetics of Cicero's Brutus: The Invention of Literary History*. Cambridge.

Vandrei, M. (2018) *Queen Boudica and Historical Culture in Britain: An Image of Truth*. Oxford.

Varner, E. R. (2001) "Portraits, Plots, and Politics: *Damnatio Memoriae* and the Images of Imperial Women," *Memoirs of the American Academy in Rome* 46: 41–93.

Varner, E. R. (2004) *Mutilation and Transformation: Damnatio Memoriae and Roman Imperial Portraiture*. Leiden.

Vervaet, F. J. (2002) "Domitius Corbulo and the Senatorial Opposition to the Reign of Nero," *AncSoc* 32: 135–93.

Vielberg, M. (1987) *Pflichten, Werte, Ideale. Eine Untersuchung zu den Wertvorstellungen des Tacitus*. Stuttgart.

Vout, C. (2007) *Power and Eroticism in Imperial Rome*. Oxford.

Waddell, P. (2013) "Eloquent Collisions: The *Annales* of Tacitus, the Column of Trajan, and the Cinematic Quick-Cut," *Arethusa* 46: 471–97.

Walker, B. (1952; 2nd edn. 1960) *The Annals of Tacitus: A Study in the Writing of History*. Manchester.

Wallace-Hadrill, A. (1981) "The Emperor and his Virtues," *Historia* 30: 298–319.

Wallace-Hadrill, A. (1982) "*Civilis Princeps*. Between Citizen and King," *JRS* 72: 32–48.

Walser, G. (1951) *Rom, das Reich und die Fremden Völker in der Geschichtsschreibung der frühen Kaiserzeit*. Baden-Baden.

Walsh, J. J. (2019) *The Great Fire of Rome: Life and Death in the Ancient City*. Baltimore.

Ward-Jackson, P. (2011) *Public Sculpture of Historic Westminster*. Vol. 1. Liverpool.

Wardle, D. (2012) "Suetonius on *Vespasianus religiosus* in AD 69–70: Signs and Times," *Hermes* 140: 184–201.

Webster, G. (1981) *Rome against Caratacus. The Roman Campaigns in Britain AD 48–58*. London.

Webster, G. (1993) *Boudica: The British Revolt against Rome AD 60*. Rev. edn. London.

Wellesley, K. (1960) "*Suggestio falsi* in Tacitus," *RhM* 103: 272–88.

Wellesley, K. (ed.) (1972) *Cornelius Tacitus. The Histories Book III*. Sydney.

Wellesley, K. (ed.) (1989) *Cornelii Taciti Libri Qui Supersunt. II: Historiarum Libri*. Leipzig.

Wellesley, K. (tr.) (2009) *Tacitus. The Histories*. Rev. edn., ed. R. Ash. London.

Wheeler, E. L. (1997) "The Chronology of Corbulo in Armenia," *Klio* 79: 383–97.

White, H. (1973) *Metahistory: The Historical Imagination in Nineteenth-Century Europe*. Baltimore.

Whitehead, D. (1979) "Tacitus and the Loaded Alternative," *Latomus* 38: 474–95.

Whitton, C. L. (2012) "'Let Us Tread Our Path Together': Tacitus and the Younger Pliny," in V. E. Pagán (ed.), *A Companion to Tacitus*. Chichester and Malden, MA: 345–68.

Whitton, C. L. (2013) *Pliny the Younger. Epistles Book II*. Cambridge.

Whitton, C. L. (2019) *The Arts of Imitation in Latin Prose. Pliny's "Epistles"/Quintilian in Brief*. Cambridge.

Whitton, C. L. (forthcoming a) "The Agrippina Plot: History and Intratext in Tacitus *Annals* 14."

Whitton, C. L. (forthcoming b) "From Memory to History: Tacitus' Octavia," in M. T. Dinter and M. Martinho de Santos (eds.), *Roman Cultural Memory under the Empire*. Cambridge.

Whitton, C. L. (forthcoming c) "*Histories* Lost and Found: Tacitus and Pliny on Vesuvius," in P. Christoforou and B. L. H. ten Berge (eds.), *Tacitus and the Incomplete*. Ann Arbor.

Whitton, C. L. (forthcoming d) "The Many Deaths of Agrippina: Associative Intratextuality in Tacitus' *Annals*."

Whitton, C. L. (ed.) (forthcoming e) *Tacitus. Annals XIV*. Cambridge.

Wildberger, J. (2015) "Senecan Progressor Friendship and the Characterization of Nero in Tacitus' *Annals*," in C. Kugelmeier (ed.), *Translatio humanitatis: Festschrift zum 60. Geburtstag von Peter Riemer*. St Ingbert: 471–92.

Wille, G. (1983) *Der Aufbau der Werke des Tacitus*. Amsterdam.

Williams, B. (1989) "Reading Tacitus' Tiberian *Annals*," *Ramus* 18: 140–66.

Williams, C. D. (2009a) *Boudica and Her Stories: Narrative Transformations of a Warrior Queen*. Newark, DE.

Williams, K. F. (2009b) "Tacitus' Germanicus and the Principate," *Latomus* 68: 117–30.

Wilson, M. (2003) "After the Silence: Tacitus, Suetonius, Juvenal," in A. J. Boyle and W. J. Dominik (eds.), *Flavian Rome: Culture, Image, Text*. Leiden: 523–42.

Winterbottom, M. and Ogilvie, R. M. (eds.) (1975) *Cornelii Taciti Opera Minora*. Oxford.

Winterling, A. (2008) "Freundschaft und Klientel im kaiserzeitlichen Rom," *Historia* 57: 298–316.

Wirszubski, C. (1950) *Libertas as a Political Idea at Rome during the Late Republic and Early Principate*. Cambridge.

Wiseman, T. P. (2002) "History, Poetry, and *Annales*," in D. S. Levene and D. P. Nelis (eds.), *Clio and the Poets: Augustan Poetry and the Traditions of Ancient Historiography*. Leiden: 331–362.

Wisse, J. (2013) "Remembering Cremutius Cordus: Tacitus on History, Tyranny and Memory," *Histos* 7: 299–361.

Wistrand, E. (1979) "The Stoic Opposition to the Principate," *StudClas* 18: 93–101.

Wolf, J. G. (1988) *Das Senatusconsultum Silanianum und die Senatsrede des C. Cassius Longinus aus dem Jahre 61 n. Chr.* Heidelberg.

Woodcock, E. C. (ed.) (1939; repr. 1992). *Tacitus Annals XIV*. Bristol.

Woodman, A. J. (1975) "Questions of Date, Genre, and Style in Velleius: Some Literary Answers," *CQ* 25: 272–306.

Woodman, A. J. (1979) "Self-imitation and the Substance of History: Tacitus, *Annals* 1.61–5 and *Histories* 2.70, 5.14–15," in D. West and T. [= A. J.] Woodman (eds.), *Creative Imitation and Latin Literature*. Cambridge: 143–56 [repr. in Woodman (1998): 70–85].

Woodman, A. J. (1988) *Rhetoric in Classical Historiography*. London.

Woodman, A. J. (1989) "Tacitus' Obituary of Tiberius," *CQ* 39: 197–205.

Woodman, A. J. (1992a) "Nero's Alien Capital: Tacitus as Paradoxographer (*Annals* 15.36–7)," in A. J. Woodman and J. G. F. Powell (eds.), *Author and Audience in Latin Literature*. Cambridge: 173–88 [repr. in Woodman (1998): 168–89].

Woodman, A. J. (1992b) "The Preface to Tacitus' *Annals*: More Sallust?" *CQ* 42: 567–68.

Woodman, A. J. (1993) "Amateur Dramatics at the Court of Nero (*Annals* 15. 48–74)," in T. J. Luce and A. J. Woodman (eds.), *Tacitus and the Tacitean Tradition*. Princeton: 10–28 [repr. in Woodman (1998): 190–217].

Woodman, A. J. (1995a) "A Death in the First Act: Tacitus, *Annals* 1.6," in R. Brock and A. J. Woodman (eds.), *Roman Comedy, Augustan Poetry, Historiography*. Papers of the Leeds International Latin Seminar, 8. Leeds: 257–73.

Woodman, A. J. (1995b) "*Praecipuum munus annalium*: The Construction, Convention and Context of Tacitus, *Annals* 3.65," *MH* 52: 111–26.

Woodman, A. J. (1998) *Tacitus Reviewed*. Oxford.

Woodman, A. J. (tr.) (2004) *Tacitus, The Annals*. Indianapolis.

Woodman, A. J. (2006a) "Mutiny and Madness: Tacitus Annals 1.16–49," *Arethusa* 39: 303–29.

Woodman, A. J. (2006b) "Tiberius and the Taste of Power: The Year 33 in Tacitus," *CQ* 56: 175–89. [repr. in A. J. Woodman (2012), From Poetry to History: Selected Papers. Oxford: 339–60].

Woodman, A. J. (ed.) (2009a) *The Cambridge Companion to Tacitus*. Cambridge.

Woodman, A. J. (2009b) "Tacitus and the Contemporary Scene," in A. J. Woodman (ed.), *The Cambridge Companion to Tacitus*. Cambridge: 31–43.

Woodman, A. J. (2010a) "*Aliena facundia*: Seneca in Tacitus," in D. H. Berry and A. Erskine (eds.), *Form and Function in Roman Oratory*. Cambridge: 294–307 [repr. in A. J. Woodman (2012), *From Poetry to History: Selected Papers*. Oxford: 361–77].

Woodman, A. J. (2010b) "Community Health: Metaphors in Latin Historiography," *Papers of the Langford Latin Seminar* 14: 43–61.

Woodman, A. J. (ed.) (2014) *Tacitus: Agricola*. With C. S. Kraus. Cambridge.

Woodman, A. J. (ed.) (2017) *The Annals of Tacitus: Books 5 and 6*. Cambridge.

Woodman, A. J. (ed.) (2018) *The Annals of Tacitus: Book 4*. Cambridge.

Woodman, A. J. (ed.) (forthcoming) *Sallust. Bellum Catilinae*. Cambridge.

Woodman, A. J. and Martin, R. H. (eds.) (1996) *The Annals of Tacitus Book 3*. Cambridge.

Woolf, G. (2011) *Tales of the Barbarians: Ethnography and Empire in the Roman West*. Chichester and Malden, MA.

Woolf, G. (2013) "Ethnography and the Gods in Tacitus' Germania," in E. Almagor and J. Skinner (eds.), *Ancient Ethnography, New Approaches*. London: 133–52.

Yardley, J. and Barrett, A. (tr.) (2008) *The Annals: The Reigns of Tiberius, Claudius, and Nero*. Oxford.

Yavetz, Z. (1998) "Latin Authors on Jews and Dacians," *Historia* 47: 77–107.

Zanker, P. (1988) *The Power of Images in the Age of Augustus*. Ann Arbor.

Zarecki, J. (2014) *Cicero's Ideal Statesman in Theory and Practice*. London and New York.

Zetzel, J. E. G. (ed.) (2017) *Cicero: On the Commonwealth and on the Laws*. 2nd edn. Cambridge.

Zetzel, J. E. G. (2022) *The Lost Republic: Cicero's* De oratore *and* De re publica. Oxford.

Index

Since the index has been created to work across multiple formats, indexed terms for which a page range is given (e.g., 52–53, 66–70, etc.) may occasionally appear only on some, but not all of the pages within the range.

Actium 42, 57–8, 124, 130–1
adulatio 9, 67, 74, 105–6, 108–9, 140, 142–4, 169–70
Aemilia Lepida 134–5, 137–41
Afranius Burrus 10, 149, 189–92, 200–2, 204–5, 211–12, 230–1
Africa 17–18, 50, 56–7, 89, 93–4, 105–6, 124, 127, 140, 145
Agricola 2–3, 13–19, 21–2, 26–7, 40, 59, 122, 145, 148–50, 153, 206–7, 211–12, 236–7
Agrippa. *See* Vipsanius Agrippa, Marcus
Agrippa Postumus 115–18, 125, 171–2
Agrippina the Elder 112, 127, 129–31, 136–40, 149–51, 154–7, 160–3, 168, 180, 207, 217–18
Agrippina the Younger 9–10, 122, 131, 137–8, 149, 157, 160, 175–7, 179–95, 200–5, 207–14, 230–2
Alexandria 64–5, 77, 89, 91–4, 98, 125–6, 130 n.33, 215–16, 233–4
Anicetus 77, 201–2, 210, 213–14
annalistic tradition 5–6, 8, 48, 90, 126–8, 133–4, 183, 196
    See also historiography: Roman
Antistius Sosianus 141, 210–11, 234
Antonius, Marcus 64–5, 70, 114–15, 128 n.21, 233–4
Antonius Primus 1–2, 76–82, 84–5, 89, 92–4, 97
Aper, Marcus 4–5, 36–7, 44–5, 146–7, 154
Aristotle 18, 21–2, 115–16
Armenia 115, 124–5, 183–5, 190–2, 205, 215, 217–20, 222, 237–8
Arminius 112, 126–8, 132
Arruntius, Lucius 119–20, 165, 171–2
Artaxata 185–6, 191
Arulenus Rusticus 147, 153–4, 236–8
Asia 1, 57, 64–6, 124, 139–40, 150–1, 188, 205, 212, 234
Asinius Gallus 119–20, 151, 167–8
Asinius Pollio 118
Augustus 6–9, 8 n.23, 28–9, 41–2, 44–5, 50–1, 57, 70, 99, 110, 112–22, 125–6, 128 n.21, 134, 138–42, 144, 146, 148, 150–1, 153–6, 160–1, 165, 167–8, 171–3, 176–7, 180–5, 221, 224, 229–34
avaritia 17, 65, 80, 148–9, 188–9, 195

Barea Soranus 91–3, 230–1, 237–8
Batavians 69–70, 89, 93, 95–9, 101–3, 107–8
Bedriacum 64, 66–7, 69–72, 76–7, 79, 85–6, 146–7, 150
Berenice 64–5, 104–6
biography 2, 4, 13–17, 46, 115–16, 153
Bithynia 121, 238
Blaesus, Junius. *See* Junius Blaesus
Boudica 10, 134, 148–9, 184, 200, 206–9, 212–13

Britain 2, 10, 13–14, 16–22, 26, 50, 55, 58, 71, 77, 175, 183–5, 187, 205
    peoples and armies of 2–4, 16–21, 105–6, 148–9, 184, 206–9
Britannicus 175–7, 180–1, 192–5, 198, 203
Brutus. *See* Junius Brutus
Burrus. *See* Afranius Burrus

Caecina Alienus 54–6, 66–8, 74, 76–7, 81–3, 98
Caecina Severus, Aulus 112, 136
Caesar, Julius 2–4, 17–21, 24–6, 28–9, 34–5, 41–2, 47, 55–7, 64–5, 69–70, 114–15, 142, 153–4, 184, 237–8
Caesellius, Bassus 230–3
Caesennius Paetus 218–19, 222
Caledonians 148–9, 184
Calgacus 2–3, 13–14, 16–17, 20–1, 148–9, 184, 206–7
Caligula 9, 51–2, 128 n.21, 131, 147, 160–1, 165, 167, 170–3, 175–6, 181, 184–5, 188, 229, 239–40
Calpurnius Piso, Gaius 10, 119, 210, 214, 226, 230–2
Calpurnius Piso, Gnaeus 125, 128–31, 133, 135–40, 143, 150–1
Calpurnius Piso, Licinianus 51–4, 60
Calpurnius Piso, Lucius 89, 93–4, 149, 197
Capri 9, 143, 145, 156–7, 160–1, 164, 167–8, 170, 240
Caratacus 183–4, 208–9
Carthage 28–9, 72, 96, 146, 197, 231–2
Cassius Dio 45 n.41, 59–60, 118, 134–6, 161, 225, 229–30, 233
Cassius Longinus, Gaius (assassin of Caesar) 64, 134, 136, 143, 153–4, 237–8
Cassius Longinus, Gaius (jurist) 209–10, 234
Catiline 69, 87, 142, 146, 197, 226
Cato the Elder 2, 5–6, 15, 17, 65
Cato the Younger 70, 134, 235–6
Celsus 66–8, 150
Celts 18–19, 27–8
Christians 109, 111, 215, 225, 229–30
    See also religion: Christian
Cicero 2, 4–5, 17–18, 20, 36–45, 197, 218
Civilis. *See* Julius Civilis
civil wars 53–4, 102, 104–5, 184–5
    imperial Roman 6–7, 48–9, 52, 54–8, 60–74, 76–98, 102, 108–9, 118–19, 146–7, 151, 167
    Jewish 101–2, 105–6
    of late Republic 34–5, 38, 50–1, 64, 67–70, 114–15, 130–1, 153–4, 171
    See also mutinies and revolts
Claudia Pulchra 155–7

Claudius 9, 19, 51–2, 135–6, 135 n.9, 143, 148, 152, 160, 164, 168–9, 172–3, 175–93, 203, 206, 208, 214, 230, 239–41
clementia 129–30, 139–41, 152, 183–5, 190–1, 195, 210–13, 238
Cleopatra 64–5, 207–9, 233–4
Clutorius Priscus 136–7, 141–2
consolatio 2, 15, 17–18, 22
constitution, Roman 5, 37–46, 138–9, 177
Corbulo. *See* Domitius Corbulo
Cornelius Sulla, Faustus 200, 212–13
Cornelius Sulla, Lucius (dictator) 114–15, 171, 181–2
Cossutianus Capito 149–50, 154, 210–11, 237–8
Cremona 76–7, 79–80, 82, 84–8, 90–1
Cremutius Cordus 46, 118, 143, 153–4, 165–6
Curiatius Maternus 2–5, 36–41, 44–6, 150, 153

Dacians 25–6, 77
delatores 9, 13–14, 120–1, 140, 142, 146–7, 152, 154–7, 237
dialogues 4–5, 36–42, 44–7, 212
Domitia Lepida 178–9, 182
Domitian 1–3, 6–8, 13–16, 20, 26, 33–4, 40, 44, 48–9, 57–8, 77–8, 89, 93–4, 99, 103, 108–9, 116, 145–7, 149, 157, 206–7, 219, 229, 236–8, 241–2
Domitius Ahenobarbus, Gnaeus 122, 157, 159–60
Domitius Corbulo 10, 183, 189–93, 195, 205, 216, 218–20, 222, 227, 231–2, 234, 240–1
Drusus, Nero Claudius (Drusus the Elder) 28–9, 128–30
Drusus Caesar (Drusus the Younger) 119–20, 127, 133, 135–41, 145–6, 149–50, 155–6, 173–4
Drusus Caesar (son of Germanicus) 131, 156–7, 163, 168–70, 172

Egypt 50, 57, 64–5, 77, 89, 91–4, 98, 104–6, 124–6, 130–1, 215–16, 233–4
eloquence 5, 13, 36–8, 41, 44–7, 190–1
Ennius 113–14, 217 n.7, 243
Eprius Marcellus 91–3, 98, 149–50, 154, 236–8
ethnography 2–4, 13–14, 17–19, 24–5, 27–30, 33–5, 103–7, 157
eulogy 13–15, 140–1, 187, 190–1, 233–4
Euripides 201–2
exemplum 2, 13–14, 21–2, 58, 70, 78, 90–1, 136, 139–40, 142–3, 152, 181, 191

Fabius Justus, Lucius 4, 36
Fabius Valens 54–8, 67, 76–7, 83, 86
Flavius Sabinus 7, 77–8, 80–2, 85–8
Florus 133–4, 140
fortuna 9, 62–3, 65, 67, 83, 127–8, 143, 146–7, 178, 231–2
freedmen and freedwomen 45–6, 52, 65–6, 70–1, 77, 85, 148, 169–70, 209, 226
  and Claudius 175–9, 181–2, 187–90
  and Nero 70–1, 192–3, 201–2, 205–7, 210, 213–15

Galba 7, 48–62, 64–6, 79, 85–6, 91–3, 96–8, 132, 167–8, 203–4, 215–16, 236–7, 240–1

Gaul 1, 25–6, 28–9, 34–5, 50, 56–7, 70–1, 77, 89, 91, 93–7, 215–16, 240–2
  armies of 54–5, 63–5, 87, 225
  peoples of 3–4, 18–20, 25, 62, 95, 98, 102, 134, 135 n.9, 177, 187, 224–5
geographies 3–4, 10, 18–19, 24–5, 28, 32, 105–7
Germanicus 9, 26, 28–9, 112, 115, 124–44, 149, 151, 155–7, 160, 163, 168, 171, 173–4, 179, 181, 189–90, 192, 203–4, 217–19, 240
Germany 25–7, 32–3, 72–3, 76–7, 89, 91, 95–9, 101–2, 112–13, 124–32, 136, 145, 148, 157, 207
  armies of 28–30, 54–5, 62–5, 102, 112–13, 118, 125–6
  peoples of 3–4, 24–34, 50, 77, 93, 95–7, 105–6, 108, 148, 166–7
  and purity 3, 24–7, 32–5
Golden House (*Domus Aurea*) 196, 215, 224–5
Granius Marcellus 121
Great Fire of Rome 10, 111, 215, 220–1, 223–5, 229–31

Helvidius Priscus the Elder 7, 91–4, 149–50, 153, 234, 236–9
Herennius Senecio 147, 153–4, 236–7
Herodotus 4, 18, 24–6, 30–5, 41, 58
Hispania. *See* Spain
historiography 24–5, 43–4, 46–7, 83, 103, 109, 112, 116–17, 164, 230
  Greek 4, 16–17, 58–9, 78
  Roman 5–7, 9, 16–18, 48–51, 57–9, 62–5, 74, 78, 90, 113–14, 134–6, 153–4, 184
  See also annalistic tradition; biography
Hortensius 38

Illyricum 50, 56–7, 73, 76–7, 91
imperialism, Roman 2–3, 19–21, 183–4

Jerome 229, 239–40
Jerusalem 6, 62, 64, 101–10
Jewish-Roman War 6–7, 62, 64, 101–3, 107–11
Jews 6–7, 64–5, 99, 101–11, 240–1
Josephus 6–7, 59, 101–2, 104–5, 107–10
Judea 56–7, 91, 98–9, 101–9
Julius Civilis 89, 95–9, 101–3, 108
Junia Tertulla 134, 136, 140–3
Junius Blaesus 77–8, 81–2, 86, 151–2
Junius Brutus 64, 134, 136, 143, 153–4, 237–8
Junius Silanus, Gaius 137, 139–41, 150–1
Junius Silanus, Lucius 179, 188
Junius Silanus, Marcus 115–16, 188, 200–1, 226

laudatio 14–15, 187, 233–4
Lepida. *See* Aemilia Lepida; Domitia Lepida
Lepidus, Marcus 119–20, 122, 136–7, 139–40, 149–51, 165
libertas 3–5, 8, 20, 24–5, 41–2, 44–5, 51–2, 112–14, 122, 127–9, 134, 140, 144, 154, 169–70, 184, 206–7, 211
  senatorial 7, 9, 91, 93–4, 141, 144, 192, 236–7
Licinius Proculus 67–8, 150
Livia 127, 136–8, 140–1, 149–51, 154–5, 159–62, 165, 173–4, 180, 182–3, 189–90, 204, 240
Livia, Claudia (Livilla) 146, 149–50, 154–6

Livy 2, 5–6, 18, 78, 86–7, 90, 113–14, 118
Locusta 182, 194
Lollia Paulina 179–80
Lucan 60, 64–5, 113–14, 235
Lucilius, Bassus 74, 81–2

Macro 166–70, 172
maiestas. See treason laws and trials
Marc Antony. *See* Antonius, Marcus
Maternus. *See* Curiatius Maternus
Memmius Regulus 159, 210
Messalina 9, 175–82, 185, 187, 193, 203
Mettius Carus 154
migrations 18–19, 28–30, 35, 105–6
models and sources, literary
    for *Agricola* 2, 16–18, 20, 22
    for *Annals* 8, 42–5, 113–14, 134–6, 142–3, 145–53,
        178, 193, 197, 212–13, 218–19, 225–7, 231–2, 235–6
    for *Dialogus de oratoribus* 5, 37–42, 44–5
    for *Germania* 3–4, 24–35
    for *Histories* 5–6, 50–1, 59–60, 65, 68–9, 80, 85–8,
        104–7, 118
Moesia 56–7, 73–4, 84–5, 121–2, 125–6
Mucianus 65–6, 72–3, 76–8, 80–1, 85, 89, 92–4,
        99, 146–7
Musonius Rufus 84, 91–3
mutinies and revolts 56, 60, 223
    in Britain 10, 134, 148–9, 183, 206–9
    in eastern provinces 102, 185, 240–2
    in Gaul 67, 79, 84, 133–4, 140, 241–2
    in Germany 49, 54–5, 89, 93–9, 101–3, 107–8,
        112–13, 118–20, 128–32, 207
    Pannonian 112–13, 118–20

Narcissus 178–9, 181–2, 188–9
Nero 6–7, 9–10, 13, 44–6, 49–54, 59, 65–6, 70–1, 86,
        91–3, 96–7, 112, 115–16, 119, 122, 128 n.21, 132, 134,
        148–50, 157, 160, 168–9, 172–3, 175–7, 179–83,
        186–98, 200–14, 219–27, 229–35, 237–42
Nero Julius Caesar 131, 150, 156–7, 161–2, 168
Nerva 1–2, 13, 15–16, 44–5, 51–2, 116, 118–19
Nicolaus of Damascus 118
Nonianus, Servilius 134–5

obituary 9, 53–4, 83, 86–7, 112, 116–17, 122, 127–8,
        133–4, 160–4, 171–4, 182–3, 201–2, 210
Octavia 10, 175, 179–81, 193, 195, 200–1, 207–9, 212–15
Octavian. *See* Augustus
Ofonius Tigellinus 200, 210–12, 216, 224, 231,
        236–8, 240–1
omens and prophecies 48, 55, 62, 64, 73, 82, 87 n.38,
        93–4, 99, 102–3, 107, 119–20, 130–1, 167, 171–2,
        181–2, 198, 205–7, 223–4, 234
oratory 9, 38, 44, 51–2, 60–1, 121
    in *Agricola* 16–17, 20–1, 152
    in *Annals* 134, 136–7, 139–40, 154–5, 160, 162,
        165–6, 177, 183–4, 187, 190–1, 207–12, 218, 220, 222
    and *Dialogus de oratoribus* 2–5, 36–8, 40–1, 44–7,
        118, 151–2

in *Histories* 53, 56, 60–1, 67–8, 72–3, 79–82, 84,
        96–7, 152
    Tacitus' reputation through 1–2, 13
    See also eulogy; *laudatio*
Orosius 109–10
Ostorius Scapula 152, 183, 206, 234
Otho 7, 48–9, 51–4, 56–60, 62, 64–72, 74, 79, 85–6,
        98, 119, 122, 149–50, 194, 202–4
Ovid 216–17

Pallas 178–9, 189–90, 192
Pannonia 25, 73, 79, 112–13, 118, 124, 183
Parthia 20, 28–9, 58, 124–5, 170, 184–5, 190–1, 215,
        217–19, 222
Petilius Cerialis 77, 89, 96–8, 108
Petronius 230–1, 235–6
Piso. *See* Calpurnius Piso, Gaius; Calpurnius Piso,
        Gnaeus; Calpurnius Piso, Licinianus;
        Calpurnius Piso, Lucius
Plancina 135–7
Plato 37, 39, 41–2, 235–6
Pliny the Elder 3, 18, 24–7, 34–5, 80, 223 n.38
Pliny the Younger 1 n.5, 13, 47, 51–2, 151 n.35, 241–2
Plutarch 14, 59–60, 67–8, 115–16
poison 81–2, 117–18, 124–8, 136–7, 149–50, 155–6, 182,
        192–4, 208–9, 211, 215, 233–4, 236–7
Polybius 78
Pompey 41–2, 44–5, 64, 67, 69, 107, 114–15
Pomponius Mela 3, 18
Poppaea Sabina 10, 122, 189–90, 193–4, 200–2, 210–14,
        220–1, 230–1, 233–4
Poppaea Sabina the Elder 175–6
Poppaeus Sabinus 121–2, 155
Posidonius 4, 18–19, 24–30, 34–5
praetorians 51–3, 56, 60, 65–6, 93–4, 150, 166–7, 190,
        204–5, 209, 211, 216, 240–1
prophecies. *See* omens and prophecies
Pytheas of Massalia 18

Quintilian 5, 36, 60–1, 113–14, 121
Quintilius Varus, Publius 28–9, 112, 115, 118, 135–6

Radamistus 185–6
religion 22, 105–6
    Christian 110–11
    Druidic 18–19, 102–3, 206–7
    Jewish 99, 101–2, 105–6, 110–11
    Roman 8, 19–20, 64, 71–2, 74, 94, 105–6, 121,
        139–41, 154, 176–7, 217–18, 221, 223–4
    See also Christians; Jews; omens and prophecies
Rhine 25–8, 32, 53–4, 89, 93, 95–8, 101–2, 112
Rhoxolani 33–4, 56
Rubellius Plautus 149, 200, 205, 212–13, 234

Sacrovir 133–4, 140
saevitia 64–5, 146–7, 149–52, 155–7, 166–7, 173–4
Sallust (historian) 2, 5–6, 15, 17–18, 20, 50–1, 60, 64–5,
        68–9, 87, 105–6, 114, 142, 146, 151–2, 193, 197,
        209, 226

Sallustius Crispus 133–4, 143
Sarmatians 25–6, 31–5
Scipio Aemilianus 40–2, 44 n.30
Scythia 25–6, 31–5
Sejanus 5–6, 9, 134–5, 137, 141–3, 145–6, 149–57, 159,
    161–70, 173–4, 189–90, 201, 205, 212, 216, 240
senate, Roman 9, 40, 42–3, 46, 113, 142, 148
    under Augustus 117, 122
    amidst civil wars 48, 54–5, 57, 60, 65–6, 68, 70,
        74, 77
    under Claudius 175–80, 184, 187
    under Nero 182, 192, 195, 201, 204–6, 209–12,
        214–15, 219–22, 231, 233, 237–8, 240–1
    under Tiberius 117–18, 125–7, 133–7, 139–42, 144,
        150–2, 154–7, 160–2, 165–7, 169–70
    under Vespasian 89, 91–4, 98
Seneca the Elder 121
Seneca the Younger 2, 10, 17–18, 22, 39 n.10, 104, 180,
    187, 189–93, 195, 200–2, 211–13, 215–16, 221–2,
    226–7, 230–1, 235–9
sententiae 21, 53–4, 60–1, 63, 70, 72–3, 81–2, 85–6,
    162, 165
Silanus. See Junius Silanus, Gaius; Junius Silanus,
    Lucius; Junius Silanus, Marcus
Silius, Gaius 151, 177–80
Soranus. See Barea Soranus
sources. See models and sources, literary
Spain 28–9, 50, 52, 56–7, 77, 91, 96, 98, 112, 154–5,
    215–16, 240–1
speeches. See oratory
Statius 243
Stoicism 84, 91–2, 167, 189–90, 192–3, 202, 208–9, 212,
    215, 230–1, 234–8
Strabo 18, 26–30, 34–5, 106–7
Suetonius 14, 21, 59–60, 67–8, 107–10, 117–18, 149, 196,
    200 n.1, 225, 229–30, 232–4, 236–7, 240–1
Suetonius Paulinus 66–8, 150, 206–7
suicide 7, 10, 59, 62, 64, 70, 85, 120–1, 125–6, 132, 151–2,
    160, 162, 165, 167–8, 171–2, 175–6, 178–9, 181–2,
    188–9, 191–2, 202, 208, 210, 216, 221–2, 226–7,
    229–31, 234–9

Suillius Rufus, Publius 152, 154, 175–6, 234
Sulla. See Cornelius Sulla, Faustus; Cornelius
    Sulla, Lucius
Sulpicius Quirinius 133–4, 140–1
Sulpicius Severus 109–10
Syria 56–7, 65–6, 72–3, 89, 91, 124–5, 128–9, 183, 222

Thrace 73–4, 122, 124–7, 145, 148–9, 155
Thrasea Paetus 7, 91–2, 149–50, 153, 189–93, 201,
    210–11, 220–2, 229–31, 234–9
Thucydides 2, 16–18, 58, 60, 78, 164, 166–7
Tiberius 8–9, 28–9, 44, 50–2, 91–2, 112–13, 115–22,
    124–52, 154–7, 159–76, 182–5, 189–90, 200–1,
    203–4, 212, 218–19, 230, 239–41
Tiridates 185–6, 219, 222, 237–8, 240–1
Titius Sabinus 151, 157, 168
Titus 1–2, 6–7, 57–8, 62–5, 70–3, 89, 99, 103–11, 229,
    236–8, 241–2
Trajan 2, 13, 15–16, 22, 28–9, 51–2, 112, 116, 118–19
treason laws and trials 73, 112, 115, 120–2, 134, 137–41,
    145, 148, 151–4, 157, 201, 210–11
    See also delatores
Troy 88, 124, 224–5

Varus. See Quintilius Varus, Publius
Velleius Paterculus 118, 141, 146, 161
Vergil 5–6, 19, 33–4, 60, 70–2, 88, 104–7, 113–14, 203,
    207, 225, 231–2, 243
Verginius Rufus 2, 13, 86, 240–1
Vespasian 1–2, 6–7, 44–6, 48, 57–9, 62–6, 72–4, 76–7,
    79–82, 84–5, 89–95, 97–9, 101–4, 108–10, 132,
    139–40, 146–7, 233, 236–8, 241–2
Vindex 54, 96–7, 215–16, 240–1
Vipsanius Agrippa, Marcus 133–4, 143, 224
Vipstanus, Messalla 4–5, 36–7, 46, 78, 93
Vitellius, Aulus 6–7, 48–9, 53–74, 76–90, 92–8, 102,
    162–3, 203–4
Vitellius, Lucius 78, 175–6, 179–80
Vologaeses I 184–5, 217–20, 222

Zenobia 185–6

About the Contributors

Rhiannon Ash is Professor of Roman Historiography and Fellow and Tutor in Classics, Merton College, Oxford University. She publishes widely on Latin prose narratives, especially Tacitus, including her first monograph, *Ordering Anarchy: Armies and Leaders in Tacitus' Histories* (1999) and two commentaries in the Cambridge "Green and Yellow" series on *Tacitus Histories 2* (2007) and *Tacitus Annals 15* (2018). She has co-edited *Classical Quarterly* and currently co-edits *Histos*, the online journal of ancient historiography. She is currently writing a monograph on Pliny the Elder *Natural History* book nine, marine creatures, and depictions of Roman emperors.

Sergio Audano is the Coordinator of the Centro di Studi sulla Fortuna dell'Antico "Emanuele Narducci" of Sestri Levante (Italy). Qualified as Full Professor of Latin Language and Literature, he is interested in the Reception of Antiquity, Ancient Consolation, *Centones Vergiliani*, and Roman Historiography. He has published extensively on these topics, including *Classici lettori di classici. Da Virgilio a Marguerite Yourcenar* (2012), and, most recently, the commentaries on Tacitus' *Agricola* (2017) and *Germania* (2020).

Salvador Bartera is Assistant Professor of Classics at the University of Tennessee, Knoxville. His main research interests focus on Roman historiography, particularly Tacitus. He is also interested in the reception of the Classics in the Renaissance. His main publications include articles on the *Annals*, the concept of *fides* in the *Histories*, the history of the commentary tradition of Tacitus, his first Italian translations and Tacitist commentators, and the neo-Latin Jesuit poet Stefonio. He is currently completing a commentary on *Annals* 16 and preparing an edition of Stefonio's *Flavia Tragoedia*.

René Bloch is Professor of Jewish Studies at the University of Bern, where he holds a joint appointment in the Institute of Jewish Studies and the Institute of Classics. After obtaining an MA in Classics from the Sorbonne, he received his PhD as well as his habilitation in Classics and Jewish Studies from the University of Basel. Bloch's research focuses on Hellenistic Judaism, ancient myth, and Tacitus. René Bloch is the author of *Ancient Jewish Diaspora: Essays on Hellenism* (2022), *Jüdische Drehbühnen: Biblische Variationen im antiken Judentum* (2013), *Moses und der Mythos: Die Auseinandersetzung mit der griechischen Mythologie bei jüdisch- hellenistischen Autoren* (2011), and *Antike Vorstellungen vom Judentum: Der Judenexkurs des Tacitus im Rahmen der griechisch-römischen Ethnographie* (2002).

Katherine Clarke is Professor of Greek and Roman History in the University of Oxford and Fellow and Tutor in Ancient History at St Hilda's College. She has published extensively in the field of Ancient Historiography and has a particular interest in the interface between geographical and historical thought. Works include *Between Geography and History: Hellenistic Constructions of the Roman World* (1999), *Making Time for the Past: Local History and the* Polis (2008), and *Shaping the Geography of Empire: Man and Nature in Herodotus'* Histories (2018). She is currently working on Tacitus, focusing on the *Annals* as a work that explores the profoundly "kingly" history of Rome.

Cynthia Damon is Professor Emerita of Classical Studies at the University of Pennsylvania. Her books include *The Mask of the Parasite* (1997), commentaries on and translations of Tacitus (*Histories* 1 [2003], *Agricola* [2017]; *Annals* [2013]), texts of Caesar's *Civil War* (2015, 2016), and, with Will Batstone, *Caesar's Civil War* (2006). Edited volumes include *Citizens of discord: Rome and its* *civil wars* (with B. Breed and A. Rossi, 2010) and *Ennius' Annals: Poetry and History* (with Joe Farrell, 2020).

Aske Damtoft Poulsen is a postdoctoral researcher in Latin at Lund University, where in May 2024 he started a four-year project on counterfactual thinking in Roman historiography. He holds a PhD in Latin from Lund University (2018) and has since worked as a postdoc at The Swedish Institute in Rome (2018–19), Bristol University (2019–21), and Aalborg University (2021–4). His main research interests are Roman historiography, Latin poetry, narratology, cognitive science, intertextuality, rhetoric, ideas of history, and history of ideas. He has co-edited a volume on *Usages of the Past in Roman Historiography*, and he has written several articles on late Republican and early imperial literature, published in *Mnemosyne, Histos*, and *The Cambridge Companion to Sallust*.

Olivier Devillers is Professor of Latin Language and Literature at the University Bordeaux-Montaigne. Since 2019, he has been the Head of the Ausonius Institute (UMR 5607), after having been the Director of Ausonius Editions (from 2011 to 2018). He is also president of the SIEN, International Society of Neronian Studies. He is a specialist on Tacitus, on whom he has written two books (1994 and 2003) and about fifty articles, as well as more generally on Roman historiography, especially of the imperial period. He has published, with B. B. Sebastiani, three collected volumes on historiography in antiquity, *Sources et modèles des historiens anciens* (2018, 2021, 2024).

Caitlin Gillespie is Assistant Professor, Department of Classical and Early Mediterranean Studies at Brandeis University, Waltham, Massachusetts. She received her PhD in Classical Studies from the University of Pennsylvania. Her scholarship focuses on women and power in Tacitus' *Annals*. She has published several articles on individual women within the imperial family as well as women who rebel against the imperial system. Her first book, *Boudica: Warrior Woman of Roman Britain*, was published with Oxford University Press in 2018.

Alain M. Gowing is Professor Emeritus of Classics at the University of Washington in Seattle. His interests include Roman memory, imperial historiography (Greek and Roman), and imperial literature and culture generally. He is the author of *Empire and Memory. The Representation of the Roman Republic in Imperial Culture* (Cambridge 2005).

Timothy A. Joseph is Professor of Classics at the College of the Holy Cross in Worcester, Massachusetts, where he has also served as the director of Peace and Conflict Studies. He is the author of *Tacitus the Epic Successor* (2012) and *Thunder and Lament: Lucan on the Beginnings and Ends of Epic* (2022), as well as numerous essays on Latin literature and the reception of the Classics in the United States.

S. P. Oakley is Kennedy Professor of Latin and Fellow of Emmanuel College in the University of Cambridge; previously he taught at the University of Reading. His principal publications are *The hill-forts of the Samnites* (1995), *A commentary on Livy, books VI–X* (4 vols., 1997–2005), and *Studies in the transmission of Latin texts* (2 vols., 2020 and 2023).

Victoria Emma Pagán is Professor of Classics at the University of Florida. She is the author of *Conspiracy Narratives in Roman History* and *Conspiracy Theory in Latin Literature* (2004, 2012), *Rome and the Literature of Gardens* (2006), *A Sallust Reader* (2009), and *Tacitus* (2017). She co-edited *Disciples of Flora: Gardens in History and Culture* (2015) with J. W. Page and B. Weltman-Aron and *Tacitus' Wonders: Empire and Paradox in Ancient Rome* (2022) with James McNamara. She is the editor of the *A Companion to Tacitus* and *The Tacitus Encyclopedia* (2012, 2023). She has also written over two dozen articles on Latin literature, including Statius, Ovid, Vergil, Pliny the Younger, Sallust, and Velleius.

Kelly E. Shannon-Henderson is Associate Professor in the Department of Classics at the University of Cincinnati. She holds a bachelor's degree in Classics from the University of Virginia, and an MSt and DPhil in Greek and Latin Languages and Literature from the University of Oxford. She is the author of *Religion and Memory in Tacitus'* Annals (2019), a commentary on Phlegon of Tralles' *On Marvels* (2022), and various articles on aspects of Greek and Roman historiography, religion, and paradoxography.

Lydia Spielberg is Assistant Professor in the Department of Classics at the University of California, Los Angeles. She has published on various aspects of Roman historiography and rhetoric and is currently preparing a monograph on quotation in the Roman historians.

Bram ten Berge is Associate Professor of Classics at Hope College in Holland, Michigan. His latest publications are *Writing Imperial History: Tacitus from* Agricola *to* Annales (University of Michigan Press, 2023) and "Tacitus' Use of Columella's *De re rustica*" (Histos, 2024). Current projects include *Tacitus and the Incomplete*, a co-edited volume that analyzes gaps, omissions, and lost portions in Tacitus' oeuvre, and a co-edited volume on envy in the Roman world.

Christopher S. van den Berg is Aliki Perroti and Seth Frank '55 Professor of Classical Studies at Amherst College and Chair of Classics. His first book was a study of Tacitus' *Dialogus de Oratoribus* (2014), his second a study of Cicero's *Brutus* (2021). He is currently writing a book on visual and material culture in Greco-Roman rhetoric and literary criticism. The project has been funded by an ACLS Burkhardt Residential Fellowship at Princeton and a Fellowship at the American Academy in Rome. Other projects include less formal work on modern rhetoric, especially right-wing extremism in American and European political discourse.

Christopher Whitton is Professor of Latin Literature at the University of Cambridge and Fellow and Director of Studies in Classics at Emmanuel College. His publications include a "Green and Yellow" commentary on Pliny *Epistles 2* (2013), *The Arts of Imitation in Latin Prose: Pliny's Epistles/Quintilian in Brief* (2019), *Roman Literature under Nerva, Trajan and Hadrian: Literary Interactions, AD 96–138* (co-edited with Alice König, 2018), and *The Cambridge Critical Guide to Latin Literature* (co-edited with Roy Gibson, 2024). Current projects include a commentary on Tacitus *Annals* 14 for Cambridge University Press.